OLMEC

COLOSSAL MASTERWORKS OF ANCIENT MEXICO

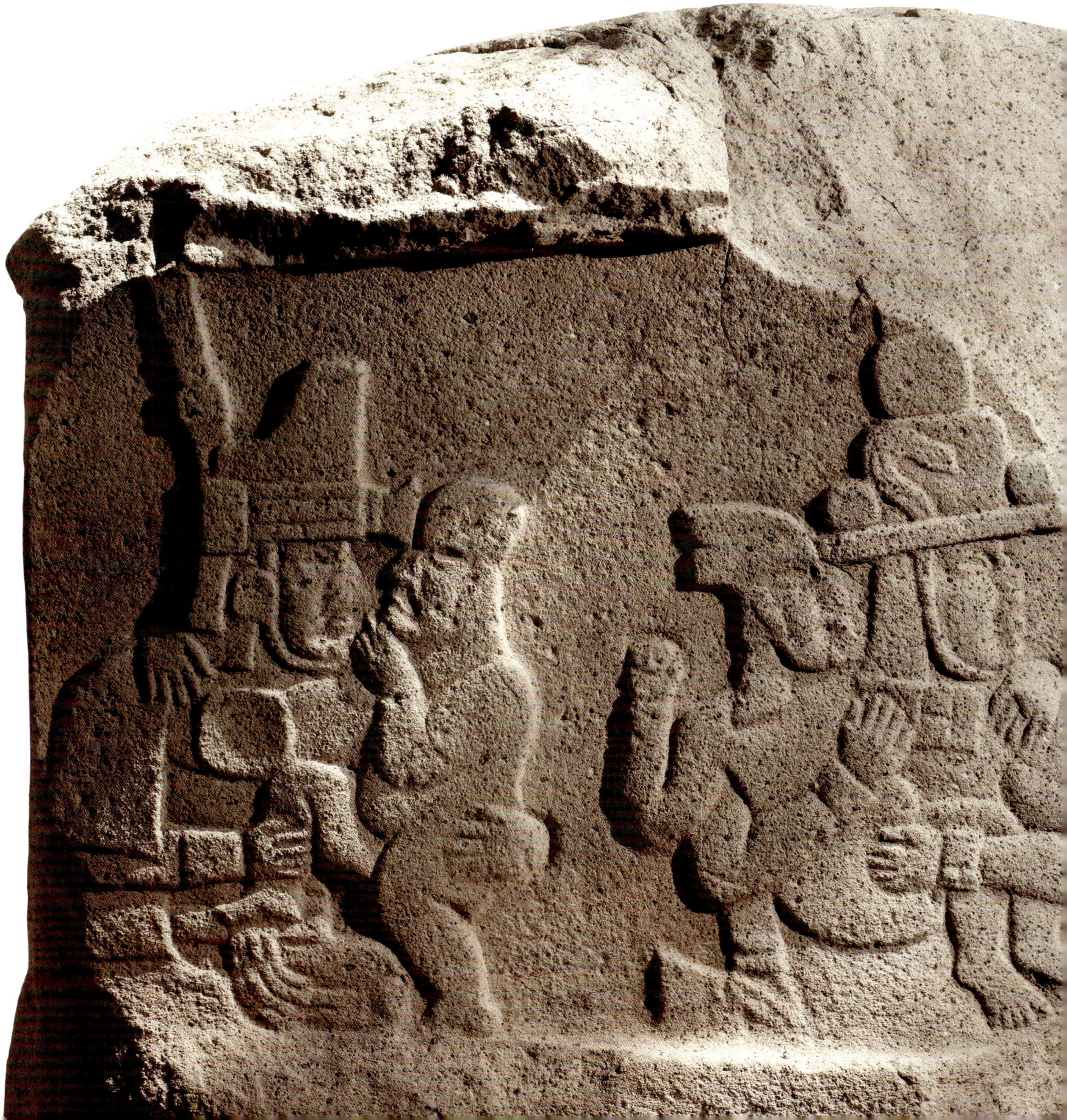

OLMEC: COLOSSAL MASTERWORKS OF ANCIENT MEXICO

Edited by Kathleen Berrin and Virginia M. Fields

FINE ARTS MUSEUMS OF SAN FRANCISCO
LOS ANGELES COUNTY MUSEUM OF ART
in association with
YALE UNIVERSITY PRESS, NEW HAVEN AND LONDON

CONTENTS

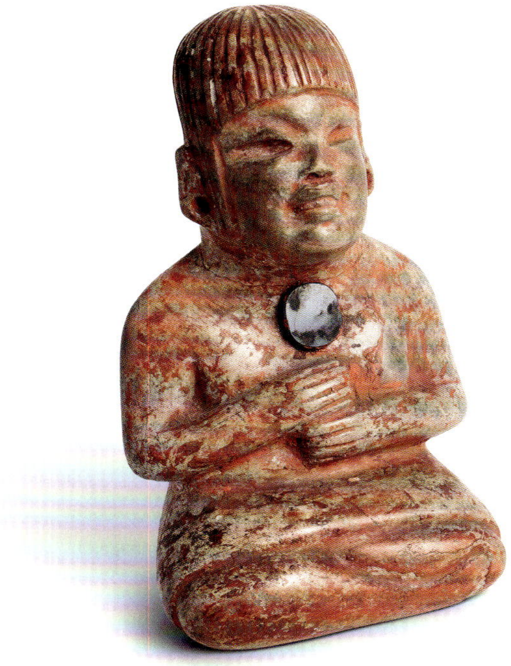

Plates
With entries by Kathleen Berrin, Marcía Castro-Leal Espino, Virginia M. Fields, Roberto Lunagómez Reyes, Patricia Ochoa Castillo, Ponciano Ortíz Ceballos, Christopher A. Pool, and Ma. del Carmen Rodríguez M.

First Discoveries in the Olmec Heartland 88

The Heartland Setting 94

The Hierarchy of Power: Capital Cities and Minor Centers 118

Mesoamerican Neighbors Near and Far 196

The Olmec Legacy in Later Mesoamerica 234

Foreword, Consuelo Sáizar 6

Foreword, Alfonso de María y Campos Castelló 7

Lenders to the Exhibition 8

Directors' Foreword, John E. Buchanan, Jr., and Michael Govan 9

Preface, Diana Magaloni Kerpel 10

Acknowledgments, Kathleen Berrin and Virginia M. Fields 14

Introduction, Kathleen Berrin and Virginia M. Fields 18

Olmec Art: Essence, Presence, Influence, and Transcendence, Sara Ladrón de Guevara 24

San Lorenzo, Ann Cyphers 34

La Venta, F. Kent Reilly III 44

Tres Zapotes: Where Olmec Archaeology Began, Christopher A. Pool 54

Olmec-Style Art outside Olman, David C. Grove 68

The Olmec Legacy in Stone: A Mesoamerican Alpha and Omega, Richard A. Diehl 76

A Note on the Naming of Olmec Monuments, Christopher A. Pool 86

Contributors 252
Works Cited 254
Photography Credits 265
Index 266

The presentation of Olmec art by the Los Angeles County Museum of Art and the Fine Arts Museums of San Francisco reflects the desire of the United States and Mexico—through their cultural institutions—to broaden the understanding of expressions that have nourished and defined today's complex world.

Holding this exhibition at such illustrious venues in the United States is a source of profound satisfaction for Mexico. It also fulfills the fundamental mission of the Consejo Nacional para la Cultura y las Artes: to coordinate the work of public institutions in Mexico to ensure the research, protection, and diffusion of our country's historical and cultural heritage. In this way we foster a cultural dialogue that promotes mutual understanding while reinforcing the bonds of friendship. As befits the open and generous spirit of exchange between Mexico and the United States, *Olmec: Colossal Masterworks of Ancient Mexico* seeks to introduce wider audiences to the rich cultural legacy of a remarkable early civilization.

Comprising loans from many important collections, the exhibition includes some of the most significant objects discovered at sites in the Olmec heartland and elsewhere in Mexico. Ranging from the portable to the monumental, they offer an unparalleled glimpse of the life of the Olmec and the authority and influence of their rulers. The expressive power of these extraordinary artifacts, about which we learn more with ongoing scholarship, has made them a source of endless fascination both in Mexico and abroad.

The success that we have achieved in this joint effort reaffirms that the sphere of collaboration and cultural exchange has no limits; it enriches shared knowledge and cultivates a respect for diversity. Mexico's loan of the finest Olmec works stands as testament to our commitment to promote understanding and partnership between our two nations.

CONSUELO SÁIZAR
President
Consejo Nacional para la Cultura y las Artes

As demonstrated by some of the essays in this splendid catalogue, it seems we are indebted to art historians for much of what we know about the Olmec style. Painstaking archaeological exploration revealed the material remains of this early people—as well as its very existence—and art historians such as Miguel Covarrubias and Beatriz de la Fuente, by defining its style and iconography, offered us a pattern or code to infer the spiritual and material life of the Olmec. At the same time, art historians have provided a frame of reference for comparative analyses with Mesoamerican cultures that succeeded that of the Olmec.

It is not by chance that I refer to these later cultures. Many aesthetic, stylistic, and iconographic studies have been sustained since 1942, when Covarrubias, Alfonso Caso, and Wigberto Jiménez Moreno first proposed the idea of the Olmec as the foundational origin, or "mother culture," of Mesoamerican civilization. Today, that perspective is no longer unanimously endorsed by specialists, and it is possible that scientific research might eventually overturn that supposed origin of Mesoamerican civilization. However, I have no doubt that the *search for origins* is a societal imperative. Whether through myth or scientific research, we humans strive to find that starting point that allows us to trace the existential coordinates of our future.

Knowing or imagining origins allows us—as a people and as a nation—to establish temporal and geographical parameters that help us to define and understand ourselves. For Mesoamerica, the Olmec formed a cradle of civilization shared by many of the peoples of ancient Mexico, including the Aztecs, the Maya, and the Teotihuacanos, to mention only three of the best-known cultural groups.

With the exhibition *Olmec: Colossal Masterworks of Ancient Mexico*, the Instituto Nacional de Antropología e Historia offers a perspective dating back more than three thousand years to the first settlements of this people, whose name for themselves remains shrouded in mystery. As Beatriz de la Fuente wrote, "There are moments in the pre-Hispanic world in which the visual rendering of the human body is expressed with pleasure and sensuality, while in others, emotion is conveyed in concepts abstracted from visual reality." The masterpieces in this exhibition will offer the international public a starting point for understanding this classic dichotomy in pre-Hispanic art.

ALFONSO DE MARÍA Y CAMPOS CASTELLÓ
General Director
Instituto Nacional de Antropología e Historia

American Museum of Natural History, New York
Bowers Museum
Centro INAH Morelos
Centro INAH Veracruz
Cleveland Museum of Art
Dallas Museum of Art
Dumbarton Oaks Research Library and Collection
Fine Arts Museums of San Francisco
Indiana University Art Museum
Instituto de Cultura de Tabasco, Dirección de Patrimonio Cultural
Los Angeles County Museum of Art
Metropolitan Museum of Art
Museo Amparo, Puebla
Museo Arqueológico de Soconusco, Tapachula, Chiapas
Museo de Antropología de Xalapa, Universidad Veracruzana
Museo de Cuauhnahuac "Palacio de Cortés," Cuernavaca, Morelos
Museo del Templo Mayor, Mexico City
Museo de Sitio de Teotihuacan
Museo Nacional de Antropología, Mexico City
Museo Regional de Antropología "Carlos Pellicer Cámara," Villahermosa, Tabasco
Museo Regional de Chiapas, Tuxtla Gutiérrez
Museo Regional de Puebla
Museo Regional de Yucatán "Palacio Cantón," Mérida, Yucatán
Museo Regional Tuxteco, Santiago Tuxtla, Veracruz
Parque-Museo de La Venta, Villahermosa, Tabasco
Peabody Museum of Archaeology and Ethnology, Harvard University

More than a century of Olmec studies have taken place since the first monumental portrait head was discovered in the Gulf Coast heartland, yet the mystique of the Olmec continues, and the questions surrounding the origins and nature of Mexico's first great civilization have in some ways grown more complex. *Olmec: Colossal Masterworks of Ancient Mexico* presents the most recent archaeological and art-historical investigations and interpretations of Olmec civilization and its widespread manifestation throughout ancient Mexico, revealing both newly discovered works of art and the new perspectives that enlighten us about this fascinating period in history.

The prospect for the Fine Arts Museums of San Francisco and the Los Angeles County Museum of Art to collaborate with Mexico's Instituto Nacional de Antropología e Historia to present *Olmec* arose in 2007, and we eagerly embraced the opportunity. Both the Fine Arts Museums and LACMA have shared lengthy relationships and unique ties with Mexico over the course of the past forty years, and this extraordinary exhibition underscores our commitment to continue to foster our mutual enthusiasm to present innovative and important projects to our public. The exhibition will not only inaugurate the Resnick Exhibition Pavilion at LACMA and grace the de Young, the home of the Fine Arts Museums in Golden Gate Park, but will also commemorate both the centennial and the bicentennial of Mexico's revolution and independence from Spain.

We are immensely grateful to the Instituto Nacional de Antropología e Historia and the national and regional museums of Mexico for so graciously sharing their works of art and artifacts that constitute Olmec civilization and its legacy. We couldn't be more honored to host these treasures, first in the southern part of our multifaceted state, and then again in the north. This exhibition is supported by an indemnity from the Federal Council on the Arts and the Humanities. The San Francisco production of the exhibition is wholly funded by and attributed to the Phyllis C. Wattis Fund for Traveling Exhibitions.

JOHN E. BUCHANAN, JR.
Director of Museums
Fine Arts Museums of San Francisco

MICHAEL GOVAN
Chief Executive Officer and Director
Los Angeles County Museum of Art

The beauty, monumentality, and expressive power of the art of the Olmec civilization continue to inspire admiration and fascination. It is amazing that works of such exquisite artistry were created in Mesoamerica as early as 1800 BC. The vast geographic reach of the Olmec is equally astounding, and the wealth of artistic expression is magnificent. Monumental basalt sculptures depict high-status individuals with naturalistic features, proportions, and forms, while massive thrones show other notable figures emerging from caves. Jade and greenstone sculptures crafted on a smaller scale portray eminent men or fantastic beings with ferocious faces; figurines of white kaolin and other fine paste ceramics depict crying or laughing babies and aquatic or land animals. Mural paintings, created with a wide range of pigments, illustrate complex scenes of ecstatic journeys that involve multiple symbolic planes; bas-reliefs on cliffsides relate creation myths. The aesthetic excellence and originality of all these works capture the imagination of the modern observer. It is thus an enormous privilege to feature objects from this culture in the exhibition *Olmec: Colossal Masterworks of Ancient Mexico*, the culmination of the joint efforts of Mexican and American cultural institutions.

The problem of the nature of Olmec society and history continues to intrigue us. Some experts agree with the idea that Olmec culture from the coastal area of the modern-day states of Veracruz and Tabasco was the "mother culture" of Mesoamerica.[1] This region, characterized by a tropical, moist climate and filled with riverine plains and rainforests, has been referred to as the Olmec heartland. It is believed that the Olmec of San Lorenzo Tenochtitlán, La Venta, and other heartland sites developed a complex hierarchical society and a system of symbols, and that they exerted a crucial influence over less-developed peoples in Mesoamerica through trade and political control of territories.

Another interpretation regards the Olmec phenomenon as a multiethnic cultural horizon. This view underscores the geographic breadth of similar artistic expressions that were chronologically contemporary to those in the Olmec heartland but were found in the central valleys of Oaxaca, the modern-day states of Morelos and Guerrero, the Valley of Mexico, and on the coast of Chiapas.[2] At times, this debate conceals a fact that is fundamental for those who study indigenous cultures of the Americas: Olmec culture coherently and powerfully crystallized fundamental principles that pervade Mesoamerican thought. Throughout the development of diverse Mesoamerican cultures—including the time of contact with the Spanish and, at times, updated in the present—we can recognize principles initially expressed in Middle Preclassic or Formative Olmec art and architecture. According to the anthropologist Marshall David Sahlins, fundamental categories of thought survive dynamically through time, serving to explain both the evolution and continuity of civilizations.[3] In this preface I focus on one of these categories: the sacred mountain.

In their pioneering research at La Venta in 1925, Frans Blom and Oliver La Farge were the first to associate the Olmec "style" with a geographic area: southern Veracruz and Tabasco. However, the authors did not define the monuments they found as being from a new culture because many of the characteristics of the monuments corresponded to objects from other Mesoamerican cultures. For example, the central figure on the front of La Venta Stela 2 **(FIG. 16)**, who wears an elaborate headdress and holds a bar at a diagonal in his arms, is today recognized as a ruler dressed as a ballplayer. But for Blom and La Farge, the figure seemed to confirm the Maya identity of the monuments.[4] In that same period, Hermann Beyer described an anthropomorphic basalt sculpture known as Monument 1, found by Blom and La Farge in the Tuxtla Mountains, as "Olmec."[5] The efforts of these important early scholars in discerning what was Olmec and tracing its origins attest to cultural continuity in Mexico's ancient past. I am referring to the juxtaposition of diversity and unity of thought, expressed culturally and artistically, that is so characteristic of Mesoamerican societies. For example, if we carefully consider Monument 1 **(FIG. 1)**, we can see that the figure has what Beatriz de la Fuente called prototypical Olmec features: thick lips with downturned corners; slanted, almond-shaped eyes; and a rounded and thick body.[6] At the same time, the context of the discovery speaks to the ancient pan-Mesoamerican cult of the sacred mountain and the cave of origin. The sculpture was found in a rocky refuge at the peak of the volcano San Martín Pajapan, in the Tuxtla Mountains, about 62 miles (100 kilometers) from San Lorenzo. It had been there for centuries, receiving offerings from the local people.[7] We know the figure is a high-status individual by his headdress, which depicts the anthropomorphic face of a fantastic creature; by the earflares decorated with human faces; and by the V-shaped cleft in his forehead, from which a form resembling a plant emerges. The amazing expressive and narrative capacity of Olmec sculptural art invites us to anticipate the actions of the individual. He sits with one leg bent and the other extended behind him. He leans forward, his hands grasping the staff in front of him, with one palm facing upward and the other down, suggesting that, in an instant, the ruler will stand and shift his arms to hold the staff of authority in a vertical position. In other words, the maker of this sculpture skillfully synthesized the lapse of time of a ritual act in which the ruler presides over the mountain and, with his staff, directs the three levels of the cosmos: upper, middle, and lower. It is a perfect sculpture in its expression, intention, and power. The association between the ruler and the sacred landscape is undeniable: the sculpture was situated at the peak of the most prominent volcano in the region and sheltered in a cave. This connection with the mountain as the sacred place of origin, and with the cave as the threshold of entrance into and emergence from the mountain for important members of a community, is a central theme in Mesoamerican thought that persists even today in regions such as Chiapas. San Martín Pajapan Monument 1, with all of its characteristics of the Olmec world, expresses concepts that became cornerstones of indigenous thought in the Americas for centuries to come.

The ritual management of water and, by extension, agriculture, and its close connection to blood offerings, the ritual ballgame, and the ruling elite, was another important symbolic complex formalized at the time; it

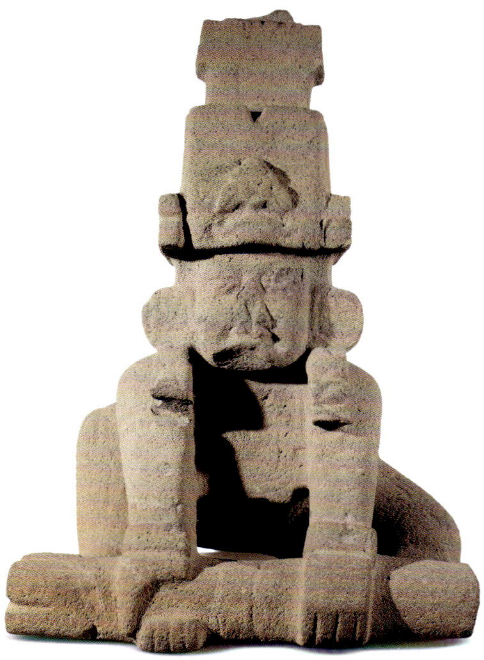

FIG. 1
MONUMENT 1 (CROUCHING FIGURE WITH HEADDRESS AND CEREMONIAL STAFF)
Mexico, Veracruz, San Martín Pajapan,
1100–900 BC
Basalt
142 x 93 x 94 in. (44⅞ x 36⅝ x 37 cm)
Museo de Antropología de Xalapa,
Universidad Veracruzana

was also associated with the mountain as a place of origin and pilgrimage. Ponciano Ortíz Ceballos and Ma. del Carmen Rodríguez M. have carried out extensive research at the Cerro Manatí in Veracruz. Their studies show that the mountain, from the interior of which emerges a spring of thermal waters, has been a site of pilgrimage and worship for the past twelve hundred years. The materials used for and the pattern of the offerings found at El Manatí make them diminutive, collective cosmograms—geometric figures representing a cosmology. Containing stone axes, rubber balls, and wood sculptures representing human busts, as well as more perishable materials such as seeds, leaves, and branches, the offerings were placed on east-west or north-south axes, facing the mountain. Ortíz Ceballos and Rodríguez M. also indicate that the mountain is associated with another important symbolic element, a red pigment made from hematite.

El Manatí clearly expressed the symbolic complex of the mountain/spring, red pigment/jade celt. This complex appeals to the sacred forces of water and the interior of the mountain, which is associated with the underworld, the origin of creative forces. All of these elements, as categories that order thought, can also be found in mural paintings dating to AD 600 in the apartment compound of Tepantitla at Teotihuacan, in the Basin of Mexico. According to María Teresa Uriarte's analysis, the Tepantitla murals represent the city of Teotihuacan as a pilgrimage site. Dominated by the color red, the paintings depict a narrative in which ballplayers from many Mesoamerican centers traveled to Teotihuacan, where they played the ritual ballgame and worshipped the cult of the sacred mountain, offering precious seeds, jade beads, and the blood of men who died in sacrifice. The mountain is depicted with a gushing spring, home to a great toad that provides water for the fields of distant communities. The blood offered after the ritual ballgame is thus transformed into the abundant verdure of cultivated fields and into sustenance for communities affiliated with the sacred mountain. The red world of the inside of time—together with its offerings, sacred water, and mountain of origin—is expressed as a fundamental principle both at El Manatí around 1600 BC and at Teotihuacan around AD 600.

These symbolic principles endured for centuries, also appearing at the Aztec Templo Mayor (AD 1300–1500) in Tenochtitlan, now Mexico City. Archaeological explorations conducted at the Templo Mayor by Eduardo Matos Moctezuma and Leonardo López Luján have demonstrated that this great temple was conceived of as a mountain of sustenance and a mountain of Aztec origin: the *altepetl* ("mountain of water") and the *tlatepetlalilli* ("hill made by men"). The offerings found at the Templo Mayor are small, collective cosmograms, just as at the site of El Manatí. Furthermore, according to sixteenth-century Nahua sources, the Templo Mayor was constructed on a location prefigured as the center of the world. On this site, the vertical axis from the upper, middle, and lower levels is articulated with the four horizontally conceived cosmic directions, in the same way that the ruler of San Martín Pajapan presided over space and time. According to myth, the world center would be located near two caves from which issued forth red and blue water. This mythical place recalls elements that archaeologists observed at El Manatí: the spring of blue water and the red pigment from hematite, with offerings placed as cosmograms. The gods' primordial act of creation was reestablished in each ritual, with each offering, as López Luján has proposed of the offerings at the Templo Mayor.

In this way, the Olmec cultural horizon establishes the foundations of Mesoamerican thought. After the Olmec, the peoples of Mesoamerica created and revered a seemingly infinite series of mountains of origin. Each archaeological site, its construction a reflection of the first act of creation, expresses this pact with the gods and with time. The mountain, brought to life through rites, continues as the dark refuge where the indigenous voices of the Americas can be still be heard. The ruler of San Martín Pajapan continues to crouch, actively prefiguring the moment he will stand up and serve as the axis of communication between the heavens and the earth.

NOTES

1 Jiménez Moreno 1942.

2 Diehl and Coe 1995: 11; Niederberger 1996a.

3 Sahlins 1985.

4 Blom and La Farge 1926: 90.

5 Benson 1996b: 18; Taube 2004: 2, 14.

6 de la Fuente 1996a: 162.

7 Ibid.

The exhibition and catalogue *Olmec: Colossal Masterworks of Ancient Mexico* resulted from the multifaceted collaborative efforts of numerous individuals and institutions in Mexico and the United States. The inspiration for and development of the project began with Mexico's Instituto Nacional de Antropología e Historia (INAH), when José Enrique Ortiz Lanz, then national coordinator of museums and exhibitions, invited us to bring this landmark exhibition to our institutions. We are grateful to our directors, John E. Buchanan, Jr., at the Fine Arts Museums of San Francisco and Michael Govan at the Los Angeles County Museum of Art, for their enthusiasm and vision in making *Olmec* a reality.

The support and encouragement of various officials in Mexico were critical to the organization of *Olmec: Colossal Masterworks of Ancient Mexico*. We are especially grateful to Consuelo Sáizar, president of the Consejo Nacional para la Cultura y las Artes (CONACULTA) and Alfonso de María y Campos Castelló, general director of INAH. Miriam Kaiser, INAH's director of international exhibitions; Lourdes Herrasti, national coordinator of museums and exhibitions; Leticia Pérez Castellanos, subdirector of exhibitions; Ileana Peña Cid, legal liaison; and the talented Miguel Báez and Erika Gómez Carbajal managed endless details. We are also indebted to Laura Pescador, former director, and Salvador Guilliem Arroyo, current director, Coordinación Nacional de Arqueología.

We owe tremendous thanks to Mexico's foremost archaeologists, who provided the intellectual substance for the exhibition and catalogue. We deeply appreciate their generosity in sharing with us their profound and nuanced knowledge of the ancient peoples of the Gulf Coast. The exhibition also benefited from the enthusiastic support of curators and directors at a number of institutions in Mexico, including Diana Magaloni Kerpel, director, Museo Nacional de Antropología, Mexico City; Sara Ladrón de Guevara, director, Museo de Antropología de Xalapa, Universidad Veracruzana; Eduardo López, Centro INAH Morelos; Juan Contreras de Oteyza, Museo de Cuauhnahuac "Palacio de Cortés," Cuernavaca, Morelos; Abraham Guerrero, Museo Regional de Yucatán "Palacio Cantón," Mérida, Yucatán; Carlos Javier González, Museo del Templo Mayor, Mexico City; Laura Filloy Nadal, Patricia Ochoa Castillo, and Marcía Castro-Leal Espino, Museo Nacional de Antropología, Mexico City; Lucia Alonso Espinosa, Museo Amparo, Puebla; Delia Martínez Cuanalo, Museo Regional de Puebla; Emiliano Gallaga Murrieta, Centro INAH Chiapas; Roberto López Bravo, Museo Regional de Chiapas, Tuxtla Gutiérrez; David Morales, Centro INAH Veracruz; Norma Lilí Cárdenas, Instituto de Cultura de Tabasco, Dirección de Patrimonio Cultural; Rebeca Perales, Museo Regional de Antropología "Carlos Pellicer Cámara" and Parque-Museo de La Venta, Villahermosa, Tabasco; Roberto Lunagómez Reyes, Museo de Antropología de Xalapa, Universidad Veracruzana; Alejandro Sarabia, director of the Archaeological Zone of Teotihuacan; Ponciano Ortíz Ceballos, Instituto de Antropología, Universidad Veracruzana; and Ma. del Carmen Rodríguez M., INAH. We also appreciate the guidance of INAH conservator Frida Montes de Oca.

At the United States Embassy in Mexico, we are most grateful to Ambassaor Carlos Pascual; James Williams, public affairs officer; Robin Smith, cultural attaché; and the incomparable Bertha Cea Echenique, senior cultural affairs specialist, whose ongoing support proved essential to our project. Mexico's ambassador to the United States, Arturo Sarukhan, was always enthusiastic and helpful. We are also thankful to Carlos Félix Carona, consul general in San Francisco, and Jonathan Chait Auerbach, and to Juan Marcos Gutiérrez, consul general in Los Angeles.

Other friends and colleagues in Mexico who provided help and encouragement include Teresa Franco, Roxana Velazquez, Virginia Classing, James Oles, Leonardo López Luján, Diana Mogóllon González, Miguel Fernández, Alejandra de la Paz, Alberto Fiero, Luz Elena Banos Rivas, María Teresa Uriarte, Marta González, and Mario Pérez Campa.

We appreciate the exhibition loans from museums in the United States, and we would like to thank the following individuals for their support: Kristen Mable, American Museum of Natural History, New York; Jennifer Ring, Bowers Museum; Susan Bergh, Cleveland Museum of Art; Carol Robbins, Dallas Museum of Art; Gudrun Bühl, Dumbarton Oaks

Research Library and Collection; Adelheid Gealt and Anita Bracalente, Indiana University Art Museum; Julie Jones, Metropolitan Museum of Art; and William Fash and Viva Fisher, Peabody Museum of Archaeology and Ethnology, Harvard University. We are also grateful to John Clark, Anatole Pohorilenko, Dorie Reents-Budet, F. Kent Reilly III, and Matthew Robb, always the sources of good advice.

We thank the authors of the catalogue essays and object entries for their insightful contributions; Javier Hinojosa for his beautiful new photography of the Mexican loans; and Debra Nagao and Rose Vekony for their exceptional translations of Spanish texts. Thanks also to the meticulous Karen Levine, editor in chief at the Fine Arts Museums, who oversaw all aspects of this catalogue; to Jennifer Boynton, who carefully edited the manuscript; to Tracey Shiffman, Alex Kohnke, and Deanne Oi for their inspired book design; and to Tony Manzella and his team at Echelon for their outstanding work on the reproductions. We are grateful to Patricia Fidler and Michelle Komie of Yale University Press for their enthusiastic partnership on the publication. Also deserving thanks are José Cabeza at *Arqueología Mexicana*, Ashley Parada at the National Geographic Society, and Stephanie Christensen and Daisy Njoku at the Smithsonian for their assistance with archival photography, and Anandaroop Roy, Ann Cyphers, Richard Diehl, Christopher Pool, David Grove, Susan Gillespie, and F. Kent Reilly III for their help with the maps.

Our two institutions divided the responsibilities for *Olmec: Colossal Masterworks of Ancient Mexico*, with LACMA organizing the exhibition logistics and the Fine Arts Museums publishing the catalogue. At LACMA, we would like to express our appreciation to Irene Martín, who tirelessly spearheaded the exhibition negotiations, assisted by Sarah Minnaert and Marciana Broiles. We are grateful to Renée Montgomery and Alexandra Moran, who coordinated the domestic and international loans. Special thanks also to exhibition designer Victoria Behner, who developed an installation plan that resonated sensitively with the elegant vocabulary of the monumental platforms designed by Michael Heizer. And thanks especially to Kim Richter, Megan Knox, and Victoria Lyall, who managed the technical intricacies of compiling and updating the crucial documentation for the exhibition and publication with graciousness and enviable skill.

At the Fine Arts Museums, we thank Renée Baldocchi, Lesley Bone, Martha Brigham, Steven Brindmore, Krista Brugnara, Therese Chen, Bob Futernick, Sarah Bailey Hogarty, Lauren Ito, Ann Karlstrom, Gary Landis, Samantha Leo, Suzy Peterson, Sheila Pressley, Allison Satre, Ashley Stropes, Richard Sutherland, William White, and the Technical Production and Marketing and Design teams. For valuable seed money in the initial stages of catalogue development in San Francisco, we sincerely wish to thank Virginia Patterson.

Finally, we mourn the recent passing of two colleagues in Mexico, Beatriz de la Fuente and Felipe Solís Olguín, whose passion, enthusiasm, and contributions to the field of Olmec studies and the larger Mesoamerican world are deeply felt and enduring.

KATHLEEN BERRIN
Fine Arts Museums of San Francisco

VIRGINIA M. FIELDS
Los Angeles County Museum of Art

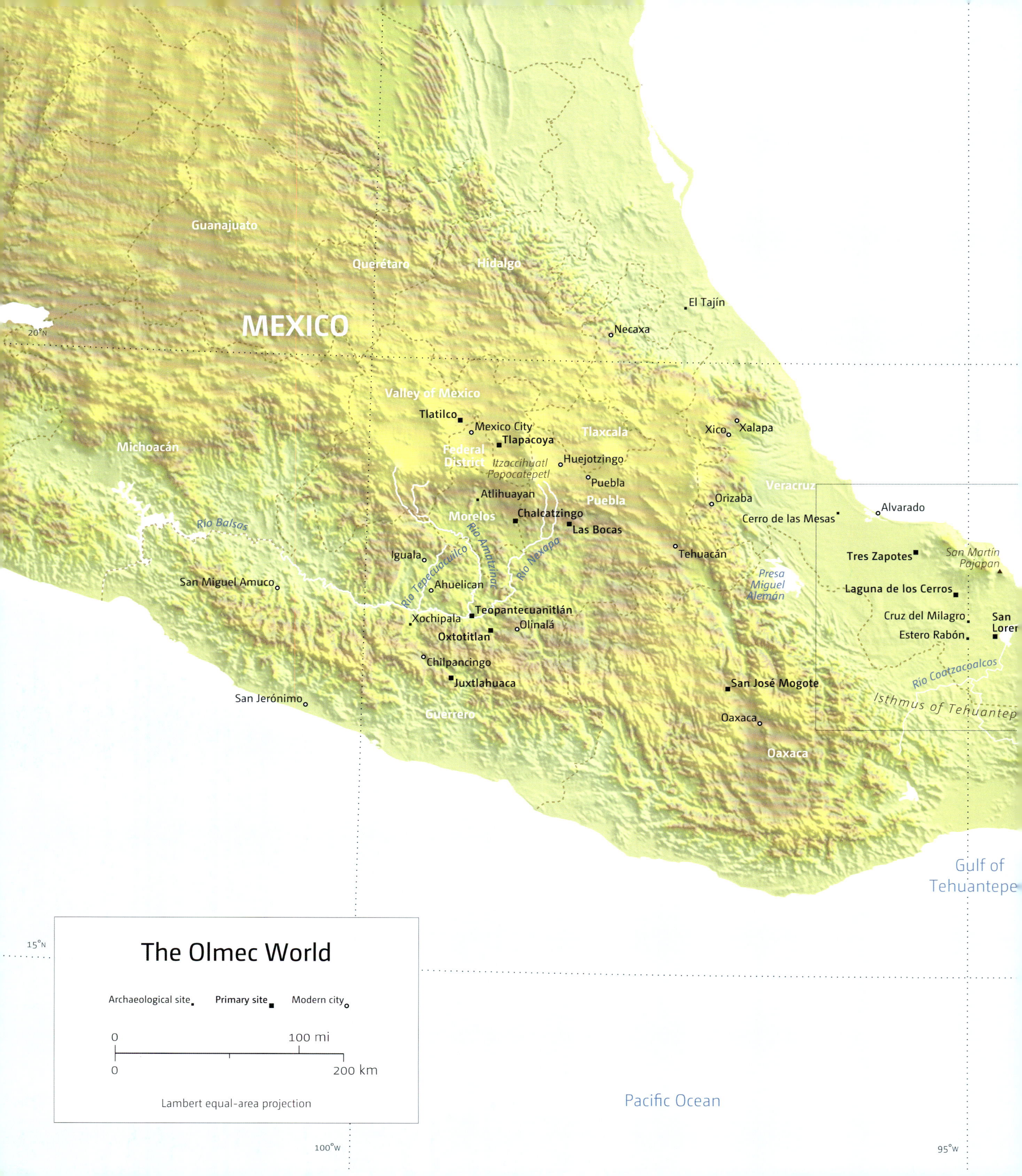

The Olmec World
Archaeological site
Primary site
Modern city
0
100 mi
0
200 km
Lambert equal-area projection
MEXICO
Guanajuato
Querétaro
Hidalgo
El Tajín
Necaxa
20°N
Valley of Mexico
Tlatilco
Mexico City
Tlapacoya
Tlaxcala
Xico
Xalapa
Michoacán
Federal District
Itzaccihuatl
Popocatepetl
Huejotzingo
Puebla
Veracruz
Atlihuayan
Puebla
Orizaba
Alvarado
Río Balsas
Morelos
Chalcatzingo
Las Bocas
Cerro de las Mesas
Río Amatzinac
Río Nexapa
Tehuacán
Tres Zapotes
San Martín Pajapan
Iguala
Río Tepecuacuilco
Presa Miguel Alemán
San Miguel Amuco
Ahuelican
Laguna de los Cerros
Teopantecuanitlán
Xochipala
Olinalá
Cruz del Milagro
San Lorer
Oxtotitlan
Estero Rabón
Chilpancingo
Río Coatzacoalcos
Juxtlahuaca
San José Mogote
San Jerónimo
Isthmus of Tehuantep
Guerrero
Oaxaca
Oaxaca
Gulf of Tehuantepe
15°N
Pacific Ocean
100°W
95°W

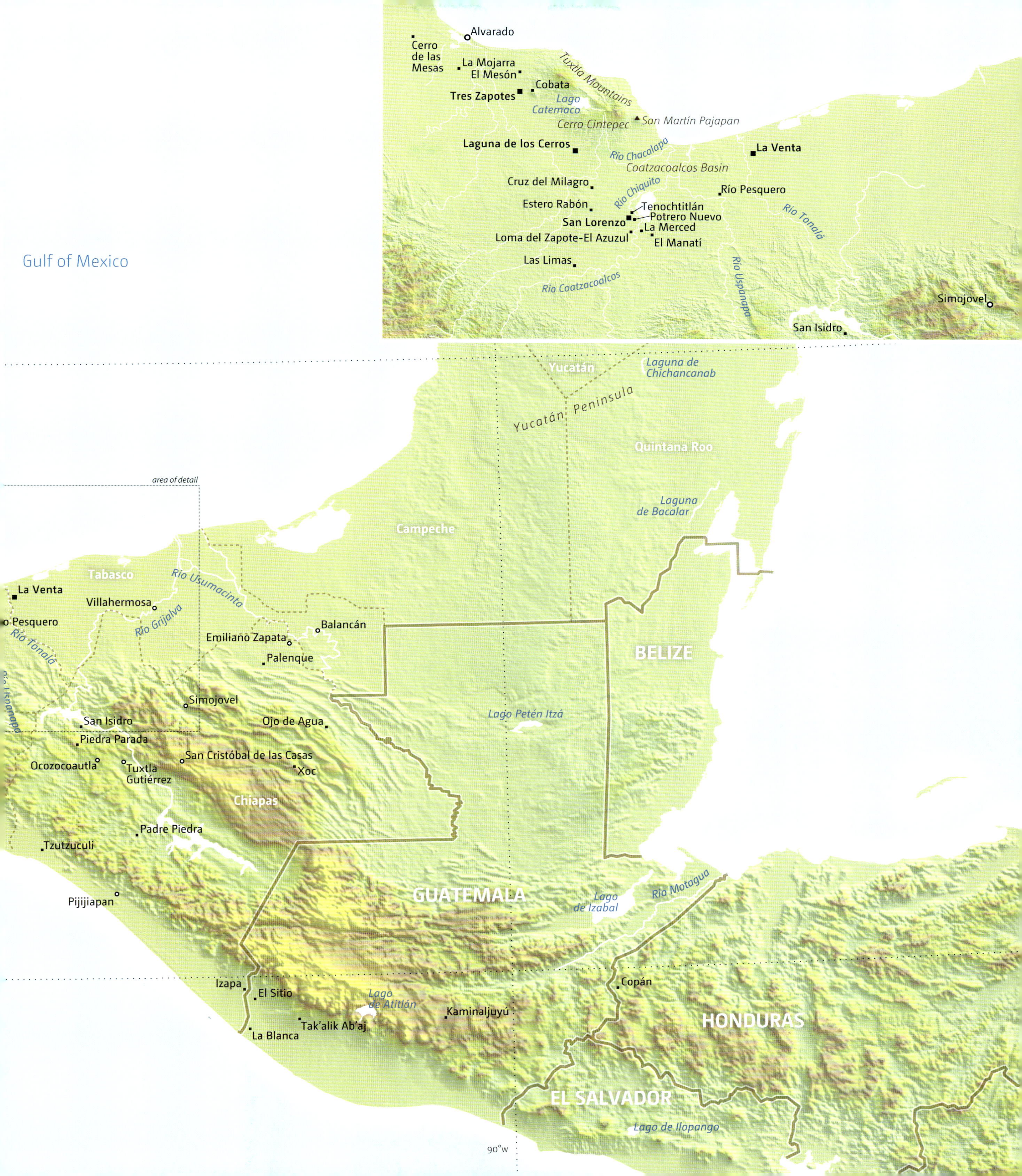

Alvarado
Cerro de las Mesas
La Mojarra
El Mesón
Tuxtla Mountains
Cobata
Tres Zapotes
Lago Catemaco
Cerro Cintepec
San Martín Pajapan
Laguna de los Cerros
Río Chacalapa
La Venta
Coatzacoalcos Basin
Cruz del Milagro
Río Chiquito
Río Pesquero
Estero Rabón
Tenochtitlán
Potrero Nuevo
San Lorenzo
La Merced
Río Tonalá
Loma del Zapote-El Azuzul
El Manatí
Las Limas
Río Uspanapa
Río Coatzacoalcos
Simojovel
San Isidro
Gulf of Mexico
Yucatán
Laguna de Chichancanab
Yucatán Peninsula
Quintana Roo
area of detail
Laguna de Bacalar
Campeche
Tabasco
Río Usumacinta
La Venta
Villahermosa
Río Grijalva
Pesquero
Río Tonalá
Balancán
Emiliano Zapata
Palenque
BELIZE
Simojovel
Lago Petén Itzá
San Isidro
Ojo de Agua
Piedra Parada
Ocozocoautla
Tuxtla Gutiérrez
San Cristóbal de las Casas
Xoc
Chiapas
Padre Piedra
Tzutzuculi
GUATEMALA
Lago de Izabal
Río Motagua
Pijijiapan
Izapa
El Sitio
Lago de Atitlán
Kaminaljuyú
Copán
Tak'alik Ab'aj
La Blanca
HONDURAS
EL SALVADOR
Lago de Ilopango
90°W

INTRODUCTION

Kathleen Berrin and
Virginia M. Fields

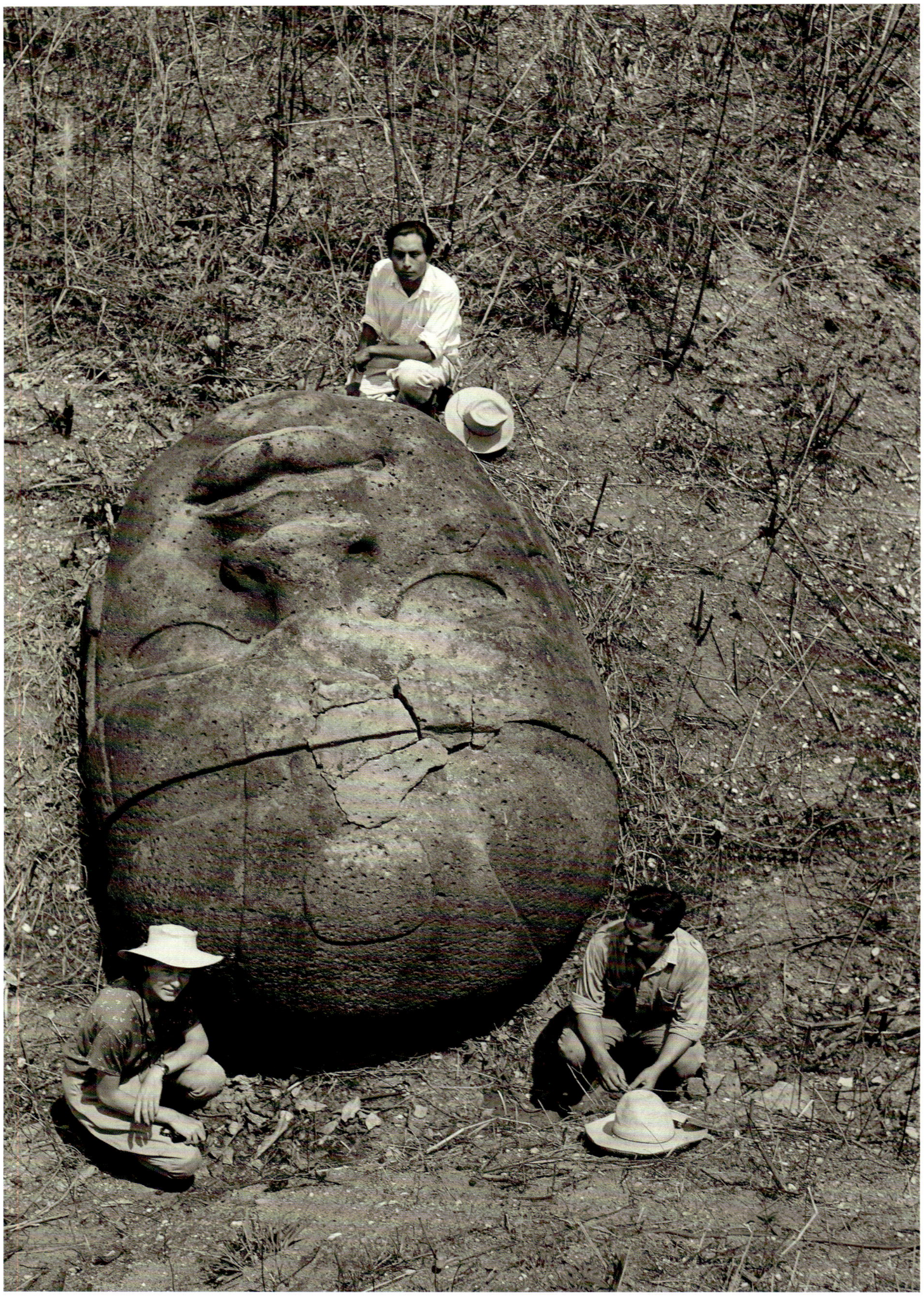

Olmec: Colossal Masterworks of Ancient Mexico marks a significant collaboration between the Instituto Nacional de Antropología e Historia, the Fine Arts Museums of San Francisco, and the Los Angeles County Museum of Art, enabling us to present the most recent knowledge about Olmec civilization, the earliest to erect monumental art and architecture in Mexico. This exhibition is not an exhaustive survey; rather, it highlights new discoveries about the nature and extent of the Olmec style as seen in the archaeological remains of the Gulf Coast heartland's major centers—San Lorenzo Tenochtitlán, La Venta, and Tres Zapotes—in minor Gulf Coast sites, and in the variety of regional and chronological expressions that appear throughout Mexico.

Olmec style is evident in powerful and impressive sculptural forms such as colossal portrait heads and massive thrones and in a wide array of exquisite greenstone figures, axes (also called celts), and masks that convey monumentality despite their smaller size. The basalt for monumental sculptures derived from the Tuxtla Mountains, some 35 miles (60 kilometers) from San Lorenzo, and it required massive amounts of manpower to transport such enormous boulders.[1] Favoring a translucent blue-green jadeite from the distant Río Motagua source in southern Guatemala, Olmec artists rendered precious greenstones into objects that symbolized elite sacred and secular authority.

The name *Olmec* also refers to an archaeological culture[2] that flourished in the tropical lowlands of present-day Veracruz and Tabasco between 1800 and 400 BC, an era roughly corresponding to the Middle Kingdom of ancient Egypt. We do not know what the peoples of the Gulf Coast called themselves, but *Olmec* came into use to refer to a number of isolated objects that came to light in the nineteenth and early twentieth centuries. Although the small-scale objects reportedly derived from Central Mexico, Guerrero, and Oaxaca, explorers and

FIG. 2
Discovery of Colossal Head 1 ("El Rey") at San Lorenzo, 1946

scholars such as Frans Blom and George Vaillant perceived the stylistic connection between these objects and the occasional discoveries of monuments in the Gulf Coast region that carried similar physical features.

Scholars also puzzled over the chronological parameters of Olmec, the last major Mesoamerican civilization to be discovered. While authors such as Miguel Covarrubias defined it as an early cultural manifestation, others disputed that Olmec preceded the better-known Maya civilization until radiocarbon dating at La Venta confirmed the great antiquity of Olmec centers.[3] One difficulty in affixing precise dates to archaeological time periods reflects the individual site histories coinciding with their respective patterns of expansion and decline. For the purposes of this volume, we include the dates provided by each author as defined by his or her research.

The traits defining Olmec began to coalesce at San Lorenzo between 1800 and 1400 BC (see Cyphers, this volume), a period referred to as the Early Formative (also known as the Preclassic). The demise of San Lorenzo and the rise of La Venta and Tres Zapotes coincide with the Middle Formative period, beginning around 1000 BC. La Venta reached its apogee between 900 and 500 BC, declining as a major center by 400 BC (see Reilly, this volume). Tres Zapotes, however, continued to flourish, adopting a new system of governance and surging into the epi-Olmec period (see Pool, this volume).

Ongoing archaeological investigations continue to refine our understanding of the fluid chronological boundaries that define the Gulf Coast centers, and recent studies further elucidate the traits that constitute Olmec and the presence or influence of Olmec style outside the Gulf Coast. Elizabeth Benson, for example, has documented where Olmec-style objects have been found across Mesoamerica.[4] *Olmec: Colossal Masterworks of Ancient Mexico* has benefited significantly from these latest reports from the field and current interpretations as well as from the guidance of a number of esteemed archaeologists in Mexico.

The history of the term *Olmec* has been recounted in numerous publications, most recently in those by Beatriz de la Fuente and Christopher Pool.[5] The word itself derives from *Olman*, which the Nahuatl-speaking Aztecs of the fifteenth century used to refer to the rubber-producing area of Veracruz and Tabasco. The term influenced pioneers of Olmec studies such as Vaillant, who first recognized the distinctive features and unity of style of objects found in diverse collections. Covarrubias adopted the term despite his concerns about its accuracy.[6] In his paper at the 1942 roundtable convened to address Olmec style, Covarrubias concluded that Olmec culture was the first true civilization to appear in Mesoamerica and promoted the idea of Olmec as Mexico's mother culture.[7] He also discussed the problem with the name *Olmec*, preferring to describe the "people of Olman" in his presentation, a phrase that has come into current usage.[8] González Lauck masterfully summarized the current knowledge about the nature of Olmec terminology, influence, and presence in Mesoamerica.[9]

The systematic studies of Covarrubias, de la Fuente, and later scholars have demonstrated consistent patterns of representation that endure throughout later Mesoamerican civilizations (see Diehl, this volume). Such studies, enriched by archaeological research that began in the 1930s and continues to the present day, have illuminated the nuanced character of the art and architecture of individual centers that fall under the Olmec rubric (see Cyphers, Reilly, and Pool, this volume). As David Grove points out in his essay in this catalogue, Olmec as an art style was neither monolithic nor static but rather subject to chronological and regional variations as demonstrated in the archaeological record.

The lack of a fully developed writing system in the Gulf Coast heartland centers hampered initial efforts to interpret Olmec style. Lyle Campbell and Terrence Kaufman first proposed that the peoples of the Gulf Coast spoke a language in the Mije-Zoque family, and they suggested that a number of words from this language served as the ancestral forms for the words for culturally significant aspects of descendant Mesoamerican civilizations.[10] Recent studies corroborate that the language of the peoples of the heartland were part of the Mije-Zoque family.[11]

The objects on view in *Olmec: Colossal Masterworks of Ancient Mexico* were found through both serendipitous and systematic archaeological investigations. The exhibition opens with objects that came to light in the nineteenth century, including a colossal portrait head from the same site as the first one to be recovered from the Hacienda de Hueyapan in the mid-nineteenth century, as well as two signature small-scale jadeite objects that influenced the initial descriptions of the origin myths of Gulf Coast peoples as descendents of human-jaguar coupling.

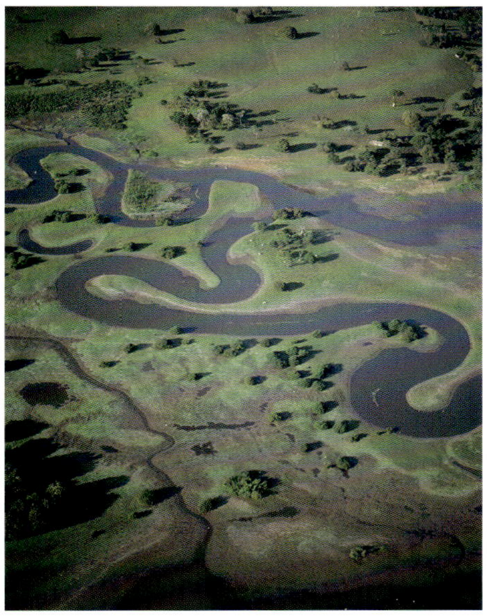

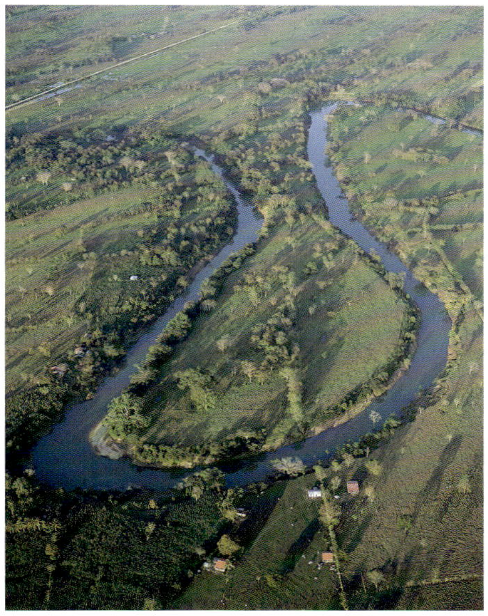

The second section focuses on the environment of the heartland, featuring objects that depict the flora and fauna essential to Gulf Coast inhabitants. The waterways that surrounded Olmec centers **(FIGS. 3–4)** were rich in the fish, turtles, caimans, manatees, and other aquatic creatures that provided a basic protein source for ancient populations. The river levees were also lush farmlands that received fertility-restoring silt deposits after annual flooding; maize eventually became a sustaining crop, and farmers comprised the majority of the population. Community leaders oversaw hydraulic systems and long-distance exchange networks; their management of such important economic responsibilities contributed to the emergence of a social elite, manifested in monumental art and architecture. Artists played an increasingly important role, because they created the objects that signified elite power and authority in sacred and secular matters.

The third section of the exhibition focuses on key objects, including monumental sculptures, that were recovered from the major centers of San Lorenzo Tenochtitlán, La Venta, and Tres Zapotes, and from the smaller centers that were part of the regional hierarchy of settlements. Cyphers (this volume) describes the importance of the location of San Lorenzo, which was established on an island surrounded by rivers and floodplains. The management of these waterways and the seasonal inundations of rain, and the development of San Lorenzo into a major center

FIGS. 3–4
Riverine landscapes in Mexico, 2004

characterized by "social zoning," in which elite residences occupied the upper terraces of the landscaped island, marked the emergence of a ruling class. To date, ten of the seventeen known colossal heads derive from San Lorenzo, each distinguished by scale, expression, and personal adornment. They constitute the first royal portraits of ancient Mexico.

The sculpture of La Venta reveals the development of narrative in public monuments, as rulers depict themselves as the central focus of ancestral sanctions, and their regalia signal that they are the embodiment of sacred and secular authority. Later Tres Zapotes sculptures show larger connections with the Mesoamerican world, for example, in Stela C, a dated monument that precedes any dated Maya monument, and in the complex imagery of Monument C, which links it to Izapa on Mexico's south coast.

Caches comprising axes (or celts) laid out in symbolically significant patterns have also been discovered at La Venta and other contemporary sites. Until 1000 BC, these axes, while beautifully shaped, were generally undecorated. At La Venta, a number of celts were found with incised imagery describing the importance of maize to the local populace. The exhibition presents a selection of greenstone objects adorned with these motifs that signaled royal authority.

The extraordinary discoveries of the shrines at El Manatí and La Merced, which came to light in 1988 and 1994, respectively, and have been carefully documented by Ponciano Ortíz Ceballos and Ma. del Carmen Rodríguez M., revealed an important dimension of Olmec religious ideology[12] focused on the intersection of landscape and ritual during the Early Formative period. The exhibition features a selection of the abundant deposits found at these two sites, including plain stone axes, wooden busts, rubber balls, and other ritually significant objects **(SEE FIG. 5)**.

Numerous populations contemporaneous with the Gulf Coast centers inhabited the diverse Mesoamerican landscape. These peoples shared in widespread exchange networks that disseminated both ideological concepts and the material goods that expressed the notions of elite prerogative. The fourth section of the exhibition concerns the regional centers in the Valley of Mexico, Guerrero, Morelos, and coastal Chiapas, and how spheres of interaction fostered commonalities in the development of social hierarchies, the use of a specific symbolic repertoire, and, most importantly, its local and regional expression.

The exhibition's fifth section presents the legacy of the Olmec as the source of symbols that legitimated elite authority. As Michael Coe noted, "We will then see how the Olmec pattern was transmitted to become the common legacy of all the native peoples of Mesoamerica."[13] Throughout the span of Mesoamerican history, various peoples adopted the symbolic references that defined their social and political systems and made them their own, while acknowledging ancestral Olmec forms. The exhibition features several of these heirloom objects that refer to Olmec sources; it concludes with objects that allude to the development of hieroglyphic writing in late Olmec times.

This exhibition and its publication mark a stage in ongoing research into the nature and extent of the civilization credited to the people of Olman, who provided the template for Mesoamerican civilizations over the course of three thousand years, and whose cosmology, rooted in the ancient landscape, continues to resonate with contemporary traditionalist communities in Mexico.

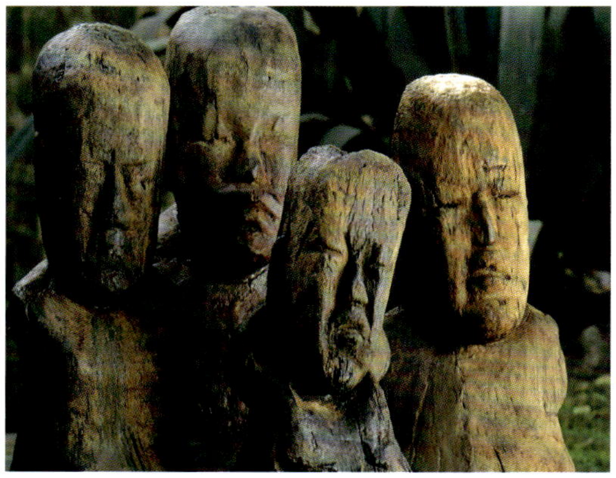

FIG. 5
Four of the eighteen wooden busts from El Manatí (see pl. 34), 1991

NOTES

1 Heizer 1966.

2 Pohorilenko 2008; Ladrón de Guevara, this volume.

3 Drucker, Heizer, and Squier 1959.

4 See for example, the essays by Paillés Hernández, Paradis, and others in Uriarte and González Lauck 2008; Benson 2008: 265.

5 de la Fuente 2008: 28–31; Pool 2007; see also Ladrón de Guevara, this volume.

6 Vaillant 1932; Covarrubias 1946b, 1957.

7 Coe 1968a: 148.

8 Covarrubias 1946b: 80; see, for example, Diehl 2004 and Pool 2007.

9 González Lauck 2008.

10 Campbell and Kaufman 1976.

11 Lacadena 2008; Wichmann, Beliaev, and Davletshin 2008.

12 Ortíz Ceballos, Rodríguez M., and Delgado C. 1997; Rodríguez M. and Ortíz Ceballos 2000.

13 Coe 1968a: 7.

OLMEC ART: ESSENCE, PRESENCE, INFLUENCE, AND TRANSCENDENCE

Sara Ladrón de Guevara

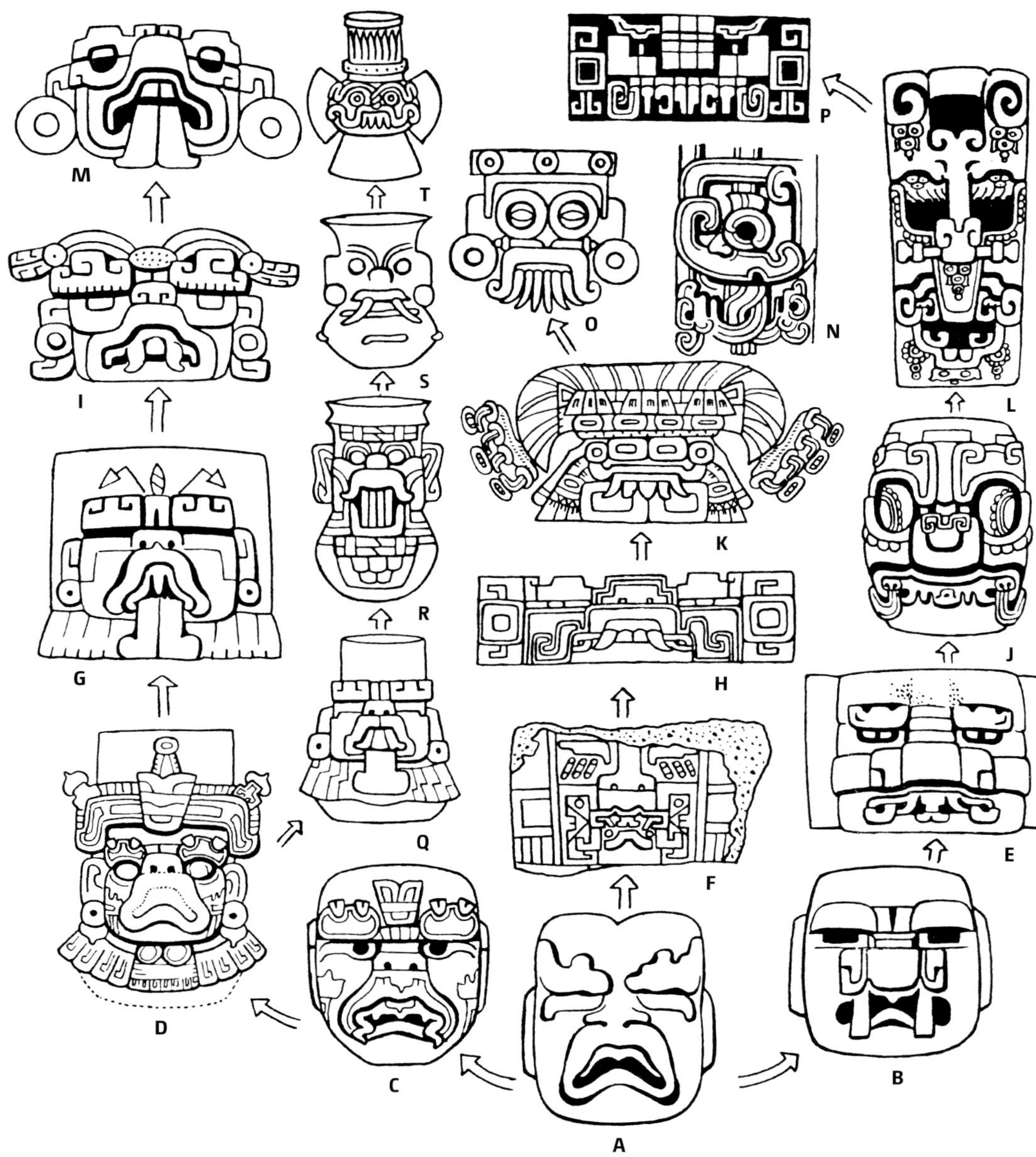

Art historians have probably been more successful in defining *Olmec* as a style than archaeologists have been in discussing it as a culture with aspects of a civilization. After all, the term *Olmec* has been best known and recognized primarily as a particular style of carving stone into magnificent sculptures. Indeed, Olmec works stand out in the three millennia of pre-Hispanic Mesoamerican art history for their superb aesthetic and technical quality.

The enormous temporal distance, three millennia, that separates us from the Olmec yields less information about this group than other, later cultures. The Aztecs and Maya were described by chroniclers in European languages; by contrast, all that remains of their ancient predecessors, the Olmec, are material vestiges of a once-vast culture. To a large extent, Olmec thought has been revealed solely through graphic, iconographic, and sculptural evidence. Olmec works display coherence with mythical discourses that are also Mesoamerican but are much later in date and therefore better known.

Certain art historians have made equal or even greater contributions than archaeologists to the knowledge and comprehension of this fascinating civilization. Here we must acknowledge the groundbreaking work of Miguel Covarrubias and the more recent, meticulous analyses of Beatriz de la Fuente.[1] Such studies, taking an aesthetic, stylistic, or iconographic point of view, have made it possible to recognize that some of the basic premises of Olmec sculpture have spread through space and transcended time. These include the focus on the human figure, the use of monumentality, the conjoining of human and animal elements in mythical beings, the representation of hierophanies—physical manifestations of the sacred—on thrones and stelae, and the symbolic association of power and the sacred. The same themes were taken up to a considerable extent throughout the development of pre-Hispanic Mesoamerica.

FIG. 6
Miguel Covarrubias's 1957 chart demonstrating Olmec influence on the evolution of the jaguar mask into rain gods

The Olmec chose to work stone of the greatest hardness: basalt[2] and andesite for large monoliths, and jade and serpentine for small pieces. The hardness of these materials has contributed to the survival of these magnificent sculptures, but it required considerable skill to carve them. The Olmec were clearly an ingenious people, able to master a technology and natural elements in their environment to transport enormous blocks of stone (up to 20 tons, or 18.1 metric tons, as in the case of the colossal head from Cobata, today in the park at Santiago Tuxtla) over great distances. They were also able to sculpt monuments without the use of metal implements, which were then unknown. Hard stones, abrasives, and technical skill were sufficient for the creation of the finest sculpture. They must have also worked more ephemeral materials, such as wood, leather, textiles, bone, and shell, that have been lost through the centuries. The fortunate exception to chemical and climatic conditions is the discovery at El Manatí of wood, textile, rope, and rubber artifacts, which grant us a mere glimpse at what must have been a thriving industry.[3]

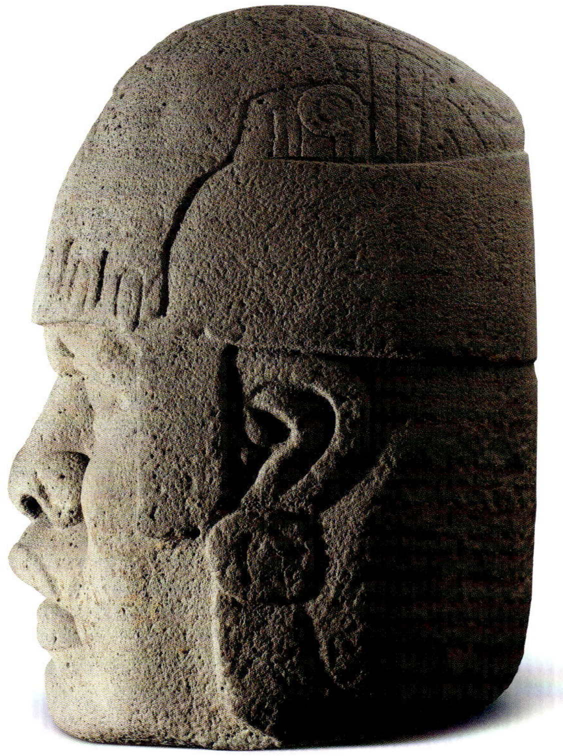

The four characteristic types of monumental Olmec sculpture are colossal heads, thrones, stelae, and full-length figures. The latter are subdivided into human beings, animals, animal-human hybrids, and fantastic creatures. The most recurrent motifs in Olmec sculpture and iconography are human figures, jaguars, and jaguar-men. Other animals are also represented, such as serpents and birds, but jaguars are of particular importance. Some scholars have proposed the Olmec had a totemic cult to these animals and have inferred the existence of myths involving jaguars in their religion. Given the absence of written documents, these theories remain in the realm of hypothesis, but the magnitude and incidence of representations of jaguars speak eloquently of the symbolic, mythical, and ritual importance of these creatures.

FIG. 7
COLOSSAL HEAD 5
Mexico, Veracruz, Municipality of Texistepec,
San Lorenzo Tenochtitlán, 1200–900 BC
Basalt
$73^{1}/_{4}$ x $56^{11}/_{16}$ x $49^{1}/_{4}$ in. (186 x 144 x 125 cm)
Museo de Antropología de Xalapa,
Universidad Veracruzana

The colossal heads, of which seventeen are known, were probably portraits of rulers **(SEE FIGS. 7, 11, 28, PLS. 1, 25–28)**. This type of monument, which has been found only in the Olmec heartland,[4] marks the beginning of the cult of the ruler and his figural representation, which would become fundamental in other pre-Hispanic contexts.[5] As a matter of fact, rulers are represented in large cities throughout Mesoamerica. Their feats are recorded and their lineage is claimed to be that of the gods. The power of the ruler is legitimated by placing him in a sacred and supernatural line of descent—a concept that seems to be the principal message of the massive Olmec monoliths.

The colossal heads found to date are all different from one another. Their specific features demonstrate that each is a true portrait. Unlike the Olmec ceramic figures known as "baby faces," which are generic representations of human beings, the colossal heads depict precise elements that would make it possible to recognize individuals. The particular shapes of the face and facial features, the depth of the wrinkles in the frown, and the proportions are all unique to each example. To reinforce these characteristics, the helmet on each head incorporates particular insignia that must have been associated with the name and identity of the wearer. These insignia are, for the most part, geometric shapes, but there are also some animal parts (from birds or jaguars); only one has human hands (Colossal Head 7 from San Lorenzo). Given that birds and jaguars are animals symbolically associated with the sky and underworld, respectively, perhaps these accoutrements represent the notion of *pars pro toto*, in which a part symbolically represents the whole, alluding to different levels as realms commanded by the ruler who wears them.

The thrones, which were mistakenly referred to as altars in the past, legitimate the ruler's lineage. Since the first discoveries, the tablelike shape of these monoliths seemed to correspond in function to an altar. But after a study by Grove (1973) showed how a mural in Oxtotitlan, Guerrero, represented a figure sitting on a shape similar to these monuments **(FIGS. 36–37)**, it has been widely accepted that they were seats from which Olmec rulers exercised authority. They are seats in a real and a metaphorical sense. Some are plain, while others display the face of a fantastic creature of enormous proportions. The most common throne shape displays a hollow or a niche from which emerges a figure, probably evoking the ancestor of the ruler who sat upon the throne **(SEE FIG. 19, PLS. 64–66)**. This cavelike opening also resembles the entrance to the underworld, "the mouth of the earth monster," which the Maya later represented on facades to emphasize the entrance to sacred precincts. The few individuals who had the right to enter these structures were either visually swallowed or spat out by the architectural monster.

Stelae—upright slabs usually bearing inscriptions—were commemorative monuments, and monumentality itself bore a connotation of prestige. Stelae were regarded as a necessary feature in later traditions, such as those of the epi-Olmec at Cerro de las Mesas and La Mojarra, and particularly in the architecture of the Maya. Olmec stelae display figures of nobility. In later cultures, these were accompanied by written inscriptions, usually dates recording specific moments in a people's history.

Olmec sculptures portraying full-length figures tend toward a more naturalistic style: soft, rounded shapes form the bodies of human beings, animals, or fantastic creatures with faces that combine characteristics of both. It is in these sculptures, above all, that the Olmec demonstrated their great mastery at carving hard, volcanic stone. They sculpted by using rock against rock, in addition to abrasives such as sand and silica, because they did not have metal technology. The sculptural qualities achieved in three-dimensional forms are unparalleled among all other Mesoamerican cultures. Outstanding and beautiful examples include Monument 1, "The Prince" from Cruz del Milagro **(PL. 85)**, and the daringly posed "Lord" from San Martín Pajapan **(FIG. 1)**, who kneels, on the verge of standing up, with a staff grasped firmly in his hand. In these sculptures, there is clearly a limited repertoire of poses that must have been codified. Figures often appear seated cross-legged, with clenched fists resting on knees or thighs. Curiously, representations of jaguars, such as those found at El Azuzul, adopt the same position as the sculptures of dignitaries. There are also figures carrying horizontal bars that might have signified power. The hands hold each side of the bar, one palm down and one palm up, as if about to raise it as a staff of authority.

It was precisely the discovery of four figures at El Azuzul (two jaguars and a pair of human twins) that transformed our understanding of Olmec sculpture, for the pieces were found arranged in a sculptural grouping **(FIG. 8, PLS. 60–62)**. This layout suggests a three-dimensional re-creation of myths through the deliberate arrangement of objects. Although we do not know the exact significance of the myth behind the El Azuzul grouping, we cannot overlook the fact that the Popol Vuh, the sacred book of the K'iché Maya, later recounted the adventures of a pair of hero twins confronting the gods of the underworld. These monuments were not to be exhibited on their own but within the coherence of a mythical account that was brought to life through stone. The tradition of representing myths in real space and time was preserved in Mesoamerican city planning. Thus, the Aztec myth of Huitzilopochtli was represented through the deliberate location of sculptural monuments in the Templo Mayor, the great temple in the heart of Mexico City, once the capital of Tenochtitlan.

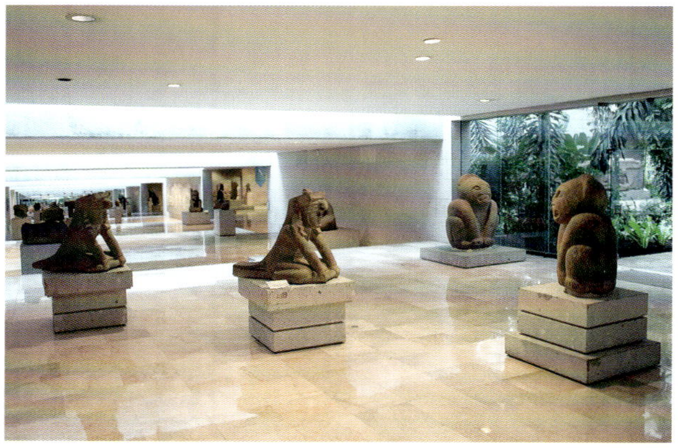

Also worthy of mention are small-scale stone objects, particularly celts, masks, and human figurines. Celts **(PLS. 88–93, 100)**—axes traditionally regarded as work tools—became sacred objects when they were used in offerings, buried as part of a sacred ritual. Their arrangement in specific aligned or radial groupings, as found at sites such as La Venta, El Manatí, and La Merced, attests to their character as a ritual symbol. Today, witnessing shamanic rituals in various indigenous societies, such as Popoluca and Nahua practices in the region of Los Tuxtlas and the Isthmus of Tehuantepec, or the Tzotziles and Tzeltales in the Chiapas highlands, allows us to observe the disposition of offerings. But the archaeological discovery of Olmec artifacts takes place in a context deprived of the paraphernalia of ceremony. We can only imagine the moment of their deposition, accompanied by the sound of prayers and chants, the scent of copal incense and flowers, and intense emotions of devotion and praise, with everyone in rapt attention around the sacred objects. Most of the axes found in offerings at sites such as El Manatí or La Merced were never used,[6] and only rare examples have been found displaying evidence of use. Very few have images of deities or other sacred symbols engraved on their surfaces to reinforce their symbolic value.

The masks from Arroyo Pesquero and Hueyapan de Ocampo are made of stone **(SEE PLS. 77–78)**. There are two types: those that correspond to human scale, and miniatures. The life-size masks must also have been used in ceremonies, for they are equipped with a hollow on the inner surface that could accommodate a human face; the majority are perforated so it is possible to see through the eyeholes and to breathe through the nose. Those that were not perforated were perhaps made as funerary masks. All of the masks represent naturalistic human faces. Some are smiling, while others display engravings of signs reiterated from Olmec iconography, which belongs to the realm of the sacred and divine. Thus, during any ritual in which the masks might have been used, they conferred upon the wearer a mystical alter-ego status, as well as a serenity arising from the immobility of the stone.

Although the Olmec tradition of carved figurines continued throughout the development of Mesoamerica, they were generally modeled in clay rather than sculpted in greenstone as the Olmec had done. Here again, we face a limited corpus in the Olmec repertoire of postures. Often, the figures are standing and display marked cranial deformation. The discovery

FIG. 8
Installation view of El Azuzul Monuments 7–10
at the Museo de Antropología de Xalapa,
Universidad Veracruzana, 2009

of Offering 4 **(FIG. 25, PL. 72)** from La Venta, which represents a group of figurines and miniature stelae arranged in what appears to be a ritual, also allows us to recognize that specific spatial arrangements of figural groups were surely intended to preserve a rite or a myth for posterity.

Alongside the monumental sculptures and magnificent miniatures, there are also medium-size sculptures in greenstone. In this category, it is worth highlighting Las Limas Monument 1 **(FIG. 9)** and "El Bebé" of La Merced **(PLS. 58–59)**. The Las Limas monument is the only sculpture found to date that shows two figures carved together from a single block of semiprecious stone. In addition to the impressive quality of the carving, the main figure displays incised details on his face, shoulders, and legs that express a specific iconographic discourse. The designs on his face have been associated with maize as a sacred element, while the faces on his extremities have been identified with the four principal deities in the Olmec pantheon. Both figures surely illustrate a myth concerning a newborn baby with the face of a jaguar. Characteristics of this composite face may be found on adult human figures in monumental sculptures, reiterating the existence of a myth now lost. These figures can only have been cult objects. The size and weight of these works, and even the manner in which they were carved, make them transportable, calling to mind the ceremonial movement of icons in religious processions today. This could explain the discovery of a sculpture of such high quality at the relatively low-ranking Preclassic site of Las Limas.

As noted above, if it were not for the survival of the artifacts themselves, the ideas and concepts they evoke would never have come down to us, and we would have been unable to form a unity that helps us to define the cultural boundaries of what is today known as Mesoamerica.[7] However, pieces that are clearly affiliated with Olmec culture, from sites distant in time and space, continue to occupy a position of sacred symbolic significance.

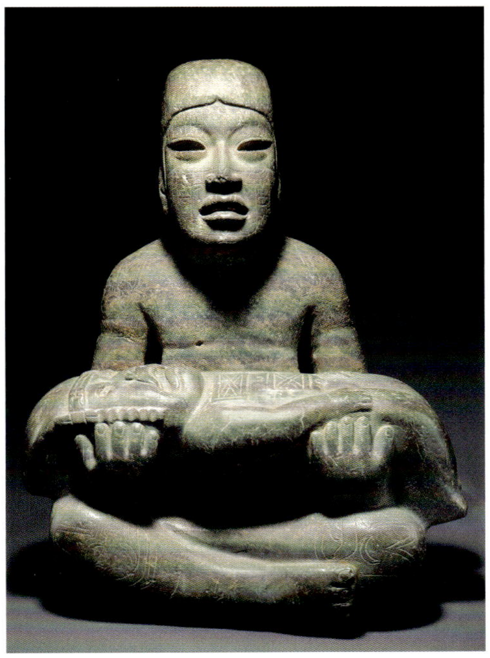

FIG. 9
MONUMENT 1 ("EL SEÑOR DE LAS LIMAS")
Mexico, Veracruz, Jesús Carranz, Las Limas,
1000–400 BC
Greenstone
21 5/8 x 16 9/16 in. (55 x 41 cm)
Museo de Antropología de Xalapa,
Universidad Veracruzana

Although the Olmec heartland is bordered by the modern-day states of Veracruz and Tabasco, the distribution of artifacts identified as Olmec extends from the Isthmus of Tehuantepec to Guatemala and El Salvador. Expressions of the Olmec style have also been recognized in Central Mexico and on the Pacific Coast, particularly in what is today the state of Guerrero.

It should be acknowledged, however, that the dissemination of objects regarded as Olmec is far from uniform. Some traits were adapted in different ways from one territory to another. For example, in Guerrero, the Olmec influence is visible in reliefs and mural paintings; in the central valley of Mexico, it is evident in ceramics, particularly vessels from Las Bocas, Puebla, and figurines from the sites of Tlatilco and Tlapacoya; and in Morelos, in the reliefs at Chalcatzingo. More recently, the discovery at Zazacatla of monolithic sculptures has confirmed the acceptance not only of these sculptural forms in the Olmec style outside the Olmec heartland but also and above all the appropriation of narratives, such as the man-jaguar legend, and the tradition of arranging sculptural monuments according to specific myths.

An interesting trajectory of Olmec influence arose from Central America (Guatemala, El Salvador, Costa Rica, and Honduras) and extended northward through Chiapas and Oaxaca. It was undoubtedly along this route that the Olmec transported one of their most important and rare commodities, jade, which has been found in the Río Motagua Valley in Guatemala and was the raw material for small- to medium-size statuary. Olmec influence is suggested by finds at a number of sites contemporary with the development of Olmec culture during the Middle Preclassic period (900–400 BC). Objects distinguished by a stylistic unity, or at least a stylistic familiarity, with Olmec material culture have been found at sites such as El Baúl, Tak'alik Ab'aj, and San Bartolo in Guatemala as well as at Río Tinto in Honduras.

The enormous spatial distribution of the Olmec style—which reaches from the state of Colima in western Mexico to Costa Rica in Central America—is surprising. What is even more amazing is that the symbolic value of the style has endured for centuries. An Olmec-style mask **(PL. 140)**, for example, was discovered in an offering at the Aztec Templo Mayor.[8] The inclusion of this object in an offering twenty-five hundred years after it was created, without its having undergone any modifications, is eloquent testimony to the care that must have been given to its preservation over three millennia. This is true even though it is undetermined whether the mask was an heirloom treasured for generations, or whether its inclusion was the result of a fortuitous find made by the Aztecs at some site of Olmec affiliation.

In the case of other artifacts, scholars have noted the modification, alteration, or transformation of the original Olmec forms. Evidence of the reworking of such pieces suggests that the message transmitted was also undoubtedly transformed. Significantly, numerous objects produced by the Olmec in greenstone and other substances have been found in the Maya area. Often they show traces of reuse by the Maya, who were known to engrave glyphic inscriptions on these heirloom pieces. Examples include the pendant from San Gervasio, Quintana Roo **(PL. 142)**; the plaque from Isla Piedras in Campeche; and the winged plaque in the collection at Dumbarton Oaks **(PLS. 149–150)**.

When murals were found at the site of San Bartolo in the Petén region of Guatemala, one figure in particular was conspicuous among the finely drawn figures in the Mayan style.[9] This figure is apparently a creator god associated with corn, and its face is rendered in the purest Olmec style with a jaguar-man mouth; it is shown receiving offerings from several individuals. Naturally, this high esteem for ancestral relics did not occur only outside the Olmec heartland; it also occurred at Olmec settlements. For example, the Tuxtla statuette from the Smithsonian Institution collection seems to be an artifact from the Olmec period, but its inscription pertains to the epi-Olmec tradition from the beginning of our era. It is not unusual to find evidence of later occupation at these sites—especially during the Classic period (AD 250–900)—even at San Lorenzo,

Tres Zapotes, and Laguna de los Cerros, among others. This has given rise to scholarly confusion, and in some cases architectural patterns have been erroneously dated; for example, mounds corresponding to Classic period patterns were dated according to ceramic materials from Olmec occupation.

Some Olmec sculptures found at these sites had also been reused, perhaps because of the scarcity of raw materials, or the need to change symbols to adjust to new political and religious circumstances, or both. Stelae were recarved and transformed, and sculpture was recycled even in Olmec times. It is now widely accepted that some thrones were remade as colossal heads. The efforts of true sculptural workshops have been identified particularly at San Lorenzo, where such tasks included recarving.[10] But we also now recognize that in later times, some Olmec sculptures were reworked, which changed the original message of the piece. A noteworthy example is the large mask from Medias Aguas (**FIG. 10**), a monumental sculpture that seems to represent a skull. Careful observation of the piece, however, suggests that the block was once a small throne showing a figure emerging from a cave—the typical form for such monuments. The mask has atypical proportions in the face, where it was necessary to adjust the carving to the shape of the original sculpture.

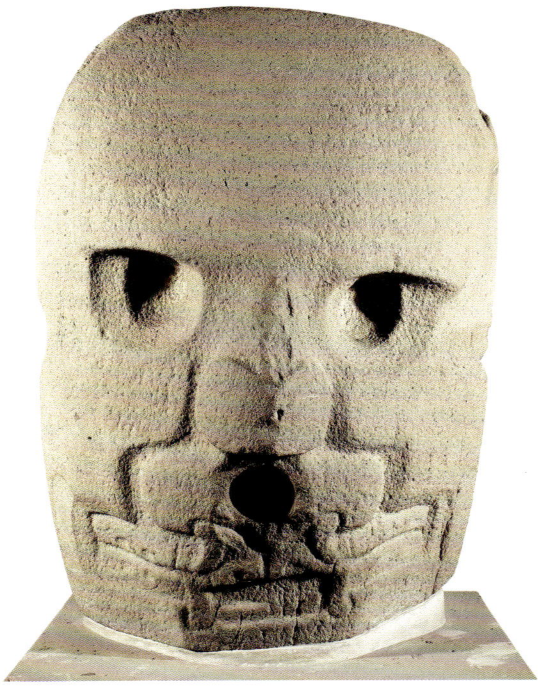

It is evident that the principal conceptual elements of the Mesoamerican worldview can be found in the corpus of Olmec sculpture. The placement of monuments—the colossal heads at San Lorenzo arranged along two north-south axes, for example, or those of La Venta in an east-west alignment—as well as some inscriptions on celts and tablets, reveal a cosmic order with four directions and a center, just as the Mesoamerican cosmos has been represented in more recent times.

The idea of superimposed levels is plausible given the thematic insistence of the Olmec on beings regarded as earthly, such as jaguars and

FIG. 10
LARGE MASK (RECARVED MONUMENT)
Mexico, Veracruz, Municipality of Sayula, Medias Aguas, AD 800–1000
Basalt
$25\frac{3}{16}$ x $31\frac{1}{2}$ x $19\frac{11}{16}$ in. (64 x 80 x 50 cm)
Museo de Antropología de Xalapa, Universidad Veracruzana

serpents, and those regarded as celestial, such as birds. The possibility of mobility between levels is suggested by San Lorenzo Monument 107 **(FIG. 14)**, which shows a man wearing a bird helmet descending in front of a jaguar, which in turn seems to be scaling the column formed by the human figure.

The deities of the Postclassic period (AD 900–1500) seem to have a mythical and visual origin in Olmec discourse, as Covarrubias demonstrated in his well-known diagram showing how the Olmec jaguar might have developed into the Aztec rain god Tlaloc **(FIG. 6)**. Indigenous traditions throughout Mesoamerica today still retain elements and symbols born in the heart of Olmec civilization more than three millennia ago. The dance of the jaguar continues to be celebrated at patron feast days in many corners of Mexico (it is particularly well known in lands formerly occupied by the Olmec in southern Veracruz, Tabasco, and Guerrero). Even though the jaguar skins have been replaced by commercial printed textiles, the spots still remind us that once upon a time, the night sky and its stars were imagined as the cosmic dance on the jaguar's pelt.

NOTES

1 In the 1940s and 1950s, the Mexican artist and intellectual Miguel Covarrubias participated in defining the Olmec style. Using illustrated charts—one, for example, showed how the image of the rain god Tlaloc might have derived from an Olmec representation of a jaguar (fig. 6)—he managed to elucidate aesthetic paths that were perhaps more convincing than the judicious writings of archaeologists. At the 1942 Tuxtla Gutiérrez roundtable, Covarrubias, Alfonso Caso, and Wigberto Jiménez Moreno jointly proposed that the Olmec be considered the "mother culture" as a result of its antiquity and impact on later Mesoamerican cultures, such as that of the Maya, Teotihuacanos, or the Zapotecs. Their proposal was based on stylistic characteristics rather than absolute dating techniques (Covarrubias 1942; Caso 1942; Jiménez Moreno 1942). From the 1960s to the end of her life, Beatriz de la Fuente systematized the study of Olmec monumental sculpture, cataloguing works and describing the fundamental principles of their style (de la Fuente 1977a).

2 The Mohs scale is used to measure the hardness of minerals, not rocks such as basalt. However, the minerals that form basalt have a hardness ranging from 6 to 6.5 on the Mohs scale, and it is possible to attribute to basalt a hardness of 6 on the Mohs scale.

3 Ortíz Ceballos, Rodríguez M., and Delgado C. 1997.

4 Olmec territory, known as the "heartland or metropolitan zone" (Bernal 1968), comprises the modern-day southern part of the state of Veracruz and the northwestern sector of the state of Tabasco, covering an area estimated to be more than 11,583 square miles (30,000 square kilometers).

5 The concept underlying the colossal heads is in that sense assimilated throughout Mesoamerica. Teotihuacan is the exception to the rule. There, the absence of this type of representation is so strange when compared to the rest of Mesoamerica that scholars have proposed different forms of collective government in which there was no single, dominant leader.

6 Pierre Masson, personal communication.

7 In 1943, Kirchhoff (1960) defined Mesoamerica as a cultural super-area based on elements shared in the territory that occupied more than half of modern-day Mexico and part of Central America as far south as Nicaragua. The use of the term has continued, albeit based on theoretical positions different from those that initially gave rise to it. López Austin (1998: 29) proposed that the unity of this territory ranging from latitude 25 degrees to latitude 10 degrees north is derived from the shared historical discourse of the groups who settled there.

8 This piece was found in Offering 20 at Templo Mayor, on the west side (that is, the back part of Templo Mayor), at the union of the two buildings that compose it (one dedicated to Tlaloc and the other to Huitzilopochtli) (Matos Moctezuma 2003: 80).

9 The murals from San Bartolo were reported in 2001 by William Saturno (Taube and Saturno 2008).

10 Cyphers 1994a.

SAN LORENZO

Ann Cyphers

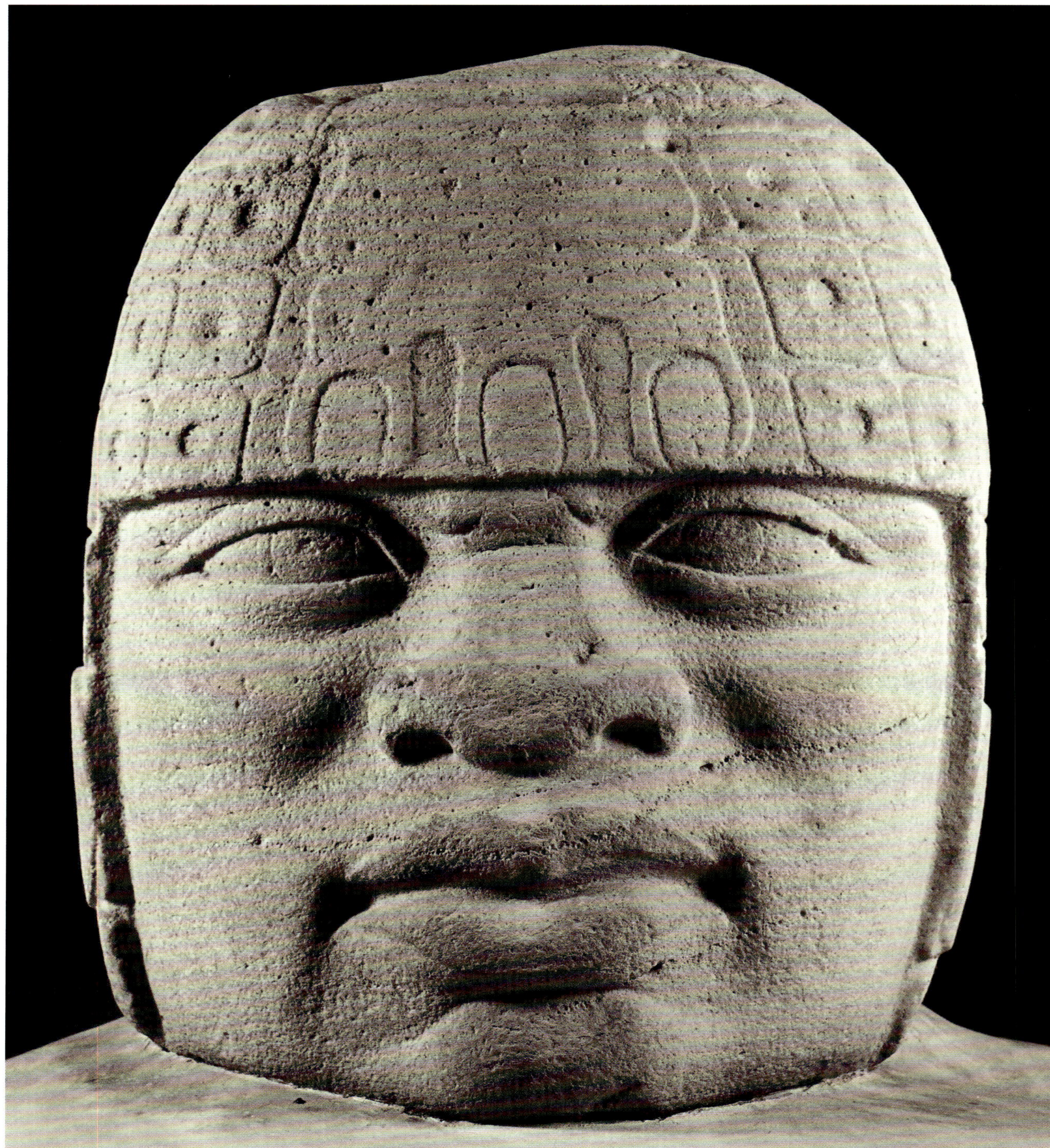

Shrouded in a thick veil of multicolored clays, the great plateau at San Lorenzo conceals the origins of early Olmec grandeur within a colossal, constructed earthen monument that rises 164 feet (50 meters) above the surrounding wetlands. Deeply incised by more than three millennia of weathering and erosion,[1] the plateau was the heart of the Olmec world for six centuries, and it cloaks the material traces of the people whose traditional beliefs, values, and lifeways underwrote its planning, creation, and embellishment. Several short- and long-term research projects[2] conducted since 1945 at the oldest Olmec capital have been able to unravel details of its Early Preclassic genesis, growth, and development.

The Olmec

Who were these early Olmec, and where did they come from? The true name of this preliterate culture born in Mexico's southern Gulf Coast has not endured in oral traditions and historic memory but is lost in time. For many decades, their borrowed name, *Olmec*, meaning "people of the rubber country," didn't seem appropriate until the discovery of rubber balls at the El Manatí site (SEE PL. 33) showed that the Olmec not only were aware of but also produced this exceptional substance from the sap of the *Castilla elastica* tree.[3] There is no scientific proof that the Olmec civilization originated from migrations of peoples from far-flung places in Asia or Africa, or from other areas in Mesoamerica. Rather, it was the Archaic period milieu of the northern Isthmus of Tehuantepec that gave birth to the Olmec.[4] As a result, their origins and accomplishments cannot be credited to others.

The Olmec's Gulf Coast heartland is easily distinguished from neighboring areas by the magnificent stone sculptures that mark both their political territory and a characteristic way of life. The heartland inhabitants also had a distinctive

FIG. 11
MONUMENT 89 (COLOSSAL HEAD)
Mexico, Veracruz, Municipality of Texistepec,
San Lorenzo Tenochtitlán, 1400–1000 BC
Basalt
70⁷⁄₈ x 36¼ x 65⅓ in. (180 x 92 x 143 cm)
Museo Comunitario de Tenochtitlán,
Municipality of Texistepec, Veracruz

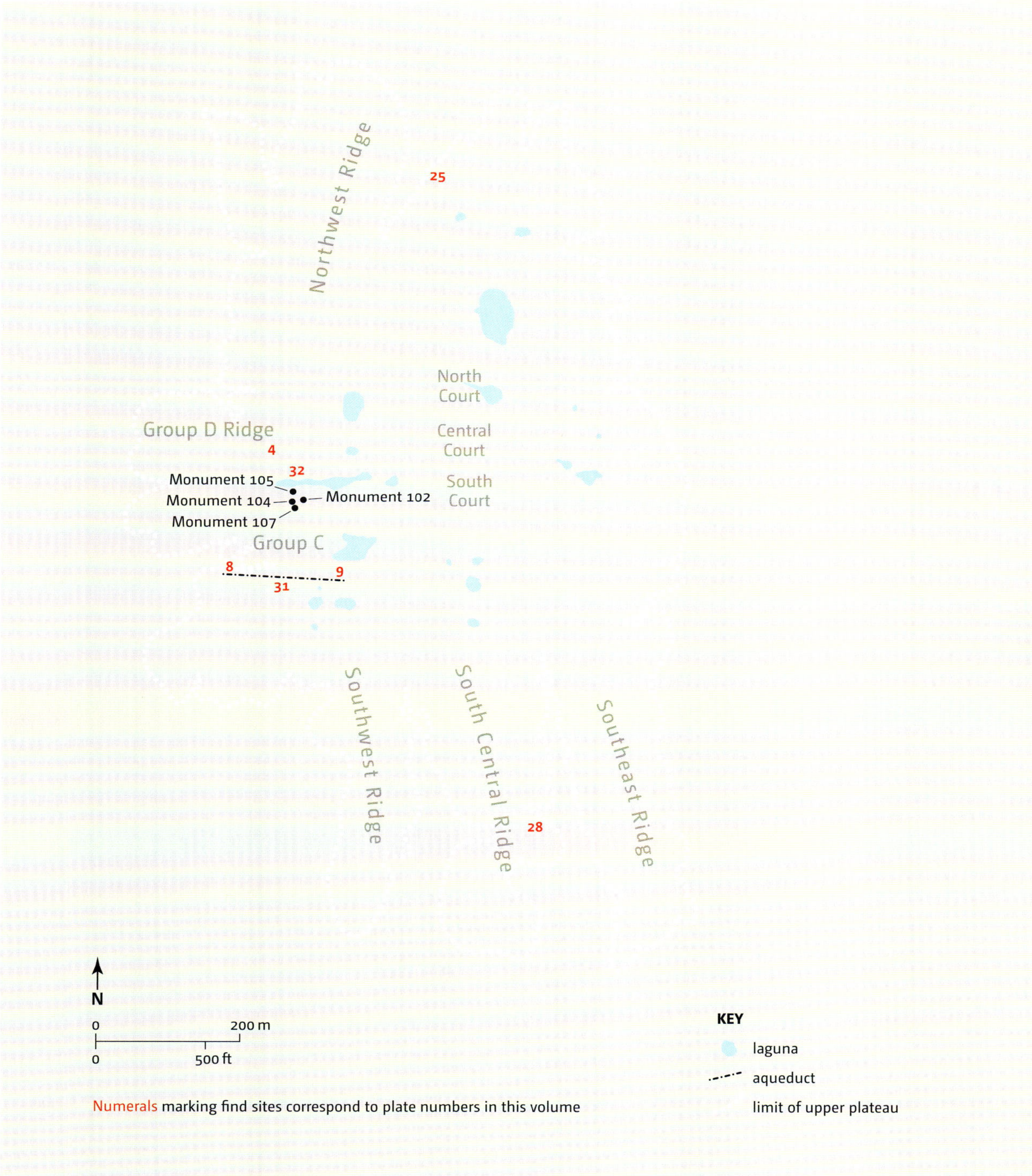

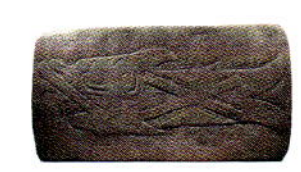

PLATE 4

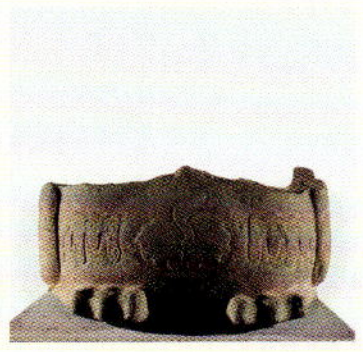

PLATE 8

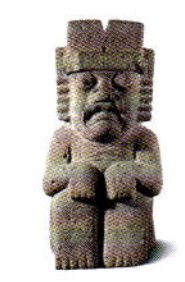

PLATE 9

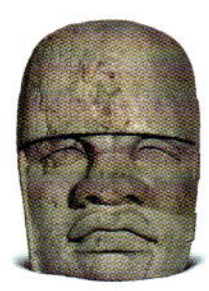

PLATE 25

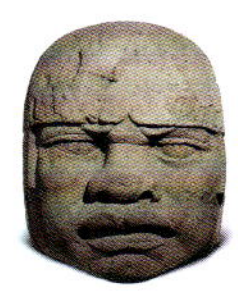

PLATE 28

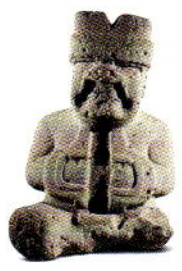

PLATE 31

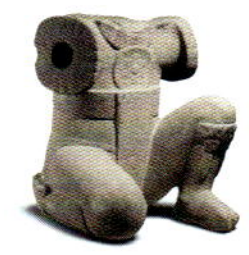

PLATE 32

physical appearance. The San Lorenzo Olmec portrayed themselves in clay and stone with a specific and intentional craniofacial deformation that created a pear-shaped head, downturned mouth, and slit eyes. The elite of the later Olmec capital of La Venta (see Reilly, this volume) continued the tradition of stone portrayals, although they adopted a new fashion in head-shaping characterized by a slanted forehead and a flattened back, as seen in clay figurines.[5]

San Lorenzo

Sometime around 1800 BC, the first settlers arrived at San Lorenzo, which is located on a large island set in the midst of branching rivers and broad, swampy floodplains.[6] These pioneers founded their village on the highest defendable ground, then covered in virgin jungle and surrounded by wetlands teeming with wildlife. In their quest for food, they moved between the jungle and the wetlands to hunt, gather, fish, and cultivate. Root crops were an early mainstay, and maize gradually increased in dietary importance during the apogee period.[7] After discovering that aquatic, protein-rich foods were exceptionally abundant in one portion of the wetlands, they built small earthen mounds in the swampy expanse to use as camps during fish, turtle, and shrimp harvesttimes.[8] These refuges were like little islands, or miniature hills surrounded by water, and represent some of the first construction efforts of the early Olmec. Their construction not only transformed the natural wetland landscape into a cultural world but also established the founder groups' claims to resources. These groups were able to extract and preserve aquatic resources and thus manage the needs of a growing community, particularly during the predictable annual drought period, a time of famine. The artificial mounds became the point of departure for setting in motion and maintaining asymmetrical rights to a productive base, with social and political advantages accruing to the founder groups.

Meanwhile, the inhabitants of San Lorenzo began giving shape to the natural hill by leveling the terrain and filling in the ravines to create a plateau. Between 1800 and 1400 BC, they moved 2.2 million tons (2 million metric tons) of earth[9] as part of the initial step in their plan to erect the first capital of the Olmec world, a sacred mountain created in homage to their principal deity, the cosmic monster. They also built a low, stepped earthen platform and a sunken patio on San Lorenzo's plateau,[10] as well as the open-air theater at the base of the nearby Cerro Manatí, which likely served as the first private and public ritual spaces for the San Lorenzo elite and other social groups. In daily life, for grinding and hammering, they used stone vessels and tools that were made of imported basalt from the Tuxtla Mountains. The origins of basic Olmec sculptural techniques undoubtedly stem from the early technologies used to make these utilitarian objects.

San Lorenzo achieved its maximum splendor between 1400 and 1000 BC. Its size increased dramatically to more than 1,700 acres (700 hectares), with a mean population of seventy-five hundred.[11] The 222-acre (90-hectare) great plateau was the gemstone of this setting. The construction of multiple levels of habitation terraces, which involved the erection of retaining walls and the addition of more earthen fill, increased its size sevenfold. Its final size, calculated at 247 million cubic feet, equivalent to 9.4 million tons of earth (7 million cubic meters or 8.5 million metric tons), is unequaled in the Early Preclassic and in fact rivals many later works. It has seven times the volume of the magnificent Pyramid of the Sun in Teotihuacan. Seen from afar, the great plateau towering above the waterlogged countryside and sluggish rivers must have commanded awe and admiration.[12]

The plateau was simultaneously an artificial hill and a monumental symbol of the cosmic monster, which is explicitly portrayed in a bas-relief block from San Lorenzo **(FIG. 12)**. In artistic representations, the Olmec rulers consecrated their founding ancestors by placing them within the jaws of this deity, a symbol of the entrance to the watery underworld, and thus legitimated their right to rule.[13] As in other Mesoamerican cosmologies, the ancestral monster floating on the primeval waters is considered the source and quintessence of the universe. Related to it are ancient notions of hills, which figure prominently in the better-known cosmologies. For these ancient peoples, there was not a clear separation between the natural and the constructed landscape, and, consequently, natural features were integrated in their worldview. The concepts of the "hill surrounded by water" and the "sacred mountain" derive from this primordial monster. They embody diverse levels of the universe and are places inhabited by the gods and ancestors and the source of wealth and power.[14] The monster was the rulers' emblem and that of their capitals throughout Mesoamerican time. Among the Maya, the association of the *witz* monster and "mountains of water" illustrates the inseparability of cosmology and sociopolitical hierarchy in ancient thought, as does the *altepetl* among Nahua peoples.

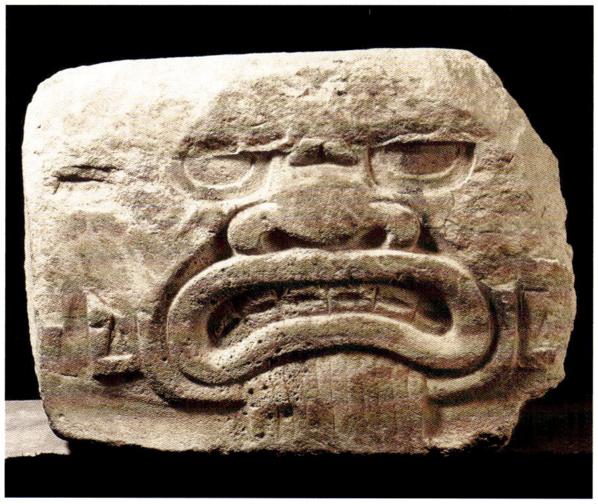

Life at San Lorenzo was highly organized. The capital shows a pattern of "social zoning" in which people built their homes in sectors that corresponded to their social status.[15] The rulers and elites used the heights and terraces of the great plateau for their residences and ceremonial and administrative buildings, while those of lesser status occupied the surrounding lower-altitude lands. Status differences contrast sharply between the inhabitants of the terraces and the periphery, the latter being the zone where the poorest residents lived. In effect, the settlement zoning shows status decreasing away from the center and by elevation, a phenomenon that replicates the cosmological concept of the sacred hill or mountain.

One of the most important examples of plateau architecture is a buried precinct known as Group E, which is located near the site's center. It is composed of four earthen platforms surrounding a sunken patio and is associated with important rulership icons such as a throne, a colossal head, and a standard bearer.[16] Rife with the symbolism of origin myths, water, fertility, and the underworld, it was the locus of early Olmec regimes, a place sanctified by a colossal portrait of a divine ancestral ruler.[17] There, each hereditary ruler sat on his throne, from which he made important social, economic, and political decisions and, in his capacity as an intermediary between the terrestrial and spiritual worlds, conducted private and public rituals at the symbolic threshold between the two.[18]

The San Lorenzo elites enjoyed a way of life unattained by their distant neighbors at this time, and their homes were at least five times larger than those at the San José Mogote site in Oaxaca.[19] Their domestic structures were not the modest one-room buildings found in Oaxaca but had several large rooms and sometimes an enclosed patio with subfloor drain. They were not built of simple wattle and daub but had thick, poured earthen walls, a sophisticated construction technique for the time. The walls and floors were vividly colored with red, orange, and yellow sand

FIG. 12
MONUMENT 104 (EARTH MONSTER)
Mexico, Veracruz, Municipality of Texistepec,
San Lorenzo Tenochtitlán, 1400–1000 BC
Basalt
$33^{1}/_{2} \times 41^{3}/_{4} \times 17^{1}/_{3}$ in. (85 x 106 x 44 cm)
Museo Comunitario de Tenochtitlán,
Municipality of Texistepec, Veracruz

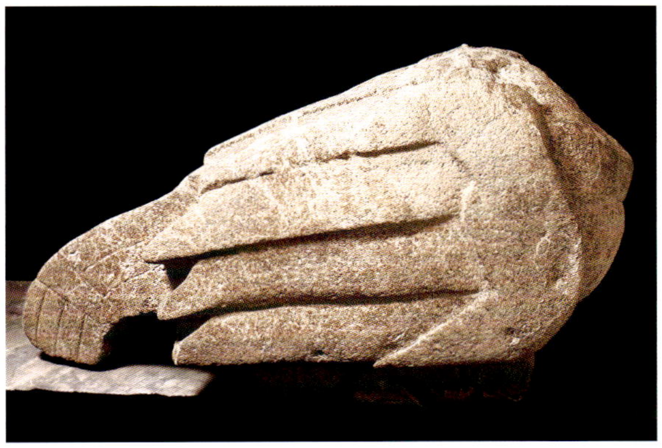

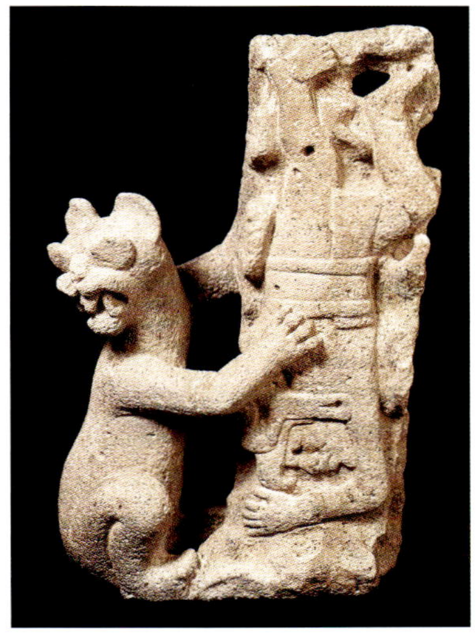

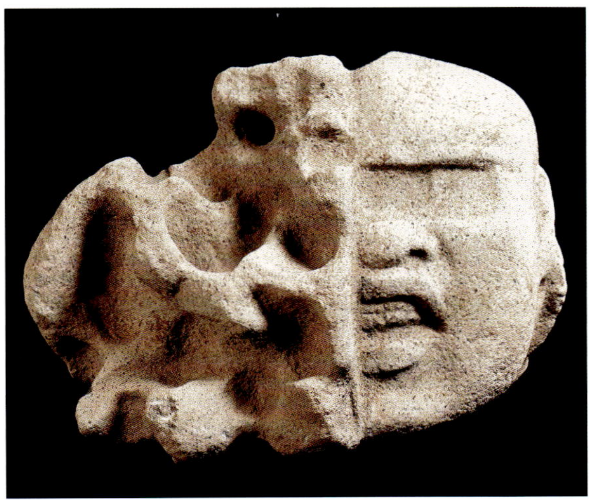

plaster. A sedimentary stone called bentonite was quarried nearby for use as the impermeable subfloor pavement of these house floors.[20]

The Red Palace, residence of an important elite family or perhaps a ruler, was built on the heights of the plateau. The home is noteworthy for its unusual size (about 21,500 square feet, or 2,000 square meters) and construction style, and its many rooms were used for diverse activities, some domestic, others ceremonial and productive.[21] The central room was a kind of inner sanctum probably used for private ceremonies such as ancestor veneration; it contains a tall basalt column, a low bench that runs along one wall, and a stone drain that winds its way beneath the blood-red floor. Another red-floored room was used for the storage of small- and medium-size sculptures that had been ceremonially mutilated by decapitation, dismemberment, and defacement, such as a beheaded bird, a composite piece showing a feline and a ballgame player, and a mutilated head **(FIGS. 13–15)**. Adjacent to this storeroom is the work area where sculptors under the patronage of the palace's owners reused and transformed sacred monuments into new objects.

FIG. 13
MONUMENT 102 (DECAPITATED BIRD)
Mexico, Veracruz, Municipality of Texistepec,
San Lorenzo Tenochtitlán, 1400–1000 BC
Basalt
36 5/8 x 70 7/8 x 39 3/8 in. (93 x 180 x 100 cm)
Museo Comunitario de Tenochtitlán,
Municipality of Texistepec, Veracruz

FIG. 14
MONUMENT 107 (COMPOSITE FELINE AND DESCENDING BALLPLAYER)
Mexico, Veracruz, Municipality of Texistepec,
San Lorenzo Tenochtitlán, 1400–1000 BC
Basalt
37 3/8 x 23 5/8 in. (95 x 60 cm)
Museo Comunitario de Tenochtitlán,
Municipality of Texistepec, Veracruz

FIG. 15
MONUMENT 105 (MUTILATED HEAD)
Mexico, Veracruz, Municipality of Texistepec,
San Lorenzo Tenochtitlán, 1400–1000 BC
Basalt
20 1/2 x 24 7/8 x 15 in. (52 x 63 x 38 cm)
Museo Comunitario de Tenochtitlán,
Municipality of Texistepec, Veracruz

The productive activities conducted at San Lorenzo also conform to a centric pattern. Elite pursuits on the top of the plateau include the recarving of large monuments to create colossal heads (**SEE FIG. 11, PLS. 25–28**).[22] Between 1100 and 1000 BC, several multiton sculptures, too large to be displayed in a residence, were recarved at select locations in the northern part of the plateau. Neither the reshaping of one large throne nor the final details of two colossal heads was ever finished. It is possible that the heads—the intended finished products of this recycling activity—were originally destined for display in a macro-scene composed of two lines of colossal ruler portraits that crowned the southern half of the plateau.[23] Was this unfinished epic scene a historical display of divine rulers or god-kings, or a commemoration of ancestral rulers who, upon their death, had turned into mythical ballplayers in the great cosmic game?

The terraces also reveal craft activities in association with less ostentatious residences. For example, one terrace workshop under elite patronage specialized in drilling and polishing imported materials. Excavations discovered greenstone polishing tools, drill bits, drilled and shaped greenstone artifacts, flakes and chunks, drilled basalt beads, and worked iron-ore ornaments, as well as one hundred and fifty thousand bearings made of a ferrous mineral called ilmenite.[24] The bearings had been used as part of a drilling apparatus and, when worn out, were stashed in underground pits rather than discarded. Why was this done? The Olmec prized ferrous minerals such as ilmenite and magnetite for a number of reasons. The physical and chemical properties of the minerals made them suitable for use as drilling and polishing tools. Also, when the minerals were polished, their brilliant shine made them a desirable material for symbolically charged and highly prestigious items such as mirrors and mosaics, which were used only by a privileged few.[25] Clearly, the worn-out materials from the workshop had to be carefully guarded, given their potential to be reworked into numerous prestige goods, the uncontrolled circulation of which in the society could undermine their meaning and value, and the social order.

The patronage of craft production by the San Lorenzo rulers extended as far as the Tuxtla Mountains. The site of Laguna de los Cerros was founded around 1300 BC as a permanent managerial post for the nearby Llano del Jícaro basalt quarry and workshop, located at the tip of the Cerro Cintepec basalt flow.[26] The Olmec did not use mining technology to extract stone from the thick, buried lava flow, but rather took advantage of large surface boulders for making sculpture pre-forms (unfinished sculptures) that were dispatched overland to the important patrons at San Lorenzo.

Trade in exotic items was not practiced exclusively by the elite. Many residents participated in regional and long-distance networks trading obsidian, cacao, basalt, rubber, iron-ore mirrors, mosaics, tools, quartz crystals, mica, greenstone, and bitumen.[27] Sadly, other sought-after but perishable tropical lowland products—such as brightly colored bird feathers, feline pelts, bone and shell items, wooden objects, flowers, fruits, spices, medicinal substances such as sulfur and plants, and live animals and birds—have left few traces in the archaeological record.

San Lorenzo in Wider Perspective

Throughout history, civilizations have arisen alongside major waterways, which are natural arteries of communication and transportation and barriers for defense. They were also vital to trade and commerce because they facilitated the rapid and low-cost transport of bulk foods, raw materials, and finished products. Key settlements were advantageously located near river crossings, confluences, islands, natural ports, and transshipment points. Networked systems of land and water transport have united neighbors and encouraged territorial integration; rivers have separated enemies and defined political territories, and ancient legends glorify or personify them. The Olmec, who inhabited the soggy coastal plains, were, accordingly, a culture of water. Their two major capitals—San Lorenzo and La Venta—arose on islands emerging from swampy terrains crisscrossed by waterways. The major rivers encircling the capitals were more than just a water supply—they also afforded natural defenses, concentrations of essential natural resources, and efficient communication and transportation. The San Lorenzo Olmec lived by water's syncopated rhythms, which touched all aspects of their existence. The rivers of the Coatzacoalcos system, lifeblood of their homeland, dictated alternating cycles of abundance and scarcity for the foods and resources that were essential to their lifeways. Springs and streams were the cherished sources of drinking water on high ground, and their levels dropped only at the peak of the dry season. The timing of rainfall was of great concern as it affected the maturation of cultivated upland crops and the predictability of the water levels necessary for the procurement of aquatic foods in the rivers and wetlands. The Olmec founded their villages on isolated promontories or elevated strands of ground set in the watery landscape, always seeking transport advantages and safety above the flood line. Dugout canoes cast upon the strong river currents were the only means of communication with distant communities scattered across the permanent wetlands.

San Lorenzo's rulers implemented a strategy intended to integrate the near and distant villages into a single political entity via the command of the political ideology, the propagation of the belief system, and the management of transportation networks that were vital to regional trade and communication.[28] Their short-lived and probably sporadic success was spatially limited to portions of the Gulf Coast. The ideology of rulership, deeply intertwined with religious beliefs, was the blueprint for social relations at all levels. From their vantage point atop the massive stone thrones that symbolized their authority, the sovereigns determined the distribution of lesser stone sculptures, which acted as emblems that transmitted clear messages about the rightful social and political order throughout the region.[29] They propitiated a diverse array of social, political, and economic relations with specific villages in order to open and manage channels of communication and transportation and maintain access to certain resources—and they marked the key points in the regional political hierarchy with one or more stone monuments. San Lorenzo and its closest satellite centers—Tenochtitlán, El Remolino, and Loma del Zapote—formed the nucleus of the regional fluvial and terrestrial transportation system. The sites of Estero Rabón and Laguna de los Cerros acted as outlying satellite centers, the former managing access to a major transportation route leading into the Tuxtla Mountains, and the latter in charge of basalt exploitation and the production of sculpture and grinding tools.[30]

Political integration and social cohesion also were promoted by region-wide religious festivities, which drew pilgrims to the San Lorenzo island from the outlying areas. A focal point of such festivities was the ritual reenactment of mythical or historical dramas via the staged display of groups of sculptures, often placed in architectural settings.[31] The scenic display of twin anthropomorphic sculptures and two felines **(FIG. 8, PLS. 60–62)** from the El Azuzul acropolis of the Loma del Zapote site is an outstanding example of the dramatization of an ancient myth. Clearly, varying the composition of such displays could modify the meaning of the individual sculptures as well as the messages transmitted by this cyclically practiced dramaturgical device. Distant communities became valued participants in regional ceremonies by periodically contributing their stone sculptures to these displays. In this way, the intensification of their religious and political bonds with the early center of the Olmec world tended to foment regional unity.

By 1000 BC, San Lorenzo was beset by numerous difficulties, and it lost its place as the capital of the early Olmec world. The causes of its decline are unclear, but competition from the rising center of La Venta may have played a significant role in undermining San Lorenzo's sociopolitical organization. The onset of a major drought period also placed stress on the subsistence needs of its dense population, and residents were forced to seek other options.[32] The recarving of stone monuments ceased, and the macro-display of colossal heads was never finished. Most inhabitants left San Lorenzo, perhaps in search of a better life in places like La Venta and other sites along the Gulf Coast. The few people who remained were slowly but surely subsumed into the political sphere of

La Venta and showed their adherence to its social values and customs by adopting the style of artificial head-shaping that was preferred there.

San Lorenzo slowly retreated into the shadows, never regaining its former splendor, but its achievements set the stage for later developments. It was the first of many celebrated sites, the earliest in the long line of great Mesoamerican capitals.

NOTES

1 Cyphers 1997d, 1997g.

2 Beverido 1970; Brüggeman and Hers 1970; Coe and Diehl 1980; Cyphers 1994c, 1997d; Stirling 1955.

3 On the discovery of rubber balls, see Ortíz Ceballos, Rodríguez M., and Delgado C. 1997; Ortíz Ceballos and Rodríguez M. 2000. On the production of rubber, see Hosler, Burkett, and Tarkanian 1999.

4 Stark 2000.

5 Cyphers 2006, 2007a, 2009; Cyphers and Villamar 2006.

6 Note that all dates are calibrated; in other words, expressed in calendar years. On San Lorenzo, see Cyphers and Ortiz 2000; Symonds, Cyphers, and Lunagómez 2002.

7 Cyphers and Zurita-Noguera 2006a, 2006b, 2007, forthcoming.

8 Cyphers and Di Castro 2009; Cyphers and Zurita-Noguera, forthcoming.

9 Cyphers et al., forthcoming.

10 For the platform, see Coe and Diehl 1980. For the sunken patio, see Cyphers n.d.

11 Cyphers n.d.; Cyphers et al., forthcoming.

12 Cyphers et al., forthcoming.

13 Grove 1970a, 1973, 1981; Reilly 1999.

14 Gillespie 1993; Bassie-Sweet 1996; Scarborough 1998; Schele 1995.

15 Cyphers, forthcoming.

16 On the discovery of the throne, see Stirling 1955. On the excavation of the colossal head, see Brüggeman and Hers 1970. On the excavation of the aqueduct, see Krotser 1973. On the interpretation of Monument 52 as a standard bearer, see Cyphers 2004a.

17 On water and underworld symbolism, see Cyphers et al. 2006. The colossal heads have been considered portraits by scholars such as Bernal 1969; Coe 1968a; de la Fuente 1992; Stirling 1955; Wicke 1971, among others.

18 Coe (1968a) proposed the existence of hereditary rulers that calculated their descent from a jaguar deity. On the ruler's role as intermediary, I follow Grove 1973, 1997; Reilly 1994, 1995, 1999.

19 Flannery and Marcus 2005.

20 Cyphers 1997d, 1997g.

21 On the Red Palace, see Cyphers 1997d, 1997g, n.d.

22 Porter 1989.

23 Cyphers 2004a.

24 Cyphers and Di Castro 1996; Cyphers n.d.

25 Di Castro, Cyphers, and Varela 2008.

26 On Llano del Jícaro, see Medellín Zeñil 1960; Gillespie 1994; Borstein 2001, 2008.

27 Cobean et al. 1971; Cobean et al. 1991; De León 2008; Pires-Ferreira and Evans 1978; Wendt and Lu 2005, among others.

28 Symonds, Cyphers, and Lunagómez 2002; Cyphers 2004a.

29 Cyphers and Zurita-Noguera 2006a.

30 Cyphers 2004b, 2008; Borstein 2008.

31 Cyphers 1993, 1994b, 1999.

32 On subsistence and risk management, see Cyphers and Zurita-Noguera, forthcoming.

LA VENTA

F. Kent Reilly III

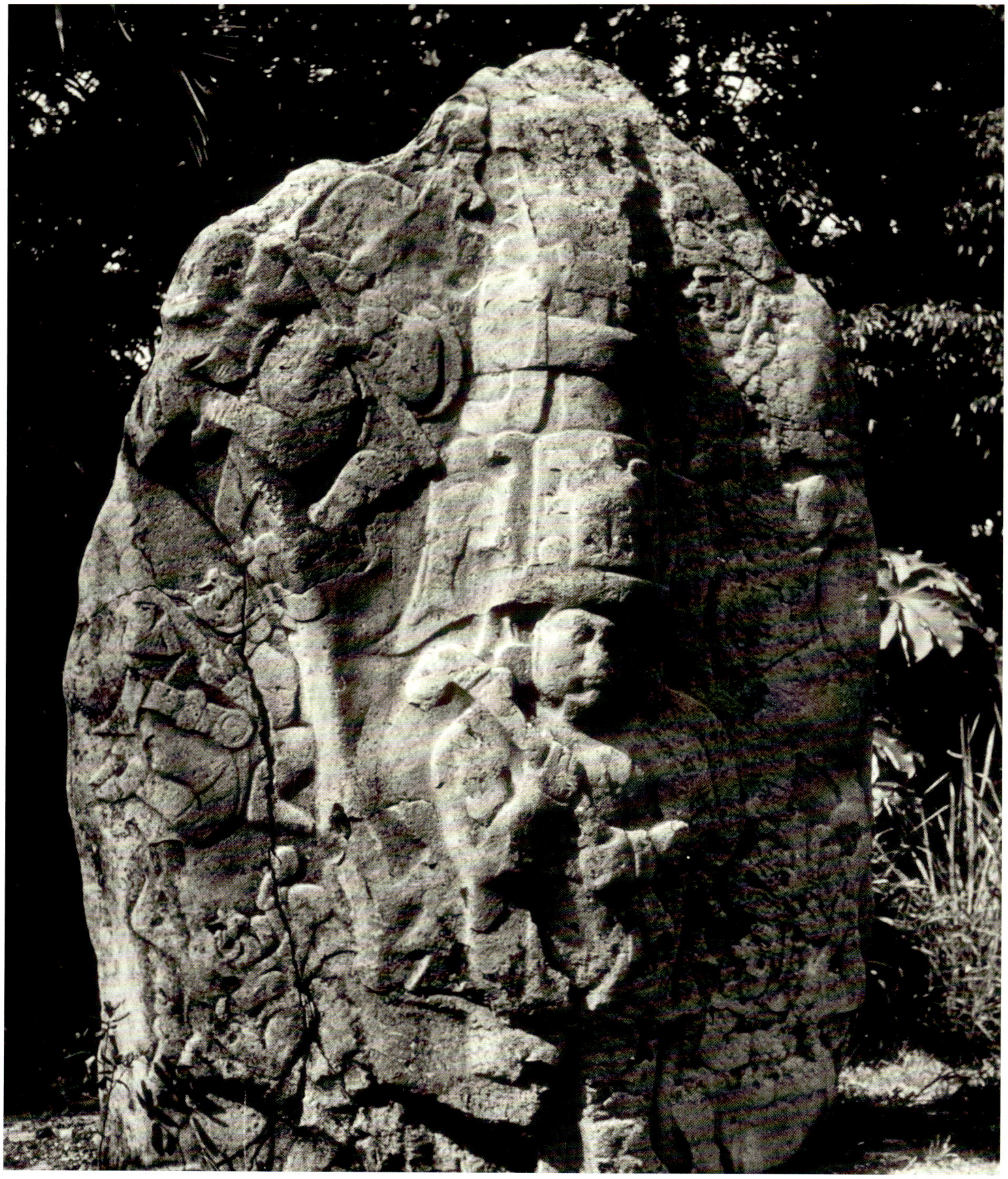

Traveling south from the volcanic Tuxtla Mountains that surround beautiful and, yes, mysterious Lago Catemaco, one rapidly descends onto the steamy plain of the Gulf Coast and its southern projection, the Bay of Campeche. The flat riverine and estuarine environment of this coastal area dominates the topography until one reaches Villahermosa, the capital of the Mexican state of Tabasco. For the traveler, this landscape is a monotonous and sultry expanse of swamps, sluggish rivers, and haze. The landscape breaks after crossing the Río Tonalá, the muddy stream that marks the boundary between Tabasco and its northern neighbor, the state of Veracruz. Soon, and prior to reaching the turnoff to the archaeological site and town of La Venta, the traveler will see the truncated mass of the great Olmec pyramid rising above the treeline.

First brought to the attention of a wider public by Frans Blom and Oliver La Farge in 1926 with the publication of *Tribes and Temples*, the record of their 1925 explorations in tropical Mexico, La Venta is one of the early, large-scale Olmec ceremonial centers, along with San Lorenzo and Tres Zapotes, that arose in Olman, the Olmec Gulf Coast heartland.[1] Since its investigation by Matthew W. Stirling in 1940 and through the current excavations and site mapping by Rebecca González Lauck, La Venta has been archaeologically researched and thematically interpreted, and its sculpture and artifacts have become templates through which scholars define Olmec culture and the Olmec style of art and architecture.

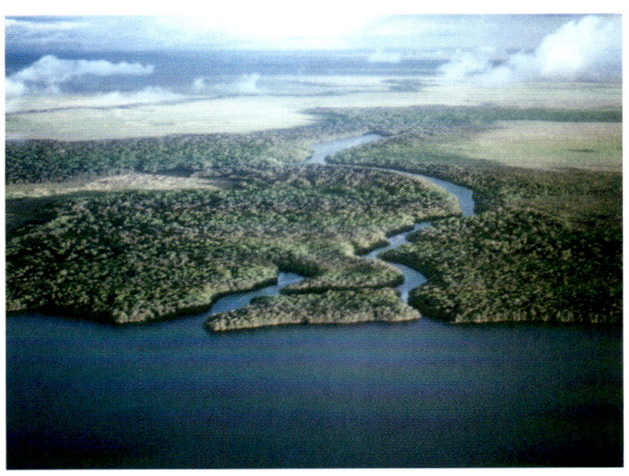

La Venta covers a large swamp island about 6 miles (10 kilometers) from the Gulf of Mexico (FIG. 17). Like many sites in Olman, La Venta is surrounded by rivers and other bodies of water (see Cyphers, this volume). Recent research has revealed that during its apogee (ca. 900–500 BC), La Venta was at the center of a rich, low-lying riverine and estuarine environment.[2] One of

FIG. 16
Stela 2, depicting a standing Olmec ruler surrounded by smaller beings, in situ at La Venta, 1940

FIG. 17
Aerial view of the coast of Tabasco, 1966

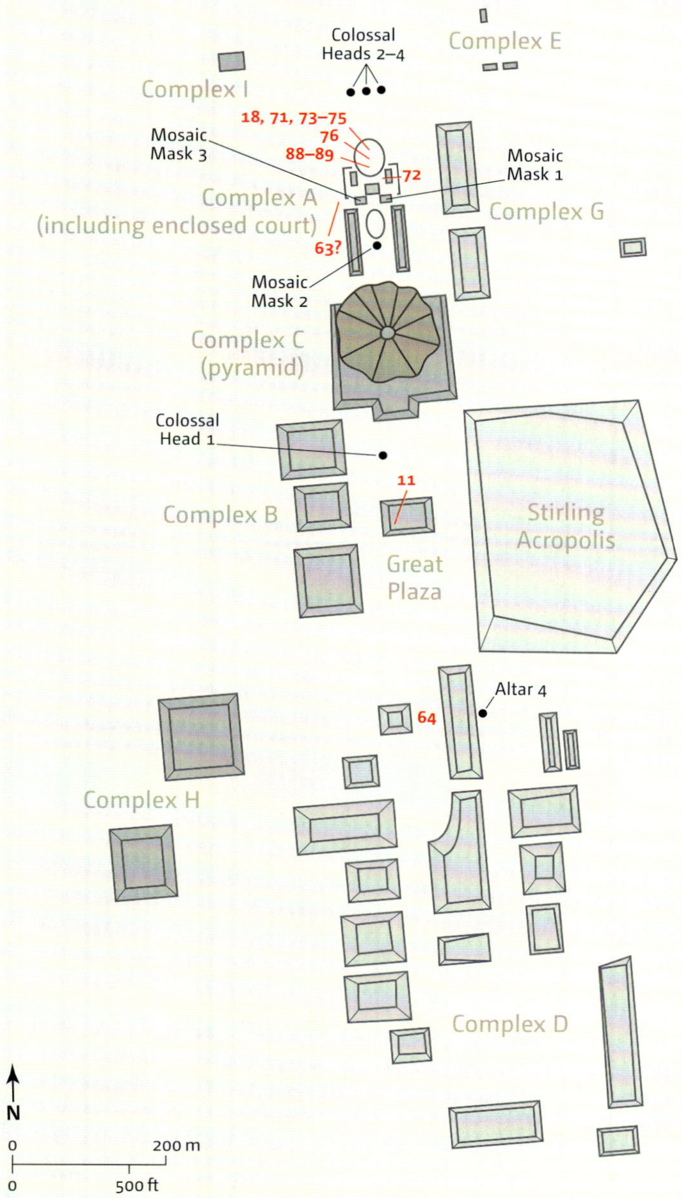

Numerals marking find sites correspond to plate numbers in this volume

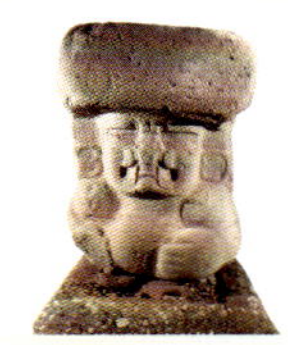

PLATE 11

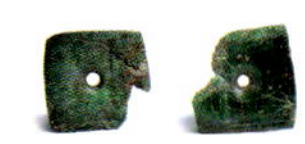

PLATE 18

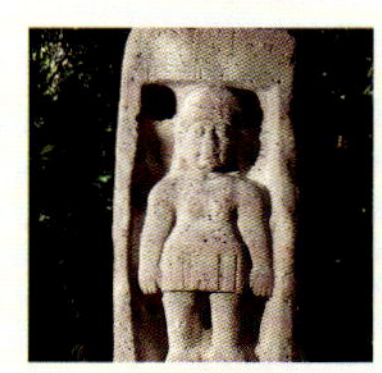

PLATE 63

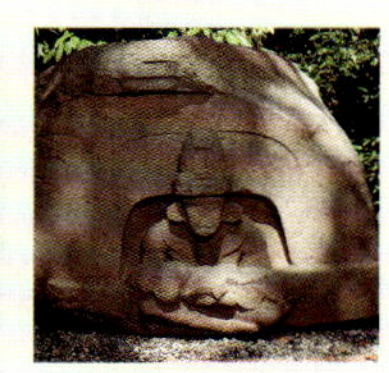

PLATE 64

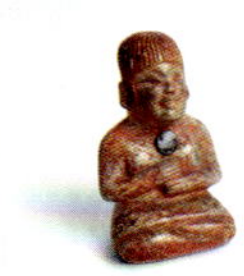

PLATE 71

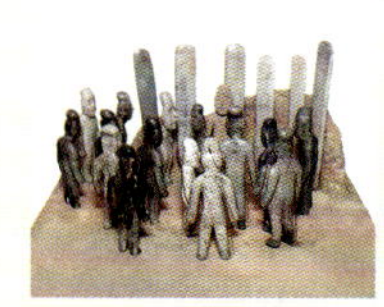

PLATE 72

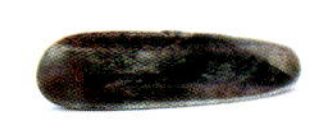

PLATE 73

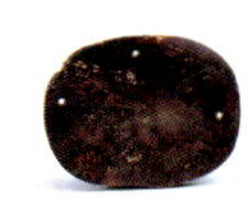

PLATE 74

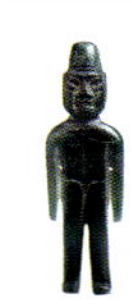

PLATE 75

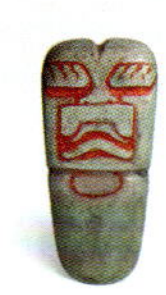

PLATE 76

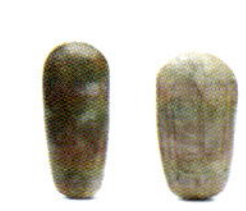

PLATES 88–89

the factors that explains La Venta's growth was the accessibility of varied nutritional resources such as several species of freshwater and saltwater fish, caimans, turtles, clams, oysters, snails, iguanas, frogs, and migratory ducks. These dietary resources were augmented with large mammals such as manatees and white-tailed deer. Archaeological and ethnobotanical research also has revealed that by 1750 BC, the diet of the people of La Venta area was complemented with corn (*Zea mays*), a domesticate that originated in the Mexican highlands.[3]

Several of the most recent excavations and site surveys, combined with a long-term mapping project directed by González Lauck, have uncovered evidence that La Venta and its environs supported a substantial population,[4] which it retained from the Early Preclassic period (ca. 2250–1150 BC) until the site's abandonment sometime around 400 BC. This demonstrates that during La Venta's apogee, its inhabitants clearly constituted "a diverse and stratified range of groups including artisans, subsistence workers such as fishers and farmers, religious specialists, and chiefly or elite families."[5]

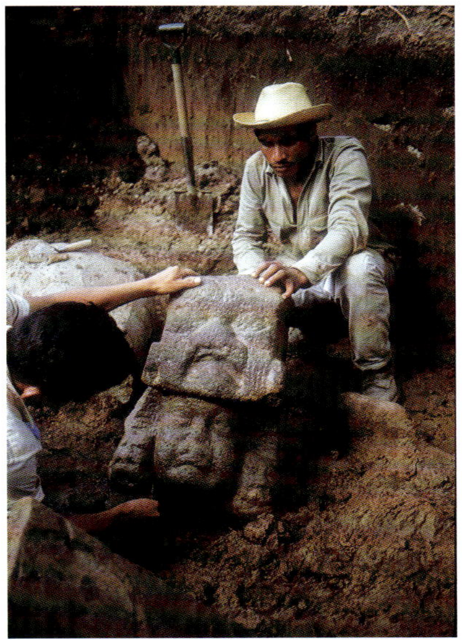

Excavations conducted in the 1940s, 1950s, and 1960s **(SEE FIG. 18)**, as well as the more recent work of González Lauck, reveal that La Venta consisted of several large complexes of earthen architecture that totaled some thirty mounds and platforms.[6] The mound groupings are currently labeled alphabetically, and this discussion focuses only on the most significant: Complexes A, B, C, and D. These architectural complexes functioned both as the residences of La Venta's elite and as the ceremonial centers for the site's entire population. La Venta's structures are positioned along a low ridge running north-south through the center of the island of La Venta. The mounds are laid along a north-south axis or centerline that runs 8 degrees west of magnetic north, dividing the several groups of earthen architecture into east-west zones in a way that makes many of their components appear to be mirror images of one another.

The site is also separated into northern and southern zones, positioned on either side of the large Great Plaza. Known as Complex B, the plaza undoubtedly served as the focus of much of La Venta's public areas, as opposed to restricted elite precincts such as Complex A, to the north. It was also studded with large monuments such as Colossal Head 1 and Stela 2 **(FIG. 16)**.[7] Public access to this area appears to have been from the south, with more restricted access along one or perhaps two processional ways that traversed Complex D, the multimound group bordering the plaza to the south.[8] Three extant mounds and one destroyed mound compose the plaza's western border, blocking access along that edge. The eastern boundary is formed by the relatively unexplored Stirling Acropolis.

Complex D, south of the Great Plaza, is a large assemblage of twenty mounds positioned on either side of what appear to be one or two processional ways or roads that led into the Great Plaza from a plaza on the southern end of the site.[9] The processional route on the west leads directly into the Great Plaza; the eastern route veers to the west, creating a distinct entrance that focuses on the Stirling Acropolis. One of the Complex D mounds, D-8, narrowly separates both processional routes at their northern end, while at the southern end of Complex D, Mounds D-7 and D-9 support sculptural tableaux. If understood thematically, these tableaux could reveal a great deal about La Venta's social order and belief system because—as Ann Cyphers's new discoveries at the archaeological site of San Lorenzo clearly illustrate—the Olmec achieved a method for conveying the narrative of ritual action through the placement or grouping of monuments.[10]

The sculptural tableau on Mound D-7 is composed of three heavily eroded, monumental sandstone figures of different sizes, in a squatting position, with arms that reach upward to hold large, helmetlike headdresses.[11]

FIG. 18
Excavation of Monument 44 at La Venta, 1968

These dwarflike figures stand in contrast to three colossal heads—Monuments 2, 3, and 4—positioned slightly beyond the northern boundary of Complex A, aligned east to west and facing north. The two sculptural groupings or tableaux seem literally to frame La Venta's architectural complexes on their north (Complex A) and south (Complex D) ends. Both tableaux undoubtedly conveyed ideological or religious messages of wonder and awe to their ancient viewers and perhaps also identified the ritual and ideological function of La Venta itself.

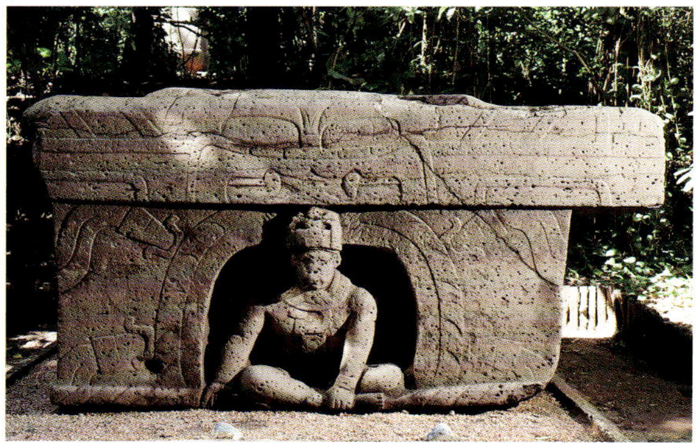

Mound D-8, positioned just south of the Great Plaza, displays one tableau that was arranged using Altars 4 and 5, two of La Venta's most important monuments. The altars, now understood to be thrones, are positioned with their backs directly opposite each other, on either side and at the middle of Mound D-8. Altar 4 ("Harpy Eagle Warrior") **(FIG. 19)** faces east, and Altar 5 ("Infant Altar") **(FIG. 33, PLS. 64–66)** faces west. Altar 4 is carved from a single block of basalt.[12] A ledge carved with symbols, among which is a prominent feline face, projects over its three undamaged sides. Altar 4's central image depicts a life-size human figure seated cross-legged, emerging from a niche, and wearing an intricate raptorial headdress. The figure holds a rope that surrounds the bottom of the throne and ends at the left wrist of a figure carved on the monument's right side. Altar 5, also made from a single block of basalt, is one of the most elegant and important objects that Olmec artists ever created. Like its counterpart, Altar 5 had an overhanging ledge, although only remnants survive. Its central carved figure emerges from a niche, holding an infant in its outstretched arms. The figure wears an elaborate headdress bearing a mask, two crossed-band motifs, and three exclamation point–shaped raindrop motifs that also appear prominently in a bas-relief at the highland site of Chalcatzingo, Morelos (see Grove, this volume). On its chest, the figure appears to wear a mirror pectoral, a recurring symbol for elite status in the corpus of Olmec regalia. Two pairs of elaborately dressed individuals, all wearing a distinctive headdress and holding a wriggling infant, are rendered in bas-relief on each side of Altar 5. The precise execution of this sculpture's carving and the quality of movement that animates the infants and the emerging niche figure identify Altar 5 as the work of an Olmec master sculptor.

Heading north, just entering Complex B's plaza and cut off by the bulk of the Stirling Acropolis, the eastern processional way narrows and shifts to the west. Altar 1, which faces east, was positioned near the narrow north entrances of the two processional routes. Altar 1 unfortunately is mutilated, but enough of the carving remains to identify the supernatural image, the Olmec dragon, that composes its body.[13]

Both Complex B (and its plaza) and the Stirling Acropolis have been the sites of only minimal archaeological investigation; in 1967, for example, limited excavations were completed in these areas by the University of California, Berkeley.[14] This work revealed that the acropolis possessed hydraulic drain lines carved from basalt, similar to those reported at San Lorenzo. Complex B and the acropolis also had large numbers of fragmented monuments. Colossal Head 1 and Stela 2 in Complex B were grouped to be understood as a tableau.[15] Monument 59 **(PLS. 10–11)**, also recovered from Complex B, may have likewise functioned in a tableau grouping. The monument depicts a zoomorph with perhaps supernatural feline attributes; a slab runs the length of the figure and overhangs its

FIG. 19
ALTAR 4
Mexico, Tabasco, La Venta, 900–400 BC
Basalt
63 x 75 x 125 1/5 in. (160 x 190 x 319 cm)
Parque Museo de La Venta, Villahermosa, Tabasco

head. A hole or channel piercing the sculpture lightens the effect of the slab. This slab itself may have served as a seat or throne or functioned in rituals for La Venta's political and religious elite.[16] Another important piece of sculpture that is thought to have been found in the vicinity of the La Venta pyramid is the three-dimensional Monument 77 **(PLS. 67–68)**. Carved from basalt, Monument 77 presents a seated figure wearing an elaborate cape and headdress, the latter bearing symbols associated with the Olmec maize deity.[17] The cape is a unique representation of Olmec elite regalia because it is divided into registers by what appear to be ropes, with each register bearing several bar-and-dot numerals. Monument 77 almost certainly composed part of a sculptural group, perhaps placed atop a throne.[18]

The La Venta Pyramid

Rising some 105 feet (32 meters) above Complex B **(SEE FIG. 20)**, the La Venta pyramid (or Complex C) is one of the earliest large pyramidal structures erected in Mesoamerica. González Lauck's recent testing reveals that the entire structure is earthen. Although the pyramid has a ridged, conical form, in the past it more closely resembled other such early pyramidal structures; centuries of erosion created the gulleys seen now.[19]

La Venta's pyramid was built atop a large earthen platform, the southern side of which was constructed in the shape of three arcs that jutted out into Complex B's plaza.[20] Access to the platform was provided by an earthen ramp that began to the north, on the east side of Complexes A and C. Atop this platform, on either side of the site's centerline and facing the Great Plaza, the Olmec builders positioned two thrones (Altars 2 and 3) and a number of large stone monuments or stelae (Stelae 4 and 5).[21] Six of these monuments were erected and evenly distributed on the pyramid's south side; at some point, however, they were broken and intentionally buried at the pyramid's base. When excavated, each fragment was assigned a separate number, and these designations stood unchallenged until González Lauck demonstrated that Monuments 25 and 26 were in fact fragments of the same monument.[22] When the fragments from the two monuments were rejoined—and newly designated as La Venta Stela 4—a comparison of the incised images revealed a zoomorphic and wrapped or bundled supernatural wearing a trefoil device in its headdress. Monument 27, also broken and excavated in the same area of the pyramidal platform, bears an identical bundled, zoomorphic image.

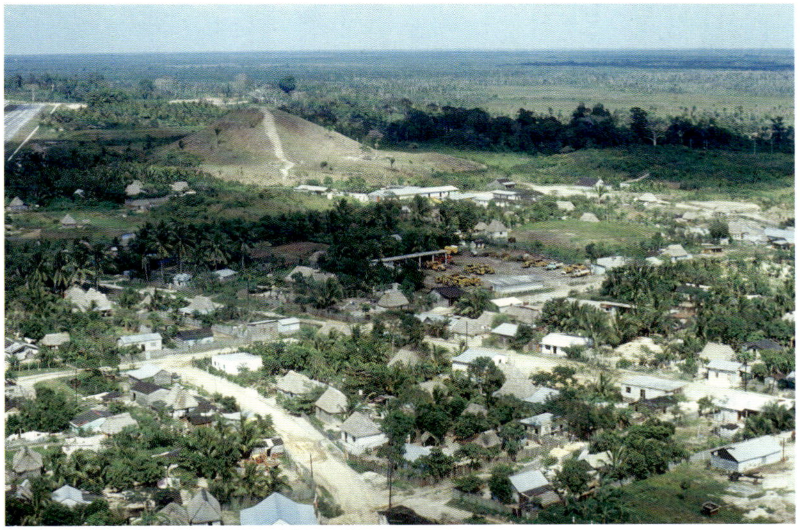

FIG. 20
Aerial view of the modern town of La Venta, dominated by the site's Olmec pyramid, 1968

Complex A: Mounds A-4 and A-5

North of the La Venta pyramid, in Complex A, builders constructed two range mounds—Mounds A-4 and A-5—that bordered an interior space (about 285 x 131 feet, or 87 x 40 meters). Within this space Blom and La Farge first located La Venta Stela 1 **(FIG. 21, PL. 63)** in 1925; it was found, along with several other monuments, in the northwest quadrant of the patio or ritual precinct formed by the mounds. Carved in relief, Stela 1 depicts what appears to be a bare-breasted female figure standing in a niche, facing forward. She wears a turbanlike headdress and a short skirt topped by an overskirt cut in a distinctive striped pattern. The lintel, or upper register of the niche enclosing the figure, is carved with familiar motifs from the Olmec symbol system.

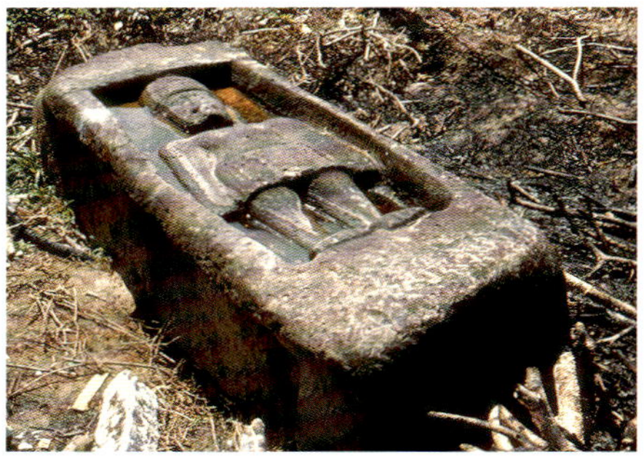

The southern entrance of the enclosed court of Complex A was augmented with bastionlike projections that contained buried mosaic masks **(SEE FIG. 22)** and enormous deposits of serpentine unique to La Venta. Even though two of the mosaic masks of Complex A were buried immediately after construction, they nonetheless served as vehicles for ideological information for initiates, much like the facade masks displayed on later mound and pyramidal structures. La Venta's buried masks identify the function of an enclosed and restricted ritual space used primarily by a private, elite audience. Therefore, the flanking masks that carry the ritual identity of that space are themselves hidden from view.

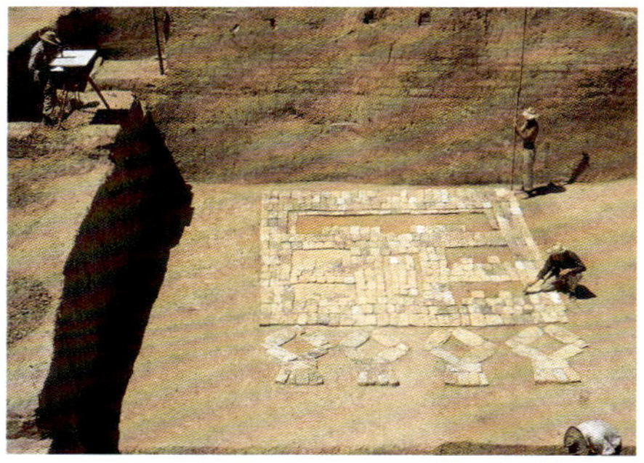

Mosaic Mask 2—the second of the three famous La Venta mosaic pavements—was also uncovered at the center of the space defined by Mounds A-4 and A-5. Large, low, and circular, Mound A-3 was positioned east to west over the site's centerline and erected over Tomb C, a stone-lined cavity harboring the burial goods of an elite personage.[23] However, before the construction of Mound A-3 and Tomb C, Mosaic Mask 2 occupied the principal central location between the mounds.

When excavated, Mosaic Mask 2 (16 x 14 feet, or 4.8 x 4.4 meters) was missing many pieces and worn smooth in several areas, indicating that, unlike the other two mosaic pavements, it had not been buried immediately upon completion.[24] The placement of this mosaic mask at the time of its construction—almost dead center in the space defined by the range mounds—strongly suggests the mask functioned as a center marker, perhaps for a ballcourt whose borders were formed by the two range mounds. Unless further evidence is obtained, however, this area's enormous size makes its function as a metaphorical rather than an actual ballcourt seem implausible. Be that as it may, this clearly demarcated and restricted area is undoubtedly a liminal space, which is further signaled by the presence of a center marker. Perhaps it functioned as another grand processional way, directing a flow of ritual movement between Complex C and the enclosed court that is the most prominent feature of Complex A.[25]

Complex A: The Enclosed Court

In Complex A, a series of three mounds—the northeast, northwest, and south-central platforms—is grouped around a plaza forming the enclosed court. Both the mounds and plaza were double-bordered by a bracket-shaped wall that in the site's later stages was topped with a basalt-column fence. Major excavations conducted in Complex A (from 1941 to 1943 and again in 1955) uncovered many of the construction details of the enclosed court, including four major construction phases, each initiated with a massive offering of serpentine blocks.[26]

FIG. 21
Stela 1 at La Venta, 1940

FIG. 22
Excavation of Mosaic Mask 3, one of three mosaic pavements found at La Venta, 1955

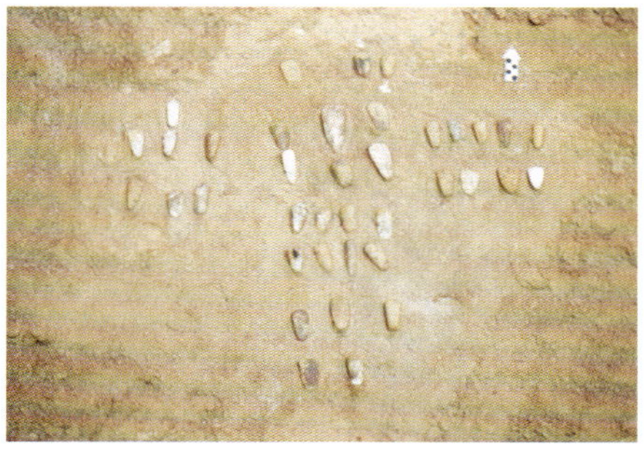

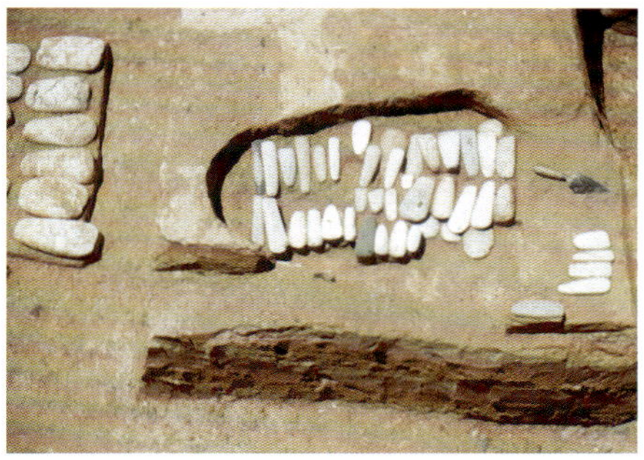

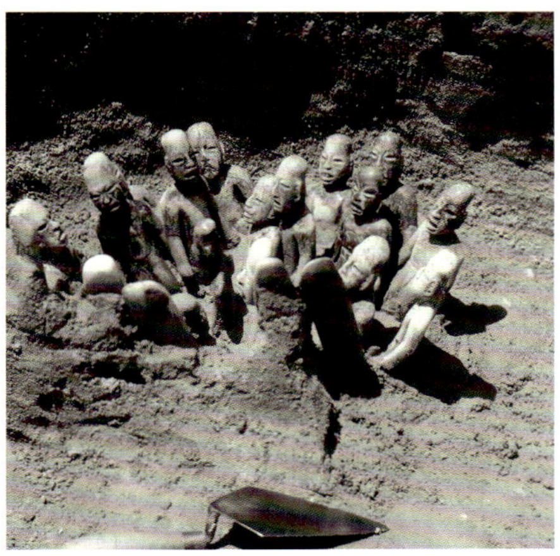

La Venta's builders sometimes deposited caches of serpentine and jadeite celts along the site's centerline, directly over these massive offerings **(SEE FIGS. 23–24)**. The most famous cache, Offering 4, was found off the centerline and directly in front of the enclosed court's northeast platform. Excavated during the 1955 season, it was buried under layers of colored clays and a single layer of white sand. Offering 4 comprises a grouping of sixteen anthropomorphic figures and six standing celts arranged in a miniature ritual tableau **(FIG. 25, PL. 72)**. Fifteen of the figures are carved from jadeite or greenstone, and they form a semicircle facing the celts. A sixteenth figure made of stone stands facing the fifteen greenstone figures, with the celts arrayed behind him. Each celt is approximately 10 inches (25 centimeters) high and was covered in red cinnabar. Of the six celts, four display incised symbolic information and appear to have been cut down from a larger incised object.[27] Carbon samples from the 1955 excavations revealed that the enclosed court was in use between 1000 and 600 BC.[28] Unfortunately, an airstrip was built through the northern end of La Venta in the late 1950s and much of Complex A was destroyed.

Over time, a series of multicolored clay floors within the court continued to be built up, raising the floor level to the top of the surrounding adobe wall and necessitating a startlingly new architectural innovation: the construction of a basalt-column fence atop the adobe wall. The addition of this fence would have restored a sense of secrecy and exclusivity to the ritual activity, which was becoming more visible with the elevation of the floor.

Complex A: Mound A-2 and Tomb A

In Construction Phase 4, the court's northern entrance was blocked almost entirely by Mound A-2 (approximately 10 x 6½ x 6 feet, or 3 x 2 x 1.8 meters), a greatly enlarged, low-lying, stepped pyramid. Initially built during earlier construction phases, Mound A-2 shielded the interior of the court and its ritual activity from public view. At the close of Phase 4, the Olmec excavated Mound A-2 to a considerable depth and, at the bottom

FIGS. 23–24
Excavation of Offering 2 (top) and Offering 10 (center) at La Venta, 1955

FIG. 25
Excavation of Offering 4 at La Venta, 1955

of this excavation, deposited a layer of bright red sand. A tightly fitted pavement consisting of a single layer of cut and polished serpentine blocks—Massive Offering 2—was placed on top of the red sand. Measuring nearly 50 feet north-south and 20 feet east-west (14.8 x 6 meters), Massive Offering 2 was covered immediately with earthen fill. A sandstone sarcophagus carved in the likeness of the Olmec dragon was placed upon this fill, directly over the center of the offering.[29] Above, and straddling the northern edge of the offering, the builders placed Tomb A.

Olmec tombs are quite rare, and those recovered archaeologically are rarer still. In the Olmec Gulf Coast heartland, La Venta is the one site where tombs have been uncovered by archaeological methods, and all of them have been excavated in Complex A. Currently, only Tomb A has been found to contain fragments that may be human remains. Positioned at the north end of Mound A-2, Tomb A was constructed of forty-four vertical and horizontal basalt columns "fitted as to present a smooth and even surface on the interior, leaving the outside rough."[30] The entrance to this structure faced north and was closed by five inclined basalt columns. When Matthew W. Stirling and Philip Drucker excavated the tomb in 1942, they found the interior tightly packed with clay. After clearing it away, they discovered that the southern 7 feet (2.2 meters) of the tomb floor were paved with eight waterworn flagstones. The flagstones were coated with what Stirling described as a thin layer of blue clay, although a decade later Drucker recalled it being a layer of heavy, olive-brown swamp muck. The remains of the bundle burials of two or perhaps three individuals (infants?) were found on top of this deposit, within two large areas of red cinnabar.[31] Also found was a remarkable set of grave goods, many of which had strong water connotations. Among the beautifully crafted jadeite objects were earflares **(PL. 18)**, perforators, figurines, and a necklace or headdress composed of a jadeite stingray and six stingray spines set with small squares of glittering hematite. Excavators also found a large shark's tooth on which had been placed a translucent blue jadeite standing figure, as well as a jadeite frog and a jadeite object described as a "realistic reproduction of a fresh-water clam shell . . . perforated for use as a pendant. Inside it was a small oval mirror of brilliant crystalline hematite"[32] **(PLS. 73–74)**. Underneath the clamshell pendant lay one of the masterpieces of Olmec jadeite carving: a seated female figure of highly polished dark jadeite, wearing on her chest a brightly polished mirror of crystalline hematite **(PL. 71)**. The high quality of the objects found in Complex A's enclosed court and Tomb A speaks poignantly of the exalted position of La Venta's now vanished elite.

Conclusions

Tomb A's layout, like the sculptural and figural tableaux erected in several locations throughout La Venta, conveyed a distinct thematic message that was accessible to at least an Olmec elite. Considering the placement and construction of Tomb A, the deliberate grouping of three colossal heads to the north of Complex A opposite the three monumental sandstone dwarf-like figures in Complex D, as well as the disposition of stelae in front of the pyramid, the brilliance of La Venta's builders comes arrestingly into focus. The evidence of La Venta's layout and its tombs, monuments, and iconography strongly support an interpretation that its overall site plan was intended to mirror the landscape of primordial creation. On this stage, the rites of world renewal and elite validation were reenacted within the supernatural landscape as well as the physical geography of the creation event. As such a stage, La Venta certainly announced itself as an important Formative period pilgrimage site.

La Venta's architecture, monuments, caches, tableaux, and tombs physically manifested the unseen supernatural powers released into the world at creation, and its rulers undoubtedly were encoding and manipulating the symbolic messages contained in Olmec legends and belief systems to increasingly spectacular effect. These supernatural powers were harnessed and revalidated on a daily basis with each ritual performance, and La Venta's art, architecture, and site layout superbly proclaimed that this power could be accessed through the rituals performed there by its divinely inspired elites. These leaders manifested in themselves the gods who had created this world, and they functioned as the fulcrums on which the oppositions, inherent in both the natural and supernatural order, were balanced and renewed.

NOTES

1 See Blom and La Farge 1926. Scholars of the Mesoamerican past continue to debate the temporal and cultural primacy of the Gulf Coast Olmec within the Preclassic period. Within these debates, different researchers often use the term Olmec in different ways. Moreover, the definition of Olmec culture and art style has changed through time as new artifacts from a limited number of archaeological excavations and art objects from unprovenienced collections have been added to the corpus. Additional ambiguity has resulted from the various emphases, biases, and viewpoints of the scholars involved in study of the Preclassic period (Coe 1965a; Flannery 1968; Grove 1989a; Reilly 1995). However, in the most commonly applied definition, Olmec refers both to an archaeological culture centered in a Mexican Gulf Coast heartland whose principal sites include La Venta in Tabasco, and San Lorenzo, Laguna de los Cerros, and Tres Zapotes in Veracruz, as well as to an early, geographically dispersed Mesoamerican art style that shares stylistic and iconographic features with stone monuments created by the Gulf Coast Olmec culture. Scholarly discussion centers particularly on whether and to what extent the Gulf Coast centers can be considered the principal place of origin for the Olmec art style and iconographic system, or whether the widespread dissemination of a shared Preclassic art style and symbol set represents more reciprocal exchange of ideologically significant valuables and associated symbols among various regional elites whose cultures were undergoing parallel paths of sociopolitical evolution.

2 Rust 1992.

3 González Lauck 1996c: 73.

4 González Lauck 1988, 1994.

5 Rust 1992: 124.

6 On the excavations, see Stirling 1940b, 1941, 1943, 1947; Drucker 1952a; Drucker et al. 1959; Heizer et al. 1968. On site exploration and mapping, see González Lauck 1988, 1989, 1995.

7 Heizer et al. 1968.

8 Grove 1995, 1996a; Reilly 1999.

9 Grove 1995, 1996a; González Lauck 1996; Reilly 1999, 2002.

10 Cyphers 1997c, 1997d.

11 Blom and La Farge 1926; Stirling 1968; González Lauck 1996. Carolyn Tate (2009) has suggested that these eroded sandstone figures may be fetuses.

12 Reilly 1995.

13 Joralemon 1976.

14 Heizer et al. 1968.

15 Reilly 2002.

16 Reilly 1995.

17 Taube 1996.

18 Cyphers 1997; Reilly 2002; Kappleman and Reilly 2001.

19 González Lauck 1996.

20 Heizer et al. 1968: 138.

21 On Altars 2 and 3, see Grove 1973.

22 On the original broken fragments, see Drucker et al. 1959. On Monuments 25 and 26 as a single work, see González Lauck 1988: 129.

23 Drucker 1952a: 65–71.

24 On the condition of the mask, see Drucker 1952a: 75.

25 Reilly 1995, 2002.

26 Stirling 1941: 321–332; Stirling and Stirling 1942: 635–661; Drucker 1952a; Drucker et al. 1959.

27 On the incised information, see Reilly 1994. On the cutting down of the celts, see Drucker et al. 1959: 27–29, 46.

28 Heizer et al. 1968: 14.

29 Joralemon 1976.

30 Stirling and Stirling 1942: 640.

31 Ibid.: 640–641; Drucker 1952a: 23.

32 Stirling and Stirling 1942: 640–642.

TRES ZAPOTES: WHERE OLMEC ARCHAEOLOGY BEGAN

Christopher A. Pool

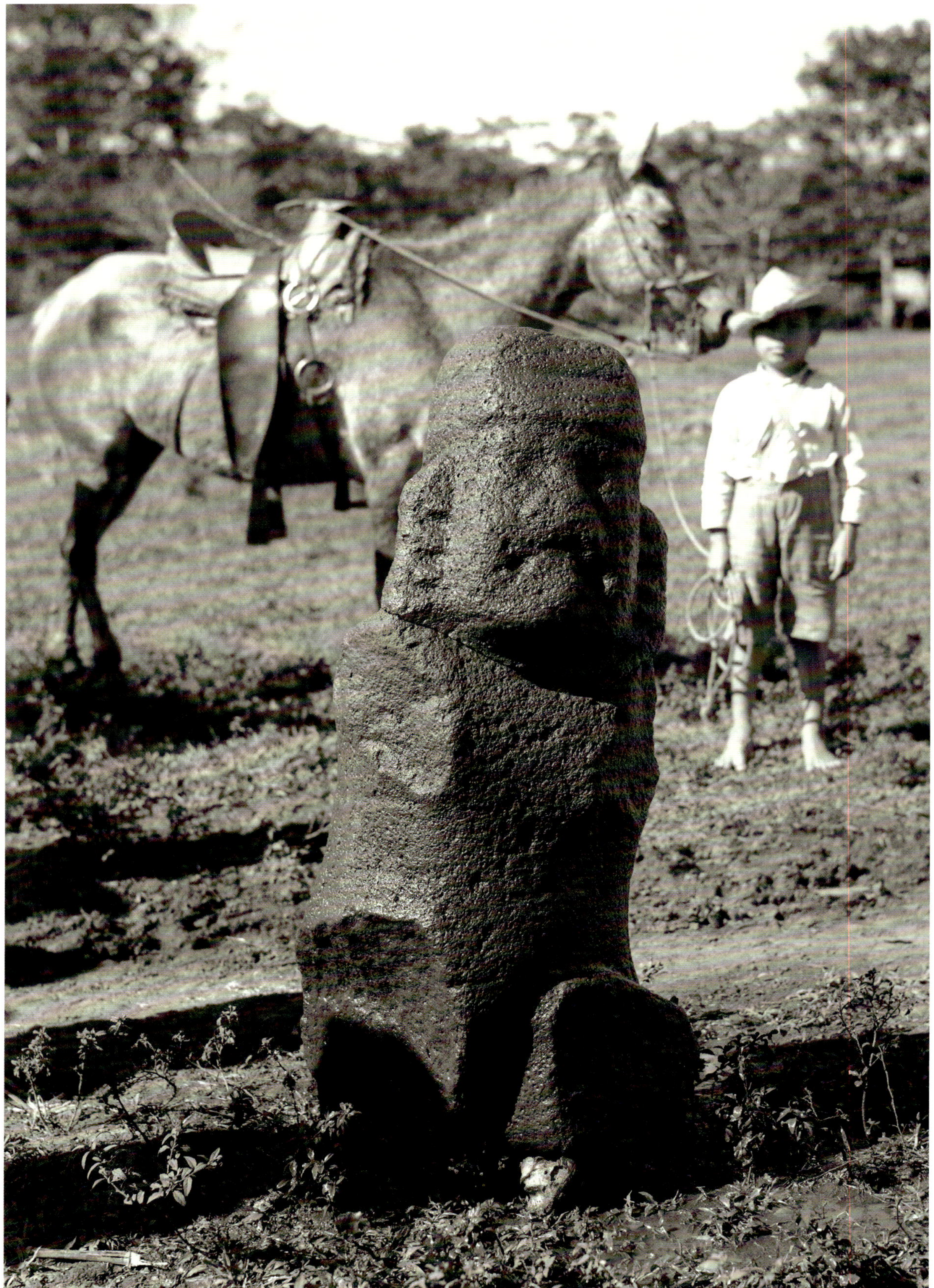

Our hearts beat a little faster when first we distinguished to the eastward the hazy volcanic peaks of the Tuxtla mountains, at the base of which lay our goal. —MATTHEW W. STIRLING, "Discovering the New World's Oldest Dated Work of Man," *National Geographic Magazine*, 1939[1]

I understand how Matthew W. Stirling felt as his launch chugged through the sluggish channels of the Papaloapan delta late in 1938. My pulse quickened, too, the first time I saw those peaks take form in the smoky haze as I bounced along Federal Highway 180 in the cab of a pickup truck,[2] and I imagine ancient travelers felt much the same as they crossed the western threshold of Olman, the "Olmec heartland" in Mexico's southern Gulf lowlands.

Stirling's goal was the archaeological site of Tres Zapotes **(FIG. 27)**, and his objective was to launch the first scientific field investigation of Olmec culture. Seven decades later, Tres Zapotes is distinguished as the one Olmec capital in Olman that continued to flourish after the collapse of La Venta in 400 BC.[3] With fifty stone monuments and a record of continuous occupation that spans two millennia, Tres Zapotes best documents the emergence of epi-Olmec culture from its Olmec roots. There the transition from Olmec to epi-Olmec involved a profound shift in political organization, toward a system of shared governance, as well as the development of sophisticated writing and calendrical systems. Contrasting with the eastern Olmec centers of San Lorenzo and La Venta in its upland setting, the details of its artistic style, and its external contacts, Tres Zapotes also challenges the notion of Olmec as a monolithic, homogenous culture within Olman.

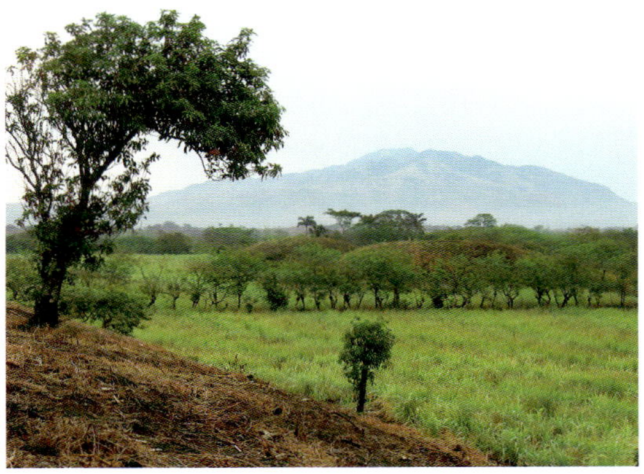

FIG. 26
Monument M (pl. 81) at Tres Zapotes, 1939

FIG. 27
View of Tres Zapotes Group 2 with the Cerro El Vigía and Tuxtla Mountains in the background, 2003

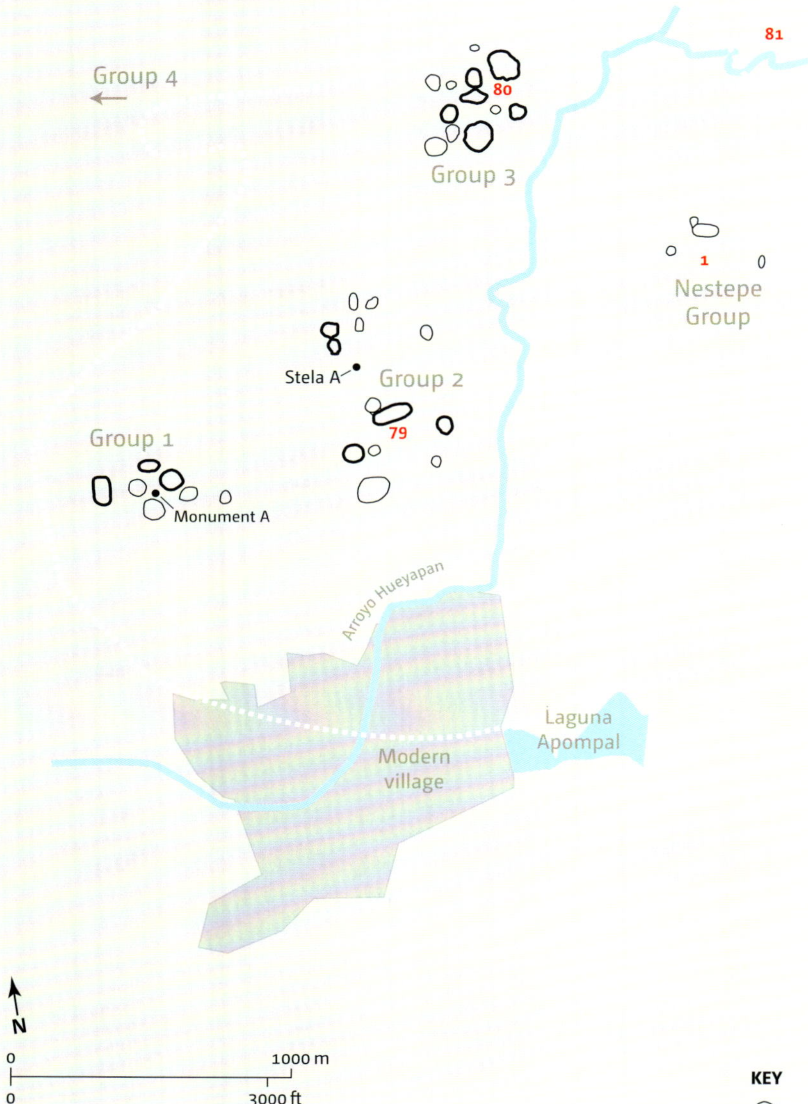

Numerals marking find sites correspond to plate numbers in this volume. Site limit indicates the maximum extent of the site as determined by the distribution of artifacts.

KEY

- mound shorter than 5 m
- mound taller than 5 m
- site limit

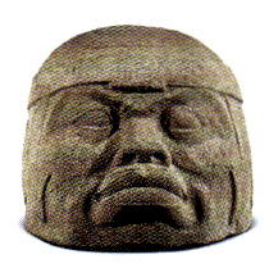

PLATE 1

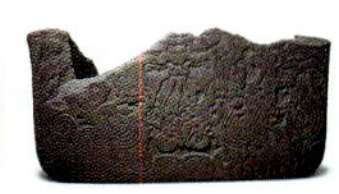

PLATE 79

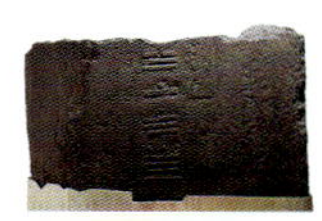

PLATE 80

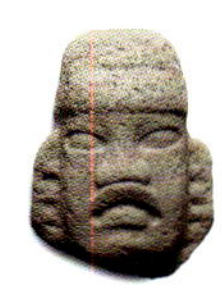

PLATE 81

A Century and a Half of Discovery

The story of Olmec studies begins around 1860 on the Hacienda de Hueyapan, at the site that would become known as Tres Zapotes. As José Melgar recounted in 1869, a worker clearing a cornfield a few years earlier found the smooth, rounded surface of what he believed to be the bottom of an iron cauldron.[4] He reported the find to the hacienda owner, who commanded him to dig out the cauldron and bring it to him. Imagine the worker's surprise when he uncovered the colossal visage instead of the rim of the vessel he had expected!

The "cabeza colosal de Hueyapan," as Tres Zapotes Monument A **(FIG. 28)** was then called, sat in the same field for another century as visitors came and went.[5] Among them were the renowned German archaeologist Eduard Seler and his photographer wife, Caecilie Seler-Sachs, who visited Tres Zapotes in 1905 and took pictures of both the colossal head and Monument C **(PL. 79)**, an elaborately carved stone box. Albert C. Weyerstall, a banana planter living in nearby Tlacotalpan between 1925 and 1927, visited Tres Zapotes and published pictures of these and three other monuments. He also wrote the first report of the many large mounds and formal plazas at the site.[6]

Impressed by Weyerstall's report, Stirling, then chief of the Smithsonian Institution's Bureau of American Ethnology, set out to reconnoiter Tres Zapotes and the surrounding region in early 1938 as part of an ambitious project to clarify the cultural and temporal relationships of the ancient Maya and their neighbors. Returning with photographs of impressive monuments and mounds, he quickly secured the support of the Smithsonian Institution and the National Geographic Society to mount full-scale field research at Tres Zapotes and, indeed, the first truly archaeological investigation of an Olmec site.[7]

Stirling returned to Tres Zapotes in December 1938 accompanied by his wife, Marion; archaeologist Clarence W. Weiant and his wife, Marian; photographer Richard H. Stewart; and artist E. G. Cassedy.[8] Although their roles were informal, the assistance of Marion Stirling and Marian Weiant was important to the success of the expedition. They maintained the camp and washed artifacts, and Marion Stirling served as bookkeeper and typed Matthew's correspondence. Ornithologist Alexander Wetmore, who was director of the U.S. National Museum and a member of the National Geographic Society's Research Committee, joined them later.[9] That first season was devoted to uncovering more stone monuments and trenching mounds to determine what they could of their construction sequences. They liberated the five previously discovered monuments from the soil that had accumulated around them, and they unearthed another sixteen stone monuments. Exhibiting an impressive variety that we now know reflected the long occupation of the site, the monuments included the colossal head, five stelae, a round altar, a numeral carved into bedrock, two rectangular boxes, two cylindrical basins, two human busts with long tenons protruding behind, two flexed arms, and six more statues of humans and composite human-animal figures carved in the round.[10]

The most exciting find of Stirling's first season was Stela C **(FIG. 29, PL. 80)**.[11] The base and the upper end of the stela had been broken off in antiquity, and the remaining piece had been set on its side behind a circular altar at the base of one of the site's tallest mounds. On its front was

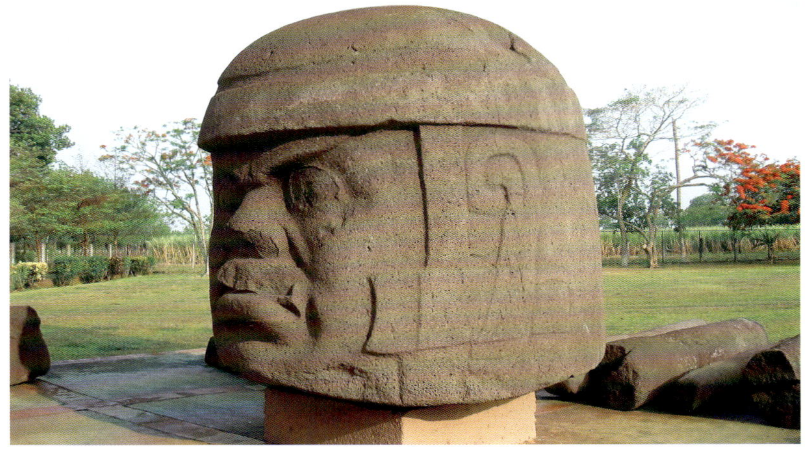

FIG. 28
MONUMENT A (COLOSSAL HEAD)
Mexico, Veracruz, Tres Zapotes, 1000–700 BC
Basalt
Height: 57 7/8 in. (147 cm)
Museo de Sitio de Tres Zapotes

carved a stylized supernatural face, which reminded Stirling of stucco masks on the facade of a Late Preclassic (ca. 300 BC–AD 100) structure at the Maya site of Uaxactun, as well as the "jaguar" faces on some Olmec jades and ceramics that were known at the time.[12] The greatest surprise, though, were the two columns of glyphs carved on the reverse face of the stela, which included part of a date in the Long Count system used by the Classic period (AD 250–900) Maya. It fell to Marion Stirling to decipher the date, using a copy of Sylvanus G. Morley's *An Introduction to the Study of the Maya Hieroglyphs*.[13] The date was incomplete, though, because the critical first coefficient had broken off with the unrecovered upper fragment of the stela. To make matters worse, the dot representing the numeral 1 in the next coefficient was just barely visible and initially went unnoticed. The resulting date of (9).15.6.16.18, 6 Etz'nab (16 Yaxk'in) fell in AD 478, respectably ancient but certainly nothing to challenge the intellectual precocity of the Maya.[14] A closer examination by Matthew Stirling, however, revealed the dot that changed the three bars of the second coefficient from 15 to 16. The only possible date with the resulting sequence of Long Count coefficients and the date of 6 Etz'nab in the 260-day sacred almanac (or "tzolkin") was (7).16.6.16.18, 6 Etz'nab (1 Wo), which was sixty-nine years earlier than the next earliest Long Count date known at the time, and a full three centuries before the beginning of the Maya Classic period.

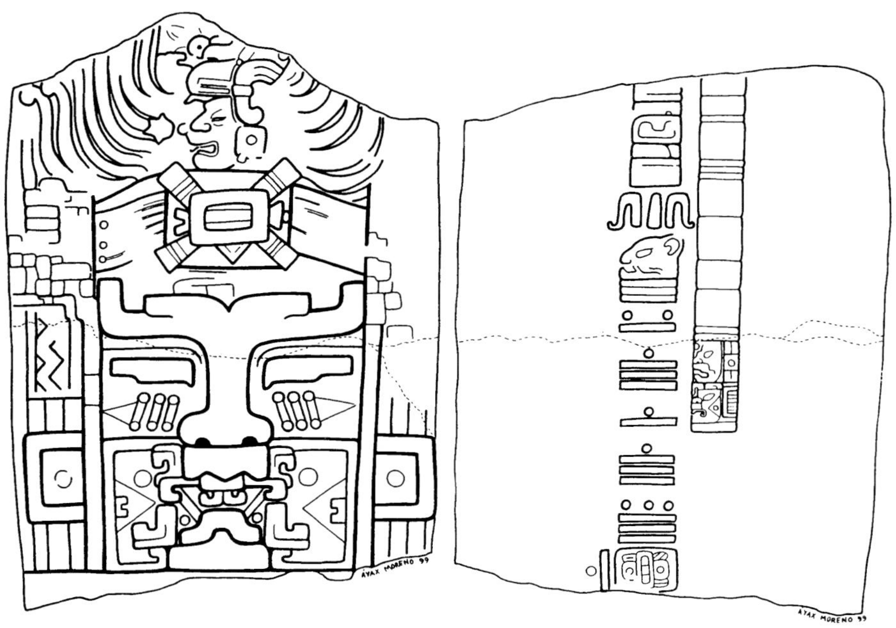

The response to Stirling's report of the "New World's Oldest Dated Work of Man" came quickly and forcefully from leading Mayanists J. Eric S. Thompson and Sylvanus G. Morley, both of whom attacked the early date,

FIG. 29
Rendering of Stela C showing the front and back of both recovered fragments

arguing that the archaeological Olmec culture belonged to the much later Postclassic period (AD 900–1500).[15] In 1969, long after radiocarbon dating had demonstrated the great antiquity of the Olmec, the Stirlings were further vindicated by the discovery of the upper fragment of Stela C, which possessed the missing Cycle 7 coefficient Marion had calculated thirty years earlier in the palm-thatched Smithsonian camp at Tres Zapotes. Today, the 32 BC Long Count date on Stela C is still the second earliest known, only four years later than that reconstructed for a fragmentary date on Chiapa de Corzo Stela 2 **(PL. 148)**.[16]

Such spectacular finds documented the artistic and intellectual accomplishments of the Olmec and their successors, and they ensured the continuing support of the National Geographic Society. Stirling also did not ignore the more tedious but essential task of classifying artifacts and using them to ascertain relative chronologies—he simply assigned them to his assistants. Consequently, the two seasons at Tres Zapotes produced two different ceramic classifications with somewhat different chronological interpretations. Weiant, who accompanied Stirling in 1938–1939, classified the artifacts recovered in the mound cuts and nonstratigraphic excavations of that season.[17] Archaeologist Philip Drucker classified the ceramics from the stratigraphic excavations he directed in the 1939–1940 field season.[18] Although Weiant had the better comparative grasp of Mesoamerican ceramics, Drucker had the advantage of stratigraphic sequences that tapped earlier levels of occupation; therefore, Drucker's sequence long stood as the standard for the southern Gulf Coast. Unfortunately, the simultaneous publication of Weiant's and Drucker's reports led to a great deal of confusion and a rancorous exchange between the two ceramicists.[19]

Following the 1939–1940 season, interest in Tres Zapotes waned as the site was overshadowed by the spectacular Olmec discoveries at La Venta and San Lorenzo.[20] Nevertheless, stone monuments continued to come to light at Tres Zapotes. A second colossal head, Monument Q **(PL. 1)**, was discovered in 1950 in the plaza of the Nestepe mound group, east of the Arroyo Hueyapan. It is linked stylistically to Monument A through the relatively plain, caplike headdress, the tapered earplugs, the triangular shape of the area between its eyebrows, the lack of irises in its eyes, and its overall proportions.[21] Monument Q is the more naturalistically carved of the two, however, and it is unique in the prognathism of its jaws, the deep carving of its features, and the birdlike shape on the top of its helmet with feathers that hang down the back of the head.

Howel Williams and Robert Heizer examined Monument Q in their pioneering petrographic study of the source rocks for Olmec monuments, concluding that it, like most of the monuments at Tres Zapotes, was carved from the porphyritic basalt with large, black, pyroxene crystals found on the extinct volcano Cerro El Vigía, whose lower slopes are a mere 3 miles (5 kilometers) away.[22] Despite the proximity of the basalt source, Tres Zapotes Monuments A and Q are among the smallest of the seventeen Olmec heads, standing a little less than 5 feet (1.5 meters) tall and weighing a mere 7.8 and 8.5 tons (7.1 and 7.7 metric tons), respectively.[23]

Fieldwork, however, still lagged at Tres Zapotes. In 1970, as part of the Tuxtlas survey directed by archaeologists Robert Squier and Francisco Beverido Pereau, Ponciano Ortíz Ceballos excavated a deep trench in the bank of the Arroyo Hueyapan, next to Drucker's trenches from the 1939–1940 season that had uncovered early deposits beneath a layer of volcanic ash.[24] Ortíz Ceballos was able to separate Middle Formative (1000–400 BC) ceramics from Late Formative (400–1 BC) ceramics, extending the occupation of Tres Zapotes some six hundred years earlier than had been thought; he also found tantalizing evidence of an even earlier occupation in a few sherds that had apparently been washed in by the arroyo. The Tuxtlas survey also recovered the largest of all the colossal Olmec heads, more than 11 feet (3.4 meters) tall and about 50 tons (45 metric tons), found at Cobata on the mountain divide separating Tres Zapotes from Santiago Tuxtla.[25]

In 1978, the construction of a natural-gas pipeline that clipped the northeast corner of Tres Zapotes provided the opportunity for Luis Millet

Cámara, under the direction of Ángel García Cook, to excavate the area around three basalt columns that were partly interred on the south side of the plaza of Group 2, the site's largest mound group.[26] Millet Cámara uncovered eight upright basalt columns surrounding a low platform that had steps made from slabs of basalt. In the middle of the platform was another slab with a hole of almost 12 inches (30 centimeters) carved through the center. The hole was placed over a short serpentine column carved with a mat design, concentric circles, and a cleft in the upper end. About 6 inches (15 centimeters) below the base of the platform was an offering of howler and spider monkey bones, two celts of jade and serpentine, a pseudocelt of petrified wood, pottery, cinnabar, and a shark's tooth. Although the basalt-column enclosure resembles La Venta Tomb A (see Reilly, this volume), minus that tomb's roof of basalt columns, it contained no human remains.

After Millet Cámara's excavations, the only fieldwork conducted at Tres Zapotes until 1995 was the occasional salvage of a burial found while plowing a field or building a road. From 1995 to 1997, I directed the Tres Zapotes Archaeological Survey (RATZ in its Spanish acronym) with the goals of producing a detailed map of the site, determining its limits, and tracing its history of settlement. In 2003, the renamed Tres Zapotes Archaeological Project (PATZ) conducted a series of excavations to investigate changes in the political economy of Tres Zapotes from Olmec to epi-Olmec times.

Despite the long history of research at Tres Zapotes, some fundamental questions remained unanswered in 1995. For example, no one knew how large the site was or how its several mound groups related to one another. Were they segments of one large town or the centers of several smaller communities? Did they operate simultaneously as the seats of powerful leaders, or did a series of rulers build and abandon them in sequence? The lack of systematically collected samples of datable pottery—or even an accurate site map—was an impediment to answering these questions.

Obtaining new data was no simple matter. There was the usual sauna-like heat and humidity of the southern Veracruz dry season, and the rains in late June and July that started to turn fields into quagmires. There was the impressive variety of ticks (*garrapatas*) and tiny chiggers (*pinolillos*) that had tormented Stirling and Drucker decades before. The seas of sugarcane had sharp-edged leaves that slashed clothing and skin, as well as stalks nearly 10 feet (3 meters) tall that obscured transit rods. As uncomfortable as these natural difficulties were, the greatest challenge—and ultimately the most rewarding—was earning the trust of the communal landholders (*ejiditarios*) in whose village we lived and in whose fields we worked. Each of the first three seasons we were there, the project had to shut down for a week or so while we resolved work-related issues in assemblies of the *ejido.*

The people of Tres Zapotes were particularly concerned about what we would do with the artifacts we found. Beginning with Stirling's removal of Stela C and Monument C to the National Museum in Mexico City, and continuing with the transport of Monument Q and others to the municipal seat in Santiago Tuxtla, generations of archaeologists and officials had taken objects from Tres Zapotes that the people believed should stay in the community. Despite the construction of a local museum in 1975, many felt that Tres Zapotes was not receiving the resources merited by its international fame. The dispute flared up around 1986 when then-governor of Veracruz, Agustín Acosta Lagunes, sent a flatbed truck to Tres Zapotes to take the first colossal head, Monument A, to the new museum he was building in the state capital, Xalapa. As related to me by a wizened woman in her eighties, she and the other *zapotecos* blockaded the road and commanded the truck driver, at the point of their machetes, to return the head to its pedestal in the Tres Zapotes museum—and she would do the same if I attempted to take any of the monuments.

We faced a potential difficulty in that Mexican law requires archaeologists to turn over everything they find to the Instituto Nacional de Antropología e Historia (INAH). We were able to resolve the matter to everyone's satisfaction by building a laboratory and storage facility in the Tres Zapotes museum, conveniently operated by INAH, enabling us to comply with the law while keeping the artifacts in the community. It goes without saying that the monuments on view in *Olmec: Colossal Masterworks of Ancient Mexico* were removed from Tres Zapotes long before our project began.

The Growth of an Olmec Capital

The research my colleagues and I have conducted since 1995 has produced a much fuller picture of how Tres Zapotes developed into a major center, how its inhabitants adapted Olmec culture to changing political environments, and how the site ultimately declined.

The village of Tres Zapotes sits on the second of two sharp bends on the Arroyo Hueyapan, where it flows from the Tuxtla Mountains onto the broad plain of the Papaloapan basin. The archaeological site stretches northward and upstream past the second bend, sprawling over 1,235 acres (500 hectares) of the alluvial plain and terraces on either side of the arroyo. The largest of the 160 earthen mounds, up to 39 feet (12 meters) in height, occur in four groups (Groups 1–3 and the Nestepe Group) set around broad plazas that are separated from one another by about five-eighths of a mile (a little less than 1 kilometer). Lower platforms that supported common residences and other buildings are interspersed between and around the formal mound groups.

The earliest in situ deposits uncovered thus far belong to the second half of the Early Formative period (ca. 1250–1000 BC).[27] At that time, Tres Zapotes appears to have been a moderately sized village that covered about 50 acres (20 hectares). The Olmec inhabitants likely practiced a mixed subsistence economy, planting maize and other crops and taking advantage of the rich wild resources of forest, field, and stream. Not all activities were devoted to subsistence, however. An offering we encountered near an Early Formative burial contained a plate on which was a single catfish spine. The spine would likely have been used in a bloodletting ritual, as were stingray spines depicted in later Olmec art. The inhabitants used pottery similar to that being made at the time at the major Olmec capital of San Lorenzo, but they also incorporated decorative techniques and motifs that were more common in pottery from the Mexican highlands. Likewise, figurines exhibit a combination of styles from the southern and central coasts of Veracruz, including both "baby-face" Olmec figures and hawk-nosed Trapiche-style figurines more common in sites north and west of Olman.[28] Volcanic obsidian glass used for cutting tools also reflects an orientation to areas north and west of Olman, because it was imported almost exclusively from two or three sources in the Mexican highlands rather than from the wide variety of Mexican and Guatemalan sources drawn upon by San Lorenzo's populace. Early Formative villagers at Tres Zapotes, however, did manage to acquire a few perforated iron-ore cubes, probably from the Río La Venta area of western Chiapas and perhaps via San Lorenzo, which imported literally tons of the enigmatic objects.[29]

It was not until the Middle Formative period (1000–400 BC), though, that Tres Zapotes grew to a size and regional importance that would support leaders with the power and authority to commission impressive stone monuments. During this period, Tres Zapotes expanded to cover a core area of 197 acres (80 hectares) with another 172 acres (70 hectares) of occupation in adjoining settlements. The earliest ceremonial platforms appear to have been constructed at this time. We have documented one such platform in excavations and deep auger tests in what would later be called Group 2. The platform, which is bracketed by radiocarbon dates of about 700–400 BC, stood around 6½ feet (2 meters) high, including a 31-inch (80-centimeter) thick cap of fine gray clay.[30] The altar with the basalt enclosure that Millet Cámara excavated also belongs to this period. A third candidate is a red-capped platform, also about 6½ feet (2 meters) high, that was later covered by Mound 5 in Group 1, the same group where Monument A was discovered.[31]

The themes expressed in the eleven Olmec sculptures currently known from Tres Zapotes reflect its importance as the capital of a Middle Formative polity.[32] Early in the period, rulers commissioned colossal heads such as Monument Q to be carved as portraits that emphasized their personal authority and power. Later, the stela became the preferred form for expressing Olmec rulership at Tres Zapotes, as it had at La Venta and other sites as far as Guerrero and Guatemala.[33] Two Olmec stelae have been found at Tres Zapotes to date: Stela A, and the recently discovered fragment of Stela F.[34] The more complete Stela A **(FIG. 30)** depicts the ruler as the axis mundi connecting the underworld and the heavens, represented by the monster masks above and below him. He is flanked by two attendants, while dwarflike supernaturals (*chaneques*) float on one side panel, similar to the diminutive figures on La Venta Stelae 2 and 3; on the other side panel, in a scene unique in Olmec iconography, a jaguar and serpent face off against each other. The face of the central figure was battered beyond recognition in antiquity.

The distribution of these monuments representing the Olmec rulers of Tres Zapotes is also revealing and contrasts with the distribution of the later epi-Olmec monuments. The two colossal heads were found at the east and west extremes of the site, in the Nestepe Group and Group 1, respectively. The two Olmec stelae were discovered within the fringes of the Middle Formative site core of Tres Zapotes. Near the center of the site was the altar with the basalt-column enclosure and serpentine column. Thus, in their final positions, these Olmec monuments exhibit a pattern of concentric zones that moves inward from the peripheries, guarded by the colossal head portraits of the most ancient rulers, to the stelae of more recent rulers, to the symbolic expression of the axis mundi in the central altar. Although the heads may have been repositioned in the Late Formative period, the fact that

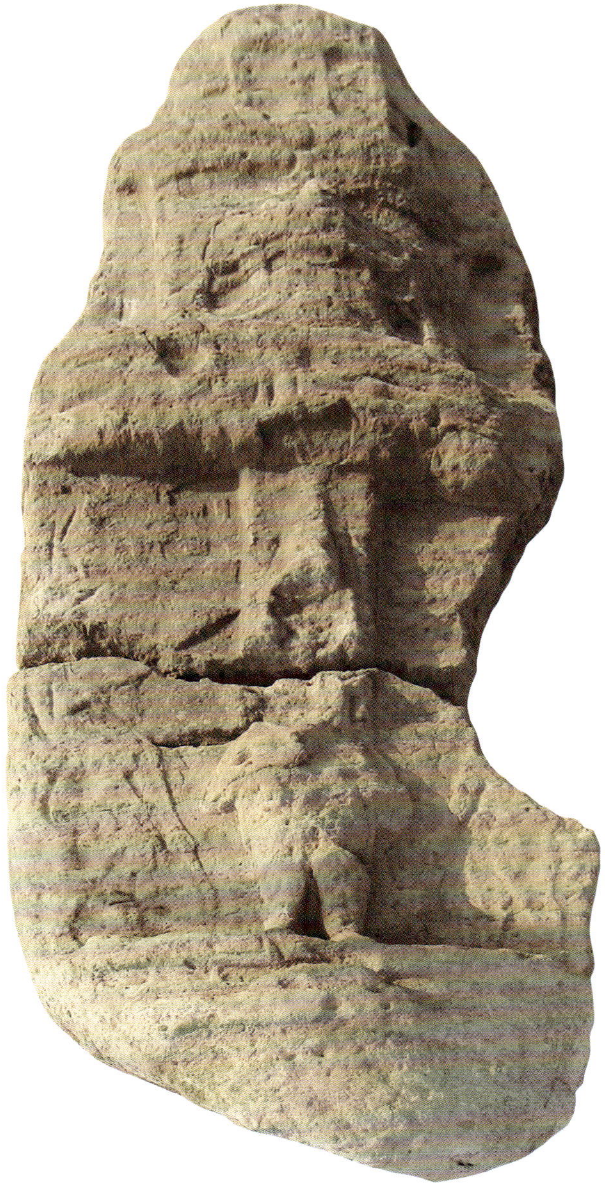

FIG. 30
STELA A
Mexico, Veracruz, Tres Zapotes, 700–400 BC
Volcanic breccia
Height: 211 1/8 in. (536 cm)
Museo de Sitio de Tres Zapotes

this concentric zoning pertains only to particular classes of Olmec monuments suggests that they were in their approximate locations by the end of the Middle Formative period when the altar (which certainly was not repositioned) was constructed.

Throughout the Middle Formative period, Olmec rulers at Tres Zapotes also commissioned sculptures in the round depicting humans and composite human-animal figures, of which Monument M **(FIG. 26, PL. 81)** is a good example. Stirling found Monument M on the west bank of the Arroyo Hueyapan, about a half mile (0.8 kilometers) upstream and east of Group 3, near Monument N, a 19-inch-tall (48-centimeter-tall) basalt cylinder with a 4-inch-deep (10-centimeter-deep) basin at one end.[35] Although the arms and legs had broken off, enough was left to see that it had been a seated figure carved in a style that reminded Stirling of some monuments at La Venta. The head was later broken off when local inhabitants attempted to move the monument to the village of Tres Zapotes. The monument then disappeared for a time, until the head resurfaced in the collection of the Museo Amparo in Puebla, where it was displayed as a piece from La Venta. Alerted by a former student, David C. Grove examined illustrations in a museum catalogue and concluded that it could be the head of the missing Tres Zapotes statue. The pattern of fracture at the neck and other imperfections in the stone confirm that it is, indeed, the missing head. It is unfortunate that someone recarved the eyes, nose, and mouth to accentuate them, perhaps in a misguided attempt to increase the aesthetic appeal or the "authenticity" of the monument; such are the dangers of acquiring unprovenienced objects. Despite the damage, however, the recovered piece is an important testament to the Olmec presence at Tres Zapotes.

The Epi-Olmec Florescence

Around 400 BC, the great Olmec center of La Venta collapsed and the surrounding area of western Tabasco was largely abandoned, echoing the fate that had befallen San Lorenzo and the Coatzacoalcos basin six hundred years earlier. Meanwhile, Tres Zapotes flourished, growing to its full extent of more than 1,200 acres (500 hectares) during the Late Formative period (400–1 BC). Major programs of mound construction were initiated, with most of the construction concentrated in the four formal plaza groups mentioned previously. Distributions of artifacts on the surface and in deep auger tests in the alluvial floodplain show that these groups were not centers of separate communities but were connected by residential occupation that extended continuously between them.[36] Another formal complex that Stirling named Mound Group 4 lies outside this continuous zone of artifacts, and so outside Tres Zapotes proper.[37]

Rather than formal architecture being heavily concentrated in a central civic-ceremonial district pattern typical in lowland sites such as La Venta and Laguna de los Cerros, the plaza groups of Tres Zapotes are widely dispersed and regularly spaced at between 3,100 and 3,230 feet (945 and 985 meters), and three of the four groups are located in the less densely settled periphery of the site. All four groups exhibit common elements—a long mound along the plaza's north side, a pyramidal or conical temple mound at the plaza's west end, and a low *adoratorio* platform on the plaza's central east-west axis—which we call the Tres Zapotes Plaza Group (TZPG) plan. Three of the four groups contain one or two additional temple mounds at the west end of the plaza that are aligned to the same axis and other ancillary mounds. Later additions to Group 3 modified this basic layout, although the original plaza was preserved.[38] Although Group 2 has the largest area and is centrally located, Group 3 rivals it in area and has a greater volume of mound construction.[39] In other words, no single plaza group of the four is clearly dominant over the others. This raises the questions of whether political rule was centralized in any one of the four mound groups, whether the mound groups were erected sequentially by successive rulers, or whether power was shared among the several leaders of a confederation.

The data we have collected most strongly supports the last model. Late Formative ceramic types are prevalent on the mounds of each plaza group, although each also exhibits Protoclassic (AD 1–300) and Classic period (AD 300–900) types. Radiocarbon dates from refuse deposits behind the long mounds in Group 2, Group 3, and the Nestepe Group likewise overlap to a substantial degree, reducing the likelihood that they were successive seats of rulership. The artifact assemblages do not reveal significant differences in access to exotic prestige goods among the four plaza groups. Craft specialists in workshops attached to each plaza group produced pottery, obsidian artifacts, and groundstone artifacts similar to those that were made and used by nonelite residents, the principal exception being evidence for the working of mica in Group 2. Indeed, the most striking difference we have detected between the elite and nonelite inhabitants of Late Formative Tres Zapotes is that the elites appear to have more often consumed dogs as food.[40] All of this evidence points to a political economy in which epi-Olmec elites downplayed their differences among one another and between themselves and their subjects, at least compared with their Olmec predecessors. Essentially, the leaders of Tres Zapotes appear to have survived the growing political competition of the Late Formative period by creating a system of cooperative government. The construction of a plaza group in the TZPG plan at El Mesón, a little more than 6 miles (10 kilometers) to the north, suggests that the Tres Zapotes confederation was also successful in expanding its territory to incorporate other settlements.[41]

Heritage and Adaptation in Epi-Olmec Tres Zapotes

The epi-Olmec monuments of Late Formative Tres Zapotes reflect key strategies used by the confederation of leaders to reinforce their authority in an increasingly competitive political landscape. One strategy was to underscore their Olmec heritage as a source of legitimacy while adapting Olmec iconography to the requirements of a more cooperative governmental structure, for example, by incorporating ancient Olmec monuments in the layouts of formal civic-ceremonial architecture.[42] The two colossal heads, Monuments A and Q, were each located on the south edges of Group 1 and the Nestepe Group, and they both looked northward toward the center of the opposing long mound. Likewise, the long mound of Group 2 was constructed opposite the altar that contained the serpentine column representing the axis mundi. The positioning of the principal administrative building and elite residence of each of these three mound groups opposite a more ancient representation of Olmec rulership seems to have been calculated to legitimate the authority of the factional leaders of epi-Olmec Tres Zapotes.[43]

The iconography of ritual and rulership in Late Formative monuments also drew on Olmec concepts. This is particularly evident in the carving on the obverse of Stela C. In the lower register on the front of Stela C is a carving recognizable as an Olmec-derived mask representative of an earth monster.[44] In the upper register, the profile head of a human emerges amid curving branches from a quadripartite medallion located above and between the flame eyebrows of the mask, a striking reference to the ruler as the axis mundi in the form of the world tree. The image of the ruler "seated" above the monster mask recalls Olmec thrones such as La Venta Altar 4 **(FIG. 19)**, and the figure of a costumed personage seated on the monster-mask throne in the Oxtotitlan mural **(FIGS. 36–37)**; the profile head on this celtiform stela also resembles profile heads carved on Middle Formative celts such as that from Río Pesquero, which F. Kent Reilly III identifies as a representation of the ruler as world tree.[45]

While clearly employing Olmec themes, Stela C also stands as an example of how the representation of rulership changed with the development of cooperative governance in Late Formative Tres Zapotes. Images of rulers in the Olmec monuments of Tres Zapotes, like those of other Olmec capitals, reveal a preoccupation with the personal power of the ruler as an individual.[46] That individualizing focus is exhibited in the portraiture of the colossal heads; the centrality, high relief, and tall stature of the rulers carved on Stelae A and F;[47] and the naturalistic modeling of human figures in some seated monuments like Monument I. By comparison, images of rulers on Late Formative sculpture at Tres Zapotes are rare and less individualized than their predecessors. The iconic profile head on the obverse of Stela C focuses on the office of ruler and his role as cosmic intermediary rather than upon his individual persona. Another Late Formative monument, Stela D, may represent the subjugation of a rival, but it is from a secondary center in the orbit of Tres Zapotes and the figures on the monument are not highly individualized. Interestingly, the "faceless" representation of governance within Tres Zapotes does not extend to Late Formative and Protoclassic monuments from other sites in the lower Papaloapan basin, such as El Mesón Stelae 1 and 2, the Alvarado Stela, or, most strikingly, the La Mojarra Stela, with its image of a richly adorned ruler accompanied by a four-hundred-character hieroglyphic text with Long Count dates in AD 143 and 156.[48] These representational contrasts suggest that the cooperation we infer among factional leaders within Tres Zapotes did not characterize relationships among competitors in the broader region.

The inscription of historical events in stone using sophisticated writing and calendrical systems is another important epi-Olmec development, represented at Tres Zapotes by the Long Count date and hieroglyphic text on the reverse of Stela C (which may have been carved some time after the obverse).[49] Although the text on Stela C is definitely in the epi-Olmec script, most of it is unfortunately illegible.[50] The Long Count date may, however, provide a clue to the event commemorated in the text. The date is usually interpreted as September 3, 32 BC, but based on his studies of other epi-Olmec inscriptions, John Justeson argues that the base of the epi-Olmec Long Count was twenty days earlier than the Maya calendar, or August 14, 32 BC, the date of a lunar eclipse that was followed two weeks later by a solar eclipse.[51] The second century AD text on the La Mojarra Stela also appears to make reference to astronomical events, while the Tuxtla statuette (AD 162) refers to rituals, although in the context of historical events surrounding the installation of the ruler depicted on the La Mojarra Stela.[52]

The development of epi-Olmec writing and the Long Count can be seen as the culmination of an increasing focus on historicity, beginning with the carving of scenes in late Olmec reliefs that appear to record mythicohistorical events (such as the meeting of two important personages in La Venta Stela 3), and continuing in Late Formative relief scenes like that on Tres Zapotes Stela D.[53] In addition to adapting an ancient Olmec heritage, the rulers of Tres Zapotes also expressed their interactions with distant and powerful polities of their own time. This is particularly evident in the use of carving styles and iconographic conventions from the Pacific slopes of Chiapas and Guatemala, although the intensity of Izapan influence at Tres Zapotes has sometimes been exaggerated.

One of the better examples of Izapan influence is the elaborately carved stone box, Monument C **(PL. 79)**. Discovered in front of the long mound in Group 2, the box depicts warriors with spears caught up in swirling scrolls of water or clouds.[54] The design completely fills the space, which is atypical for Olmec style but similar to some monuments from Izapa, such as Stela 5. The incised flat relief of the carving is characteristic of the Izapan style, as are the scrolls along the lower edge of the best-preserved side A. The dots within these basal scrolls are unusual, but they are also present in the equally intricate scene on Izapa Stela 5.[55] Izapan influence can also be seen in Stela D, particularly in the long-lipped serpents carved on the sides of the monument, the downward-facing figure at the top of the scene, and the overall narrative composition.[56] The use of the monster's maw to frame the figures recalls Izapa Miscellaneous Monument 2 and a niche figure from Tiltepec.[57] The depiction of a two-headed serpent hanging from the monster's mouth resembles both Izapan and earlier Olmec monuments, however, and the softly rounded contours of the relief carving are very different from the plano-relief style of most Izapa stelae.

Protoclassic Reorganization and Classic Decline

During the Protoclassic period (AD 1–300), natural disaster and increasing political tensions contributed to significant changes in the settlement pattern and ceremonial programs at Tres Zapotes, especially after about AD 100.[58] People had begun to build their houses away from the banks of the Arroyo Hueyapan by the beginning of the Protoclassic period, and a volcanic eruption late in the period further accelerated abandonment of large parts of the floodplain as the volcanic ash accumulated to depths of 13 feet (4 meters) in lower elevations.[59] As a result, the area of residential occupation was slightly reduced, although not the overall extent of the site. The four plaza groups continued to be used, but the leaders ensconced in Group 3 initiated a new construction program with a north-south plaza that diverged from the standard Tres Zapotes Plaza Group plan.

Stela C enters the story of Tres Zapotes once again at this point, having been broken some time after the carving of the 32 BC date. Its lower fragment was erected behind an irregular circular altar at the southern foot of Mound 23, which encloses the north end of the newer plaza and is the largest mound in Group 3.[60] The stela, however, was set on its side, just as Stirling found it, with no attention paid to the correct orientation of the monster mask or the carved date. That is, it was employed in a similar fashion to Monument 44, an irregular slab of unworked basalt that was placed as a plain stela just south of Stela C with accompanying offerings of pottery and obsidian. A bowl in one of these offerings contained charcoal that produced a calibrated radiocarbon date of AD 135,[61] firmly in the Protoclassic period. What irony that the lords of Tres Zapotes should treat one of the oldest inscriptions in the epi-Olmec stela so cavalierly, at virtually the same time Harvester Mountain Lord was inscribing his deeds on the La Mojarra Stela and the Tuxtla statuette!

During the Early Classic period (AD 300–600), substantial mound construction in Groups 1, 2, and 3 suggests that Tres Zapotes continued to hold a prominent position in the eastern lower Papaloapan basin.[62] The ancient capital had already begun a slow decline, however. Residential settlement was reorganized into discontinuous zones of intensive settlement separated by more sparsely inhabited areas, resulting in an overall decline in the population of the site while populations were growing on the plains to the north around El Mesón, and while Cerro de las Mesas held sway on the western side of the lower Papaloapan basin.[63] By the end of the Late Classic period (AD 600–1000), after more than two thousand years of continuous occupation, Tres Zapotes was abandoned. Early Postclassic people would inter the cremated remains of their dead there, but Tres Zapotes would never regain its regional preeminence.

NOTES

1 Stirling 1939: 183–218.

2 In May 1983, with Robert S. Santley in a University of New Mexico pickup truck on the way to San Andrés Tuxtla for the Matacapan Archaeological Project.

3 All dates in this article are given in calendar years, as opposed to uncalibrated radiocarbon years. The difference is insignificant at 400 BC, but, for example, 900 BC in radiocarbon years calibrates to about 1000 BC in calendar years. I use *Olmec* to refer specifically to the archaeological culture that flourished in southern Veracruz and western Tabasco (Olman) between 1400 and 400 BC.

4 Melgar 1869. Stirling (1939: 183) gives the date of the initial discovery by a workman on the Hacienda de Hueyapan as 1858. However, Melgar (1869: 292) writes only, *"Estaba en 1862 avecindado en San Andrés Tuxtla... supe de una cabeza colosal que habia desenterrado pocos años antes..."* without specifying the precise year of the discovery.

5 Clewlow et al. 1967: 28.

6 On the 1905 visit, see Seler-Sachs 1922. For the Weyerstall publication, see Weyerstall 1932.

7 Stirling 1968: 3.

8 Stirling 1943: 2.

9 Pugh 1981: 3.

10 Stirling 1943: 11–25.

11 Stirling 1940a, 1939.

12 Stirling 1940a: 5–8. The Preclassic structure at Uaxactun was E-VII-sub, which at the time had been excavated only a few years before.

13 Pugh 1981: 6. Working outside the Maya area, it is notable that the Stirlings had the foresight to pack Morley's 1915 *Bureau of American Ethnology Bulletin*.

14 Long Count dates were inscribed by the epi-Olmec and the Maya using a modified vigesimal (base 20) place system with bar-and-dot numerals arranged in columns. By convention, epigraphers represent the dates horizontally, beginning with the largest unit of time (the baktun) on the left and the numerals for the other units in descending order separated by dots. The Goodman-Martinez-Thompson correlation is used here, which accords best with radiocarbon dates and astronomical events. In his *National Geographic* article, Stirling (1939) reported the actual date of (7).16.6.16.18, 6 Etz'nab (1 Wo) on Stela C as November 4, 291 BC, using the Spinden correlation. Neither Marion Stirling nor Matthew Stirling in his formal report (1940a) attempted to correlate the Stela C date with the western calendar. Basing their work on Morley, the Stirlings used the spelling *Eznab*; contemporary scholars tend to prefer *Etz'nab* (see Coe and Van Stone 2001).

15 Stirling 1939: 183; 1940a; Thompson 1941; Morley 1946.

16 Justeson and Kaufman 2008.

17 Weiant 1943.

18 Drucker 1943a.

19 Wauchope (1950) drew attention to the inconsistencies in the two reports. The responses came from Drucker (1952b) and Weiant (1952).

20 For La Venta, see Drucker, Heizer, and Squier 1959; Stirling 1940b, 1942, 1943: 48–60. For San Lorenzo, see Stirling 1955: 1–23; Coe 1968b; Coe and Diehl 1980.

21 Clewlow et al. 1967: 57–58.

22 Williams and Heizer 1965.

23 Clewlow et al. 1967: table 17.

24 Ortíz Ceballos 1975.

25 Beverido Pereau 1987.

26 Millet Cámara 1979.

27 Pool, Ortíz Ceballos, and Rodríguez M. 2010.

28 The name *Trapiche style* is used for hawk-nosed, solid figurines most common in south-central Veracruz (that is, north and west of Olman). See García Payón 1971: figs. 16a–e.

29 On the iron-ore cubes, see Weiant 1943: 21, pl. 76. On the Río La Venta, see Agrinier 1984. On the importation of objects, see Di Castro Stringher 1997.

30 Davidson 2009; Pool and Ortíz Ceballos 2008.

31 Weiant 1943: 6–7.

32 Ortíz Ceballos 2008.

33 See Grove, this volume.

34 On Stela A, see Pool, forthcoming; Stirling 1943: 11–14; compare with Coe 1965c: 773; Pool 2000: 149, 151. On Stela F, see Pool, forthcoming.

35 Stirling 1943: 24.

36 Pool and Ohnersorgen 2003: 25.

37 Stirling 1943: 14; Pool and Ohnersorgen 2003: 19–21.

38 Pool 2008: 138–139; Sullivan 2002.

39 Sullivan 2002: 91–97.

40 Peres 2009.

41 Loughlin 2009.

42 Pool 2008, forthcoming.

43 Pool 2008: 145.

44 Coe 1965c: 769.

45 Reilly 1995: 26–45; Pool 2000: 150.

46 Blanton et al. 1996.

47 de la Fuente 1996b, 2000; Pool, forthcoming.

48 Stuart 1993: 1700.

49 Graham 2005.

50 Justeson and Kaufman 2008: 167.

51 John Justeson, personal communications, 2003, 2007; compare with Malmström (1997: 141–144), who speculates on the discrepancy between the solar eclipse and the September 3 date.

52 Kaufman and Justeson 2001; Houston and Coe (2004: 151–161) dispute Kaufman and Justeson's decipherment of the epi-Olmec script. For a partial response, see Justeson and Kaufman 2008: 162, 187, 190.

53 Pool 2000: 152–153.

54 On the discovery location, see Stirling 1943: 14.

55 Norman 1976: 296.

56 On Stela D, see Coe 1965c: 773; Norman 1976: 293.

57 Norman 1976: figs. 5.25, 5.26, 5.27.

58 Pool 2008: 138, 141; forthcoming.

59 Pool and Ohnersorgen 2003: 25; Wendt 2003: 36, 38.

60 Stirling 1940a: 1.

61 The date given is the calibrated intercept for the radiocarbon age of 1870 ± 50 B.P. The calibrated 2σ error range is AD 55–255 (using Calib Rev 4.4.2 computer calibration program with the intcal98 calibration curve).

62 Drucker 1943a: 144–146; Weiant 1943: 6–7, 12–15; see also Pool 2008.

63 Coe 1965a: 710–711; Drucker 1943a: 123.

ACKNOWLEDGMENTS

Fieldwork at Tres Zapotes was conducted with the permission of the Instituto Nacional de Antropología e Historia, the institutional support of the University of Kentucky and Ithaca College, and financial support from the National Science Foundation (grant numbers SBR-9405063, SBR-9615031, and BCS-0242555). I am indebted to the many students and colleagues who have collaborated on the Tres Zapotes project and whose work is cited herein, but especially to Ponciano Ortíz Ceballos for his unwavering support and invaluable advice. Special credit and thanks go to David Grove for recognizing that the head in the Museo Amparo, Puebla, was that of Tres Zapotes Monument M and for including me in the discussion. Finally, I thank Kathleen Berrin and Virginia Fields for their invitation to contribute this essay.

OLMEC-STYLE ART OUTSIDE OLMAN

David C. Grove

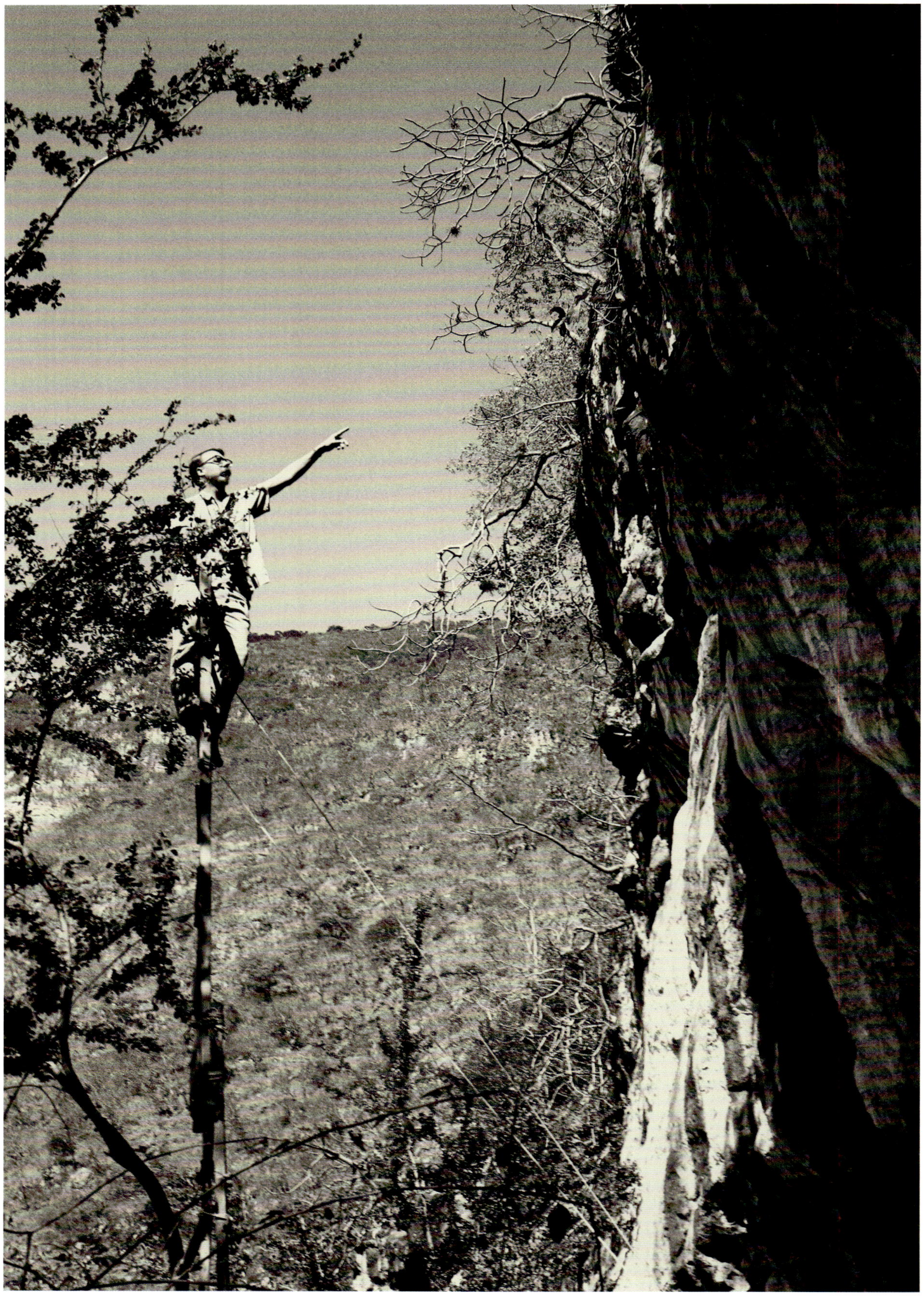

Although archaeological evidence securely identifies Mexico's southern Gulf Coast as the domain of the Olmec, Olmec-like artifacts and iconographic motifs are often found at the contemporaneous settlements and centers of non-Olmec societies across much of Mesoamerica. The term *Olmec style*, or sometimes simply *Olmec*, has frequently been used to characterize such art and artifacts,[1] resulting in two separate meanings for the word: (1) a Formative (Preclassic) period archaeological culture of southeastern Mexico, and (2) a diverse and far more widely spread art style. Because the two meanings are not identical, the term *Olmec* can be confusing to both scholars and the public.[2] Furthermore, even after seven decades of research, scholars have not reached agreement regarding the relationship between the Olmec archaeological culture of Mexico's Gulf Coast and the widespread art style bearing the same name.

This essay provides my archaeologist's perspective on some important Formative period sites in non-Olmec areas of Mesoamerica where various examples of the Olmec art style have been found. I begin with a significant but often overlooked point: What is termed the Olmec art style was neither monolithic nor static. It changed over time; thus, the traits comprising the Olmec style at 1000 BC are different from those at 800 or 500 BC. In addition, as the objects in this exhibition illustrate (and as this essay reiterates), the Olmec style shows significant regional and subregional variations. Whatever its origins, the style was adopted, adapted, manipulated, and elaborated upon by creative artisans of many non-Olmec societies.

Between ca. 1150 and 900 BC—the Early Formative period time span contemporaneous with the zenith of the Olmec center of San Lorenzo—the Olmec art style in Olman and elsewhere appeared primarily as a distinctive set of symbols incised or engraved on pottery vessels **(PLS. 23–24)**, and as solid and hollow

FIG. 31
Author David C. Grove examining the polychrome cliff mural (fig. 36) at Oxtotitlan cave, Guerrero, 1968

"baby-face" figurines **(PL. 132)**. It is significant that during this early period of Olmec prehistory, the most distinguishing feature of Olmec culture—stone sculpture such as colossal heads, thrones, and three-dimensional statuary—is found only at sites in Olman. In the subsequent Middle Formative period (ca. 900–500 BC), when La Venta and Tres Zapotes were the predominant centers in Olman, the widespread Olmec art style underwent significant transformations. Motifs on pottery and ceramic baby figurines gave way to iconography on elite objects such as greenstone (especially jadeite) figurines and celts. Furthermore, during this period Olmec-like stone carvings were created at some sites in west-central and southern Mexico.[3] Because the Early and Middle Formative periods are so different, they are discussed separately below.

Early Formative Period Sites

Tlatilco and Tlapacoya

Modern Mexico City sprawls across the large, flat floor of the Basin of Mexico and into the surrounding foothills. Until the sixteenth century, the basin's floor was dominated by a large lake; thirty centuries ago, small Formative period villages ringed the shores of the lake. Although the archaeological remains of most of the villages were destroyed long ago by the urban expansion of Mexico City, a small number of sites did receive archaeological attention before disappearing. The two most prominent of these are Tlatilco and Tlapacoya, both of which attained fame from the Olmec-style ceramic vessels and figurines found there.

Tlatilco, situated a few miles inland from the western shore of the lake, was discovered by accident. San Luis Tlatilco, the location of twentieth-century brickyards, was being intensively "mined" for the clay needed to make bricks. Workers digging the clay often found pottery fragments, clay figurines, and sometimes human skeletons associated with funerary offerings of clay figurines and bowls. Collectors of pre-Columbian antiquities, including the famed Mexican artists Diego Rivera and Miguel Covarrubias, visited the Tlatilco brickyards frequently to purchase artifacts found by the workers. Covarrubias recognized that some of the site's pottery was "in the purest Olmec style,"[4] and he helped bring about the first archaeological research there. Four archaeological excavations were carried out at Tlatilco between 1942 and 1969 on plots of land not yet destroyed by the brickyards.[5] That research uncovered nearly five hundred burials and their associated offerings, and perhaps an equal or greater quantity had been found by brickyard workers.

Covarrubias noted that "baby-face" figurines and vessels decorated with Olmec-style motifs occur at Tlatilco. It is now possible to determine that such objects compose three to five percent of the site's ceramics and that the motifs are usually executed on highland vessel forms, informing us that those pots were locally produced, not imported. The most numerous decorated pottery vessels at Tlatilco—the "local style"—are earthenware bowls and bottles, often in exotic forms, with simple red geometric and linear designs. Similarly, the site's most abundant clay figurines are primarily in the highland "pretty lady" style **(PLS. 116–117, 119)**.

Although our knowledge of Tlatilco comes from its burials and offerings, it was not a graveyard. The site contains the remains of one or several Early Formative period villages, and the burials are deceased villagers who had most probably been interred beneath or adjacent to their house structure in the settlement.[6] Furthermore, even though Tlatilco is a famous site, it is not unique. Early Formative villages and hamlets with identical red-on-brown ceramics, "pretty lady" figurines, and Olmec-style pottery existed in the western lake area of the Basin of Mexico as well as throughout the entire state of Morelos to the south.[7] A selection of the rich variety of ceramic vessels and figurine types from Tlatilco and Morelos can be seen in this exhibition.

The site of Tlapacoya (also known as Zohapilco) is located approximately 24 miles (39 kilometers) southeast of Tlatilco, edged against the base of a large hill near the extreme southeastern margin of the lake. Archaeological excavations at Tlapacoya[8] did not seek or uncover burials, thus the Tlapacoya data are not comparable to Tlatilco's. From the richness and quantity of the ceramic bowls and figurines recovered through both illicit and professional excavations at Tlapacoya, however, the site's Olmec-style ceramics *seem* to have been more abundant and diverse than Tlatilco's. Although Tlatilco (the western lake area) and Tlapacoya (the southeastern lake area) have many ceramic vessel types and figurines in common, there are also some noticeable regional differences in their ceramic assemblages. One of the most striking to me is that most of the resist-decorated red-on-brown vessels in exotic forms found at Tlatilco and at sites in Morelos are rare or nonexistent at Tlapacoya.[9] Some of the loveliest ceramic bowls from Tlapacoya, in fact, are whitewares with Olmec-style motifs executed in a smudge resist (black on white), which is a vessel type rare at Tlatilco **(PL. 112)**.

While the southeastern basin has historically been an important communication and trade route gateway to the southeast (Puebla, Oaxaca, and Veracruz states), we have little archaeological evidence of the role that Tlapacoya played in the basin's Early Formative lifeways. Tlapacoya's lakeside location suggests that it could have been an active port for canoe trade with the western lake region. Like Tlatilco, Tlapacoya was not unique in its region of the basin but merely one of the few sites that we know about. In fact, the ceramic complex of Tlapacoya seems to be characteristic of the pottery of other southeastern basin villages as well.[10]

Las Bocas

The site of Las Bocas is 50 air miles (80 kilometers) to the southeast of Tlapacoya, in the Izúcar de Matamoros valley of the state of Puebla. Las Bocas has been famed for decades for its very beautiful and imaginative Olmec-style pottery vessels and figurines **(SEE PLS. 24, 130, 132)**, but little is known about the settlement itself.[11] When archaeological research was attempted in 1966 (and recently), the site had already been largely destroyed by clandestine digging.[12] Nonetheless, Las Bocas was smallish in size, and it seems unlikely that the many ceramic vessels and figurines attributed to the site were actually found there. It is probable that these vessels were illicitly excavated at other Early Formative sites within that region of southwestern Puebla and attributed to Las Bocas for convenience and because they fall within that regional style.[13] Likewise, many vessels labeled as originating from Tlapacoya may have come from other southeastern basin sites. Names such as Tlatilco, Tlapacoya, and Las Bocas have become generic labels characterizing regional ceramic styles rather than describing actual proveniences for specific objects.

Southwestern Mesoamerica: Chiapas

The northwestern portion of the state of Chiapas adjoins the domain of the Olmec in southern Veracruz and western Tabasco, and the Early Formative period ceramics throughout Chiapas show many similarities to those from Olman.[14] A recent discovery of very elegant Olmec-style ceramics and "baby-face" figurines at the site of Cantón Corralito have led a few to speculate that the site had been a San Lorenzo Olmec colony.[15] However, the data from Cantón Corralito are not yet published, and the colony hypothesis remains to be tested. Like Tlapacoya and Las Bocas, Cantón Corralito may simply be another example of a site where non-Olmec artisans created their own ornate regional variations of the general Olmec art style.

The Middle Formative Period

By ca. 900 BC, the population across Mesoamerica had grown significantly. In most regions there was an increasing demand for a variety of nonlocal commodities such as greenstone and cacao, which appears to have led to a restructuring and expansion of trade networks. Although we do not know what sorts of alliances were made between distant network centers to provide or acquire commodities, it is intriguing that after 900 BC, Olmec-like stone carvings and art began to occur at a limited number of sites in west-central Mexico and at a second set of sites along the Pacific coastal region of southern Mesoamerica. Most of those sites were situated along major trade routes, and their adoption of the Olmec innovation of stone carving certainly marks them as having had a special relationship with Olman. But how did those distant centers learn the techniques and skills necessary to create Olmec-like stone monuments? Did the artisans somehow learn directly from Olmec sculptors? We don't yet know. Nevertheless, it is clear from the carvings in Morelos, Guerrero, Chiapas, and elsewhere that each center mastered the techniques and also expressed some of their own stylistic canons and motifs in their art.

Chalcatzingo, Morelos

The important Central Mexico Formative period site of Chalcatzingo is located 50 miles (80 kilometers) to the southeast of Mexico City and the Basin of Mexico. Thirty-six Olmec-like carvings, whole and fragmentary, have been recorded there, a quantity that is surpassed for the period only at the Olmec center of La Venta. The site's carved art occurs in two distinct areas. Thirteen bas-reliefs are executed directly onto the exposed rock faces and boulders of the Cerro Chalcatzingo, a mountain that looms over the site. The other twenty-three, primarily statuary and stone stelae, were found amid the house remains and stone-faced platforms of the Middle Formative period village at the base of the mountain.[16]

Chalcatzingo's most famous carving, Monument 1 **(FIG. 32)**, is on a large, vertical stone face high on the mountainside, overlooking a gully that carries rainwater down the mountain. The bas-relief depicts a personage seated within a U-shaped cave-niche, above which are trilobed rain clouds and exclamation point–shaped falling raindrops. Large scroll motifs issue outward from the cave-niche. Both in content and location, the symbolism of rain and fertility on this magnificent relief (and several smaller carvings nearby) is obvious. What is less apparent, however, is that the carving is essentially a two-dimensional depiction of the same basic symbolism covertly expressed in certain large, three-dimensional Olmec thrones.[17] An excellent example is La Venta Altar 5 **(FIG. 33, PLS. 64–66)**, in which a personage (a ruler, living or ancestral) sits within a cave-niche in the throne's front face. Pre-Hispanic Mesoamericans commonly believed caves to be entrances to the underworld and to supernatural forces related to agricultural fertility. Chalcatzingo's Monument 1, with its cave, clouds, and raindrops, depicts that relationship more explicitly than do the stone thrones of Olman.

One of the most significant stone monuments within the ancient village area is Monument 22, the only Olmec-style throne known outside Olman.[18] The throne, which sat within a large, stone-faced sunken patio, is unquestionably Olmec in form although its execution is very different. Whereas thrones in Olman were sculpted from individual boulders, Chalcatzingo's was constructed of stacked stone slabs, even though suitable boulders lay only 100 yards (91 meters) away. It also lacks the frontal niche common to thrones within Olman. Its front is instead carved with a stylized serpent face,[19] a similar version of which occurs in a contemporaneous mural at Oxtotitlan cave in Guerrero (discussed below).

Several motifs in Chalcatzingo's carvings are seen only at La Venta, thus demonstrating a sig-

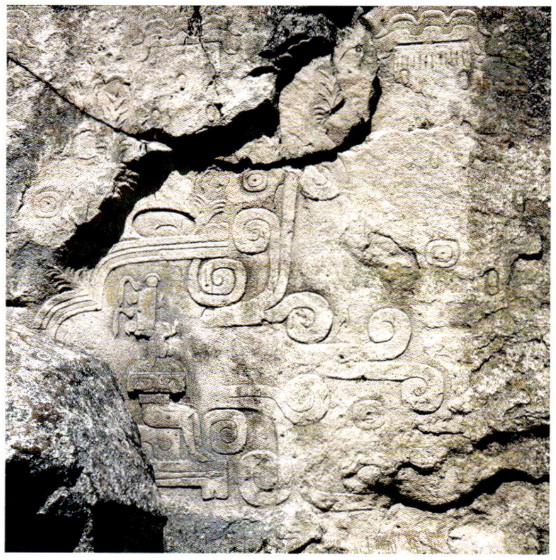

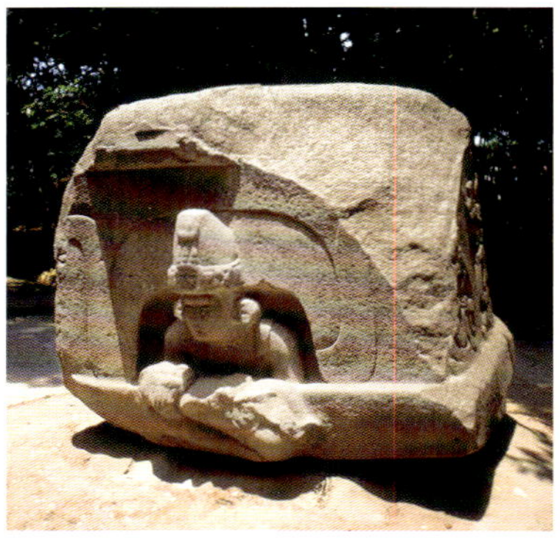

FIG. 32
MONUMENT 1
Mexico, Morelos, Chalcatzingo, 700–500 BC
Granodiorite
Approx. 96 x 120 in. (243.8 x 304.8 cm)

FIG. 33
ALTAR 5
Mexico, Tabasco, La Venta, 900–400 BC
Basalt
61 x 80 x 60¼ in. (155 x 203 x 153 cm)
Parque Museo de La Venta, Villahermosa, Tabasco

nificant connection between the two centers.[20] Nevertheless, some carvings at Chalcatzingo, such as the site's throne, are quite different from counterparts at La Venta, and many of the site's carvings contain local motifs that do not appear in any art in Olman. Several other traits and features at Chalcatzingo seem to link it to sites in Guerrero and the Pacific Coast of southern Mesoamerica.[21]

Teopantecuanitlán, Guerrero

So many Olmec-style objects were found in the state of Guerrero that some scholars once explored the idea that the style might have originated there.[22] Today, however, we recognize that most of those objects date to the Middle Formative period. It also now seems likely that various centers in Guerrero were creating stone and shell artifacts in the Olmec style, and that some of those objects had ultimately been dispersed to other regions via Middle Formative period trade networks. Guerrero may also have been an important source of raw materials such as greenstone.[23] Some of the artifacts and raw materials from Guerrero probably moved northward to other parts of Mesoamerica via the center of Teopantecuanitlán.[24] Situated at the junction of the Amacuzac and the Balsas—two major Central Mexico rivers that were important access and communication routes through mountainous northeastern Guerrero and into the Central Highlands—Teopantecuanitlán was well positioned to control this trade.

Although there is strong evidence that Teopantecuanitlán interacted with Chalcatzingo, its carved art is very different. The significant Olmec-style carvings at Teopantecuanitlán are four large and nearly identical bas-relief faces that project upward from the walls of a large, stone-faced sunken patio[25] **(SEE FIG. 34)**. The site's two other major sculptures—a frog "altar" and a large, non-Olmec stone head[26]—are more akin to carvings from the Pacific slopes of southern Mesoamerica.[27]

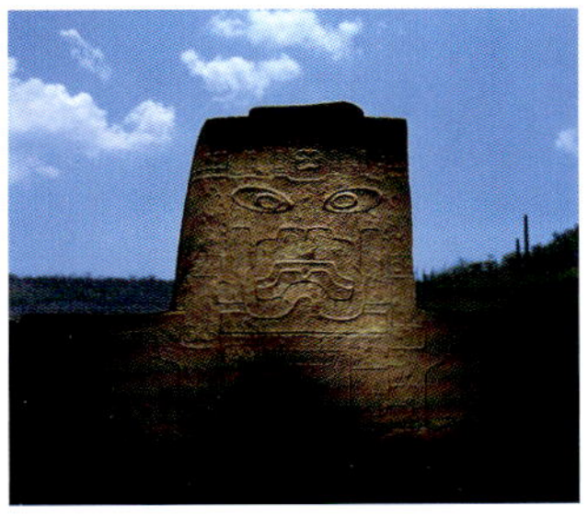

Oxtotitlan and Juxtlahuaca Caves, Guerrero

An extraordinary manifestation of Olmec-style art found in the state of Guerrero consists of highly sophisticated mural paintings preserved in caves at the sites of Oxtotitlan and Juxtlahuaca. Oxtotitlan cave is situated on a mountainside 18 miles (29 kilometers) south of Teopantecuanitlán. Its paintings were executed within two large but relatively shallow grottoes and on exposed rock faces between the grottoes. They range from small, Olmec-style images in the north grotto to simple red geometric designs in the south grotto.[28] The north grotto's masterpiece is the painted image of an upright yellow jaguar with black spots and a red mouth. It is the earliest known painting of a jaguar in Mesoamerica. A human figure, executed almost entirely in black, stands behind the feline **(FIG. 35)**.[29] However, the most spectacular painting is found outside, high on the cliff face between the two grottoes: a large, multicolored mural depicting a personage wearing an elaborate feathered cape and an "owl" headdress-mask **(FIGS. 36–37)**.[30] The owl mask is cut away to reveal the person's face, a convention used in later Maya art to indicate that it is a costume rather

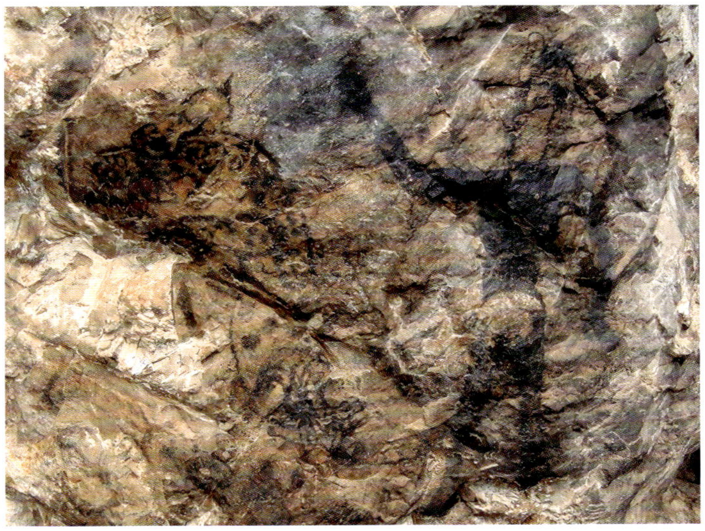

FIG. 34
SCULPTURE 4
Mexico, Guerrero, Teopantecuanitlán,
700–500 BC
Travertine
Height: approx. 51 in. (129.5 cm)

FIG. 35
PAINTING 1-D (HUMAN AND JAGUAR)
Mexico, Guerrero, Oxtotitlan, North Grotto,
700–500 BC
Pigment on limestone
Approx. 60 x 60 in. (152.4 x 152.4 cm)

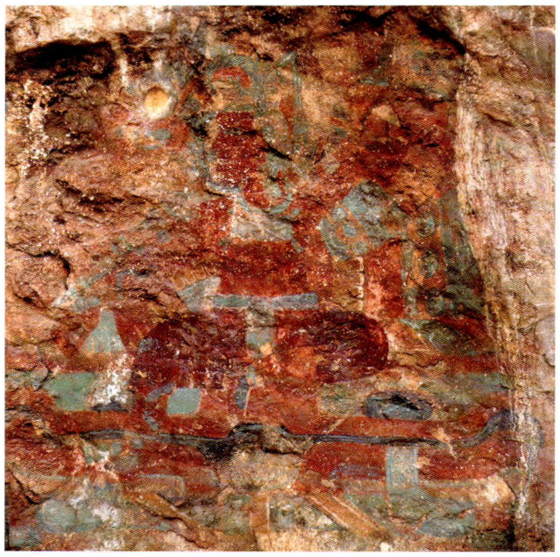

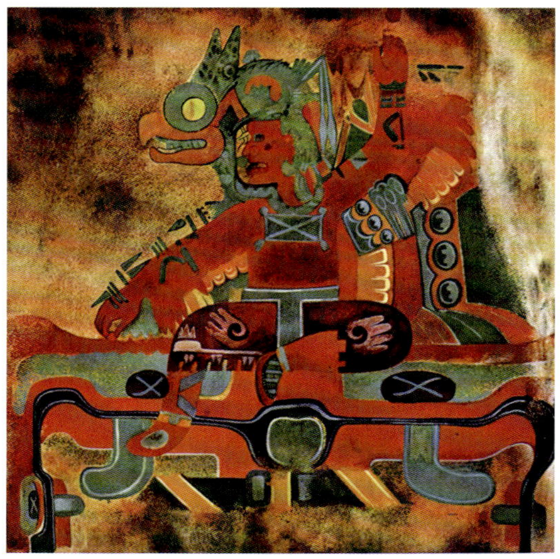

than a supernatural animal. The figure is seated atop the large, blocky face of a stylized serpent supernatural, with Olmec-style elongated eyes rendered in a turquoise blue pigment. The figure's right leg dangles over the face, suggesting that he is actually seated on a throne. Perhaps not coincidentally, the front of Chalcatzingo's throne, as mentioned previously, is adorned with a nearly identical supernatural serpent face.[31] While the faces of stone thrones in Olman have symbolic cave-niches, the possible throne depicted in the Oxtotitlan mural, 350 miles (563 kilometers) to the west, has an actual cave below it.

Juxtlahuaca cave lies 20 very mountainous miles (32 kilometers) south of Oxtotitlan. Unlike the Oxtotitlan images, which are found in shallow grottoes and easily accessible, those at Juxtlahuaca were executed deep within the lengthy cave system. Juxtlahuaca's major mural depicts a standing figure wearing a multicolored striped garment and a headdress with plumes; a much smaller individual sits in front of the figure.[32]

Southwestern Mesoamerica: Chiapas

Olmec-style stone carvings occur at a few Middle Preclassic centers along Mesoamerica's southern Pacific slopes, from Chiapas, Mexico, to El Salvador.[33] Those centers were presumably part of a trade route involved in the exploitation and movement of cacao and Guatemalan jadeite. The stone carvings at these sites also exhibit some regional stylistic differences from the art of both Olman and Central Mexico. Those differences can be seen in objects from Chiapas displayed in this exhibition **(PLS. 133–139)**. Unfortunately, the Chiapas sites where those objects were found have not been extensively studied and thus the context of their Olmec-style art is unclear.

FIG. 36
POLYCHROME MURAL (FIGURE IN FEATHERED CAPE AND HEADDRESS SEATED ON A THRONE)
Mexico, Guerrero, Oxtotitlan, 700–500 BC
Pigment on limestone
Approx. 96 x 144 in. (243.8 x 365.8 cm)

FIG. 37
Contemporary rendering of the Oxtotitlan polychrome mural (fig. 36) by Felipe Davalos

NOTES

1 Coe 1965c; Covarrubias 1942; Covarrubias 1946a. Also relevant is Joralemon 1971.

2 For comments on the confusion, see Clark and Pye 2000b, and Grove 1989b.

3 The differences and changes between the Early and Middle Formative periods are discussed in greater detail in Grove 1993.

4 Covarrubias 1943: 41.

5 Covarrubias 1943; García Moll et al. 1991; Niederberger 2000: 173–174; Piña Chan 1958; Porter 1953.

6 Tolstoy 1989: 102, fig. 6.7.

7 Grove 1974: 3–4; Grove 2006; Grove 2007: 213–219.

8 Niederberger 1976; Niederberger 2000: 174–179; Porter Weaver 1967; Tolstoy and Paradis 1970: 347.

9 The resist technique involves the application of wax or a similar substance to the body of a clay vessel or figure before slipping or painting it. The wax prevents the slip or paint from adhering to those areas of the ceramic body.

10 For example, the site of Temamatla, 12 miles (about 19 kilometers) southeast of Tlapacoya (Ramírez, Gámez, and González 2000).

11 Figurines and vessels attributed to Las Bocas are illustrated in Coe 1965b.

12 The 1996 excavations at Las Bocas were never published. Research there in 2000 is reported in Paillés Hernández 2007.

13 Grove 1996a: 108–109.

14 Clark and Cheetham 2005.

15 Cheetham 2006.

16 Córdova Tello and Meza Rodríguez 2007; Grove 1984: 49–68, 109–122; Grove and Angulo V. 1987 (also available online; see Grove 1987).

17 Grove 1989a: 132–136.

18 Fash 1987: 82–94 (also available online; see Grove 1987).

19 Grove 1984: 65–67, fig. 15, col. pl. 7; Grove 1989a: 137–139, figs. 7.10, 7.11; Grove 2000: 287–289, figs. 16, 17.

20 Grove 1989a: 132–136.

21 Grove 1989a: 141–145.

22 Covarrubias 1957: 76; Gay 1972; Paradis 1981: 203–204; Piña Chan 1955: 26.

23 Niederberger 2002; Niederberger 1996c: 101–102; Reyna Robles and Schmidt Schoenberg 2006.

24 Martínez Donjuán 1994: 154–162; Niederberger 1996c: 97–101, figs. 9.10–9.20.

25 Martínez Donjuán 1994: figs. 9.12–9.14.

26 Ibid.: figs. 9.16–9.17.

27 See, for example, Pye and Gutiérrez 2007: 234–239.

28 Grove 1970a; Grove n.d.

29 Painting 1-d. Grove 1970a: 17–18, fig. 13.

30 Mural 1. Grove 1970a: 8–11, frontispiece.

31 Grove 1973; Grove 2000: 287–289.

32 Gay 1967; Grove 1970a: 29–34, fig. 34.

33 Major sites include Pijijiapan, Chiapas; La Blanca and Tak'alik Ab'aj, Guatemala; and Chalchuapa, El Salvador. Stone carvings in Chiapas are discussed and illustrated in Lee 1989: 216–221; and Lowe 1994.

THE OLMEC LEGACY IN STONE: A MESOAMERICAN ALPHA AND OMEGA

Richard A. Diehl

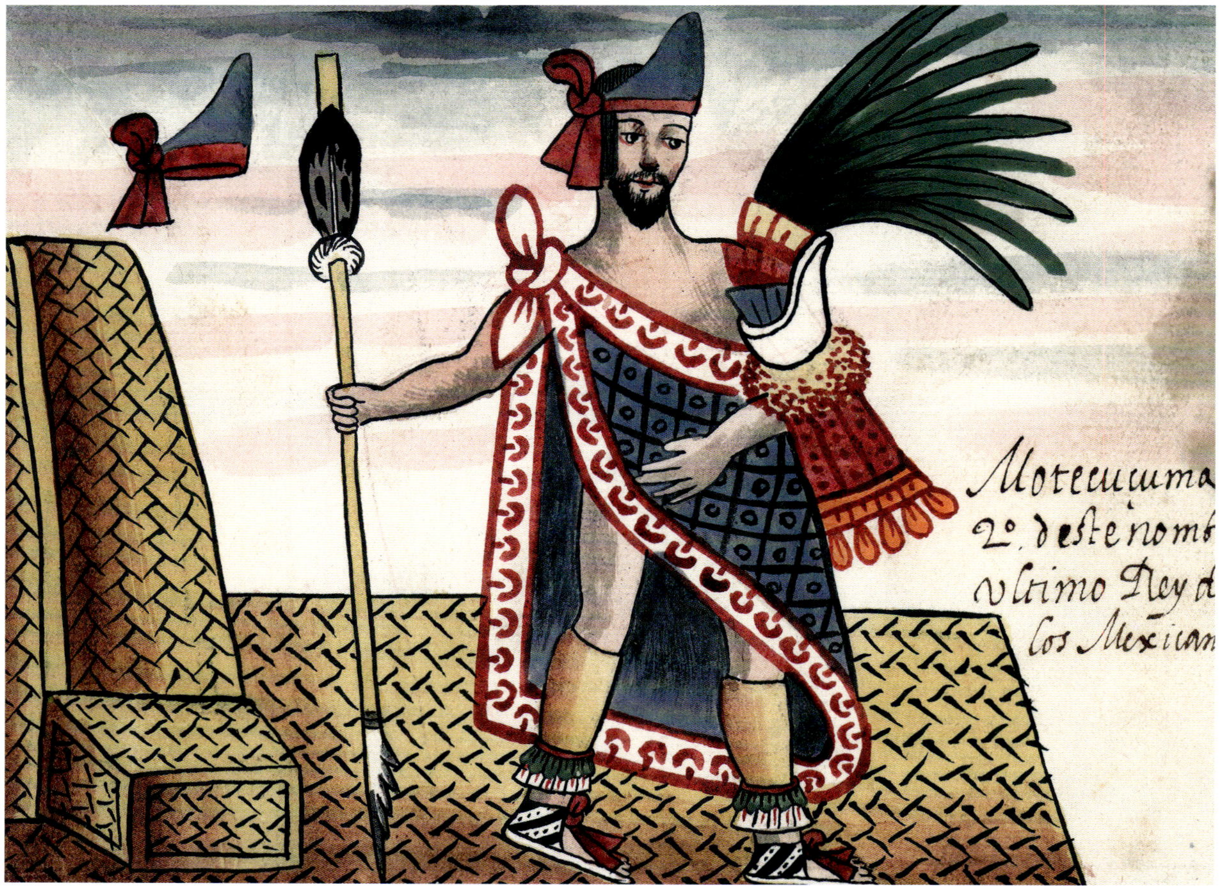

Legacy: material or immaterial thing handed down by predecessor

Alpha and Omega: beginning and end —*The Concise Oxford Dictionary of Current English,* 1988

Introduction

In the year 12 Reed on the day 1 Crocodile (June 11, 1503, in our calendar), a renowned warrior and priest named Moctezuma Xocoyotzin ("he who speaks like an angry lord") was inaugurated as the new Huey Tlatoani, or sovereign of the Aztec empire.[1] After his monthlong coronation, during which he underwent many trials, privations, and rituals, he was invested with the symbols of his exalted office. As seen in a Colonial painting of the investiture of one of his predecessors **(FIG. 38)**, they included a pointed, turquoise-colored crown or *xiuhuitzolli*, a netted royal cloak replete with precious greenstones, and other splendid regalia. He was seated on a high-backed reed throne covered with jaguar skins, a refined version of the woven mat used by the earliest rulers. Moctezuma Xocoyotzin knew that his symbols of office were ancient in concept and design, but he could not have known that many of them first came into vogue in Olmec culture twenty-five hundred years earlier.

Sixteen years and five months later (November 8, 1519), Moctezuma Xocoyotzin had the great misfortune to meet face-to-face with Hernán Cortés and his small band of Spaniards at the south edge of Tenochtitlan, the Aztec capital situated in the middle of a large lake. One Spaniard later recalled the scene and the city as being "like the enchantments they tell of in the legend of Amadis,...some of our soldiers even asked whether the things that we saw were not a dream."[2] On that occasion, the Aztec ruler honored Cortés by offering him one of the most precious gifts imaginable, a necklace of the greenstones much more highly valued

FIG. 38
THE INVESTITURE OF MOCTEZUMA XOCOYOTZIN
From the Codex Tovar (fol. 117), ca. AD 1585
Watercolor
6 x 8¼ in. (15.2 x 21 cm)
John Carter Brown Library, Brown University

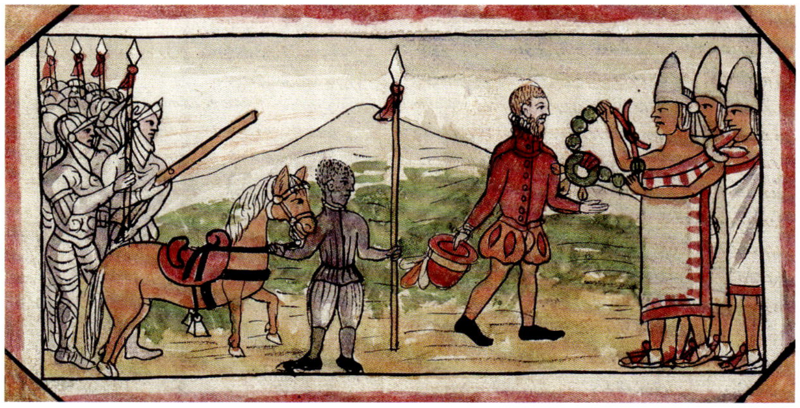

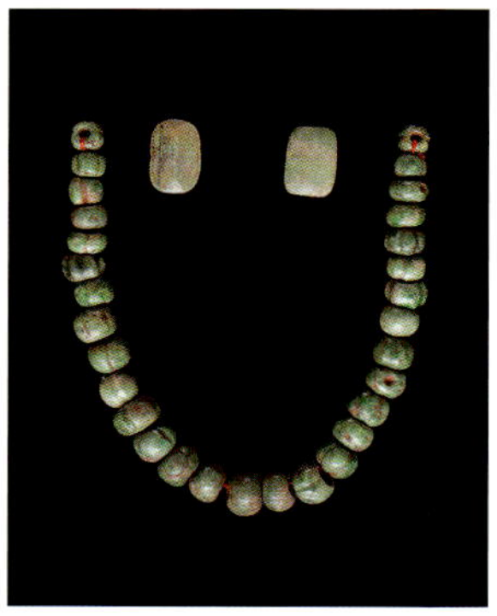

by the Aztecs than the gold that obsessed the Spaniards (**FIG. 39**). Neither man could have known that the concept of preciousness signified by greenstones strung on necklaces was also an Olmec invention (**FIG. 40**).

If the mighty Aztecs, overlords of the largest tributary empire that ever existed in Mesoamerica, owed these symbols of wealth, power, and royalty to the Olmec, what else formed the Olmec legacy? I have written on this topic before[3] and will not repeat myself here. Instead, I focus on two facets of the Olmec legacy: objects that became heirlooms in later cultures, and similarities in monumental stone sculpture and small lapidary objects created by two civilizations separated by two millennia and hundreds of miles. If I do these topics justice, I will leave the reader with more questions than answers. As always, the past is an unknown country.

What Is the "Olmec Legacy"?

As discussed earlier in this book, Olmec culture lasted approximately a thousand years. After its demise, it left visible imprints on art, religion, governance, culinary preferences, and many other Mesoamerican practices and concepts for the next two thousand years. Many of these imprints appear superficial, but others signal much deeper influences on the basic nature of the affected cultures. These "material and immaterial" imprints are the legacy the Olmec unknowingly bequeathed to their successors. They include heirlooms, actual Olmec *objects* found in later contexts as well as the *meanings* behind these objects. The most important of these included concepts of rulership and its associated regalia, religious beliefs, practices, and rituals, and a basic understanding of the cosmos and the place of humans in it.

Heirlooms

Heirlooms are objects reused by later people in one fashion or another and finally redeposited in archaeological contexts that date to this subsequent phase of their use. A few have been recovered in archaeological excavations; others were looted in modern times and later entered

FIG. 39
THE MEETING OF HERNÁN CORTÉS AND MOCTEZUMA XOCOYOTZIN
From the Codex Durán (fol. 208v), AD 1579
Watercolor and ink
11 x 7 1/2 in. (28 x 19 cm)
Biblioteca Nacional de España, Madrid

FIG. 40
NECKLACE
Mexico, Tabasco, La Venta, ca. 500 BC
Greenstone
Width of largest bead: 3/4 in. (1.9 cm)
Museo Nacional de Antropología, Mexico City

the antiquities market. Those found in archaeological excavations were complete surprises to the excavators. In a few cases they were part of later ritual caches, perhaps serving as the crowning element that added additional sanctification to a collection of contemporary objects. Others occurred on the floors of humble peasant homes and in similar perplexing circumstances.

Some heirlooms were reworked, modified, or perhaps even broken by the later users. Many were reused a few centuries after their original manufacture; others appeared in settings as much as two thousand years later. We do not know when these precious relics from the past were obtained by successive cultures. Some may have been passed down from one generation to another over centuries, perhaps as special gifts to important individuals, while others may have been fortuitous finds by people digging in the ground. The looting of ancient ruins is not a modern invention; almost every Mesoamerican archaeological site has graves, altars, and ruined buildings that show signs of the ancient search for old and venerated objects.

The first examples of Olmec heirlooms to be identified as such were a figurine and a "canoe," both of fine jadeite, found in a Classic period offering at Cerro de las Mesas, Veracruz, Mexico. This cache is the stuff of archaeological legend. In 1941, Matthew W. Stirling and his National Geographic Society/Smithsonian Institution team discovered it and its seven-hundred-plus objects on the very last day of fieldwork at the Classic period (AD 300–600) regional capital in southern Veracruz.[4] Even today it remains the largest collection of jadeite objects ever found by archaeologists in Mexico. Two Olmec heirlooms were especially notable among the hundreds of Classic period beads, earspools, and other ornaments: a beautifully polished figurine that depicts a standing dwarflike creature with the face of a crying baby, and a canoe-shaped vessel with blunt bow and stern reminiscent of the punts that ply Cambridge University's River Cam today **(PLS. 143–144)**.

The pendant from Cozumel **(PL. 142)** was part of a later offering in a burial crypt that contained two adult human skeletons; several Maya pots, at least some of which were centuries-old heirlooms themselves; and several jadeite and shell beads.[5] At least a millennium and perhaps more separated the manufacture of the pendant from its final resting place.

The final object recovered by archaeologists that we will consider here is a fascinating Olmec mask **(PL. 140)** uncovered in a cache in the heart of Tenochtitlan, the Aztec capital. The highest priests reverentially deposited it in a dedicatory offering during a rebuilding of the Templo Mayor, their great temple, in AD 1470. Along with it they placed an heirloom stone mask from Teotihuacan, shells, turtles, sawfish remains, sacrificial knives, Mezcala-style stone objects, and images of Aztec gods with ancient lineages. The offering contents suggest a concern with uniting the ancient and the physically distant worlds with the Aztec world's central and sacred locale, the heart of the burgeoning empire.

Having dealt, therefore, with Olmec objects whose heirloom status is securely proven, what can we say about the many pieces of unknown history in museums and private collections? In a few cases they can be identified by the presence of post-Olmec modifications. The winged plaque with the were-jaguar face in the Dumbarton Oaks collection **(PLS. 149–150)** provides an especially clear example. Said to have been purchased by a missionary in a village in Yucatán, Mexico, its actual provenience and date of last use are, of course, unknown.[6] What we do know is that a powerful and exquisitely carved green quartzite ornament was modified at least twice after its original manufacture. One modification involved drilling the two funnel-shaped holes in the wings. The second came when some very early Protoclassic or Early Classic period Maya ruler had his portrait and a hieroglyphic text inscribed into the back of the piece. The latter modification, surely done before AD 100, may be the oldest known Mesoamerican example of a practice found all over the world, that of later rulers bolstering their claims to legitimacy by appropriating the works of their predecessors.

Aztec Omega: Parallels in Olmec and Aztec Visual Representations

Despite the great distance in time that separated the Aztecs from the Olmec, their art is an excellent example of the full flowering of the Olmec legacy. Nowhere is this more evident than in Aztec monumental stone sculpture. As H. B. Nicholson observed almost fifty years ago, when speaking about the rise of the Aztec state and its associated monuments, "One of the most important results of this final central Mexican era of power and prosperity was a production of major works of sculpture such as the world has rarely seen."[7] No Mesoamerican civilization ever created so many fine sculptures, to say nothing of the fact that they did it in less than a hundred years! No comprehensive catalogue of this sculptural corpus exists, but the number of *known* pieces must exceed one thousand and new examples are found beneath Mexico City and its environs almost weekly. This incredible achievement in monumental sculpture was accompanied by equally notable production of small, portable objects, personal adornments, costumes, and ritual paraphernalia. No wonder the Spanish conquistadors constantly marveled at what they saw and experienced in their first two years in this truly New World of Mexico! However, it is not simply the quantity of Aztec sculpture that impresses; the quality of many pieces is comparable to that of the ancient world's most highly acclaimed stone-carving traditions.

In the early 1990s, Felipe Solís, longtime director of Mexico's Museo Nacional de Antropología and an Aztec expert, began organizing and fostering spectacular national and international exhibitions highlighting heretofore poorly known examples of Aztec art.[8] The latest of these, the British Museum's *Moctezuma: Aztec Ruler* (2009–2010), reawakened two questions that first occurred to me in my student days fifty years ago: How did the Aztecs manage to create so much sculpture in such a short time? And what was the inspiration for the unique Aztec sculptural style's combination of faithful realism and otherworld fantasy, especially as expressed in three-dimensional carvings designed to be viewed from every possible angle? We can explore these issues by turning to a few concrete examples that show how that Aztec artisans frequently harked back to Olmec norms, even if we cannot explain how or why they did so.

Three-Dimensional Human Portrayals

We begin our examination of Olmec and Aztec works of art with two true masterpieces: La Venta Monument 77 **(FIG. 41, PLS. 67–68)** and an Aztec personification of the sun god, Tonatiuh, presently housed in Basel **(FIG. 42)**. Both were carved from hard, volcanic stone using only tools made of stone and infinite patience. The seated Olmec man appears to depict a local lord or ruler, while Tonatiuh is either a deity or deity-impersonator identified by the solar shield on his back and other regalia connected with this high member of the Aztec pantheon. Both display relaxed but alert positions that project a certain tension lacking in most Mesoamerican stone sculpture. Both fully human figures seem to radiate power and the self-confidence it brings, so different from the blank stares often found on most other Mesoamerican sculpture. These men know what they are doing, understand their places in the cosmos and its earthly realm, and are prepared to carry out their respective duties on behalf of the people they protect.

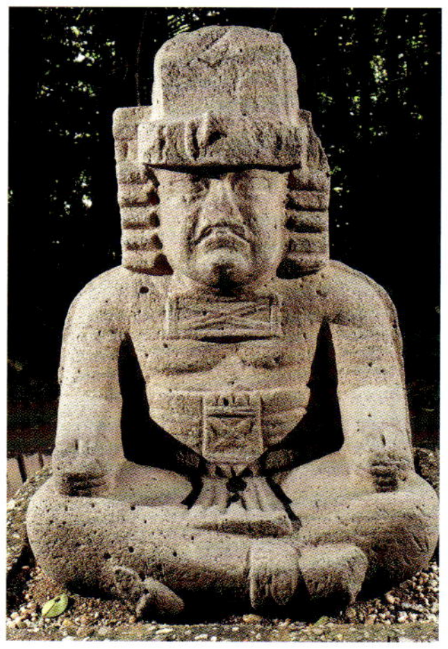

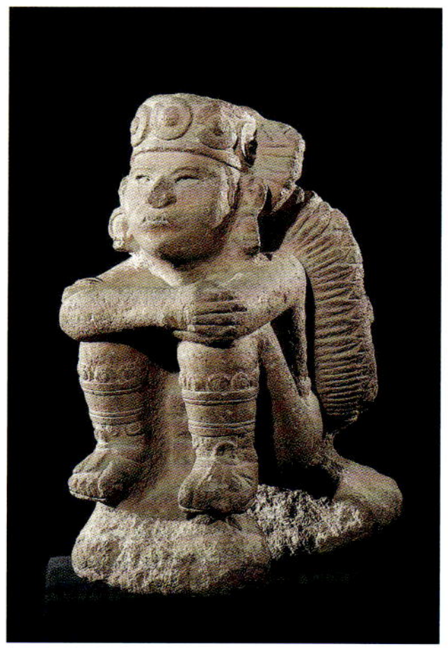

FIG. 41
MONUMENT 77 (SEATED FIGURE WEARING CAPE)
Mexico, Tabasco, La Venta, 900–400 BC
Basalt
41 5/16 x 30 11/16 x 28 3/8 in. (105 x 78 x 72 cm)
Parque-Museo de La Venta, Villahermosa, Tabasco

FIG. 42
TONATIUH
Mexico, Aztec, dates unknown
Volcanic stone with pigment
12 3/8 x 6 3/8 x 9 5/8 in. (31.5 x 16.2 x 24.5 cm)
Museum für Völkerkunde, Basel

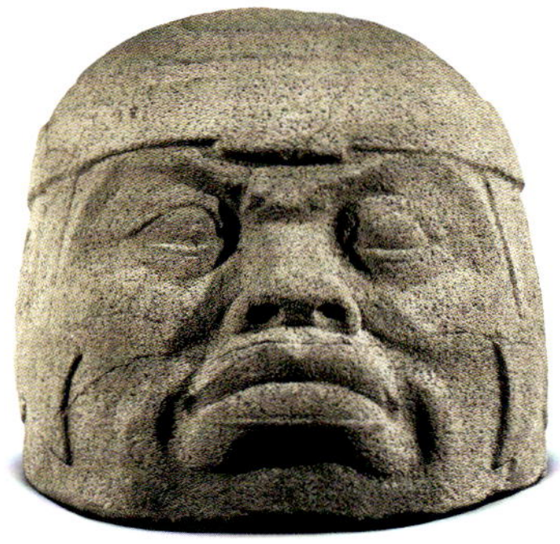

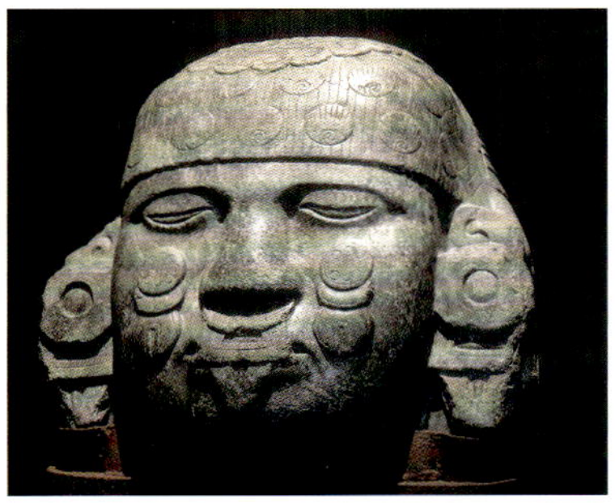

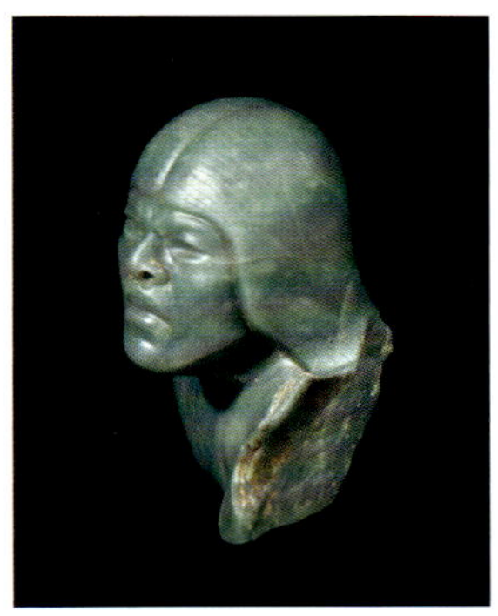

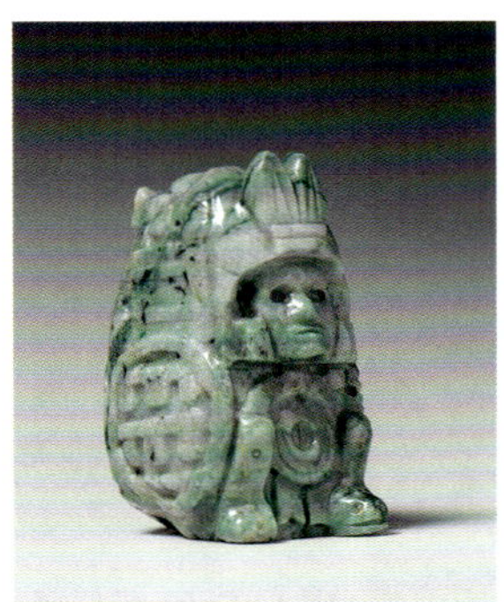

Colossal Heads

Both the Olmec and the Aztecs depicted human heads as complete sculptures carved in the round, a rare art form in intervening Mesoamerican cultures. Colossal heads **(FIG. 43, PLS. 1, 25–28)** have become the trademark of Olmec civilization. Although the Aztecs created relatively few three-dimensional heads isolated from their torsos, the Coyolxauhqui illustrated here **(FIG. 44)** is a true masterpiece in its own right. It depicts the goddess who played a pivotal role in the birth of Huitzilopochtli, the Aztec patron god of war. Like many Aztec monuments, it has a carved image hidden on its base where only supernaturals could see it, a practice of Olmec sculptors as well.

Realistic Lapidarian Works

Skilled lapidaries existed in most Mesoamerican societies, but Olmec and Aztec artisans were unique in their abilities to create objects of great realism from small greenstones and semiprecious minerals, works fully comparable to those of their sculptor colleagues. A fragmentary Olmec bust in the Dumbarton Oaks collection **(FIG. 45, PLS. 97–98)** and an intact portrayal figure of the Aztec war god Huitzilopochtli **(FIG. 46)** are outstanding examples. Today both are approximately the same size, but the Olmec piece originally crowned a human body of unknown dimensions. It is almost certainly the portrait of a living person, although the gender is the subject of considerable debate. The sensitivity and maturity of the Olmec figure's expression contrast sharply with that of Huitzilopochtli's steely-eyed warrior, which seems to be following an unfolding battle. His identification as the Aztec war god—whose name translates as "Hummingbird-on-the-Left," denoting the fierce battles these tiny birds conduct against their own kind—is signaled by his feathered costume, a spear-thrower in his left hand, a shield in his right, and a knife worn on his left shoulder.

FIG. 43
MONUMENT Q (COLOSSAL HEAD)
Mexico, Veracruz, Tres Zapotes, 1000–800 BC
Basalt
$59^{7}/_{16}$ x $59^{1}/_{16}$ x 63 in. (151 x 150 x 160 cm)
Museo Regional Tuxteco, Santiago Tuxtla, Veracruz

FIG. 44
COYOLXAUHQUI
Mexico, Mexico City, Convento de la Concepción, ca. AD 1500
Diorite
$31^{1}/_{2}$ x $33^{1}/_{2}$ x $26^{3}/_{4}$ in. (80 x 85 x 68 cm)
Museo Nacional de Antropología, Mexico City

FIG. 45
FRAGMENTARY FIGURE
Mexico, Olmec, 900–400 BC
Jadeite
$2^{5}/_{8}$ x $1^{1}/_{2}$ in. (6.6 x 3.8 cm)
Dumbarton Oaks Research Library and Collection

FIG. 46
ANTHROPOMORPHIC FIGURE OF HUITZILOPOCHTLI
Mexico, Aztec, ca. AD 1500
Jadeite
$2^{1}/_{2}$ x $1^{5}/_{8}$ x $1^{7}/_{8}$ in. (6.4 x 4 x 4.7 cm)
Musée du Quai Branly, Paris

The Natural and Cultural World

All ancient Mesoamericans depicted the most salient elements of their natural and culturally relevant worlds in their art, but few achieved the mastery that characterizes Olmec and Aztec creations. Two comparisons from among the many that might be made will suffice as examples: maize, the Mesoamerican staff of life and a plant so drastically modified by them and their ancestors that it has lost the ability to reproduce without human cultivation, and the jaguar, *Felis onca*, and its close relatives, denizens of the tropical forests and isolated mountain ranges of Mexico.

Maize was domesticated in Mexico beginning in the third millennium BC and spread from there to Argentina and southern Canada.[9] In Olmec times, its productivity and significance increased dramatically between 1200 and 600 BC. The maize cob deeply incised into the surface of a diopside jadeite celt designed to be worn as a horizontal pectoral **(FIG. 47, PL. 91)** is one of the earliest representations of that crucial plant known in Mesoamerican art. The spearhead-shaped cob emerges from its surrounding husk on top of what may be the handle of a maize fetish used in ritual. The stylization of the entire design is so severe that scholars can identify it as maize only by tracing the minor changes in maize imagery back through time from later cultures.[10]

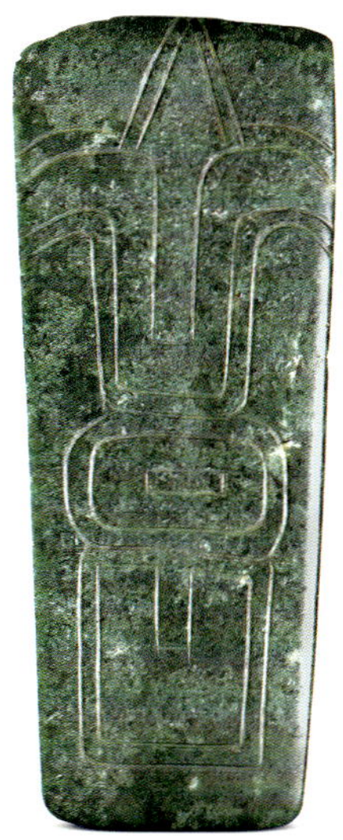

On the other hand, anyone familiar with maize can easily identify the four cobs that embellish each side of a small Aztec altar carved from basalt **(FIG. 48)**. The goodly sized cobs with their even-rowed, plump kernels show the great strides made by ancient farmers in "genetically engineering" this major food crop as well as the way Aztec sculptors viewed it. Husks encircle the cob bases while cornsilk emerges from their tops.

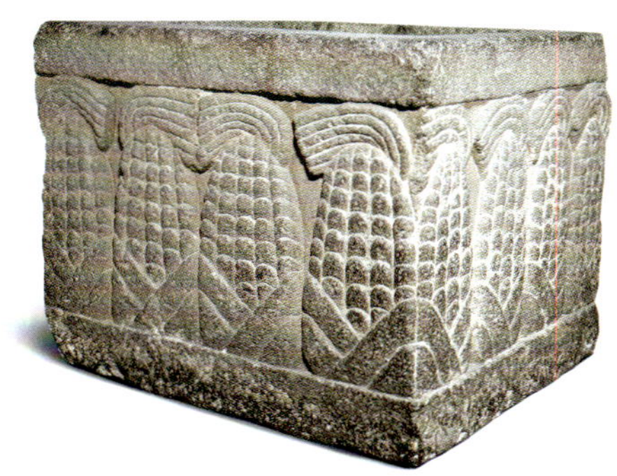

One denizen of the natural world all Mesoamericans feared and never came to dominate was the jaguar. A native of the tropical forests of the Olmec homeland, it became symbolic of a host of implacable supernatural forces even in lands where it had never existed, including the

FIG. 47
CELT PENDANT
Mexico, Olmec, 900–300 BC
Diopside jadeite
6 1/2 x 2 1/2 x 1/4 in. (16.5 x 6.4 x 0.6 cm)
Dumbarton Oaks Research Library and Collection

FIG. 48
ALTAR
Mexico, Aztec, AD 1325–1521
Basalt
22 7/8 x 25 1/4 x 29 1/2 in. (58 x 64 x 75 cm)
Museo Nacional de Antropología, Mexico City

Aztec heartland. For the Olmec it personified a deity who could possess humans, becoming their symbol of rulership. The Aztecs deified it as Tezcatlipoca, one of their most feared gods; it also served as the avatar of a highly regarded military corps of accomplished warriors. Both societies depicted felines in various ways, but their naturalistic portraits stand out from other Mesoamerican depictions of this top predator.

San Lorenzo Monument 107 **(FIG. 49)** portrays a jaguar and a human (perhaps a ballplayer) in a highly charged scene that we do not yet understand. Is the jaguar attacking the human, or should some deeper meaning be considered? The feline is completely naturalistic except for the enlarged eyes that add to the terror implicit in the scene. The Aztec reclining jaguar **(FIG. 50)** is equally naturalistic, although its relaxed posture and engaging smile make it seem almost like a domesticated tabby.

Rain Deities

Rain, the beneficence of the supernaturals who rule the cosmos, was the most critical and most unpredictable element in Mesoamerican farming. If it came too early or too late, too little or too much, hunger and even famine were certain to follow. Thus it is only natural that propitiation of the water gods first revered by the Olmec was a central tenet of all later native religions and continues in Mesoamerican folk Catholicism in the region even today.

Near the end of La Venta's Middle Formative period climax, a greenstone celt with a highly abstracted rain or water god image **(FIG. 51, PL. 76)** was deposited in Tomb E north of the site's great pyramid. This small masterwork features a were-jaguar face with typical Olmec flame eyebrows, cleft cranium, downturned lips, toothless gums, and a flattened nose. During the centuries that followed, the concepts and depictions of this deity gradually changed into the Aztec rain god Tlaloc, a fanged creature with round "goggle" eyes and a prominent mustache.

This final pre-Columbian expression of the rain god cult was one of two high deities worshiped in the Templo Mayor, the largest and most centrally located structure in Tenochtitlan. The twin temples atop the single pyramid base were dedicated to the two most prominent members of the Aztec pantheon, Tlaloc and Huitzilopochtli. Tlaloc's charge was to provide water for locally grown sustenance, while the war god Huitzilopochtli oversaw the conquests that filled Aztec coffers with food for humans, sacrificial victims to nourish the gods, and luxury goods from

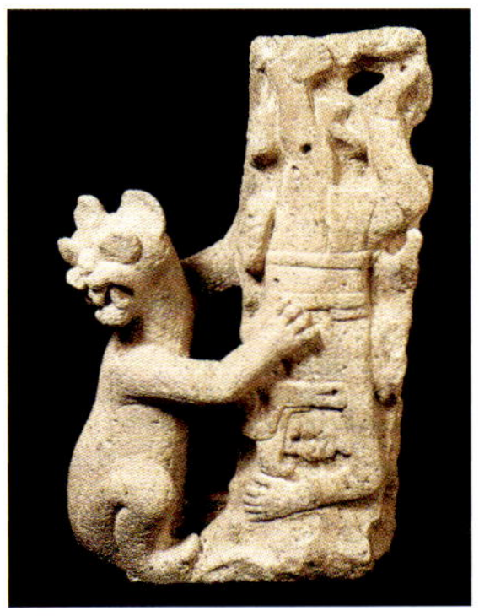

FIG. 49
MONUMENT 107 (COMPOSITE FELINE AND DESCENDING BALLPLAYER)
Mexico, Veracruz, Municipality of Texistepec, San Lorenzo Tenochtitlán, 1400–1000 BC
Basalt
$37^{3}/_{8}$ x $23^{5}/_{8}$ in. (95 x 60 cm)
Museo Comunitario de Tenochtitlán, Municipality of Texistepec, Veracruz

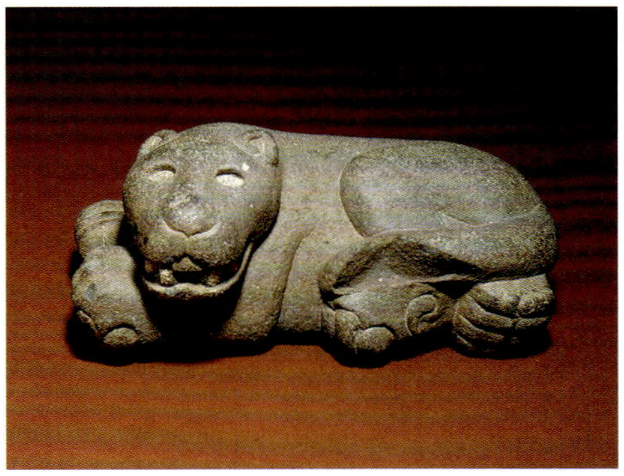

FIG. 50
RECLINING JAGUAR
Mexico, Aztec, AD 1440–1521
Volcanic stone
5 x 11 x $5^{3}/_{4}$ in. (12.7 x 27.9 x 14.6 cm)
Brooklyn Museum, Carll H. de Silver Fund

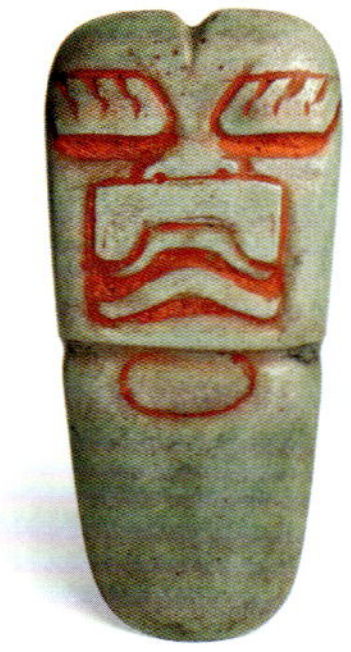

FIG. 51
VOTIVE AXE
Mexico, Tabasco, La Venta, Mound A-2, Tomb E, 900–400 BC
Jadeite with pigment
$4^{3}/_{8}$ x 2 x $^{1}/_{2}$ in. (11.1 x 5.1 x 1.2 cm)
Museo Nacional de Antropología, Mexico City

foreign lands. Near the foot of this temple, Mexican archaeologists uncovered Offering 60, a cache of precious objects deposited in honor of Tlaloc. Among them was a beautifully carved stone vase depicting him **(FIG. 52)**; its accompanying lid was painted blue, his identifying watery color.[11]

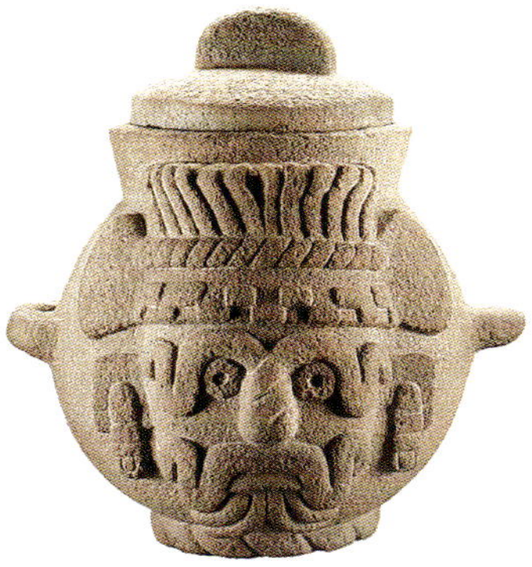

Another offering nearby contained well-made and decorated flint knives of the type employed in human sacrifice. The knife shown here **(FIG. 53)** depicts the visage of Tlaloc with his circular eyes. That is a long way from the Olmec celts described above. Although two thousand years of stylistic change left these Tlalocs looking very different from their Olmec predecessors, the Mexican artist Miguel Covarrubias could trace the gradual changes through time, from Olmec item A to Aztec item T, in his famous chart showing the lineages of Mesoamerican rain deities through the pre-Columbian period **(FIG. 6)**. Despite their stylistic differences, on occasion sets of Olmec celts and Aztec flint knives deposited in offerings were deliberately set upright in the ground, perhaps symbolizing lightning bolts striking the earth.

Concluding Thoughts

How can we account for the similarities seen above? The question can be answered in several ways, and several generations of dedicated scholars have managed to unravel the basic tenets of Olmec religion and belief systems as reflected in their rich body of art and iconography. Their work allows us to connect the dots of the visual imagery.

However, that does not answer the two questions that have bothered me for almost fifty years: How was it that knowledge of the sculptural techniques, procedures, and approaches invented by the Olmec apparently disappeared for a thousand years only to reappear suddenly in the mid-fifteenth century? And how did Aztec society produce enough master sculptors and lapidaries to account for such an incredible outpouring of masterpieces? Or did the Aztecs use the same techniques, procedures, and approaches as the Olmec? Only future studies will tell. One thing we *can* say is that it is extremely doubtful that any Aztec sculptor ever saw an Olmec monument "in the flesh" because, until recently, they all remained buried underground in distant jungles.

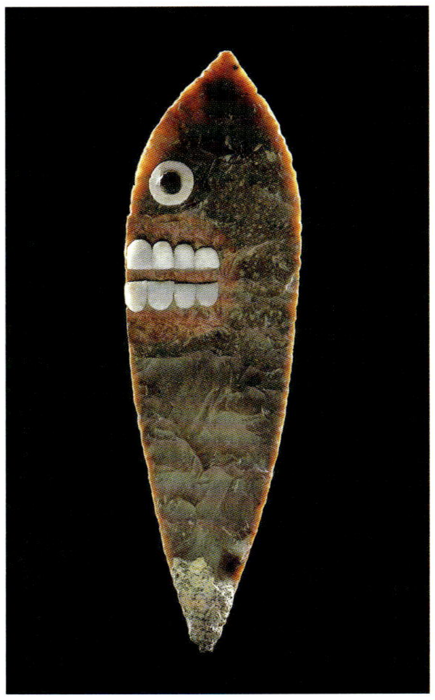

FIG. 52
TLALOC VASE
Mexico, Templo Mayor, Offering 60,
AD 1469–1481
Basalt with pigment
11 x 9⅝ x 9⅝ in. (28 x 24.5 x 24.5 cm)
Museo del Templo Mayor, Mexico City

FIG. 53
KNIFE
Mexico, Templo Mayor, House of the Eagles
Offering B, AD 1325–1521
Flint, obsidian, and resin
10⅜ x 2⅞ x ⅜ in. (26.5 x 7.3 x 1.1 cm)
Museo del Templo Mayor, Mexico City

NOTES

1 Matos Moctezuma 2009.

2 Díaz del Castillo 1956: 190–191.

3 Diehl 2004; Diehl and Coe 1995.

4 Stirling 1941.

5 Rathje, Sabloff, and Gregory 1973.

6 Coe 1966.

7 Nicholson 1971: 115.

8 Royal Academy of Arts 2002; Solís Olguín 2004; McEwan and López Luján 2009.

9 Piperno and Flannery 2001.

10 Joralemon 1971; Fields 1989; Taube 1996, 2000.

11 López Luján 1994: 313.

This essay is dedicated to the memory of Beatriz de la Fuente (1929–2005) and Felipe Solís (1944–2009), outstanding scholars of Olmec and Aztec art, especially stone sculpture, and friends and mentors from whom so many of us learned so much.

A Note on the Naming of Olmec Monuments

Olmec monuments are named according to a bewildering set of alphabetic and numeric designations, which generally follow the order in which the monuments were found at a site. Early in the history of Olmec studies, Frans Blom and Oliver La Farge (1926) assigned numbers to the various monuments they encountered in La Venta and other sites they visited during the 1925 Tulane expedition, giving separate sequences of numbers to stelae, altars (most of which probably served as thrones), and "idols" from each site. Albert Weyerstall (1932) also assigned a series of numbers to the monuments he encountered at Tres Zapotes, although he didn't distinguish the different monument types. It was Matthew W. Stirling (for example, 1943) who had the greatest influence on the labeling of Olmec monuments, because he found and reported so many of them at Tres Zapotes, La Venta, San Lorenzo, and other sites. Stirling continued Blom and La Farge's practice of giving different numbering series to stelae, altars, and other "monuments" (dropping the already outdated title of "idol"). Stirling retained the numbers Blom and La Farge had assigned to the La Venta monuments, but changed the designation of Altar 1 to Stela 3. Although Stirling generally preferred numbers, he used letters to designate stelae and monuments at Tres Zapotes, apparently to avoid confusion with Weyerstall's numeric sequence. Subsequently, C. William Clewlow and colleagues (1967) gave separate numeric designations to the four colossal heads from La Venta, the six colossal heads then known from San Lorenzo, and the two colossal heads from Tres Zapotes, which they identified as Tres Zapotes 1 and Nestepe 1.

By the end of the 1960s, the proliferation of monument names and numbering sequences was already becoming bewildering. Beatriz de la Fuente tried to bring some order to the picture in her 1973 catalogue of Olmec monumental sculpture. She gave each monument a sequential catalogue number, regardless of its location, and reported the various names that had been assigned to it in the literature, although in the figure captions she preferred to use the alphabetic or numeric sequences begun by Stirling. On occasion, and particularly where there might be confusion among different names, writers have sometimes used de la Fuente's catalogue numbers, but this practice has not caught on widely, particularly as new monuments have been discovered and are therefore not listed in the catalogue. Moreover, researchers have continued to redesignate monuments to conform to new data, reinterpretations of site boundaries, or a desire to simplify the system for a particular site. For example, Ann Cyphers (1997f, 2004b) has renamed Potrero Nuevo Monuments 1–4 as Loma del Zapote Monuments 1–4 to accord with her assessment, based on archaeological survey, that Loma del Zapote encompassed the village mound site of Potrero Nuevo as well as the high ground to the west of the village, where three of the monuments were actually found. At Tres Zapotes, James Porter chose to replace the alphabetic designations of Monuments A–R assigned by Stirling and others with numbers in the same order, because the many monuments discovered since 1965 exhausted the alphabet. Because of the prevalence of Stirling's alphabetic designations in the literature and the potential confusion of Porter's and Weyerstall's numbers, I use Stirling's letters for Monuments A–R and continue Porter's numbering sequence for Monuments 19 and above in my contribution to this volume and other publications.

PLATES

Introductions by Kathleen Berrin and Virginia M. Fields

Authors of individual object entries are designated by initials, as follows:

KB: Kathleen Berrin

MC-LE: Marcía Castro-Leal Espino

VMF: Virginia M. Fields

RLR: Roberto Lunagómez Reyes

POC (OCHOA): Patricia Ochoa Castillo

POC (ORTÍZ): Ponciano Ortíz Ceballos

CAP: Christopher A. Pool

MCRM: Ma. del Carmen Rodríguez M.

Also abbreviated:

INAH: Instituto Nacional de Antropología e Historia

Olmec civilization, which flourished in the tropical forests and waterways of south central Mexico, is considered by many to be the oldest civilization in the Americas. The term *Olmec* was coined in the early twentieth century to refer to an art style that came to light in the mid-nineteenth century, after a farmworker discovered the first colossal head in a cornfield. At the time, not much was known about the great diversity and antiquity of Mesoamerican civilizations, and this enormous sculpture was perceived as unique, not only for its size but also for the realism of its features.

Archaeologists refer to the tropical rainforests, swamps, and watery savannahs located in the southern Gulf lowlands of the present-day Mexican states of southern Veracruz and western Tabasco as the Olmec heartland. It was here that the major Olmec centers—San Lorenzo Tenochtitlán, Tres Zapotes, and La Venta—and a number of secondary sites established in regional hierarchies flourished between 1800 and 400 BC. This region is also referred to as *Olman*, a Nahuatl name derived from the word *ollin*, meaning "land of rubber" and referring to an important natural resource of the area.

Votive axes, considered impressive examples of stone carving linked to the same mysterious culture, were the next Olmec objects to be discovered and published after the first colossal portrait head. Early-twentieth-century studies began to define Olmec style as representing not only powerful human portraits but also composite jaguar-humans with slanting, oval eyes, thick lips, and a snarling mouth. This sophisticated carving style was rendered in both monumental and small scale, and in volcanic stone such as basalt as well as precious jadeite and other greenstones. Strongly anchored in the human form, Olmec style is also represented by composite supernatural creatures ranging from realistic to abstract.

During a major roundtable conference on the Olmec question at Tuxtla Gutiérrez in 1942, Alfonso Caso and Miguel Covarrubias designated Olmec as the mother culture of all succeeding Mesoamerican civilizations, rather than solely as an art style, because many cultural patterns originated on the Gulf Coast that continued over time. The antiquity of Olmec civilization was not fully appreciated until the second half of the twentieth century, when convincing radiocarbon dating of samples from the site of La Venta clearly demonstrated the fact. Today, the term *Olmec* continues to be utilized to refer to both an art style and an archaeological culture centered in the Gulf Coast states of Veracruz and Tabasco. While fragmentary texts hint at the existence of Olmec writing, no definitive body of written records has yet been discovered. The corpus of Olmec art, however, speaks dramatically and eloquently to the artistic and cultural genius of these amazing ancient peoples.

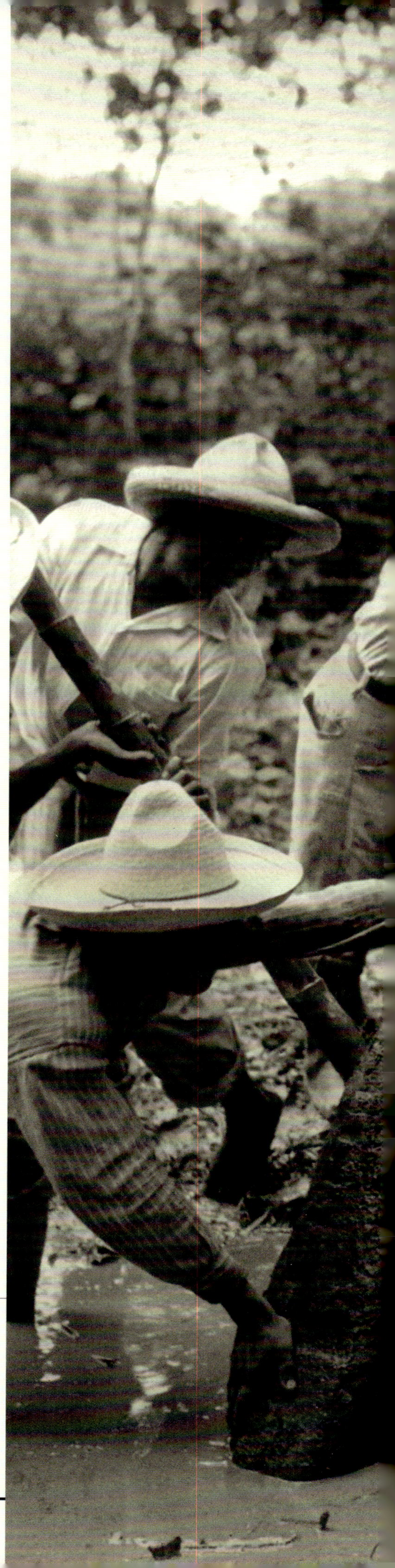

Workers raise Stela D from the mud at Tres Zapotes, 1939

FIRST DISCOVERIES IN THE OLMEC HEARTLAND

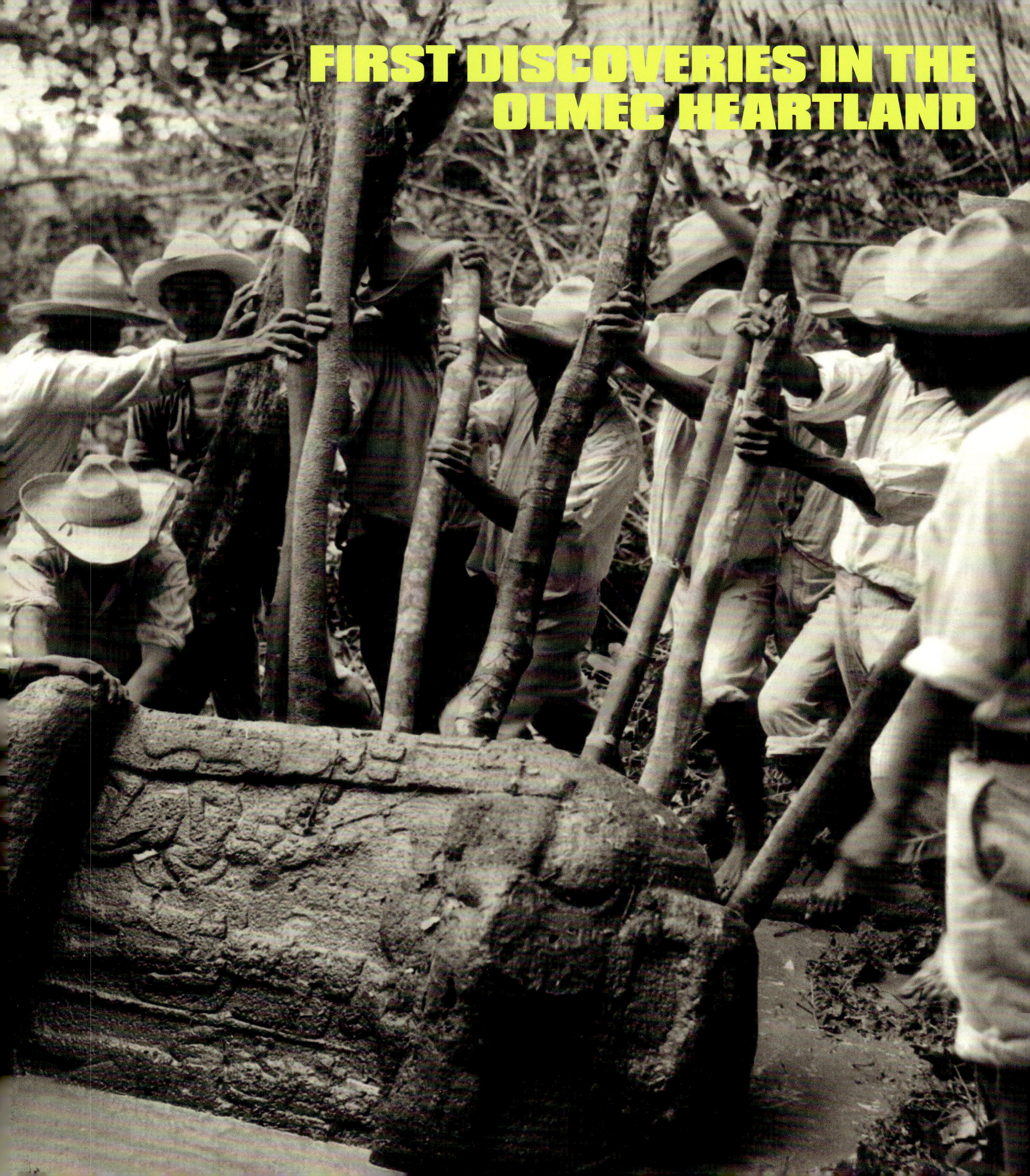

Also known as Tres Zapotes Colossal Head 2 and Nestepe Monument 1, Monument Q was the second colossal head to be discovered at Tres Zapotes. It was found on the south edge of the mound group known as Nestepe and was transported in 1950 to Santiago Tuxtla, where it still resides. Fieldwork conducted in the 1990s confirmed that the Nestepe Group was part of the Tres Zapotes site. Monument Q was carved from a distinctive porphyritic basalt obtained about 3 miles (5 kilometers) away on the slopes of the Cerro El Vigía, as were most of the Tres Zapotes monuments. Both Monument Q and Tres Zapotes Monument A (fig. 28) are small as colossal heads go, weighing "only" 8.5 and 7.8 tons (7.7 and 7.1 metric tons), respectively.

The lower face of Monument Q projects forward more than that of other Olmec colossal heads. Also distinctive are the seven elements that hang down the back of the head. Sometimes interpreted as beaded braids, these elements emerge from the back of a bird-shaped cap and are more likely intended to be long tail feathers. Both Monument Q and Monument A display the wide headband; the earflares with a wide, concave front; the triangular shape of the nasion (the area immediately above the nose); and the eyes with lids that overlap at sharp outer corners, all of which distinguish the Tres Zapotes heads from those of San Lorenzo and La Venta (Clewlow et al. 1967: 29, 32). CAP

PLATE 1

MONUMENT Q (COLOSSAL HEAD)
Mexico, Veracruz, Tres Zapotes, 1000–800 BC
Basalt
59 7/16 x 59 1/16 x 63 in. (151 x 150 x 160 cm)
Museo Regional Tuxteco, Santiago Tuxtla, Veracruz (10-4795)

See also:
de la Fuente 1973: 252–254
de la Fuente 1977a: 289–291
Heizer, Smith, and Williams 1962
Pool 2007: 106, fig. 4.3
Porter 1989: 119–122

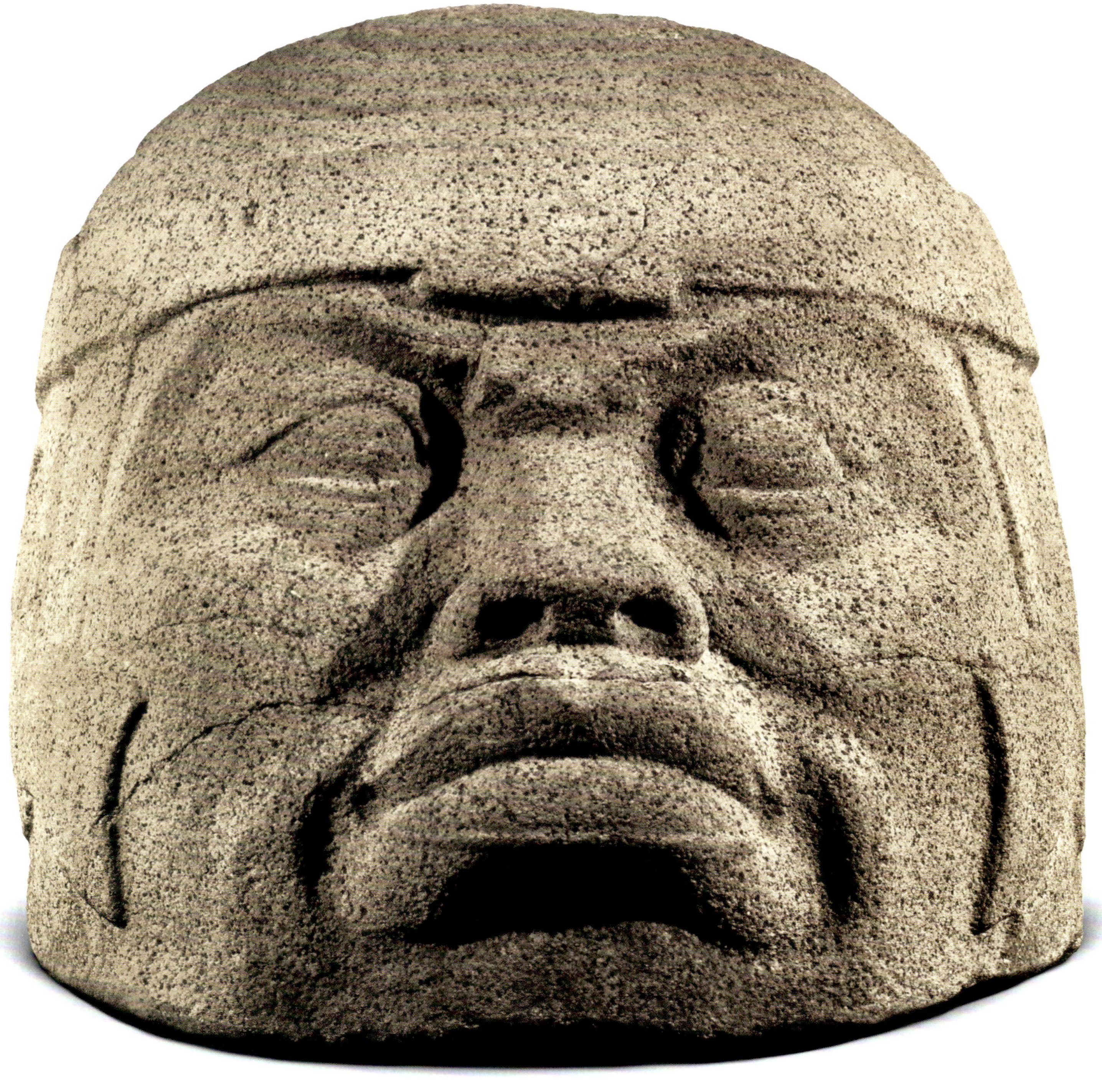

According to Marshall Saville (1929: 269), the votive axe described by geologist George Kunz (1890) may have come from the modern state of Oaxaca and been transported to New York by a sailor around 1869. Saville compared the Kunz Axe to other known examples of the form: one in the British Museum and another, published by Chavero (1888), which ended up at the American Museum of Natural History when its director purchased it in Switzerland as part of a "small but splendid collection of unique Mexican antiquities" (Saville 1929: 266).

Elizabeth Easby (1968: 88) noted that portions had been removed from the reverse of the axe where large veins of imperial green jade were visible, suggesting that jadeite was such a rare resource in ancient times that it was utilized sparingly. The extraordinary techniques for carving and incising such objects, as Kunz (1890: 278) first pointed out, represented long-distance exchange and enormous artistic skill, which led Easby (1968: 88) to propose a close connection between the Olmec area and Costa Rica.

Kunz (1890: 278) described his namesake axe as having "grotesque human" features, but Saville (1929: 268) noted that the "carving on the front represents the conventional mask of a tiger," which he concluded pertained to "a phase of worship of the god Tezcatlipoca" (ibid.: 287), a fourteenth-century Aztec deity. His study set the stage for the interpretation that the features consistently found on these forms combine the traits of a human infant and a jaguar, or a "were-jaguar" being; that is, almond-shaped eyes, prominent canine teeth, small nostrils, an unusually large and flaring upper lip, and, on the British Museum example, a central cleft in the forehead and a feature that came to be known as "flame eyebrows."

Saville was among the first scholars to attribute the votive axes and other greenstone objects to the "ancient Olmecan culture," which he located in the San Andrés Tuxtla area around Lago Catemaco and down the coast to the Gulf of Mexico in the southern part of Veracruz (ibid.: 285). The chronology of ancient Mexico was not well understood at the time, and Saville erroneously aligned Olmecan culture with the tenth-century Toltec civilization.

The concept of the were-jaguar dominated Olmec studies for much of the twentieth century (see, for example, Covarrubias 1946b; Coe 1968a; and various authors in Benson and de la Fuente 1996 and Princeton University 1995, among others). Matthew W. Stirling (1955) further promoted the idea after recovering an eroded sculpture in the San Lorenzo region (see pl. 86), which he proposed represented the mating of a jaguar and a human female.

Alternative interpretations emerged in the 1970s, suggesting that the were-jaguar was more likely modeled on a serpent (Luckert 1976: 14–19) or a toad (Furst 1981). Joralemon's study (1971) defined a series of deities whose traits combined those of various biological creatures into distinctive mythical beings. Scholars currently acknowledge that the so-called were-jaguar is more properly understood as a composite supernatural being (F. Kent Reilly III, personal communication, November 2009) whose physical features are drawn from multiple sources in the natural world. VMF

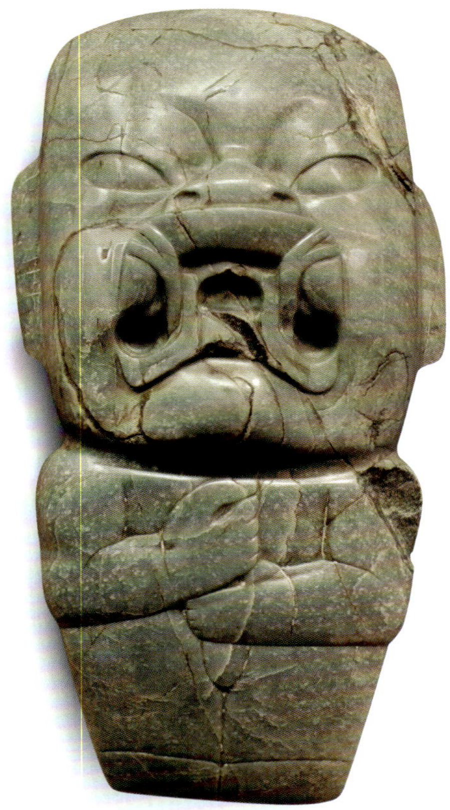

PLATE 2

KUNZ AXE (VOTIVE AXE)
Mexico, Oaxaca, 1000–400 BC
Jadeite
11 13/16 x 6 in. (30 x 15.2 cm)
American Museum of Natural History, New York (30/7552)

See also:
Benson 1996c: cat. 110

This unique figurine, which washed out of a mound in 1909 in the town of Necaxa during construction of a dam (Ekholm 1970; Benson 1996c: cat. 73), wears an elaborate costume that includes a woodpecker-like crest across the top of its head and the pleated ear ornaments that often adorn the headdresses of rulers and mythic beings associated with water. The figure sits in a pose associated with rulers, with his left foot under his right knee and his right leg bent back; his back is richly decorated with foliation-like streamers and an X motif on the belt, similar to the costume depicted on La Venta Monument 77 (pls. 67–68). The U motif incised on his back suggests an interpretive link with other Olmec-style objects that pair the U and X motifs (see pl. 70; Fields and Reents-Budet 2005: cat. 54).

The figure's almond-shaped eyes and snarling mouth had led to its early identification as a were-jaguar. Michael Coe (1968a: 45) suggested, however, that both the Kunz Axe (pl. 2) and this figure represented the Olmec rain god. Karl Luckert (1976: 14–16, fig. 2) proposed that, rather than a were-jaguar, the figure was more properly recognized as a serpent man.

While curator at the American Museum of Natural History, George Vaillant (1932: 512) applied the name *Olmec* to the culture that produced it. The wealth of detail offered by the scale, pose, and richness of adornment, as well as the lack of comparative examples in the Olmec sculptural corpus, makes a specific identification of the figure difficult, although its characteristics place it firmly within the canons of Olmec artistic production (Easby and Scott 1970: cat. 42). VMF

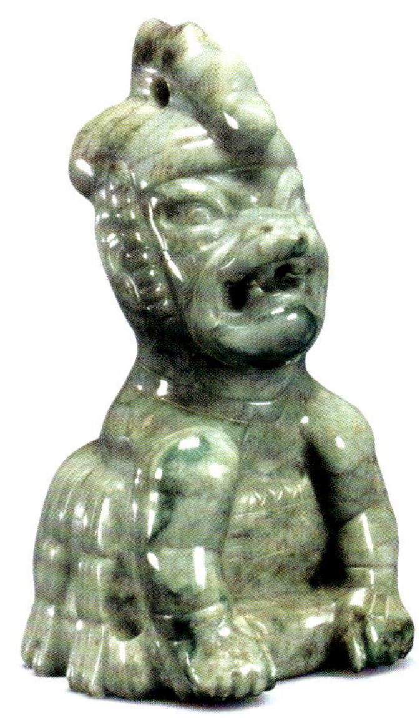

PLATE 3

SEATED ZOOMORPH WITH CREST AND PLEATED EAR DECORATIONS
Mexico, Puebla, Necaxa, 1000–400 BC
Jadeite
3 7/16 x 1 15/16 x 1 7/8 in. (8.7 x 4.9 x 4.7 cm)
American Museum of Natural History, New York (30.1/2168)

Olman's tropical lowlands have always been a challenging and changing environment. Today, and in ancient times, rivers, streams, and lagoons affect every aspect of life in the heartland region. Before twentieth-century highways and bridges were constructed, hollowed-log canoes were the main source of transportation. People lived as fishermen, farmers, hunters, artists, warriors, or merchants adjacent to the water sources that provided fertile agricultural land and aquatic foods such as fish, turtles, caimans, manatees, and shellfish. The region's most productive farmlands were natural levees that received fertility-restoring silt after annual floods. Domesticated crops and animals, as well as hunting and gathering of wild foods, were essential to the livelihood of these peoples. Images of animals, creatures of the sea, and humans are consistently reflected in objects fashioned by Olmec artists, works that express the world in which they lived and represent complex beliefs in metaphorical forms.

The Tuxtla Mountains, the main source of the volcanic stone used by Olmec architects and artists for structures and large monuments, were an important presence in the Olmec world, visible from every major center. Volcanoes dominated the landscape and, along with water, played an important role in Olmec cosmology, or worldview.

Olmec urban centers contained impressive temples, mounds, plazas, palaces, ballcourts, hydraulic systems, and living areas. Olmec society seems to have been ruled by powerful members of royal lineages. These elite lords, who resided in the central core of the major capitals, commanded the support of a regional hierarchy of smaller towns and villages, including the use of waterways, human power, and other resources. Ceremonial structures were constructed in relationship to cardinal directions and strongly keyed into features of the sacred landscape, such as springs, caves, and mountaintops. Olmec religious practices focused on the powerful natural and supernatural forces of their dynamic, changing universe, which required significant custodianship and care by means of rituals performed in constructed and natural settings. Olmec supernatural beings as seen in their art were often represented as composite creatures that embodied characteristics of birds, fish, and other creatures of the water and land, as well as life-sustaining foods such as maize.

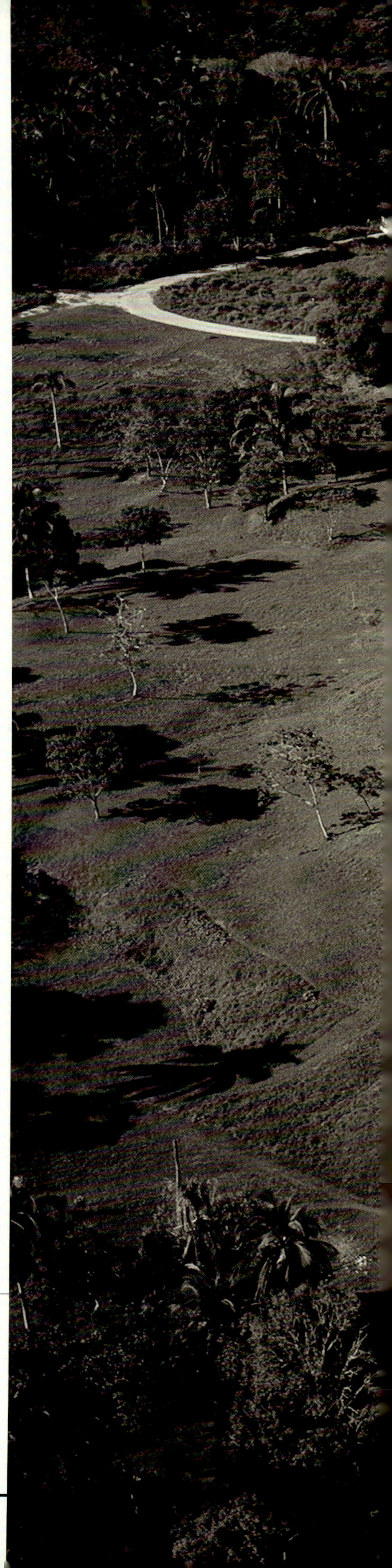

Aerial view of the pyramid of Complex C
at La Venta, 2002

THE HEARTLAND SETTING

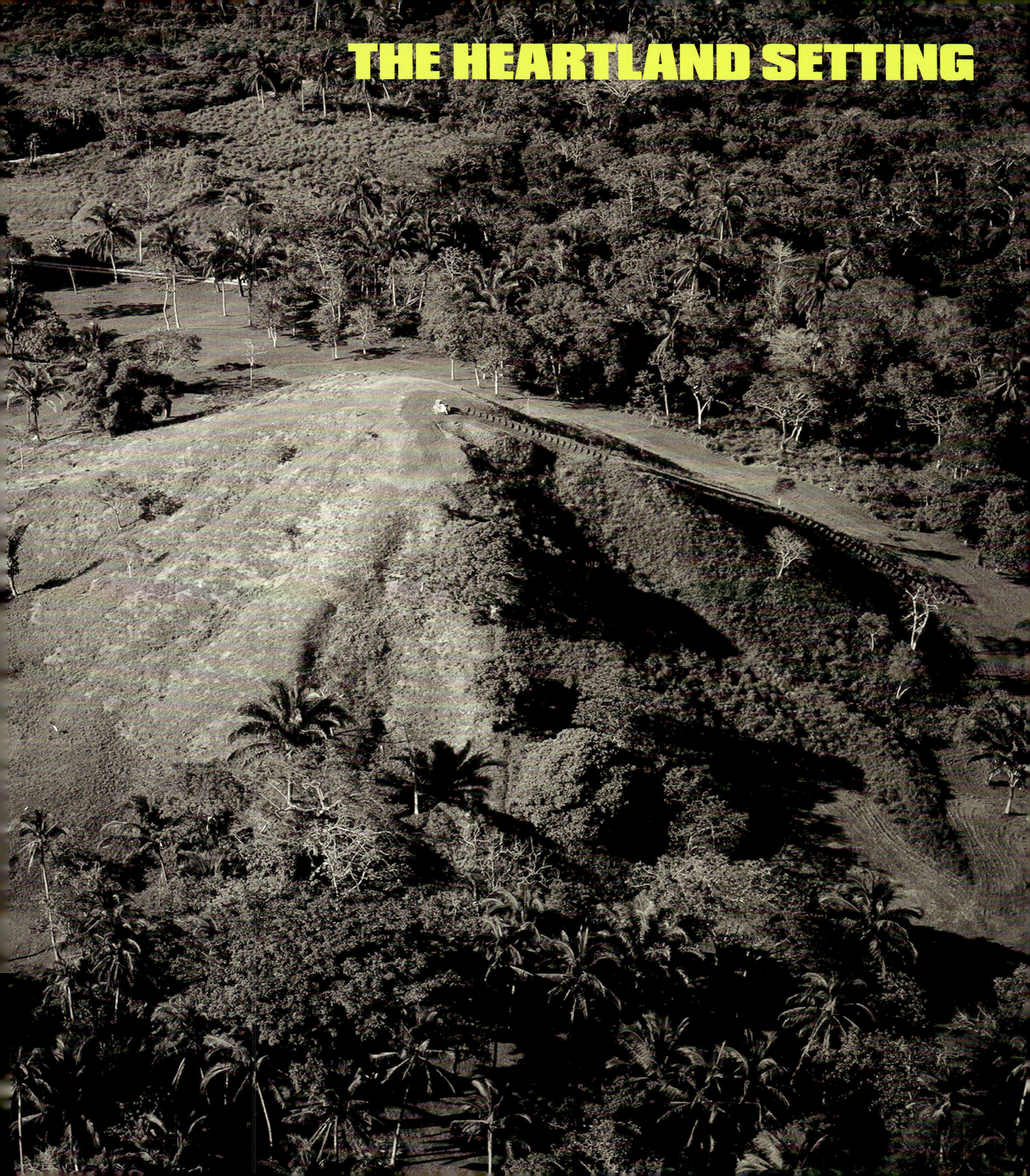

This rectangular slab may have served as a lid for a large stone box (Cyphers 2004b: 123). Discovered by Roberto Gallegos in 1969 during the INAH excavation project in Pit 11 on San Lorenzo's Group D ridge (Coe and Diehl 1980, vol. 1: 364), this weighty sculpture embodies the complex relationship of the Gulf Coast Olmec with the sea, rivers, and lagoons of their homeland and implies the importance of marine animals for food.

Because of its distinctive pointed tooth, the hybrid creature carved on the surface has been characterized as a composite fish-feline-human (de la Fuente 1984: 102) and as a shark (Cyphers 2004b: 123–124). Other features include a curved eye, which appears closed, and a human-style nose above an accentuated upper lip. In combination with the reduced lower lip, a buccal (or mouth) mask may be implied (ibid.). A large X covers the body of the creature, which ends in a bifurcated tail. The sculpture weighs about 661 pounds (300 kilograms) and is undecorated on its back and sides. MC-LE

PLATE 4

MONUMENT 58 (RELIEF OF COMPOSITE CREATURE)
Mexico, Veracruz, Municipality of Texistepec, San Lorenzo Tenochtitlán, 1400–1000 BC
Basalt
27 9/16 x 52 3/4 x 11 1/4 in. (70 x 134 x 28.5 cm)
Museo Nacional de Antropología, Mexico City (10-627693)

See also:
Castro-Leal 1996: cat. 16
Cyphers 1997d: 204–205, fig. 8.6
de la Fuente 1977a: 102–103, ill. 5

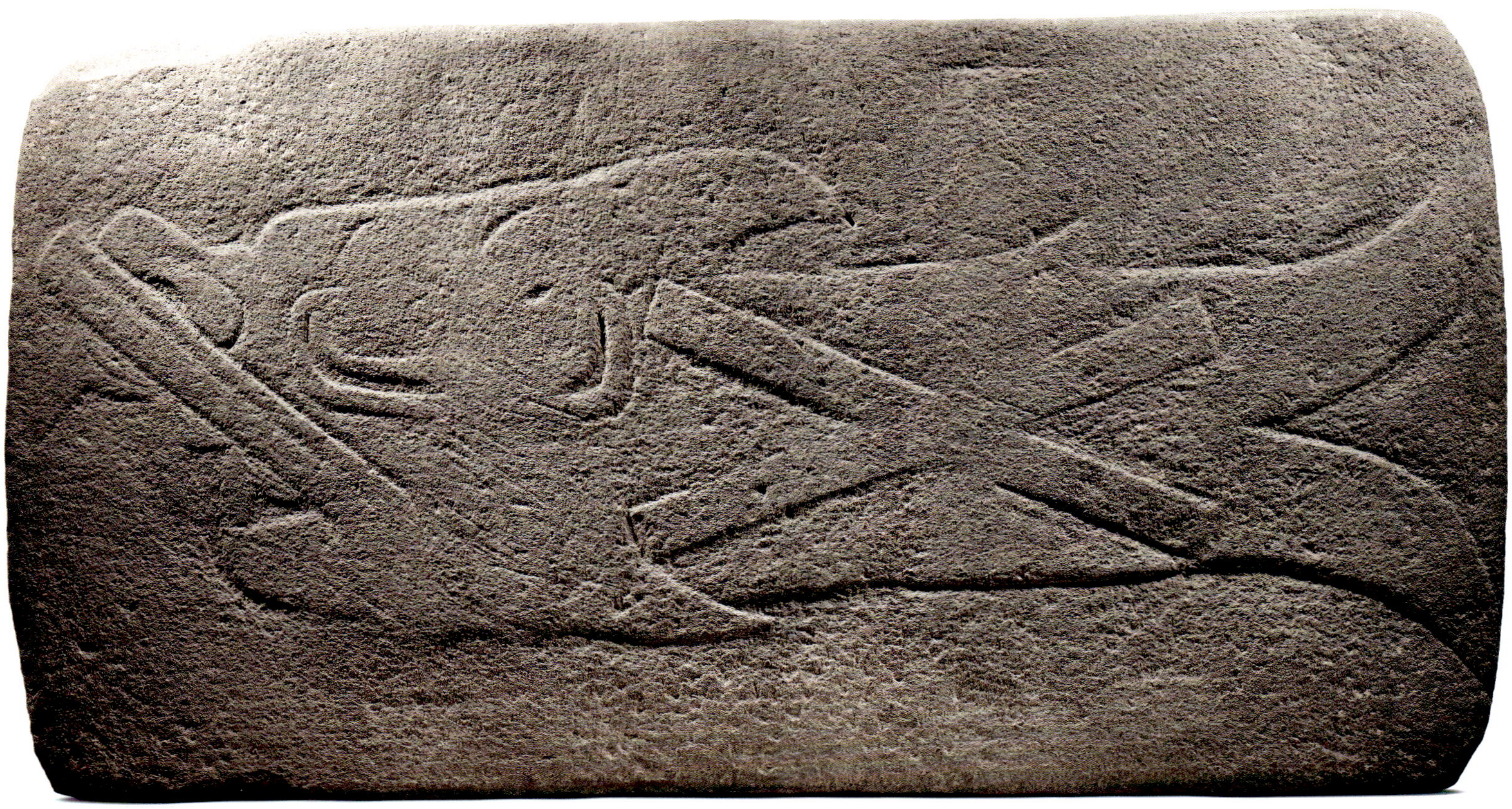

This sculpture in the shape of a fountain is part of a score of monuments discovered in 1946 by Matthew W. Stirling (1955: 13–14, pls. 17b–18), and it was created using a combination of fine and rough hammering. Representing a bird of prey or waterbird with a hollowed-out body, it has stylized wings with five feathers on each of its sides, and webbed feet with three toes and talons. It has no head, suggesting that there might once have been a lid or cover on the upper part. The U-shaped opening on the right side is similar to the silhouette of aqueduct sections at San Lorenzo, and it is possible that this monument was associated with part of the site's aqueduct system. Apparently, water circulated through a small orifice behind the U-shaped opening and into the rounded interior. The trilobed iconographic elements associated with water—two on the front and one on the back—are also present on other monuments at San Lorenzo. RLR

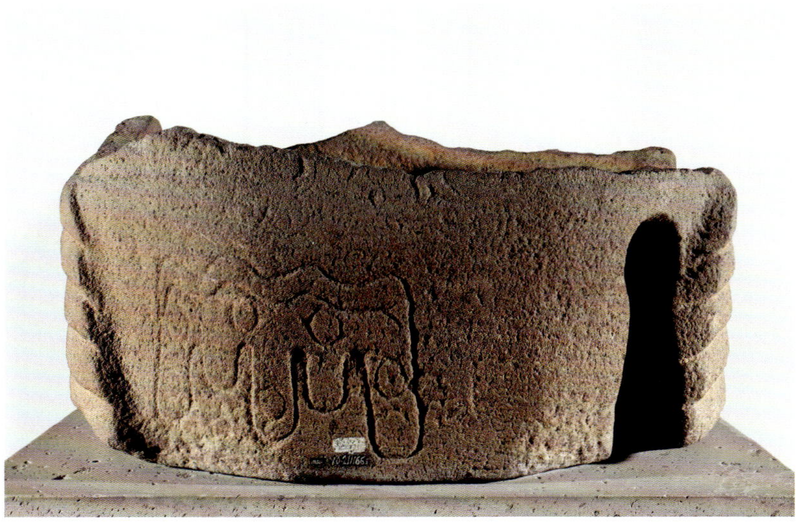

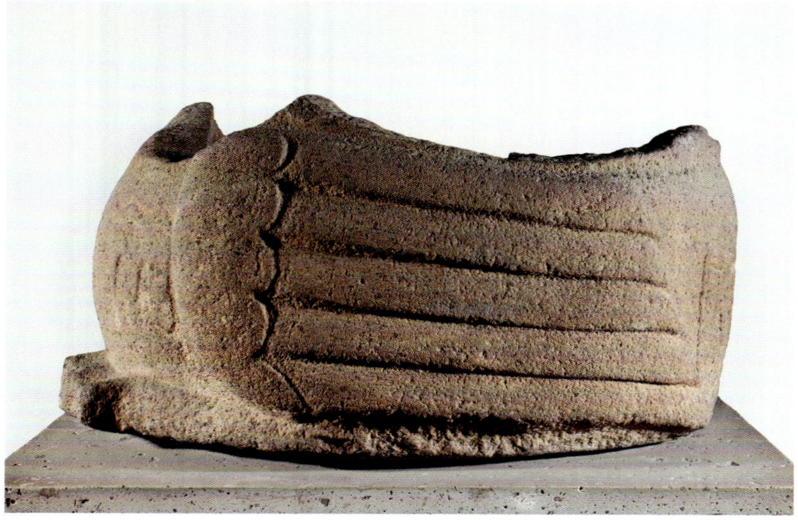

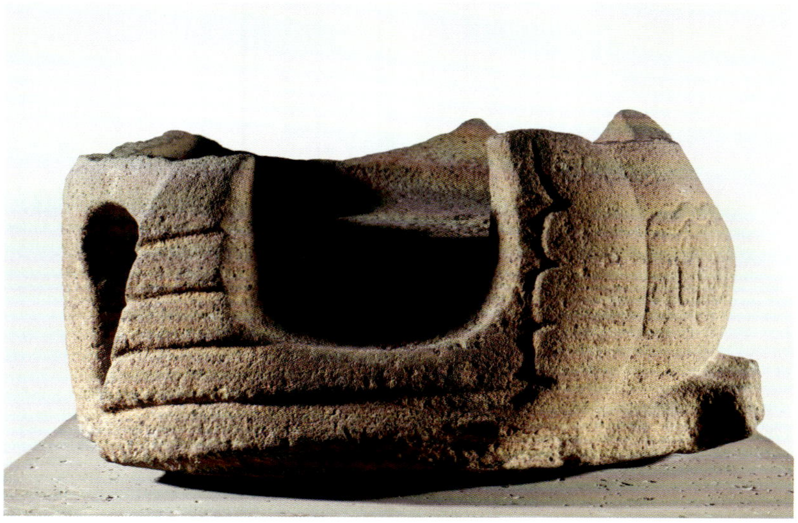

PLATES 5–8

MONUMENT 9 (WATERBIRD)
Mexico, Veracruz, Municipality of Texistepec, San Lorenzo Tenochtitlán, 1200–900 BC
Basalt
18⅞ x 37 x 37 in. (48 x 94 x 94 cm)
Museo de Antropología de Xalapa, Universidad Veracruzana (Reg. 49 P.J. 331)

See also:
Coe and Diehl 1980, vol. 1: 314–315, figs. 432–433

Cyphers 2004b: 59–61, figs. 19–21

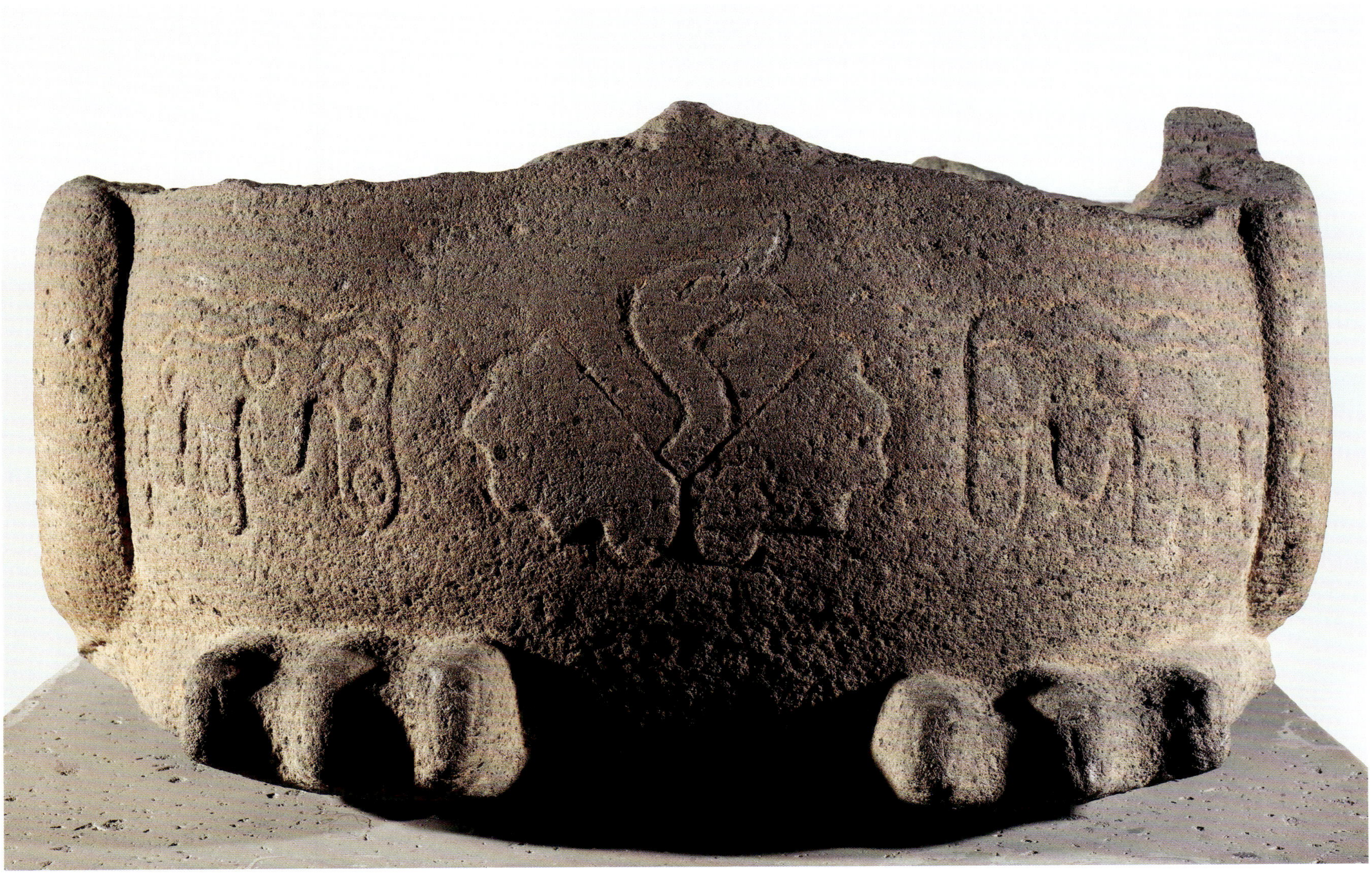

This sculpture, discovered during the 1968–1969 excavation season under the direction of Michael Coe, was deeply buried about 3 feet (1 meter) north of the head of the main basalt drain line at the western edge of the San Lorenzo plateau. Matthew W. Stirling had located numerous stone troughs or drain conduits in this area during his 1946 season, although none that were intact (Coe and Diehl 1980, vol. 1: 35). Coe's team excavated 69 feet (21 meters) of the aqueduct during the 1967 season, and work continued in 1968. Ultimately, they found that an east-to-west main line (558 feet, or 170 meters long) had three branches that extended south-to-north. The system, constructed of U-shaped basalt troughs with flat basalt covers, distributed water from a shallow lagoon on the surface (ibid.: 118). The symbolism on this monument, which was found lying on its back, may pertain to the importance of managing rain and/or water at this site.

The crouching figure with his hands resting on his knees has the cleft head, almond-shaped eyes, and snarling mouth that define both monumental and small-scale composite creatures in Olmec art. Flanking the face are the pleated ear ornaments that Coe and Peter Joralemon (in Coe and Diehl 1980, vol. 1: 363) associate with the Olmec water deity. Ann Cyphers (2004b: 112) suggests, however, that the figure's features, which are both human and zoomorphic, imply it is undergoing transformation. The headdress is marked with a pair of the scalloped designs also seen on the Cleveland Museum of Art axe (pl. 92), and the figure wears a pendant with the X motif. The back of the monument is hollowed out into a U shape, similar to one of the trough stones of the drain line (Coe and Diehl 1980, vol. 1: 363). Alternatively, Cyphers (2004b: 112) proposes that the figure may have been attached to a stake, since the proportions of the U shape do not conform to any of the known drains at San Lorenzo. MC-LE

PLATE 9

MONUMENT 52 (ZOOMORPHIC SCULPTURE)
Mexico, Veracruz, Municipality of Texistepec, San Lorenzo Tenochtitlán, 1000–400 BC
Andesite
36 3/16 x 18 7/8 x 15 3/16 in. (91.9 x 47.9 x 38.5 cm)
Museo Nacional de Antropología, Mexico City (10-81268)

See also:
Castro-Leal 1996: cat. 12
Cyphers 1994c: 49–51, fig. 4.6
Cyphers 1997d: 202–204, fig. 8.5
de la Fuente 1977a: 98–100, pl. 1, figs. 11–11a, ill. 3
Easby and Scott 1970: cat. 34
Reilly 1994: 245–246, fig. 15.11

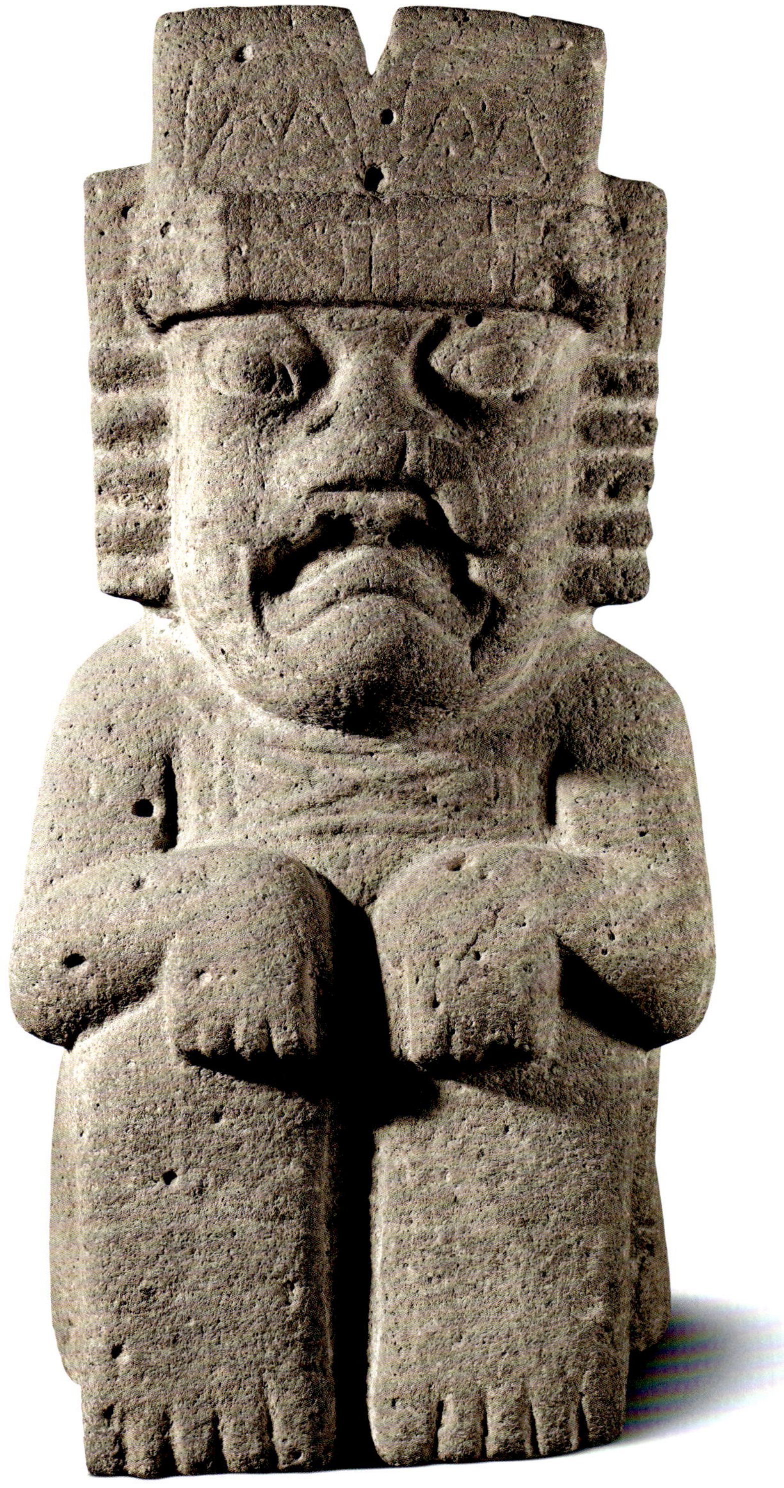

This throne depicting a crouching composite jaguar creature was found on Mound B-4 at La Venta, directly centered on the pyramidal substructure of Complex A (Clewlow and Corson 1968: 178–179) and clustered together with five other monuments. Weighing about 2,200 pounds (998 kilograms), the throne combines the physical traits of human and jaguar, especially visible in the horizontal eyes, downturned mouth with fangs, and jaguar ears. Although no ritual defacement appears to have occurred, the right hand has broken away, leaving only a human-looking hand on the left.

The tabletop throne has a projecting ledge. It was once thought that such objects served as altars, but David Grove (1981), based on his 1968 discovery and interpretation of a mural in Oxtotitlan cave in Guerrero (Grove 1970a), has demonstrated that they essentially function as thrones. Olmec thrones seem to have been seats of power for rulers and sources of political patronage. They established a visual administrative hierarchy by their very weight and size; hence, the larger and heavier thrones were reserved for the most important Olmec rulers (Cyphers 2008). KB

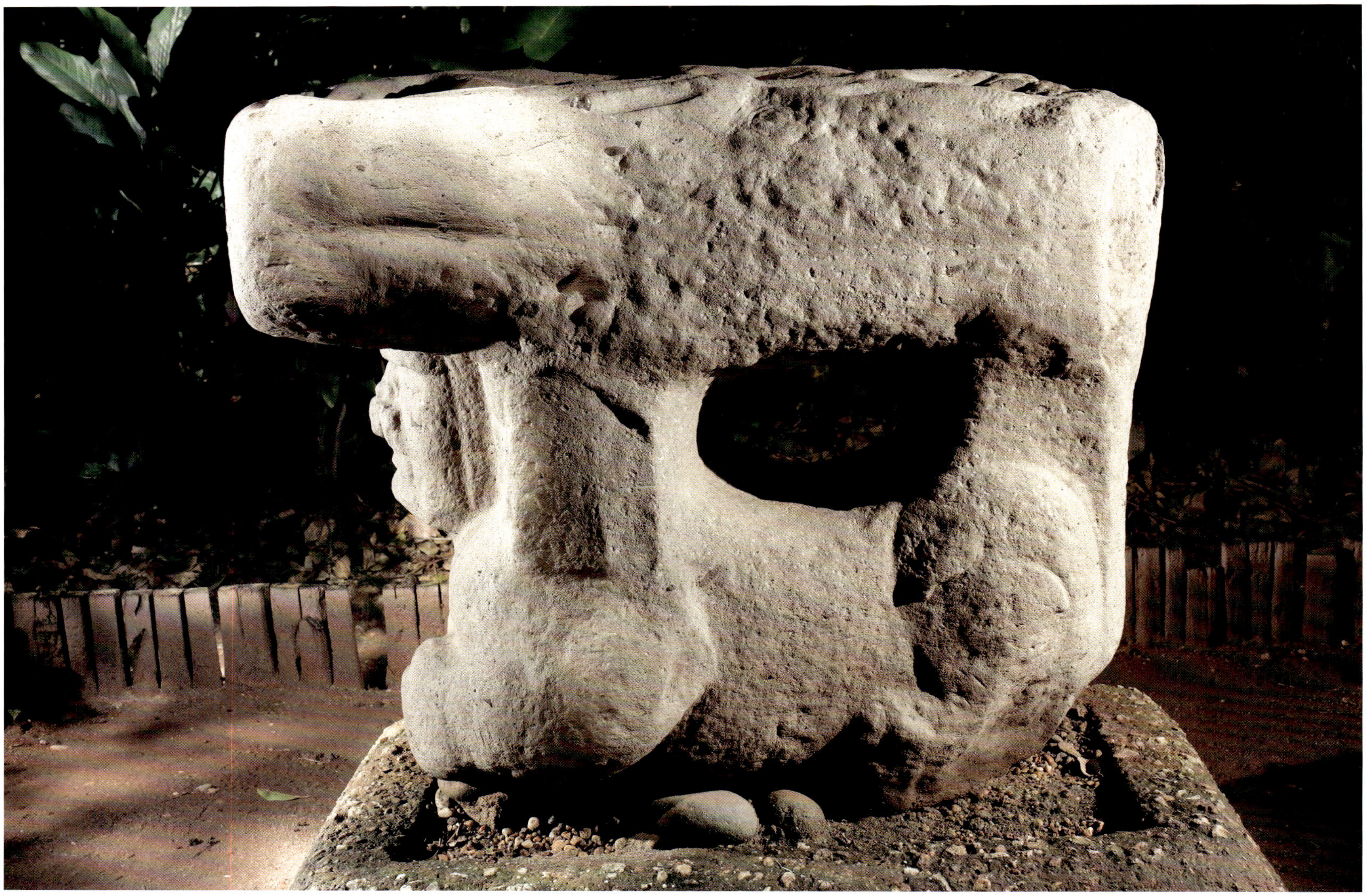

PLATES 10–11

MONUMENT 59 (THRONE)
Mexico, Tabasco, La Venta, 900–400 BC
Basalt
40 9/16 x 31 1/8 x 44 1/8 in. (103 x 79 x 112 cm)
Parque-Museo de La Venta, Villahermosa, Tabasco (PMV-016)

See also:
Reilly 1995: 43, fig. 33

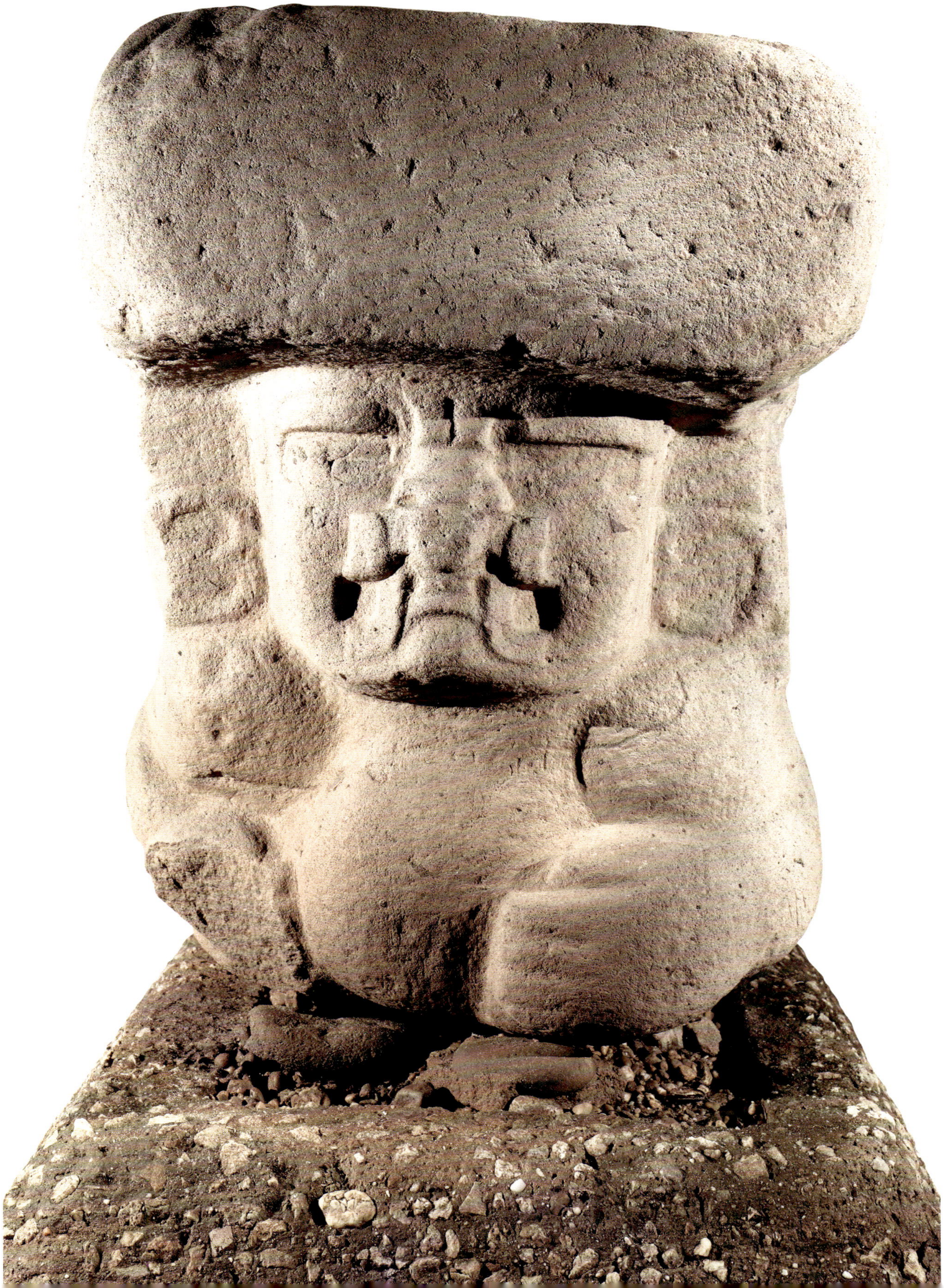

There is evidence at Zohapilco, Tlapacoya, of one of the earliest settlements in Mesoamerica that created ceramics, and its material remains reveal one of the most complete chronological sequences of cultural development that arose in the Formative period in Central Mexico. The renowned Zohapilco figurine—a small, torso-shaped piece with a bulging stomach, minimal facial features, and no arms or legs—was found here. The archaeological sequence at this site ends with the ceremonial center at Tlapacoya. Also found were ceramics with a series of iconographic themes associated with Gulf Coast Olmec groups.

Composite silhouette vessels such as this plate, with incised decoration on the inner surface and a double, broken, incised line on the rim, can be dated stylistically to 1000–800 BC. This example was recovered from excavation unit 7B (Niederberger 2000: fig. 1b), and its decoration reflects the strong relationship between the Zohapilcans and their environment. Water, which surrounded Zohapilco, is magnificently evoked here in the incised design of two highly realistic, swimming fish against a white bath that covered the pinkish clay beneath. POC (OCHOA)

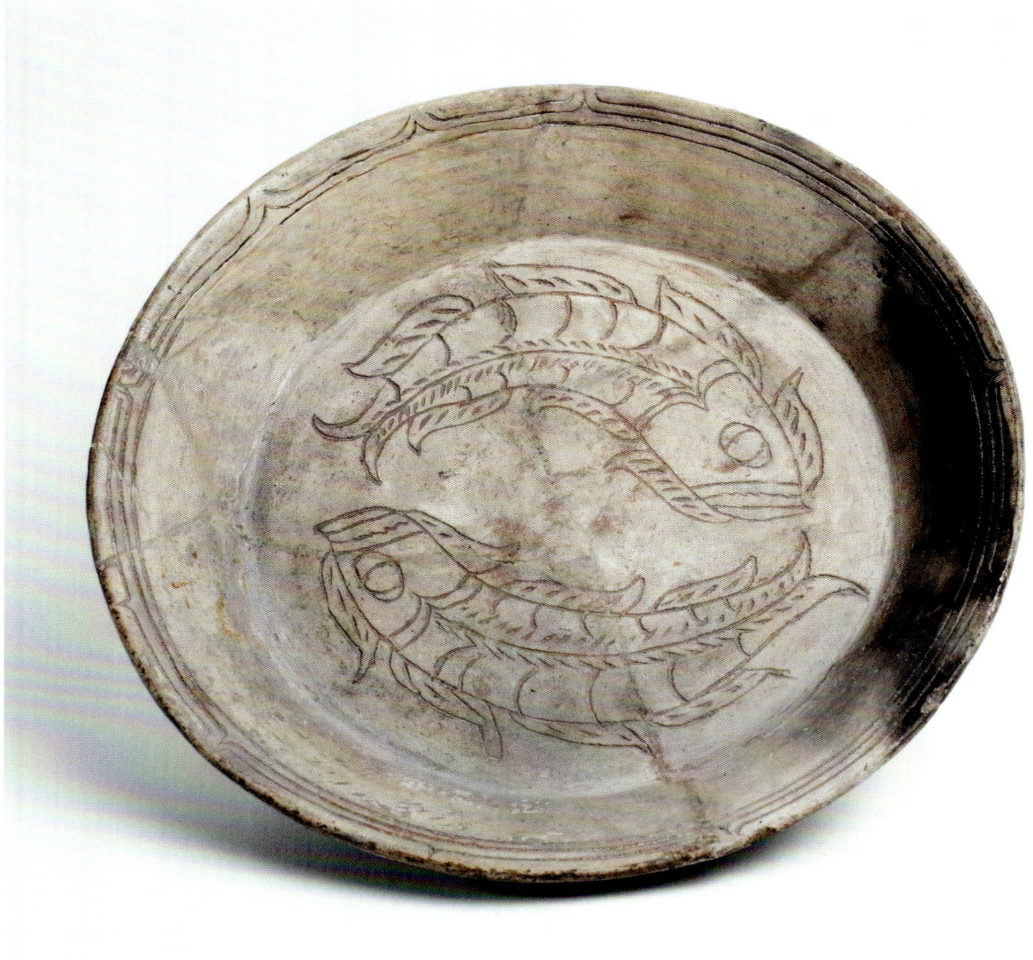

PLATE 12

PLATE WITH TWO FISH
Mexico, Tlapacoya, Zohapilco, 1000–600 BC
Earthenware
$2^{3}/_{16}$ x $11^{7}/_{16}$ in. (5.5 x 29 cm)
Museo Nacional de Antropología, Mexico City
(10-357234)

The potters of the Middle Preclassic period drew inspiration from a wide variety of natural forms to visualize design elements that reflected their surroundings. This dish has a composite silhouette, convex base, and curved and angular body, and it is covered with a white wash that allows the beige clay to show through the incised lines and grooves of the decoration. The dish's inner surface is incised with a series of cut shells; the double row of incised, broken lines on the rim—recalling the jaguar's gums or eyes—links the dish to Olmec iconography. Composite silhouette plates with linear decoration on the rim were common at several Mesoamerican sites during this period. Local ceramics also displayed highly distinctive characteristics, such as the gray paste wares of Izúcar and Epatlán in Puebla.

This vessel was recovered in the fourth field season at Tlatilco, a site known for its superb pottery. This piece, which falls slightly later in the archaeological sequence at Tlatilco, displays naturalistic elements that characterize ceramics from settlements in the Basin of Mexico. POC (OCHOA)

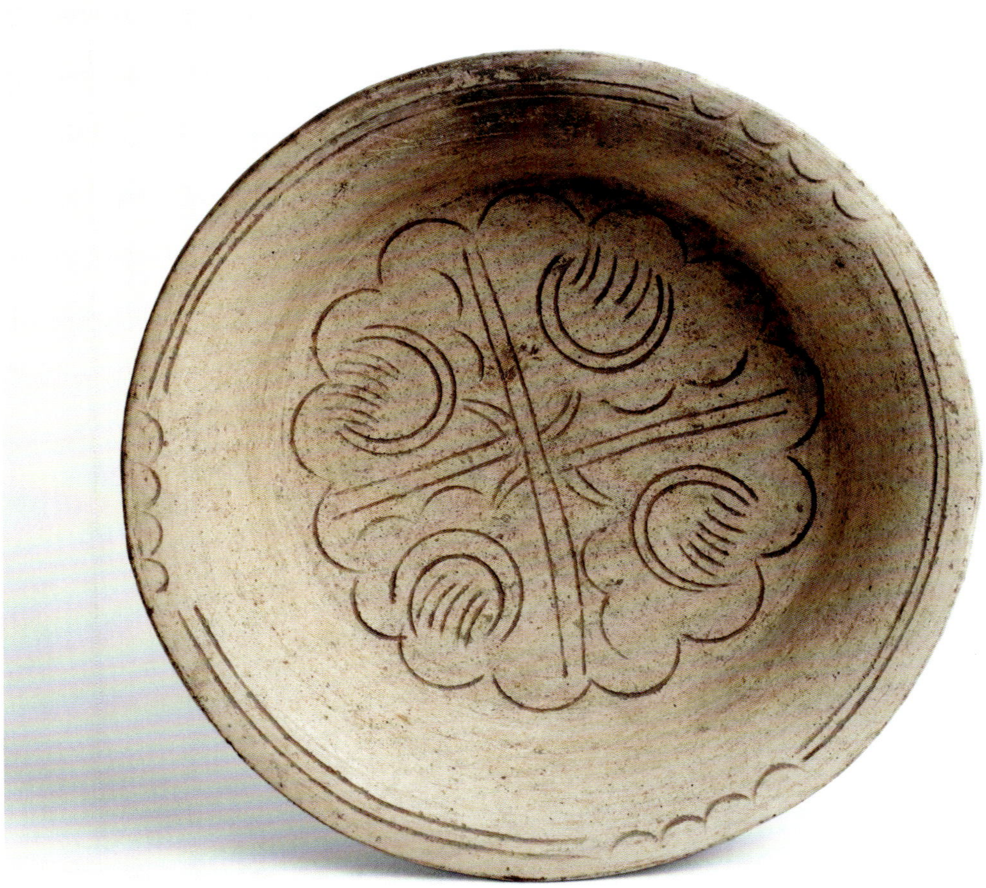

PLATE 13

PLATE WITH CUT SHELLS
Mexico, Tlatilco, 1000–600 BC
Earthenware
$2^{1}/_{2} \times 9^{13}/_{16}$ in. (6.3 x 25 cm)
Museo Nacional de Antropología, Mexico City
(10-341580)

This piece, with its fine, highly polished black slip finish, exemplifies the artistry of Early Preclassic period potters. In the shape of a fish with an open mouth at the top to form a spout, the vessel has features rendered as grooves; a round object was used to mark the deeper parts of the design. The rough texture of the belly and mouth areas was produced by scraping the piece after firing and then rubbing it with red pigment. These elements are often present in Early Preclassic ceramics associated with Olmec groups, as are other decorative motifs such as the *ilhuitl* (opposing volutes).

Early Preclassic peoples developed a cult of the dead, and bodies were buried with belongings intended to accompany them on their afterlife journey. More than five hundred burials were explored at Tlatilco, the majority of which contained rich offerings in the Olmec style. During the second excavation season, project director Román Piña Chan discovered this vessel in Burial 53. It was associated with other objects including vessels decorated with the typical "Tlatilco panel," a series of parallel lines forming triangles. POC (OCHOA)

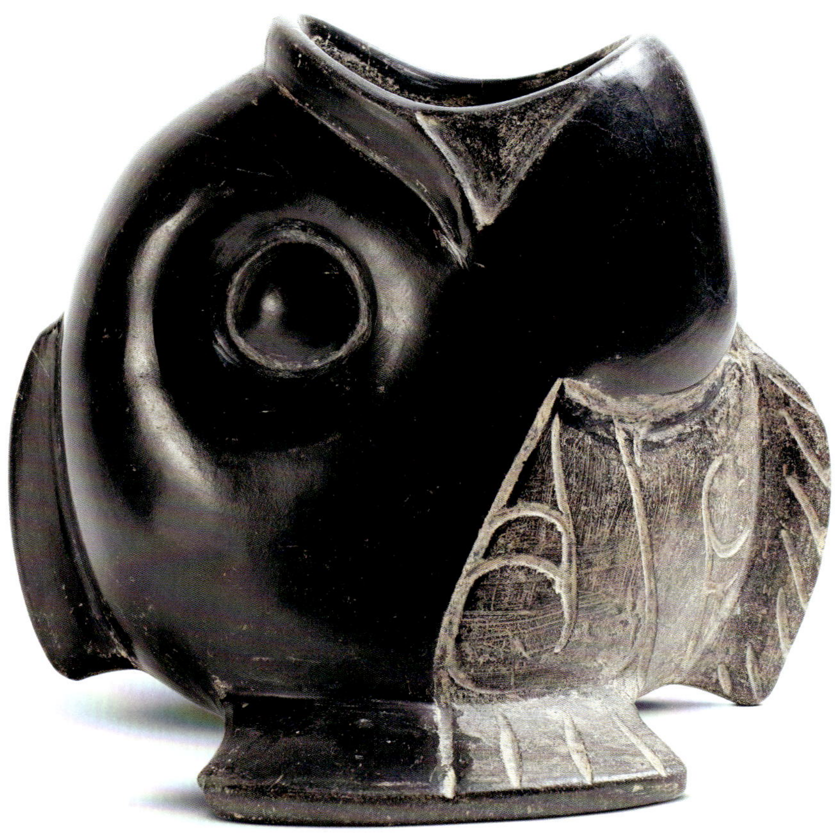

PLATE 14

FISH EFFIGY VESSEL
Mexico, Tlatilco, Burial 53, Offering 3, 1200–600 BC
Black earthenware
$5^{1}/_{16}$ x $4^{1}/_{2}$ in. (12.8 x 11.5 cm)
Museo Nacional de Antropología, Mexico City (10-50)

See also:
Ochoa Castillo 1996: cat. 26

Tlatilco, a site located in the modern-day state of Mexico, developed during the Early and Middle Preclassic periods (1400–600 BC). It may be regarded as one of the most important in the Central Highlands during the Formative period, not only for the number of objects found during four seasons of fieldwork but also for the beauty and quality of the objects. Many of these pieces are noteworthy because they are stylistically related to those of Gulf Coast Olmec groups, whose culture is regarded by many as the earliest civilization in Mesoamerica.

The vessels at Tlatilco and other early sites in the Central Highlands, such as Los Molinillos, display a wide variety of shapes. Among the many styles of bowls are some with a convex base and curved walls, their edges modeled to create bird shapes. In this piece, modeling, incising, and grooving the clay defined the features of the bird's head, wings, and tail. POC (OCHOA)

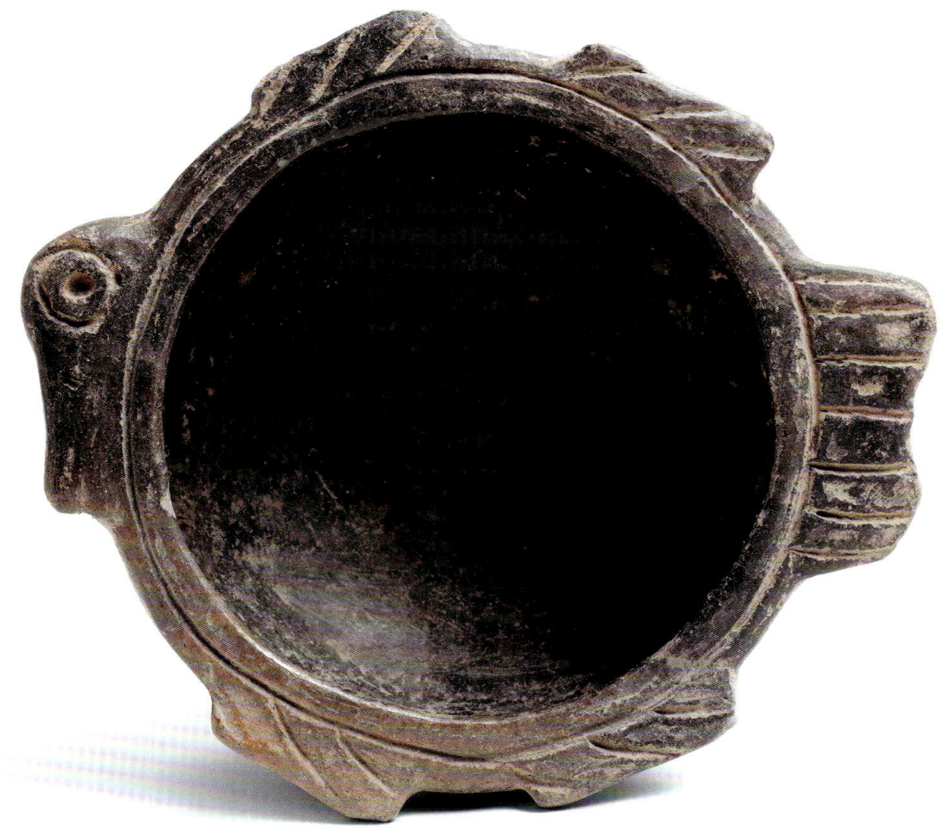

PLATE 15

BIRD-SHAPED EFFIGY VESSEL
Mexico, Central Highlands, Los Molinillos, 1200–600 BC
Earthenware
$2\frac{3}{16}$ x 6 in. (5.6 x 15.2 cm)
Museo Nacional de Antropología, Mexico City (10-394996)

Aquatic animals played an important role in the lives of the peoples of the Gulf Coast, whose capitals were essentially islands and whose success in managing water was reflected in the growth and development of their communities. This pectoral is carved in the form of a turtle carapace, with an image of the Olmec maize god carved and incised on its surface. A distinctive form of the Olmec-style maize plant emerges from the cleft head of the snarling visage of the deity, whose face is flanked by the pleated-paper ear ornaments commonly seen adorning the headdresses of both humans and supernatural beings (pls. 9, 67–68).

Although the significance of the turtle in early cosmologies is unknown, turtles appear in later Maya art and culture in various contexts, such as musical instruments and monumental altars, and as a metaphor for the earth's surface. An intriguing depiction on the west wall mural at San Bartolo, Guatemala, for example, dating to around 100 BC, shows supernatural participants in a specific ritual action, which takes place on a giant turtle shell (Taube and Saturno 2008: 312–313). Corresponding to the image on this pectoral may be the later Maya depictions of the maize god rising up through a crack in the back of a turtle carapace representing the surface of the earth (ibid.: 314, fig. c). VMF

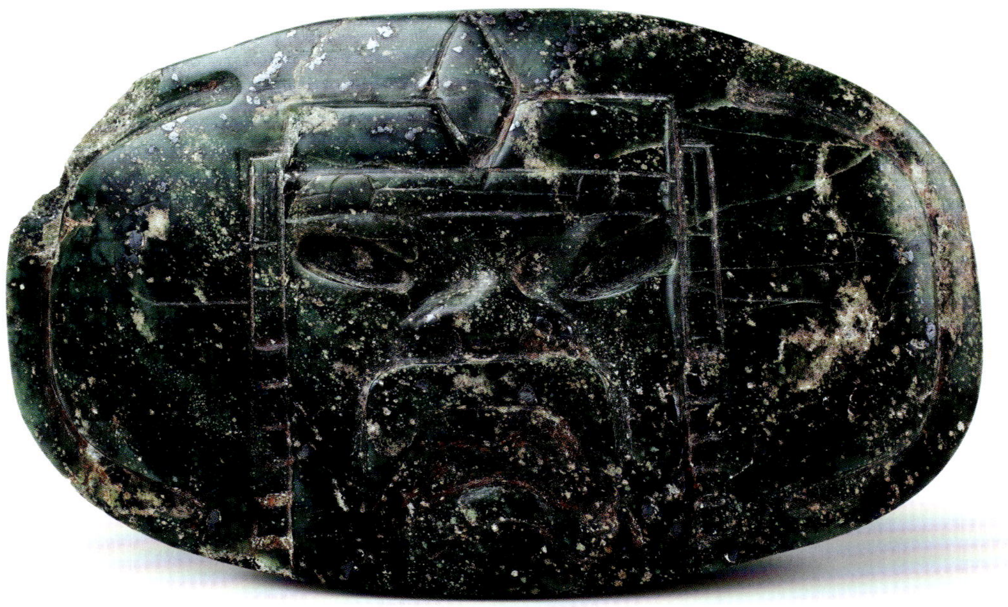

PLATE 16

PECTORAL
Mexico, La Encrucijada, 900–500 BC
Greenstone
3 3/8 x 5 3/8 x 1 in. (8.5 x 13.6 x 2.5 cm)
Instituto de Cultura de Tabasco, Dirección de Patrimonio Cultural (B-4531)

See also:
Diehl 1990: cat. 12
Gómez Rueda and Courtes 1987: 73–88

Although lacking a specific archaeological context, this plaque apparently derives from the Motozintla area of Chiapas, which constitutes a major passageway from the Pacific Coast to the inland river valleys on the northern side of the Sierra Madre chain (Clark and Pye 2000b: 226, fig. 12b). The plaque depicts two cross-legged men wearing elaborate costumes that include bird masks and headdresses (held in place with a chin strap), necklaces, earflares, hipskirts, and belts, which attach their back shields. They face each other within a distinctive oval frame decorated with a geometric pattern, and their upraised arms suggest they are engaged in a lively conversation or negotiation. Gareth Lowe (1994: 123–124, fig. 7.12) described the figures as deities seated in a terrestrial environment, possibly a cave, and he linked their identifications to paired deities in the Olmec pantheon defined by Peter Joralemon (1971), specifically Gods I and III.

There are, however, a number of depictions of humans wearing similar avian regalia, including on monumental sculptures such as La Venta Altar 4 (fig. 19) and Chalcatzingo relief I-B-2 (Angulo V. 1987: 142, fig. 10.13), on the mural in Oxtotitlan cave (figs. 36–37), and on small-scale precious objects such as this pendant. The consistent appearance of avian regalia on figures portrayed as members of the ruling elite asserts their status and authority in their communities. This metaphoric use of the characteristics of powerful creatures from the natural world to express equivalent powers in the human world represents the well-established pattern of defining royal authority in Mesoamerica. VMF

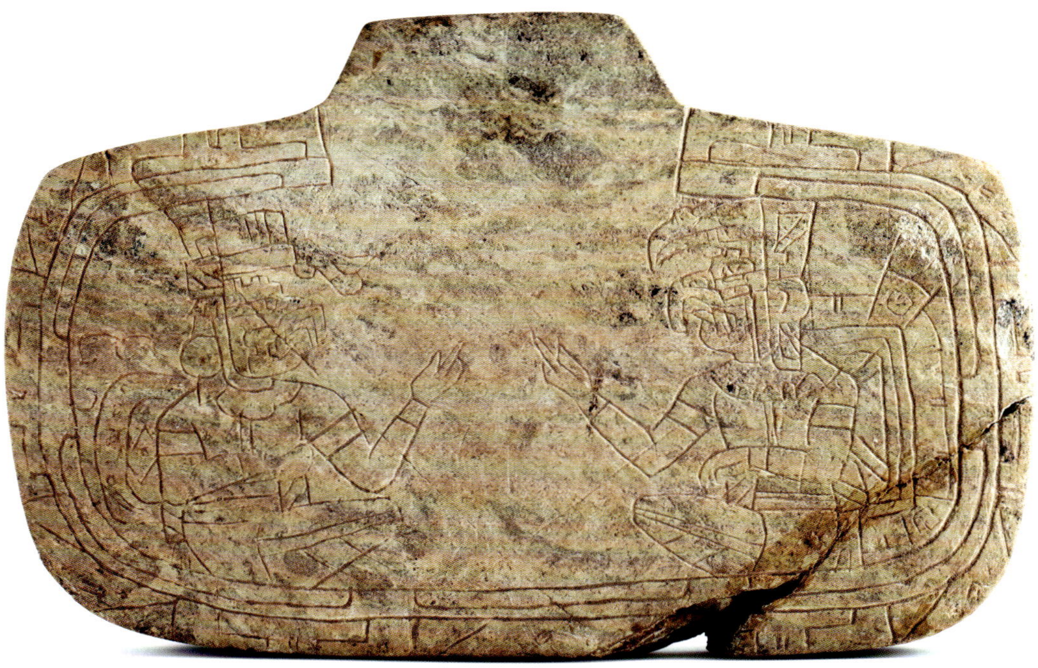

PLATE 17

PENDANT WITH TWO MEN WEARING BIRD MASKS
Mexico, Chiapas, 600–400 BC
Serpentine
$3^{3}/_{8}$ x $5^{1}/_{8}$ x $1^{15}/_{16}$ in. (8.5 x 13 x 5 cm)
Museo Regional de Chiapas, Tuxtla Gutiérrez
(10-623898)

During their investigations in 1942, Matthew W. Stirling and Philip Drucker discovered an extraordinary tomb composed of basalt columns (Drucker 1952a: 23–26, 154–155, pls. 46, 47; see also Reilly, this volume). Clay had been used to fill and cover the tomb, resulting in the mound now referred to as A-2 (Diehl 1990: 59). Inside, on the tomb's limestone floor, the archaeologists discovered the remains of two bundled burials that had been coated with red pigment. Each bundle contained fragmentary bones and teeth, suggesting that each had held a juvenile, and was accompanied by offerings, primarily of jadeite, indicating elite status. Bundle 1 contained this pair of ear ornaments, as well as a pendant and a mirror (pls. 73–74), among its offerings (Drucker 1952a).

The slight depression on the interior surface of the ornaments indicates that they were reworked from a larger jadeite object, most likely a canoe-shaped pendant (Diehl 1990: cat. 8). The profile of a crested raptor was incised onto the surface of each ornament; the drilled hole for attaching the ornament doubles as the eye of the bird. MC-LE

PLATE 18

PAIR OF EARFLARES
Mexico, Tabasco, La Venta, Mound A-2, Tomb A (Columnar Tomb), 900–500 BC
Jadeite
2 5/16 x 2 5/16 x 9/16 in. (5.9 x 5.9 x 1.5 cm)
Museo Nacional de Antropología, Mexico City (10-3096 a, b)

See also:
González Lauck 2007: 52
Stirling 1942: 640–643, pl. 1

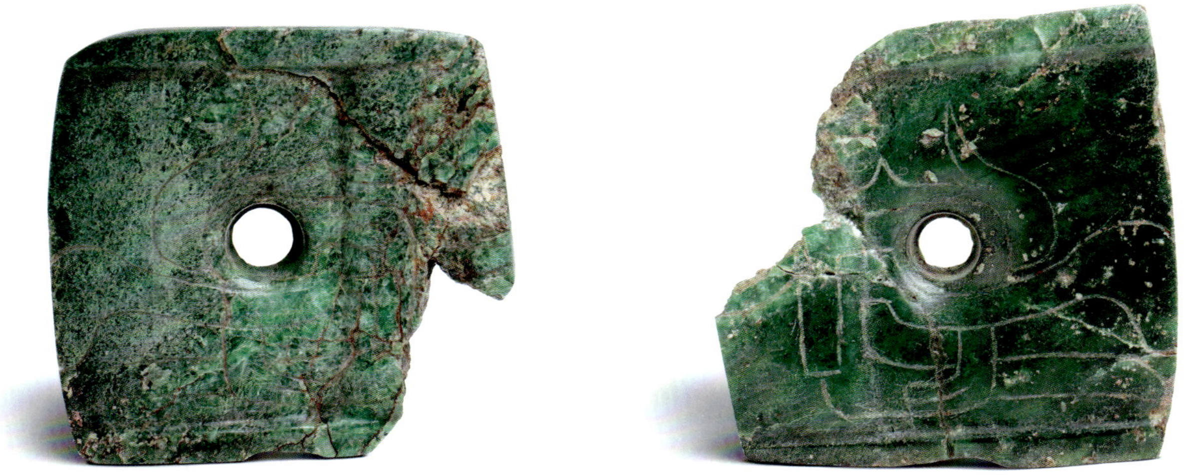

Preclassic period effigy vessels seem to have been used both in daily life and for ceremonial purposes. Gray-colored clay typical of Puebla and Oaxaca was used in this piece, which has a fine surface finish covered with slip of the same color. It was perhaps made by modeling the clay as if shaping a sculpture that was intended to be hollowed out later. It depicts a fantastic animal, a common subject in Olmec symbolism and one primarily seen on vessels. This piece in particular is an outstanding example of abstraction in Olmec art, for it shows the combination of jaguar and reptile elements to create a creature resembling a dragon.

The stylized elements include the modeled flame brows. The eyes, represented as hollowed-out and inverted L shapes, must have signified underground water associated with agricultural fertility. The nose is wide and bulbous, the upper lip is modeled, and the gums are in the shape of hooks. Two appliqués fall over the upper lip, and these elements are present in other pieces as well. Four feet end in stylized claws and display round incisions along the body that might symbolize the animal's pelt markings. The vessel's spout, which was originally on the back, is now broken.

Between 1963 and 1964, George Pepper donated twelve magnificent vessels and figurines, some in the Olmec style, to the Museo Nacional de Antropología. Based on the information obtained at the time, these pieces originally came from Tlapacoya. POC (OCHOA)

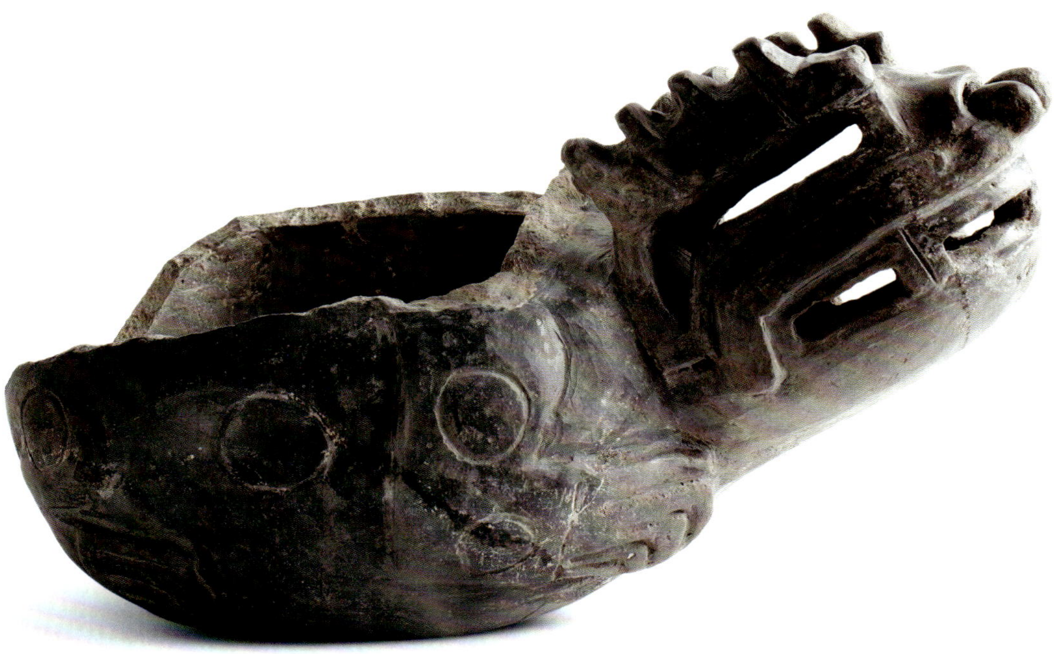

PLATE 19

ZOOMORPHIC EFFIGY VESSEL
Mexico, Tlapacoya, 1200–600 BC
Earthenware
$5^{1}/_{2} \times 6^{1}/_{8} \times 10^{5}/_{16}$ in. (14 x 15.5 x 26.2 cm)
Museo Nacional de Antropología, Mexico City, donation of George Pepper (10-77760)

See also:
Ochoa Castillo 1996: cat. 29

Beautifully modeled and covered with a brown slip polished to a fine luster, this vessel is in the shape of an opossum; the snout, which doubles as a spout, is pointed upward. The object displays the skill of the potters of this period in rendering different attitudes and positions. Opossums, especially, were represented in highly varied poses. They were frequently depicted by Tlatilco potters, perhaps because of their importance in daily life or because they were always present near fields and houses. We know that the environmental conditions of the Basin of Mexico at that time must have been quite different from those of the present day. There were more forests long ago, and the large lake (later transformed into five smaller lakes) must have had a wealth of fauna. Deer, as well as many other animals including the tapir, must have once roamed the forests, given evidence that they were fully exploited for their hides, antlers, bones, meat, and ligaments. Wildlife populations, however, were drastically reduced, especially after the trees in the immense forests surrounding the lake were felled to clear fields and provide fuel during the Preclassic period. POC (OCHOA)

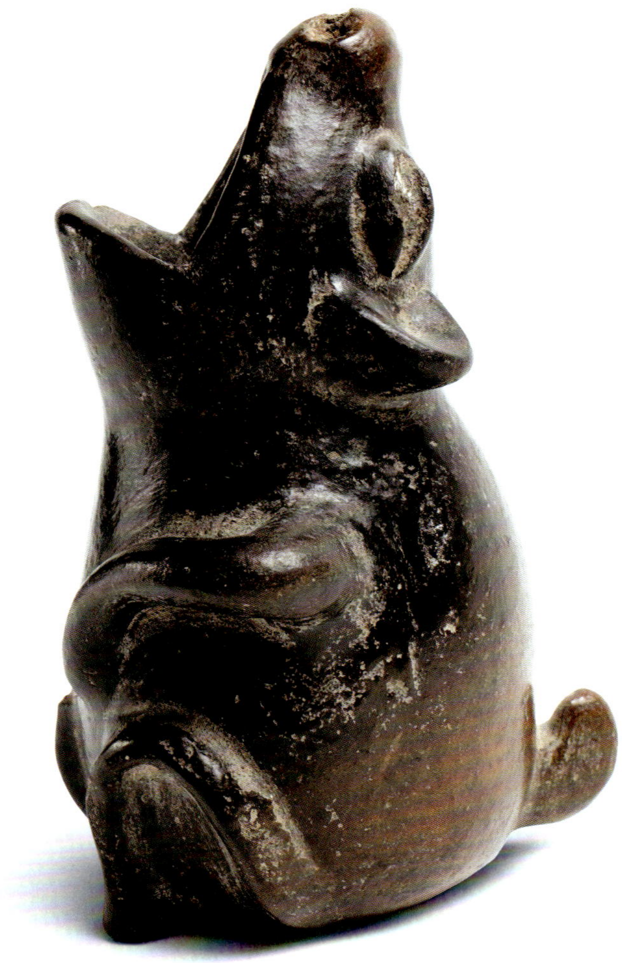

PLATE 20

ZOOMORPHIC VESSEL
IN THE FORM OF AN OPOSSUM
Mexico, Central Highlands, 1200–600 BC
Earthenware
4 3/4 x 2 3/4 in. (12 x 7 cm)
Museo Nacional de Antropología, Mexico City
(10-77583)

This object was unearthed in 1952 at Atlihuayan, an important and strategically located site in Morelos that lies within the complex trade network the Olmec had established in the Central Highlands. The vessel represents a seated male figure leaning forward with arms bent; the left hand and foot are broken, as is the right leg. The composite eyes with deep incisions, wide nose, and downturned mouth are all features found in the characteristic Olmec face.

After constructing this object in sections and joining them together, the artist formed the figure's elaborate cape, which resembles a stylized jaguar skin or zoomorph (Pohorilenko 1990: 85). The head of the animal covers the head of the man like a helmet, and its hook-shaped upper gums cover the man's ears. The nose is small; the eyebrows are flames; the claws are humanized by five fingers. Crosses made by incision cover the skin, as do three hook motifs. A wide tail falls in folds (Benson and de la Fuente 1996: 186–187). POC (OCHOA)

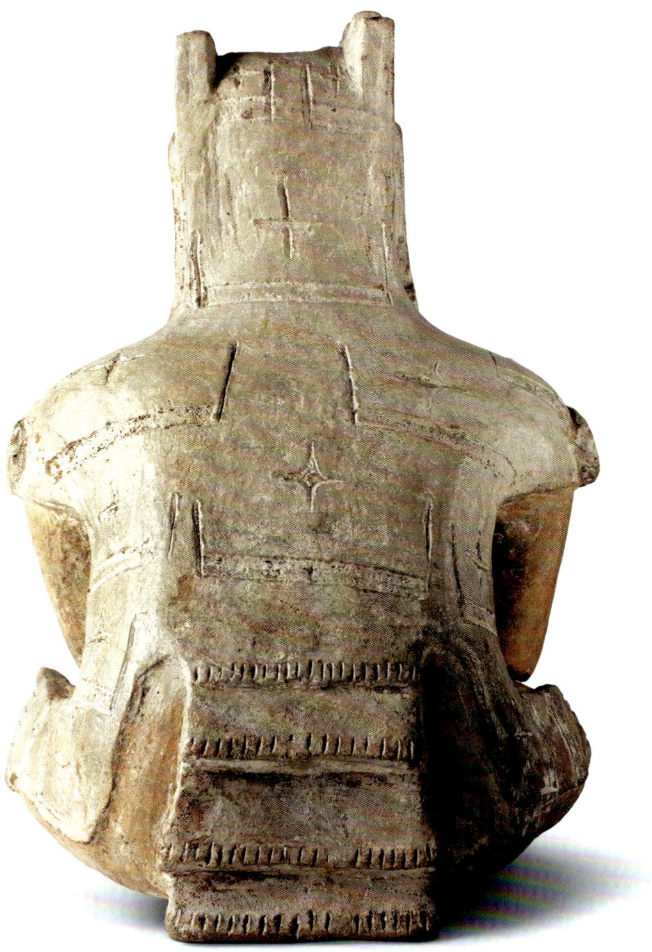

PLATES 21–22

PERSONAGE OF ATLIHUAYAN
Mexico, Morelos, Atlihuayan, 1200–900 BC
Earthenware with pigment
11⅝ x 8⅜ in. (29.5 x 21.3 cm)
Museo Nacional de Antropología, Mexico City
(10-3060)

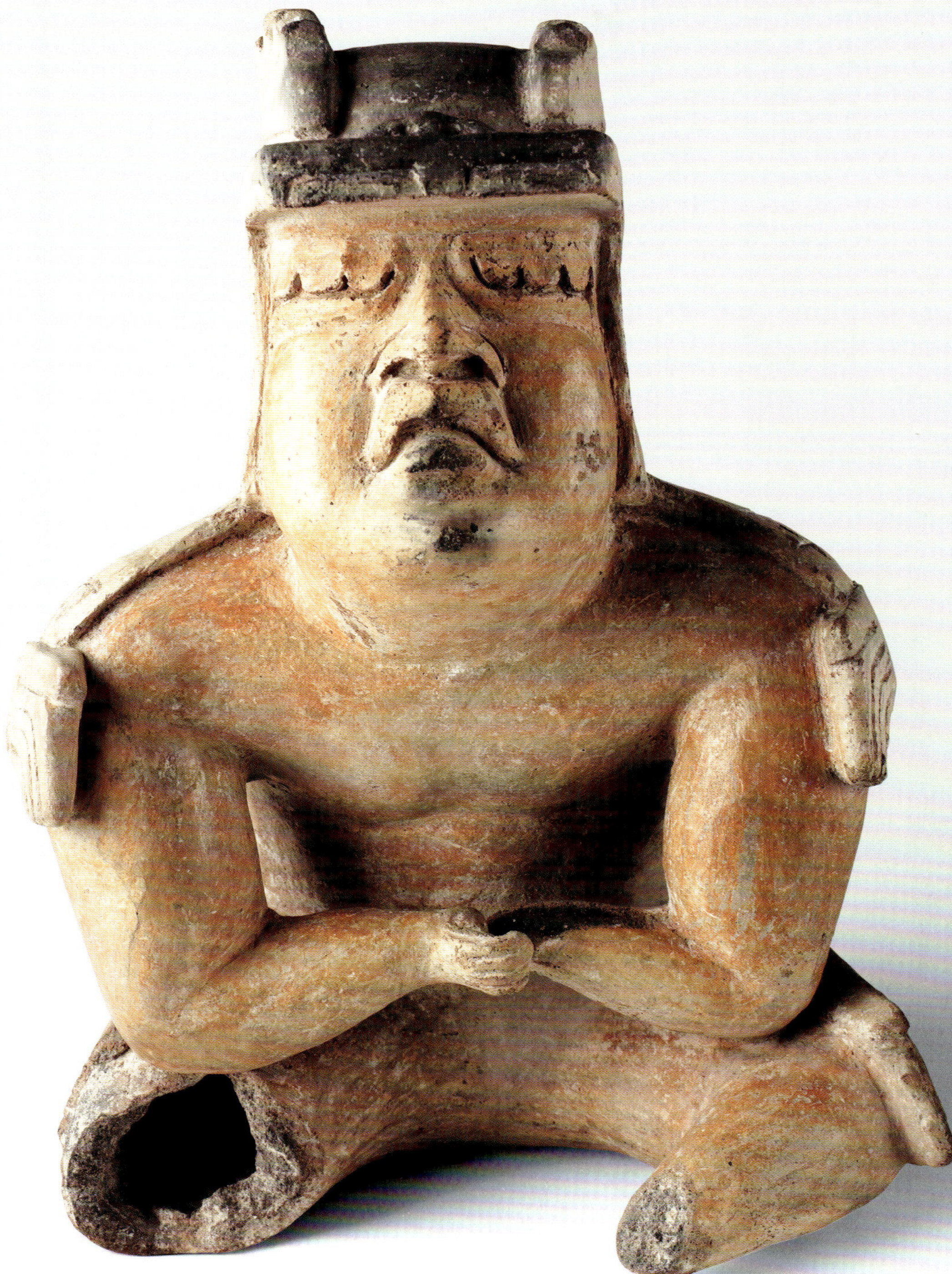

The Preclassic (also known as the Formative) period is characterized by superb ceramics, particularly those identified with Gulf Coast Olmec groups. Bottles, especially abundant in the Basin of Mexico, are less common in the Gulf Coast. Bottles from the latter area generally have a flat base and straight-sided body and neck.

This bottle displays an extremely fine, polished, black surface finish. The decoration—grooves made before the piece was fired, and incised designs added after firing and rubbed with red pigment—highlights the complex iconography associated with the Gulf Coast Olmec. These groups developed a sophisticated system of symbols based on stylized elements derived from nature. The design represents an animal-like monster in profile (Pohorilenko 1990: 86), a fantastic creature with a flame brow, rectangular eyes and nose, hook-shaped gums, and a stylized jaguar tail. Many scholars consider this creature to be an abstract representation of the Olmec dragon (Joralemon 1976).

This piece was in the collection of Miguel Covarrubias, which was donated to the Museo Nacional de Antropología. Covarrubias, who participated in the first field season at Tlatilco, noted the importance of the Olmec component at this Central Mexican site. POC (OCHOA)

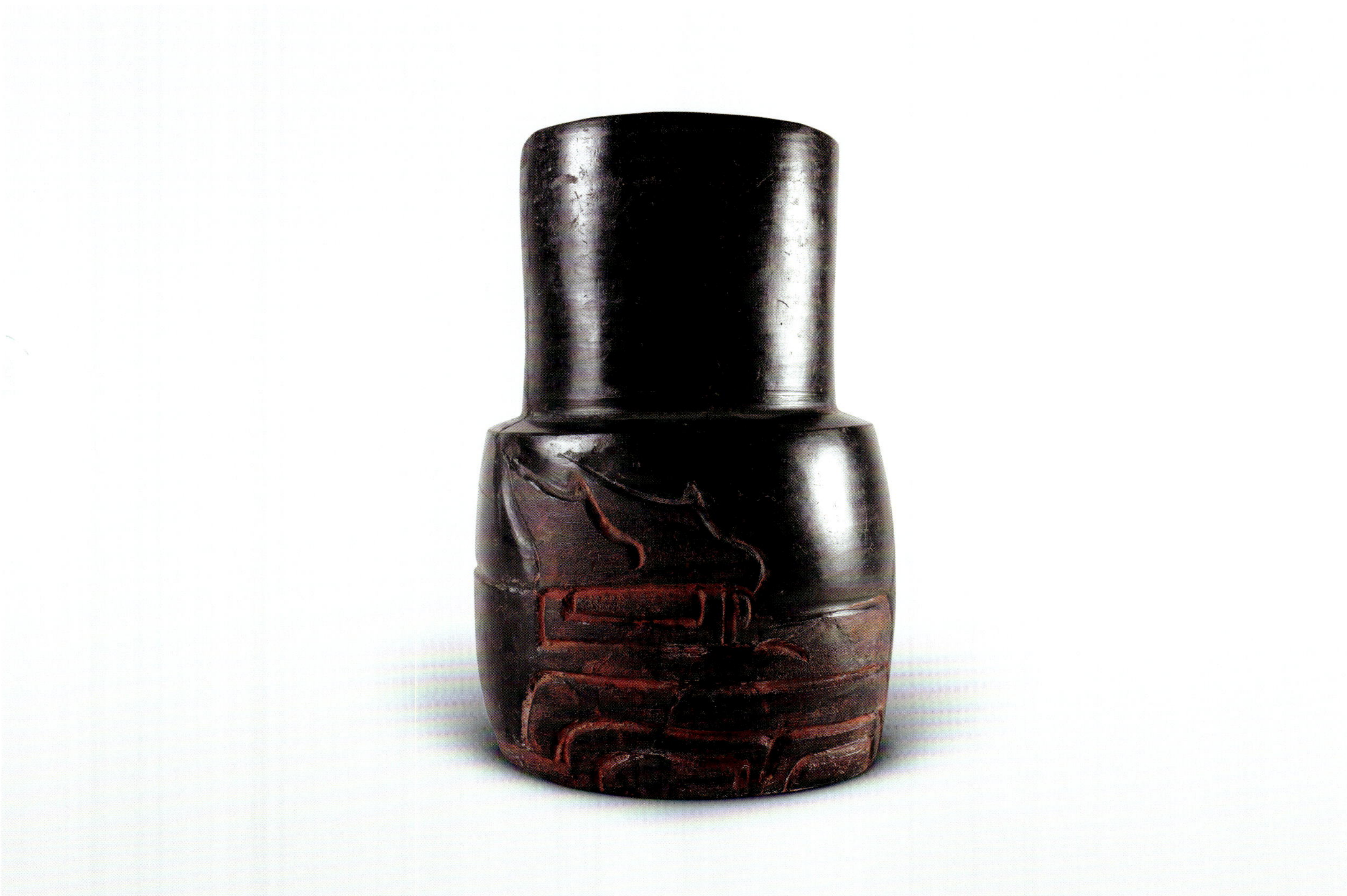

PLATE 23

BOTTLE WITH CARVED RELIEF
Mexico, Central Highlands, 1200–600 BC
Earthenware/blackware
$6^{9}/_{16}$ x $3^{15}/_{16}$ in. (16.7 x 10 cm)
Museo Nacional de Antropología, Mexico City, Covarrubias collection (10-2190)

See also:
Ochoa Castillo 1996: cat. 36

The distinctive flame brows, crossed bands, and upturned paw-wing carved deeply into the surface of this bowl imply that this composite creature aligns itself with the celestial realm in the Olmec cosmos (Fields and Reents Budet 2005: cat. 30). Although it was once thought to be a fire serpent (Coe 1968a: 148–149), Román Piña Chan (1960 59, fig. 8) hypothesized that the flame-browed aquatic serpent represented a celestial dragon, and Karl Taube (1995: 84) provided additional criteria for defining it as an avian serpent. The serrated brow, however, can also be seen on four-footed saurians with crocodilian snouts, such as the La Venta sarcophagus, Monument 6 (Stirling 1943: pl. 47). This creature also constitutes the cape on the Atlihuayan figure (pls. 21–22), which portrays a man in a trance state.

The bowl reportedly derives from Las Bocas in western Puebla, a highland site that was heavily looted in the 1950s (Pool 2007: 210). It reveals the crisp and sure-handed carving that characterizes early Olmec-style ceramics from 1200 to 950 BC, which are known primarily from non–Gulf Coast sites in Central Mexico and the Pacific Coast (Clark and Pye 2000b: 237). VMF

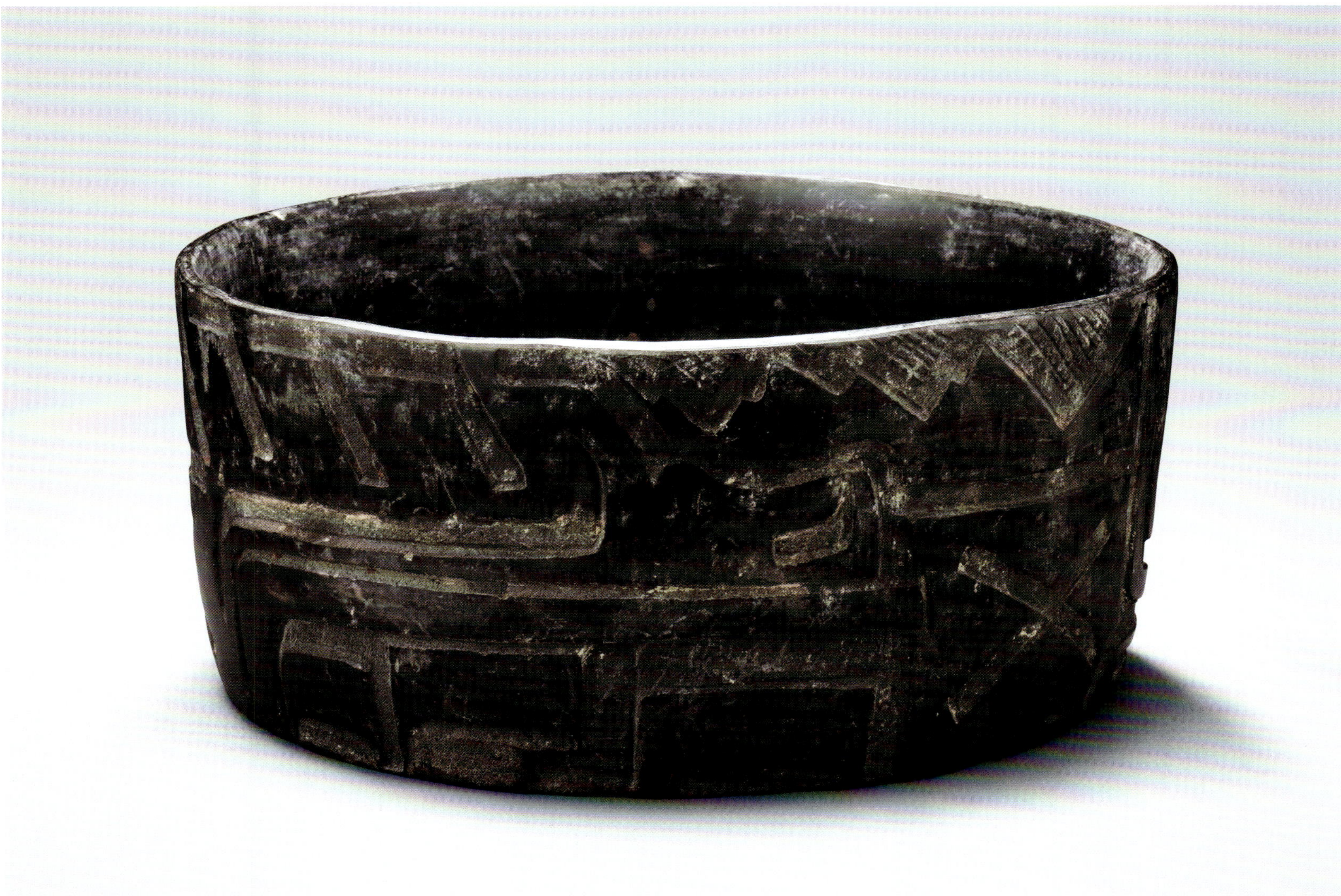

PLATE 24

BOWL CARVED WITH IMAGE OF A CELESTIAL BEING
Mexico, Puebla, Las Bocas, 1200–900 BC
Reduce-fired ceramic with traces of pigment
4 x 9 1/8 in. (10.2 x 23.2 cm)
Los Angeles County Museum of Art, purchased with funds provided by Camilla Chandler Frost (M.2002.13)

Over the course of fifteen hundred years, large and small settlements ebbed and flowed throughout Olman. Monumental stone sculpture and architecture, whether in capital cities or minor centers, formed an important basis for rulership. The three primary Olmec sites were San Lorenzo Tenochtitlán, which reached its zenith between 1200 and 900 BC; La Venta, which rose to prominence between 900 and 400 BC; and Tres Zapotes, whose trajectory began around the same time as La Venta but which continued to flourish until around the fourth century. While we know neither the specific interactions of Olman settlements nor the names of their rulers or dynasties, the presence of mutilated and recarved monuments at the sites signals the eventual waning of authority or change in rulership that occurred.

At San Lorenzo, colossal portrait heads memorialized at least ten rulers between 1400 and 1000 BC. The hard basalt stone used to produce these heads (as well as large-scale thrones and other massive sculptures) was quarried in multiton boulders and transported from the volcanic slopes of the distant Tuxtla Mountains. Noteworthy at San Lorenzo were long lines of U-shaped stones that served as aqueducts, directing the flow of water in the city and reflecting the power of the ruler to control this precious commodity. Evidence of craft specialization at San Lorenzo is reflected in workshops, adjacent to the palaces or elite residences, where basalt monuments were recarved. San Lorenzo's rulers oversaw a number of sites and villages, and the rituals held there undoubtedly promoted great political integration and social cohesion. Sacred water shrines at the nearby sites of La Merced and El Manatí were also the focus of San Lorenzo ritual activity, as was Loma del Zapote-El Azuzul, a secondary center where four sculptures, two human and two feline, were found grouped in a staged encounter.

Dramatic and intriguing finds have characterized La Venta, where powerful individuals were laid to rest in elaborate tombs with massive offerings of jadeite and serpentine objects. The sculptural corpus at La Venta is one of the largest and most diverse, exceeded only in number by the monuments at San Lorenzo. The sculptural arts at La Venta shifted from sculpture in the round to flatter relief carving. Like those at San Lorenzo, large stone monuments at La Venta were arranged in changing tableaux or clustered in groups. Thousands of stone votive axes (also known as celts) have been found at La Venta, and their arrangement, individually or positioned in groups or layers, provides insights into ritual or ceremonial behavior. Arroyo Pesquero, a smaller site in the vicinity of La Venta, has yielded an immense cache of greenstone masks, celts, figurines, ornaments, and ritual paraphernalia, revealing its status as a shrine rather than as a major settlement.

The third Olmec site, Tres Zapotes, has the longest cultural sequence. Its proximity to water transportation throughout many regions played an important role in the site's history. Tres Zapotes has fifty stone monuments of various types: stelae (vertical monuments), tenoned busts, basins, and rectangular boxes. Another western site of major importance is Laguna de los Cerros, strategically located near the foothills south of the Tuxtla Mountains. Although no colossal heads have been found there, it seems to have had a distinctive school of monument carving and surely provided other Olmec centers with either raw material or finished sculptures.

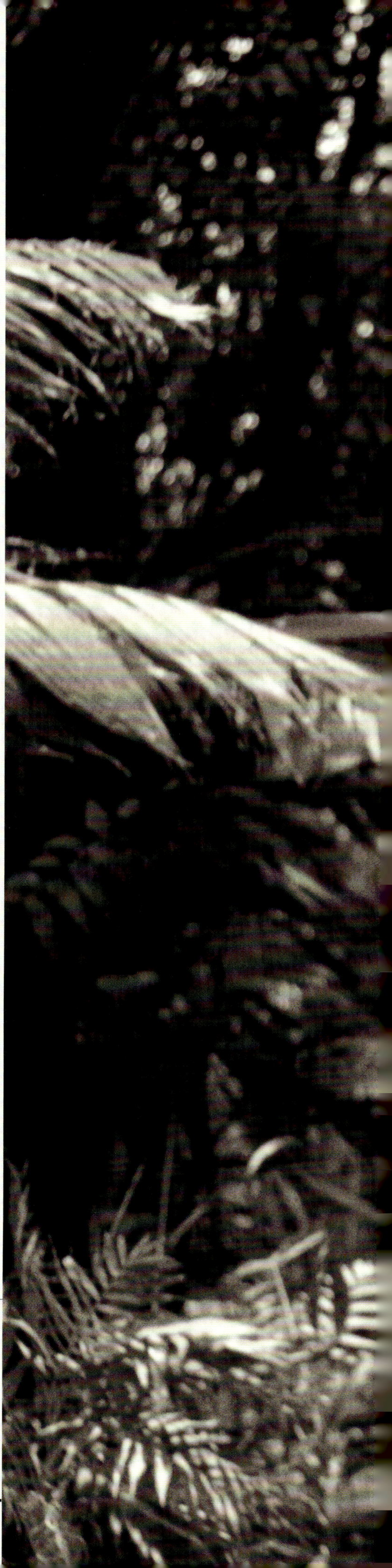

La Venta Monument 1 (colossal head) in situ at the Parque-Museo de La Venta, ca. 1985

THE HIERARCHY OF POWER: CAPITAL CITIES AND MINOR CENTERS

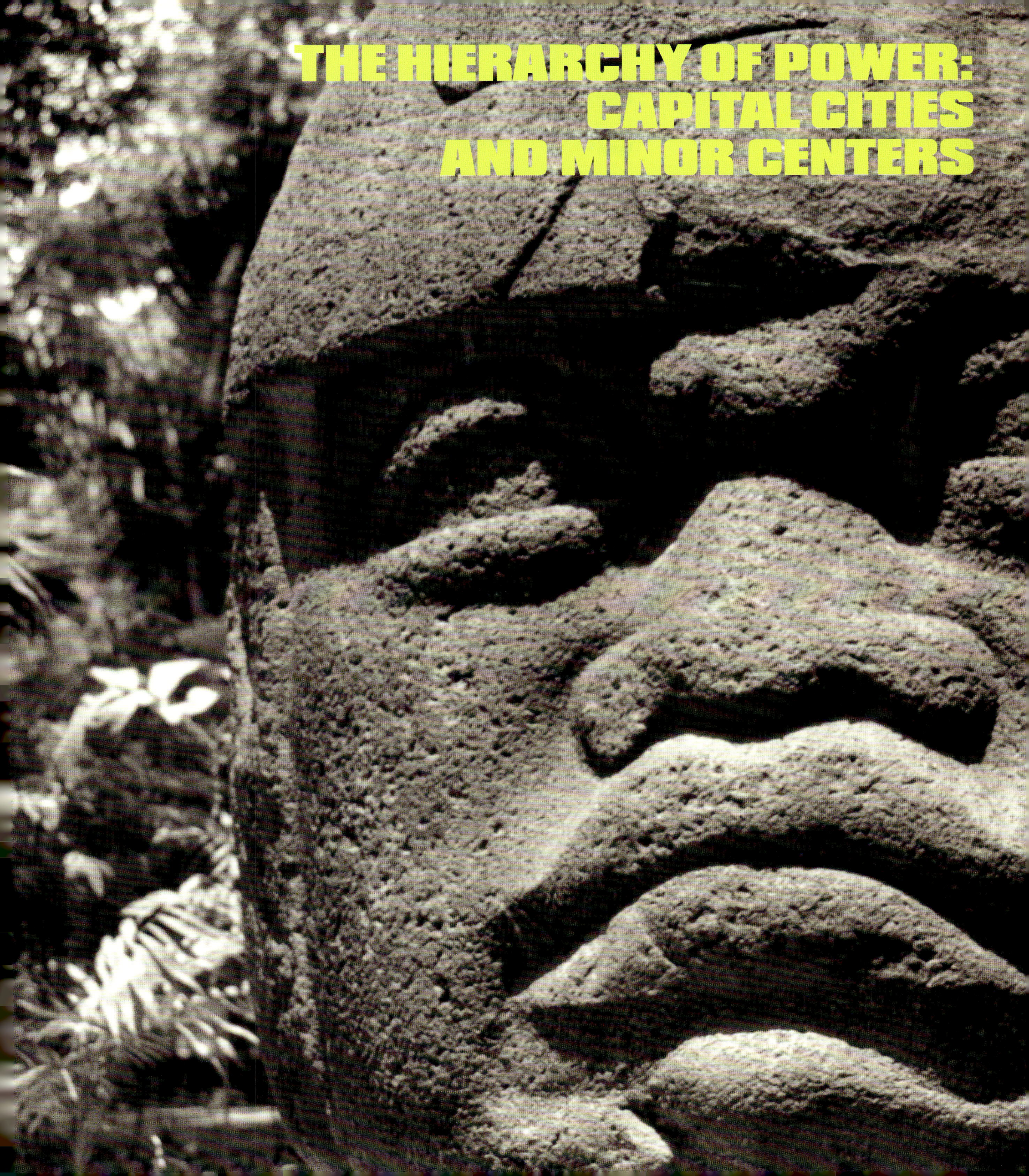

According to the late, acclaimed art historian Beatriz de la Fuente (1984: 133), this sculpture is the most harmoniously proportioned of the seventeen colossal heads that have been found to date. It is also one of the smallest heads from San Lorenzo (where ten have been found), and it is one of the best-preserved colossal heads known from any site (Coe and Diehl 1980, vol. 1: 306). Although it has not endured any mutilations, there are twenty-six circular depressions and three grooves on the back (Cyphers 2004b: 53), quite likely made for ritual purposes.

Matthew W. Stirling (1955: 4) found this head during his 1946 excavations in deep jungle some 600 yards (548.6 meters) northwest of the primary mound. Ann Cyphers (in Benson and de la Fuente 1996: 156) identifies this ruler as wearing a three-part tassel composed of rods and cords hanging down the front of the helmet. Four parallel ropes are horizontally placed across the helmet and two others serve as a strap on the right side. The individual is shown with his right ear visible, bearing an ornament that is embellished with a curved decorative element. The left side of the head is completely covered by the helmet. The ruler's face is sincere and individualized, and it appears to epitomize a mature male. This colossal head weighs 8,043 pounds (3,656 kilograms). KB

PLATE 25

COLOSSAL HEAD 4
Mexico, Veracruz, Municipality of Texistepec,
San Lorenzo Tenochtitlán, 1200–900 BC
Basalt
73¼ x 50¾ x 45¼ in. (186 x 129 x 115 cm)
Museo de Antropología de Xalapa,
Universidad Veracruzana (10-21157)

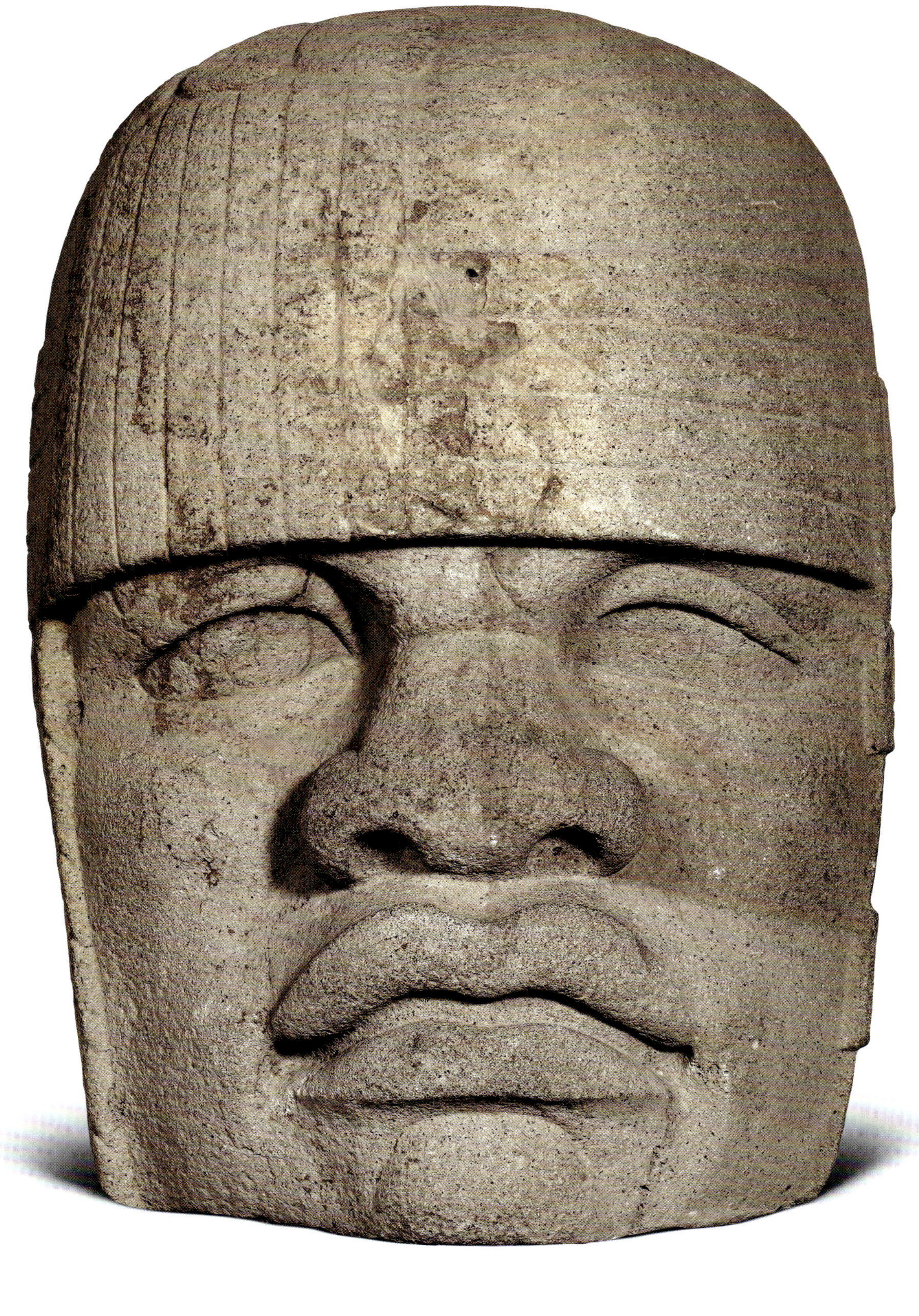

This monument, the last of the five colossal heads discovered by archaeologist Matthew W. Stirling in 1946 (Stirling 1955: 12–13, pls. 12–13), was moved to the Museo de Antropología de Xalapa by Alfonso Medellín Zeñil in 1960. It was created using a combination of polishing and fine and rough hammering. The back side is flat, a trait seen in some colossal heads, suggesting that it might have been recarved from an earlier monument. The furrowed brow, almond-shaped and slightly crossed eyes with an epicanthic fold, flaccid cheeks, flat nose, and thick mouth display great realism and suggest an individual of mature age who is related to activities of leadership. His helmet displays iconographic elements found on the other San Lorenzo heads, such as the horizontal band topped by a woven motif with circular forms. It has been proposed that the colossal heads represent portraits of individuals at the apex of power at Olmec centers such as San Lorenzo Tenochtitlán and La Venta. Unique to this head are details in the shape of three-toed bird feet or feline paws, each with a talon; these might represent iconographic elements associated with the figure's name-insignia or lineage. RLR

PLATES 26–28

COLOSSAL HEAD 5
Mexico, Veracruz, Municipality of Texistepec, San Lorenzo Tenochtitlán, 1200–900 BC
Basalt
$73\frac{1}{4} \times 56\frac{11}{16} \times 49\frac{1}{4}$ in. (186 x 144 x 125 cm)
Museo de Antropología de Xalapa, Universidad Veracruzana (Reg. 49 P.J. 4026)

See also:
Coe and Diehl 1980, vol. 1: 308–309, fig. 428
Cyphers 1994c: 51–54, fig. 4.20
Cyphers 2004b: 53–56, fig. 15
de la Fuente 1977a: 126–127, pl. 4, fig. 4b, ill. 18
de la Fuente 1981: 93, fig. 13

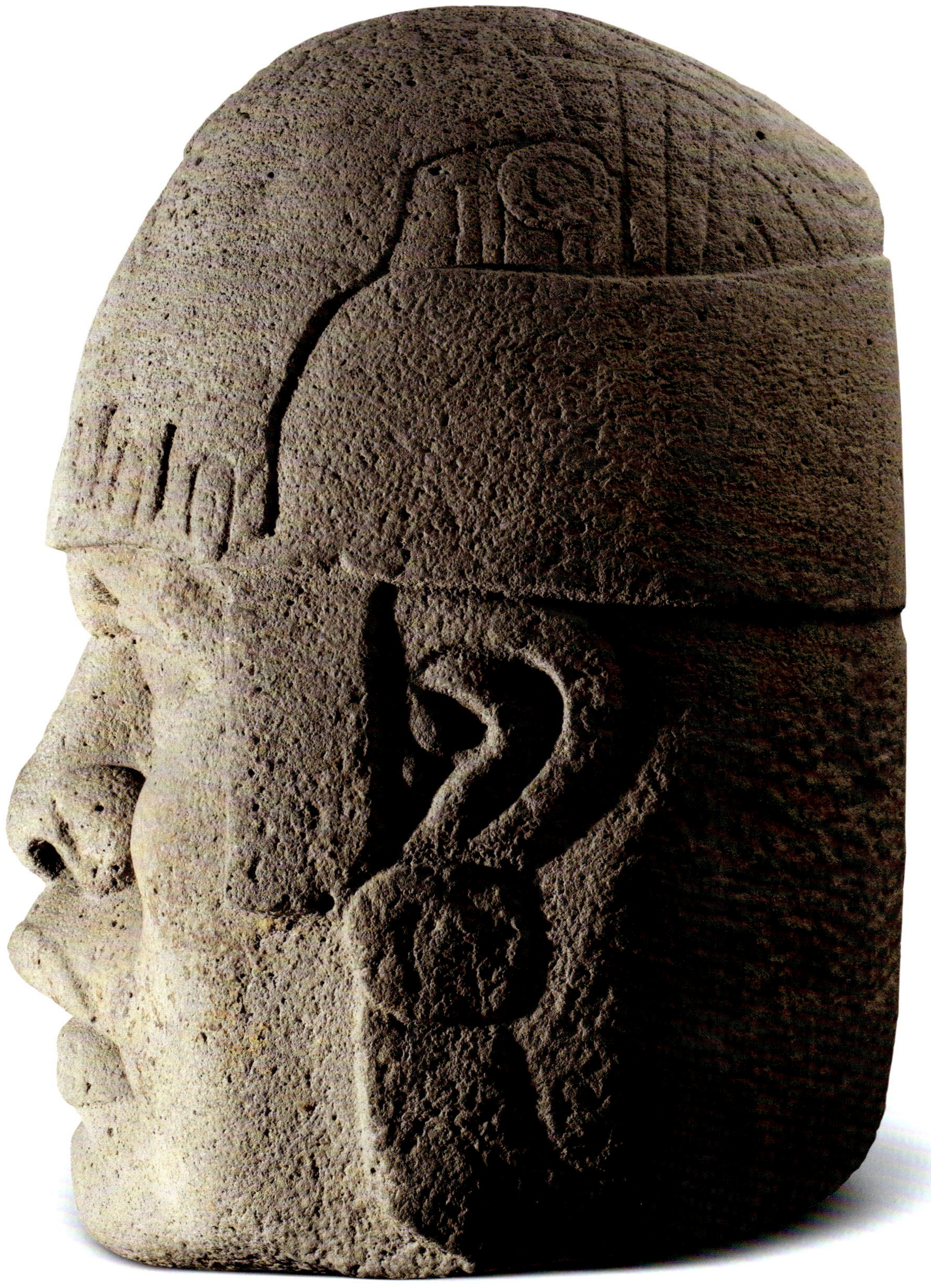

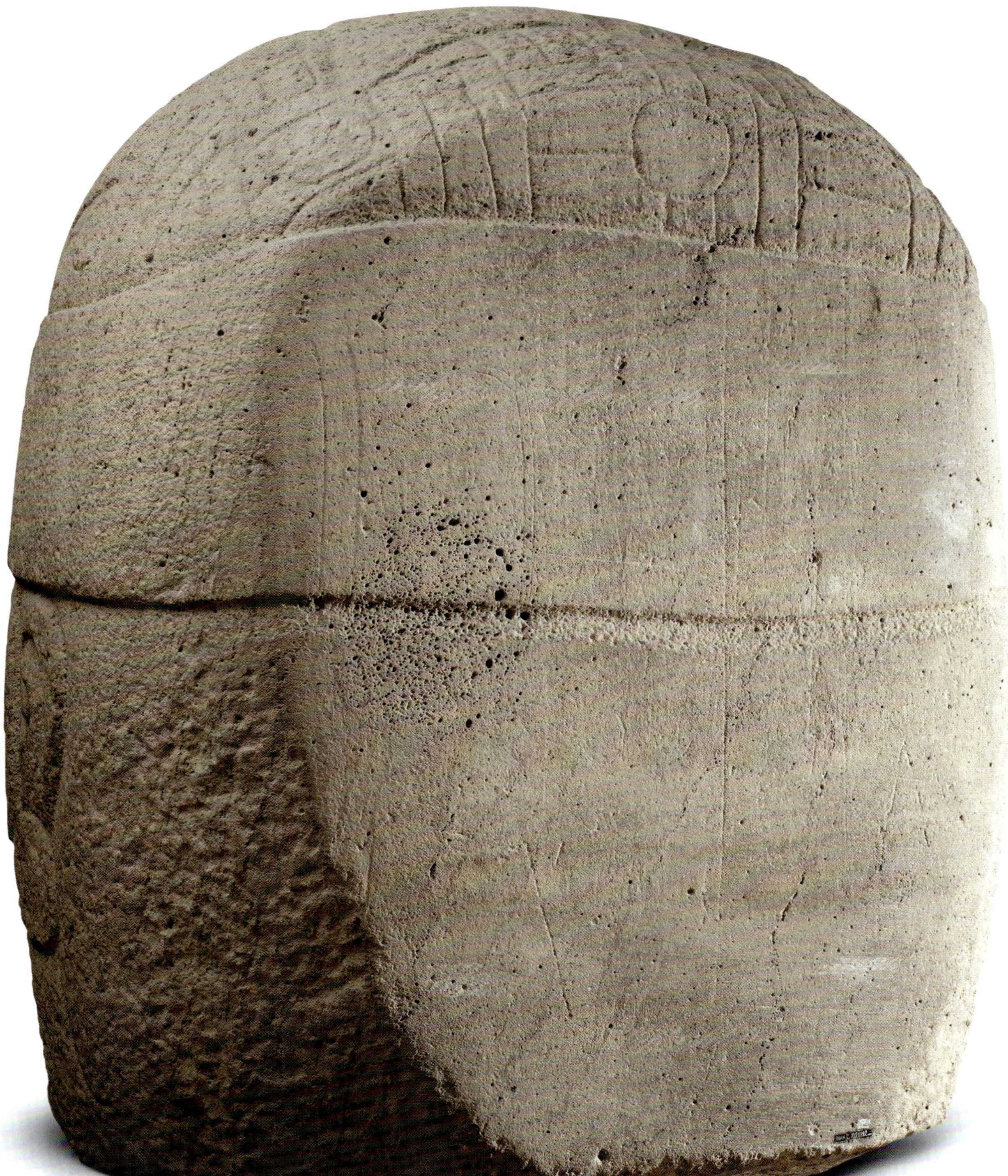

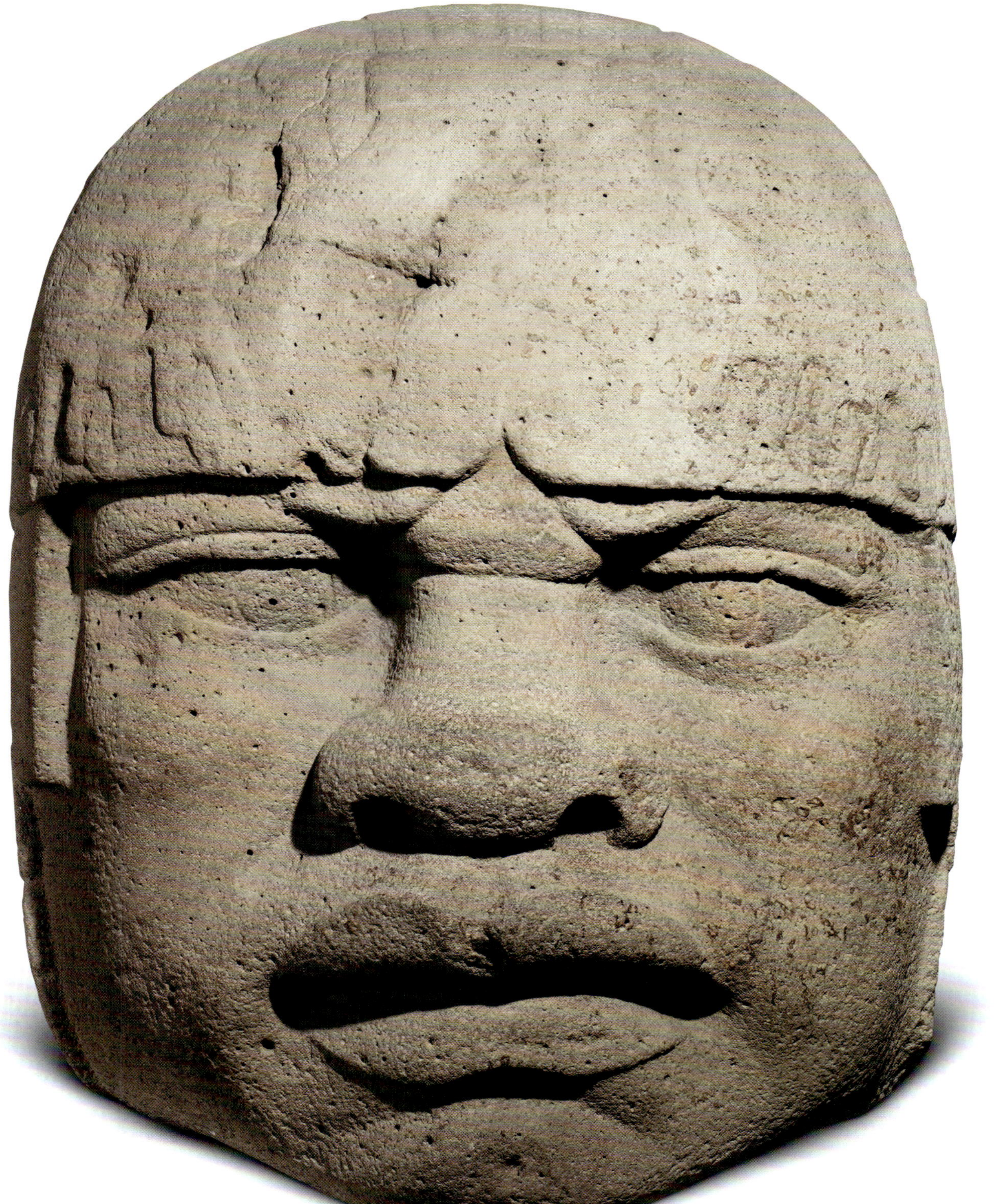

This sculpture was discovered by Matthew W. Stirling (1955: 13) during his 1946 investigations. Its exact archaeological context is unrecorded, aside from Stirling's comment that it was found about 1 mile (1.6 kilometers) south of the central mound of San Lorenzo. The extraordinary scale of the head implies that, when attached to its body, the full figure may well have exceeded 6½ feet (2 meters) in height (Coe and Diehl 1980, vol. 1: 310–311). Michael Coe and Richard Diehl suggest that the monument's headband, slit eyes, and neck shape are more akin to San Lorenzo phase figurines than to the colossal heads, although they consider the head to portray a powerful ruler. In addition to being fractured from the body, the head has been heavily battered. Such acts of mutilation and destruction apparently coincided with the end of the "San Lorenzo phase," when many monuments were destroyed and buried along the Group D ridge (ibid.: 298).

Originally catalogued as San Lorenzo Monument 6, this enormous head has been reclassified as Loma del Zapote Monument 12, reflecting the better understanding of the relationship between San Lorenzo and the secondary centers surrounding it, as well as the actual locations where sculptures were discovered (Cyphers 2004b: 22–25). Ann Cyphers describes a regional hierarchy of economic, political, and religious administration, with San Lorenzo at its apex, over a network of sites including Loma del Zapote, Estero Rabón, Tenochtitlán, and El Remolino. Dominating a confluence of ancient rivers (Cyphers 1996c: 62), Loma del Zapote had a terraced acropolis featuring stone monuments and two low, earthen causeways along which extended a large residential zone. MC-LE

PLATE 29

MONUMENT 12
Mexico, Veracruz, Municipality of Texistepec, Loma del Zapote, 1200–900 BC
Basalt
38⅛ x 25½ x 27⅜ in. (96.8 x 64.8 x 69.5 cm)
Museo Nacional de Antropología, Mexico City (10-627692)

See also:
Cyphers 2004b: 258–260

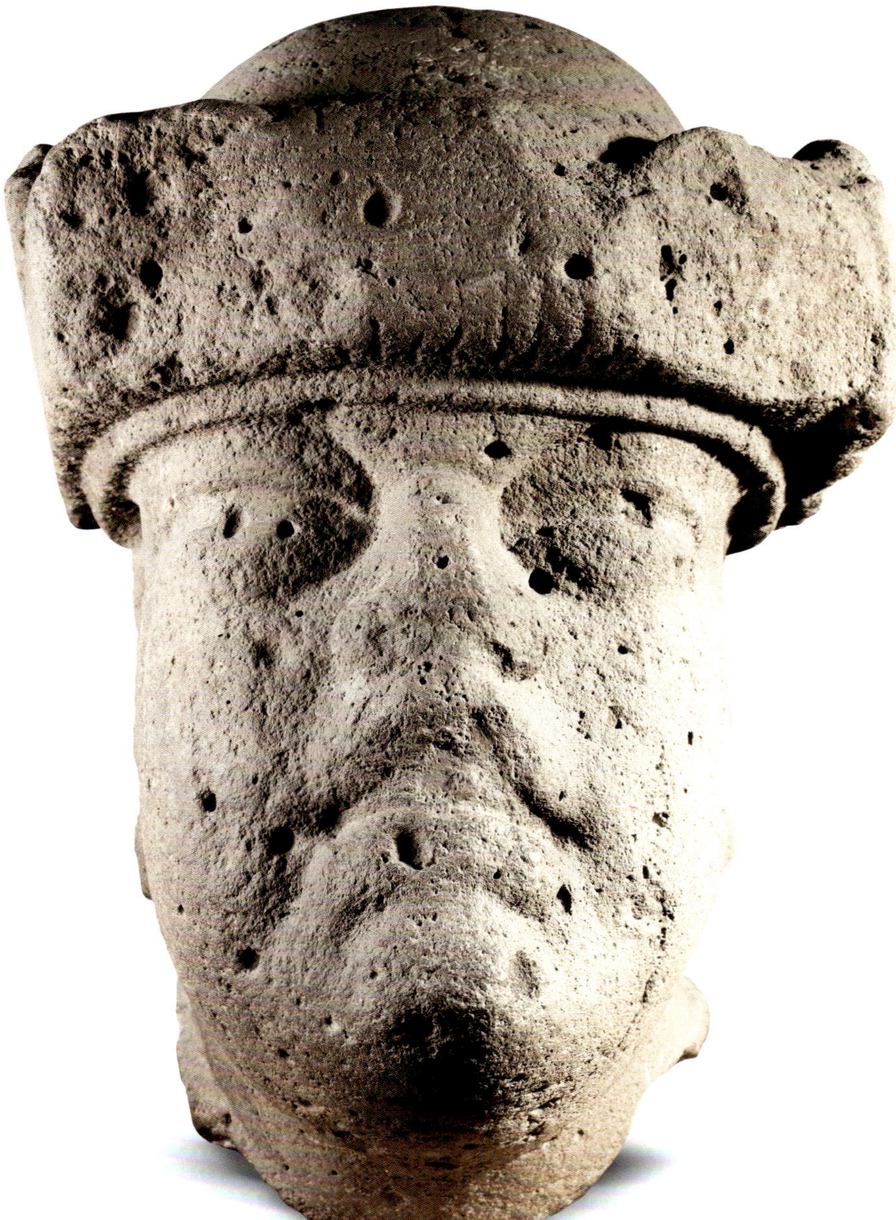

Based on its accoutrements, this sculpture represents either a seated human in transformation or a fantastic figure; it was found, along with a score of monuments, by Matthew W. Stirling in 1946. On the upper part of the headdress is a V-shaped cleft. The figure also wears a mask or a stylized feline face with L-shaped eyes, a snoutlike nose, and a roaring mouth with the corners of the lips turned downward and two large, bifurcated fangs turned outward. The pair of D-shaped objects in the figure's hands has been identified as *manoplas* (knuckledusters), used either as protective devices in the ritual ballgame, as weapons in warfare, or as implements at court. The legs have been broken at the knees. RLR

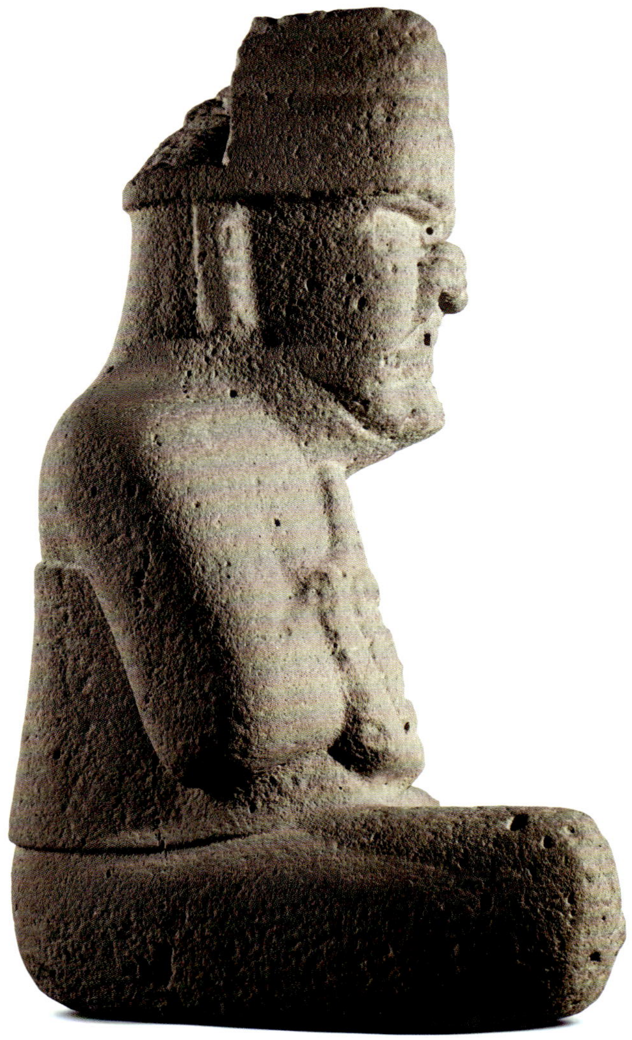

PLATES 30–31

MONUMENT 10 (SEATED FIGURE WITH KNUCKLEDUSTERS)
Mexico, Veracruz, Municipality of Texistepec, San Lorenzo Tenochtitlán, 1200–900 BC
Basalt
$59^{7}/_{8} \times 53^{9}/_{16} \times 27^{1}/_{8}$ in. (152 x 136 x 69 cm)
Museo de Antropología de Xalapa, Universidad Veracruzana (Reg. 49 P.J. 328)

See also:
Coe and Diehl 1980, vol. 1: 316, fig. 434
Cyphers 2004b: 62–64, figs. 22–23
de la Fuente 1977a: 96–98, figs. 9, 9a, ill. 2
de la Fuente 1981: 86, figs. 2, 4
Milbrath 1979: 10–11, fig. 21
Stirling 1955: 14, pl. 15b

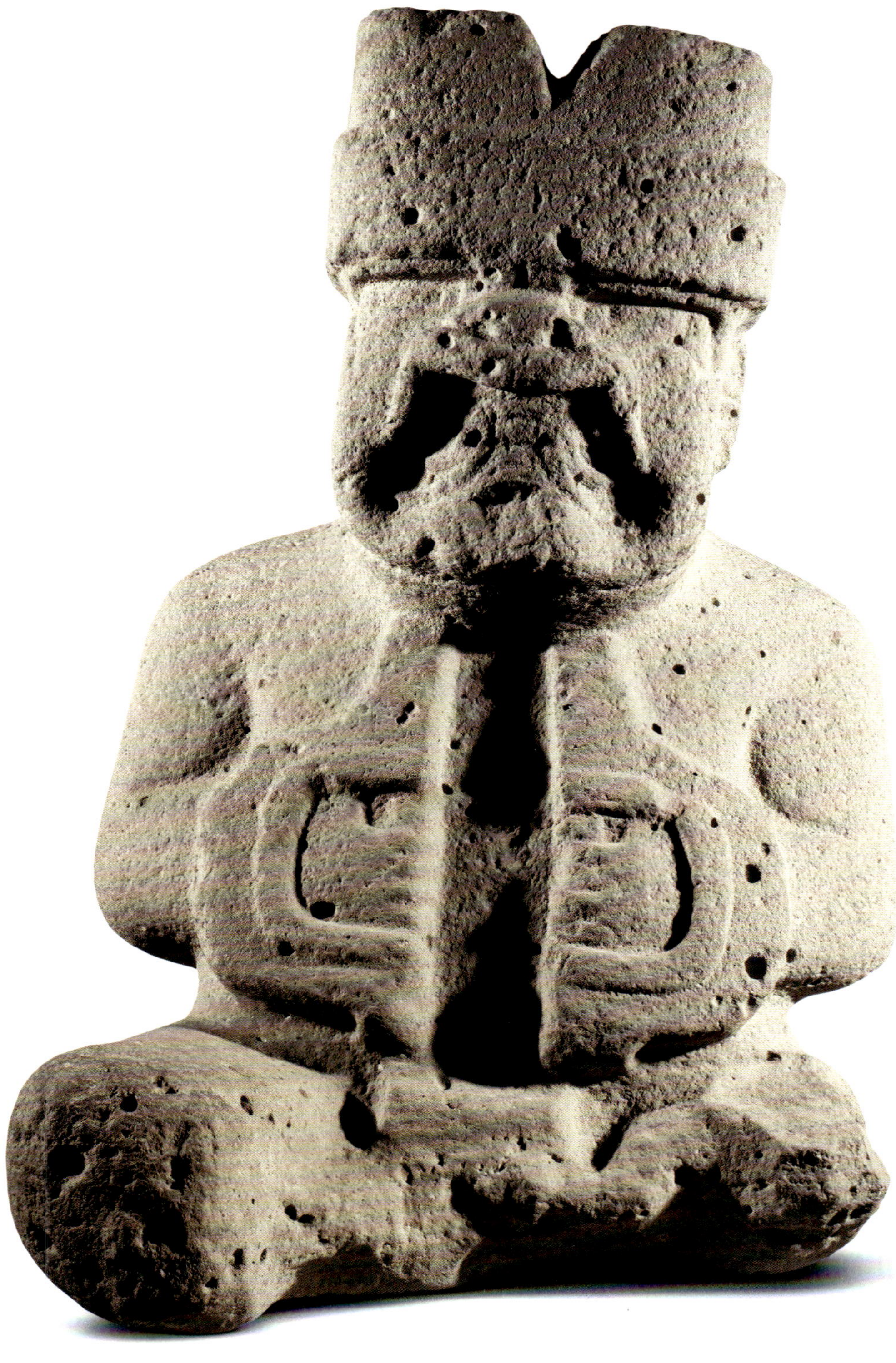

This magnificent, highly realistic example of Olmec stone sculpture depicts a half-kneeling figure adorned with items of social distinction, including a large pectoral that may represent a concave iron-ore mirror (Coe and Diehl 1980, vol. 1: 343). His high-waisted belt and the bands below his knees imply that this may be the portrait of an Olmec ruler in his role as ballplayer (ibid.). The ballcourts at Teopantecuanitlán in Guerrero and Paso de Amado in Chiapas indicate a Formative period awareness of the ballgame, and the presence of rubber balls in offerings at the water shrines of El Manatí, in the vicinity of San Lorenzo, attests to the early knowledge of processing latex.

As with many Olmec monuments, the head was broken from the body; the arms, which are also missing, may have once been moveable, as implied by the unique socketed holes carved into the figure's shoulders. Potentially made of wood, the arms could have been altered to reflect the figure's activities in the various mythic or historic scenes conveyed by sculptural groupings (Cyphers 2004b: 96), although Beatriz de la Fuente (1984: 146) proposes that moveable arms would have contradicted the element of dignity that characterizes Olmec portraiture. The head and arms of this figure were never located.

The sculpture, deposited as an offering during ancient times, was discovered by Michael Coe on the Group D ridge on the western side of San Lorenzo in 1967. It had been placed on a red gravel floor facing east and covered with a special fill containing yellow clay, limestone, and bentonitic rock; numerous potsherds were placed between the legs of the figure and around its left foot (Coe and Diehl 1980, vol. 1: 113–114). Nearby, Monument 23, a plain basalt stela, was embedded in the same type of floor. MC-LE

PLATE 32

MONUMENT 34
(HALF-KNEELING FIGURE)
Mexico, Veracruz, San Lorenzo Tenochtitlán, 1400–1000 BC
Basalt
30 9/16 x 26 x 25 9/16 in. (77.7 x 65.8 x 65 cm)
Museo Nacional de Antropología, Mexico City (10-81348)

See also:
Coe 1968a: 79

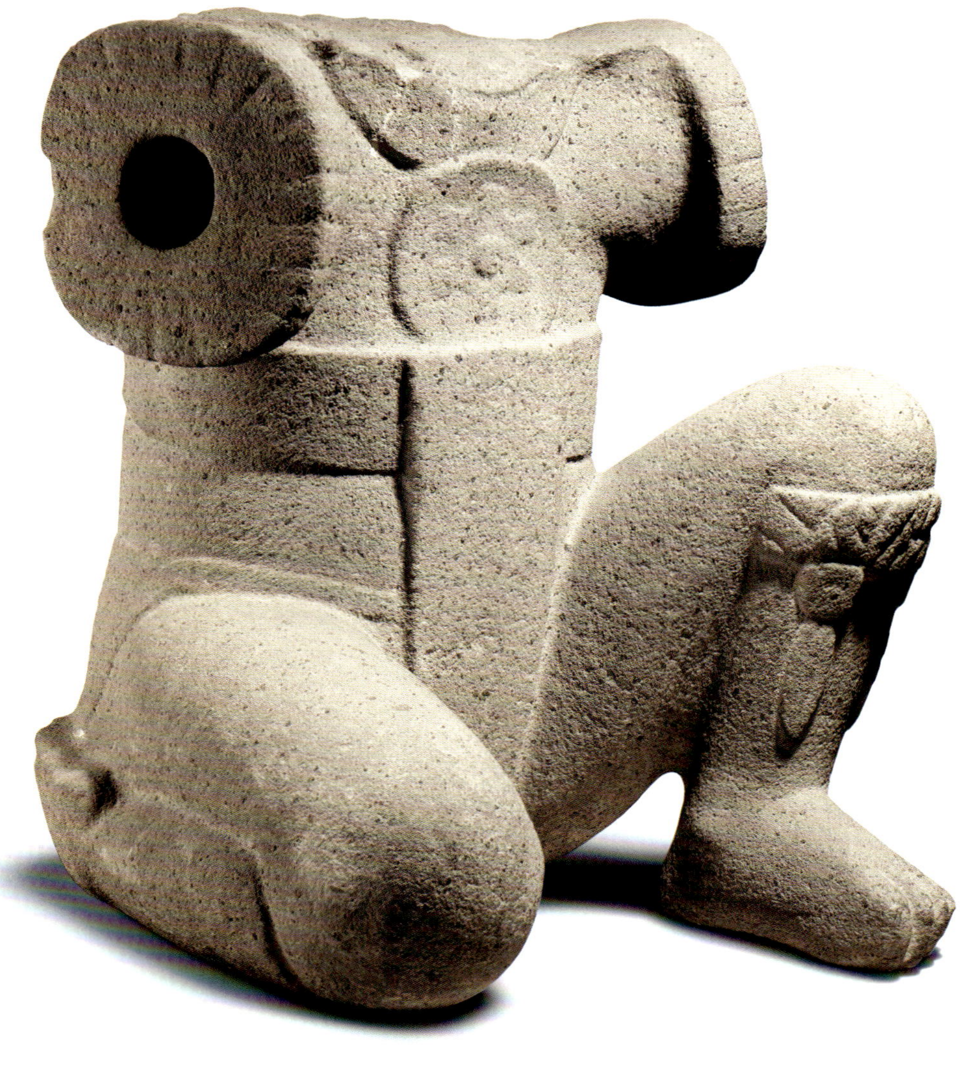

The Cerro Manatí is a saline dome that, together with El Mije and La Encantada, rises from the coastal plain of Veracruz; they are the only promontories in the entire Coatzacoalcos river basin. The town of El Manatí is in the municipality of Hidalgotitlán, Veracruz, in the Olmec heartland, a little more than 9 miles (15 kilometers) due west of San Lorenzo Tenochtitlán. Both the town and its lagoon were named for the manatees that live off the coast.

We now know that the site served as a sacred space for several centuries, and that its use varied through time. Data indicate that the first offerings date to 1600 BC and consist primarily of axes worked in greenstone (jadeite, serpentine, and varieties of schist); these were distributed randomly, lacking any clear pattern. Later (from 1500 to 1200 BC), offering deposits ranged from simple piles to careful, symmetrical placement on a north-south or east-west axis. Noteworthy in this latter group are offerings in which axes were positioned like flower petals, with the wider blade ends pointed upward.

The first, earlier offerings also included rubber balls (pl. 33). One of the most important finds was a group of seven balls of different sizes (the largest with a diameter of about 12 inches, or 31 centimeters) associated with more than forty magnificently worked stone axes. The data suggest that the Olmec discovered that the sap of a plant known as *Ipomoea alba*, which is rich in sulfur, could be used in the process of vulcanization. The fifteen rubber balls found to date are undeniable evidence that the Olmec began the ritual ballgame at this early time.

Equally noteworthy is the recovery of a wide variety of seeds as well as some turtle and white-tailed deer bones (Pérez 1996). Recent studies of the residue from a vessel interior revealed the presence of cacao (or chocolate), significant because it shows its use as early as 1600 BC.

By 1200 BC (based on radiocarbon dates from two wooden structures), another important and much more complex offering event had taken place, which included an abundance of paraphernalia. Many human busts carved from wood (fig. 5, pl. 34) were buried in varied positions along the north-south axis, either individually or in groups of two or three. Additional associated elements were also buried, all of which suggest a preconceived plan. Most of the busts were placed on top of or beside wooden lance- or serpent-shaped "staffs," along with bunches of plants tied with string at both ends. Some of the sculptures were also accompanied by skeletal remains of newborn infants or perhaps fetuses, most of them dismembered. Only two of the infant burials were primary deposits placed in the fetal position.

The significance of this sacred event is noteworthy not only for the complexity that may be inferred from the associated paraphernalia but also because of the quantity of buried sculptures: in addition to the thirteen busts originally discovered, eighteen complete busts were recovered in context, and two fragments (heads) were found in the ground by local farmers. MCRM/POC (ORTÍZ)

PLATE 33

RUBBER BALL
Mexico, Veracruz, El Manatí, 1600–1500 BC
Rubber and fibers
Diam.: approx. 6 in. (15.2 cm)
Centro INAH Veracruz

See also:
Ortíz Ceballos and Rodríguez M. 2000: 75–93, 155–167

and numerous other publications by these authors in the list of works cited (pp. 254–264)

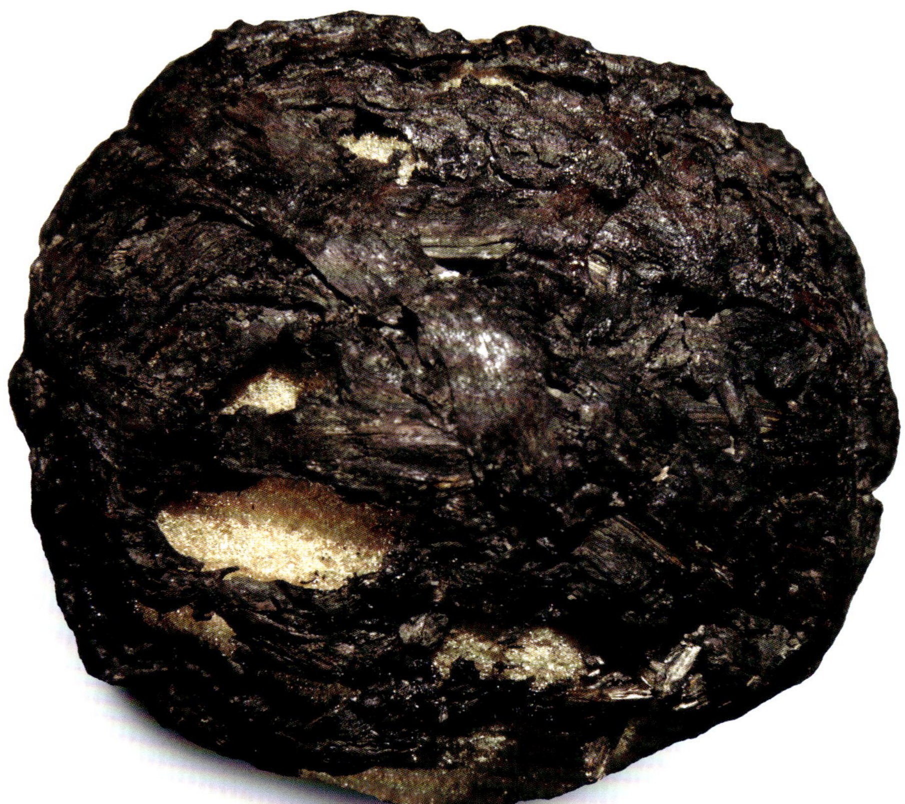

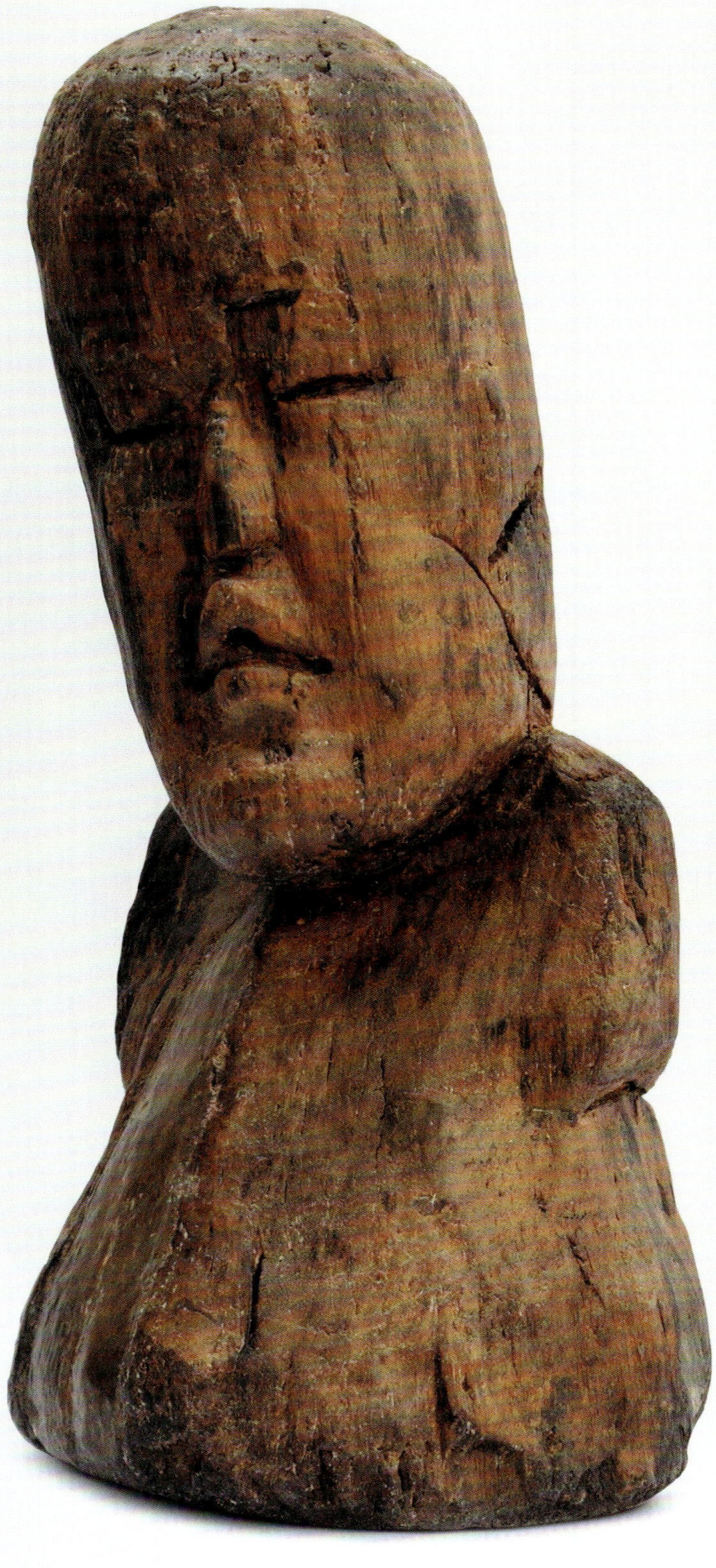

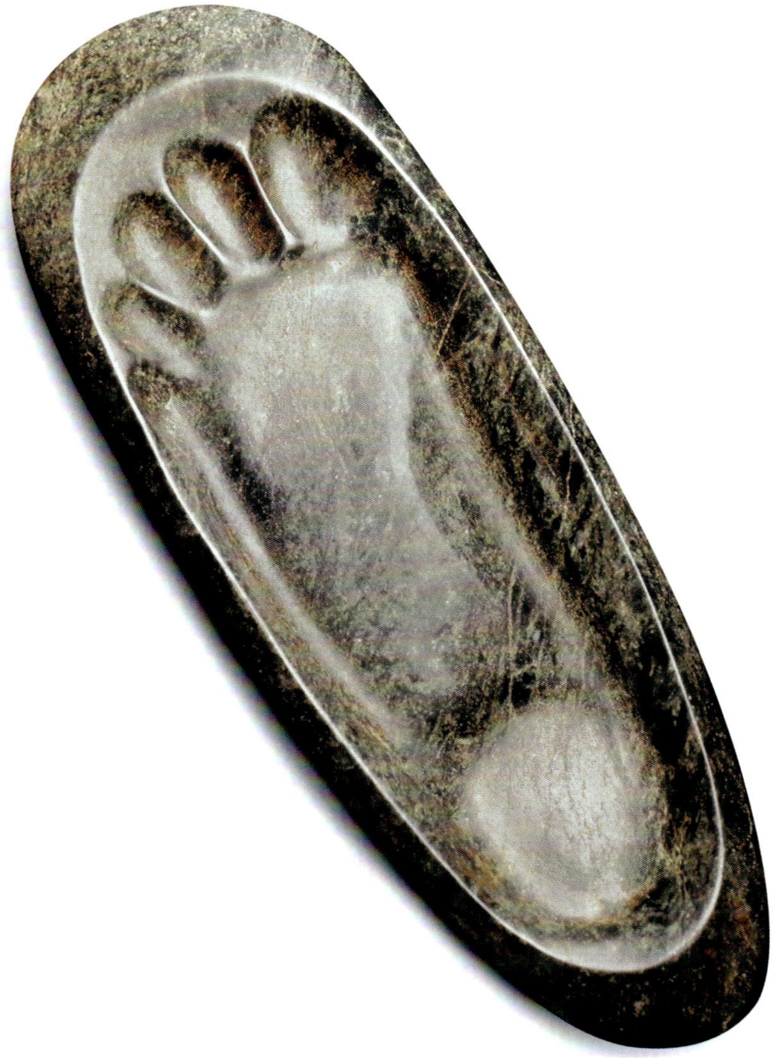

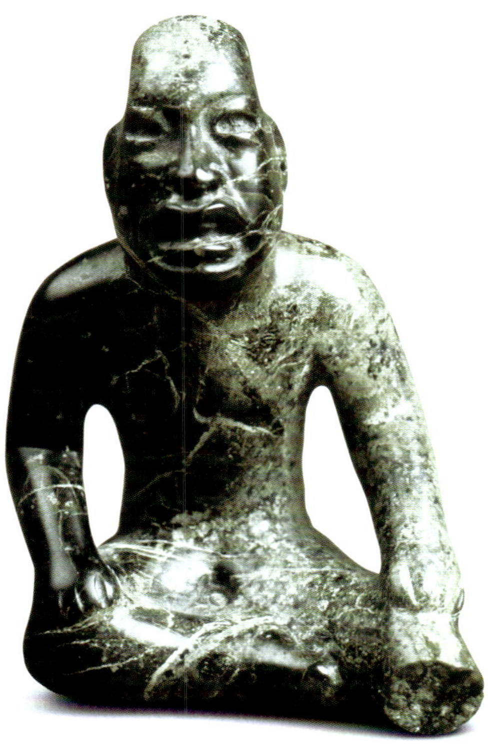

PLATES 34–36

HUMAN BUST
Mexico, Veracruz, El Manatí, 1200–900 BC
Wood
Approx. 20 x 7 x 8 in. (50.8 x 17.8 x 20.3 cm)
Centro INAH Veracruz

SEATED FIGURE
Mexico, Veracruz, El Manatí, 1200–900 BC
Greenstone
$4\frac{15}{16}$ x $3\frac{1}{8}$ in. (12.5 x 8 cm)
Centro INAH Veracruz (10-582852)

AXE WITH FOOTPRINT
Mexico, Veracruz, El Manatí, 1200–900 BC
Jadeite
$9\frac{5}{8}$ x $3\frac{1}{2}$ x $1\frac{3}{8}$ in. (24.5 x 8.8 x 3.5 cm)
Centro INAH Veracruz (10-522838)

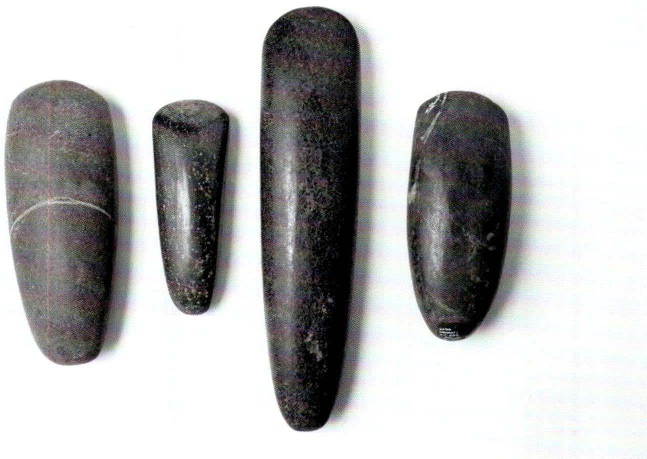
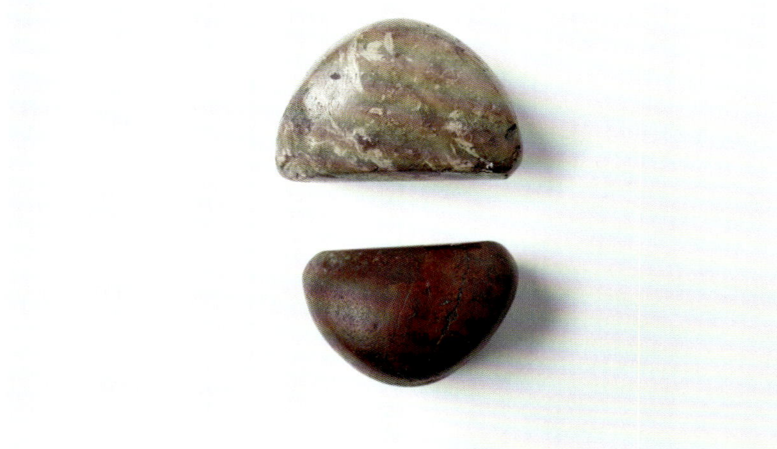
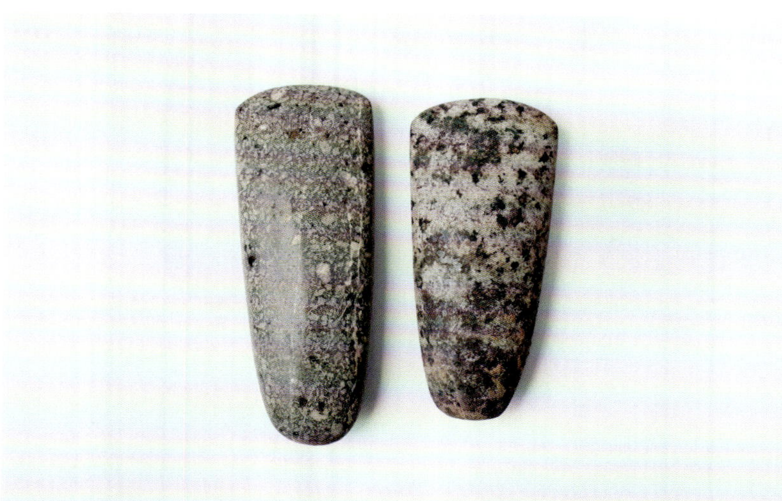
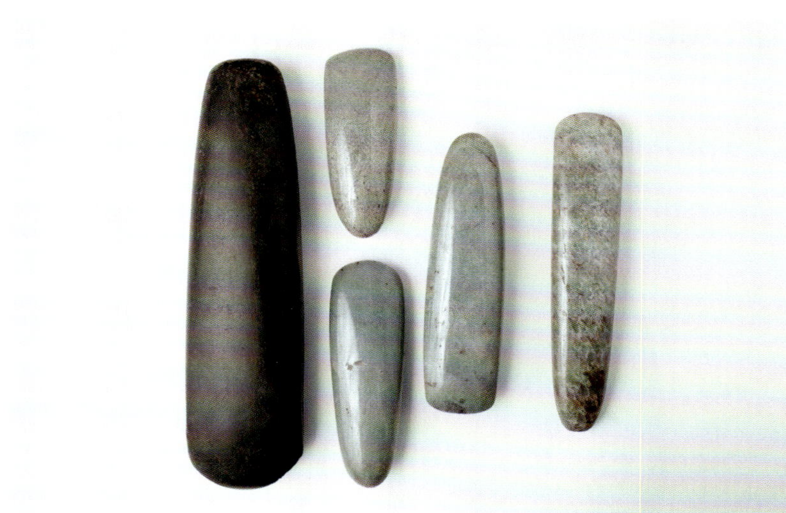
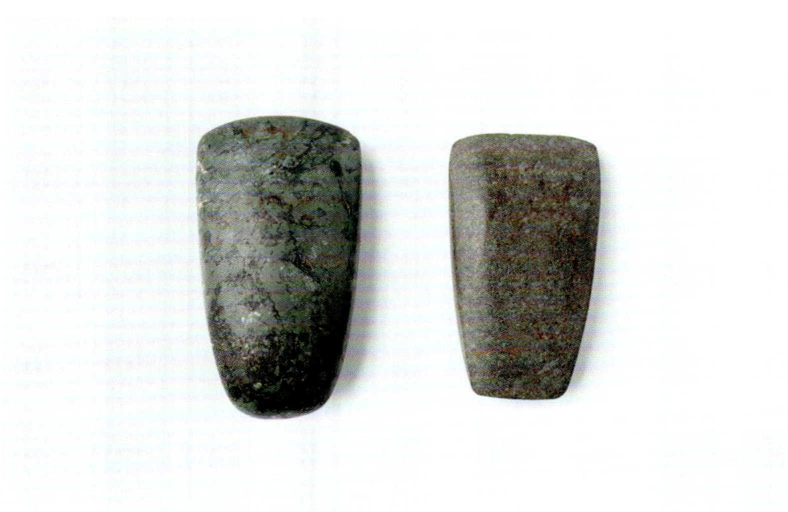
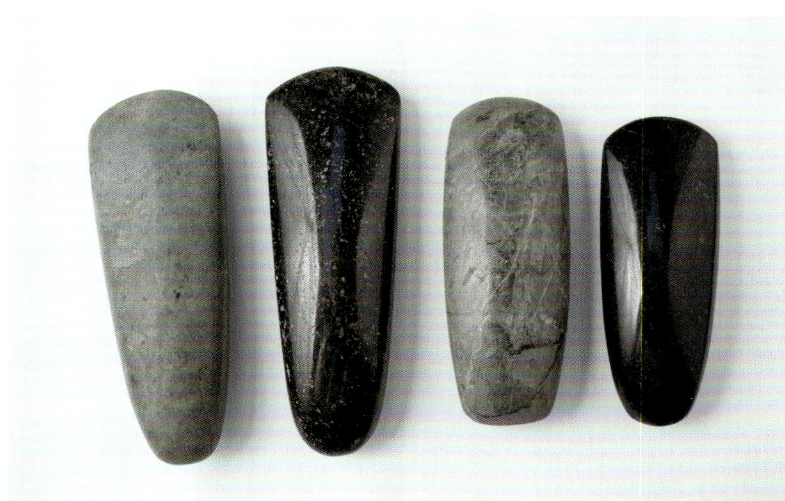

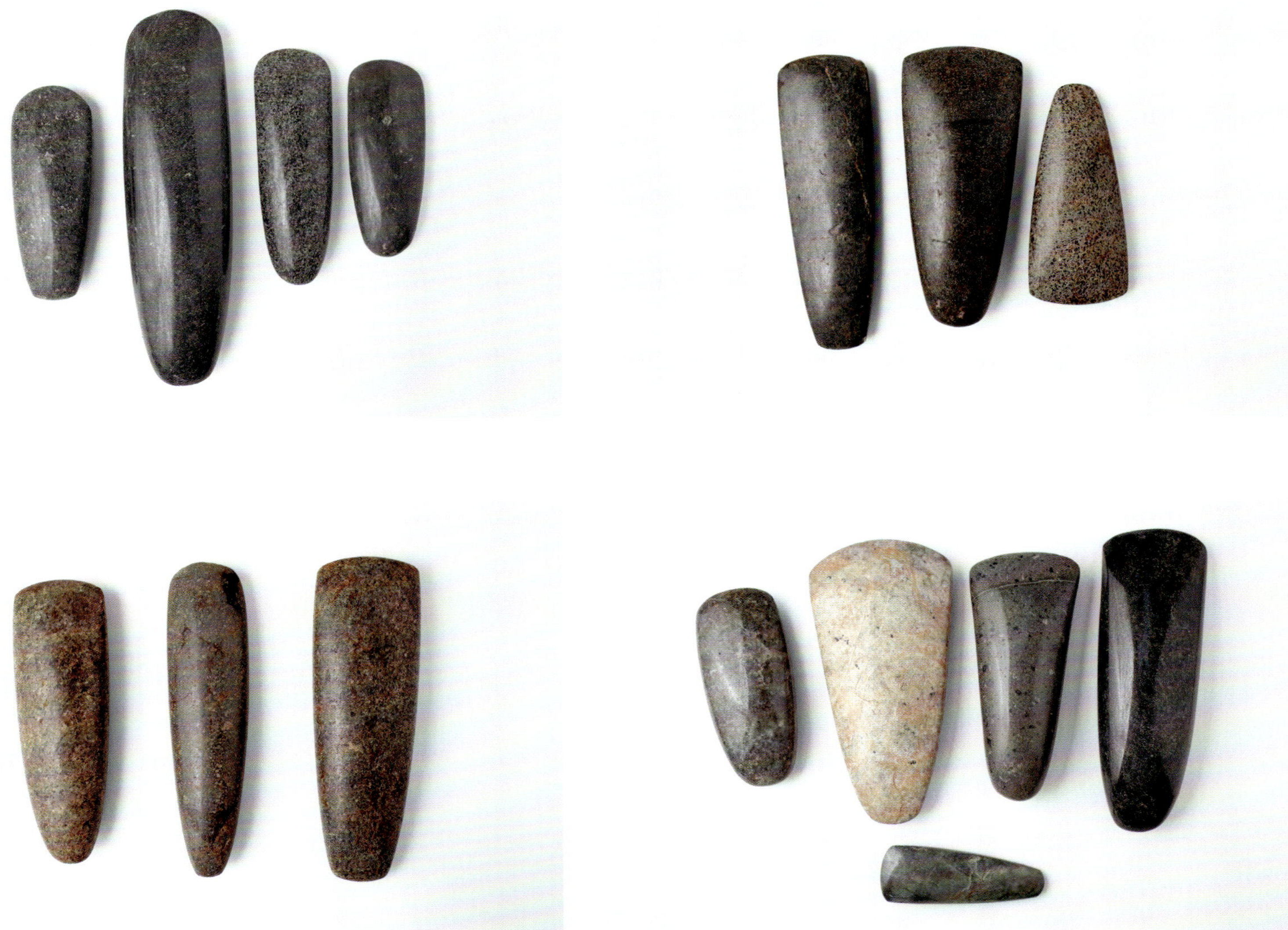

PLATES 37–48

SELECTION OF AXES AND AXE FRAGMENTS
Mexico, Veracruz, El Manatí, 1600–1200 BC
Serpentine, greenstone, and gray, green, black, and veined stones
Length: approx. $3^{1}/_{2}$–$4^{13}/_{16}$ in. (8.9–12.2 cm)
Centro Regional Veracruz, Veracruz, Mexico

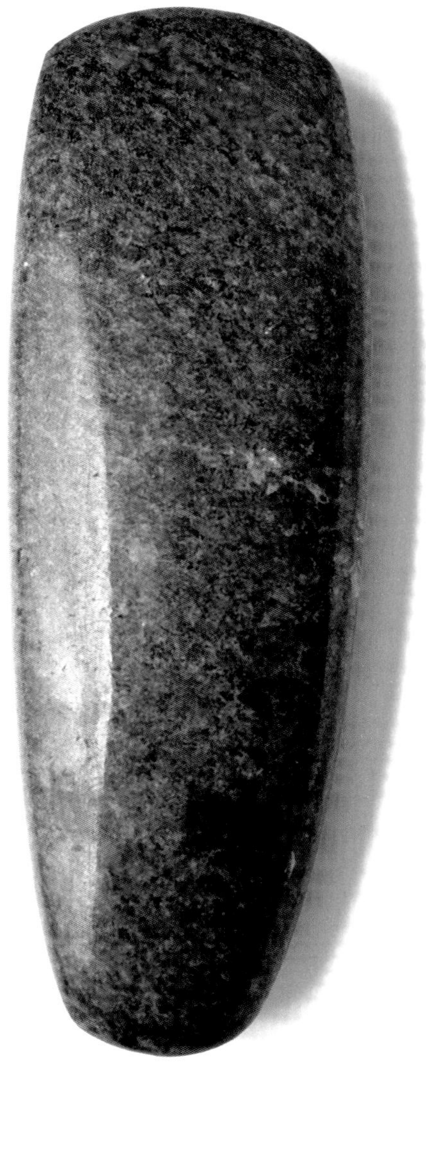

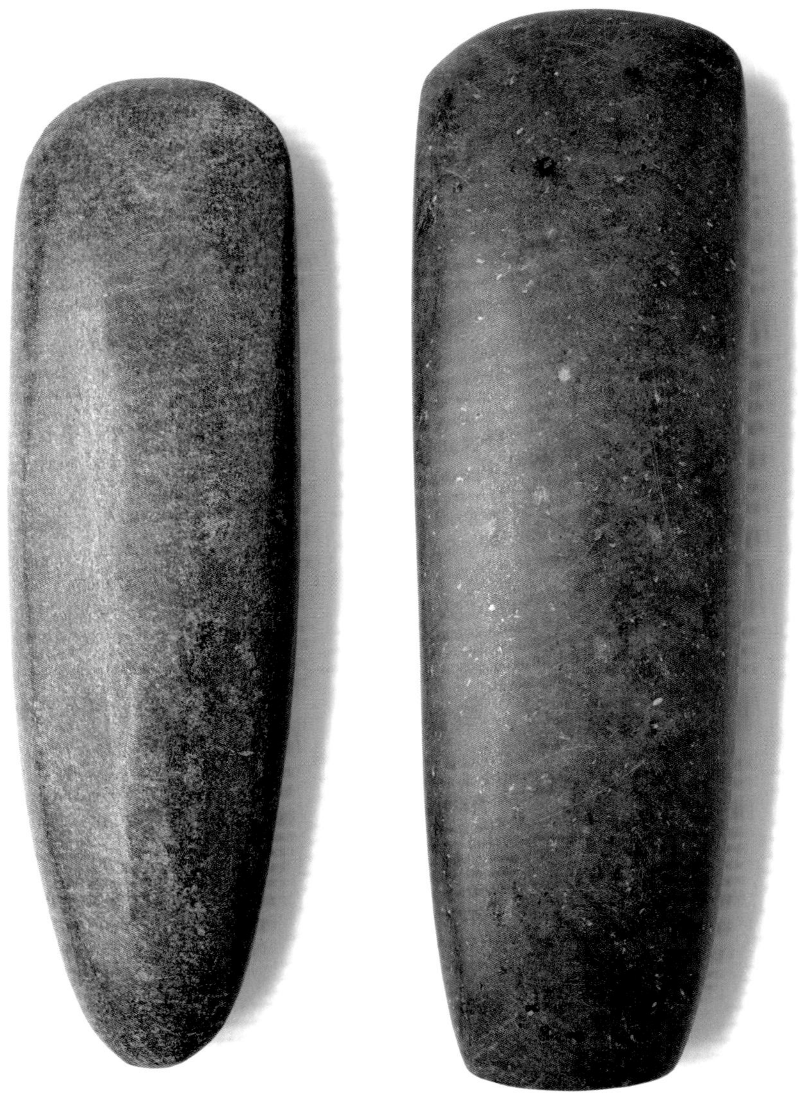

La Merced, about 3 miles (5 kilometers) northeast of El Manatí, also served as an Olmec sacred space for religious ceremonies but, unlike El Manatí, it was used almost exclusively for the massive burial of axes, most made of serpentinite. A few axes were crafted of jadeite, but they are white or cream in color, also unlike those found at El Manatí. The soil conditions have not preserved any organic matter or objects carved in wood that might also have been offered.

The La Merced offering was composed of more than nine hundred axes that occupied a space of almost 1,744 square feet (162 square meters). It must have been deposited at three separate times, distinguishable by the variations in associated objects, their placement, and quality; all three offerings occurred after a domestic occupation represented by a trash deposit. Radiocarbon dates show that the space was used for ceremonies from about 1300 BC to 900 BC.

The first and oldest offering—composed of smaller axes with narrow, well-defined shapes—was limited to a small area to the north. The axes were deposited individually or arranged in groups of four or five as open semicircles. One small axe bears the relief of a human figure; another has a partially worked image of a human-feline figure that we have nicknamed "The Ocelot."

Perhaps the most important period was the second phase, based on the quantity of objects and the presence of an anthropomorphic axe known as "El Bebé" (the baby) (pls. 58–59). "El Bebé" was surrounded by more than fifty axes placed vertically in the ground, with their broader blade ends facing upward, and other artifacts including globular pottery vessels associated with hematite mirrors. This discovery is significant for Olmec archaeology, because it is the first time that a sculpture of this type has been excavated in situ. The majority are from looted contexts and thus devoid of scientific value.

The third offering marked a change in the variety of objects deposited. The people continued to bury axes with the blades facing upward, but they increased the proportion of pre-forms and began to include raw material and several rectangular slabs or material with undefined shapes. Significantly, the proportion of axes in comparison to artifacts from the preceding phase is much smaller. Also noteworthy is the serpentinite slab carved with a typically Olmec face (Monument 1) that was placed vertically and facing slightly to the northeast.

The offering was apparently associated with agricultural cults intended to be propitiatory; for example, to maintain balance during heavy rainfall, or to save or improve harvests. It may have been near a spring or water channel, now dry, or an entry point of water from the lagoon. If the axes represented maize, the offering might have been symbolic of the sowing of corn; this could explain why most axes were positioned vertically with their narrower sides down and wider blades pointing upward.

PLATE 49

GOURD-SHAPED BOWL (*TECOMATE*)
Mexico, Veracruz, La Merced, 1000–800 BC
Ceramic
5 11/16 x 6 5/16 in. (14.5 x 16 cm)
Centro INAH Veracruz

See also:
Ortíz Ceballos and Rodríguez M. 2000: 75–93, 155–167

Rodríguez M. and Ortíz Ceballos 2000: 154, 158, 162, figs. 7, 15

and numerous other publications by these authors in the list of works cited (pp. 254–264)

These activities must have been carried out at the most critical moments, in response to a lack or an excess of water.

The many objects in this offering represented a huge appropriation of nonlocal raw materials that involved numerous inhabitants, quarrymen, and artists. It appears, however, that the quality of the objects was not the priority; many pieces were left unfinished, simply carved into the general shape of an axe to be deposited. Ultimately, their symbolic or ritual significance took precedence over their function as items for domestic or luxury use. Furthermore, the raw materials were equally as important as the finely wrought jadeite objects. At La Merced, the axe achieved its most sublime level as a divine symbol, because it was personified to allude to the human form. MCRM/POC (ORTÍZ)

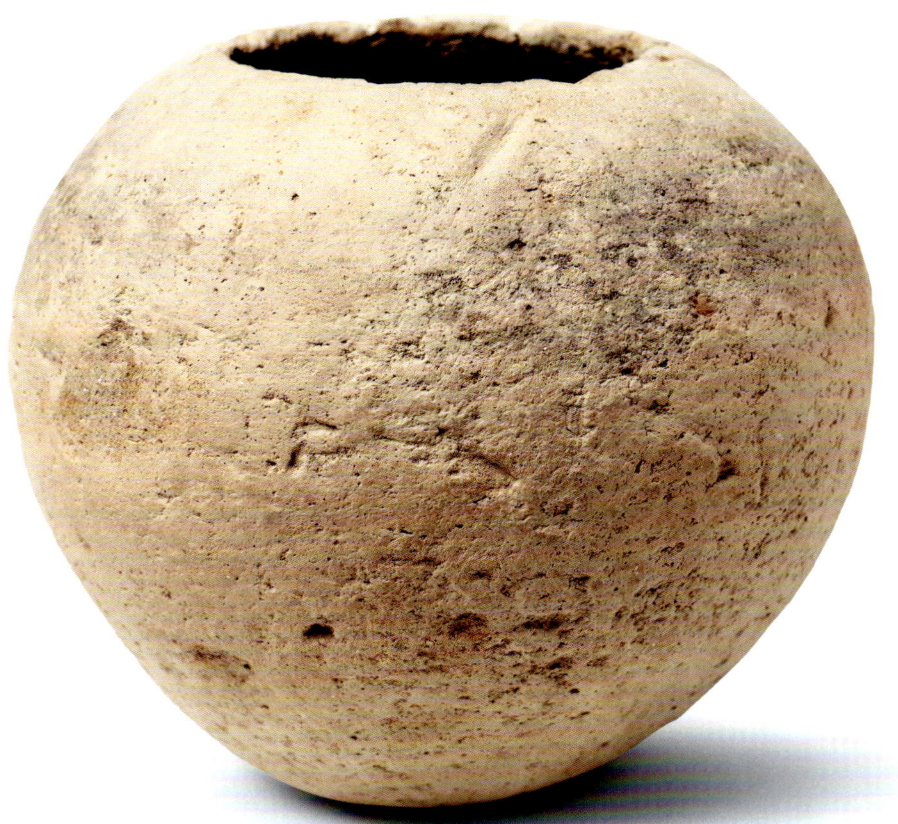

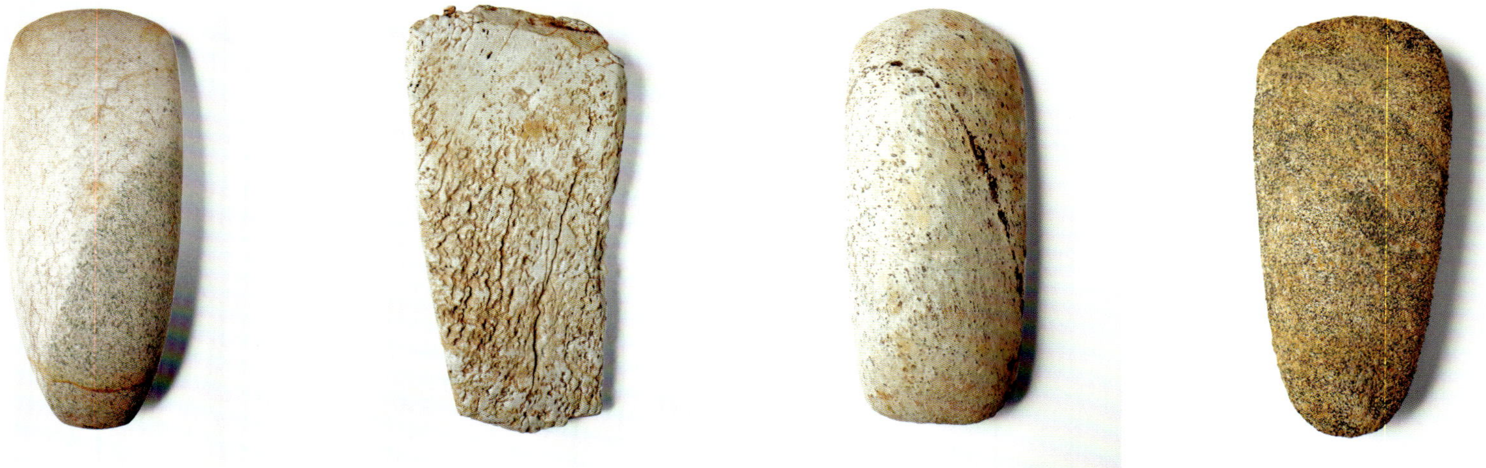
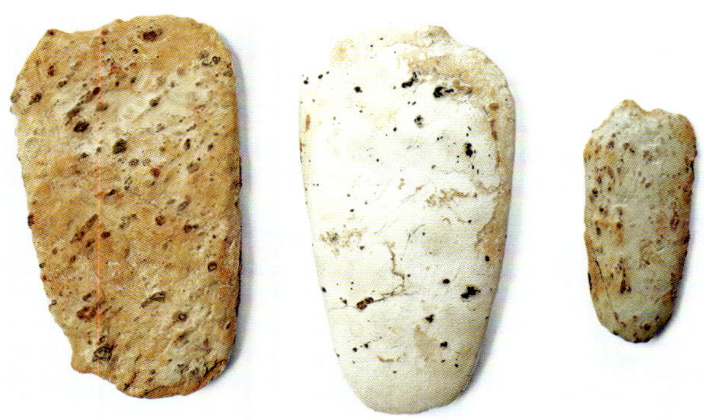
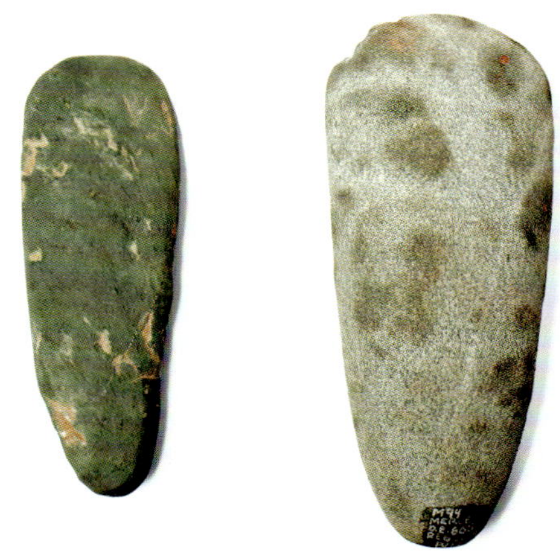
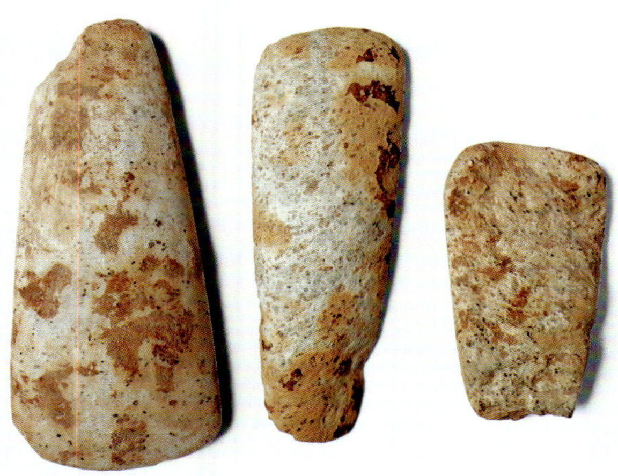
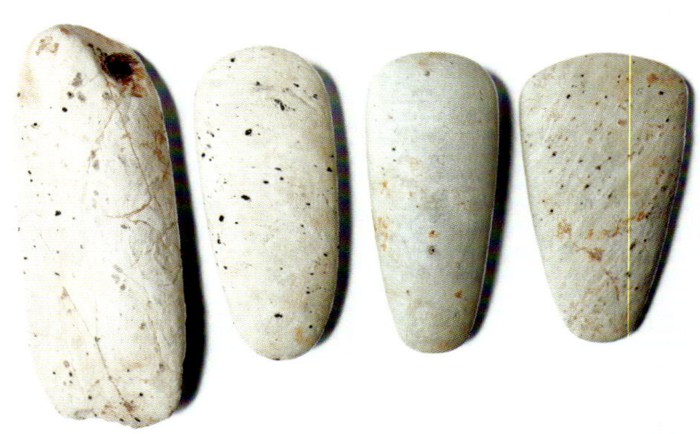

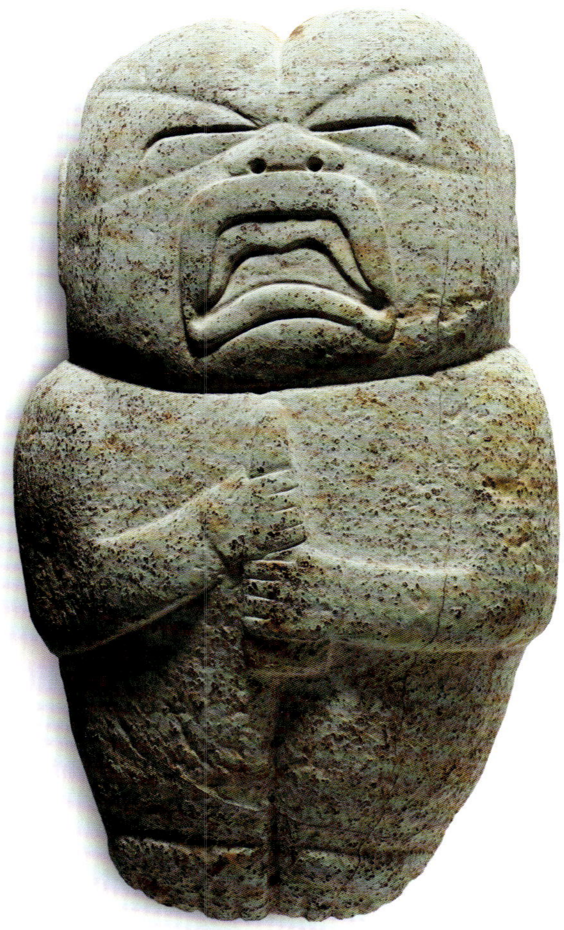

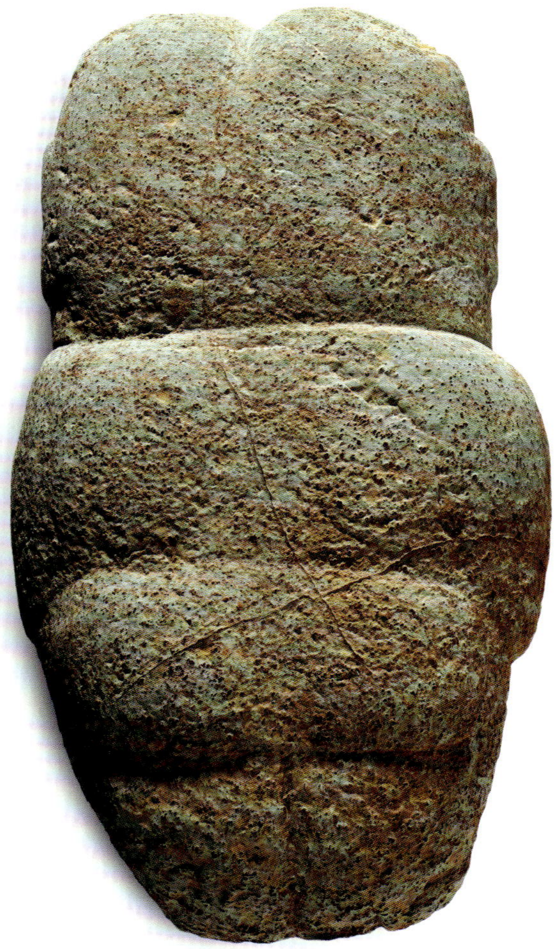

PLATES 50–59

SELECTION OF AXES
Mexico, Veracruz, La Merced, 1000–800 BC
Primarily serpentinite, with white jade, dark metamorphic stones, and sandstone
Length: $1^{1}/_{2}$–$14^{1}/_{4}$ in. (3.8–36.1 cm)
Centro INAH Veracruz

MONUMENT 2 ("EL BEBÉ")
Mexico, Veracruz, La Merced, 1000–800 BC
Stone
$15^{3}/_{4} \times 9^{1}/_{16} \times 3^{1}/_{8}$ in. (40 x 23 x 8 cm)
Centro INAH Veracruz (10-581031)

The Olmec created Monuments 7–9 (pls. 60–62) as part of a four-figure sculptural grouping for the so-called acropolis at the secondary site at San Lorenzo, known as Loma del Zapote-El Azuzul. Farmer Atanacio Vasconselos discovered this sculptural complex in 1987 when he stuck his digging stick into the ground to plant grass. Ann Cyphers found the group in its original archaeological context as positioned by the Olmec: on a pavement of bentonite, a local sedimentary rock, on the east side of the acropolis. The human figures gazed reverentially at the small feline, which was in turn watched over by a large feline behind it (the latter is not included in this exhibition). A sculptural representation of two young Olmec rulers paying homage to a feline-jaguar deity as part of a discourse of power, it is the first Mesoamerican representation of human twins involved in sacred activity, as exemplified centuries later by a pair of hero twins in the Popul Vuh, the sacred book of the K'iché Maya. It was moved to the Museo de Antropología de Xalapa in 2003 (see fig. 8).

The small feline was made by hammering the raw material arkose, a conglomerate of local sandstone. The sculpture represents a feline-jaguar in a seated position, leaning forward slightly as it roars. A mark on the right knee in the shape of an arch suggests that this piece was carved from a previously recycled monument. Among the Olmec, representations of feline-jaguars were of high symbolic value and focused on a ruler's discourse of power.

The twins were created from light-colored andesite that was finely polished and exceptionally carved. Monument 8 is a male Olmec figure in a kneeling position, with a stick or staff of authority in his hands, suggesting an attitude of reverence toward the small feline. The face shows extraordinary sculptural qualities in the treatment of the almond-shaped eyes, straight nose, firm cheeks, and fleshy mouth, all features characteristic of a young man. Attached to the front of his headdress is what might be a pyrite mirror; attached to the back is a cape. Folded decorations fall from both sides of the headdress, perhaps suggesting decorations made from bark paper. He also wears a pectoral with interlaced bands or an X motif, a belt, and a loincloth. Both the position of the figure and the folded decorations are similar to other Olmec monuments from San Lorenzo Tenochtitlán, La Venta, Tabasco, Los Soldados near Arroyo Pesquero, and San Martín Pajapan in the Tuxtla Mountains. Of slightly smaller dimensions than its twin, Monument 9 displays great attention to details such as the pupils of the eyes and the nails on the feet and hands. The pair of sculptures might represent heirs to the greater hierarchy of San Lorenzo, or the sons of an older Olmec ruler of higher rank (one of the individuals represented in the colossal heads). RLR

PLATE 60

MONUMENT 7 (SMALL FELINE)
Mexico, Veracruz, Municipality of Texistepec, Loma del Zapote-El Azuzul, 1200–900 BC
Arkose
$43^{1}/_{4}$ x $30^{11}/_{16}$ x $19^{5}/_{8}$ in. (110 x 78 x 50 cm)
Museo de Antropología de Xalapa, Universidad Veracruzana (10-573558 3/3)

See also:
Cyphers 1994a: 49–51, figs. 4.8–4.12
Cyphers 2004b: 246–255, figs. 163–169, 171
de la Fuente 2000: 257–261, figs. 7, 15, 18
León and Sánchez 1991–1992

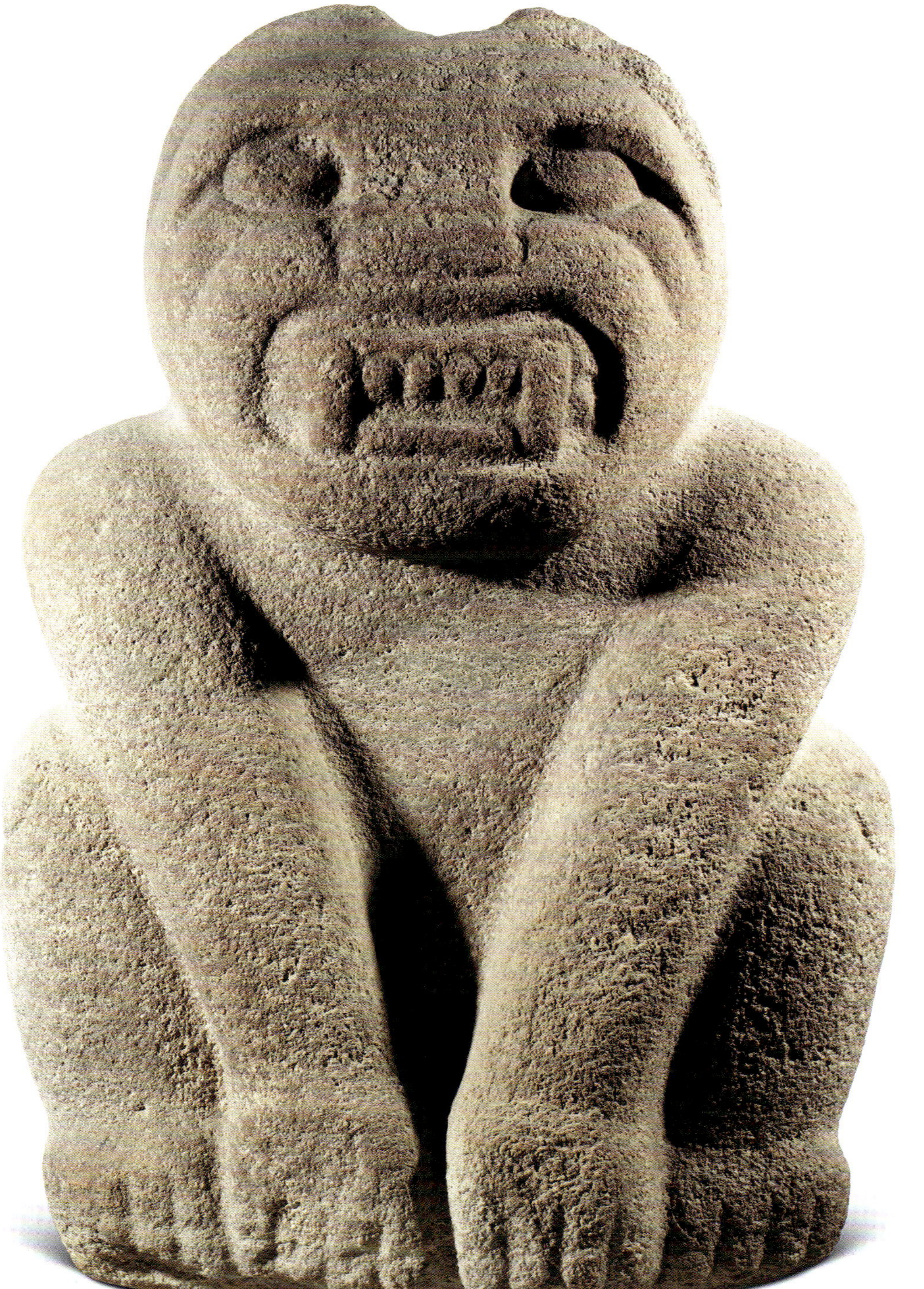

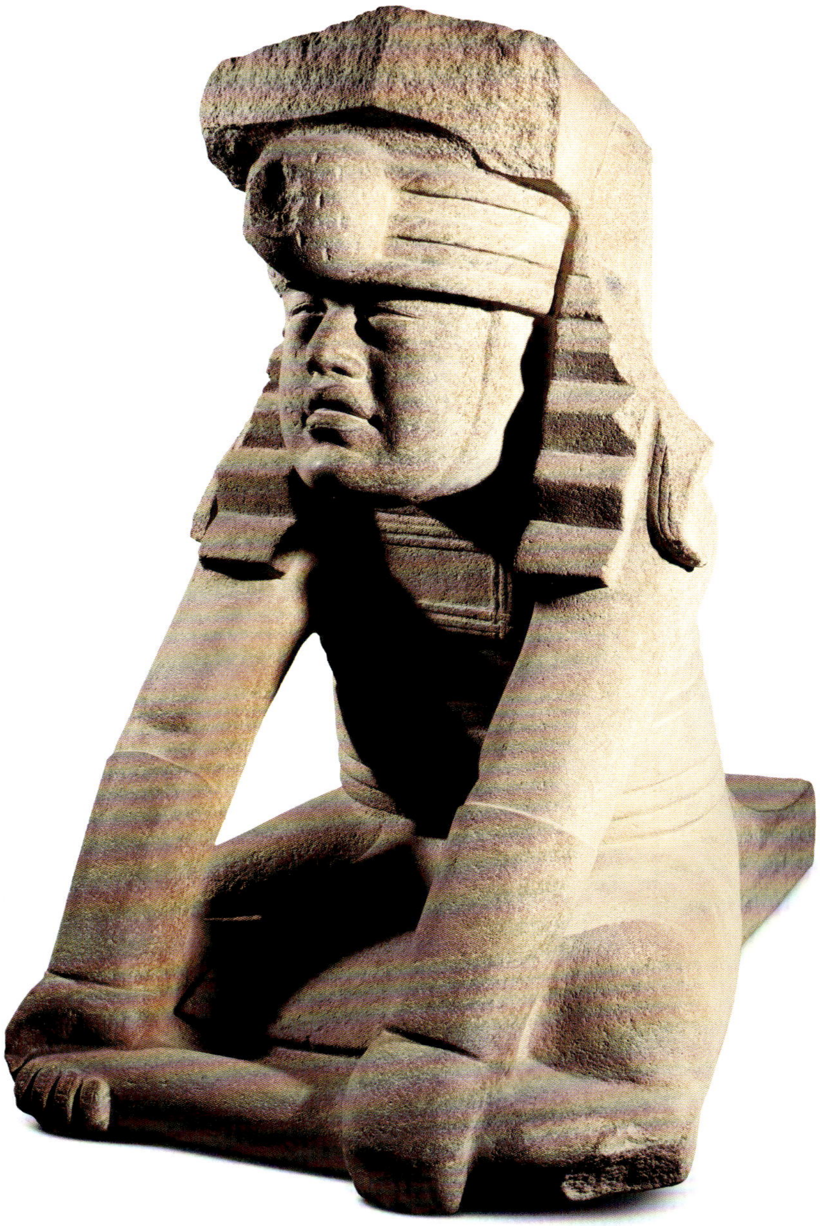

PLATES 61–62

MONUMENT 8 (TWIN I)
Mexico, Veracruz, Municipality of Texistepec, Loma del Zapote-El Azuzul, 1200–900 BC
Andesite
$39^3/_8$ x $33^7/_{16}$ x $49^3/_{16}$ in. (100 x 85 x 125 cm)
Museo de Antropología de Xalapa, Universidad Veracruzana (10-573558 2/3)

MONUMENT 9 (TWIN II)
Mexico, Veracruz, Municipality of Texistepec, Loma del Zapote-El Azuzul, 1200–900 BC
Andesite
$39^3/_8$ x $33^7/_{16}$ x $47^1/_4$ in. (100 x 85 x 120 cm)
Museo de Antropología de Xalapa, Universidad Veracruzana (10-573558 1/3)

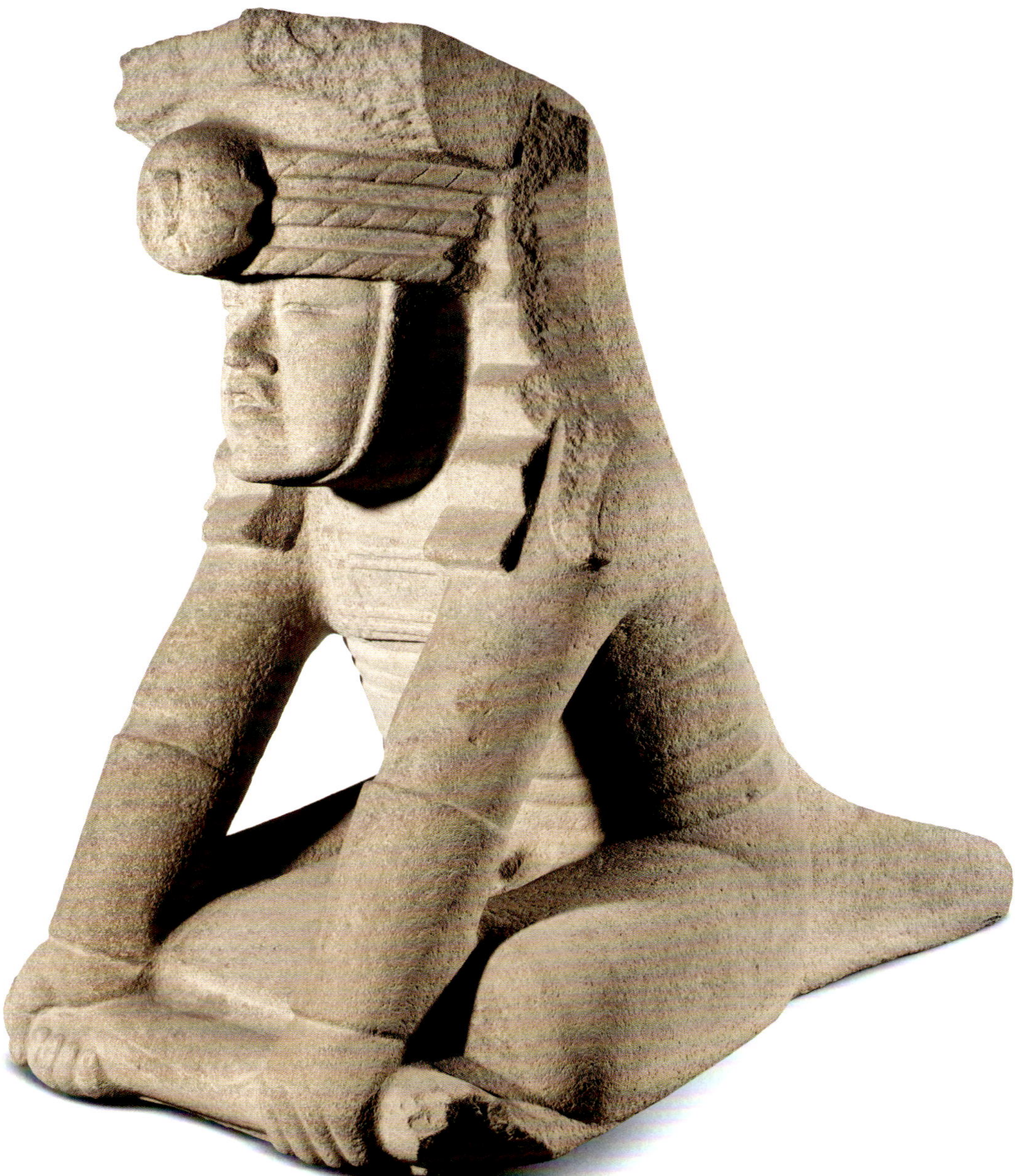

First documented by Frans Blom and Oliver La Farge, who visited La Venta in 1925, this monument was lying on its back between Mounds A-4 and A-5, north of the Complex C pyramid (González Lauck 2007: 52). The individual standing in a niche on this relief is considered to be female (Stirling 1943: 50; Milbrath 1979: 15) and appears surprisingly naturalistic; we do not know if she is a historical individual, an idealized ancestor, or a goddess. At the top border of the niche are geometric bands like those on La Venta Altar 4 (Pool 2007: 166). This may signify a cave or the open mouth of a supernatural being. The figure wears a short, pleated skirt and a headband, and there is a suggestion of breasts and long hair. Despite the apparent naturalism of the image, the face and body were not purposefully mutilated or effaced.

As Tatiana Proskouriakoff (1968: 121) noted, the La Venta stelae, which present historic scenes in a narrative manner, differ dramatically from the earlier San Lorenzo monuments, which do not. Despite being labeled as stelae, not all of the large stone monuments at La Venta are the typical stela form—that is, flat, carved slabs, like the limestone monuments from later Maya sites—but rather are boulderlike (Rebecca González Lauck, personal communication, August 2009). Many later Mesoamerican civilizations used stelae to commemorate or recall major events of the past. They were set upright in the ground, usually outdoors, and placed in relation to ceremonial structures.

At least six other stelae have been found at La Venta, and these were placed along the southern base of the mound covering the pyramid known as C-1 (González Lauck 1997: 91). KB

PLATE 63

STELA 1 (FEMALE FIGURE)
Mexico, Tabasco, La Venta, 900–400 BC
Basalt
98 7/16 x 38 9/16 x 27 9/16 in. (250 x 98 x 70 cm)
Parque-Museo de La Venta, Villahermosa, Tabasco (PMV-033)

See also:
Benson 1996b: 18, fig. 2
de la Fuente 1977a: 237–239, ill. 66

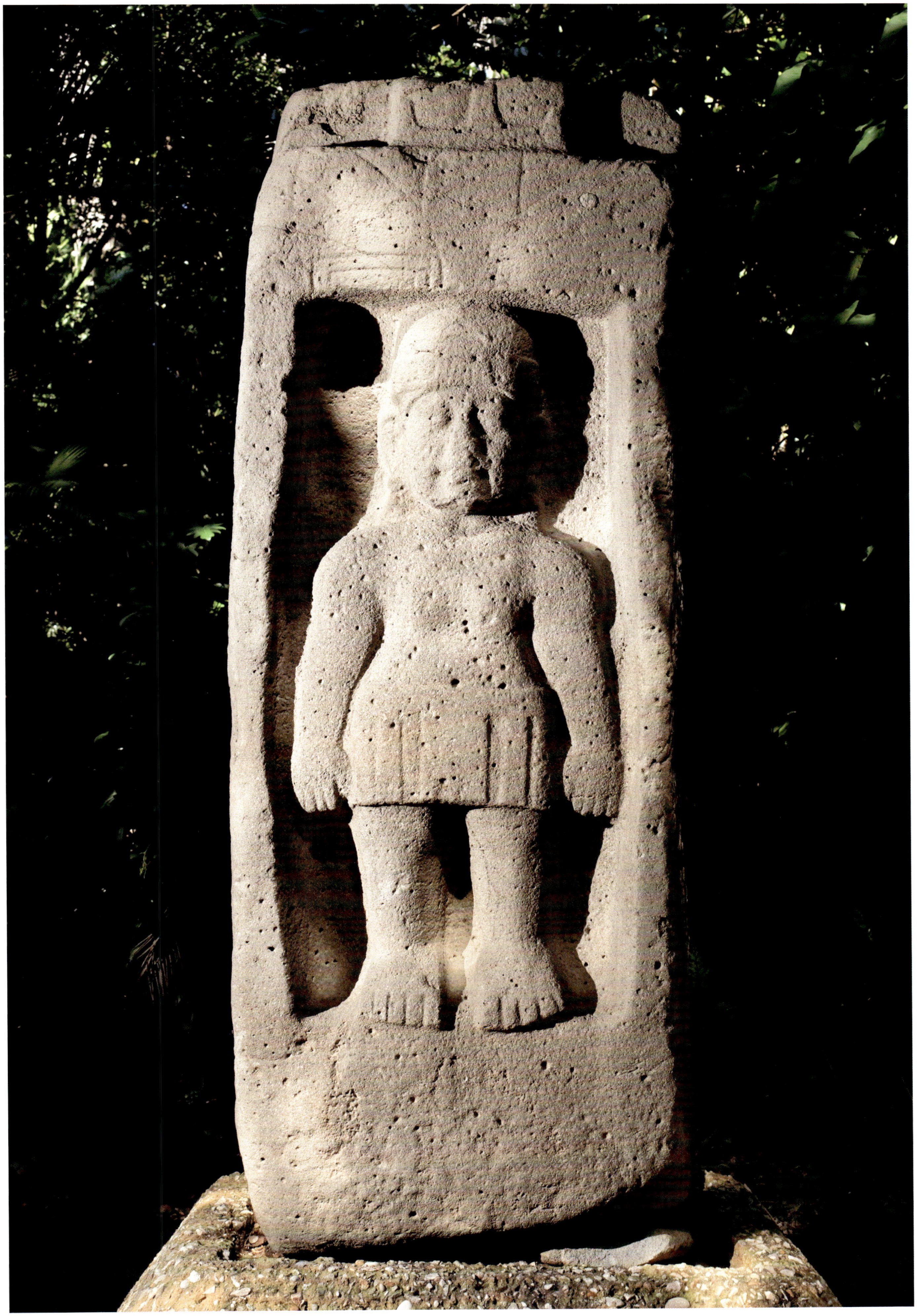

For many years, this object was identified as an altar, despite Howel Williams and Robert Heizer's comment that "while certain rectangular, flat-topped stone sculptures from the sites of La Venta and San Lorenzo look like what are usually called 'altars,' there is not the slightest evidence that they were so employed. We retain the term as a purely descriptive one" (1965: 25). Scholars now consider that they probably functioned as thrones (Grove 1973). Weighing more than 10 tons (9 metric tons), this La Venta monument was found paired with another twice its size, known as Altar 4 (fig. 19). The monuments were placed on either side of a long mound (D-8); Altar 4 was facing east, and Altar 5 was facing west (Stirling 1943: 54–55).

Altar 5 depicts a cross-legged figure seated in a central niche or symbolic cave and cradling what appears to be an infant. The projecting tabletop ledge has been battered off (ibid.). The central figure, who wears earspools and a conical headdress, is carved in high relief and leans forward. Around his neck he wears a two-banded flat collar with a large, square pendant. The facial features of the central figure and the infant appear to have been partially erased. On both sides of Altar 5 are incised scenes showing two seated adult figures, each richly garbed and holding an animated infant in an upright pose. Both pairs of figures face toward the front of the throne and appear to be moving in that direction. Perhaps these reliefs are secondary themes; the sculptor's main emphasis clearly focused on the more deeply carved frontal figure holding the prone infant.

Like Altar 5, Altar 4 depicts a central figure wearing a headdress or a helmet and sitting cross-legged, with most of his body inside a recessed cave or niche. He does not hold an infant but instead bends forward and clasps in each hand the end of a thick rope (Stirling 1943: 54), which runs along the bottom of the altar. The rope reaches around the south end of the altar and is attached to the wrist of a figure carved in low relief, variously described as a captive or an ancestor; the remains of a similar figure are on the north side. The frontal face of the ledge above the figure depicts a composite supernatural creature with oval eyes and an X-shaped motif between a pair of fangs. The top of the monument has a raised area that may be intended to suggest that a jaguar skin had been thrown on it. KB

PLATES 64–66

ALTAR 5
Mexico, Tabasco, La Venta, 900–400 BC
Basalt
61 x 79 15/16 x 60 1/4 in. (155 x 203 x 153 cm)
Parque Museo de La Venta, Villahermosa, Tabasco (PMV-012)

See also:
González Lauck 1994: 105–109, figs. 6.27–6.28
González Lauck 1996b: 47

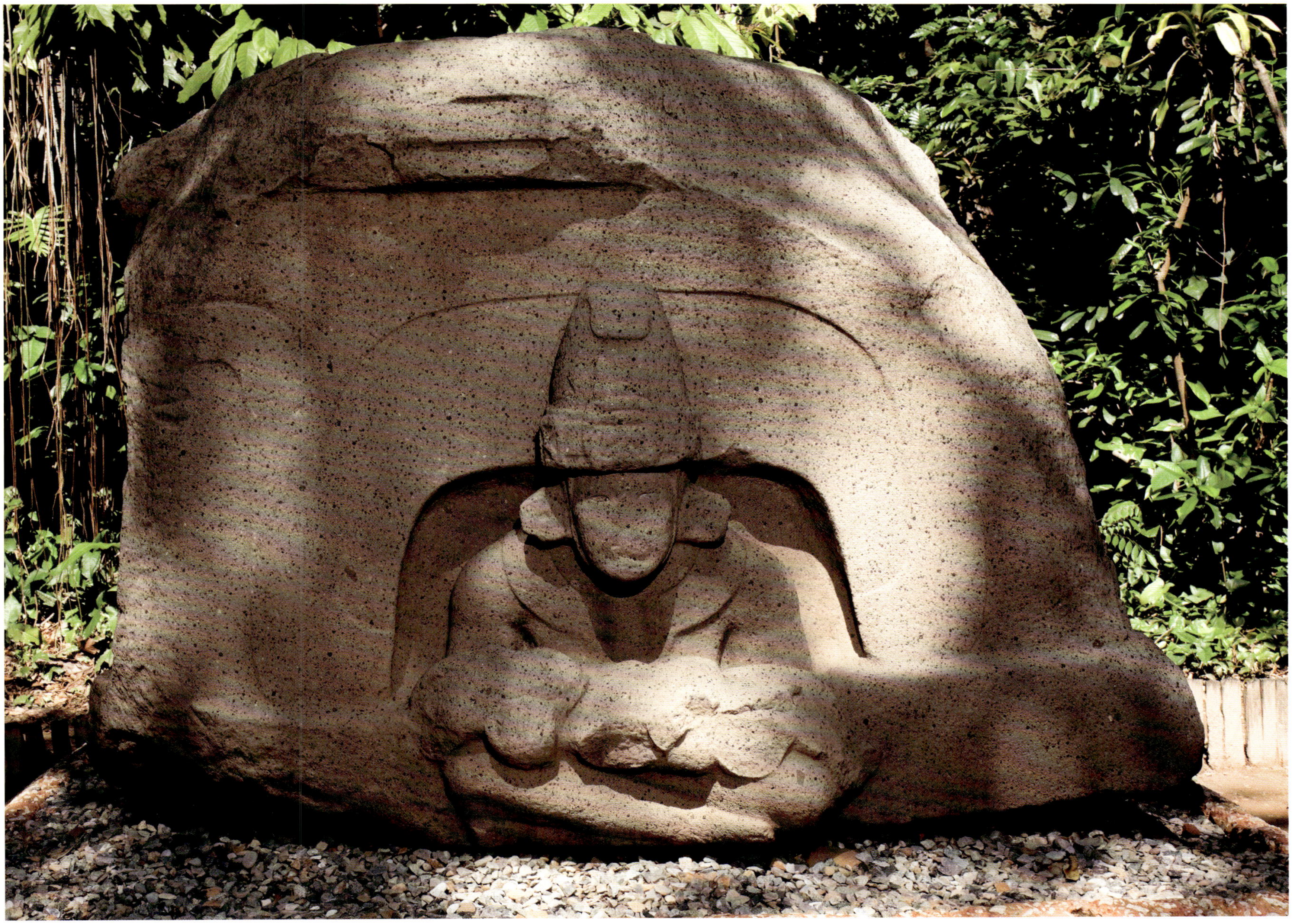

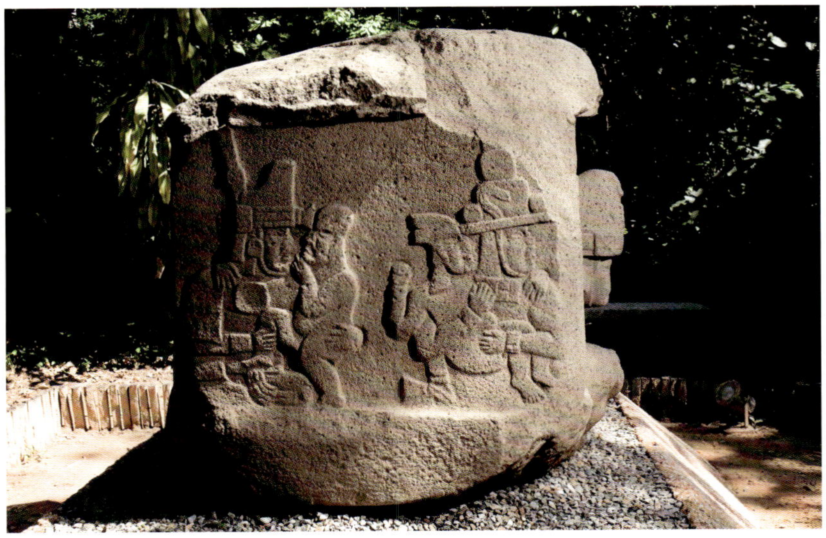

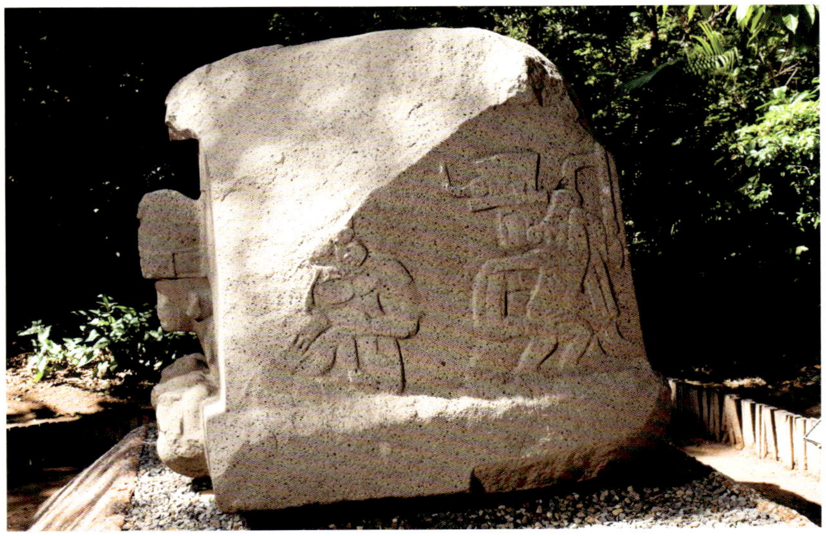

The weight, power, and balance of this imposing sculpture of an aristocrat—informally called "The Governor" in modern times—give it a solid presence, and one can easily imagine the cross-legged figure raised and seated on a throne. His arms extend in front of him, and his fists rest symmetrically on each knee. The attire is majestic: an elaborate, short cape draped across his back appears to bear important textile motifs. The figure also wears a rectangular pectoral marked with the X motif, as well as a loincloth, a sash, bracelets, and anklets. His face is framed by pleated-paper ornaments, which are attached to a headband composed of tubular beads. The headdress rises above the headband and falls to the back, where it is ends in a quadripartite cleft pattern. Weighing some 28,000 pounds (1,200 kilograms), this substantial monument was found by itself in Complex C, in front of the enormous fluted pyramid (C-1). KB

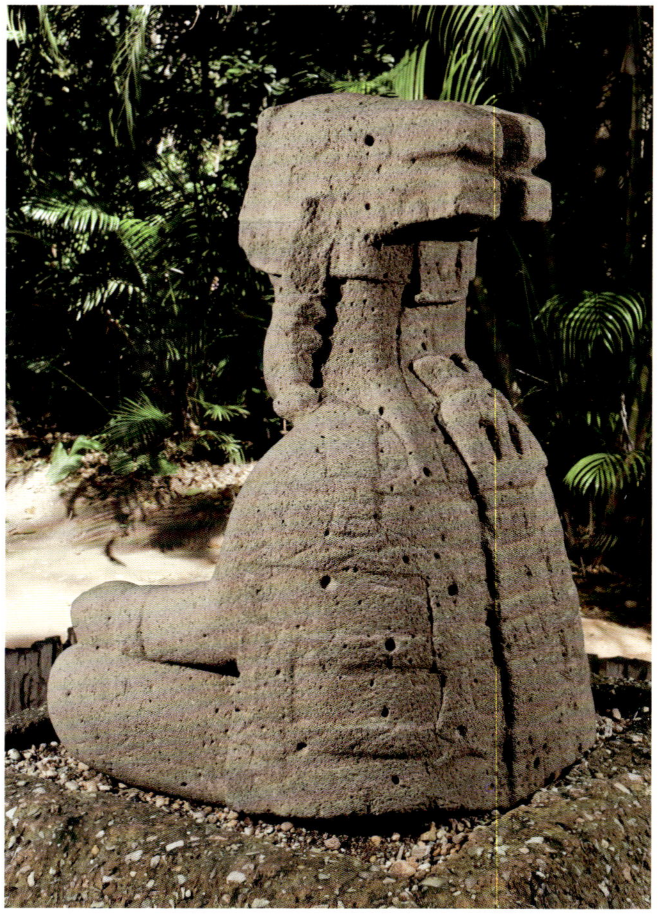

PLATES 67–68

MONUMENT 77
(SEATED FIGURE WEARING CAPE)
Mexico, Tabasco, La Venta, 900–400 BC
Basalt
41 5/16 x 30 11/16 x 28 3/8 in. (105 x 78 x 72 cm)
Parque-Museo de La Venta, Villahermosa, Tabasco (PMV-013)

See also:
González Lauck 1996a: cat. 10
González Lauck 2007: 53

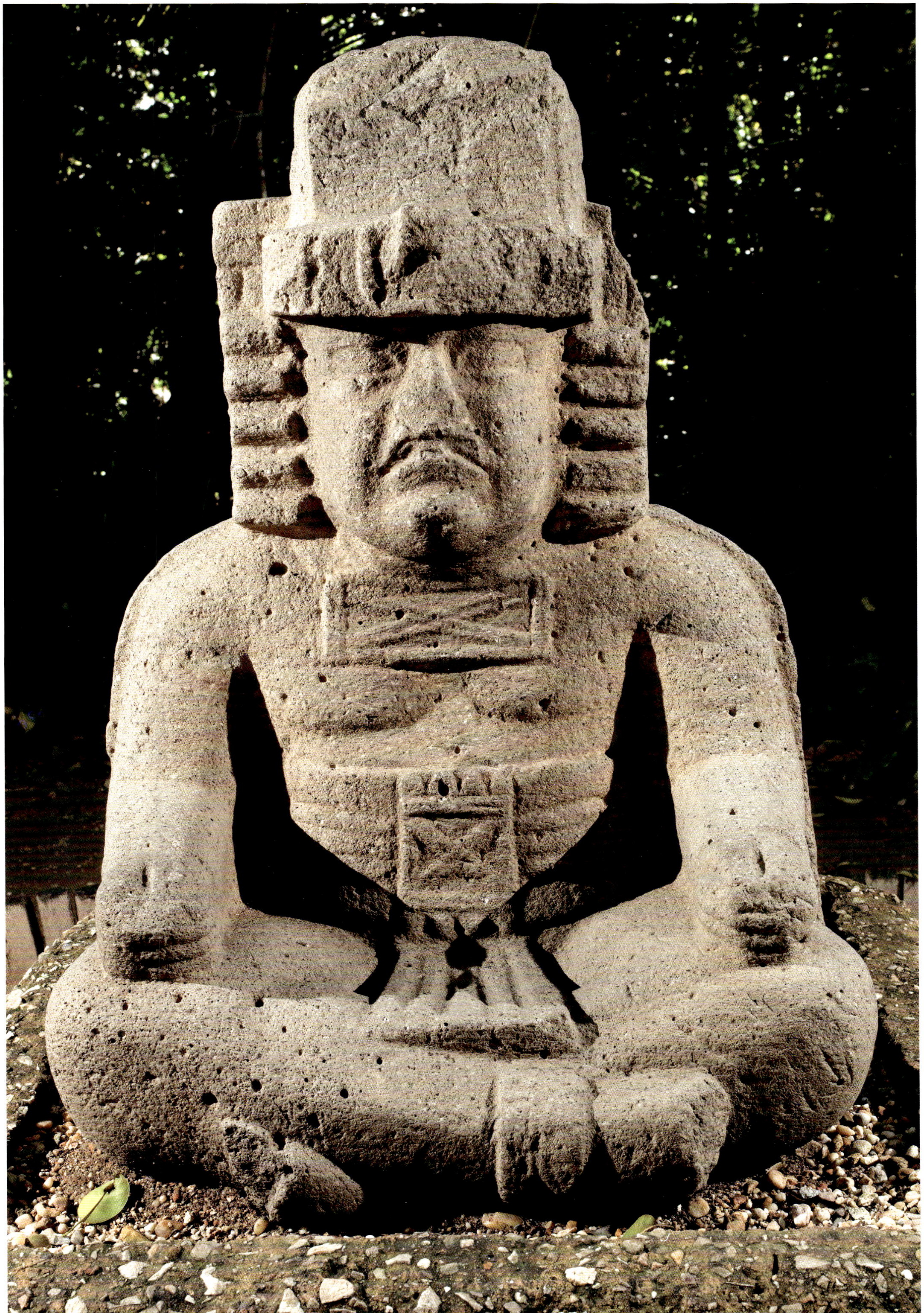

The seated body of this powerful hybrid creature thrusts forward, its rigid arms extending over legs with clawlike feet. The head tilts far back, at almost a right angle, and the face looks upward toward the sky. The open mouth of this fanged creature covers almost one-third of the face. Above the eyes, flame forms are depicted instead of eyebrows. The forehead merges with the headdress, giving the impression of an extended head with a V-shaped cleft. In the back of the monument is a feature indicating four curved branches. The right arm of the figure was completely restored (González Lauck 1996a: cat. 6). KB

PLATE 69

MONUMENT 11
(SEATED SUPERNATURAL BEING)
Mexico, Tabasco, La Venta, 900–400 BC
Basalt
$35^{13}/_{16}$ x $26^{3}/_{4}$ x $32^{11}/_{16}$ in. (91 x 68 x 83 cm)
Museo Regional de Antropología
"Carlos Pellicer Cámara," Villahermosa, Tabasco (A-0091)

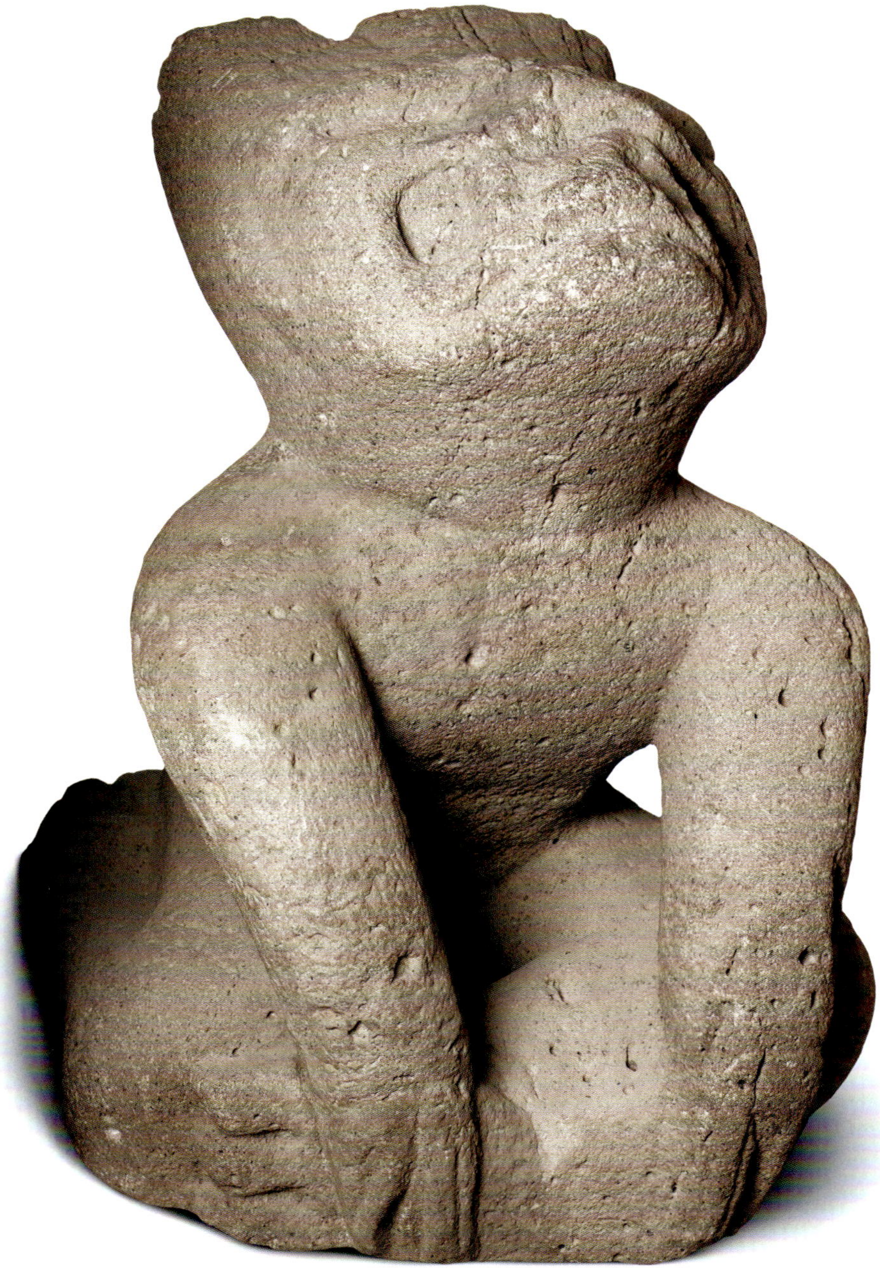

It is easy to imagine this large, rearing head once attached to a powerful feline body. The creature probably sat, and its gaze would have been directed slightly upward; it may have been part of a larger assemblage of interrelated sculptures depicting a specific mythic scene.

Many Olmec objects were decapitated or mutilated in ancient times, probably for a variety of reasons. This type of decapitation could not have been easy to accomplish. The creature's face is beautifully carved with a cleft head, flattened or sloping forehead, and grimacing features. Especially emphasized is the fearsome, open mouth, apparently a buccal plaque (González Lauck 1996a: cat. 13). Also noteworthy are the masklike ears, the X element above the right eye, and a circle enclosed in a U motif above the left eye. The X and U elements are often combined in large and small works from various Olmec sites. KB

PLATE 70

MONUMENTAL HEAD OF SUPERNATURAL CREATURE
Mexico, Tabasco, La Venta, 900–400 BC
Volcanic stone
24 13/16 x 18 1/8 x 18 7/8 in. (63 x 46 x 48 cm)
Museo Regional de Antropología "Carlos Pellicer Cámara," Villahermosa, Tabasco (A-0667)

See also:
Diehl 1990: cat. 3

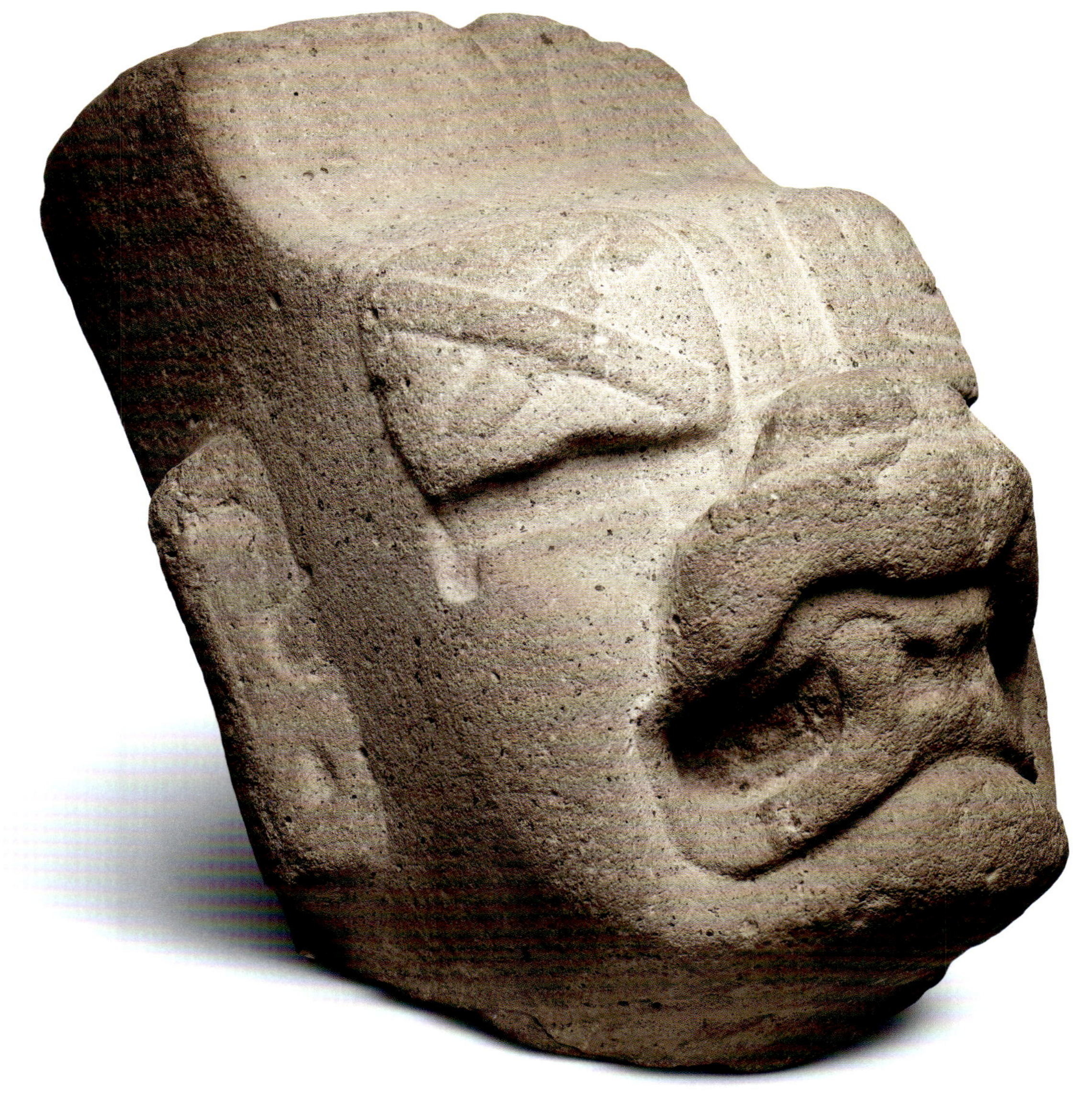

The Olmec were the earliest civilization in Mexico to craft large amounts of jadeite into a variety of objects of extraordinary value. They created items of personal finery including necklaces, earflares, and pectorals, as well as votive axes and figurines, such as this fine example of a female wearing a hematite mirror as a pectoral. The figurine was among the offerings found with the remains of a burial, Bundle 2, in the Columnar Tomb (see pl. 18). She sits in a cross-legged pose with her hands clasped at her chest, and her hair, cut in a fringe that frames her face, resembles that of the figure depicted in La Venta Stela 1 (pl. 63). She may once have worn inlaid circular ear ornaments. Intriguingly, a small hematite mirror was part of the offerings with the Bundle 1 burial, raising the possibility that the remains were those of an elite female. MC-LE

PLATE 71

SEATED FEMALE FIGURE WITH POLISHED HEMATITE DISK
Mexico, Tabasco, La Venta, Mound A-2, Tomb A (Columnar Tomb), 900–500 BC
Jadeite and hematite
3 x 1 7/8 x 1 1/2 in. (7.7 x 4.7 x 3.8 cm)
Museo Nacional de Antropología, Mexico City (10-9652)

See also:
Castro-Leal 1996: cat. 51
Drucker 1952a: 23–26, 154–155, pls. 46–47
González Lauck 2007: 52

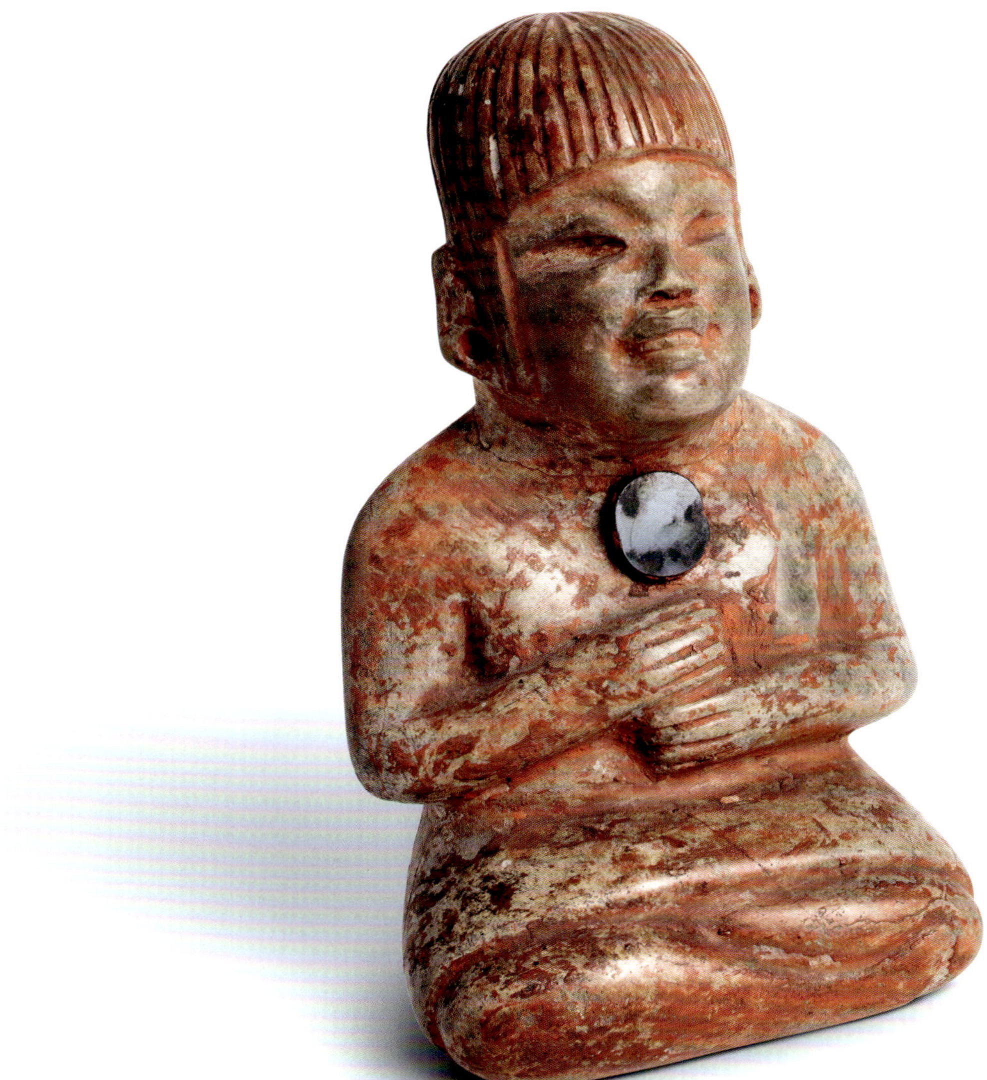

One of the most extraordinary discoveries in the Gulf Coast heartland came to light in 1955, when Mexican archaeologist Eduardo Contreras unearthed this offering beneath the patio of the northeast platform at La Venta (Drucker, Heizer, and Squier 1959: 152–161, pls. 30–36). Unlike any found in any other region of pre-Hispanic Mexico, this incomparable offering represents a ceremonial scene. Six slender serpentine celts are placed in a row to form a wall. A central human figure, possibly made of granite, stands with his back to the celts. Two jadeite and thirteen serpentine male figurines stand opposite him (characteristic of Olmec figurines, their heads are shaved). Four celts bear Olmec-style motifs incised on their surfaces.

The figurines and celts were embedded in a matrix of reddish-brown sand and covered with a layer of white sand. The entire offering was carefully deposited below a series of multicolored floors (white, yellow, rose, and orange from top to bottom). Sometime after the offering was placed, an elliptical hole centered on it was dug down to the level of the figurines' heads, and then refilled with a slightly different matrix, further confirming the sacred significance of the offering. MC-LE

PLATE 72

OFFERING 4 (GROUP OF STANDING FIGURES AND CELTS)
Mexico, Tabasco, La Venta, 900–400 BC
Jadeite, serpentine, and an atypical stone (possibly granite)
Sixteen figurines, height: 6–7 7/8 in. (15.3–20 cm); six celts, height: 9 3/8–10 in. (23.8–25.5 cm)
Museo Nacional de Antropología, Mexico City (10-9650 0/22)

See also:
Castro-Leal 1996: cat. 42
Coe 1968a: 67–69
González Lauck 1994: 104, fig. 6.20
González Lauck 2007: 52
Pool 2007: 163–164, fig. 5.7

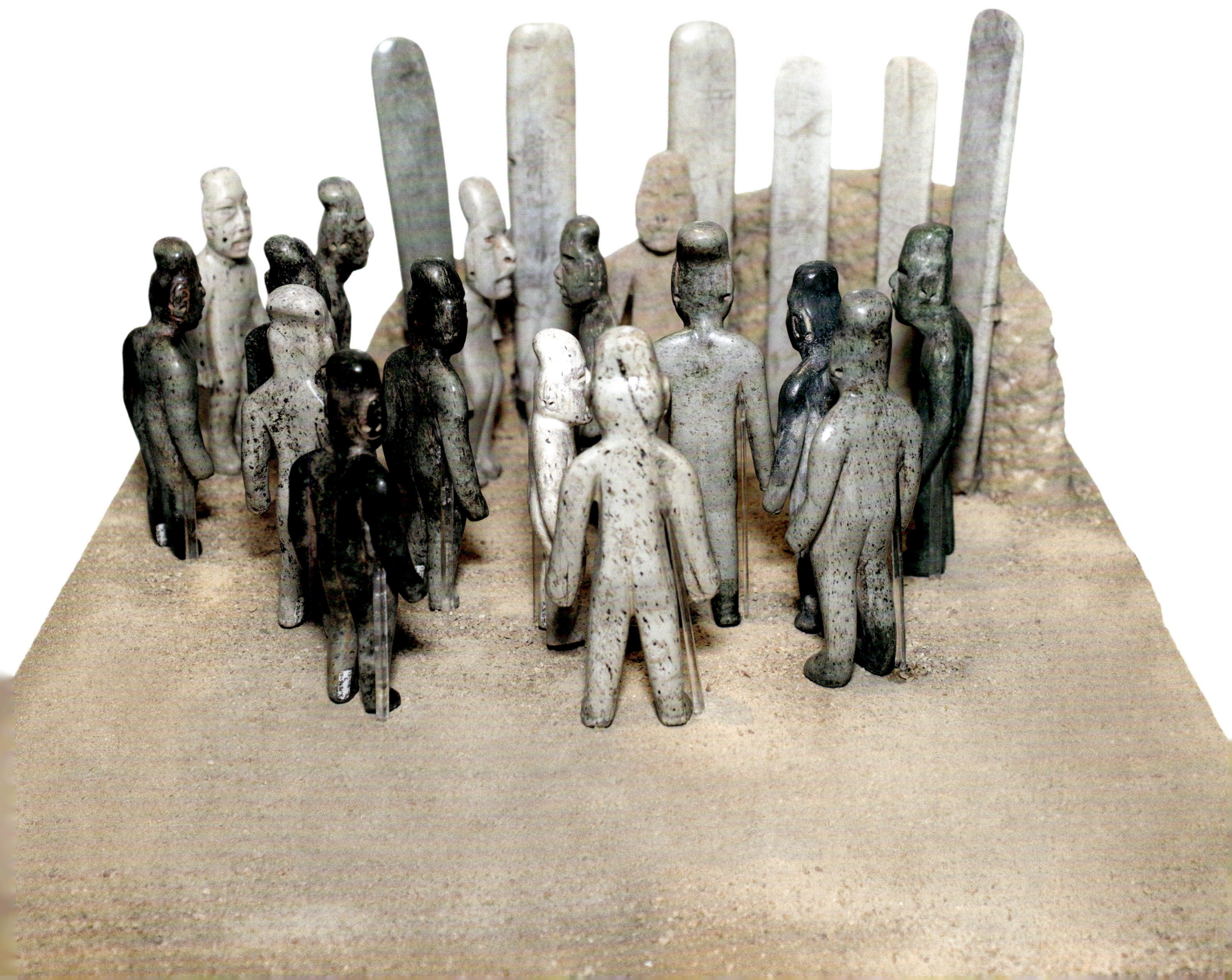

Among the rare resources sought by the Gulf Coast Olmec were iron-oxide ores, especially magnetite, ilmenite, and hematite. Caches of ilmenite blocks have been recovered from San Lorenzo, while at La Venta archaeologists have discovered seven iron-ore mirrors in various offerings (Diehl 1990: cat. 7). The reflective and refractive properties of mirrors made them tools for secular and sacred purposes. MC-LE

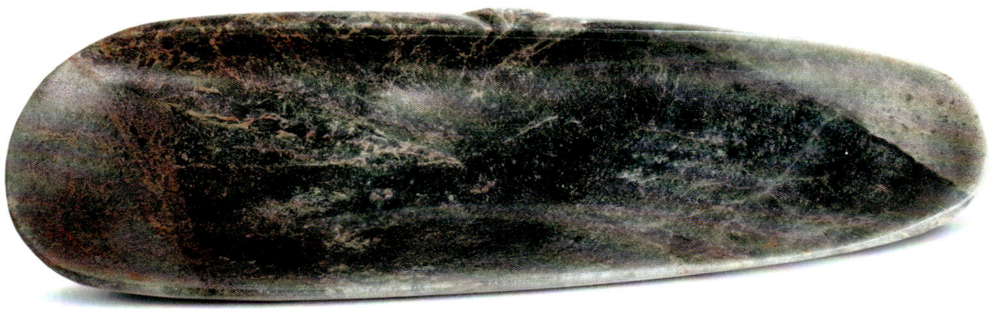

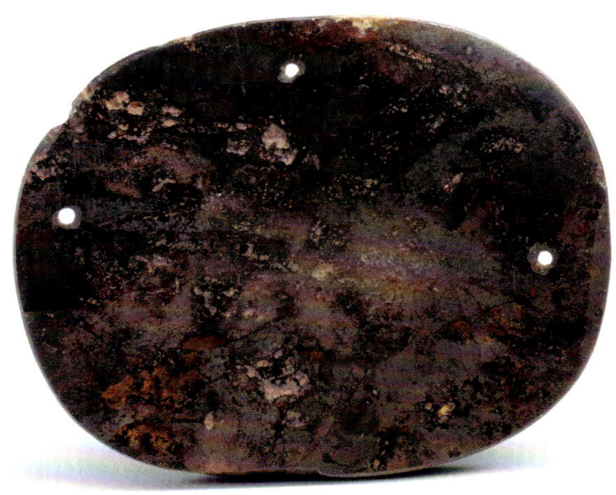

PLATES 73–74

CLAMSHELL PENDANT
Mexico, Tabasco, La Venta, Mound A-2, Tomb A (Columnar Tomb), 900–500 BC
Jadeite
2 1/2 x 7 1/8 x 11/16 in. (6.4 x 18 x 1.7 cm)
Museo Nacional de Antropología, Mexico City (10-3072)

MIRROR
Mexico, Tabasco, La Venta, Mound A-2, Tomb A (Columnar Tomb), 900–500 BC
Magnetite
1 13/16 x 2 5/16 x 1/8 in. (4.6 x 5.9 x 0.3 cm)
Museo Nacional de Antropología, Mexico City (10-7452)

See also:
Drucker 1952a: 23–26, 163, pl. 53

Stirling 1942: pl. 1

Together with the pendant and mirror opposite, this small sculpture was found among the offerings in the Columnar Tomb at La Venta. Part of Bundle 1 (see pl. 18), it depicts a male figure whose face was given a masklike quality. While adhering to the criteria of Gulf Coast style with its simply delineated arms and legs, the figure has an unusual feature in that the arms are not fully separated from the body. Rather, they have holes drilled through at the elbow, suggesting that this figure may have been worn as a pendant (Diehl 1990: cat. 6). MC-LE

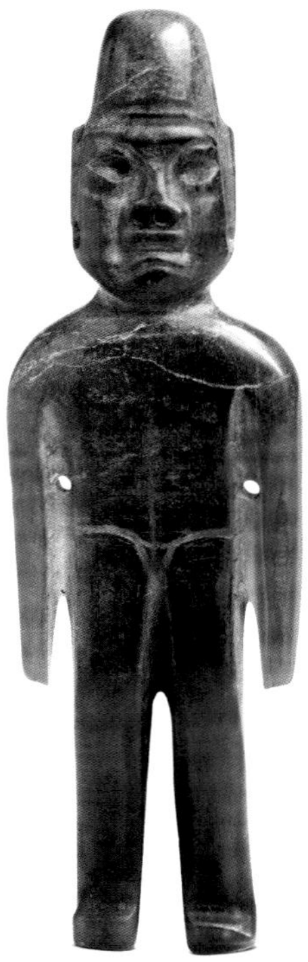

PLATE 75

STANDING FIGURE
Mexico, Tabasco, La Venta, Mound A-2, Tomb A (Columnar Tomb), 900–500 BC
Jadeite
4 5/16 x 1 5/16 x 3/8 in. (11 x 3.3 x 0.9 cm)
Museo Nacional de Antropología, Mexico City (10-3062)

See also:
Castro-Leal 1996: cat. 45
Drucker 1952a: 23–26, 155–156, pls. 47–48
Stirling 1942: pl. 1

This axe was part of a large cache containing 108 jade axes, ornaments, and other objects. Found in the southwest corner of the offering, it was the only object to be decorated (Wedel 1952: 64, 164–166, pl. 56). The upper half of the axe displays the well-known Gulf Coast facial features of flame eyebrows, downturned mouth, and cleft head. The body in the lower half is completely unworked aside from an oval shape suggesting a pendant. Red pigment has been rubbed into the carved and incised lines.

Located to the south of Tomb A (the Columnar Tomb), the slightly rectangular area containing the offering was also covered by basalt columns, but they were irregularly placed and no skeletal remains were found (ibid.). Jadeite ornaments were placed as if adorning a human body, however, leading to the identification of the offering as a tomb (Diehl 1990: cat. 10). MC-LE

PLATE 76

VOTIVE AXE
Mexico, Tabasco, La Venta, Mound A-2,
Tomb E, 900–400 BC
Jadeite with pigment
4 3/8 x 2 x 1/2 in. (11.1 x 5.1 x 1.2 cm)
Museo Nacional de Antropología, Mexico City
(10-9668)

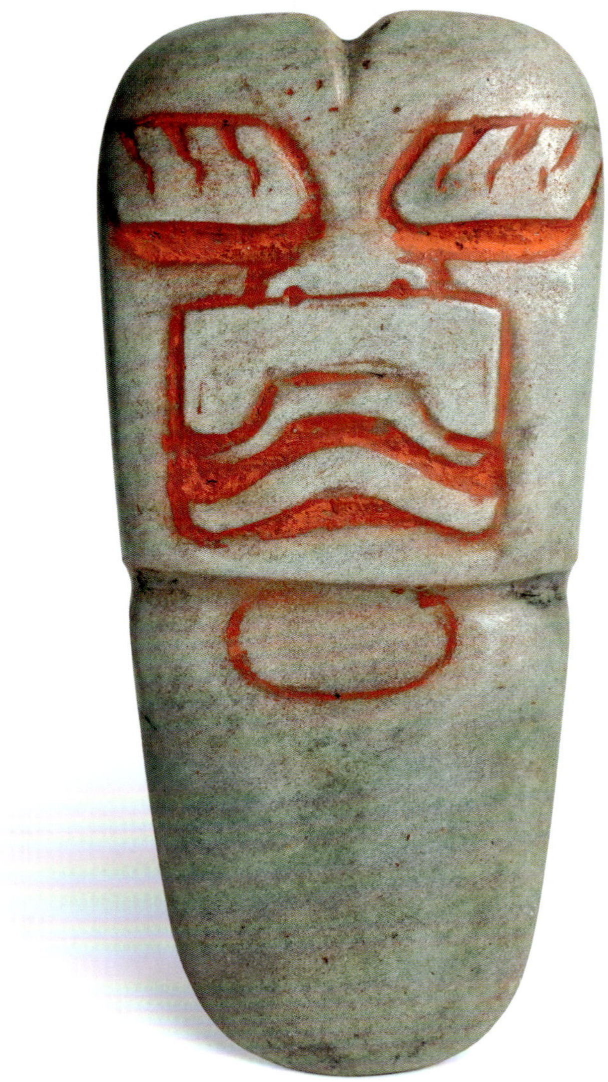

This life-size mask formed part of an offering of jade masks and celts recovered from the Hueyapan stream near La Isla, an Olmec site on the spurs of the Tuxtla Mountains. The piece was originally finely polished to produce a glossy surface; however, it has oxide spots caused by immersion in the water. Both the perforated, almond-shaped eyes and the holes on the sides suggest that the mask was intended to be worn, perhaps for ceremonies. The nose is straight and sharp, and the half-open lips reveal evidence of dental mutilation on the upper incisors. The Olmec and later cultures in Mesoamerica, such as the Maya and the Aztecs, prized jadeite for its color, which varies from jet black to milky white. RLR

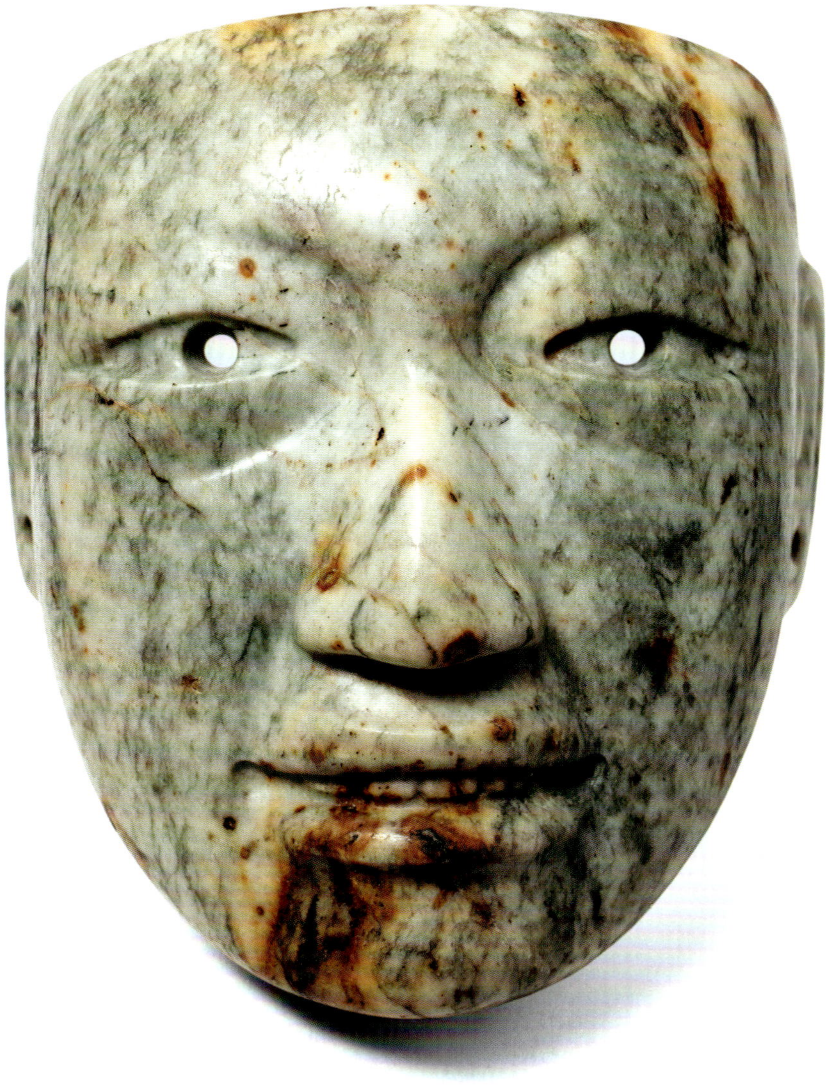

PLATE 77

MASK
Mexico, Veracruz, Hueyapan de Ocampo, 900–400 BC
Jadeite
$6^{3}/_{4} \times 5^{7}/_{8} \times 3^{7}/_{8}$ in. (17 x 15 x 10 cm)
Museo de Antropología de Xalapa, Universidad Veracruzana (10-582842)

This small mask was part of a large offering of jade masks, celts, and figurines found in the Arroyo Pesquero, a rivulet in the swamps of southern Veracruz near La Venta. The discovery was reported by local residents in 1969; archaeologists from the Instituto de Antropología, Universidad Veracruzana, recovered the cache and moved it to the Museo de Antropología de Xalapa. The mask has almond-shaped eyes, a straight, sharp nose, and a half-open mouth expressing laughter. Evidence of dental mutilation can be seen on the upper incisors. It does not have perforated eyeholes, suggesting that it might have been intended for funerary use. The surface of the mask was finely polished and burnished. The ocher tonality of the jadeite was caused by the mask's submersion in water.

For the Olmec, jadeite or greenstone—a stone of metamorphic origin with sources in the Motagua river valley in Guatemala—was of high symbolic value, a result of its association with water or rain. It has been found in large offerings at other Olmec sites including La Venta, Tabasco, and El Manatí and La Merced, Veracruz. RLR

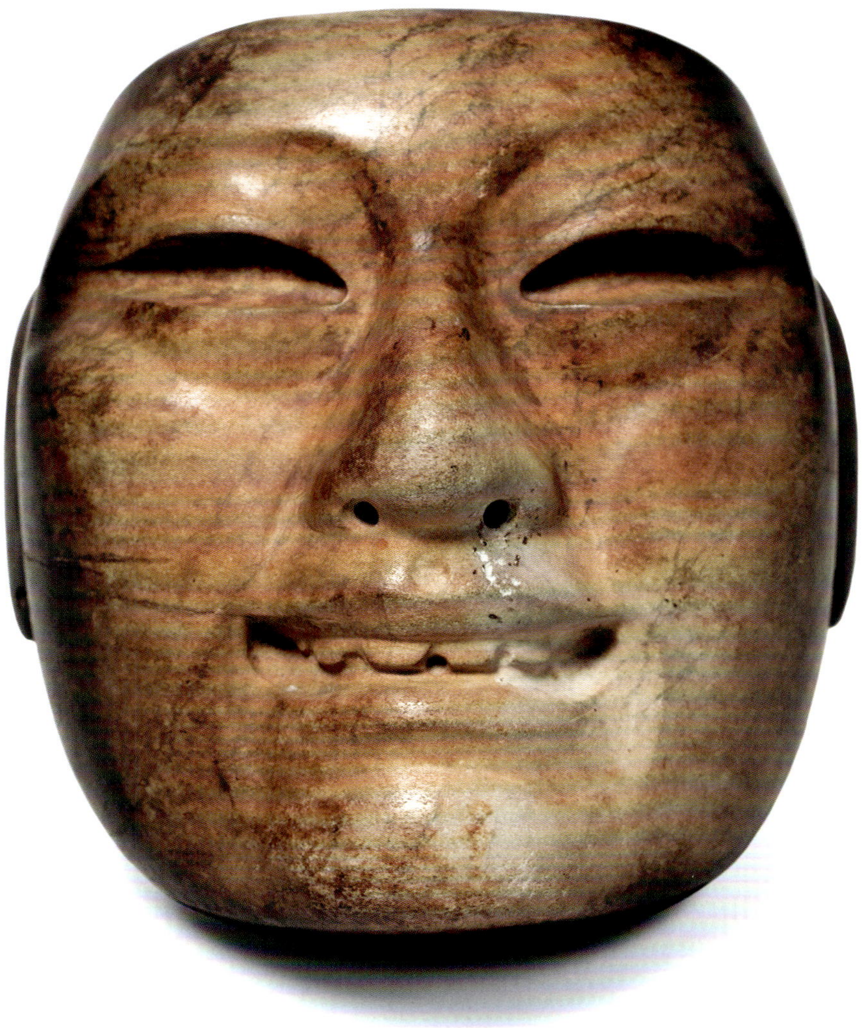

PLATE 78

MASK
Mexico, Veracruz, Municipality of Agua Dulce,
Arroyo Pesquero, 900–400 BC
Jadeite
$5^{1}/_{8}$ x $4^{1}/_{2}$ x $3^{1}/_{8}$ in. (13 x 11.5 x 8 cm)
Museo de Antropología de Xalapa,
Universidad Veracruzana (Reg. 49 P.J. 4009)

First photographed and described by Caecilie Seler-Sachs (1922) and Albert Weyerstall (1932), this elaborately carved stone box was located by Matthew W. Stirling (1943: 18–21, pls. 5–6) in front of the long mound that borders the north side of the plaza of Group 2 at Tres Zapotes. The complex scene, carved in incised plano-relief on all four sides, shows warriors with spears and clubs amid large scrolls that may represent water or clouds. On side A, the best preserved, a deity mask with a wide nose, from which hangs a three-pointed ornament, can be seen at the top. James Porter (1989) sees this deity mask as the elaborate belt ornament of a standing figure. Smaller, fanged deity heads appear amid the scrolls on either side of the central design. A series of small scrolls along the base of this scene and that on the opposite side of the box can be interpreted confidently as representing water.

Monument C is a prime example of the involvement of epi-Olmec Tres Zapotes in trans-isthmian networks of interaction that included Izapa and other prominent sites on the Pacific slope of Chiapas and Guatemala. Very different from earlier Olmec carvings or other Late Formative monuments at Tres Zapotes, the box has several elements—primarily the plano-relief carving technique and the small water scrolls—that link it to the Izapan style of the Pacific Coast and Piedmont of Chiapas and Guatemala. The lack of negative space likewise is profoundly non-Olmec but has a parallel in the "supernarrative" Stela 5 of Izapa.

The function of this and similar boxes from Tres Zapotes is unknown, although it has been suggested that they were receptacles for water, blood offerings, or human remains. Other stones with recessed borders, and in the size and shape to have served as box covers, offer some support for the use as a sarcophagus or altar containing ancestors' remains, though none were found near Monument C. The positioning of the monument at the base of a civic-ceremonial building, as well as its surface location, suggests an altar or ritual receptacle, while the carving is consistent with a theme involving water.

CAP

PLATE 79

MONUMENT C (BOX WITH ELABORATE CARVING)
Mexico, Veracruz, Tres Zapotes, 400–1 BC
Basalt
18 3/8 x 58 1/16 x 39 3/4 in. (46.6 x 147.5 x 101 cm)
Museo Nacional de Antropología, Mexico City (10-1327)

See also:
Coe 1965c: 773
Ortiz Ceballos and Rodriguez M. 1994: 74, fig. 5.1
Pool 2007: 255, fig. 7.7
Williams and Heizer 1965: 15

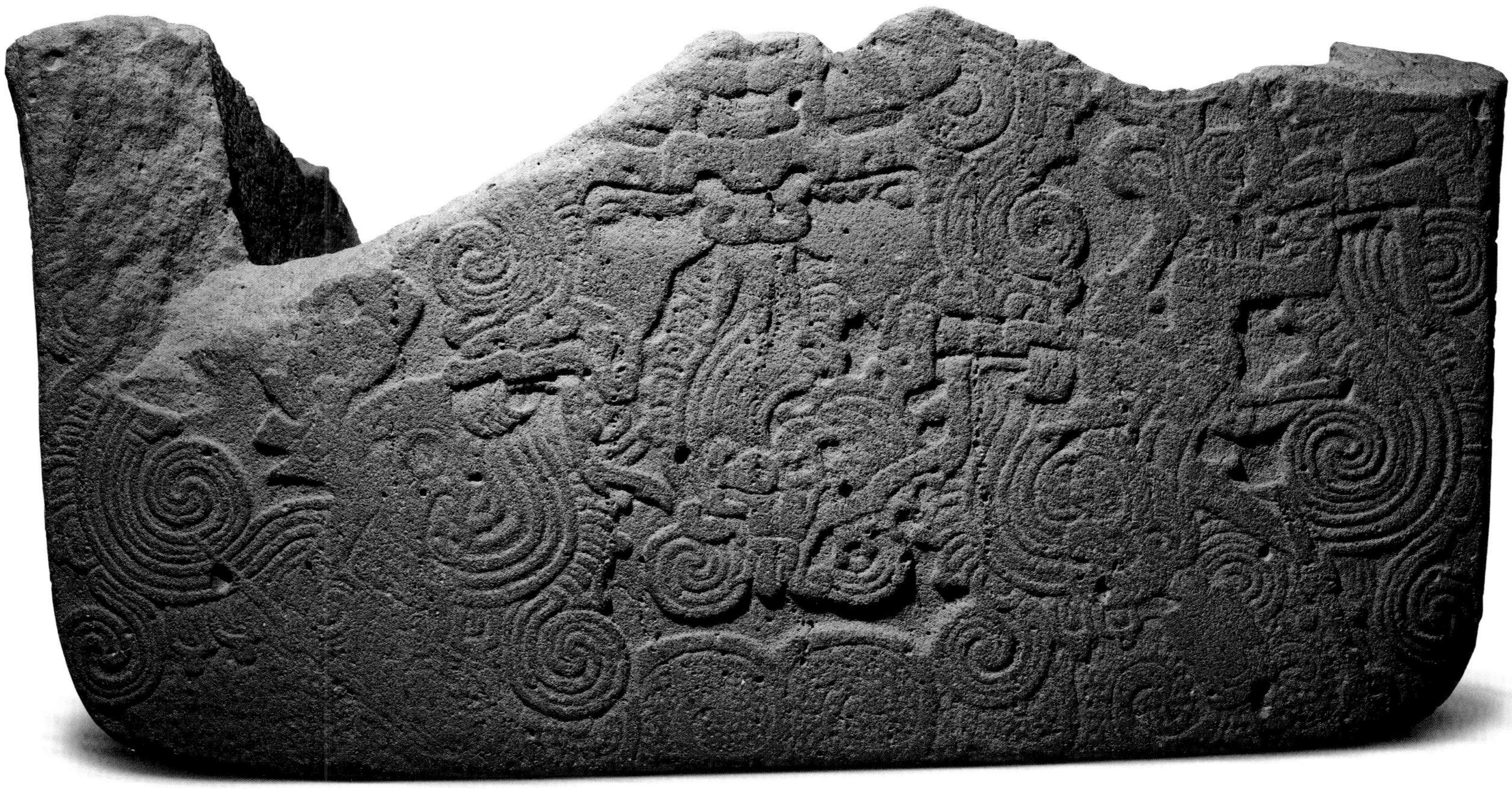

The most famous monument from Tres Zapotes, Stela C was broken into at least three parts in antiquity. This segment was the first to be found by Matthew W. Stirling in 1939. It is the lowest segment to have been recovered, but the fracture at its base indicates a lower segment existed at one point. The uppermost segment was recovered thirty years later in the same general area of Tres Zapotes (see fig. 29 for renderings of both sections, front and back). Stirling found this section at the foot of the largest mound in Group 3, then the northernmost group at Tres Zapotes. It had been set on its side behind a rough, round altar, and no apparent concern was shown for the orientation of the mask on the front of the stela or the inscription on its back.

The front (not shown) bears the relief carving of a stylized earth monster mask, clearly derived from Olmec imagery. The monster's bifurcated eyebrows appear on the upper segment. Above them is a quadripartite medallion from which emerges a human head in profile amid curving branches—a forceful image of the ruler as the central world tree, or axis mundi, connecting the underworld, the earthly surface, and the heavens.

Stela C owes its fame, however, to the date in the Long Count calendrical system carved on its back, possibly long after the carving of the front. The first coefficient of the date was broken off with the upper segment, but Marion Stirling reconstructed it as the numeral 7, resulting in a date of 7.16.6.16.18 6 Etz'nab, which, by the most commonly accepted correlation of the Long Count and western calendars, fell on September 3, 32 BC. This made it the earliest dated monument from Mesoamerica recovered to that time, causing considerable consternation among Mayanists. The date was confirmed in 1969 when the upper portion of the monument was recovered.

CAP

PLATE 80

STELA C
Mexico, Veracruz, Tres Zapotes, 32 BC
Basalt
Middle section: 32 7/16 x 43 1/8 x 13 1/16 in.
(82.4 x 109.5 x 33.1 cm)
Museo Nacional de Antropología,
Mexico City (10-320)

See also:
Arnold 2000: 136, 138, 147, 149–150, figs. 2, 18
Bernal 1969: 95–96, pls. 18b, 46
Coe 1968a: 141–143
Pool 2007: 41–42, fig. 2.3
Stirling 1940a

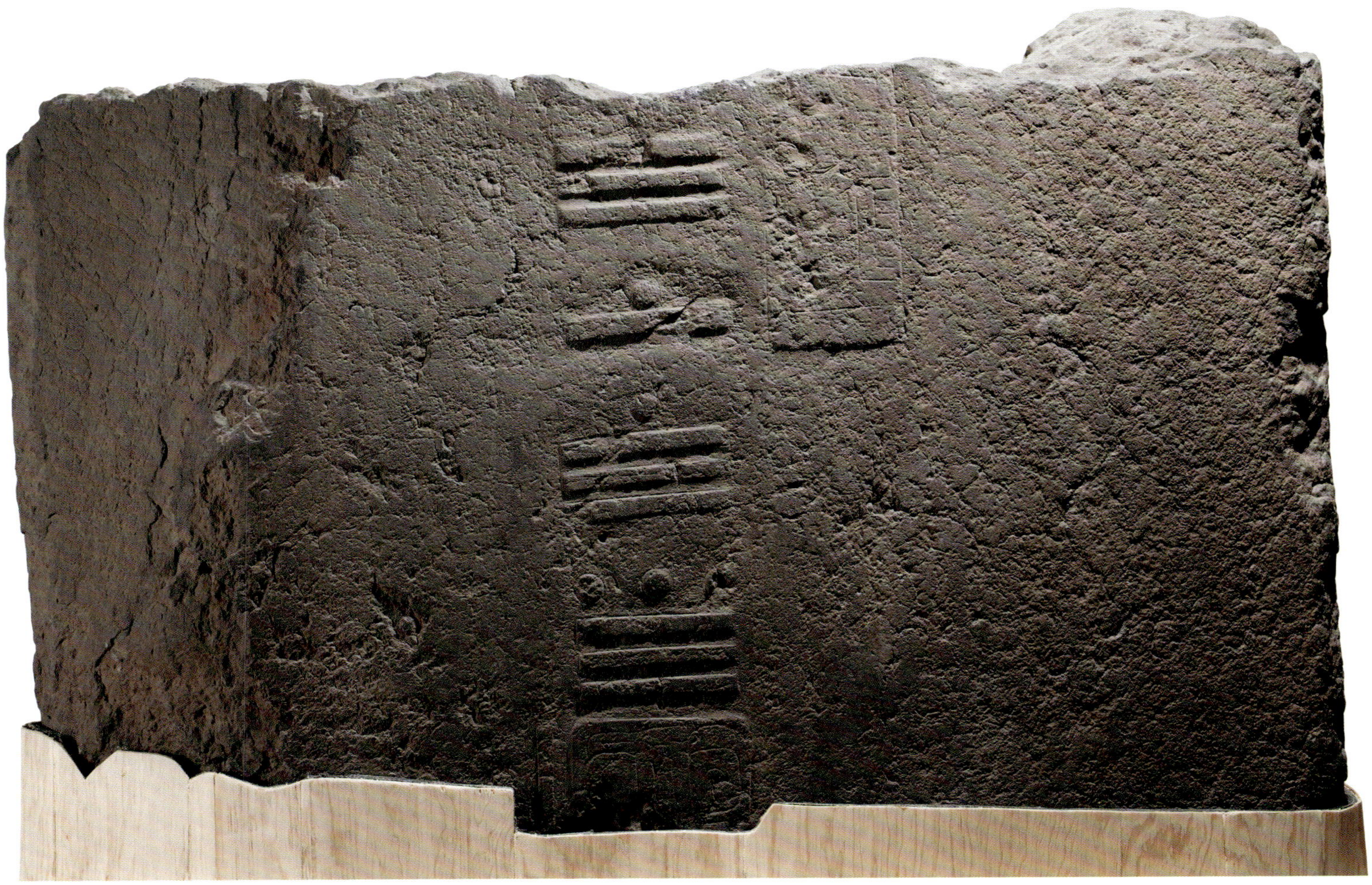

Matthew W. Stirling found Monument M in winter 1938–1939, on level ground between "a good-sized mound" and the west bank of the Arroyo Hueyapan, about half a mile upstream from Group 3. He photographed it and described it as

> a seated figure, somewhat reminiscent in style of that from La Venta.... The features, although somewhat eroded, are of modified "baby-face" style. The head is rather long and flat. It is about 4 feet high. The arms and legs were broken off, presumably in ancient times. During the interval between our two seasons...one of the natives dragged it by means of oxen to the edge of the village, where the head broke off and where the figure now lies [Stirling 1943: 24].

Art collectors acquired the head in the 1950s, and Monument M was lost to the academic world until 2009. Whoever sold the head likely identified it as coming from La Venta, because Olmec archaeology at that time focused on Philip Drucker's excavations there, and such a provenance would have enhanced the object's value.

In the 1990s, Perry Draper suggested to his professor, David Grove, that the head, now in the Museo Amparo, belonged to Tres Zapotes Monument M. Early in 2009, Grove contacted me to ask my opinion. We found fractures and imperfections strongly suggesting that the Amparo head and the monument in Stirling's photographs (1943: pls. 11b–d; fig. 26, this volume) were the same. In summer 2009, I was able to examine the monument closely, confirming the existence of the imperfections and that the monument's basalt was consistent with basalts near Tres Zapotes. Most important, however, the reddish patina—still evident on the back, sides, and top of the head—had been removed from the face, demonstrating that it had been recarved, perhaps to enhance its aesthetic appeal.

Recarving removed material above and below the lips, accentuating them and separating them from the nose and the chin. The nose was slightly reshaped to emphasize the flare of the nostrils. The eyes were heavily recarved, apparently to restore their original outline; their slight almond shape is not evident in Stirling's photographs. The front was retouched overall to remove the patina and allow the recarved features to blend in with the rest of the face. The original patina is still evident in aspects of the cheeks and depressions in the ear tabs.

The head nonetheless retains its rectangular-block shape. The V-shaped fracture at the head's base perfectly matches a crack seen in Stirling's photograph, as does an imperfection curving across the head's upper right corner. Not shown or mentioned by Stirling is a shallow depression in the top, apparently original to the piece, that is reminiscent of the V-shaped notch occurring frequently in Olmec monuments, including San Lorenzo Monument 52 (pl. 9) and the Las Limas "were-jaguar" baby. CAP

PLATE 81

MONUMENT M (ANTHROPOMORPHIC HEAD)
Mexico, Veracruz, Tres Zapotes, 500–300 BC
Basalt
$19\frac{1}{2} \times 13\frac{3}{4} \times 13\frac{13}{16}$ in. (49.5 x 35 x 34.5 cm)
Museo Amparo, Puebla (MA FA 57PJ 1084)

See also:
Bonifaz Nuño 1993: 82–83
Cervantes 2008: 43–44
de la Fuente 1973: 303–304

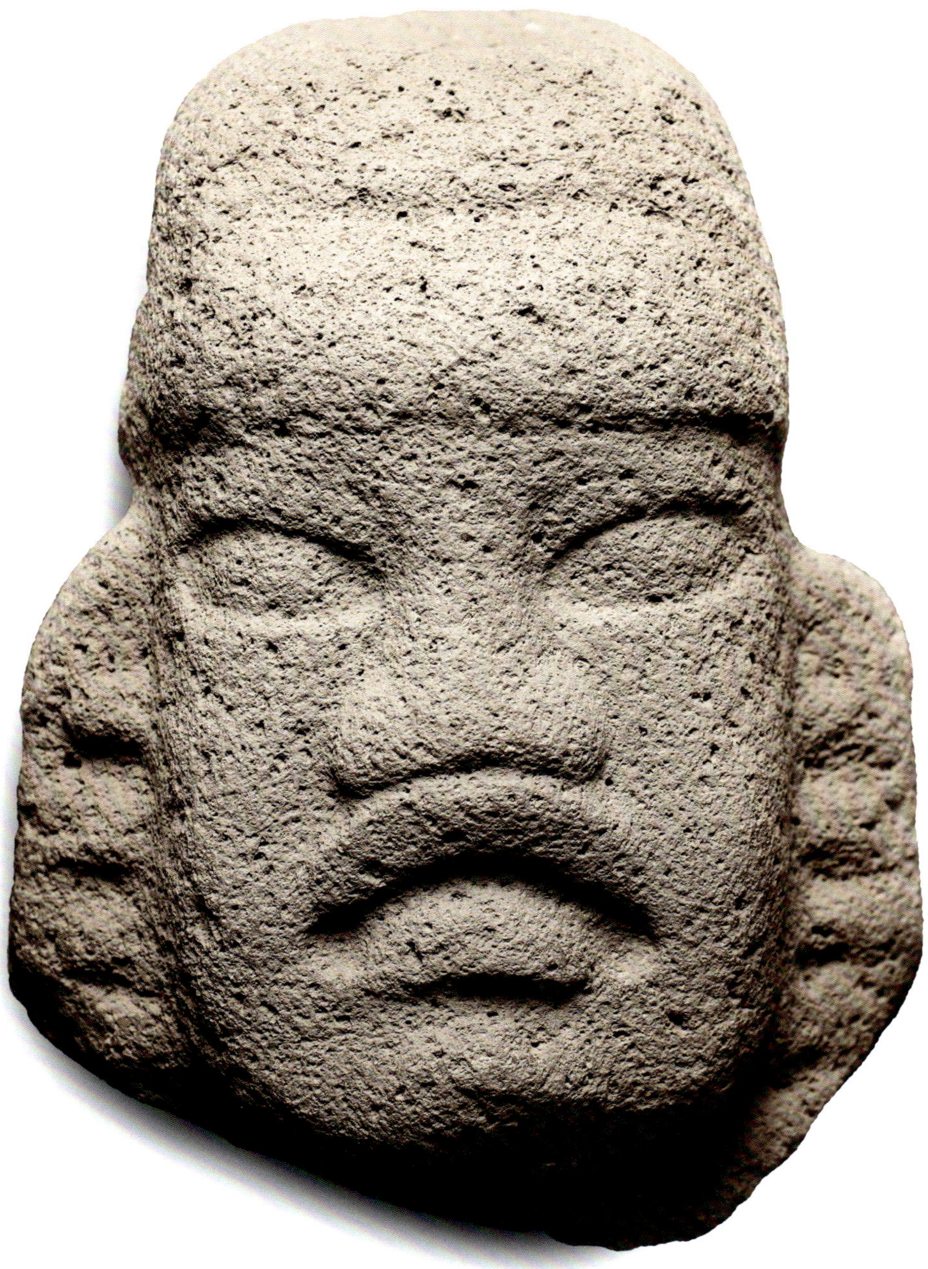

This monument has amorphous contours on the upper and back sides; a cavity in the top might be related to its use as an incense burner. Typical Olmec facial features include an eye in the shape of an X motif, the down-turned mouth with thick lips, two bifurcated fangs pointed slightly outward, and a cleft tooth. Another head at Laguna de los Cerros, Monument 2, is similar to this, although it has different designs on the eyes and snout. Because the site of Laguna de los Cerros lacks the colossal head-throne complex found at the heartland sites of San Lorenzo Tenochtitlán and La Venta, it may be classified as a secondary Olmec center. This head was discovered between 1959 and 1960 by the archaeologist Alfonso Medellín Zeñil and was moved to the Museo de Antropología de Xalapa in 1960.
RLR

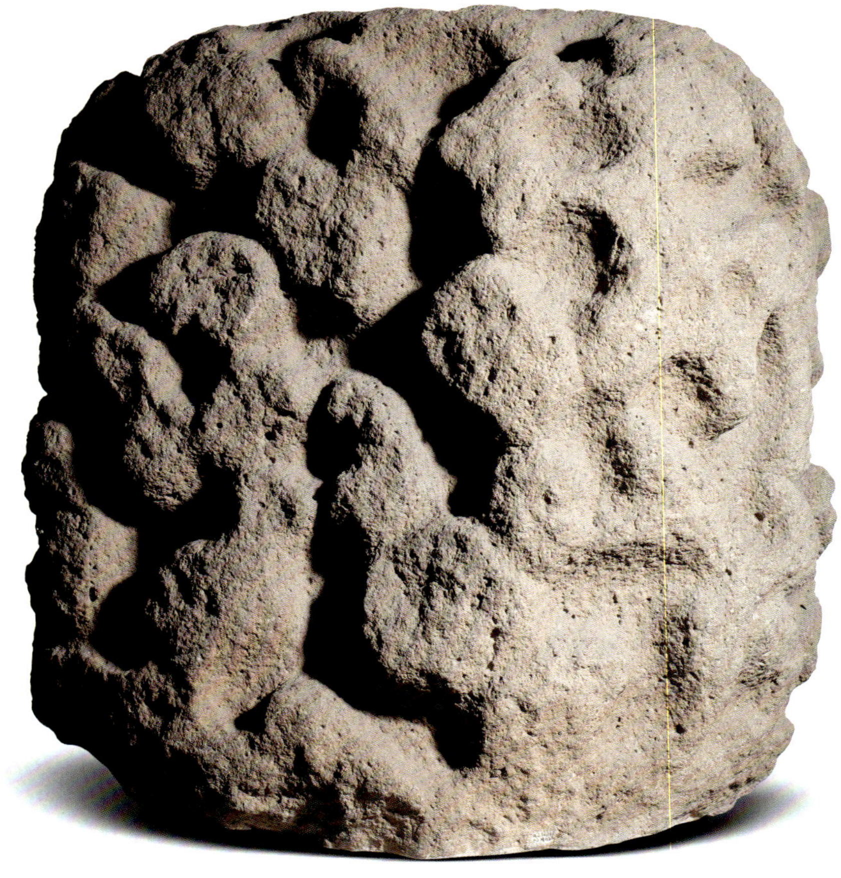

PLATES 82–83

MONUMENT 1 (HEAD OF SUPERNATURAL BEING)
Mexico, Veracruz, Municipality of Acayucan, Laguna de los Cerros, 1200–900 BC
Basalt
$31\frac{1}{8} \times 26\frac{3}{4} \times 27\frac{9}{16}$ in. (79 x 68 x 70 cm)
Museo de Antropología de Xalapa, Universidad Veracruzana (Reg. 49 P.J. 4022)

See also:
de la Fuente 1977a: 261–263, pl. 18, ill. 70
de la Fuente 2000: 258, fig. 13

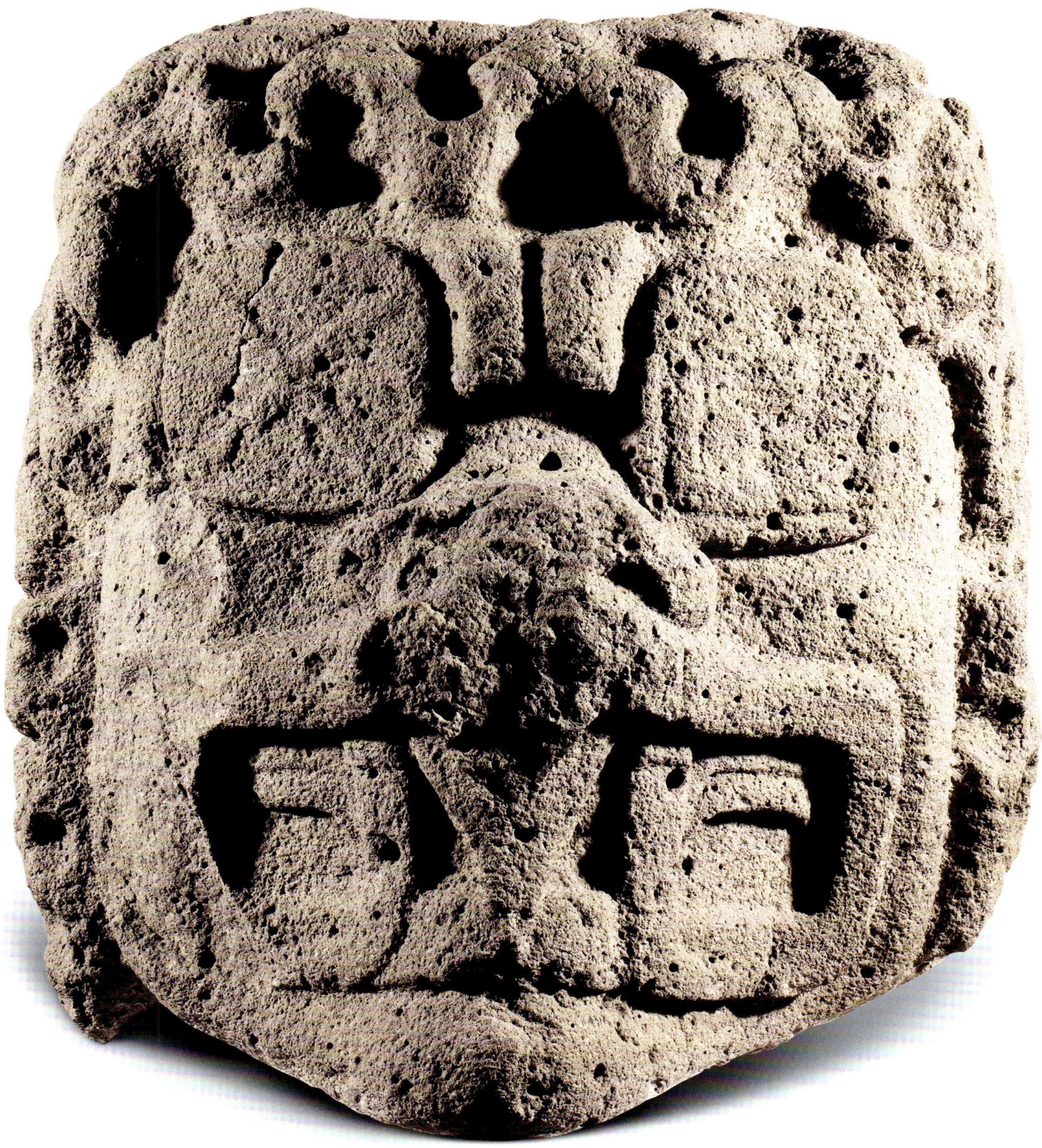

This monument is the only known representation of a life-size, standing Olmec male figure. It was decapitated and dismembered in ancient times, perhaps during an event marking the transfer of power. The figure's cape is knotted at the neck with a tie that has four Olmec dragon heads on its sides. The belt or sash is made of cords that fall in the front to form the figure's loincloth. The arms, which are broken at the elbows, might once have held an object such as an offering. On the upper part of the back can be seen braided hair. The unique standing position of this monument may indicate that the figure represented someone with high status, perhaps a ruler or leader of Laguna de los Cerros. Discovered between 1959 and 1960 by Alfonso Medellín Zeñil, the figure was moved to the Museo de Antropología de Xalapa in 1960. RLR

PLATE 84

MONUMENT 19 (STANDING FIGURE)
Mexico, Veracruz, Municipality of Acayucan, Laguna de los Cerros, 1200–1000 BC
Basalt
61⅞ x 30$^{5}/_{16}$ x 21¼ in. (157 x 77 x 54 cm)
Museo de Antropología de Xalapa, Universidad Veracruzana (Reg. 49 P.J. 333)

See also:
de la Fuente 1977a: 273–274, 280, ill. 78
de la Fuente 1994: 209, fig. 13.3
de la Fuente 2000: 258, fig. 11
Proskouriakoff 1968: 126, fig. 6

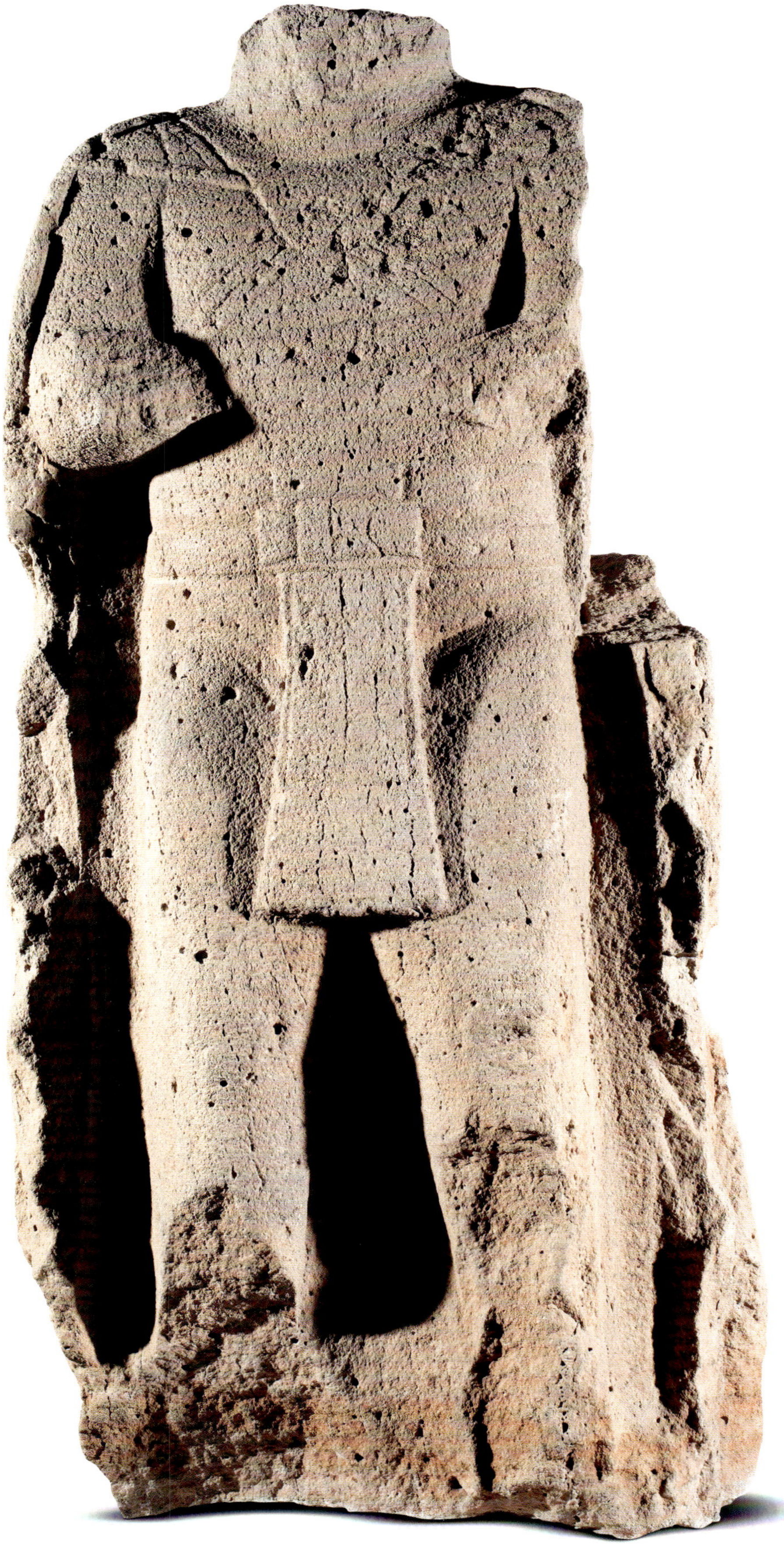

Referred to as "The Prince," this sculpture was found in 1960 by residents of the town of Cruz del Milagro while they were digging a pit to store water; it was moved to the Museo de Antropología de Xalapa by Alfonso Medellín Zeñil that same year. The figure represents a human male seated with his legs crossed and his arms resting lightly in front of his body. He wears earflares and a helmet, which covers his entire head and seems to be made of rigid leather with a vertical projection and an emblem associated with the planet Venus in the front. His almond-shaped eyes, wide nose, and thick lips display great realism, as does the sculptural quality of his muscular body, which is similar to the monument known as "The Wrestler" from Antonio Plaza, Veracruz. The figure here may represent a local leader or ruler under the control of a more important site such as San Lorenzo or the nearby Laguna de los Cerros. RLR

PLATE 85

MONUMENT 1 (SEATED FIGURE)
Mexico, Veracruz, Municipality of Sayula de Alemán, Cruz del Milagro, 1200–900 BC
Basalt
$49^{3}/_{16}$ x $33^{1}/_{16}$ x $39^{3}/_{8}$ in. (125 x 84 x 100 cm)
Museo de Antropología de Xalapa, Universidad Veracruzana (Reg. 49 P.J. 4023)

See also:
de la Fuente 1996a: cat. 7
de la Fuente 1996b: 41
Easby and Scott 1970: cat. 4

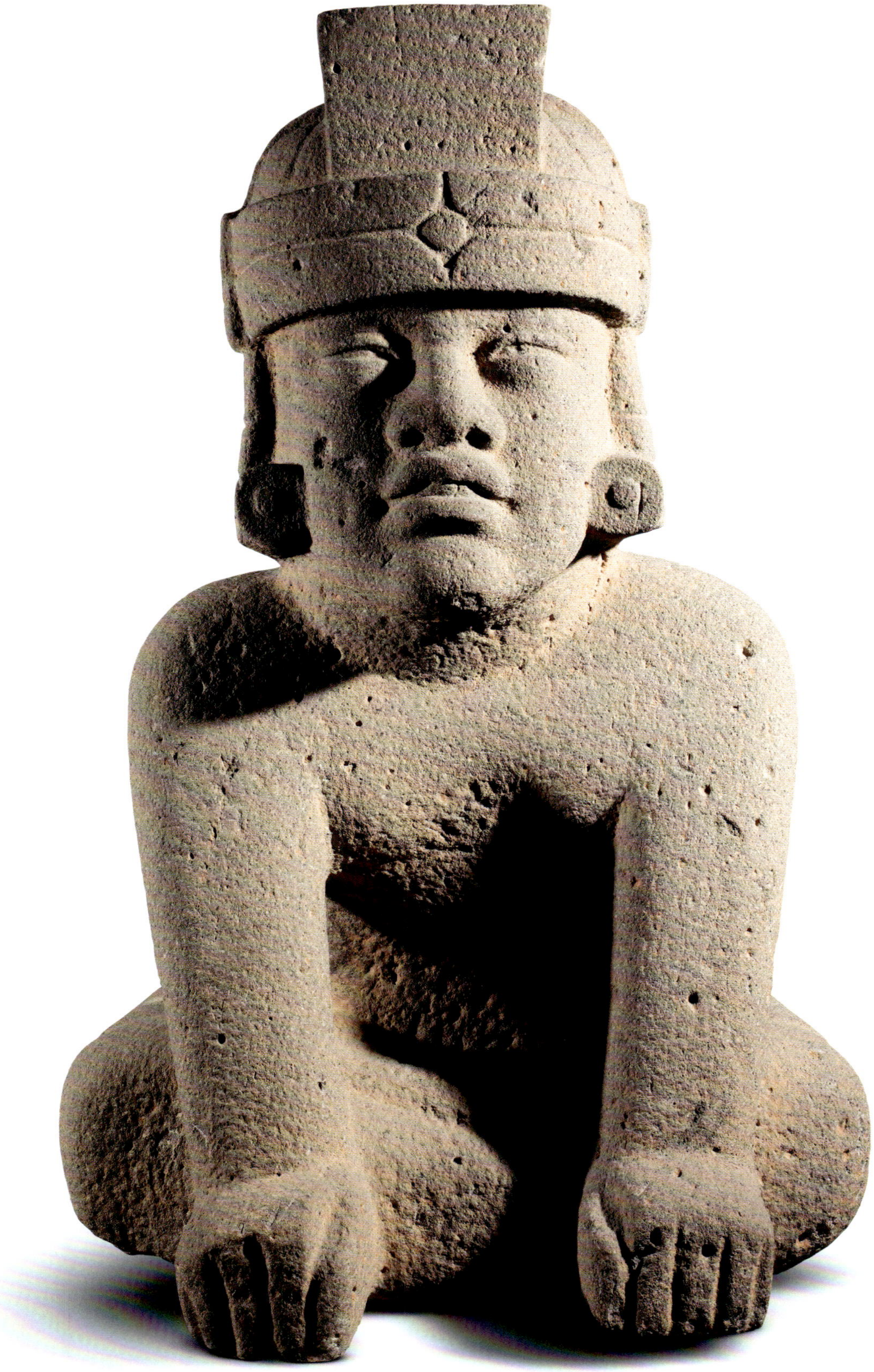

Matthew W. Stirling (1955: 8) first saw this monument in 1945 in the village of Tenochtitlán, but its specific archaeological context is unknown (Coe and Diehl 1980, vol. 1: 370–372). Michael Coe and Richard Diehl suggest that, although the monument is heavily damaged, it may depict a female figure lying on a base with a half-kneeling male figure—who wears a mirror-shaped pendant, belt, and loincloth—on top of her. Stirling's initial impression was that the monument signified a scene of copulation between an anthropomorphized jaguar and a human woman. Alfonso Medellín Zeñil (1960: 95) and subsequent scholars (Davis 1978; Reilly and Garber 2003) contend that it portrays a victor dominating a captive, a more convincing argument in light of such depictions in later Mesoamerican civilizations (Cyphers 2004b: 219–221). MC-LE

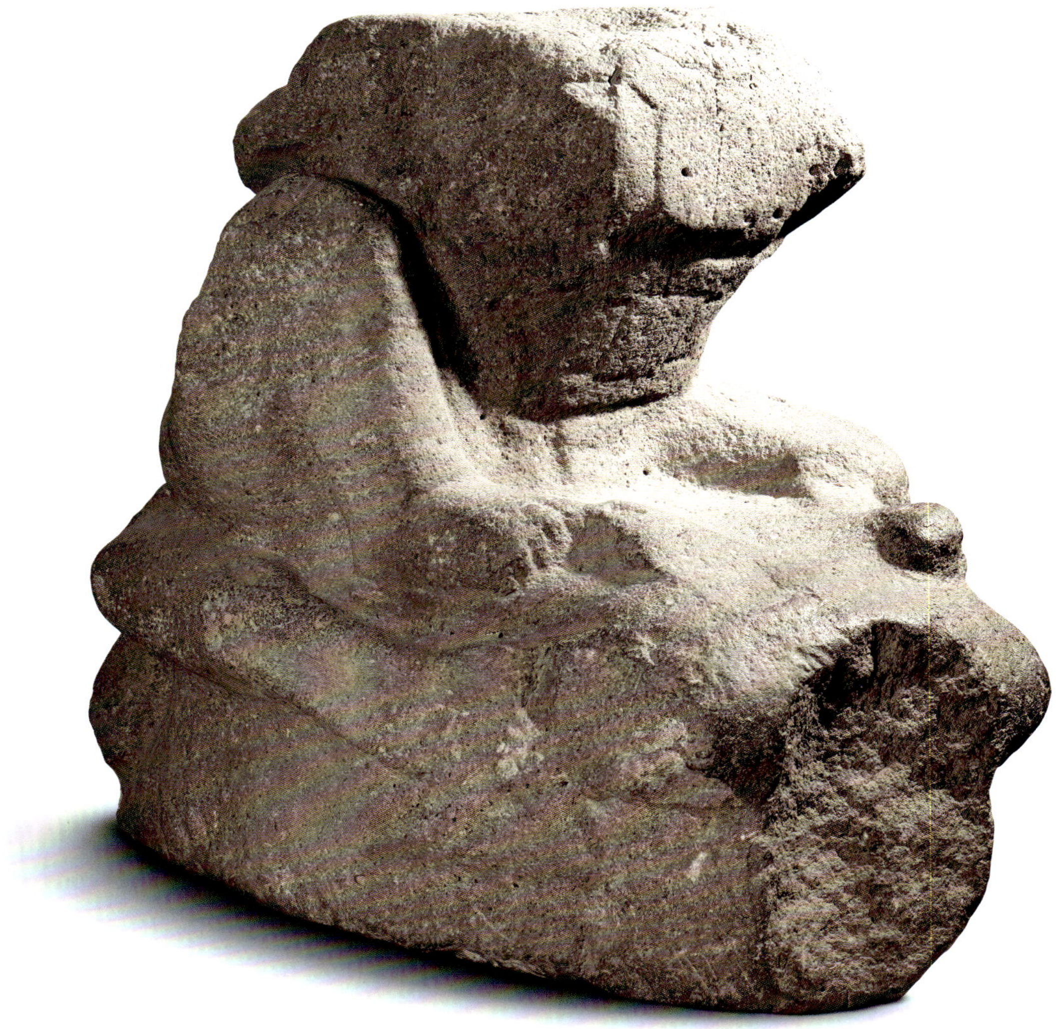

PLATE 86

MONUMENT 1
(VICTOR AND CAPTIVE)
Mexico, Veracruz, Municipality of Texistepec, San Lorenzo Tenochtitlán, 1000–400 BC
Basalt
$31\frac{1}{2} \times 33\frac{7}{16} \times 20\frac{7}{8}$ in. (80 x 85 x 53 cm)
Museo Nacional de Antropología, Mexico City
(10-627804)

This sculpture shows a human figure in an unusual position, with his feet on his head. It may have been rendered as part of a ceremony; play, music, and dance came together in rituals and were connected in religious contexts in Olmec life. Contortionists participated in these ceremonies, as seen in this bas-relief and in several other circular monuments depicting figures in a similar pose (Pérez Suárez 2008).

Alfonso Medellín Zeñil (1978) first published the monument, noting that it seemed to come from the site of Arroyo Pesquero, located in the present-day town of Las Choapas, southwest of the ancient city of La Venta (Pérez Suárez 2008: 116–117). The pose of the figure was compared to a similar relief published by Roberto García Moll (1979), and both were related to the well-known acrobat figure excavated from Tlatilco Burial 164. This monument is intended to be perceived as a three-dimensional acrobat, although it is rendered as a two-dimensional relief. Karl Taube (2005) has suggested that the acrobatic pose characterizes the maize god in both Olmec and early Maya depictions. MC-LE

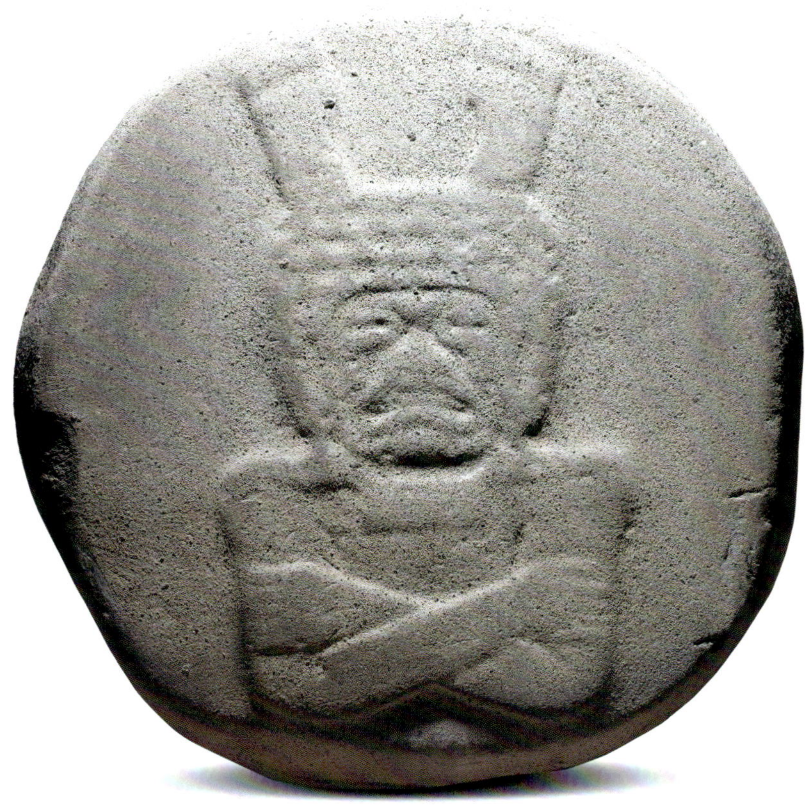

PLATE 87

CONTORTIONIST
Mexico, Veracruz, Las Choapas, 1200–600 BC
Stone
$22^{11}/_{16}$ x $6^{5}/_{8}$ in. (57.7 x 16.8 cm)
Museo Nacional de Antropología, Mexico City
(10-162410)

These celts, or axelike forms, were part of a cruciform offering of thirty-seven celts that was deeply buried in Mound A-2. Over the course of two seasons of excavation, caches containing several hundred celts were discovered at La Venta, but only four were incised. Earlier deposits of plain axes at El Manatí and La Merced connoted agricultural ritual (see pls. 37–48, 50–57). After 900 BC, celts were occasionally incised with symbolic motifs and laid out in caches in specific ritual patterns (Drucker 1952a; Taube 2000). The motifs most commonly allude to metaphors of maize as the life-sustaining plant of Mesoamerican societies and as the defining royal symbol for Mexico's earliest rulers (Fields 1989; Taube 1996).

These axes are incised with motifs associated with the Olmec maize god. One axe displays a distinctive pattern consistently found on celts: a stylized maize cob and flanking leaves above a central bar with four scalloped elements that signal the four-cornered cosmos, itself a metaphor for the maize field. The central axis simultaneously represents the world tree that links the layered cosmos, a maize plant, and the ruler himself in the guise of the maize god, presiding over this sacred realm.

The other axe is personified and shows a pair of eyes below a headband with a stylized maize plant in the center flanked by a pair of smaller cobs. Two hands clutch two cut-shell objects. This horizontal arrangement of the four-part motif and central axis equally describes the unparalleled significance of maize to Mesoamerican societies and the royal responsibility to ensure its ongoing abundance. VMF

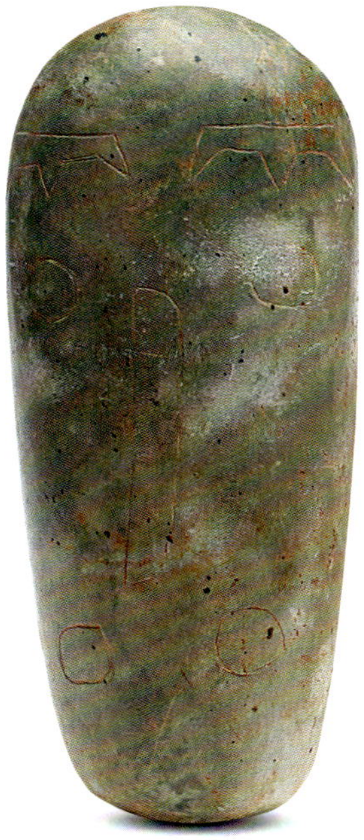

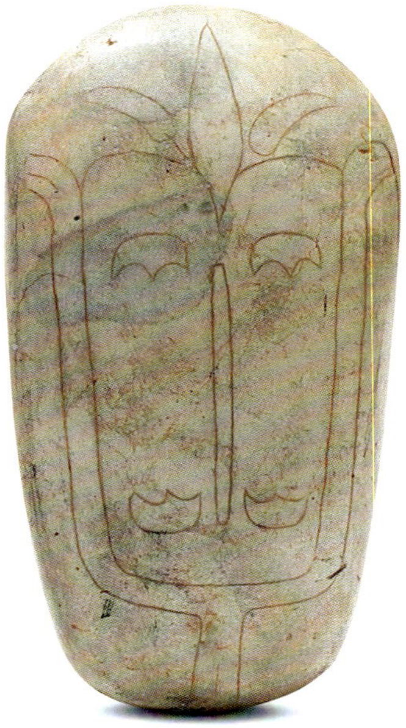

PLATES 88–89

INCISED CELTS
Mexico, Tabasco, La Venta, Mound A-2, 900–400 BC
Jadeite
5 7/8 x 2 7/16 x 1 5/8 in.; 5 1/2 x 3 x 1 1/4 in.
(14.9 x 6.2 x 4.1 cm; 14 x 7.6 x 3.1 cm)
Museo Nacional de Antropología, Mexico City
(10-3069, 10-9623)

See also:
Benson 1971: 22, 26, fig. 30
Bernal 1969: 80, fig. 11
Diehl 1990: cat. 11
Drucker 1952a: 27, 165–166, figs. 10b, 47a–b

The face of the Olmec maize god dominates the top half of this celt. A banded maize plant emerges from the cleft of his head, branching into three representations of the Olmec-style maize seed. The X motif above the god's brow, extending in four directions, may refer to the ritual circuit performed during the first planting of the maize crop, a practice continued by traditionalist Maya farmers in highland Guatemala (Allen Christenson, personal communication, June 2005). The banded maize plant emerging from the center of the X motif simultaneously represents the central axis of the four-cornered cosmos/maize field, signaling that the incised design may be perceived in three dimensions (Reilly 1995: 39). VMF

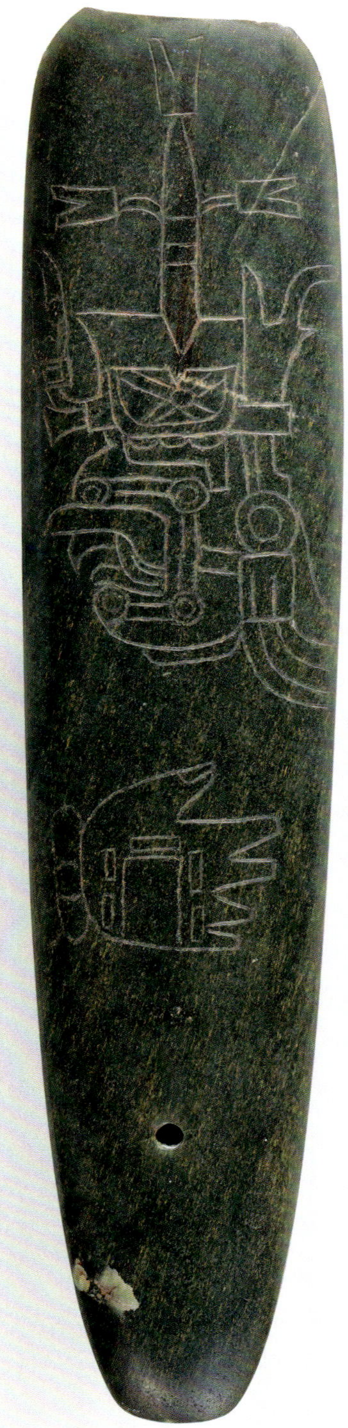

PLATE 90

CELT WITH INCISED HUMAN PROFILE AND HAND MOTIF
Mexico, Tabasco, 1000–400 BC
Jadeite
$14^{3}/_{8}$ x $3^{1}/_{8}$ in. (36.5 x 7.9 cm)
Metropolitan Museum of Art, The Michael C. Rockefeller Memorial Collection, gift of Nelson A. Rockefeller, 1963 (1978.412.5)

See also:
Fields and Reents-Budet 2005: cat. 13

Joralemon 1996: cat. 116

This pendant is pierced with two drilled, biconical holes so that it may be worn horizontally (Taube 2004: 132). The incised design shows three well-known Olmec motifs joined in a vertical column. As described by Karl Taube, the top motif is the trefoil maize plant, the central circle is defined as a maize seed-corn dot, and the squared U at the bottom may itself constitute a variant of the cleft celt motif.

The upper half of the larger axe is dominated by the Olmec-style snarling face, here shown with the squared eyes and simple headband also seen on San Lorenzo Monument 10 (pls. 30–31). The lower half depicts a quincunx pattern of four dots and a central axis. Above the quincunx are two inverted serrated motifs that also adorn the cleft element above San Lorenzo Monument 52 (pl. 9). VMF

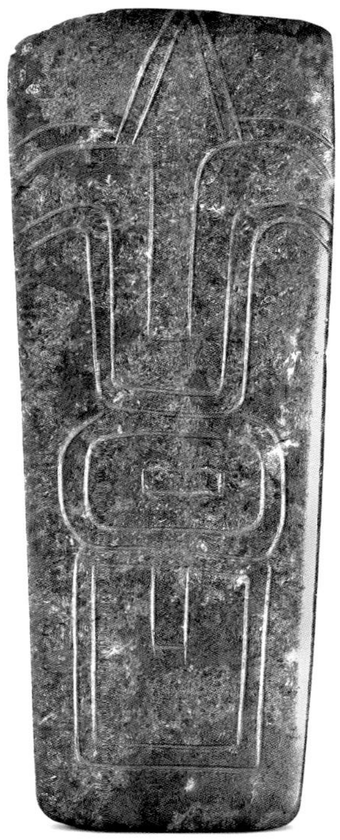

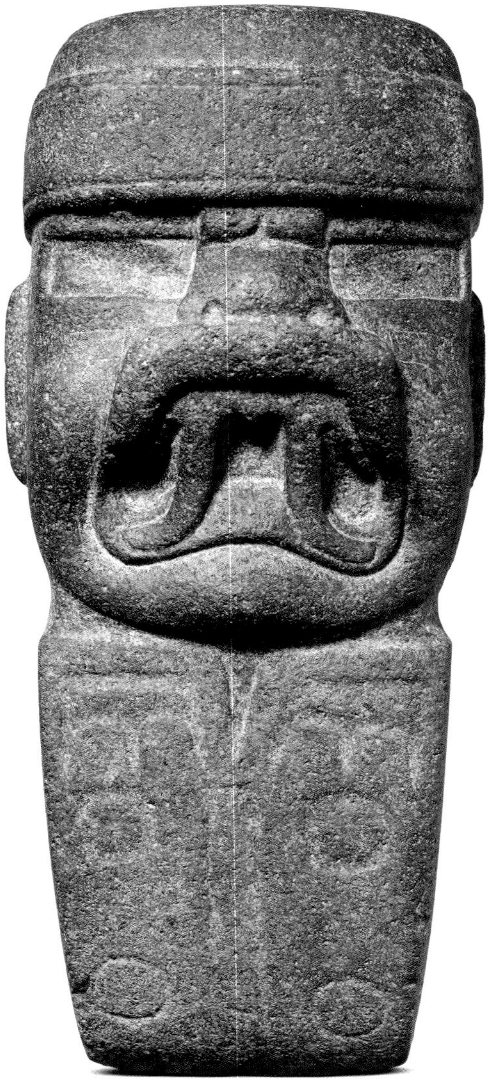

PLATES 91–92

CELT PENDANT
Mexico, 900–300 BC
Diopside jadeite
$6^{1}/_{2}$ x $2^{1}/_{2}$ x $^{1}/_{4}$ in. (16.5 x 6.4 x 0.6 cm)
Dumbarton Oaks Research Library and Collection (B-23)

CELT WITH DEITY
Mexico, Guerrero, 1000–300 BC
Stone
$12^{11}/_{16}$ x $5^{1}/_{2}$ x $4^{1}/_{2}$ in. (32.2 x 14 x 11.5 cm)
Cleveland Museum of Art, gift of the Hanna Fund (1954.856)

The image on this axe differs from most others in depicting the full figure of an elaborately dressed man striding forward and carrying a staff or other implement (Joralemon 1996: cat. 119). The figure wears a hipcloth and belt, knee and ankle bands, and a short, feathered cape associated with avian symbolism (see pl. 17). His face is in profile, a squared element covers his mouth, and a symbol that resembles the Maya *kan* cross, associated with maize abundance and the color yellow, covers his eye. He wears a headband adorned with two maize seeds; the other side of his headband would have depicted two more, separated by a central medallion signified by the oval element floating in front. His stacked headdress features a profile face above the headband, which may be a compressed figure of a supernatural shown with a hand clutching two implements. At the top of the headdress is a simplified version of the maize god with a cob emerging from his central cleft. The image resembles that on a vessel from the Valley of Mexico (pl. 129), on which can be seen the X motif in the mouth, oval eye, and cleft forehead. VMF

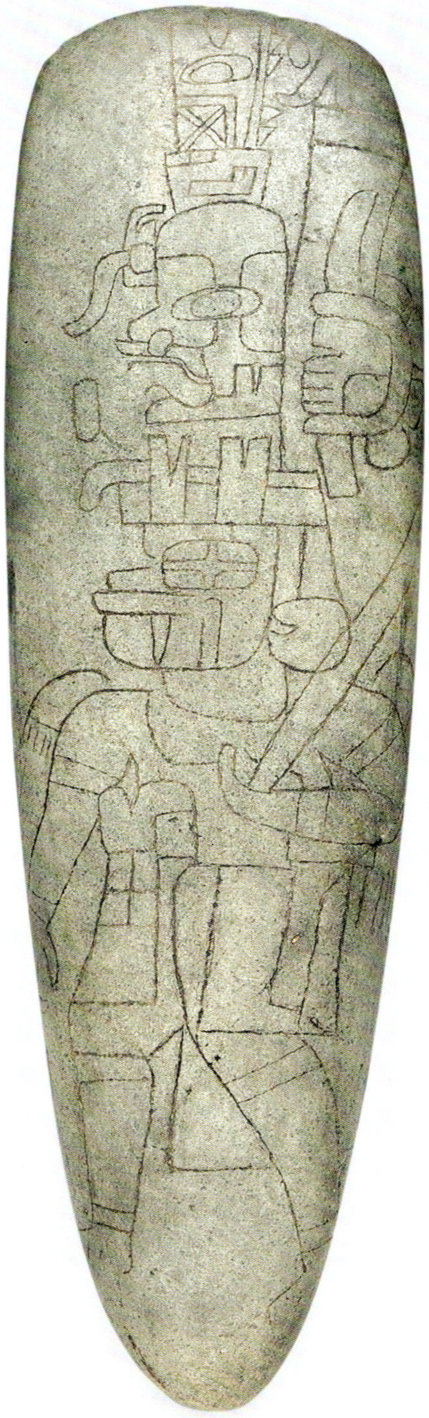

PLATE 93

INCISED CELT
Mexico, Guerrero, 900–500 BC
Jadeite
11 x 3 1/8 x 1 1/2 in. (27.9 x 7.9 x 3.8 cm)
Dallas Museum of Art, Dallas Art Association purchase (1970.18)

See also:
Princeton University 1995: cat. 216

Realistic portraiture is a defining feature of Olmec sculpture, seen in both monumental scale in the colossal heads and in exquisite, small-scale figurines and stone masks. Ceramic figurines are abundant in the archaeological record from the Early Formative period (1200–900 BC), portraying males and females in distinctive clothing, such as the ballplayers from Central Mexico described by Christine Niederberger (2000). During the subsequent Middle Formative period (900–400 BC), Olmec artists rendered the human figure in jadeite, most often as standing figures with their arms at their sides, minimal incised decoration on the body, and elongated heads with delicately carved features. Many monuments were deliberately mutilated, resulting in headless figures (see pl. 84), and the occasional monumental head is found without its body (pl. 29). The smaller jadeite figures suffered similar breakage unless they were carefully protected like the tableau of figures in La Venta Offering 4 (pl. 72). These heads—with their almond-shaped or slightly downturned eyes, elongated foreheads, and downturned, fleshy mouths—individually capture the signature theme of portraiture and the essence of the Olmec artistic style. VMF

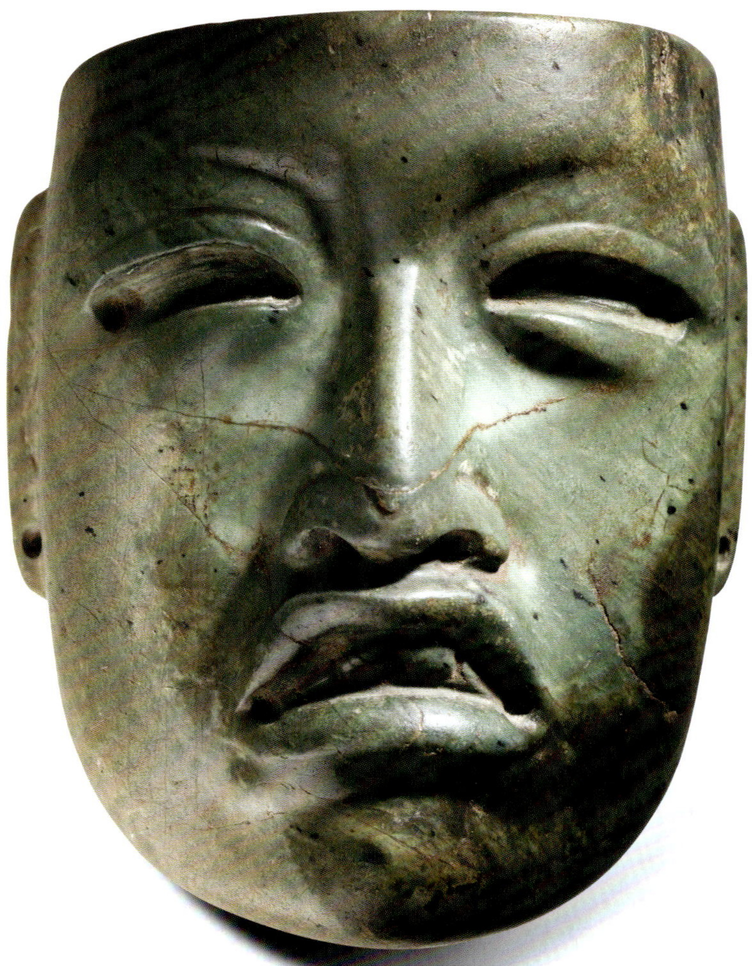

PLATE 94

MASK
Mexico, 900–600 BC
Jadeite with traces of cinnabar
Height: 4 in. (10.2 cm)
Los Angeles County Museum of Art, gift of Constance McCormick Fearing (AC1992.134.2)

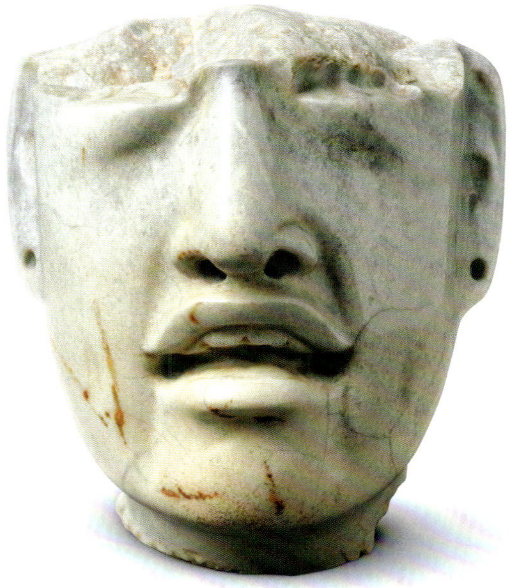

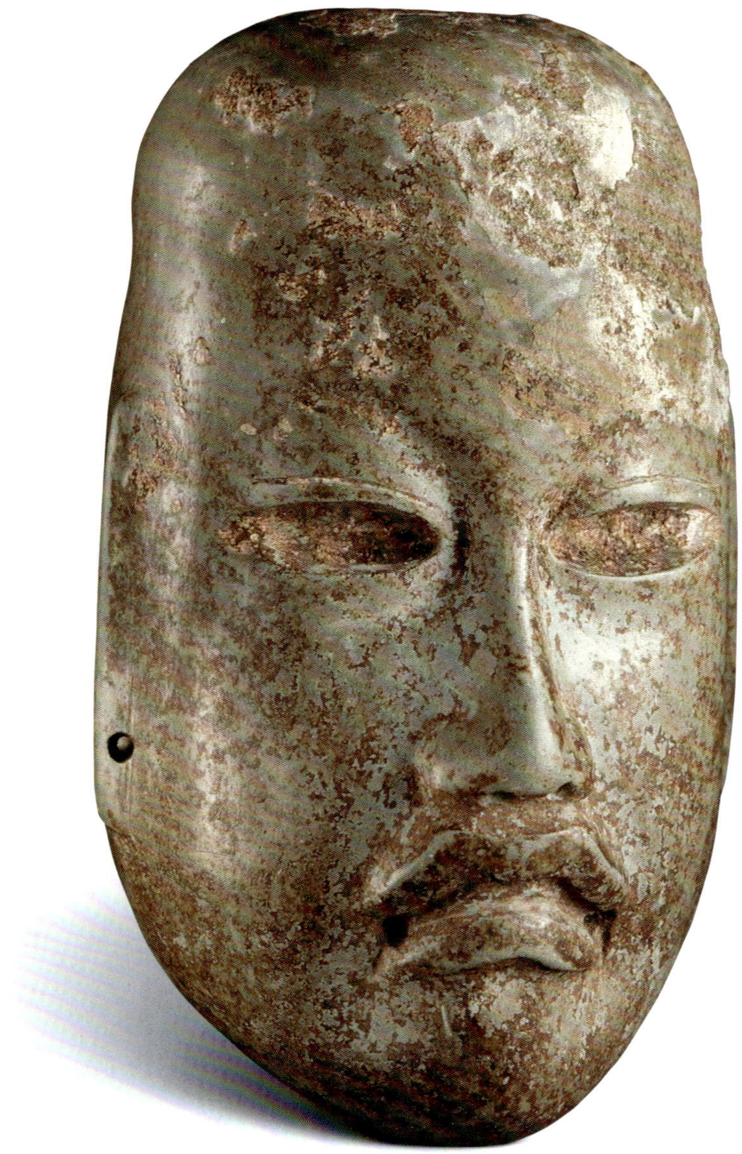

PLATES 95–96

HEAD FRAGMENT WITH INCISED DESIGN
Mexico, 900–400 BC
Jadeite
$2^{7}/_{8} \times 2^{7}/_{16} \times 1^{15}/_{16}$ in. (7.3 x 6.2 x 4.9 cm)
Cleveland Museum of Art, purchase from the J. H. Wade Fund (1961.31)

HEAD
Mexico, Tabasco, 900–400 BC
Greenstone
$4^{3}/_{4} \times 2^{15}/_{16} \times 3^{1}/_{4}$ in. (12.1 x 7.5 x 8.2 cm)
Los Angeles County Museum of Art, gift of John Gilbert Bourne (M.79.100)

As a portrait, this extraordinary fragment compares to the Olmec colossal heads (Benson 2008: fig. 3). Matthew W. Stirling (1964: fig. 6) suggested that it may have been broken from a figure in the vicinity of Tututepec, on the coast of Oaxaca. Its incredibly animated features and exquisite workmanship, despite its fragmentary state, led Karl Taube (2004: 100–101, pl. 16) to describe it as "among the most outstanding examples of portable Olmec sculpture." KB

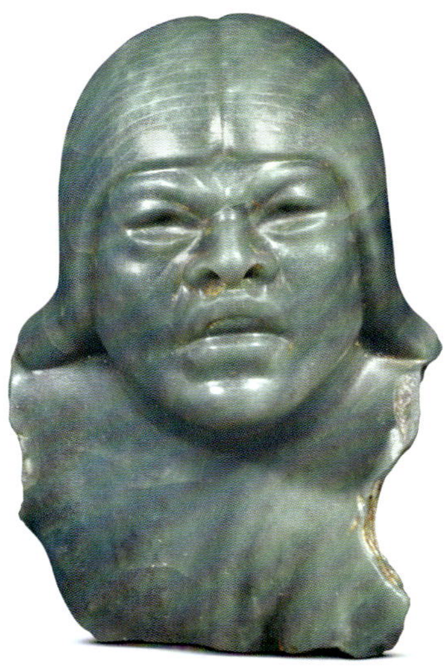

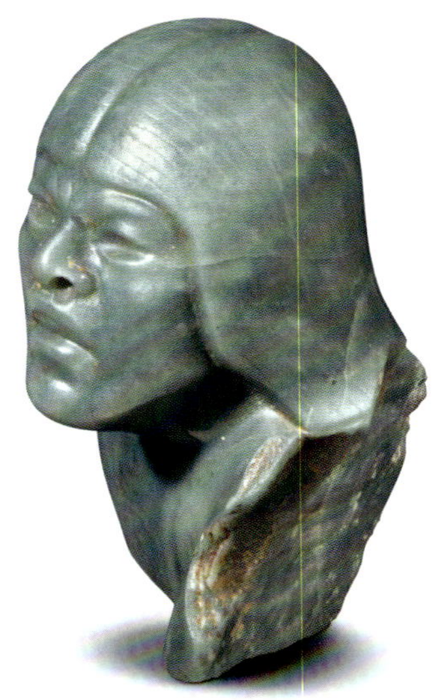

PLATES 97–98

FRAGMENTARY FIGURE
Mexico, 900–400 BC
Jadeite
$2\frac{5}{8} \times 1\frac{1}{2}$ in. (6.6 x 3.8 cm)
Dumbarton Oaks Research Library and Collection (B-19)

See also:
Benson 1981b: 99–100, fig. 4
Benson 1996a: cat. 58
Benson and Coe 1963: no. 30
Covarrubias 1946b: pl. 11
de la Fuente 1977b: 5–10

Although its exact archaeological provenience is unknown, this plaque has been in the collection of the Museo Nacional de Antropología since 1943 (Castro-Leal 1996: cat. 90). The plaque, which pertains to the Gulf Coast Olmec, is slightly later in the sequence, dating to approximately 800 BC.

Three cleft-headed incised profiles are strategically placed on the profile human face: one facing upward, one facing to the left at the level of the human ear, and one bracketing the mouth. A fourth profile head is attached to the forehead of the human face and wears the trefoil motif associated with maize. MC-LE

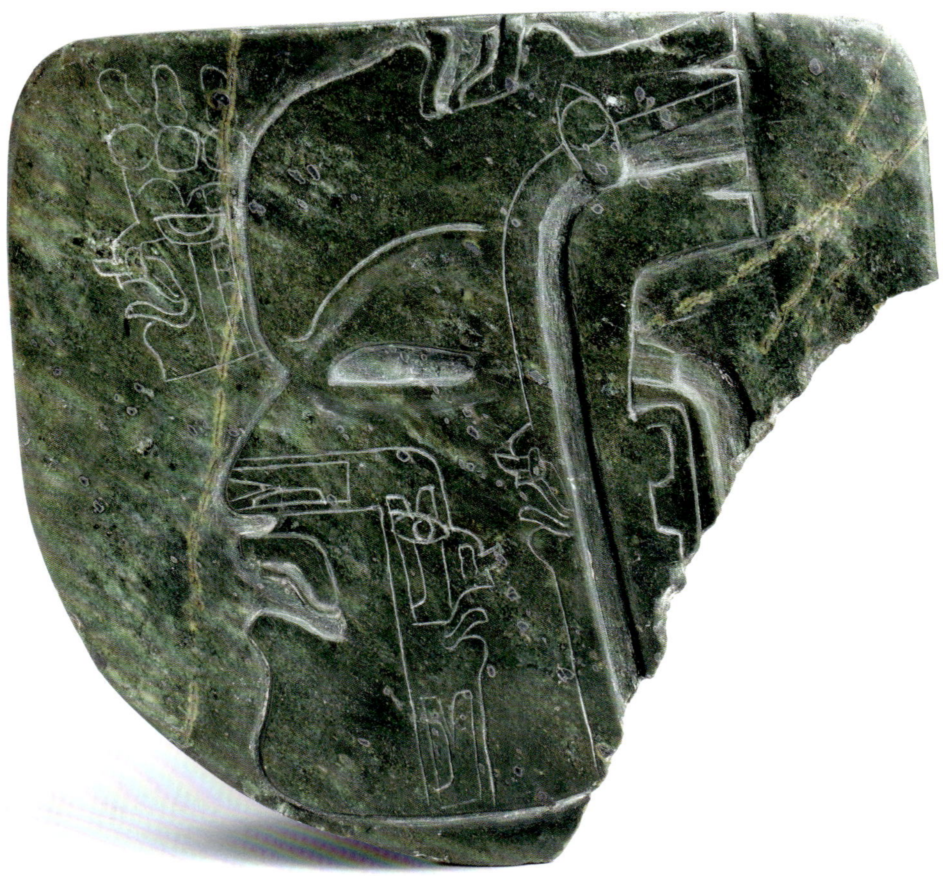

PLATE 99

PLAQUE WITH CARVED HUMAN PROFILE
Mexico, ca. 800 BC
Greenstone
$6^{7}/_{16}$ x $6^{1}/_{16}$ in. (16.3 x 15.4 cm)
Museo Nacional de Antropología, Mexico City
(10-9656)

Discovered in a cave in Simojovel, this object bears a complex design laid out in three vertical groups of elements distributed along its central axis (Benson 1971: 20–21, fig. 28; Castro-Leal 1996: cat. 115). A human face in profile appears in the center, adorned with a spool in his left ear and a cloth turban with a chin strap. On the headdress is a series of motifs related to vegetation. The face has the pronounced mouth and almond-shaped eyes associated with the Gulf Coast Olmec style, but its overall composition suggests a later regional expression and may reflect the penetration of Olmec peoples into the northeastern frontier of Chiapas (Lowe 1994: 124–125). MC-LE

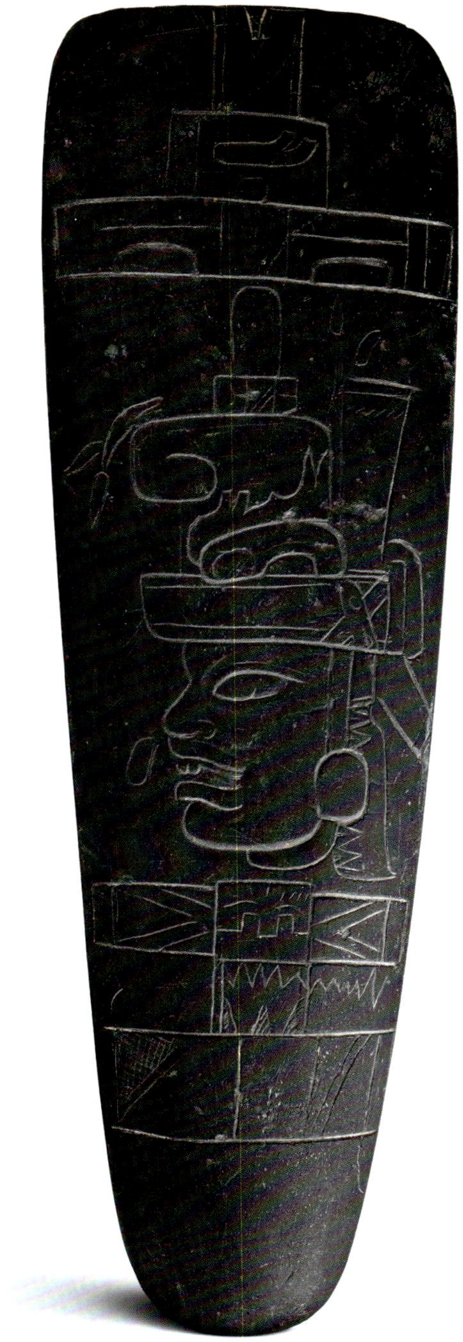

PLATE 100

CELT WITH CARVED HUMAN PROFILE
Mexico, Chiapas, Simojovel, 900–400 BC
Black slate
12 3/16 x 3 11/16 x 1 3/8 in. (31 x 9.3 x 3.5 cm)
Museo Nacional de Antropología, Mexico City
(10-9674)

Although several Olmec-style monuments show figures holding scepters or staffs, including La Venta Stela 2 (fig. 16), this is the only complete example that has been discovered (González Lauck 1996a: cat. 104). The scepter was part of an offering that contained more than a hundred celts and was found during the 1950s, some 10 miles (16 kilometers) north of La Venta (ibid.). Carlos Navarette (1974: 17) described scepter fragments from various contexts in Chiapas, Veracruz, and Guatemala, suggesting that they were easily carried objects that may have served to mark the status of the bearer. Long-distance travel by merchants or other emissaries from the Gulf Coast is one model that explains the presence of Olmec-style monumental and small-scale art over an enormous area of Mesoamerica, as demonstrated by Gareth Lowe (1969), whose surveys revealed an ancient road that linked the region of Ocozocuautla, Chiapas, with the Gulf Coast by both land and water.

The snarling visage at the top of the scepter has a cleft element from which protrudes a banded cone shape, similar to the face and emerging cone on La Merced Monument 1 (Rodríguez M. and Ortíz Ceballos 2000: fig. 13). Karl Taube (1996: fig. 5d) described the image as the head of the Olmec maize god. The midsection is striated with three horizontal cleft motifs, not unlike the three banded elements that appear below the maize god depicted on La Venta Monuments 25/26 and 27. The bottom is shaped into a profile head of a serpent. Individually, these features carried great symbolic significance for Gulf Coast peoples; combined in this single object, they must have signaled the elevated stature of its owner. VMF

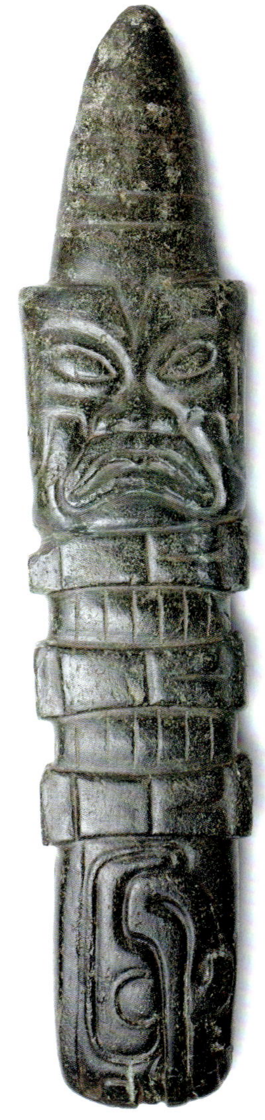

PLATE 101

SCEPTER
Mexico, Tabasco, Cárdenas, Ejido Ojoshal,
900–400 BC
Blackstone
$9\frac{13}{16}$ x $1\frac{7}{8}$ x $\frac{7}{8}$ in. (25 x 4.7 x 2.2 cm)
Museo Regional de Antropología
"Carlos Pellicer Cámara," Villahermosa,
Tabasco (A-0055)

Monumental sculptures of human figures often show them seated cross-legged, a pose associated with rulers in later Maya depictions, where a royal title, *ah pop* ("he of the mat"), referred to the woven cover placed on stone thrones. A greater variety of seated poses occurs in the corpus of Olmec-style small-scale figurines such as this one, in which the figure sits with its right leg bent and placed on a low bench and its left leg hanging over the edge, not unlike the pose of the enthroned figure on the mural at Oxtotitlan cave (figs. 36–37).

The figure holds an object of ceremonial significance in each hand. His right hand grasps a tapered, incised object, variously described as a torch or maize motif (Joralemon 1996: cat. 54) or as a feather bundle (Taube 1995: fig. 8b). His left hand holds a D-shaped implement referred to in Olmec studies as a knuckleduster; it may represent a cut conch shell (Andrews V 1987), a rare and precious material that may also signify maize fertility (Joralemon 1996: cat. 54). VMF

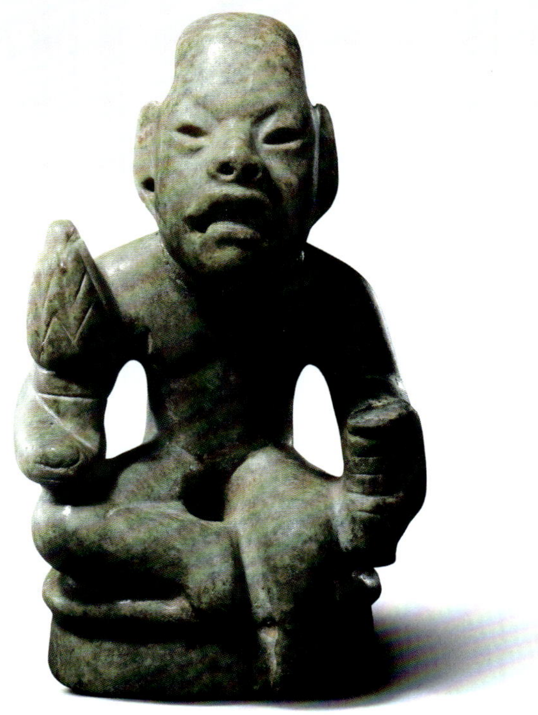

PLATE 102

SEATED FIGURE
Mexico, 900–400 BC
Albite
$4\frac{5}{16} \times 2\frac{7}{16} \times 1\frac{1}{2}$ in. (11 x 6.2 x 3.9 cm)
Cleveland Museum of Art, purchase from the J. H. Wade Fund (1941.390)

This figure, shown holding the rigid body of an infant or a small child, sits upon a stone bench referred to as a cloud throne because of its curved edges (Joralemon 1996: cat. 53). Comparisons between this figure, those on La Venta Altar 5, and Las Limas Monument 1 have been pointed out previously (ibid.; Princeton University 1995: cat. 34), because all depict a similar subject. There are, however, important distinctions in the three portrayals. The monumental Altar 5 (fig. 33, pls. 64–66) presents a narrative centered on the frontal image of a cross-legged man holding an inert child, while the sides of the monument are carved with reliefs depicting men holding animated children. The Las Limas figure (Coe 1968a: 111, 114–115; fig. 9, this volume), also a cross-legged male, is adorned with incised motifs that convey the symbolic context of the figure and child. Although the hair of the figure shown here is incised in a manner similar to the close, caplike style of the Las Limas man, the rest of the body is plain. In addition, the head is more rounded than the typical elongated heads of Olmec-style figurines.

This is the only known bench figure shown with a child. Two monumental examples and one small-scale version depict a male seated on a bench, with legs hanging down in front and hands resting on the bench surface. On La Venta Monument 40 (Clewlow and Corson 1968: 175, pl. 11a), the figure is headless and wears a short, triangular cape; the bench figure from San José Pinula, Guatemala, wears a helmet and short cape (Milbrath 1979: fig. 58); and the small-scale figure, which derives from Río Arriba, Chiapas, has a mustache and a beard (ibid.: fig. 60). VMF

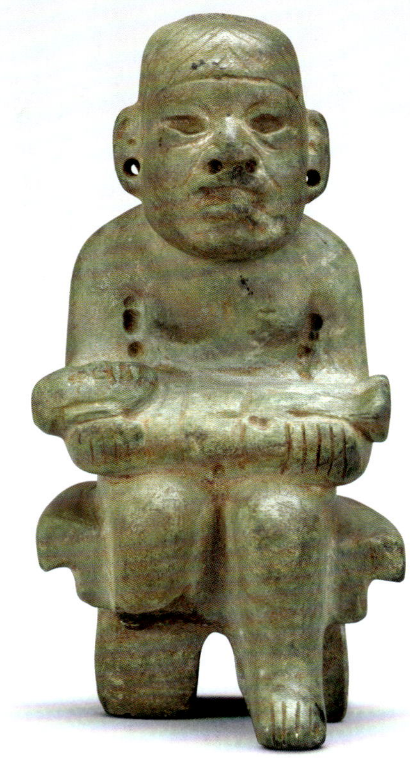

PLATE 103

SEATED FIGURE HOLDING INFANT
Mexico, Tabasco, 900–500 BC
Serpentine
$4^{7}/_{16} \times 2^{1}/_{4} \times 2^{1}/_{8}$ in. (11.3 x 5.7 x 5.4 cm)
Metropolitan Museum of Art, The Michael C. Rockefeller Memorial Collection, bequest of Nelson A. Rockefeller, 1979 (1979.206.940)

A profusion of symbolic motifs adorns this cross-legged figure's costume. Reportedly found as part of a cache containing stone masks and celts (Benson 1971), the figure has been compared to La Venta Monument 77 (pls. 67–68), an equally elaborate depiction of an Olmec ruler (Benson 1996a: cat. 52). Karl Taube identifies the figure as a female and gives a detailed analysis focusing on the wealth of maize symbolism and the correlation of maize with the precious feathers and jadeite that adorn the figure (2004: 105–121, pl. 18).

Maize symbolism dominates the upper portion of the figure, from the back-turned headdress divided into four sections, to the mask of the Olmec maize god topped with the trefoil maize motif and flanked by knuckledusters, to the headband. On the back of the maize god face appears the quincunx motif of four dots and a central bar, itself a metaphor for the four-sided cosmos and its central axis mundi (Reilly 1994: 227–228; Marcus 1989: 172–173). An identical quincunx pattern, also topped by a scalloped motif, appears on the Cleveland Museum of Art axe (pl. 92).

The headband, composed of a central circular element and flanked by pairs of celts, illustrates the ability of Olmec artists to manipulate metaphorically the powerful imagery that appears in the landscape, in architecture, and in art in both three-dimensional forms and two-dimensional designs. The horizontal headband conveys the same idea as the quincunx pattern on the back of the headdress; it also corresponds to the cruciform patterns of caches that dedicate sacred space and signify the ruler's capacity to center the cosmos (Reilly 1995: 38–39; Taube 2003: 461–464). Here, the headband's circular element, identified as a mirror (Reilly 1994: 189), resonates with the pattern of a massive offering at La Venta (Coe 1968a: 63) in the form of a great mosaic mask. A layer of multicolored clays covered the mask; atop the clays was an additional offering of twenty jade and serpentine celts arranged in a cruciform pattern, with a centrally placed concave mirror.

The elaborate cape and wrist and ankle ornaments, in combination with the symbolically laden designs on this extraordinary figure's headband and headdress, are the ultimate testament to the wealth and authority commanded by Olmec rulers. VMF

PLATE 104

SEATED FIGURE WEARING ELABORATE HEADDRESS AND CAPE
Mexico, Veracruz, 900–400 BC
Diopside
Height: 6 7/16 in. (16.3 cm)
Dumbarton Oaks Research Library and Collection (B-592)

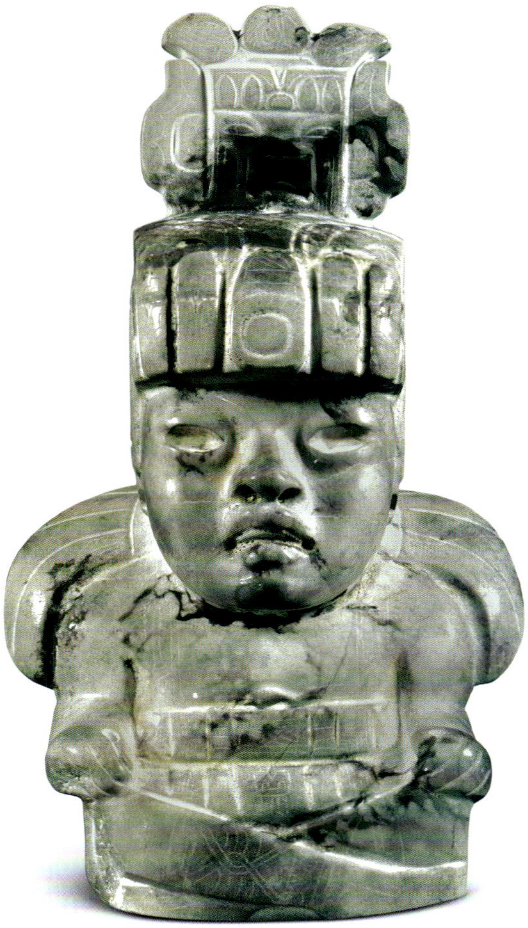

The precocious architectural and artistic developments on the Gulf Coast, reflecting a changing cultural environment of emerging social hierarchies, played out in a Mesoamerican landscape inhabited by a diverse array of peoples in both lowland and highland environments. Typical characteristics of these regional centers included an agricultural economy, a hierarchical society, and the long-distance trade and exchange of exotic materials. The possession of rare resources such as jadeite and shell ornaments and iron-ore mirrors signaled social rank. The three primary centers of greenstone production apparently included the Pacific Coast of Chiapas and Guatemala, the area comprising the modern state of Guerrero, and the Gulf Coast. As David Grove (1996a) has pointed out, between 1200 and 900 BC monumental sculpture appears only on the Gulf Coast; beginning around 900 BC, regional styles of monumental sculpture appear in the Central Highlands of Mexico, at the site of Chalcatzingo in the modern state of Morelos, at Teopantecuanitlán in Guerrero, and along the Pacific Coast. Simultaneously, the production of elegant ceramic forms, many with Olmec-style designs carved, incised, and painted on their surfaces, was the key feature of regional centers in the Central Highlands of the Basin of Mexico.

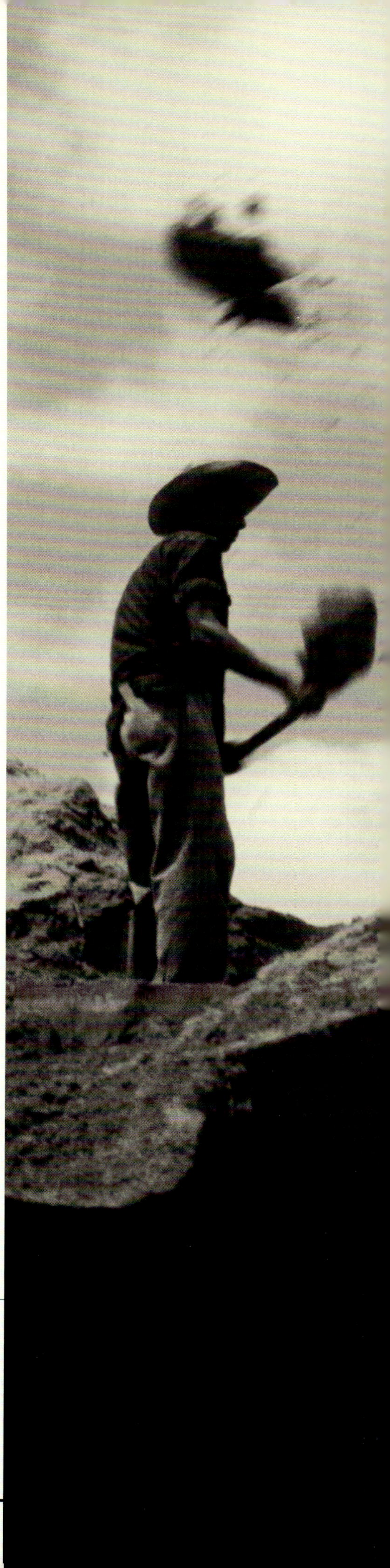

Workers excavate the Columnar Tomb at
La Venta, 1943

MESOAMERICAN NEIGHBORS NEAR AND FAR

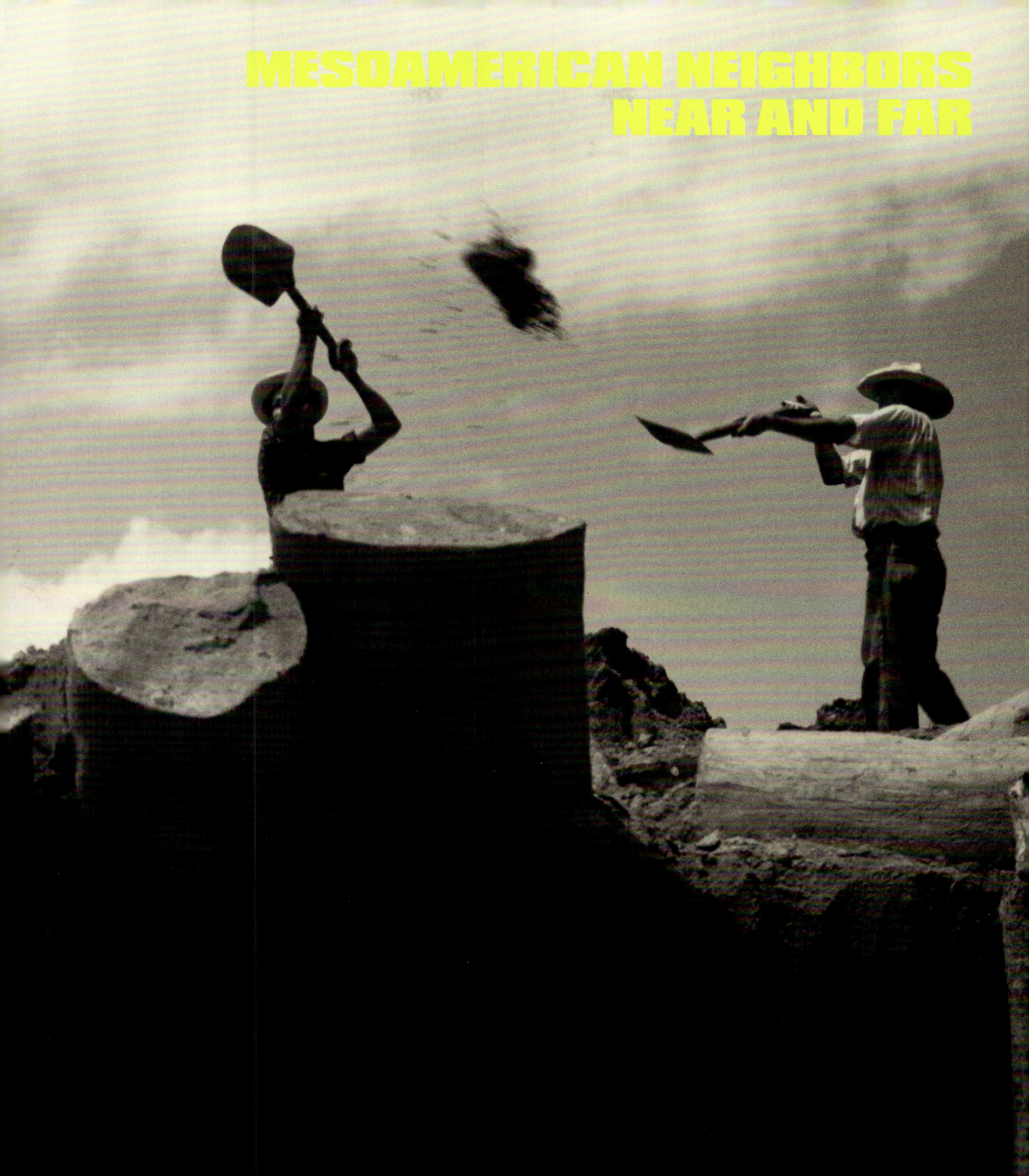

Between the 1870s and 1940s, a large number of Olmec-style polished greenstone objects (primarily of jadeite and serpentine) from Guerrero and Oaxaca in southern Mexico came to light, leading Miguel Covarrubias (1957: 76) to propose that the region was the birthplace of the distinctive Olmec art style. He suggested that the "most archaic forms" appeared there, moved up into Central Mexico, and reached a florescence on the Gulf Coast before moving into Chiapas and down the coast to Guatemala. Subsequent archaeological investigations throughout Mexico, however, have demonstrated clearly that, rather than a chronological sequence of areas coming under the influence of the Olmec style during the Formative period, Mesoamerica supported a lively landscape of diverse cultures engaged in spheres of interaction in which ideas and objects traveled widely.

The varied topography of Guerrero ranges from the humid slopes of the Pacific Coast to the forested mountains of the Sierra Madre del Sur, which extend from western Guerrero to south-central Oaxaca. Largely composed of igneous and metamorphic rocks such as basalt and serpentine, the range is also home to vast limestone cave systems, which were the locus of extraordinary Olmec-style murals found in the 1960s (Grove 1970; figs. 35–37, this volume). Teopantecuanitlán in northeastern Guerrero is one of only a handful of sites outside the Gulf Coast area where monumental art and architecture occur (Martínez Donjuán 1994). To date, Olmec-style artifacts have been recovered from fourteen sites in ancient Guerrero (Paradis 2008: 537).

The precocious expertise in lapidary technology that existed in Guerrero gave rise to local and regional styles manifested in stone vessels, figures, and jewelry, and numerous examples demonstrate the fluidity of form and technical mastery that characterizes Olmec-style art. The surface of this bowl, for example, was incised with reliefs of open-mouthed crested iguanas and then rubbed with a red pigment to highlight the design. VMF

PLATE 105

BOWL
Mexico, Guerrero, Mezcala, 1000–600 BC
Stone with pigment
4 1/8 x 9 1/4 in. (10.5 x 23.5 cm)
Los Angeles County Museum of Art, Shinji Shumeikai Acquisition Fund (M.2000.54.1)

See also:
Paradis 2008

Princeton University 1995: cat. 14

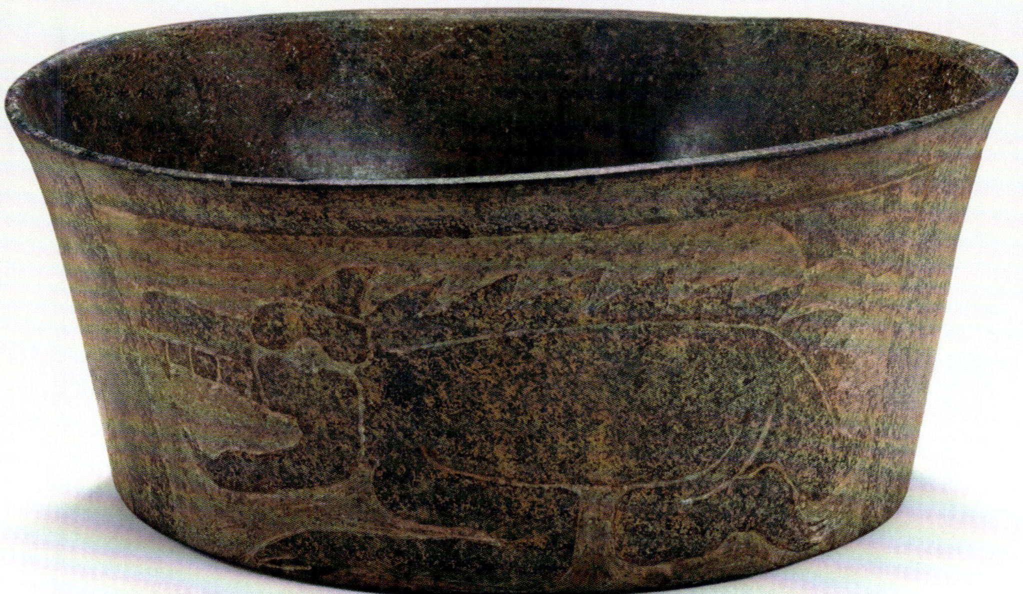

Masks bearing the image of a person or a deity were often placed on a human body. Plate 107 depicts a human face; to protect the wearer, the artist included bas-relief details alluding to a jaguar supernatural, particularly around the mouth and eyes. Masks were also frequently used in burials to cover the faces of high-status individuals. MC-LE

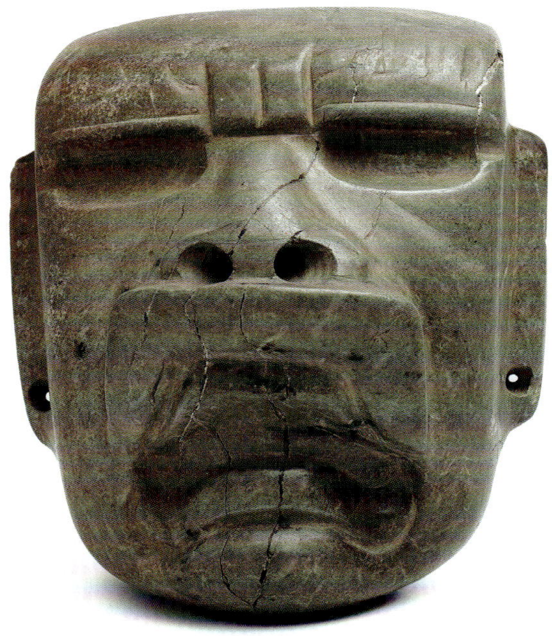

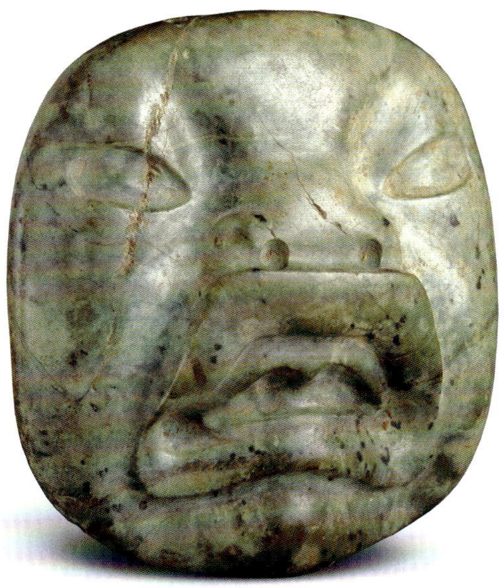

PLATES 106–107

MASK
Mexico, probably Guerrero, 1000–600 BC
Serpentine
$3^{1}/_{2}$ x 3 in. (8.9 x 7.6 cm)
Los Angeles County Museum of Art, gift of Constance McCormick Fearing (M.86.311.1)

MASK
Mexico, Guerrero, 1000–600 BC
Greenstone
$4^{1}/_{16}$ x $3^{1}/_{2}$ x $2^{1}/_{16}$ in. (10.3 x 9 x 5.2 cm)
Museo Nacional de Antropología, Mexico City (10-2504)

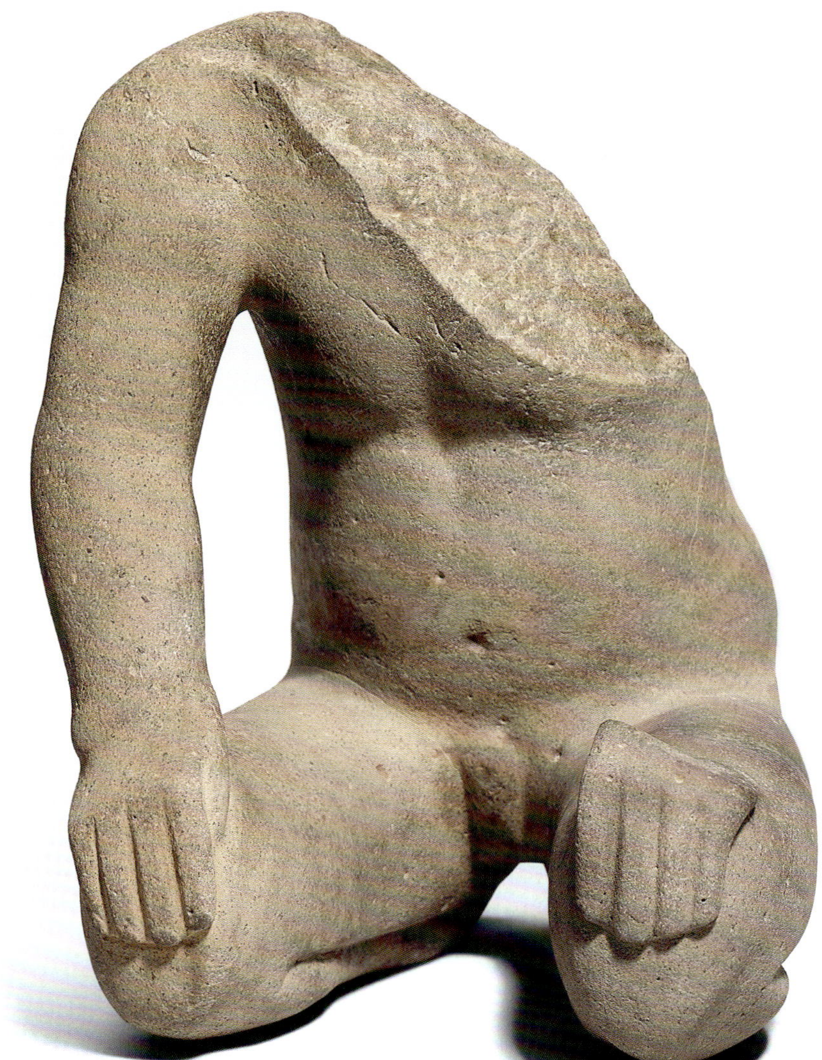

PLATE 108

KNEELING FIGURE
Mexico, 1200–600 BC
Stone
10 3/8 x 7 7/8 x 8 3/8 in. (26.3 x 20 x 21.3 cm)
Cleveland Museum of Art, the Norweb Collection (1951.179)

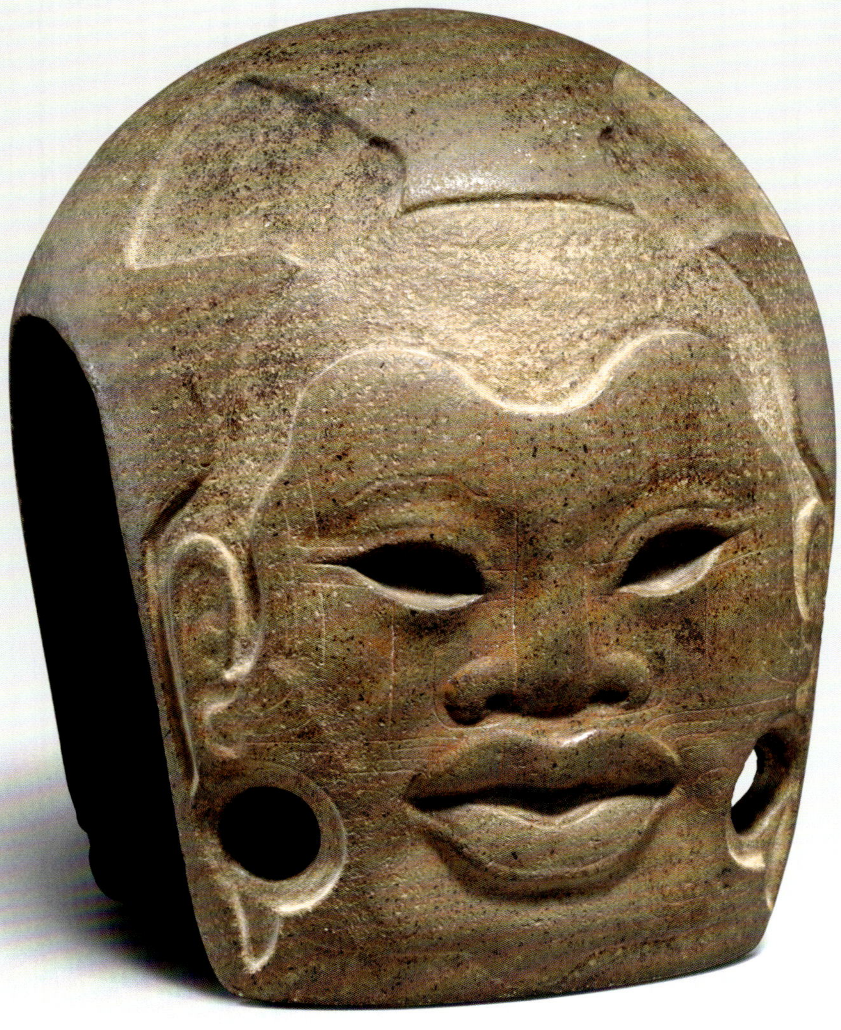

Part of the collection of Miguel Covarrubias, which entered the Museo Nacional de Antropología in 1957 (Castro-Leal 1996: cat. 109), this small yoke has an Olmec-style face carved on the front, which is framed by an incised cleft motif. Large earspools can be seen on either side of the face.

In the example opposite, the forehead area is cut away from the surface of the stone as if to frame the low-relief face with a helmet. Resembling the type of portraiture seen on the colossal heads, the face has unusually slanted eyes; fine, incised patterns cover its entire surface. Below the ears are large holes that may once have held earspools (Princeton University 1995: cat. 138). MC-LE/VMF

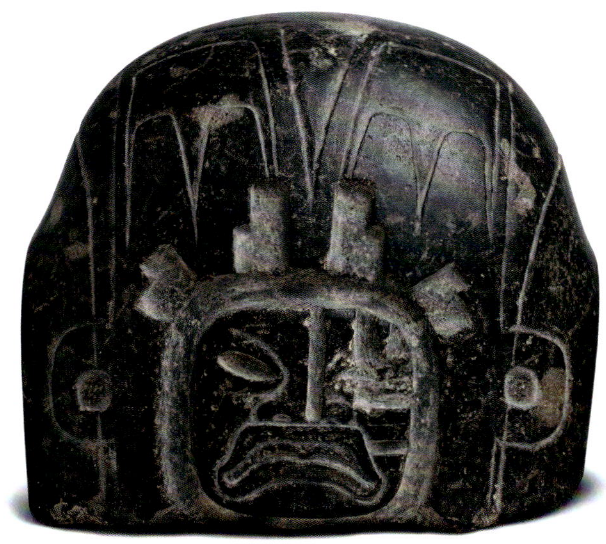

PLATES 109–110

SMALL YOKE WITH CARVED FACE AND INCISIONS
Mexico, Guerrero, Tlacotepec, 900–600 BC
Stone with pigment
$7^1/_2$ x $5^7/_8$ x 6 in. (19 x 14.9 x 15.2 cm)
Metropolitan Museum of Art,
The Michael C. Rockefeller Collection,
gift of Nelson A. Rockefeller, 1969
(1978.412.39)

SMALL YOKE
Mexico, Guerrero, Tlacotepec, 1000–600 BC
Diorite
$4^1/_2$ x $5^1/_{16}$ x $5^1/_2$ in. (11.5 x 12.9 x 14 cm)
Museo Nacional de Antropología,
Mexico City, Covarrubias collection (10-2441)

Chalcatzingo, an important regional center during the Early Formative period, was situated on a series of low terraces at the base of the Cerro Delgado and the Cerro Chalcatzingo in the Amatzinac river valley, near the eastern border of the modern state of Morelos. By 900 BC, the people of Chalcatzingo had begun carving monumental reliefs on boulders and other rock surfaces that illustrate close stylistic ties to the Olmec heartland (Grove, Hirth, and Bugé 1987; Grove 1996a).

An elite residential structure on the uppermost terrace of Chalcatzingo was home to generations of the ruling lineage, and several burials in stone-lined crypts were discovered beneath the floor. This figure had been placed at the midpoint of a body found in a crypt that was directly below another crypt (Grove 1996a: 111–112).

Its characteristics distinguish it from the jadeite figures of La Venta (Thomson 1987: 297, fig. 17.1). The figure portrays an adolescent male (ibid.); its head tilts backward and its shoulders are not defined. The foreshortened arms, held out in front of the body, differ from the straight arms held at the sides of the body of Gulf Coast area figures, although the pose is not unknown (see Taube 2004: pl. 8; pl. 75, this volume). Thomson detected incrustations of a red pigment on the face that she suggested may indicate a beard, another unusual feature of this figurine. VMF

PLATE 111

STANDING FIGURE
Mexico, Morelos, Chalcatzingo, Burial 33, 700–500 BC
Gray serpentine with pigment
4 3/4 x 1 15/16 x 1 15/16 in. (12 x 5 x 5 cm)
Centro INAH Morelos (1838 P.J. 1621)

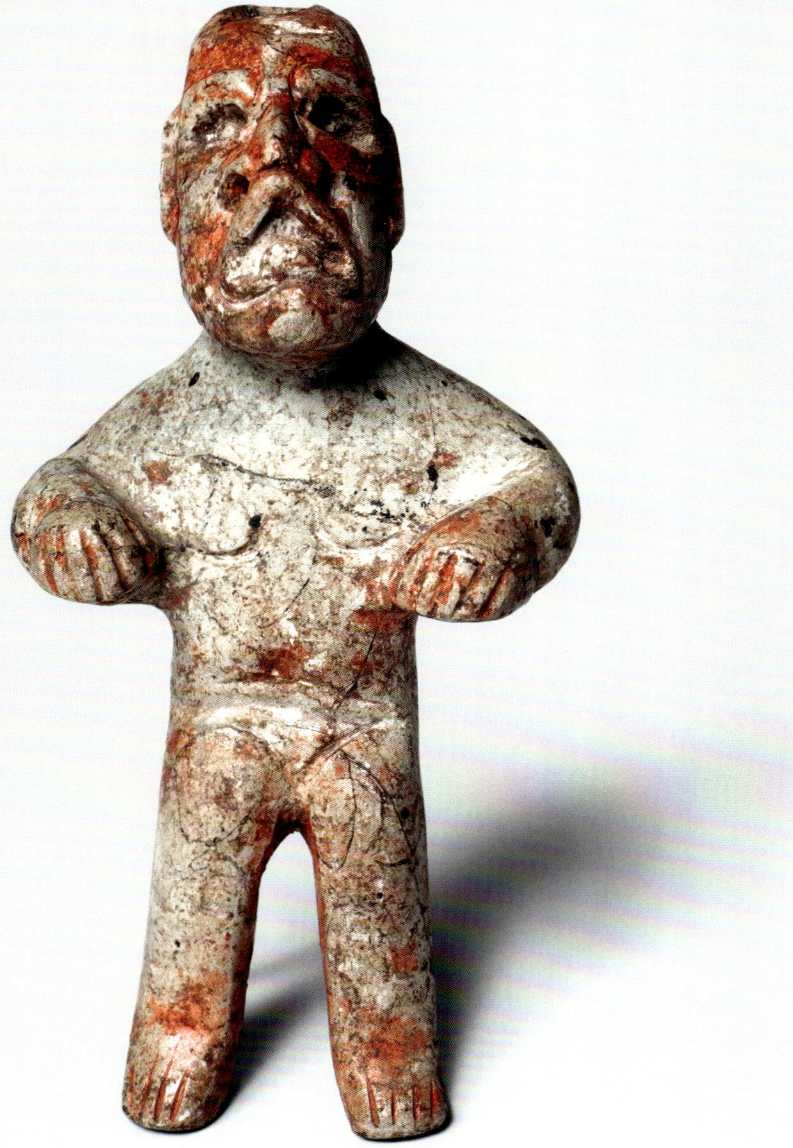

This bowl's cream slip and incised profile face represent hallmarks of the Olmec art style, although the vessel derives from Central Mexico. Comparing the image to one carved on the tabletop throne at Chalcatzingo, David Grove (2000: 289, fig. 20b) suggests that the vessel portrays a saurian earth supernatural. The ceramic ware is closely aligned with bowls from the nearby site of Tlapacoya, which feature similar profile faces that Christine Niederberger (2000: 185, fig. 9a) links to sacred and political expressions of power and authority. VMF

This figure is one of two nearly identical sculptures discovered during an INAH archaeological salvage project that began in 2006, after a construction crew came across the remains of an ancient wall (Pérez de Lara n.d.). From the ceramic data recovered during the project, it was determined that Zazacatla, a site located outside Cuernavaca in the modern state of Morelos, was occupied between 800 and 500 BC.

According to Jorge Pérez de Lara (ibid.), a facade uncovered in one of the last test pits to be explored was the northern edge of a pair of adjacent platforms separated by an earthen stairway. The facade held four niches, each containing a sculpted figure; only two of the figures, including this one, display Olmec-style carving. The sculpture depicts a cross-legged individual, human in form, with arms straight and hands resting on his knees. His face reveals the familiar Olmec-style downturned and snarling mouth, flattened nostrils, and exaggerated brow; a cleft curves up from the back of his headdress, which has a squared shape. VMF

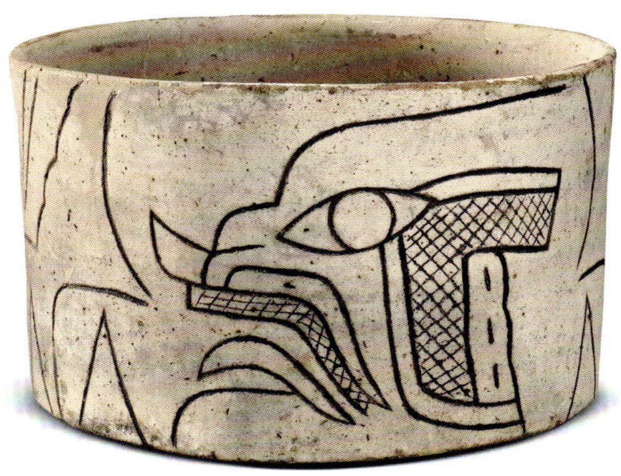

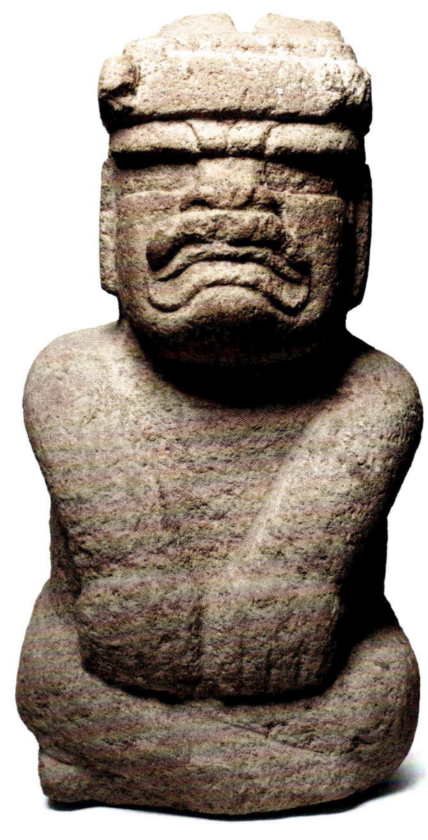

PLATES 112–113

INCISED BOWL
Mexico, Morelos, 1200–900 BC
Slip-painted ceramic with pigment
4 7/16 x 7 1/4 in. (11.2 x 18.4 cm)
Indiana University Art Museum, Raymond and Laura Wielgus Collection (IUAM81.32.3)

See also:
Princeton University 1995: cat. 98

FIGURE
Mexico, Morelos, Zazacatla, 800–500 BC
Stone
25 1/4 x 10 1/4 x 11 13/16 in. (64 x 26 x 30 cm)
Centro INAH Morelos (10-344907)

Because of its strategic location in the Amatzinac river valley in Morelos, Chalcatzingo was an important locus of trade and commercial contact between northeastern Guerrero, the Basin of Mexico, the Valley of Oaxaca, and the Gulf Coast. The site might also have housed an ethnic enclave of Olmec people, an interpretation suggested by the bas-reliefs with mythical and religious subject matter carved on the cliff walls nearby (see fig. 32).

This decapitated and dismembered sculpture, the first evidence of monumental sculpture in the highlands, was found in excavations at Chalcatzingo conducted by Eulalia Guzmán. The figure is shown seated with legs crossed; the missing hands presumably would have rested on the knees. The pose and the accoutrements indicate that the sculpture represents a human. He wears a rectangular pectoral with a band of crossed motifs on the chest; at his waist is a wide band decorated with five dots on the upper part; and a tunic covers his back.

David Grove (1981) has suggested that monuments could have been mutilated for various reasons: the end of calendrical periods or ritual cycles, similar to the fifty-two-year cycle used during the Postclassic period; a change in leadership or dynasty; or the death of a ruler, when the monuments that represented him were destroyed to diminish his supernatural power. POC (OCHOA)

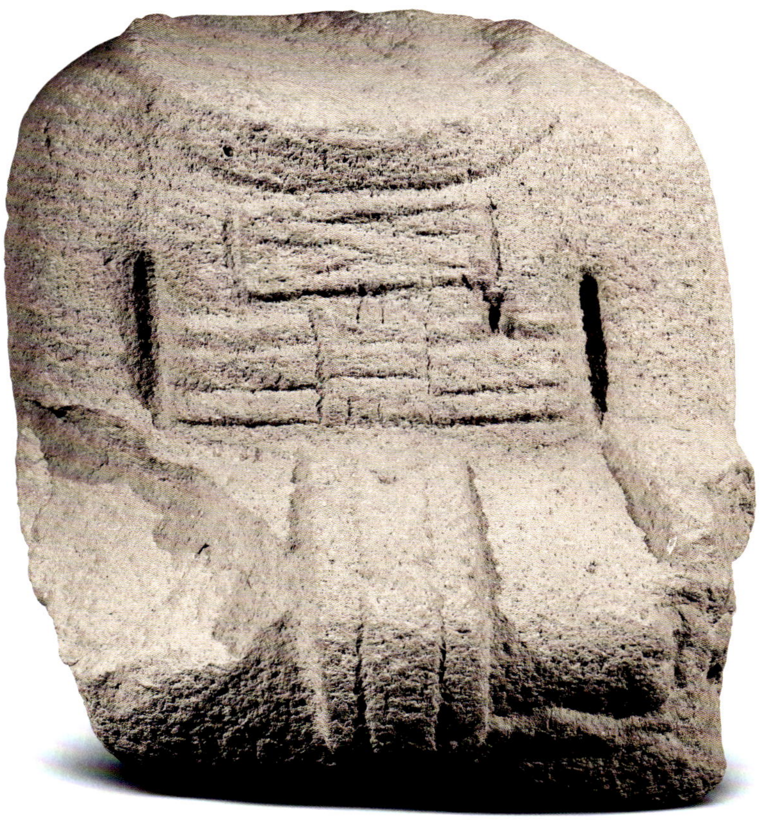

PLATE 114

MONUMENT 16
(SEATED HEADLESS FIGURE)
Mexico, Morelos, Chalcatzingo, 800–600 BC
Basalt
$20^{11}/_{16}$ x $21^{1}/_{16}$ x $23^{1}/_{4}$ in. (52.5 x 53.5 x 59 cm)
Museo Nacional de Antropología, Mexico City
(10-74394)

The site of Tlatilco, located on the plains and foothills of the Río Hondo in the northwestern outskirts of Mexico City, first came to public attention in the 1930s after it had been used for decades as a source of clay for making bricks. Initially thought to be a necropolis because of the hundreds of burials excavated at the site, Tlatilco, between 1200 and 700 BC, was actually a large town with earthen platforms and a sizable population (Niederberger 2000: 173). A series of excavations between 1942 and 1969 (Covarrubias 1950, 1957; García Moll et al. 1991) revealed evidence for a hierarchical society and craft specialists, with numerous burials yielding locally produced objects such as ceramics as well as imported objects of shell, jadeite, quartz, and iron ore.

By 1200 BC, agricultural settlements had sprung up around Mesoamerica that depended on the staple crops of maize, beans, and squash. Artists in these areas were involved in weaving, stoneworking, and pottery making. Ceramic figurines are a hallmark of this period, ranging in size from large to small, either hollow or solid, and showing local features of form and dress. Each of these solid female figurines displays elaborate details of costume and coiffure. VMF

PLATES 115–117

FEMALE FIGURE CARRYING CHILD
Mexico, Tlatilco, 1200–900 BC
Ceramic
Height: 3½ in. (9 cm)
Los Angeles County Museum of Art, promised gift of Constance McCormick Fearing (L.83.11.533)

FEMALE FIGURE WITH TOPKNOT COIFFURE
Mexico, Tlatilco, 1200–900 BC
Slip-painted ceramic
Height: 3¾ in. (9.6 cm)
Los Angeles County Museum of Art, promised gift of Constance McCormick Fearing (L.83.11.496)

FEMALE FIGURE WITH INCISED FLARING SKIRT
Mexico, Tlatilco, 1200–900 BC
Slip-painted ceramic
Height: 3⅜ in. (8.6 cm)
Los Angeles County Museum of Art, promised gift of Constance McCormick Fearing (L.83.11.518)

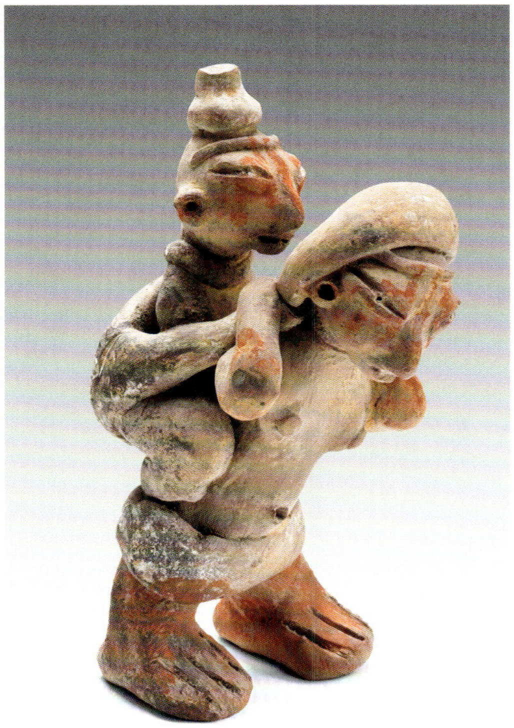

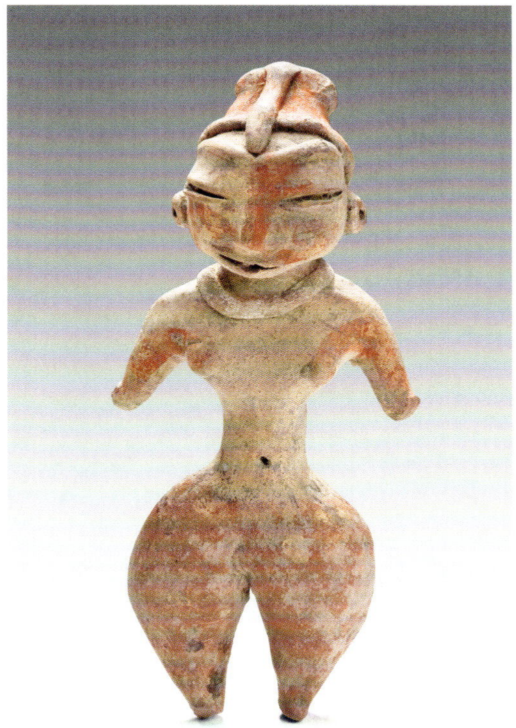

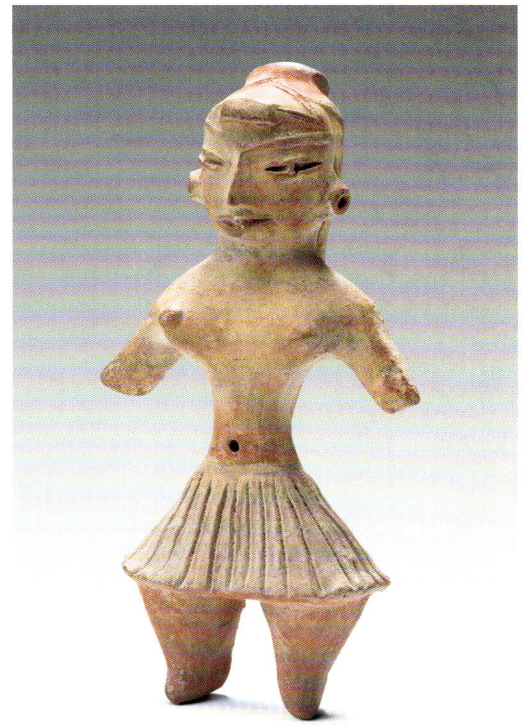

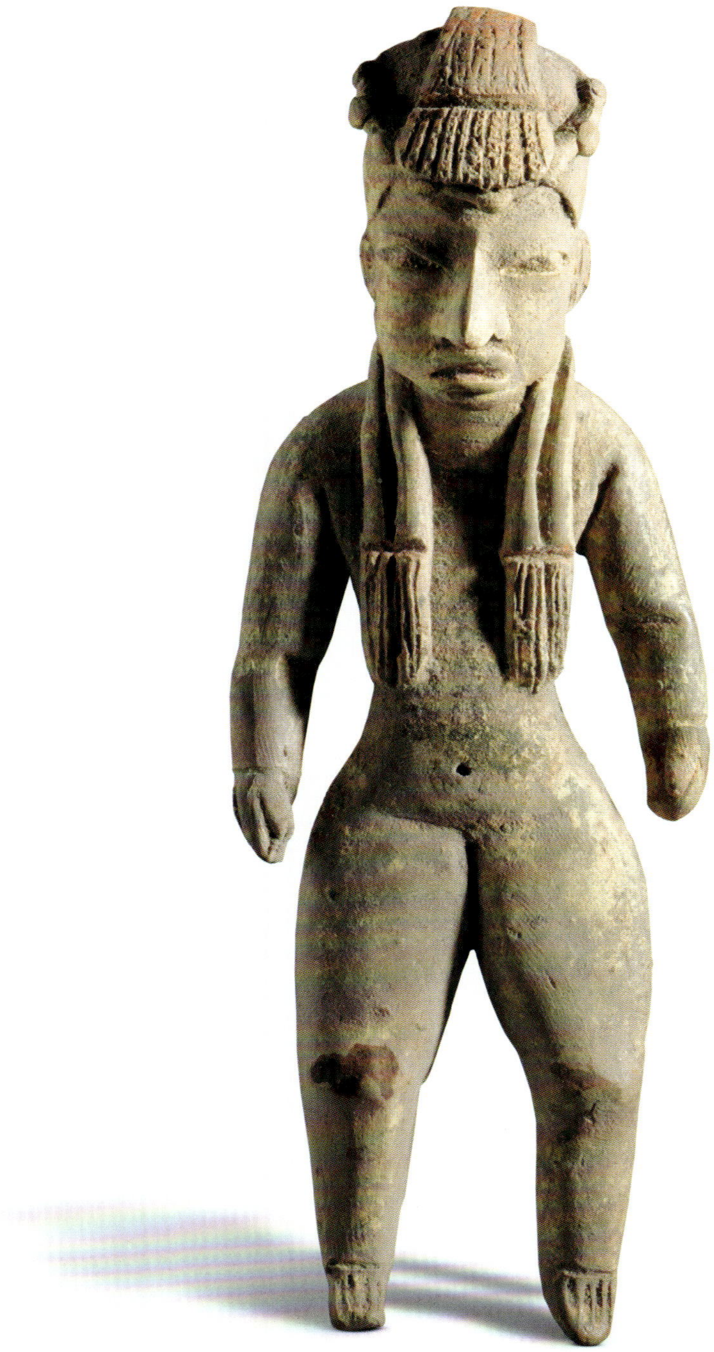

PLATE 118

FEMALE FIGURE WITH ELABORATE HAIR AND HEADDRESS
Mexico, Tlatilco, 1200–900 BC
Slip-painted ceramic
Height: 4 9/16 in. (11.6 cm)
Los Angeles County Museum of Art,
promised gift of Constance McCormick Fearing
(L.83.11.507)

Hand-modeled Preclassic period sculptures that depict female figures are popularly known as "pretty ladies." They have well-shaped, voluptuous bodies and are generally shown nude, as seen here. The heads display cranial deformation, which was a common practice at that time; some figures show dental mutilation as well. Many retain the pigments with which they were originally decorated, suggesting that this was a popular custom of this period. The figures are adorned with coiffures, headdresses, and ornamental objects. This example also wears a pyrite mirror, which might have had ritual significance. The presence of pyrite, a mineral from the Valley of Oaxaca, is evidence of the exchange of raw materials at this time.

Tlatilco was a village in the Early and Middle Preclassic periods that is noteworthy for the beauty of its material culture as well as for the many burials found near its residential areas. This tiny figure came from Burial 162, excavated during the second field season, when distinguished archaeologists and anthropologists from Mexico and abroad participated in the project. POC (OCHOA)

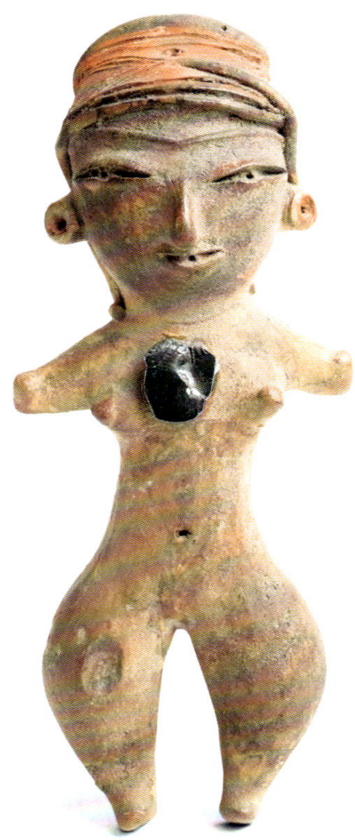

PLATE 119

FEMALE FIGURINE WITH MIRROR
Mexico, Tlatilco, Burial 162, Offering 3,
1200–600 BC
Earthenware and pyrite
$3\frac{3}{4} \times 1\frac{9}{16} \times \frac{3}{8}$ in. (9.5 x 4 x 1 cm)
Museo Nacional de Antropología, Mexico City
(10-1888)

More than five hundred burials were investigated during the four field seasons at Tlatilco, and most of them contained abundant offerings. Burial 12, excavated during the second season, is noteworthy because two almost identical human figures, known as "The Twins," were found there. They are reminiscent of Olmec "baby-face" figures, which are generally shown seated, legs apart, without clothing or ornaments; display cranial deformation and often have shaved heads, although some have tufts of hair; and show dental mutilation, a common practice at this time. "Baby-face" figures are usually plump, although the examples shown here are not noticeably so. These beautiful pieces of Olmec art are unique among the "baby-face" type because their facial expressions subtly differentiate them from each other. A white pigment covers the surface of these sculptures. POC (OCHOA)

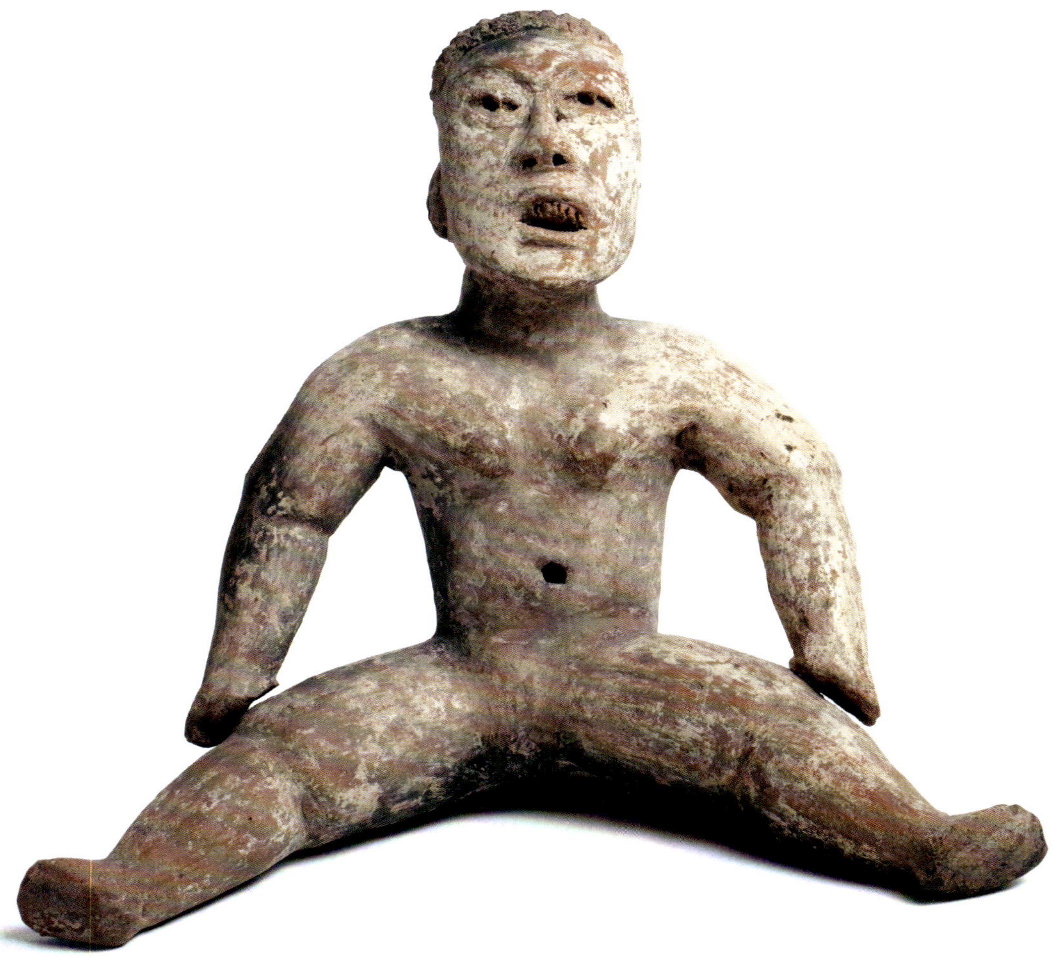

PLATE 120

TWIN FIGURE
Mexico, Tlatilco, Burial 12, Offering 6,
1200–600 BC
Earthenware with pigment
$8\frac{5}{8}$ x 10 x $5\frac{11}{16}$ in. (22 x 25.5 x 14.5 cm)
Museo Nacional de Antropología, Mexico City
(10-15742)

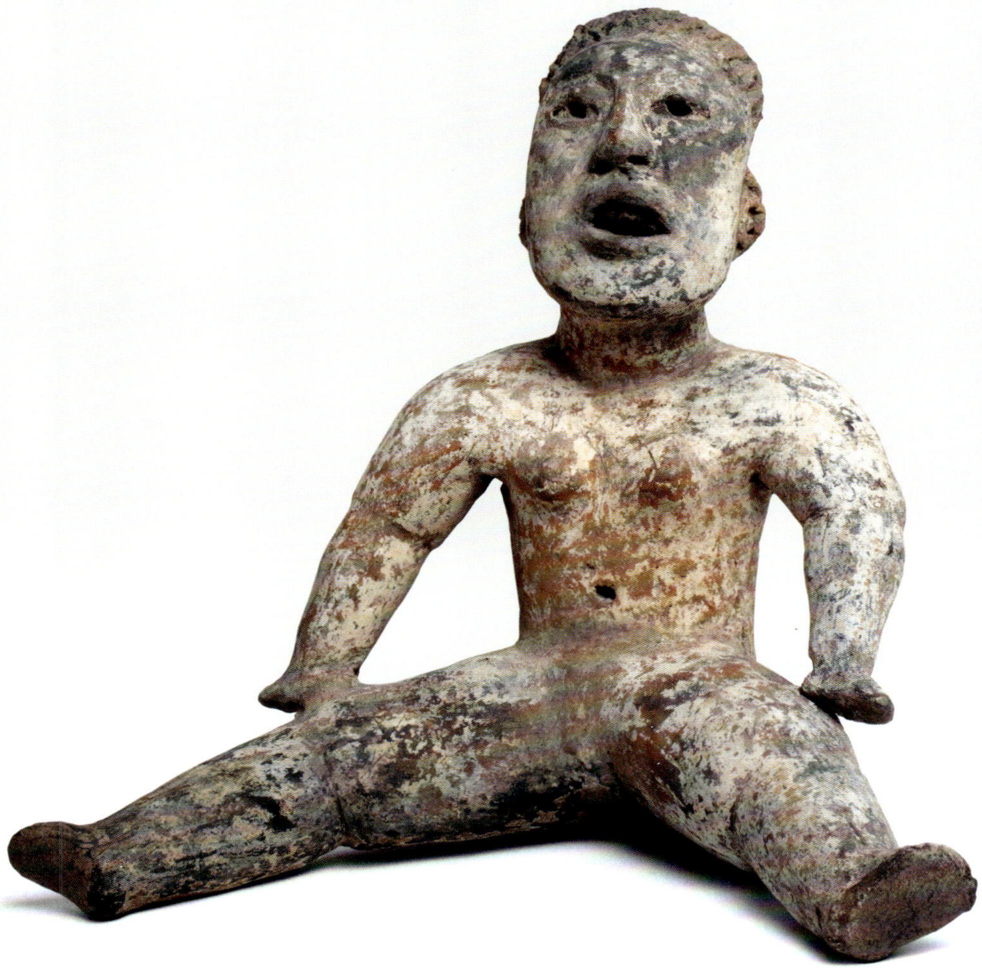

PLATE 121

TWIN FIGURE
Mexico, Tlatilco, Burial 12, Offering 6,
1200–600 BC
Earthenware with pigment
$8^{5}/_{8}$ x $9^{11}/_{16}$ x $6^{1}/_{2}$ in. (22 x 24.6 x 16.5 cm)
Museo Nacional de Antropología, Mexico City
(10-15739)

The modeling of this spectacular gourd-shaped bowl, or *tecomate*, is the epitome of elegance. The potters were probably inspired by natural forms, such as the gourds they must have used to transport liquids and foods prior to the development of pottery. Early pieces such as this might have been shaped using tools such as sticks or leather, or were simply created by the hands of the potter, for no molds have been found from the Early Formative period. Kaolin, an extremely fine white clay, was used for pottery manufacture. This piece displays attributes that make it one of the most beautiful expressions of Formative period ceramics. Found during the fourth excavation season at Tlatilco (García Moll et al. 1991), it was part of the offering in Burial 179, which belonged to a man displaying dental mutilation and cranial deformation. The latter practice was possibly carried out to identify high-status individuals. POC (OCHOA)

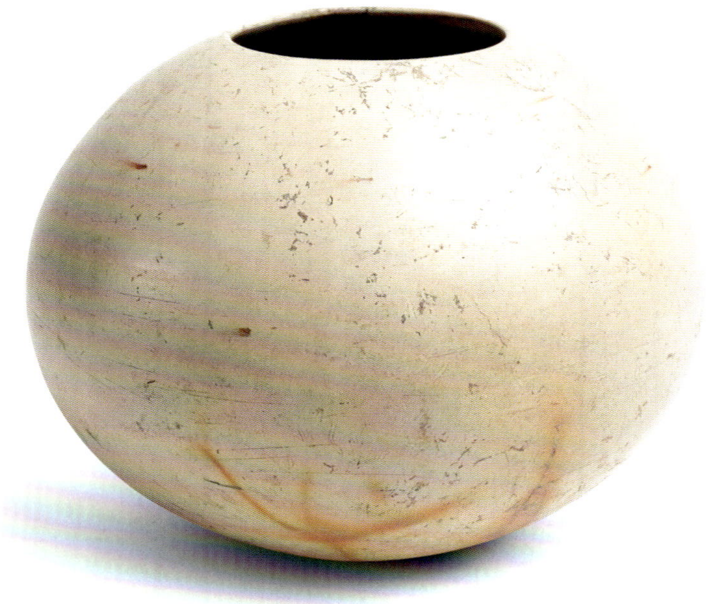

PLATE 122

GOURD-SHAPED BOWL (*TECOMATE*)
Mexico, Tlatilco, Burial 179, Offering 7,
1200–600 BC
Earthenware
4 9/16 x 5 13/16 in. (11.6 x 14.8 cm)
Museo Nacional de Antropología, Mexico City
(10-342225)

Vessels with flat bottoms, straight walls, and rims are common in pottery associated with Olmec groups, as are certain elements of grooved or incised decoration, such as the X-shaped motif and the jaguar claw, among others.

This bowl had red pigment applied after firing. It also has large quantities of pigment on its inner surface, which might imply that the bowl was a container with ritual significance. The pigment itself could have come from Guerrero, and its color may have symbolized the infusing of life wherever it was applied. The majority of burials at Tlatilco contain traces of red pigment, which suggests that it may have been intended to infuse the deceased with life. This vessel was part of the offering in Burial 80, found during the fourth and final excavation season at Tlatilco. Pertaining to the body of an adult woman, Burial 80 included figurines, stone artifacts, ceramic bowls, and a bottle. POC (OCHOA)

Spouted vessels are found at some sites in Central Mexico, particularly at Las Bocas, Puebla, and at Tlatilco, in the state of Mexico. The form, however, does not occur in the Gulf Coast Olmec area, making it more interesting that this example, from the fourth excavation season, is decorated with elements characteristic of Olmec iconography. Formed by grooves, a repetitive series of rectangles that might represent the jaguar's gums or eyes can be seen on the vessel's outer surface. It has traces of red pigment that contrast with the object's cream color. The repetitive design is typical of Olmec-style ceramic decoration. POC (OCHOA)

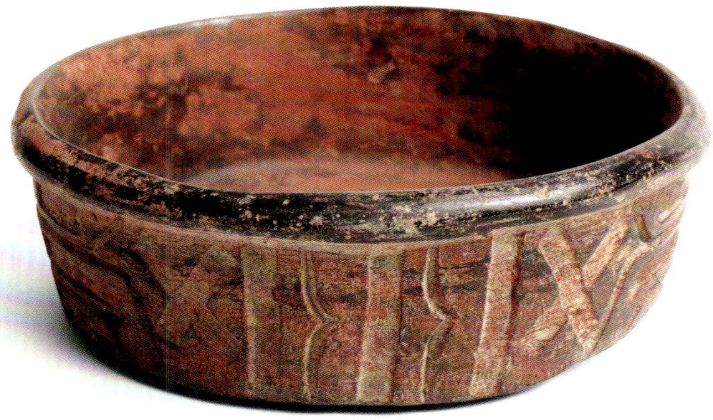

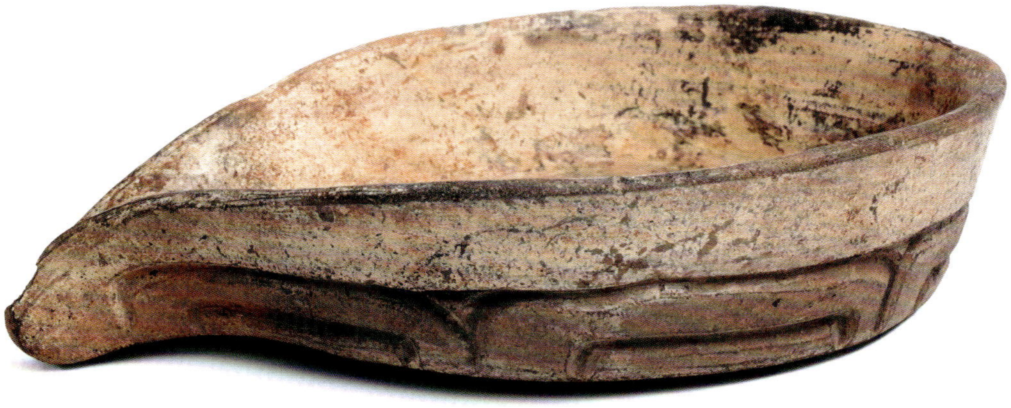

PLATES 123–124

INCISED BOWL
Mexico, Tlatilco, Burial 80, Offering 10,
1200–600 BC
Earthenware with pigment
$1^{3}/_{8}$ x $4^{1}/_{2}$ in. (3.5 x 11.5 cm)
Museo Nacional de Antropología, Mexico City
(10-341598)

VESSEL WITH SPOUT
Mexico, Tlatilco,
1200–600 BC
Earthenware with pigment
$1^{1}/_{8}$ x $6^{3}/_{8}$ in. (2.8 x 16.2 cm)
Museo Nacional de Antropología, Mexico City
(10-341916)

The early ceramics at Tlatilco, Las Bocas, and other sites in Central Mexico are often decorated with incised images of supernatural beings on a highly lustrous surface—a source of information about the cosmological beliefs of these early peoples. Bottles are particularly abundant in this region, where they display a wide variety of forms, in contrast with the Gulf Coast, where bottles are scarcer and tend to have flat bases and straight necks, and sometimes straight bodies as well.

This superb piece with a lustrous black slipped surface is decorated with one of the most frequently represented motifs in Olmec art: the claw-wing. Although they are sometimes shown with four phalanges, here five of them emerge from the palm. The artist utilized the decorative technique of carving, which reveals the original color of the clay beneath and shows traces of the red pigment with which the motif was covered.

The second example has a globular body and straight neck that displays a double rectangle motif containing another, smaller rectangle with crisscrossed lines. Three shapes, all of which are rendered schematically, can be seen on one of the sides, including a central triangular form that might represent a plant element. The carved decoration was created after

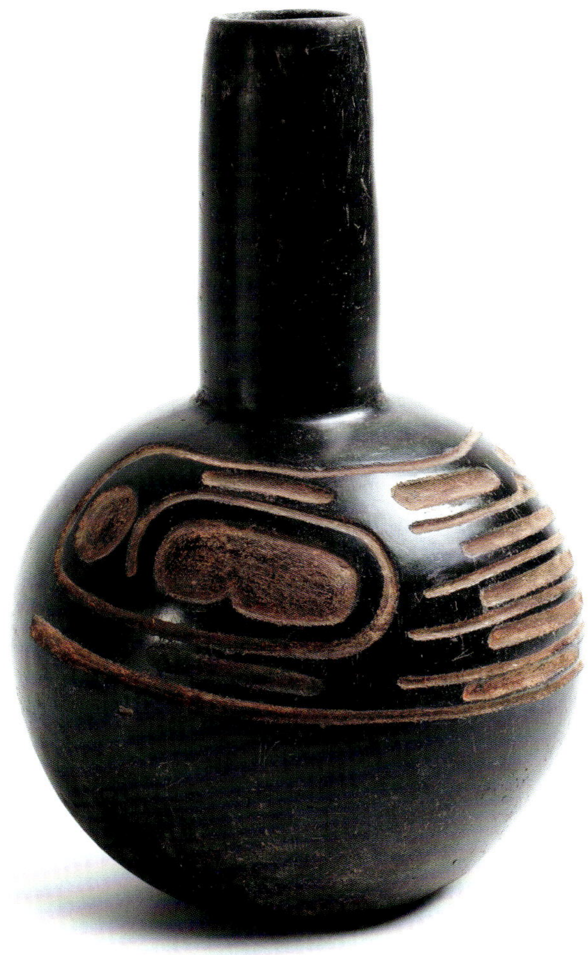

PLATE 125

INCISED BOTTLE
Mexico, Tlatilco, 1200–600 BC
Earthenware with pigment
7 1/2 x 4 15/16 in. (19 x 12.5 cm)
Museo Nacional de Antropología, Mexico City
(10-2192)

the piece was fired to produce a rough appearance; red pigment was then applied to the surface.

This bottle was part of the offering in Burial 131, excavated during the fourth and final field season at Tlatilco. Belonging to an adult woman with cranial deformation, the offering included stone objects as well as ceramics typical of Central Mexico, such as pots with long "spider" supports that were common at Tlatilco. Also found were four Olmec-style vessels with flat bases, straight walls, and carved, linear decoration, one of which displayed a netlike design. POC (OCHOA)

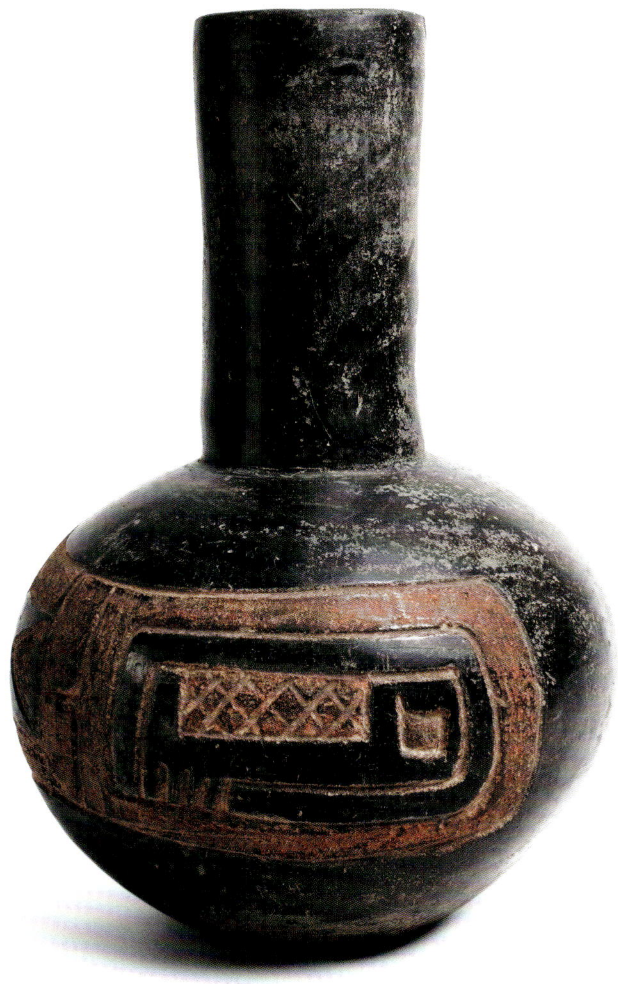

PLATE 126

INCISED BOTTLE
Mexico, Tlatilco, Burial 131, Offering 5,
1200–600 BC
Earthenware with pigment
8⅝ x 5½ in. (22 x 14 cm)
Museo Nacional de Antropología, Mexico City
(10-342071)

One of the distinguishing characteristics of the Preclassic period is the abundance of clay objects such as ceramics, figurines, ornaments, medical objects, and seals, among many others. The human figurines, all of which are different, seem to be portraits of people from the time. The forms suggest the practices that were then prevalent, including cranial deformation, dental mutilation, and facial and body paint. Even these small sculptures display traces of yellow and red color, although the designs are now barely visible. Seals can provide an idea of the types of geometric, naturalistic, or symbolic motifs that were used to create designs on skin or textiles. Flat seals had projecting pegs for handles. The Olmec are associated with the cylindrical form of roller seal seen here. The seals generally express symbolic elements, such as this example with curved and hook-like motifs. No traces of pigment are visible.

The second seal evokes the environment essential for the survival of the Gulf Coast Olmec. Among the animals represented during this period are birds, seen here rendered with grooves and deeper incisions. The head is in profile, with a long beak, and the eye was possibly created with a round object.

POC (OCHOA)

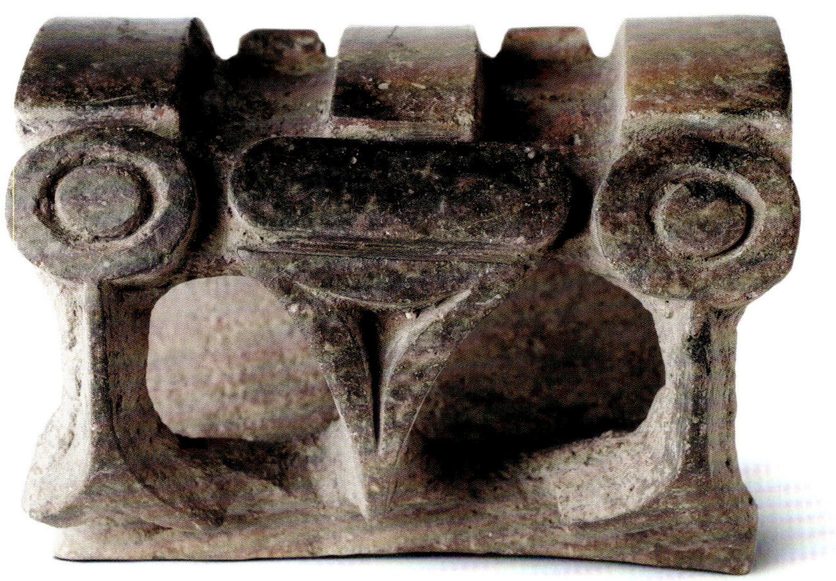

PLATE 127

ROLLER SEAL
Mexico, Central Highlands, 1200–600 BC
Earthenware
4⅝ x 3¾ in. (11.7 x 9.5 cm)
Museo Nacional de Antropología, Mexico City, gift of Frederick Field (10-78073)

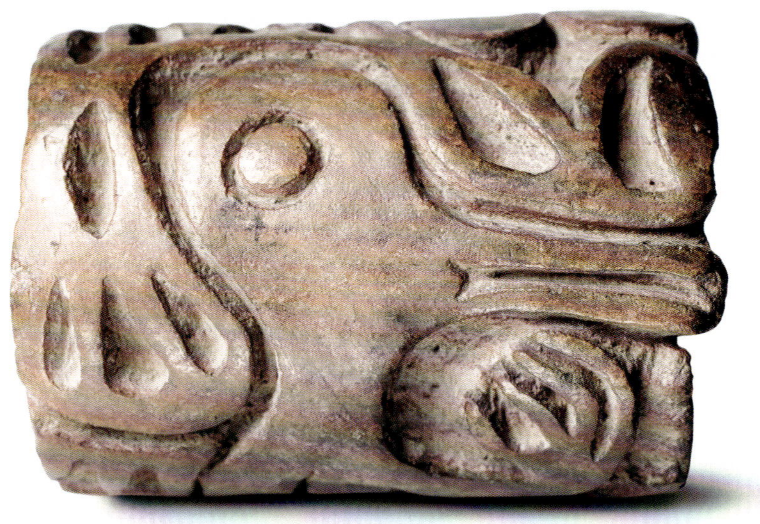

PLATE 128

ROLLER SEAL
Mexico, Central Highlands, 1200–600 BC
Earthenware
$3^{11}/_{16}$ x $2^{15}/_{16}$ in. (9.4 x 7.5 cm)
Museo Nacional de Antropología, Mexico City,
gift of Frederick Field (10-78071)

The exchange of goods, ideas, and products was firmly established by the Preclassic period, and intrusive Olmec groups distributed cultural items decorated with iconography based on the forces of nature. They also venerated certain animals such as the jaguar, which represented the earth.

This vessel is one of the key objects in Olmec iconography. Made of white clay and irregularly fired, this beautiful piece has a combination of lines and rectangles that depict the jaguar in profile and facing front. On one side, the animal is shown with a cleft on its head, a flame brow, and the X motif in its open mouth. The eyes rest on the upper lip, and the sides of the face are framed by two bands with three circles. The jaguar appears in profile on the other side, where one can see the cleft in the head, the eyebrow and eyes, the mouth, and the fangs that emerge from the lip. POC (OCHOA)

PLATE 129

INCISED VESSEL
Mexico, Valley of Mexico, 1200–600 BC
Earthenware
6 5/16 x 6 3/16 in. (16.1 x 15.8 cm)
Museo Nacional de Antropología, Mexico City, donation of George Pepper (10-77761)

See also:
Castro-Leal 1996: cat. 39
Reilly 1995: 36–37, figs. 17, 21a

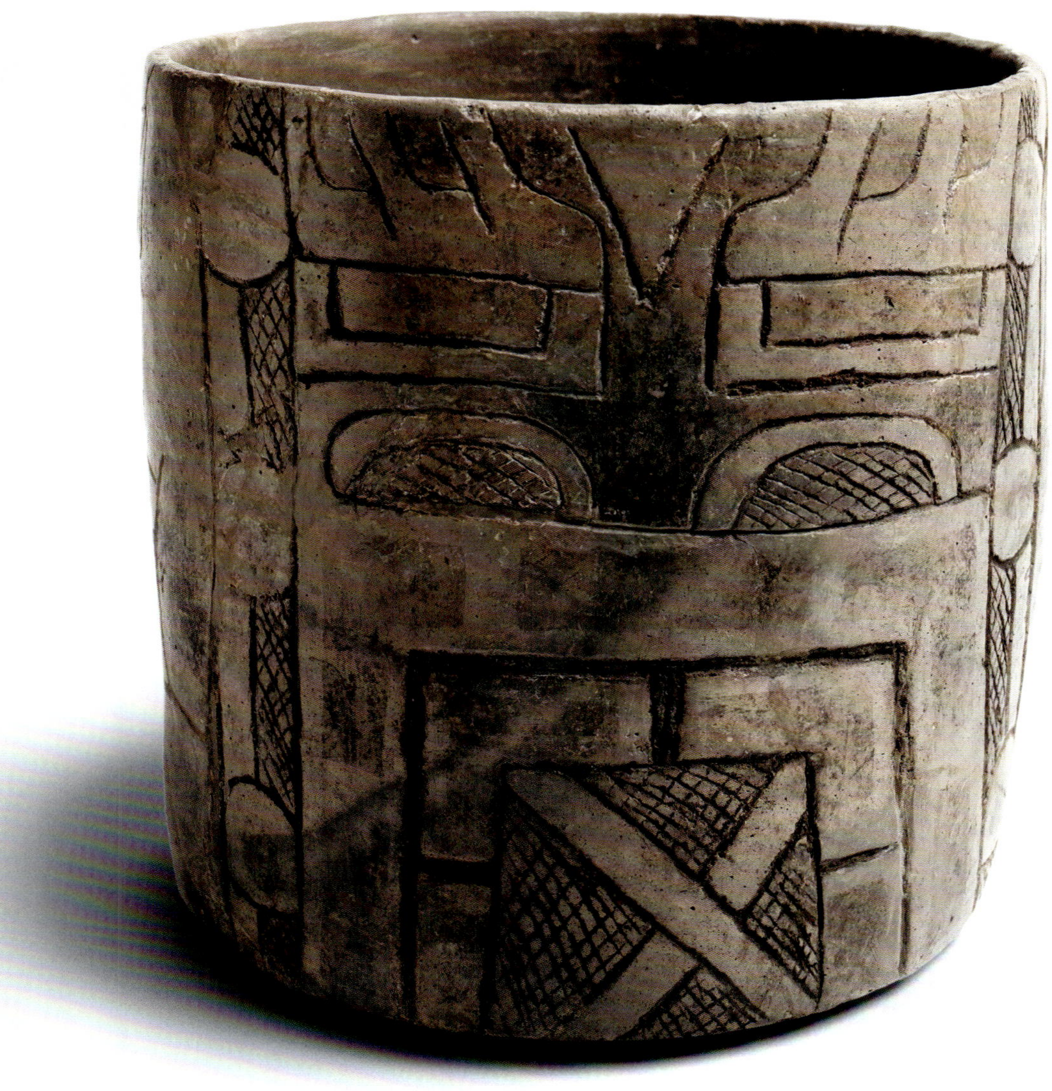

Las Bocas refers to an archaeological region in southern Puebla that occupied a key location along the routes linking the Gulf Coast, Guerrero, Morelos, and Oaxaca in ancient times. A recent archaeological survey located Formative period settlements along two fluvial terraces of the Rio Atotonilco, at the southwestern edge of the town of Caballo Pintado (Paillés Hernández 2007), documenting the remains of floors and other architectural features as well as abundant ceramic sherds and fragments of stone implements. The area was heavily looted in the 1950s and early 1960s, and a large corpus of beautifully constructed ceramic figures and vessels, many carved or incised with Olmec-style motifs, have since been attributed to the region (Coe 1965b). A local specialty was the use of a fine white clay known as kaolin for ceramic wares, as seen in the vessel and figure here.

The expressive figure, seated in a cross-legged position, rests his head on his left hand in a somewhat musing posture. Such figures are generally male and covered with a thick white slip, a suspension of kaolin clay in water, and bear an ivory-like polish (Niederberger 1996b: cat. 18). VMF

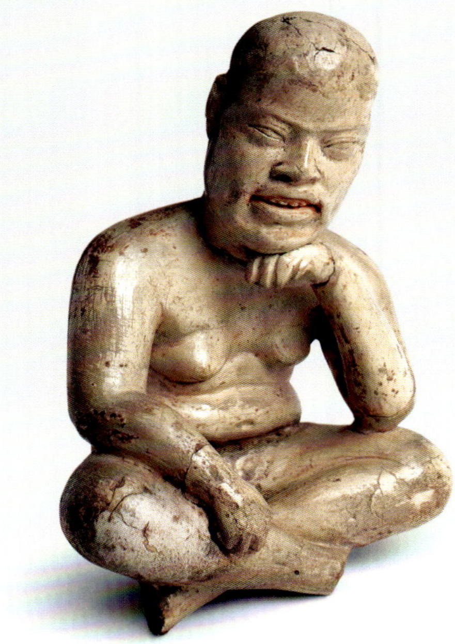

PLATES 130–131

SEATED FIGURE WITH HEAD RESTING ON HAND
Mexico, Puebla, Las Bocas, 1200–800 BC
Kaolin ceramic
$5^{1}/_{8}$ x $3^{1}/_{2}$ x 3 in. (13 x 9 x 7.5 cm)
Museo Amparo, Puebla (MA FA 57 PJ 866)

See also:
Cervantes 2008: 48–49

JAR
Mexico, Central Highlands, 1000–800 BC
Kaolin ceramic
$8^{1}/_{2}$ x $6^{1}/_{2}$ x $6^{1}/_{2}$ in. (21.6 x 16.5 x 16.5 cm)
Bowers Museum (BMCA #F74.4.1)

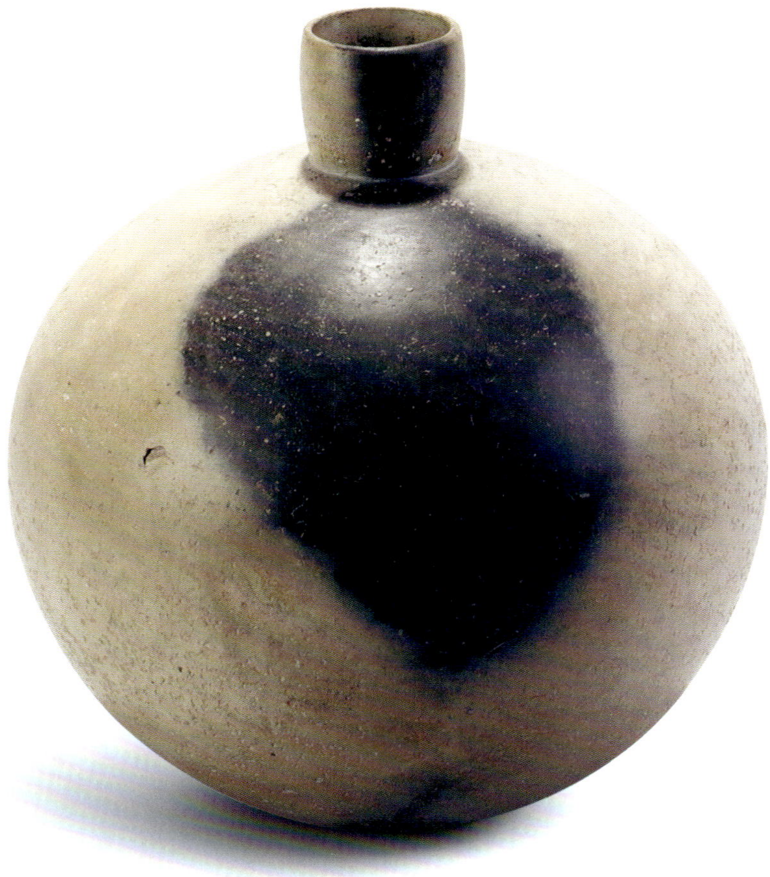

Ceramic hollow-baby figures, which appear to represent fleshy babies or infants with Olmec features, seem to have been found primarily in the Central Highlands of Mexico, especially in Morelos and Puebla. The provenience for many of these figures is unknown because they rarely have been scientifically excavated, although most are thought to date to between 1200 and 800 BC (Blomster 1998). Quite often these figures appear to have been deliberately or ritually broken or smashed in ancient times and then reassembled much later for museums and private collectors.

The figures, which often have no evident gender, are typically posed sitting with legs apart, although they have also been found in crawling positions. One or both arms may be raised, as if depicting a moment of action; sometimes the hands are animated in a particular way. In its raised right hand this figure balances a hollow ball decorated with incised lines and remains of red pigment, as if about to throw it. The form of the figure's head may evoke the custom of cranial elongation to create an ideal head shape. The particular shaved coiffure with textured designs seems to be found most often in figures unearthed at Las Bocas. On this example, an artist's thumbprint is barely discernible in the clay on the left side of the coiffure.

Some hollow babies may have been placed in elite burials, while others may have served as iconic items for display or for use in a public ceremony. One hollow baby, excavated from a bell-shaped pit in the Mixteca Alta of Oaxaca, had been placed there as ritual paraphernalia, possibly representative of some type of regional cult. It was found in a nonfunerary context with other artifacts and a canine skeleton (ibid.). KB

PLATE 132

HOLLOW-BABY FIGURE HOLDING BALL
Mexico, Puebla, probably Las Bocas, 1200–800 BC
Slip-painted ceramic with pigment
$11^1/_4$ x 10 in. (28.6 x 25.4 cm)
Fine Arts Museums of San Francisco, gift of Lewis K. and Elizabeth M. Land (2009.1.90)

See also:
Coe 1965b: 184

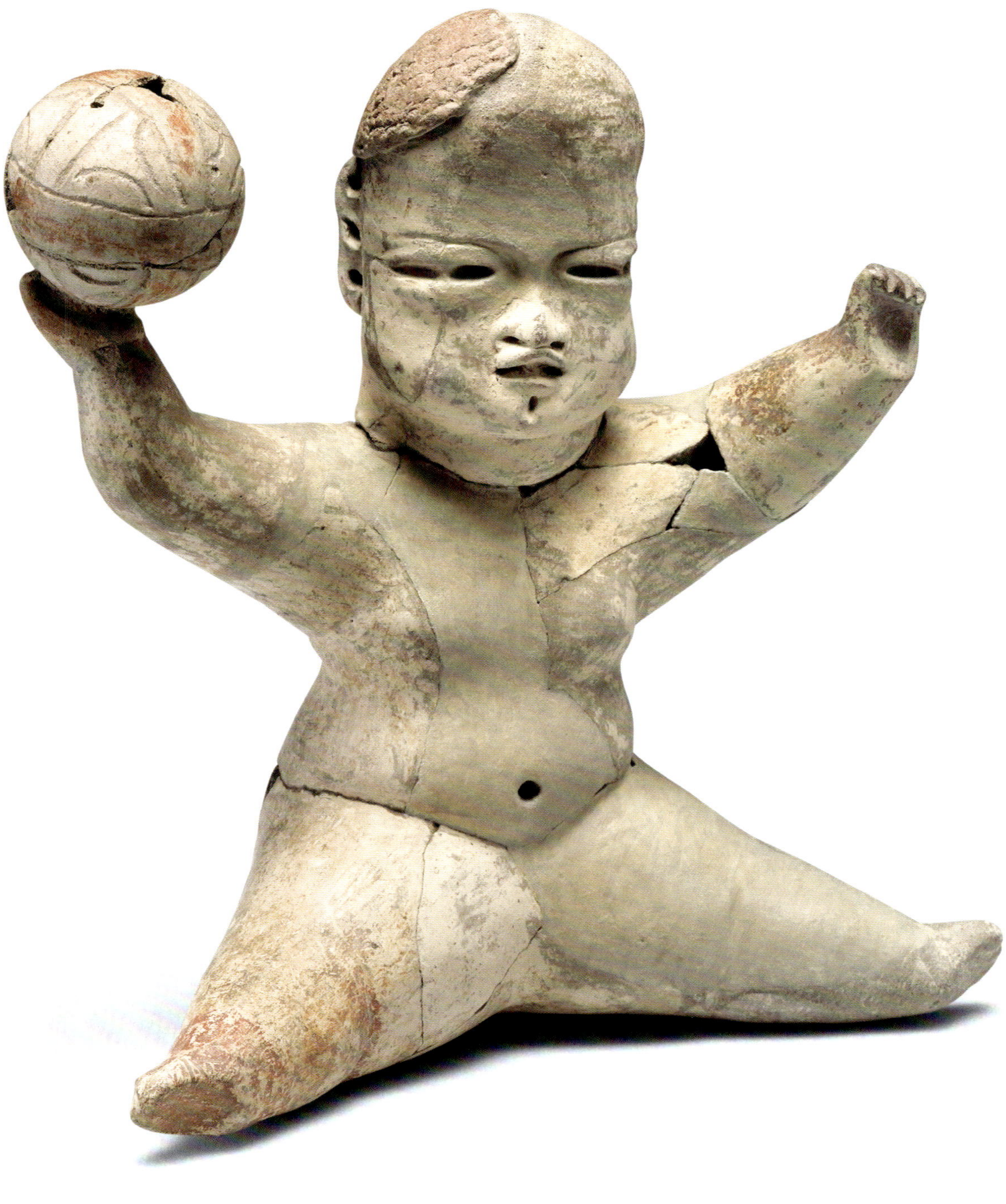

The modern state of Chiapas encompasses a variety of environmental zones ranging from the Pacific coastal plain to the highlands in the north and east to a region known as the Grijalva Depression through which runs the Río Grijalva, a major waterway linking this region to the Gulf Coast (Valverde Valdés 1992: 17). Olmec-style monuments executed in a variety of regional styles, greenstone objects, and ceramic vessels with carved motifs have been found in sites on the Pacific Coast extending from Chiapas to Guatemala, suggesting that by 1200 BC this region was actively participating in long-distance networks of trade and exchange of both goods and ideas (Navarette 1974; Clark and Pye 2000b: 237). While monumental sculpture appears to be limited to the Gulf Coast during the Early Formative period (1400–1000 BC), the beginning of the Middle Formative witnessed the creation of monumental three-dimensional and relief sculpture in both the Central Highlands of Mexico, at the site of Chalcatzingo, and along the Pacific Coast, from Chiapas to Guatemala.

Discovered some 12 miles (19 kilometers) northeast of Ocozocuautla (Navarette 1971: 69), this standing figure has the typical Olmec-style features of elongated head, downturned mouth, and incised lines indicating a plain belt and loincloth, but the sloping shoulders resemble those on the figure from Chalcatzingo, Morelos (pl. 111). The eyes, nose, and mouth are deeply drilled, and perforated holes through the earlobes suggest that the figure may have been adorned in the past. The right arm is broken above the elbow; the left arm terminates in a hand with light incisions indicating fingers.

The pectoral, which has two holes drilled through it at the level of the ears, may also have been utilized as a belt ornament (Navarette 1971: 70). VMF

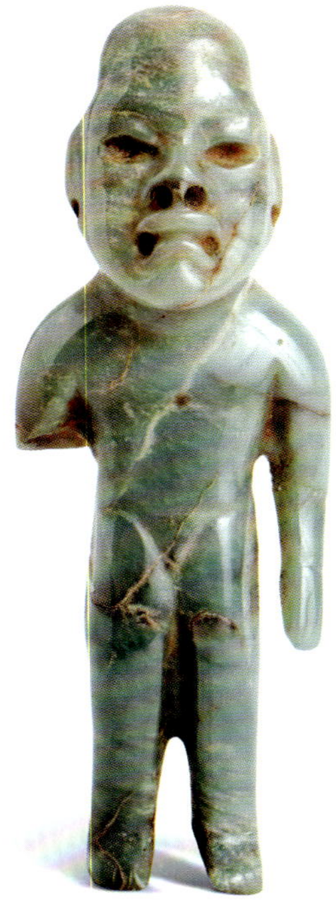

PLATE 133

STANDING FIGURE
Mexico, Chiapas, Ocozocuautla, 1000–400 BC
Jadeite
3¼ x 1³⁄₁₆ in. (8.3 x 3 cm)
Museo Regional de Chiapas, Tuxtla Gutiérrez
(10-409530)

See also:
Navarrete 1974: 13–14, figs. 12, 14
Stirling 1947: 140–142

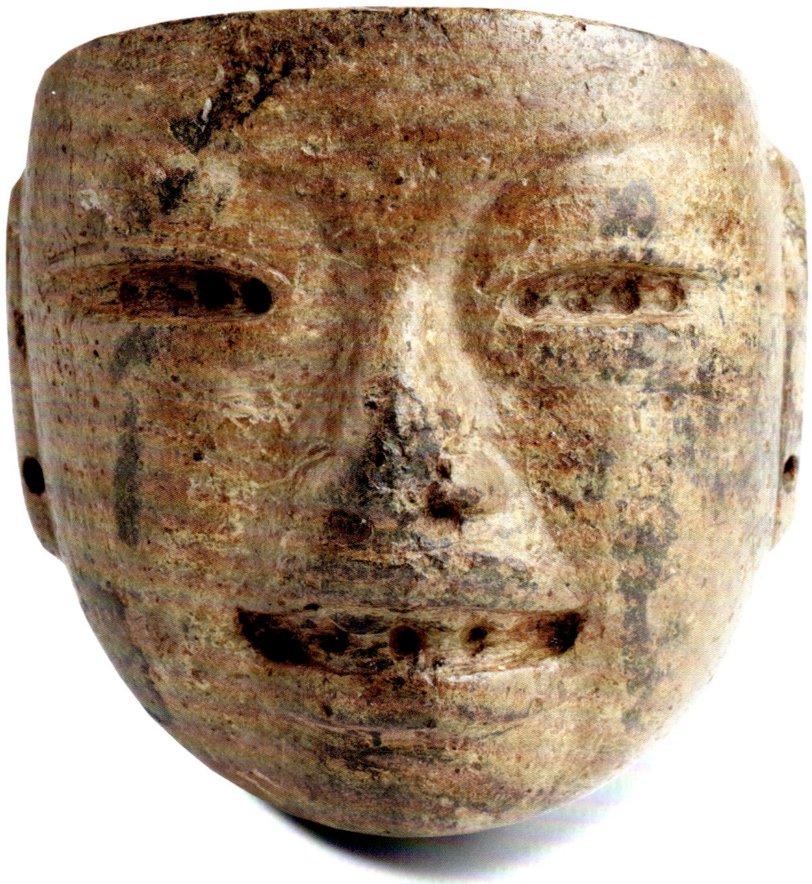

PLATE 134

PECTORAL
Mexico, Chiapas, Soconusco, 1000–400 BC
Greenstone with brown veins
$4^{3}/_{4}$ x $4^{5}/_{16}$ x $1^{15}/_{16}$ in. (12 x 11 x 5 cm)
Museo Regional de Chiapas, Tuxtla Gutiérrez
(10-409511)

Though discovered in a Late Classic period context (John Clark, personal communication, January 2010), the form of this two-part vessel implies that it was made during the Early Classic, when such types were more common. The ivory-colored slip, found on pottery from lowland Tabasco and adjacent areas of Chiapas well into the Classic period, most likely continues the characteristic Formative period tradition seen on ceramics from the Gulf Coast heartland and the Central Highlands of Mexico (Dorie Reents-Budet, personal communication, January 2010). As such this vessel may have served as a treasured heirloom. VMF

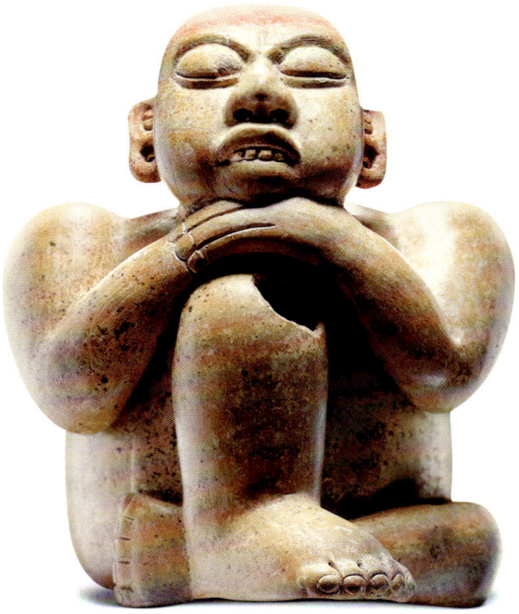

PLATE 135

FIGURAL JAR WITH LID
Mexico, Chiapas, Guajilar, AD 300–500
Slip-painted ceramic
8 x 5$^{9}/_{16}$ x 7$^{5}/_{16}$ in. (20.3 x 14.2 x 18.5 cm)
Museo Regional de Chiapas, ¯uxtla Gutiérrez
(10-338427)

See also:
Whiting in Schmidt, de la Garza, and Nalda 1998: cat. 486

This sculpture, recently discovered on private property in fragmented condition, represents the localized style of boulder relief sculpture in sites along the Pacific Coast. The squared face of this composite creature is framed by rectangular ear ornaments with circular flares at the bottom. The downturned mouth reveals two fangs, while the eyes are horizontal slits. The chin is especially pronounced, and the top of the head appears to be covered by a cap with deep vertical grooves. The same type of grooves can be seen on the Ojo de Agua monument (pl. 138) as the crested brow of the cleft-headed pectoral, possibly signifying a regional trait in Chiapas. VMF

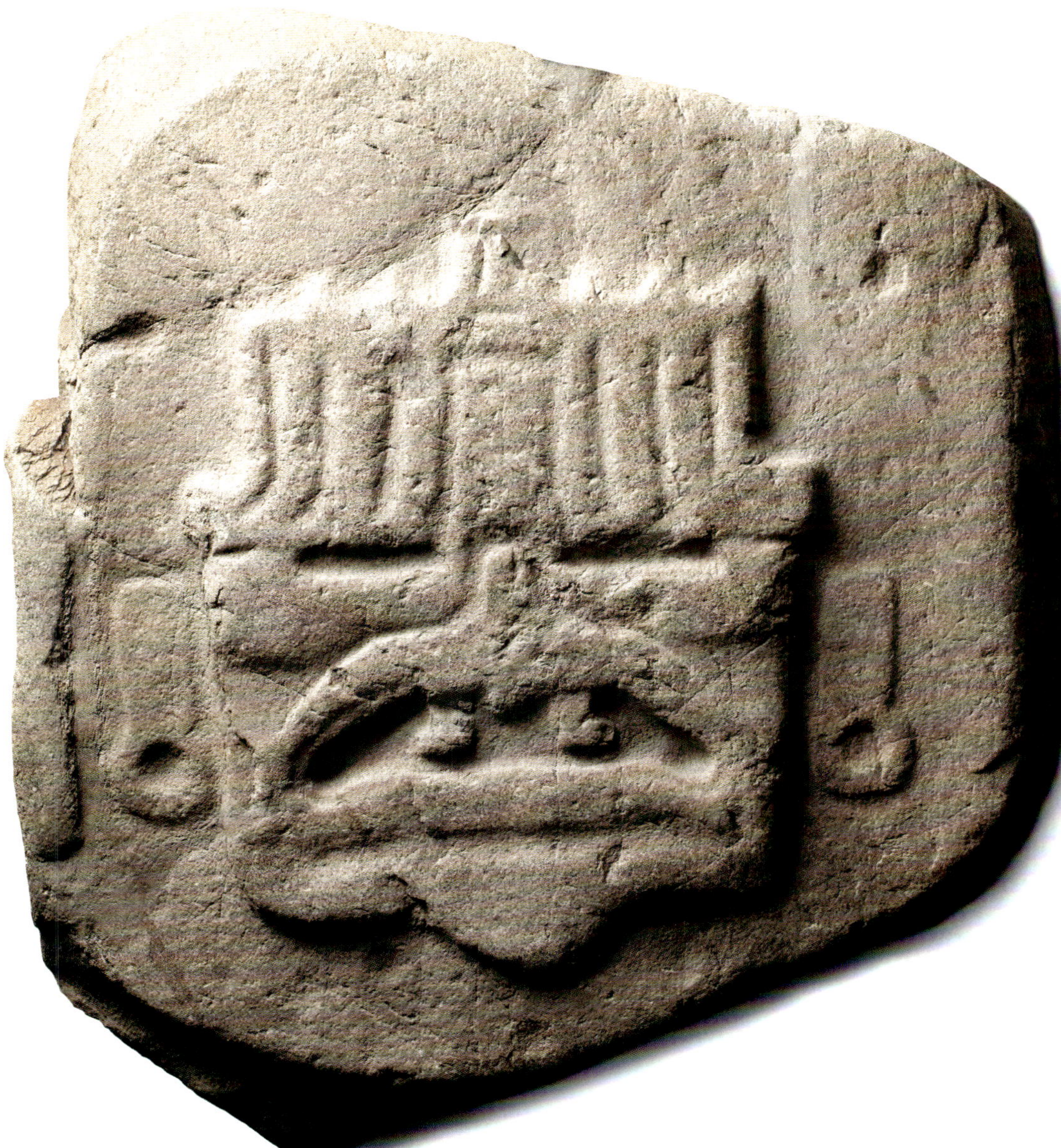

PLATE 136

MONUMENT 1
(COMPOSITE CREATURE)
Mexico, Chiapas, Villaflores, ca. 300 BC
Sandstone
$42^{1}/_{2}$ x $35^{7}/_{16}$ x $15^{3}/_{4}$ in. (108 x 90 x 40 cm)
Museo Regional de Chiapas, Tuxtla Gutiérrez
(10-461883)

Tuxtla Chico, located on the Pacific Coast of Chiapas near Izapa, may have participated in the widespread trade networks that moved luxury commodities such as cacao around Mesoamerica. Referred to as the "Dancing Jaguar" because of his crouched pose, the figure wears an elaborate headdress and headband and a cloth belt that is gathered in four loops at his back. As David Grove (1996b: cat. 4) notes, the headdress lacks the V-shaped cleft that characterizes those from the Gulf Coast. The grooved incisions down the back of the figure suggest that the headdress may be made of plumes. The figure also wears thick, curved ear ornaments and anklets that resemble shell. The cutaway area around the figure's face suggests that he may be wearing a mask. VMF

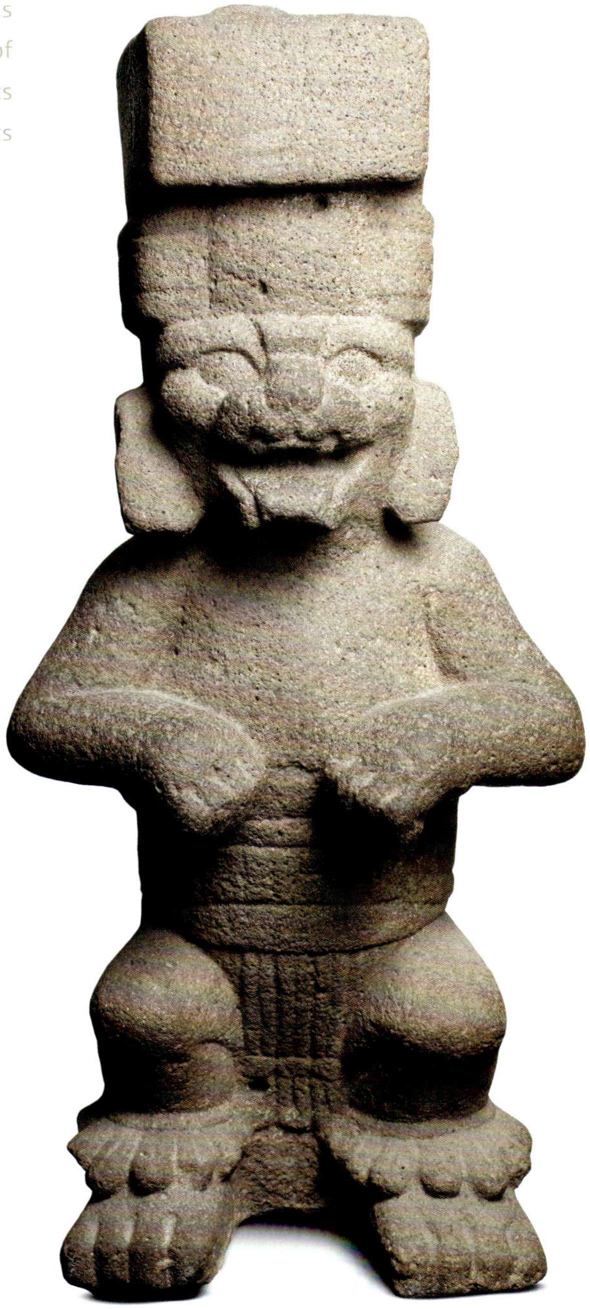

PLATE 137

ANTHROPOMORPHIC JAGUAR FIGURE
Mexico, Chiapas, Tuxtla Chico, 600–300 BC
Basalt
$39^3/_4$ x $18^1/_8$ x $15^3/_4$ in. (101 x 46 x 40 cm)
Museo Regional de Chiapas, Tuxtla Gutiérrez
(10-40941)

See also:
Clark and Pye 2000b: 223–224, 229, fig. 9
Easby and Scott 1970: cat. 35

Although this sculpture lacks specific archaeological context (Clark and Pye 2000b: 221, fig. 4), it reveals a fascinating and unique compilation of Olmec-style traits. Carlos Navarette (1974: 17) considers it the most impressive Olmec sculpture found on the Chiapas coast, aside from the relief sculptures at Pijijiapan. Ojo de Agua is a ranch located $1\frac{1}{5}$ miles (2 kilometers) south of Álvaro Obregón in the municipality of Mazatan, and the sculpture was broken in a few places by the plow that uncovered it near some mounds (Navarette 1971: 75). The figure's face, while too badly destroyed to make out its features, is framed by the pleated-paper headdress associated with the rain god. A plaque or large, rectangular pectoral completely covers the body of the figure. The plaque is in the form of a cleft-headed creature similar in shape to the incised celts from the Gulf Coast (pls. 88–89). Superimposed on the pectoral is a cross-legged Olmec-style figure seated on a throne, not unlike the figures seated within niches on the thrones from La Venta and other heartland sites (see fig. 20, pl. 64). This smaller figure also has a cleft head, and he wears a pectoral with an X motif. VMF

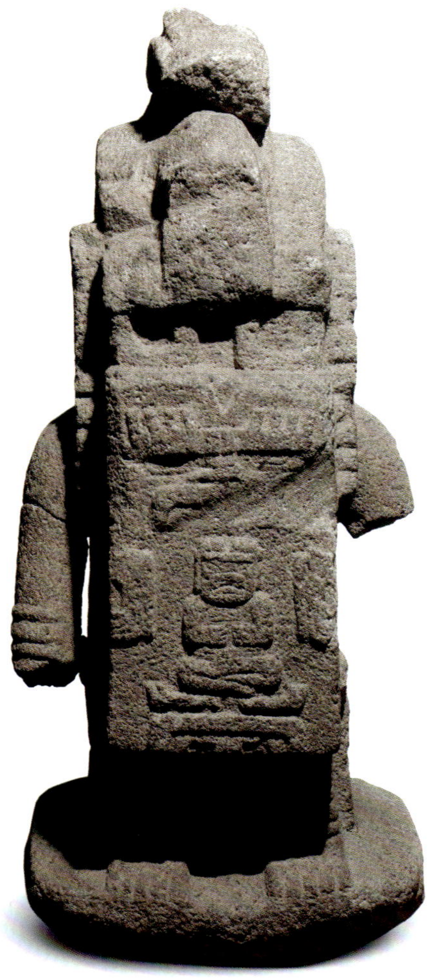

PLATE 138

STANDING FIGURE
Mexico, Chiapas, Ojo de Agua, 950–850 BC
Andesite
$26\frac{3}{8}$ x $10\frac{1}{4}$ x $8\frac{1}{4}$ in. (67 x 26 x 21 cm)
Museo Arqueológico de Soconusco, Tapachula, Chiapas (10-457456)

See also:
Milbrath 1979: 26, fig. 49

Discovered in the center of the modern city of Tonalá, this relief sculpture depicts a man simply dressed in the loincloth and helmet associated with ballplayer figurines in the Basin of Mexico (Niederberger 2000).

Although the origins of the Mesoamerican ballgame have not yet been discovered, the earliest ballcourts had been located in Chiapas, dating between 900 and 500 BC (Hill 1999: 42–47). Excavations in 1990 at the site of Paso de la Amada on the coastal plain of Chiapas, however, revealed the remains of an earthen ballcourt, constructed over an earlier playing field that dates to approximately 1400 BC. The court consisted of two parallel mounds measuring between 243 and 256 feet (74 and 78 meters) long and nearly 5 feet (1.5 meters) high. The court framed a playing alley that measured 253 feet (77 meters) in length and 22 feet (6.8 meters) wide (ibid.: 95–96). The concept of the ballgame disseminated rapidly throughout Mesoamerica, resulting in a variety of ballcourt types, from open-ended to enclosed I-shaped courts. VMF

PLATE 139

BALLPLAYER RELIEF SCULPTURE
Mexico, Chiapas, Tonalá, 1000–400 BC
Stone
22 1/16 x 15 3/4 x 7 1/16 in. (56 x 40 x 18 cm)
Museo Regional de Chiapas, Tuxtla Gutiérrez
(10-456453)

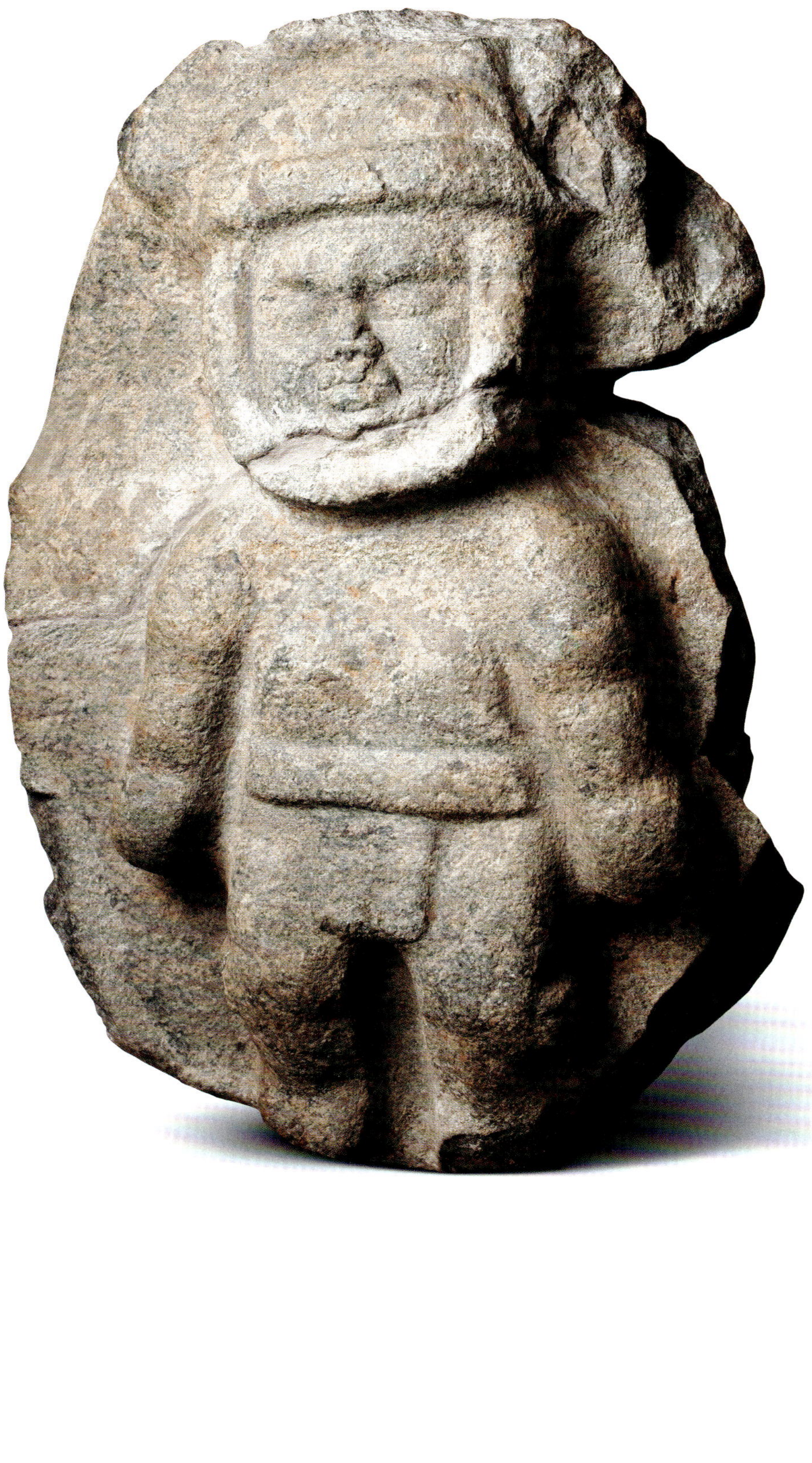

Despite the trajectory of Mesoamerica's three-thousand-year history, the civilizations that followed the Olmec apparently retained a sense of their pioneering significance in establishing the social, artistic, and cosmological patterns that resonated throughout the region. While a handful of objects from diverse areas of Mesoamerica reflect knowledge of Olmec style, deeper patterns of awareness can be seen in the layout of cities and their structures within specific landscapes and in the veneration of ancestors, natural forces, and supernatural beings.

A few objects also intimate that the idea of writing or systematic notation originated among the peoples of the Gulf Coast, as did the sacred calendar consisting of 260 days. The practice of naming individuals for the day on which they were born may have been among the early uses of this calendar, which itself corresponds to a woman's gestational period. The metaphors perceived in the cycles of nature, from seasonal weather patterns to the annual appearance of food sources, provided the basis for the enduring social and cosmological patterns expressed by Mesoamerican peoples over the course of their history.

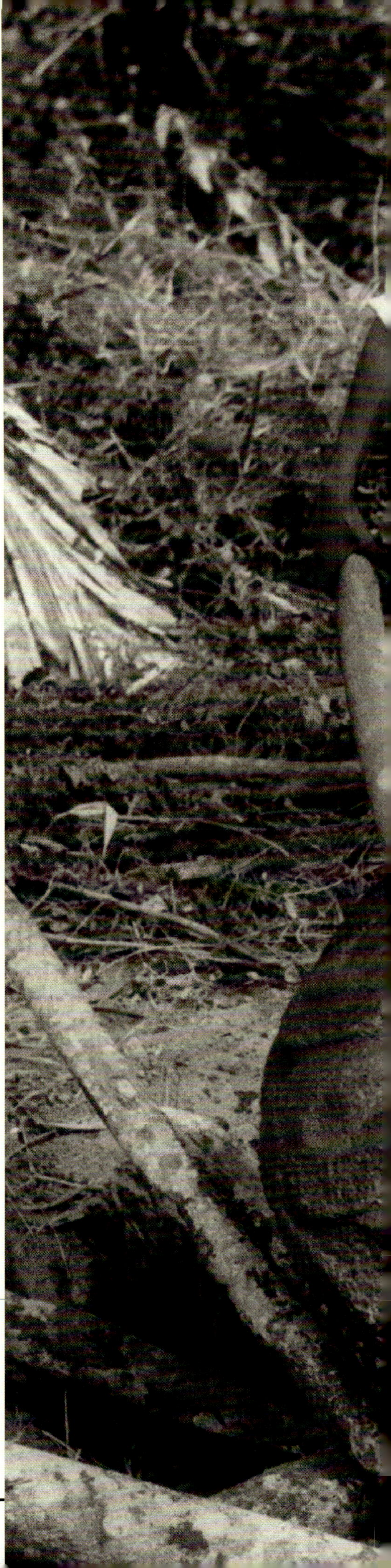

Workers pose alongside Monument 2
at Cerro de las Mesas, ca. 1940

THE OLMEC LEGACY IN LATER MESOAMERICA

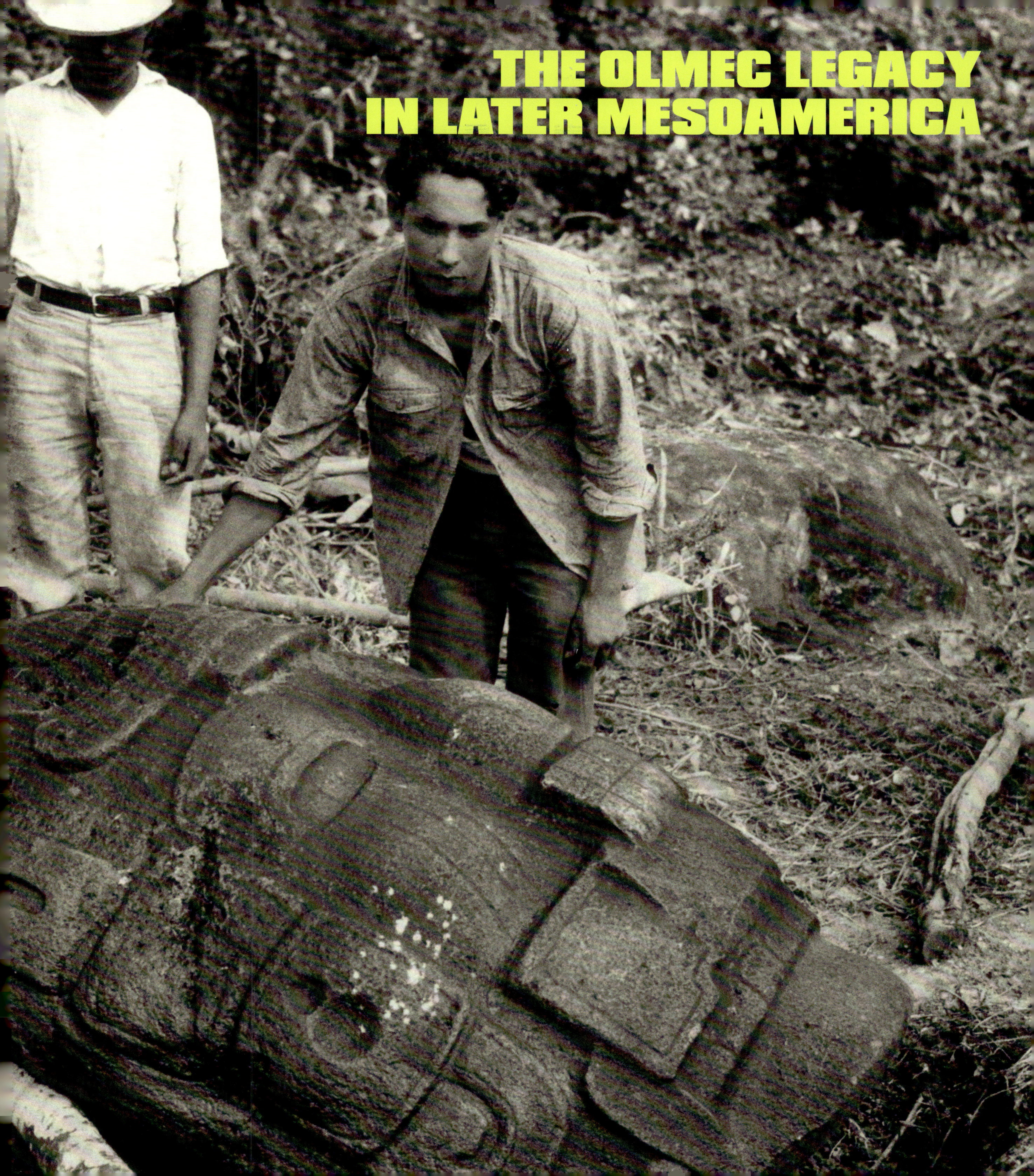

Although its style corresponds to the Middle Formative period (1000–400 BC), this mask was part of an offering excavated by archaeologists in November 1978 at the Aztec Templo Mayor (Matos Moctezuma 1999: 155). Eduardo Matos (1996: cat. 94) compares the form of the nose on the mask to other objects in the Olmec style that derive from the state of Guerrero in southern Mexico. He identifies the material as hornblende, a metamorphic rock that is found in the region bordering Guerrero, Puebla, and Oaxaca. Further lapidary analyses are being carried out at the Museo del Templo Mayor to identify when and where the mask was made, that is, in Guerrero or on the Gulf Coast. It is unusual for an Olmec-style mask to have holes drilled in the forehead, as this one does, but this feature may indicate its use as an heirloom pendant for the owner. VMF

Once part of the Holm collection of Mexican antiquities (Caso and Bernal 1952: fig. 489), this cream ware incense burner with a modeled Olmec-style face attests to widespread interaction spheres during the Middle Formative period. VMF

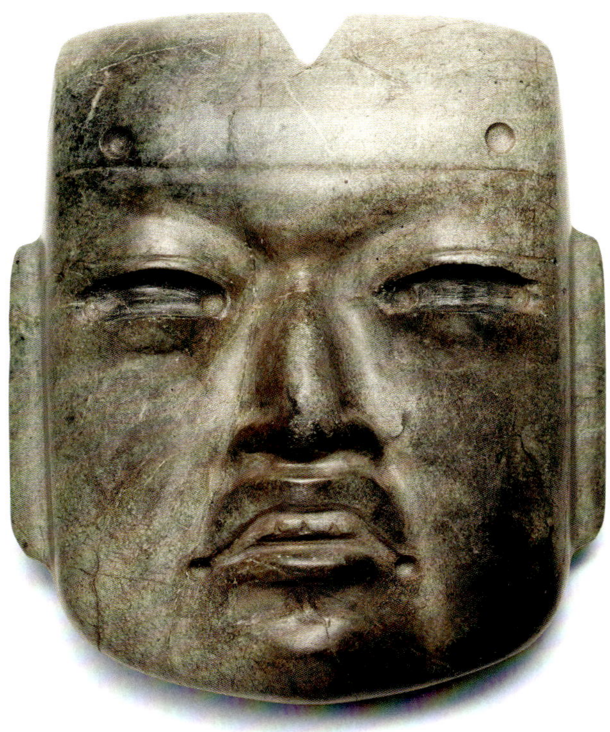

PLATES 140–141

MASK
Mexico, Templo Mayor, Offering 20, AD 1470
Hornblende
4 x 3 3/8 x 1 1/4 in. (10.2 x 8.6 x 3.1 cm)
Museo del Templo Mayor, Mexico City
(10-168803)

EFFIGY HEAD BRAZIER
Mexico, Oaxaca, 500–200 BC
Ceramic
Height: 8 1/2 in. (21.6 cm)
Los Angeles County Museum of Art,
gift of Constance McCormick Fearing
(AC1992.134.27)

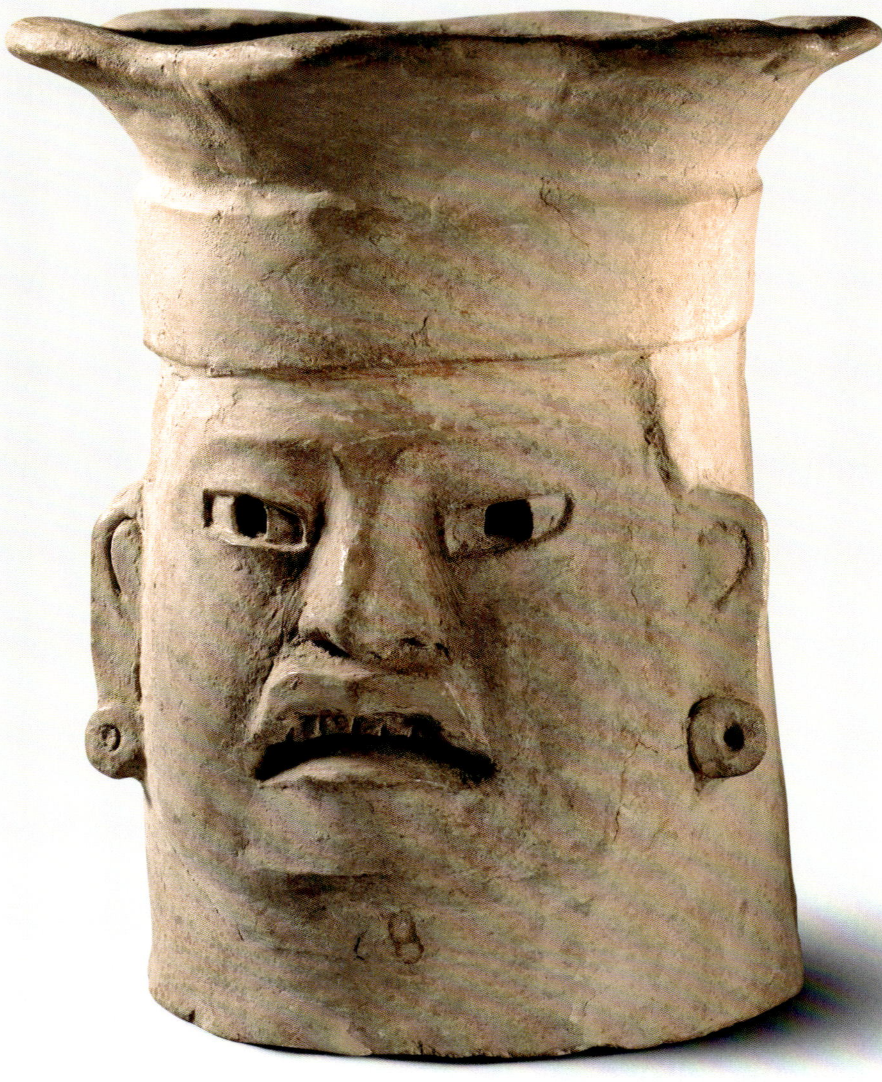

This pendant, made from the translucent blue-green jadeite that typifies the finest Olmec-style objects, was found in a crypt containing the remains of two individuals as well as several ceramic vessels and jade and shell beads (Rathje, Sabloff, and Gregory 1973). The crypt apparently dates to around AD 800, based on the types of ceramic vessels found in it, underscoring the importance of heirlooms in Mesoamerican civilizations. The pendant depicts an Olmec-style face framed within an oval form that ends with a pair of miniature maskettes flanking the cheeks. Three cleft elements emerge from the top and sides of the frame (Pohorilenko 1996: cat. 95).

The site of San Gervasio is located near the northern coastline of Cozumel. The pendant was found during investigations of the architectural Group VI, which comprised in part a large platform with seven smaller platforms resting atop it. The crypt containing the pendant was beneath a plaster floor centered on the entryway of the remains of a rectangular structure (Gregory 1975: 103–104). VMF

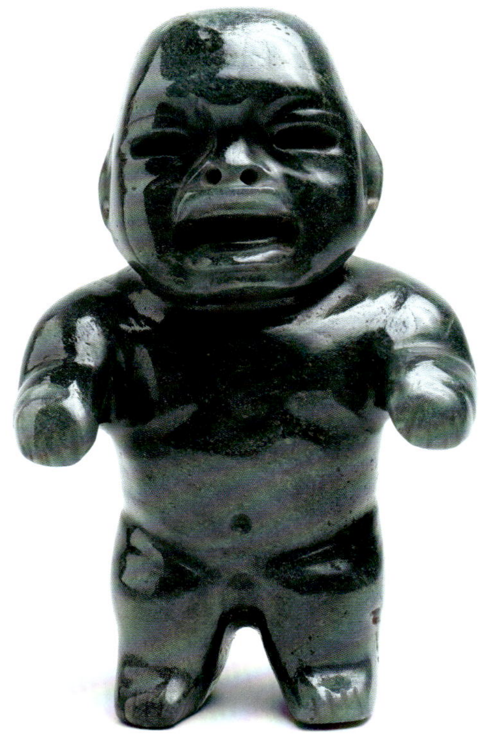

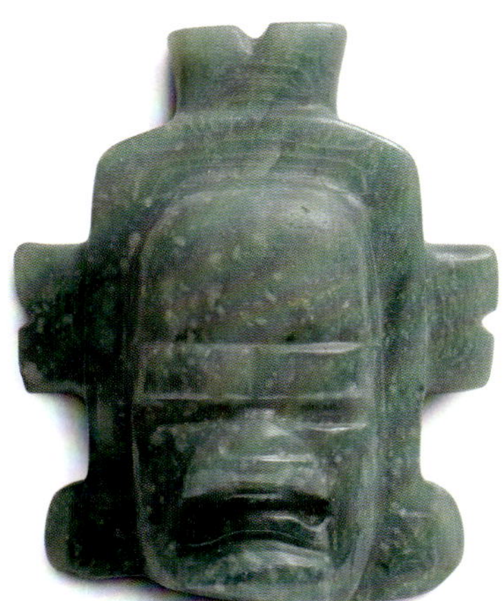

PLATE 142

PENDANT WITH WERE-JAGUAR HEAD FRAMED WITH CLEFT ELEMENTS
Mexico, Yucatán, Cozumel, San Gervasio, 1000–400 BC
Jadeite
2⅝ x 21⅝ in. (6.7 x 55 cm)
Museo Regional de Yucatán "Palacio Cantón," Mérida, Yucatán (10-152738)

See also:
Fernández Souza 1998: cat. 236
Fields and Reents-Budet 2005: cat. 78

The ancient city of Cerro de las Mesas, located west of the heartland centers in the Papaloapan basin, was occupied during the Middle Formative period but is better known for its later constructions and carved monuments, some with hieroglyphic writing, that date to the Early Classic period (AD 250–550). Matthew W. and Marion Stirling conducted excavations there in 1941, and at the very end of the season they made an amazing discovery of a cache containing 782 stone objects, primarily earspools and beads worked in a variety of jades (Pugh 1981: 7). The cache was found when Miguel Baltazar, the project foreman, was removing a wheelbarrow ramp to fill in an excavation trench. It was located beneath the steps of an Early Classic temple mound, where it may have been placed as a dedicatory offering (Easby and Scott 1970: cat. 40). Among its contents were this anthropomorphic figure and pectoral in the form of a dugout canoe.

Philip Drucker (1955: 31–32) describes the figure as "an outstanding product of Olmec art," probably representing an infant with the typical Olmec-style physical features and worked with the utmost skill in carving (Castro-Leal 1996: cat. 61). The pectoral is drilled with four biconical suspension holes (Drucker 1955: 47–48). Incised with a pair of cleft-headed supernatural beings at either end, the pendant has a hollowed-out center large enough to accommodate the feet of the figure, which may have once stood upright in the canoe (ibid.: 48). Both objects are made from a translucent bluish jadeite that was especially prized by the Gulf Coast Olmec. MC-LE

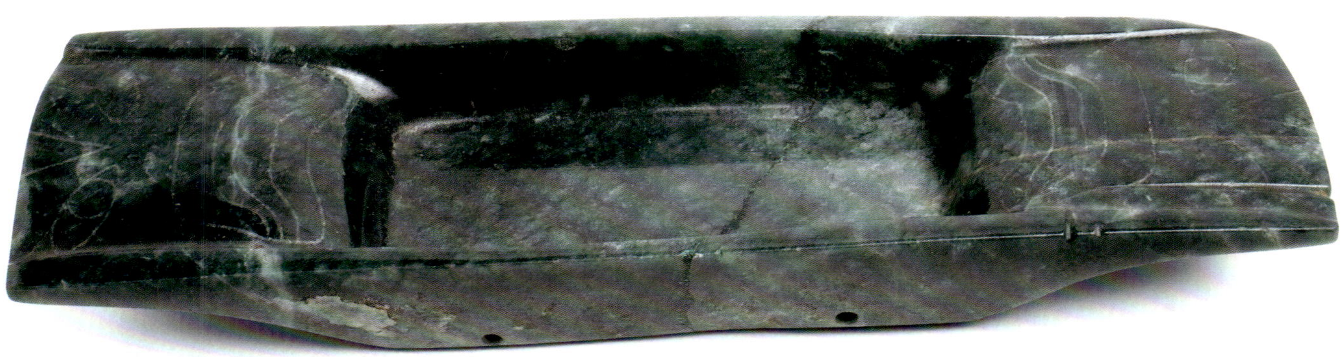

PLATES 143–144

ANTHROPOMORPHIC FIGURE
Mexico, Veracruz, Cerro de las Mesas, 1000–400 BC
Jadeite
$4^{3}/_{4}$ x $2^{15}/_{16}$ x $1^{11}/_{16}$ in. (12 x 7.5 x 4.3 cm)
Museo Nacional de Antropología, Mexico City (10-4511)

CANOE-SHAPED PECTORAL
Mexico, Veracruz, Cerro de las Mesas, 1000–400 BC
Jadeite
$1^{1}/_{16}$ x 8 x $2^{1}/_{4}$ in. (2.7 x 20.4 x 5.7 cm)
Museo Nacional de Antropología, Mexico City (10-10966)

See also:
Castro-Leal 1996: cat. 103

Olmec traditions seem to have continued long after the fall of the heartland sites. Certain figures that bear a striking facial resemblance to the Olmec style have been found in contexts of subsequent pre-Columbian civilizations. On this example, the cupped hands attached to the hips are a feature more typical of Teotihuacan; however, the downturned, curled, thick lips and the fleshy or muscular quality of the body may signal remembered Olmec traditions carried forward in time. Artists at the great city of Teotihuacan in Central Mexico (AD 150–750) continued to fashion minimally clothed or unclothed standing sculptures from very hard stones, and they utilized many of them in religious-civic rituals, temples, or residences near the Street of the Dead (Pasztory 1993). This example was found in a residential context in the Ciudadela compound, the city's religious and political center. KB

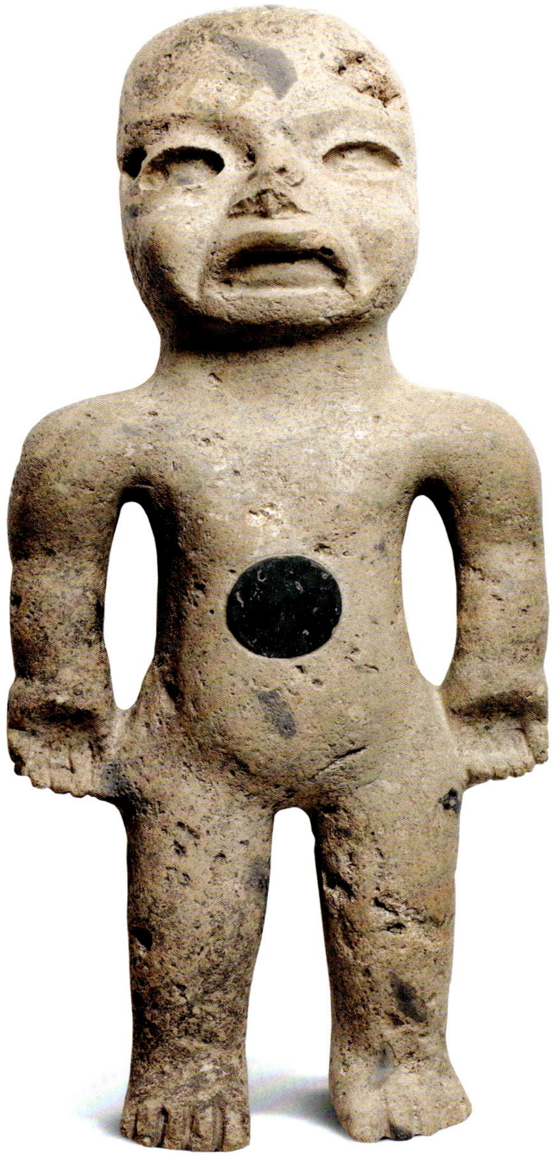

PLATE 145

STANDING FIGURE WITH CUPPED HANDS
Mexico, Teotihuacan, AD 550
Sandstone with slate inlay
17 13/16 x 11 5/16 x 3 11/16 in.
(45.3 x 28.8 x 9.4 cm)
Museo de Sitio de Teotihuacan

See also:
Berrin and Pasztory 1993: cat. 15

The elegant, sweeping design on the surface of this vessel evokes the profile of the Olmec crested creature (see pls. 23–24). The design is incised over the fire-cloud on the vessel's exterior, indicating that it was drawn on the surface after it was fired. VMF

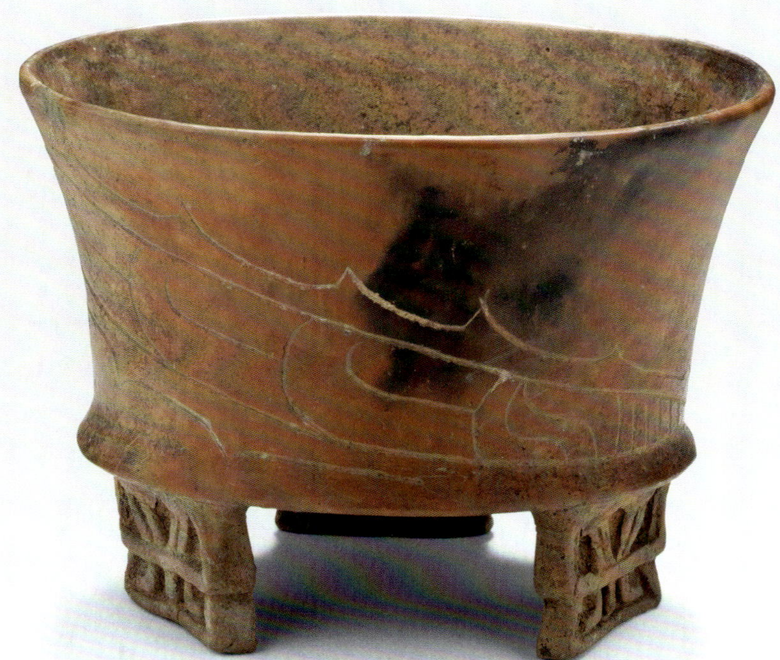

PLATE 146

TRIPOD VESSEL WITH INCISED DESIGN
Mexico, Teotihuacan, AD 400–650
Thin Orange ceramic
Height: 4 5/16 in. (11 cm)
Los Angeles County Museum of Art,
promised gift of Constance McCormick Fearing
(L.83.11.1016)

Once nicknamed the "Ambassador relief" (Coe 1968a: 148), this anomalous circular monument depicts a bearded figure striding toward a column of three hieroglyphs. A netlike turban covers his head; a hank of hair, folded over and tied, is visible at the back of his neck. He also wears a beaded necklace, bracelets at his wrists, and a nose bead as well as a loincloth and sandals. The figure carries a banner, and the isolated foot behind him may function as a fourth hieroglyph (Lacadena 2008: 615).

Discovered in 1943 by Philip Drucker and Waldo Wedel (Drucker 1952a: fig. 61; Drucker, Heizer, and Squier 1959), the monument was associated with Structure A-2 of Complex A (Lacadena 2008: 610). Archaeologists disagree over the monument's date. Some associate it with the last phase of construction of the site, between 600 and 400 BC (Pohl, Pope, and von Nagy 2002: 1986), and the final sculptural phase of the Olmec (Millbrath 1979: 38–39). Others have questioned the monument's Middle Formative heartland style attribution, given its distinctive characteristics (de la Fuente 1973: 262–264; Taube 2004: 45), and consider it Late Formative.

Many scholars have assumed that the hieroglyphic column that ends with a profile bird head names the individual (for example, Kelley 1966: 745). Alfonso Lacadena (2008: 619–620) proposes that the first hieroglyph, in the form of a circle, represents the number 1 and that the second sign may be a day name from the Olmec calendar. He suggests that the lobed shape of the sign implies certain well-known Mesoamerican day names corresponding to wind, water, earthquake, cloud, or flower.

The third glyph is the head of a bird, which may signify a title, and Lacadena (ibid.: 622) considers the footprint behind the figure to be verbal. In his analysis, the syntax of date, noun, and verb implies that the spoken language at the time the monument was carved was either Totonac, a remote possibility, or among the Mije-Zoquean family. Because Mije-Zoque speakers inhabited the Olmec nuclear area since at least ethnohistoric times, he finds that the most likely probability (ibid.: 25). VMF

PLATE 147

MONUMENT 13
Mexico, Tabasco, La Venta, 1000–400 BC
Basalt
39¾ x 35⁷⁄₁₆ x 39⅜ in. (101 x 90 x 100 cm)
Parque-Museo de La Venta, Villahermosa, Tabasco (PMV-001)

See also:
de la Fuente 1977a: 239–242, pl. 17, ill. 67
González Lauck 1996b: 47
González Lauck 2007: 54
Pool 2007: 169, fig. 5.12

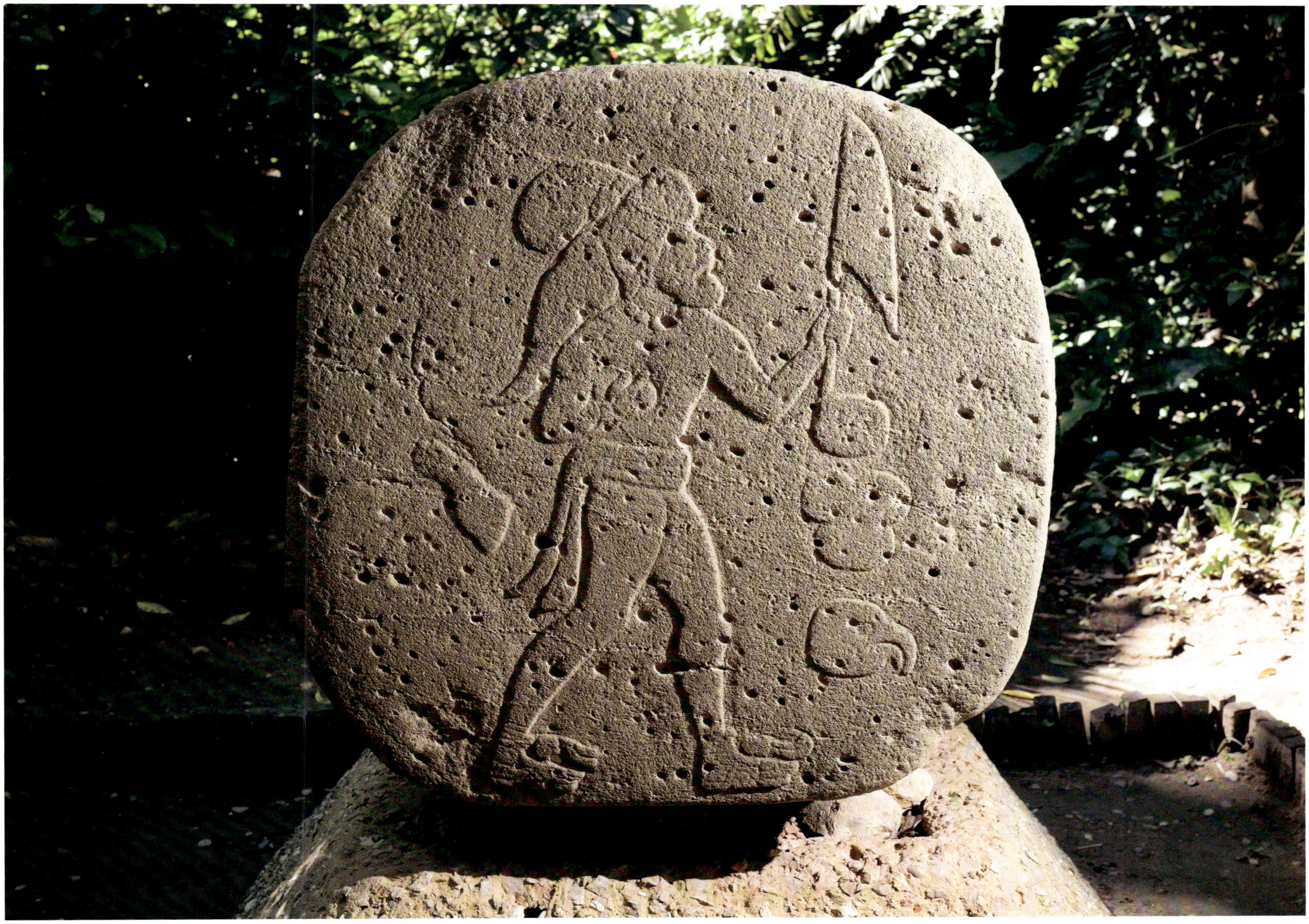

Discovered during a brief season of investigations at Chiapa de Corzo in 1961, this fragment contains a partial date in the calendrical system known as the Long Count. The history of Chiapa de Corzo, centrally located in the Grijalva Depression, extends from around 1000 to 300 BC, and the site was in continual contact with the Gulf Coast (Pool 2007: 272). Gareth Lowe (1962: 186, 192, fig. 7) reports that fragments of five monuments were found on the surface of Mound 5b, which housed a succession of structures over a long period of time.

The Long Count is primarily associated with the Classic period Maya (AD 250–900), where it recorded the dates of historic events in the lives of the members of the royal courts. Long Count dates were expressed in a vigesimal (or base 20) system of positional notation, enumerating the number of days that had elapsed from a mythological starting point in 3114 BC. This fragment contains the earliest dated notation yet discovered in Mesoamerica. Although incomplete, enough remains of the calendrical information to reconstruct the sequence of bars and dots as recording a date in 37 BC (Coe 1976: 112, fig. 3).

Alfonso Lacadena (2008: 613) considers both this monument and Tres Zapotes Stela C (pl. 80) as part of the Late Formative period writing tradition centered on the Isthmus of Tehuantepec. VMF

PLATE 148

STELA 2 (WITH PORTION OF LONG COUNT DATE: 7.16.3.2.13)
Mexico, Chiapas, Chiapa de Corzo, 37 BC
Limestone
8⅝ x 7½ x 1⁹⁄₁₆ in. (22 x 19 x 4 cm)
Museo Regional de Chiapas, Tuxtla Gutiérrez (10-342633)

See also:
Lowe 1990: cat. 26

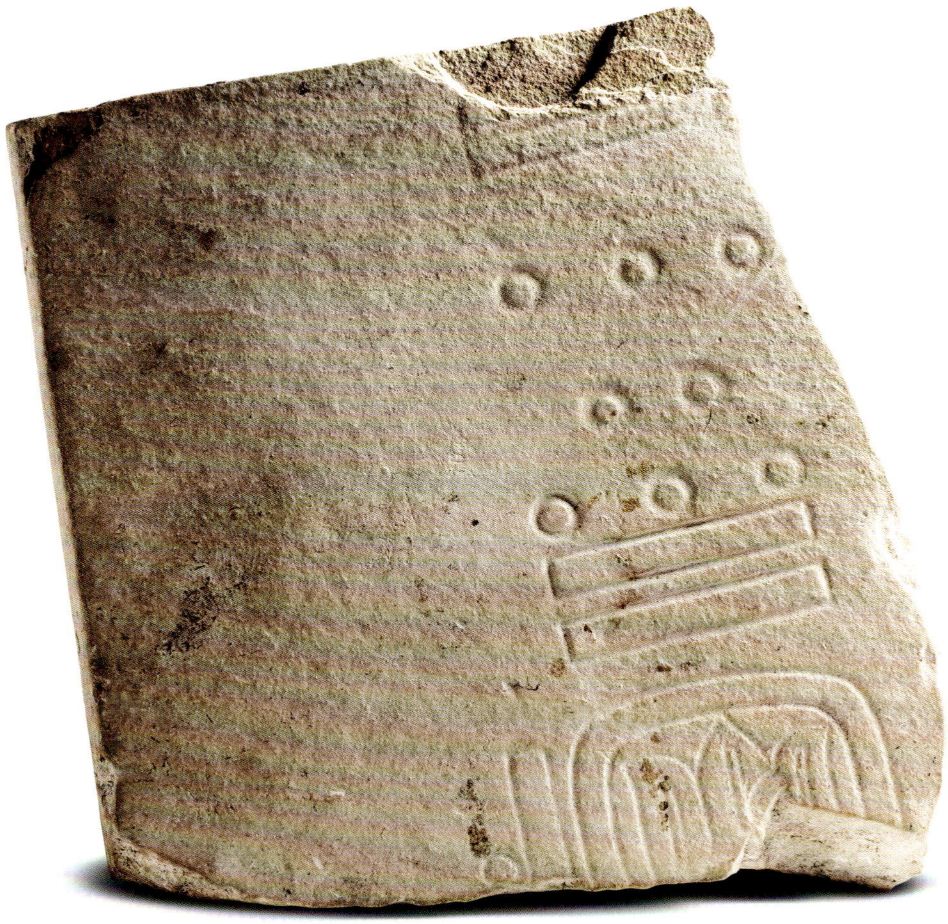

This substantial plaque is widely acknowledged as an heirloom, displaying a typical Olmec-style face on the recto side and an early Maya incised figure and hieroglyphic text on the verso. The plaque may derive from the region around Mérida on the Yucatán Peninsula (Coe 1966: 6). Michael Coe's study and that of Karl Taube (2004: 179–183) detail the techniques of carving the signature Olmec-style features on the recto surface. The cross-legged profile figure incised on the reverse depicts an early Maya king, whose accession to office is recorded in the adjacent four-column text (Schele and Miller 1986: 119–120; Fields and Reents-Budet 2005: cat. 90). Virginia Fields and Alexandre Tokovinine (forthcoming) note the uncanny resemblance of the profile figure to that of a young king who is undergoing an accession ceremony in a scene painted on the upper portion of the west wall of San Bartolo Structure 1, Sub-1. He is seated on a scaffold and is about to receive the crown of his office (Saturno 2006: 75). The mural, which has been securely dated to 100 BC (ibid.), provides a chronological anchor for dating the incised image on this remarkable object. VMF

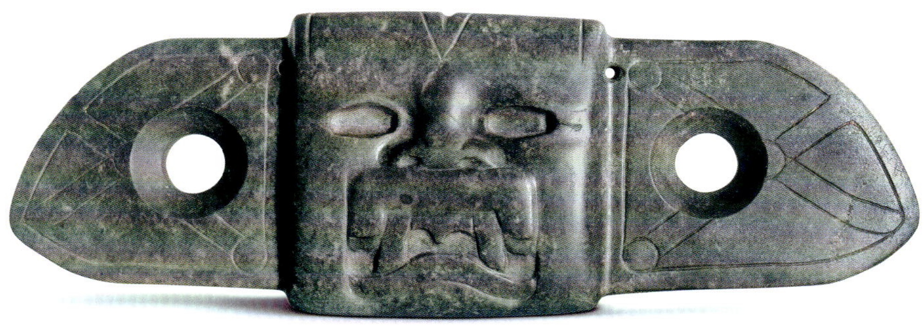

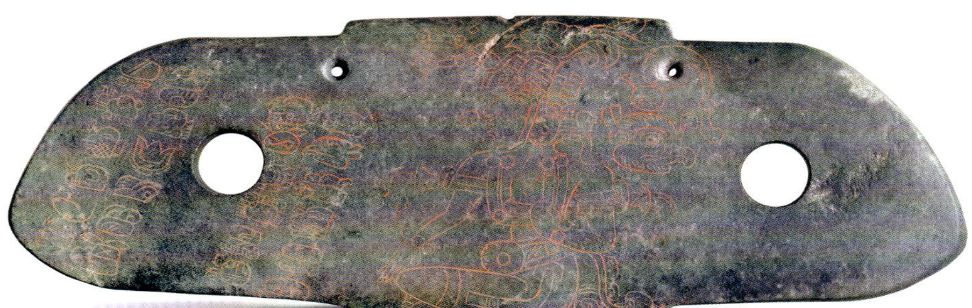

PLATES 149–150

WINGED PLAQUE
Mexico, recto: 900–400 BC, verso: 100 BC
Quartzite
$3^{1}/_{2}$ x $10^{1}/_{2}$ x $1^{1}/_{8}$ in. (9 x 26.7 x 2.8 cm)
Dumbarton Oaks Research Library
and Collection (B-538)

See also:
Benson 1996a: cat. 97

This unusually large figure wears a fringed loincloth incised with motifs that may point to a slightly later date of execution than the Middle Formative period. As Elizabeth Benson (1996a: cat. 47) notes, the features are conventional for Olmec-style standing figures despite the scale. She suggests that the central motif on the sash, which hangs down in front, resembles a feathered bundle, although Karl Taube (2004: fig. 32c) describes it as a maize fetish. The doubled motif above it, referred to as a knuckleduster, may signify a cut shell (Andrews V 1987).

On either side of the figure's skirt are paired signs that Benson (ibid.) suggests imply a cosmic diagram with the figure himself as the central axis, or world tree. The upper part of each sign resembles the well-known double-merlon motif, which Taube (1995: 89–91) identified as the Olmec sign for "green." The same sign appears on other very early Olmec-style objects, such as the roller stamp from San Andres (Pohl, Pope, and von Nagy 2002) and the cylinder seal from Tlatilco (Kelley 1966), in contexts implying royal status. VMF

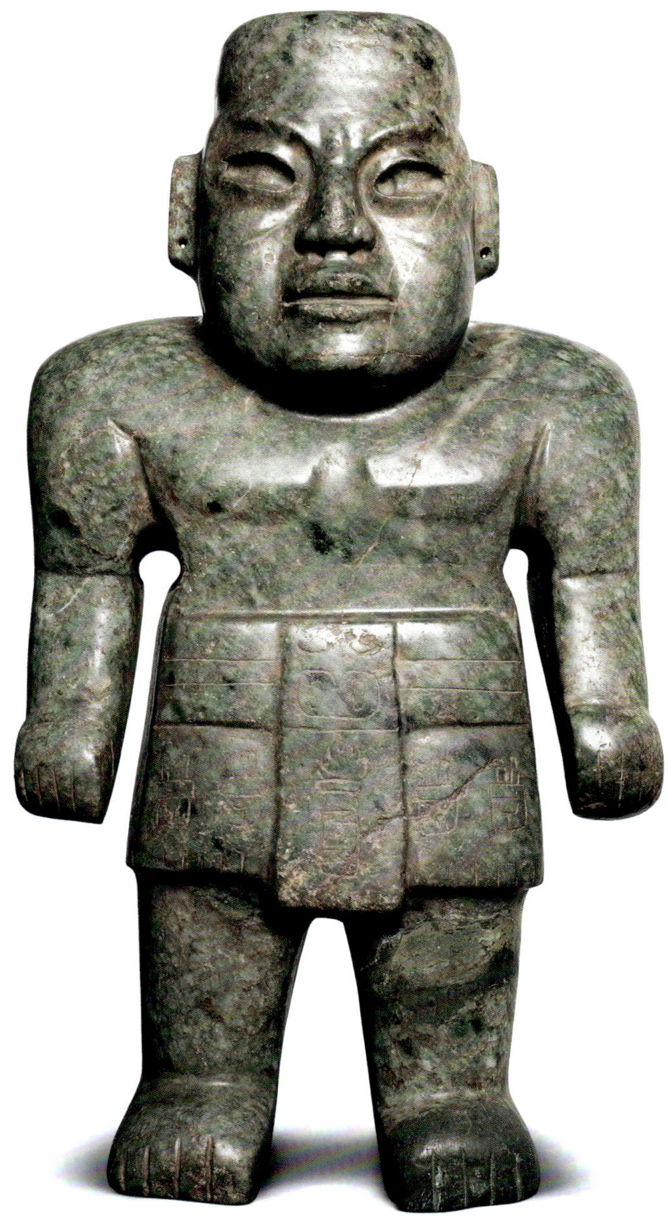

PLATE 151

FIGURE WEARING INCISED LOINCLOTH
Mexico, Puebla, 900–400 BC
Greenstone
20 11/16 x 11 7/16 in. (52.5 x 29 cm)
Museo Regional de Puebla (10-203321)

See also:
Piña Chan and Covarrubias 1964: 39, fig. 32

The nature of the florid incisions on this mask implies that they were a later addition to a Middle Formative period object (Pohorilenko 1996: cat. 93). The triangle motif in the center of the forehead, flanked by vegetal scrolls, represents a maize plant (ibid.), which is consistent with the many versions of this trefoil pattern found in the headbands of human rulers and supernatural beings (see pls. 67–68, 88–89, 153). VMF

Several stone monuments, including this one, were discovered in the Tiltepec region, and they share stylistic features with late La Venta monuments and possibly with monuments from the important coastal site of Izapa (Milbrath 1979: 27–28, figs. 50–51). The boulder-shaped stone, worked in low relief, depicts a central cartouche framing a face with a circular mouth, a flattened nose, and closed eyes. Above the cartouche is the trefoil motif consisting of a triangular form flanked by leaves. Above that is a smaller but identical representation of the cartouche and trefoil.

A pair of crossed arms is visible below the central cartouche, recalling the acrobatic representation of the Olmec and early Maya maize gods (Taube 1996, 2000). The appearance of this specific pose on monuments in Chiapas raises intriguing questions about the origin and dispersal of iconographic influences in Formative period Mesoamerica. VMF

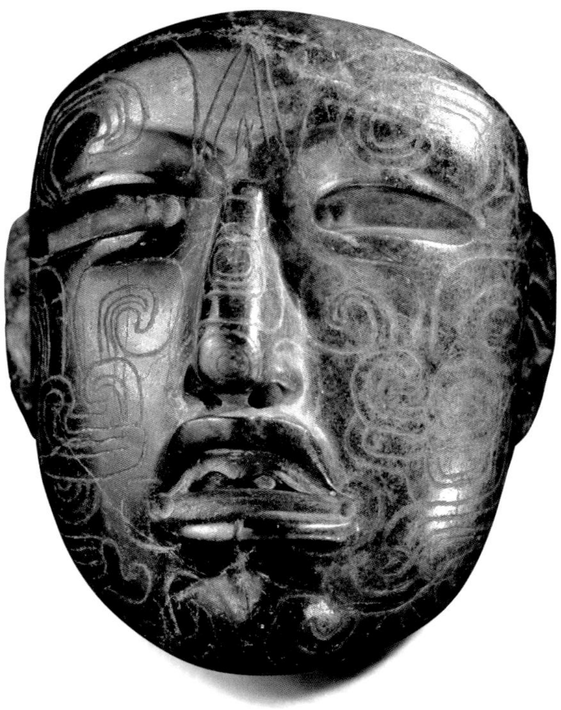

PLATES 152–153

MASK WITH INCISED DESIGN
Mexico, Oaxaca, 900–400 BC, with incisions dating to 400 BC–AD 200
Greenstone
$7^{7}/_{8} \times 5^{1}/_{8}$ in. (20 x 13 cm)
Peabody Museum of Archaeology and Ethnology, Harvard University (22-23-20/C9596)

See also:
Fields and Reents-Budet 2005: cat. 15

Princeton University 1995: cat. 152

CARVED MONUMENT
Mexico, Chiapas, Tiltepec, Rancho Nueva Rosita, AD 200–400
Stone
Approx. $59^{1}/_{16} \times 27^{9}/_{16} \times 22^{7}/_{16}$ in. (150 x 70 x 57 cm)
Museo Regional de Chiapas, Tuxtla Gutiérrez (10-409940)

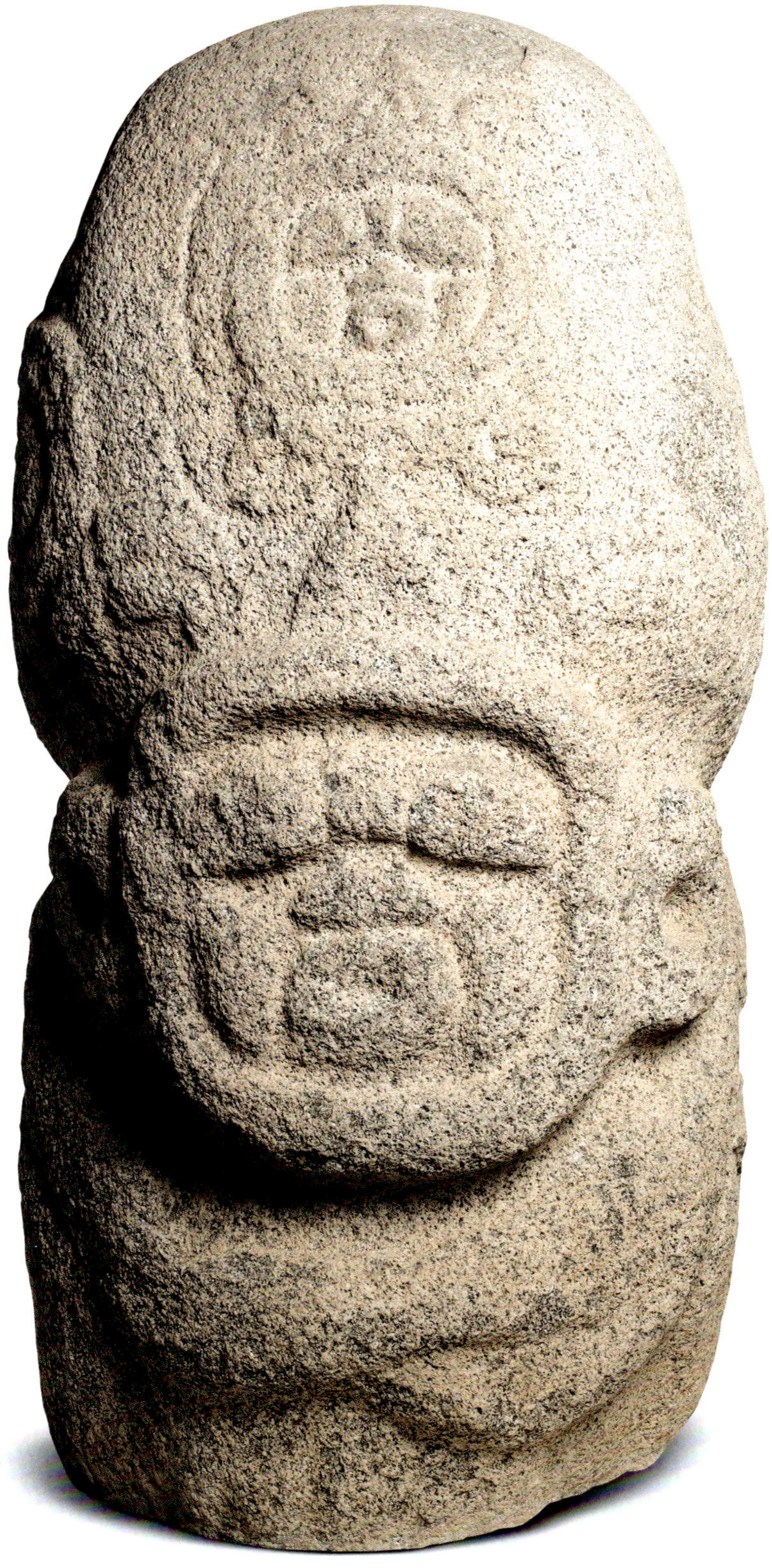

Matthew W. Stirling (1943: 35, fig. 10b) compared this monument, which has no known archaeological provenience, to a stela from Cerro de las Mesas, an important site near the south bank of the Río Blanco. The stela may have been discovered in the vicinity of San Miguel Chapultepec in the 1920s, when oil prospectors removed some monuments (ibid.: 32); it eventually ended up at the Museo Nacional de Antropología. Compositionally, the stela resembles those from the Maya area that depict royal figures attired in the clothing and paraphernalia of kingship.

Marcía Castro-Leal (2007: cat. 234) links the figure's elaborate costume to the central Mexican deity of wind, Quetzalcoatl-Ehecatl; she regards the mask covering his mouth to be a forerunner of the beaklike mask associated with that deity. The elements of dress compare to those worn by the figure on Cerro de las Mesas Stela 3 (Stirling 1943: fig. 10c). Both figures face toward the left and appear to be striding in that direction with their right hands pointed downward and left hands upraised; in this example, he holds a knotted cloth. Both wear fringed skirts with a four-lobed central design and a knotted cloth belt, a long cape with dotted and geometric patterns, and sandals. The cape appears to be tied in front, and on both figures the sash extends down the front from the chin. A knee guard in the form of an open-mouthed feline appears on each figure's right leg, and two leaves drop from the front of each skirt. Both figures wear headdresses of three stacked elements, including a long-nosed creature topped by a squared element that may signify a scaffold or other architectural feature, above which is another long-snouted creature. An open-mouthed jaguar, attached to the lowest element of the headdress, faces right.

The Gulf Coast version of the Maya royal headband trefoil jewel is attached to the scaffold element of each figure's headdress. Here, the trefoil is the pointed cone flanked by leaves, and it occurs both on top and in front of a cartouche that appears to signify the Maya day sign and title *ajaw*, or king. The column of hieroglyphs has not yet been deciphered but may carry the names and titles of the royal figure.

MC-LE/VMF

PLATE 154

STELA DEPICTING ROYAL FIGURE
Mexico, Central Veracruz, AD 500–800
Basalt
55½ x 32¼ x 23⅝ in. (141 x 82 x 60 cm)
Museo Nacional de Antropología, Mexico City
(10-627796)

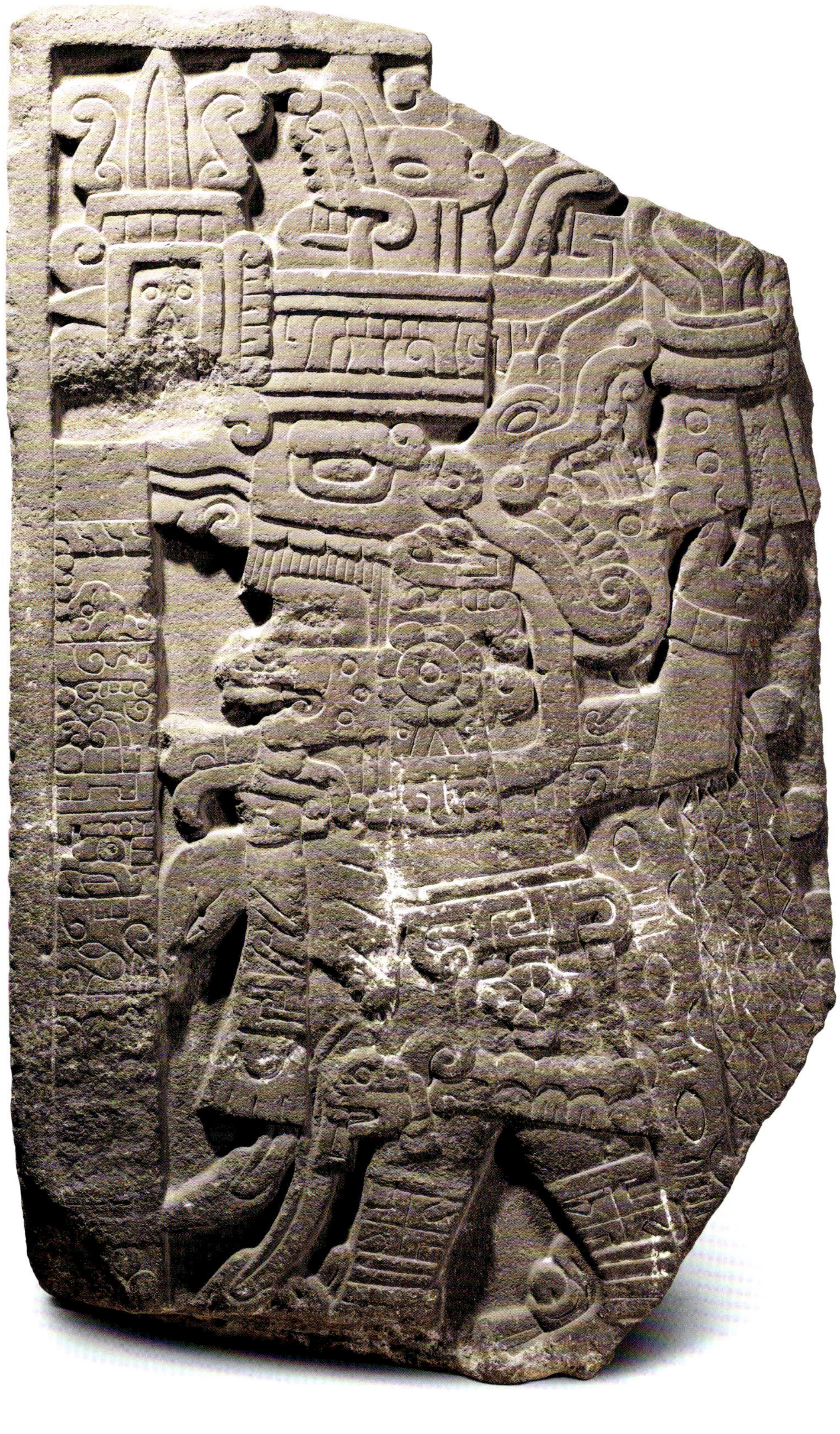

Kathleen Berrin is curator in charge of Africa, Oceania, and the Americas at the Fine Arts Museums of San Francisco. Berrin has organized several exhibitions focusing on pre-Columbian art, including the groundbreaking conservation and exhibition of the Harald Wagner Collection of Teotihuacan Murals and *Courtly Art of the Ancient Maya*. Her published works include *Feathered Serpents and Flowering Trees: Reconstructing the Murals of Teotihuacan* and *Teotihuacan: Art from the City of the Gods* (with Esther Pasztory).

Marcía Castro-Leal Espino is curator of the Sala del Golfo at the Museo Nacional de Antropología in Mexico City. Her research has focused on decapitation in the Mesoamerican ballgame as well as power and the sacred in Mesoamerican culture. Among her publications are *Archaeological Guide of the Park-Museum of La Venta* (with Lorenzo Ochoa), *Olmec Art of Ancient Mexico* (with Elizabeth P. Benson and Beatriz de la Fuente), and a contribution to *Olmeca: Balance y perspectivas: Memoria de la Primera Mesa Redonda* (edited by María Teresa Uriarte and Rebecca B. González Lauck).

Ann Cyphers is director of the San Lorenzo Tenochtitlán Archaeological Project, senior research scientist at the Universidad Nacional Autónoma de México, and a research associate in the department of anthropology at the University of Illinois at Urbana-Champaign. She specializes in Formative period archaeology of Mesoamerica, particularly that of the Central Mexican Highlands and Gulf Coast regions. She has performed fieldwork in the midwestern United States as well as in the Mexican states of Morelos and Veracruz.

Richard A. Diehl is professor emeritus of anthropology at the University of Alabama, Tuscaloosa, where he served as executive director of the University of Alabama Museums and director of the Alabama Museum of Natural History. He has conducted archaeological investigations in Mexico at Tula and the Basin of Mexico as well as San Lorenzo Tenochtitlán, La Mojarra, and Matacapan in southern Veracruz. His books include *The Olmecs: America's First Civilization*; *In the Land of the Olmec* (with Michael D. Coe); *Tula: The Toltec Capital of Ancient Mexico*; and *Mesoamerica after the Decline of Teotihuacan: AD 700–900* (edited with Janet Catherine Berlo).

Virginia M. Fields is senior curator of art of the ancient Americas at the Los Angeles County Museum of Art. Fields has taught pre-Columbian and Native American art history at several universities in California and currently serves as a senior fellow in pre-Columbian studies at Dumbarton Oaks Research Library and Collection in Washington, D.C. Among her publications are the exhibition catalogues *Lords of Creation: The Origins of Sacred Maya Kingship* (with Dorie Reents-Budet), which received the annual book award from the Association for Latin American Art, and *The Road to Aztlan: Art from a Mythic Homeland* (with Victor Zamudio-Taylor).

David C. Grove is Courtesy Professor of Anthropology at the University of Florida and professor emeritus of anthropology and Jubilee Professor of Liberal Arts and Sciences at the University of Illinois at Urbana-Champaign. Grove's primary research interest is the Mesoamerican Early and Middle Formative/Preclassic periods. He is best known for his fieldwork at Chalcatzingo, Morelos, and the cave at Oxtotitlan, Guerrero. His published works include *Regional Perspectives on the Olmec* (edited with Robert J. Sharer) and *San Pablo, Nexpa, and the Early Formative Archaeology of Morelos, Mexico*.

Sara Ladrón de Guevara is director of the Museo de Antropología de Xalapa, Universidad Veracruzana. Ladrón de Guevara has taught at the Universidad Veracruzana and the Universidad de Guadalajara and has been a visiting professor at Smith College and the Sorbonne. She has participated in numerous archaeological projects in both Mexico and Europe, with a special emphasis on the iconography and symbolism of Mesoamerica. She has published more than sixty texts, among them *Imagen y pensamiento en El Tajín* and *Diseños precolombinos de Veracruz*.

Roberto Lunagómez Reyes is curator of the Acervo Olmeca at the Museo de Antropología de Xalapa, Universidad Veracruzana. Lunagómez Reyes has focused his research on San Lorenzo Tenochtitlán as well as Medias Aguas. Among his published works are *Asentamiento prehispánico en San Lorenzo Tenochtitlán* (with Stacey Symonds and Ann Cyphers) and *Olmec to Aztec: Settlement Patterns in the Ancient Gulf Lowlands* (edited by Barbara L. Stark and Philip J. Arnold III).

Diana Magaloni Kerpel is director of the Museo Nacional de Antropología in Mexico City. A specialist in Mesoamerican and sixteenth-century indigenous pictorial techniques, she has conducted interdisciplinary research that draws on chemistry, physics, archaeology, ethnography, and art history to understand how mural paintings and codices were created. Her publications include *Materiales y técnicas de la pintura mural Maya* and *Images of the Beginning: The Painted Story of the Conquest of Mexico in Book XII of the Florentine Codex*.

Patricia Ochoa Castillo, curator of the Sala Preclásico at the Museo Nacional de Antropología in Mexico City, studied at the Universidad Nacional Autónoma de México and the Escuela Nacional de Antropología e Historia. Specializing in the Preclassic period, she has conducted archaeological fieldwork in Central Mexico. Her published works include *Tlatilco, el lugar donde hay cosas ocultas* and *Secuencia cronológica-cultural de Tlatilco, México*.

Ponciano Ortíz Ceballos, a researcher at the Instituto de Antropología, Universidad Veracruzana, is also affiliated with the Centro INAH Veracruz. Ortíz Ceballos has conducted fieldwork in several areas of Veracruz and at Tres Zapotes and Laguna de los Cerros. He has received grants from the National Geographic Society and Harvard University and was codirector, with Ma. del Carmen Rodríguez M., of the Manatí Project in Veracruz. His published works include *Las investigaciones arqueológicas en el cerro sagrado Manatí* (with Rodriguez M. and Alfredo Delgado C.) and *El Manatí: Un espacio sagrado olmeca* (with Rodriguez M.).

Christopher A. Pool is professor of anthropology at the University of Kentucky, where his research focuses on complex societies in the tropical lowlands of southern Veracruz, including the Olmec and their successors. He has investigated the archaeological sites of Matacapan and Bezuapan, and since 1995 he has directed excavations at Tres Zapotes. His publications include *Classic Period Cultural Currents in Southern and Central Veracruz* (edited with Philip J. Arnold III); *Debating with Robert: Papers on Mesoamerican Archaeology in Memory of Robert S. Santley* (edited with Patricia McAnany); *Settlement Archaeology and Political Economy at Tres Zapotes, Veracruz, Mexico*; and *Olmec Archaeology and Early Mesoamerica*.

F. Kent Reilly III is professor of anthropology and director of the Center for the Arts and Symbolism in Ancient America at Texas State University, San Marcos. He served as guest curator of *The Olmec World: Ritual and Rulership* at the Art Museum, Princeton University; was a member of the advisory board for *Hero, Hawk, and Open Hand: American Indian Art of the Ancient Midwest and South* at the Art Institute of Chicago; and contributed to the accompanying catalogues. Reilly is primarily a prehistorian, and his interests converge around religion, art, and visual validation of elite authority in New World chiefdoms and early states.

Ma. del Carmen Rodríguez M. is a researcher at the Instituto Nacional de Antropología e Historia, Mexico. She has conducted fieldwork in several areas of Veracruz as well as in Chiapas and Oaxaca. She has received grants from the National Geographic Society and Harvard University and was codirector, with Ponciano Ortíz Ceballos, of the Manatí Project in Veracruz. Her published works include *El Manatí: Un espacio sagrado olmeca* (with Ortíz Ceballos) and contributions to *Olmec Art and Archaeology in Mesoamerica* (edited by John E. Clark and Mary E. Pye).

Agrinier, Pierre. 1984. *The Early Olmec Horizon at Mirador, Chiapas, Mexico.* Papers of the New World Archaeological Foundation 48. Provo, UT: Brigham Young University.

Andrews, E. Wyllys, V. 1987. "Spoons and Knuckle-Dusters in Formative Mesoamerica." Paper presented at the Third Texas Symposium, "Olmec, Izapa, and the Development of Maya Civilization," University of Texas at Austin.

Angulo V., Jorge. 1987. "The Chalcatzingo Reliefs: An Iconographic Analysis." In Grove 1987, pp. 132–158.

——. 1994. "Observaciones sobre su pensamiento cosmogónico y la organización sociopolítica." In Clark 1994c, pp. 222–237.

Arnold, Philip J., III. 2000. "Sociopolitical Complexity and the Gulf Olmecs: A View from the Tuxtla Mountains, Veracruz, Mexico." In Clark and Pye 2000a, pp. 116–135.

Bassie-Sweet, Karen. 1996. *At the Edge of the World.* Norman: University of Oklahoma Press.

Benson, Elizabeth P., ed. 1968. *Dumbarton Oaks Conference on the Olmec.* Washington, D.C.: Dumbarton Oaks.

——. 1969. *Supplement to the Handbook of the Robert Woods Bliss Collection of Pre-Columbian Art.* Washington, D.C.: Dumbarton Oaks.

——. 1971. *An Olmec Figure at Dumbarton Oaks.* Studies in Pre-Columbian Art and Archaeology 8. Washington, D.C.: Dumbarton Oaks.

——. 1981a. *The Olmec and Their Neighbors: Essays in Memory of Matthew W. Stirling.* Washington, D.C.: Dumbarton Oaks.

——. 1981b. "Some Olmec Objects in the Robert Woods Bliss Collection at Dumbarton Oaks." In Benson 1981a, pp. 95–108.

——. 1996a. Catalogue entries. In Benson and de la Fuente 1996.

——. 1996b. "History of Olmec Investigations." In Benson and de la Fuente 1996, pp. 17–27.

——. 2008. "La iconografía olmeca." In Uriarte and González Lauck 2008, pp. 265–286.

Benson, Elizabeth P., and Michael D. Coe. 1963. *Handbook of the Robert Woods Bliss Collection of Pre-Columbian Art.* Washington, D.C.: Dumbarton Oaks.

Benson, Elizabeth P., and Beatriz de la Fuente, eds. 1996. *Olmec Art of Ancient Mexico.* Washington, D.C.: National Gallery of Art.

Bernal, Ignacio. 1968. *El mundo olmeca.* Mexico City: Editorial Porrúa.

——. 1969. *The Olmec World.* Translated by Doris Heyden and Fernando Horcasitas. Berkeley: University of California Press.

Berrin, Kathleen, and Esther Pasztory. 1993. *Teotihuacan: Art from the City of the Gods.* New York: Thames & Hudson.

Beverido Pereau, Francisco. 1970. "San Lorenzo Tenochtitlán y la civilización olmeca." Master's thesis, Facultad de Antropología, Universidad Veracruzana, Xalapa.

——. 1987. "Breve historia de la arqueología olmeca." *La Palabra y el Hombre* 64: 161–194.

Blanton, Richard, Gary M. Feinman, Stephen A. Kowalewski, and Peter N. Peregrine. 1996. "A Dual-Processual Theory for the Evolution of Mesoamerican Civilization." *Current Anthropology* 37: 1–14.

Blom, Frans, and Oliver La Farge. 1926. *Tribes and Temples: A Record of the Expedition to Middle America Conducted by the Tulane University of Louisiana in 1925*, 2 vols. Middle American Research Institute Publication 1. New Orleans: Tulane University of Louisiana.

Blomstser, Jeffrey P. 1998. "Context, Cult, and Early Formative Period Public Ritual in the Mixteca Alta: Analysis of a Hollow-Baby Figurine from Etlatongo, Oaxaca." *Ancient Mesoamerica* 9: 309–326.

Bonifaz Nuño, Rubén. 1993. *El Museo Amparo: Colección prehispánica.* Puebla: Fundación Amparo.

Borstein, Joshua. 2001. "Tripping over Colossal Heads: Settlement Patterns and Population Development in the Upland Olmec Heartland." PhD diss., Department of Anthropology, Pennsylvania State University.

——. 2008. "El papel de Laguna de los Cerros en el mundo olmeca." In *Sociedad e ideología en el periodo Formativo: Ensayos en honor al doctor David C. Grove*, edited by Kenneth G. Hirth and Ann Cyphers, pp. 153–176. Mexico City: Instituto de Investigaciones Antropológicas, UNAM.

Brüggeman, Jürgen, and Marie Areti Hers. 1970. "Exploraciones arqueológicas en San Lorenzo Tenochtitlán." *Boletín del Instituto Nacional de Antropología e Historia* 39: 18–23.

Campbell, Lyle C., and Terrence Kaufman. 1976. "A Linguistic Look at the Olmecs." *American Antiquity* 41: 80–89.

Caso, Alfonso. 1942. "Definición y extensión del complejo olmeca." In Sociedad Mexicana de Antropología 1942, pp. 43–46.

Caso, Alfonso, and Ignacio Bernal. 1952. *Urnas de Oaxaca.* Memorias del Instituto Nacional de Antropología e Historia 2. Mexico City: INAH.

Castro-Leal, Marcía. 1996. Catalogue entries. In Benson and de la Fuente 1996.

——. 2007. Catalogue entry 234. In *Isis y la serpiente emplumada: Egipto faraónico, México prehispánico*, edited by Magali Tercero. Monterrey: Fundación Monterrey.

Cervantes, Miguel. 2008. *Museo Amparo: Obras selectas.* Puebla: Fundación Amparo.

Chavero, Alfredo. 1888. *Historia antigua y de la conquista.* Bk. 1 of *México a través de los siglos*, edited by D. Vicente Riva Palacio. Mexico: Ballescá; Barcelona: Espasa.

Cheetham, David. 2006. "The Americas' First Colony?" *Archaeology* 59 (1): 42–46

Clark, John E. 1994a. "El sistema económico de los primeros olmecas." In Clark 1994c, pp. 189–201.

——. 1994b. "Los olmecas, pueblo del primer sol." In Clark 1994c, pp. 15–19.

——, ed. 1994c. *Los olmecas en Mesoamérica.* Mexico City: Citibank.

Abbreviations:

Dumbarton Oaks: Dumbarton Oaks Research Library and Collection

INAH: Instituto Nacional de Antropología e Historia

UNAM: Universidad Nacional Autónoma de México

Clark, John E., and David Cheetham. 2005. "Cerámica Formativo de Chiapas." In *La producción alfarera en el México antiguo,* vol. 1, edited by Beatriz Leonor Merino Carrión and Ángel García Cook, pp. 285–433. Colección científica 484. Mexico City: INAH.

Clark, John E., and Tomás Pérez Suárez. 1994. "Los olmecas y el primer milenio de Mesoamérica." In Clark 1994c, pp. 261–275.

Clark, John E., and Mary E. Pye, eds. 2000a. *Olmec Art and Archaeology in Mesoamerica.* Washington, D.C.: National Gallery of Art.

———. 2000b. "The Pacific Coast and the Olmec Question." In Clark and Pye 2000a, pp. 217–251.

Clewlow, C. William, and Christopher R. Corson. 1968. "Appendix II: New Stone Monuments from La Venta." In *Papers on Mesoamerican Archaeology,* pp. 171–182. Contributions of the University of California Archaeological Research Facility 5. Berkeley: University of California.

Clewlow, C. William, Richard A. Cowan, James F. O'Connell, and Carlos Beneman. 1967. *Colossal Heads of the Olmec Culture.* Contributions of the University of California Archaeological Research Facility 4. Berkeley: University of California.

Cobean, Robert H., Michael D. Coe, Edward A. Perry, Jr., Karl K. Turekian, and Dinkar P. Kharkar. 1971. "Obsidian Trade at San Lorenzo Tenochtitlán, Mexico." *Science* 174 (4010): 666–671.

Cobean, Robert H., James R. Vogt, Michael D. Glascock, and Terrance L. Stocker. 1991. "High-Precision Trace-Element Characterization of Major Mesoamerican Obsidian Sources and Further Analyses of Artifacts from San Lorenzo Tenochtitlán, Mexico." *Latin American Antiquity* 2 (1): 69–91.

Coe, Michael D. 1965a. "Archaeological Synthesis of Southern Veracruz and Tabasco." In *Archaeology of Southern Mesoamerica,* pt. 2, edited by G. R. Willey, pp. 679–715. Vols. 2–3 of *Handbook of Middle American Indians*, edited by Robert Wauchope. Austin: University of Texas Press.

———. 1965b. *The Jaguar's Children: Pre-Classic Mexico*. New York: Museum of Primitive Art.

———. 1965c. "The Olmec Style and Its Distribution." In *Archaeology of Southern Mesoamerica,* pt. 2, edited by G. R. Willey, pp. 739–775. Vols. 2–3 of *Handbook of Middle American Indians,* edited by Robert Wauchope. Austin: University of Texas Press.

———. 1966. *An Early Stone Pectoral from Southeastern Mexico.* Studies in Pre-Columbian Art and Archaeology 1. Washington, D.C.: Dumbarton Oaks.

———. 1968a. *America's First Civilization*. New York: American Heritage in association with the Smithsonian Institution.

———. 1968b. "San Lorenzo and the Olmec Civilization." In Benson 1968, pp. 41–78.

———. 1976. "Early Steps in the Evolution of Maya Writing." In Nicholson 1976, pp. 107–122.

Coe, Michael D., and Richard A. Diehl. 1980. *The Archaeology of San Lorenzo Tenochtitlán*, vol. 1 of *In the Land of the Olmec*, 2 vols. Austin: University of Texas Press.

Coe, Michael D., Douglas Newton, and Roy Sieber. 1986. *African, Pacific, and Pre-Columbian Art in the Indiana University Art Museum*. Bloomington: Indiana University Art Museum.

Coe, Michael D., and Mark Van Stone. 2001. *Reading the Maya Glyphs*. London: Thames & Hudson.

Córdova Tello, Mario, and Carolina Meza Rodríguez. 2007. "Chalcatzingo, Morelos: Un discurso sobre piedra." *Arqueología Mexicana* 87: 60–65.

Covarrubias, Miguel. 1942. "Origen y desarrollo del estilo artístico 'olmeca.'" In Sociedad Mexicana de Antropología 1942, pp. 46–49.

———. 1943. "Tlatilco, Archaic Mexican Art and Culture." *Dyn* 4/5: 40–46.

———. 1944. "La Venta, Colossal Heads and Jaguar Gods." *Dyn* 6: 24–33.

———. 1946a. "El arte 'olmeca' o de La Venta." *Cuadernos Americanos* 28 (4): 153–179.

———. 1946b. *Mexico South: The Isthmus of Tehuantepec*. New York: Alfred A. Knopf.

———. 1950. "Tlatilco: El arte y la cultura Preclásica del valle de México." *Cuadernos Americanos* 51 (3): 149–162.

———. 1957. *Indian Art of Mexico and Central America*. New York: Alfred A. Knopf.

———. 1961. *Arte indígena de México y Centroamérica.* Mexico City: UNAM.

———. 1980. *El Sur de México.* Mexico City: Instituto Nacional Indigenista.

Cyphers, Ann. 1993. "Escenas escultóricas olmecas." *Antropológicas* 6: 47–52.

———. 1994a. "Nuevos descubrimientos en la zona olmeca." *Antropológicas* 12.

———. 1994b. "Olmec Sculpture." *National Geographic Research and Exploration* 10 (3): 294–305.

———. 1994c. "San Lorenzo." In Clark 1994c, pp. 43–67.

———. 1996a. Catalogue entries. In Benson and de la Fuente 1996.

———. 1996b. "Catalogue of Colossal Olmec Heads." In *Olmecs: Special Edition, Arqueología Mexicana*, front foldout.

———. 1996c. "Reconstructing Olmec Life at San Lorenzo." In Benson and de la Fuente 1996, pp. 61–71.

———. 1996d. "The Colossal Heads." In *Olmecs: Special Edition, Arqueología Mexicana*, pp. 48–55.

———, ed. 1997a. *Población, subsistencia y medio ambiente en San Lorenzo Tenochtitlán.* Mexico City: Instituto de Investigaciones Antropológicas, UNAM.

———. 1997b. "Crecimiento y desarrollo en San Lorenzo." In Cyphers 1997a, pp. 255–274.

———. 1997c. "El contexto social de monumentos en San Lorenzo." In Cyphers 1997a, pp. 163–194.

———. 1997d. "La arquitectura olmeca en San Lorenzo Tenochtitlán." In Cyphers 1997a, pp. 91–118.

——. 1997e. "La gobernatura en San Lorenzo: Inferencias del arte y patrón de asentamiento." In Cyphers 1997a, pp. 227–242.

——. 1997f. "Los felinos de San Lorenzo." In Cyphers 1997a, pp. 195–225.

——. 1997g. "Olmec Architecture at San Lorenzo." In *Olmec to Aztec: Settlement Patterns in the Ancient Gulf Lowlands,* edited by Barbara L. Stark and Philip J. Arnold III, pp. 96–114. Tucson: University of Arizona Press.

——. 1999. "From Stone to Symbols: Olmec Art in Social Context at San Lorenzo Tenochtitlán." In *Social Patterns in Pre-Classic Mesoamerica*, edited by David C. Grove and Rosemary A. Joyce, pp. 155–182. Washington, D.C.: Dumbarton Oaks.

——. 2004a. "Escultura monumental olmeca: Temas y contextos." In Uriarte and Staines Cicero 2004, pp. 51–74.

——. 2004b. *Escultura olmeca de San Lorenzo Tenochtitlán.* Mexico City: Instituto de Investigaciones Antropológicas, UNAM, and the Coordinación de Humanidades.

——. 2006. "Olmec Figurines, c. 3000 BP." Paper presented at the annual meeting of the European Archaeological Association, Kraków, Poland.

——. 2007a. "Middle Preclassic Olmec Figurines." Paper presented at the annual meeting of the European Archaeological Association, Zadar, Croatia.

——. 2007b. "Surgimiento y decadencia de San Lorenzo, Veracruz: Del Ojochi al Nacaste." *Arqueología Mexicana* 15 (87): 36–42.

——. 2008. "Los tronos y la configuración del poder olmeca." In *Sociedad e ideología en el periodo Formativo: Ensayos en honor al doctor David C. Grove,* edited by Kenneth Hirth and Ann Cyphers, pp. 311–341. Mexico City: Instituto de Investigaciones Antropológicas, UNAM.

——. 2009. "Face to Face, Head to Head: Exploring the Significance of Olmec Figurines." Paper presented at the Braunstein Figurine Symposium, Las Vegas, Nevada.

——. Forthcoming. "Beautiful Theories and Ugly Facts: The Early Preclassic Olmec." In *Origins of Maya States*, edited by Robert J. Sharer and Loa Traxler. Philadelphia: University of Pennsylvania Press.

——. n.d. "Las excavaciones en San Lorenzo Tenochtitlán." Manuscript.

Cyphers, Ann, and Anna Di Castro. 1996. "Los artefactos multiperforados de ilmenita de San Lorenzo." *Arqueología* 16: 3–14.

——. 2009. "Early Olmec Architecture and Imagery." In *The Art of Urbanism,* edited by William Fash and Leonardo López Luján, pp. 21–52. Washington, D.C.: Dumbarton Oaks.

Cyphers, Ann, and Mario Arturo Ortiz. 2000. "Geomorphology and Ancient Cultural Landscapes of Southern Veracruz." In *Mounds, Modoc, and Mesoamerica: Papers in Honor of Melvin L. Fowler,* edited by Steven Ahler, pp. 99–110. Illinois State Museum Scientific Papers 28. Springfield: Illinois State Museum.

Cyphers, Ann, Alejandro Hernández, Marisol Varela, and Lilia Grégor. 2006. "Cosmological and Sociopolitical Synergy in Preclassic Architectural Precincts." In *Precolumbian Water Management: Ideology, Ritual and Power*, edited by Lisa Lucero and Barbara Fash, pp. 17–32. Tucson: University of Arizona Press.

Cyphers, Ann, Timothy Murtha, Joshua Borstein, Judith Zurita-Noguera, Roberto Lunagómez, Stacey Symonds, Gerardo Jiménez, Mario Arturo Ortiz, and José Manuel Figueroa. Forthcoming. "Arqueología digital en la primera capital olmeca, San Lorenzo." *Thule* (Journal of the Centro Studi Americanistici "Circolo Amerindiano"), Perugia, Italy.

Cyphers, Ann, and Enrique Villamar. 2006. "La representación del modelado cefálico en las figurillas de San Lorenzo." In *Presencia zoque: Una aproximación multidisciplinaria*, edited by Dolores Aramoni Calderón, Thomas A. Lee Whiting, and Miguel Lisbona Guillén, pp. 257–272. Mexico: Universidad de Ciencias y Artes de Chiapas; Consejo de Ciencia y Tecnología del Estado de Chiapas; Universidad Autónoma de Chiapas; UNAM.

Cyphers, Ann, and Judith Zurita-Noguera. 2006a. "A Land that Tastes of Water." In *Precolumbian Water Management: Ideology, Ritual, and Power*, edited by Lisa Lucero and Barbara Fash, pp. 33–50. Tucson: University of Arizona Press.

——. 2006b. "Lo monumental en San Lorenzo." Paper presented at the annual meeting of the Society for American Archaeology, Puerto Rico.

——. 2007. "Tempranos conceptos cosmológicos en San Lorenzo." Paper presented in Encuentro Pueblos y Fronteras 2007, "Arte y religión en el período Formativo: México y Centroamérica," San Cristóbal de las Casas, Chiapas, Mexico.

——. Forthcoming. "Early Olmec Risk Management." In *The Origins of New World Monumentality*, edited by Richard L. Burger and Robert M. Rosenswig. Gainesville: University Press of Florida.

Davidson, Matthew. 2009. "Using Auger Testing to Understand Residential Site Structure at Tres Zapotes, Veracruz, Mexico." Master's thesis, University of Kentucky.

Davis, Whitney. 1978. "So-Called Jaguar-Human Copulation Scenes in Olmec Art." *American Antiquity* 43 (3): 453–457.

de la Fuente, Beatriz. 1973. *Escultura monumental olmeca: Catálogo.* Mexico City: Instituto de Investigaciones Estéticas, UNAM.

——. 1977a. *Los hombres de piedra: Escultura olmeca.* Mexico City: UNAM.

——. 1977b. "Pequeña obra maestra de la escultura olmeca." *Anales del Instituto de Investigaciones Estéticas* 47: 5–10.

——. 1981. "Toward a Conception of Monumental Olmec Art." In Benson 1981a, pp. 83–94.

——. 1984. *Los hombres de piedra: Escultura olmeca.* 2nd ed. Mexico City: UNAM.

——. 1992. *Cabezas colosales olmecas.* Mexico: El Colegio Nacional.

——. 1994. "Arte monumental olmeca." In Clark 1994c, pp. 203–221.

——. 1996a. Catalogue entries. In Benson and de la Fuente 1996.

——. 1996b. "Homocentrism in Olmec Monumental Art." In Benson and de la Fuente 1996, pp. 41–49.

——. 1996c. "Olmec Art." In *Olmecs: Special Edition, Arqueología Mexicana*, pp. 28–37.

——. 2000. "Olmec Sculpture: The First Mesoamerican Art." In Clark and Pye 2000a, pp. 253–263.

——. 2008. "¿Puede un estilo definir una cultura?" In Uriarte and González Lauck 2008, pp. 25–38.

De León, Jason. 2008. "The Lithic Industries of San Lorenzo-Tenochtitlán: An Economic and Technological Study of Olmec Obsidian." PhD diss., Department of Anthropology, Pennsylvania State University.

Díaz del Castillo, Bernal. 1956. *The Discovery and Conquest of Mexico, 1517–1521*. Translated by Irving A. Leonard. Edited by Genaro García. New York: Farrar, Straus and Cudahy.

Di Castro Stringher, Anna. 1997. "Los bloques de ilmenita de San Lorenzo." In Cyphers 1997a, pp. 153–160.

Di Castro, Anna, Ann Cyphers, and Marisol Varela. 2008. "Los espejos de San Lorenzo." In *Tributo a Jaime Litvak King*, edited by Paul Schmidt Schoenberg, Edith Ortiz Díaz, and Joel Santos Ramírez, pp. 167–176. Mexico City: Instituto de Investigaciones Antropológicas, UNAM.

Diehl, Richard A. 1990. Catalogue entries. In *Mexico: Splendors of Thirty Centuries*. New York: Metropolitan Museum of Art.

———. 2004. *The Olmecs: America's First Civilization*. New York: Thames & Hudson.

Diehl, Richard A., and Michael D. Coe. 1995. "Olmec Archaeology." In Princeton University 1995, pp. 11–25.

Drucker, Philip. 1943a. "Ceramic Sequences at Tres Zapotes, Veracruz, Mexico." *Bureau of American Ethnology Bulletin* 140. Washington, D.C.: Smithsonian Institution.

———. 1943b. "Ceramic Stratigraphy at Cerro de las Mesas, Veracruz, Mexico." *Bureau of American Ethnology Bulletin* 141. Washington, D.C.: Smithsonian Institution.

———. 1947. "Some Implications of the Ceramic Complex of La Venta." *Smithsonian Miscellaneous Collections* 107, no. 8. Washington, D.C.: Smithsonian Institution.

———. 1952a. "La Venta, Tabasco: A Study of Olmec Ceramics and Art." *Bureau of American Ethnology Bulletin* 153. Washington, D.C.: Smithsonian Institution.

———. 1952b. "Middle Tres Zapotes Pottery and the Pre-Classic Ceramic Sequence." *American Antiquity* 17: 258–260.

———. 1955. "The Cerro de las Mesas Offering of Jade and Other Materials." *Bureau of American Ethnology Bulletin* 157. Washington, D.C.: Smithsonian Institution.

Drucker, Philip, Robert F. Heizer, and Robert J. Squier. 1959. "Excavations at La Venta, Tabasco, 1955." *Bureau of American Ethnology Bulletin* 170. Washington, D.C.: Smithsonian Institution.

Durán, Diego. 1994. *The History of the Indies of New Spain*. Translated and edited by Doris Heyden. Norman: University of Oklahoma Press.

Easby, Elizabeth Kennedy. 1968. *Pre-Columbian Jade from Costa Rica*. New York: André Emmerich.

Easby, Elizabeth Kennedy, and John F. Scott. 1970. *Before Cortés: Sculpture of Middle America*. New York: Metropolitan Museum of Art.

Ekholm, Gordon F. 1970. *Ancient Mexico and Central America*. New York: American Museum of Natural History.

Elliot, John H. 2009. "The Overthrow of Moctezuma and His Empire." In McEwan and López Luján, pp. 218–235.

Fash, William. 1987. "The Altar and Associated Features." In Grove 1987, pp. 82–94.

Fernández Souza, Lilia. 1998. Catalogue entry 236. In Schmidt, de la Garza, and Nalda 1998.

Fields, Virginia M. 1989. "The Origins of Divine Kingship among the Lowland Classic Maya." PhD diss., University of Texas at Austin.

Fields, Virginia M., and Dorie Reents-Budet. 2005. *Lords of Creation: The Origins of Sacred Maya Kingship*. Los Angeles and London: Los Angeles County Museum of Art in association with Scala Publishers.

Fields, Virginia M., and Alexandre Tokovinine. Forthcoming. Catalogue entry. In *Maya Art at Dumbarton Oaks*, edited by Joanne Pillsbury, Reiko Ishihara, Miriam Doutriaux, and Alexandre Tokovinine. Pre-Columbian Art at Dumbarton Oaks 4. Washington, D.C.: Dumbarton Oaks.

Flannery, Kent V. 1968. "The Olmec in the Valley of Oaxaca: A Model for Inter-Regional Interaction in Formative Times." In Benson 1968, pp. 79–117.

Flannery, Kent V., and Joyce Marcus. 2000. "Formative Mexican Kingdoms and the Myth of the 'Mother Culture.'" *Journal of Anthropological Archaeology* 19 (1): 1–37.

———. 2005. *Excavations at San José Mogote 1: The Household Archaeology*. Prehistory and Human Ecology of the Valley of Oaxaca 13. Ann Arbor: Museum of Anthropology, University of Michigan.

Freidel, David A. 1993. "The Jade Ahau: Toward a Theory of Commodity Value in Maya Civilization." In *Precolumbian Jade: New Geological and Cultural Interpretations*, edited by Frederick W. Lange, pp. 149–165. Salt Lake City: University of Utah Press.

———. 1995. "Preparing the Way." In Princeton University 1995, pp. 2–9.

Furst, Peter T. 1981. "Jaguar Baby or Toad Mother: A New Look at an Old Problem in Olmec Iconography." In Benson 1981a, pp. 149–162.

García Moll, Roberto, Daniel Juárez Cossio, Carmen Pijoan Aguade, María Elena Salas Cuesta, and Marcela Salas Cuesta. 1991. *Catálogo de entierros de San Luis Tlatilco, México: Temporada IV*. Serie antropología física-arqueología. Mexico: INAH.

García Payón, José. 1971. "The Archaeology of Central Veracruz." In *Archaeology of Northern Mesoamerica*, pt. 2, edited by Gordon F. Ekholm and Ignacio Bernal, pp. 505–542. Vol. 11 of *Handbook of Middle American Indians*, edited by Robert Wauchope. Austin: University of Texas Press.

Gay, Carlo T. E. 1967. "Oldest Paintings of the New World." *Natural History* 76 (4): 28–35.

———. 1972. *Xochipala: The Beginnings of Olmec Art*. Princeton, NJ: Princeton University Press.

Gillespie, Susan D. 1993. "Power, Pathways, and Appropriations in Mesoamerican Art." In *Imagery and Creativity: Ethnoaesthetics and Art Worlds in the Americas*, edited by Dorothea S. Whitten and Norman E. Whitten, pp. 67–107. Tucson: University of Arizona Press.

———. 1994. "Llano del Jícaro: An Olmec Monument Workshop." *Ancient Mesoamerica* 5: 231–242.

———. 2000. "The Monuments of Laguna de los Cerros and Its Hinterland." In Clark and Pye 2000a, pp. 95–115.

Gómez Rueda, Hernando, and Valérie Courtes. 1987. "Un pectoral olmeca de La Encrucijada, Tabasco: Observaciones sobre piezas menores olmecas." *Arqueología* 1: 73–88.

González Lauck, Rebecca B. 1988. "Proyecto arqueológico La Venta." *Arqueología* 1 (4): 121–166.

——. 1989. "Recientes investigaciones en La Venta, Tabasco." In *El Preclásico o Formativo: Avances y perspectivas*, edited by Martha Carmona Macías, pp. 81–90. Mexico: INAH, Museo Nacional de Antropología.

——. 1994. "La antigua ciudad olmeca en La Venta, Tabasco." In Clark 1994c, pp. 93–111.

——. 1995. "La Venta: Una gran ciudad olmeca." *Arquelogía Mexicana* 2 (12): 38–42.

——. 1996a. Catalogue entries. In Benson and de la Fuente 1996.

——. 1996b. "La Venta: A Great Olmec City." In *Olmecs: Special Edition, Arqueología Mexicana*, pp. 42–47.

——. 1996c. "La Venta: An Olmec Capital." In Benson and de la Fuente 1996, pp. 73–81.

——. 1997. "Acerca de pirámides de tierra y seres sobrenaturales: Observaciones preliminares en torno al edificio C-1, La Venta, Tabasco." *Arqueología* 2 (17): 79–97.

——. 2000. "La zona del Golfo en el Preclásico: La etapa olmeca." In vol. 1 of *Historia antigua de México*, 2nd ed., edited by Linda Manzanilla and Leonardo López Luján, pp. 363–406. Mexico: INAH/UNAM/Editorial Porrúa.

——. 2004. "Observaciones en torno a los contextos de la escultura olmeca en La Venta, Tabasco." In Uriarte and Staines Cicero 2004, pp. 75–105.

——. 2007. "El Complejo A: La Venta, Tabasco." *Arqueología Mexicana* 15 (87): 49–54.

——. 2008. "La arqueología del mundo olmeca." In Uriarte and González Lauck 2008, vol. 2: 397–410.

Graham, John A. 2005. "Reading the Past: Olmec Archaeology and the Curious Case of Tres Zapotes Stela C." Paper presented at the Mesa Redonda Olmeca, Mexico City.

Gregory, David A. 1975. "San Gervasio." In *A Study of Changing Pre-Columbian Commercial Systems: The 1972–1973 Seasons at Cozumel, Mexico*, edited by Jeremy A. Sabloff and William L. Rathje, pp. 88–106. Peabody Museum Monographs 3. Cambridge, MA: Peabody Museum of Archaeology and Ethnology, Harvard University.

Griffin, Gillett G. 1981. "Olmec Forms and Materials Found in Central Guerrero." In Benson 1981a, pp. 209–222.

Grove, David C. 1970a. *The Olmec Paintings of Oxtotitlan Cave, Guerrero, Mexico*. Studies in Pre-Columbian Art and Archaeology 6. Washington, D.C.: Dumbarton Oaks.

——. 1970b. *Los murales de la cueva de Oxtotitlan, Acatlán, Guerrero: Informe sobre las investigaciones arqueológicas en Chilapa, Guerrero, noviembre de 1968*. Serie investigaciones 23. Mexico City: INAH

——. 1973. "Olmec Altars and Myths." *Archaeology* 26 (2): 128–135.

——. 1974. *San Pablo, Nexpa, and the Early Formative Archaeology of Morelos*. Vanderbilt University Publications in Anthropology 12. Nashville, TN: Vanderbilt University.

——. 1981. "Olmec Monuments: Mutilation as a Clue to Meaning." In Benson 1981a, pp. 48–68.

——. 1984. *Chalcatzingo: Excavations on the Olmec Frontier*. New York: Thames & Hudson.

——. 1987. *Ancient Chalcatzingo*. Austin: University of Texas Press. Also available online at http://www.famsi.org/research/grove/chalcatzingo/index.html (accessed May 9, 2010).

——. 1989a. "Chalcatzingo and Its Olmec Connection." In Sharer and Grove 1989, pp. 122–147.

——. 1989b. "Olmec, What's in a Name?" In Sharer and Grove 1989, pp. 8–14.

——. 1993. "'Olmec' Horizons in Formative Period Mesoamerica: Diffusion or Social Evolution?" In *Latin American Horizons*, edited by Don S. Rice, pp. 83–111. Washington, D.C.: Dumbarton Oaks.

——. 1994. "La Isla, Veracruz, 1991: A Preliminary Report, with Comments on the Olmec Uplands." *Ancient Mesoamerica* 5: 223–230.

——. 1995. "Monumental Art and Preclassic Sacred Landscapes." Paper presented at the Maya Weekend, University Museum, University of Pennsylvania, Philadelphia, April 8.

——. 1996a. "Archaeological Contexts of Olmec Art outside of the Gulf Coast." In Benson and de la Fuente 1996, pp. 105–117.

——. 1996b. Catalogue entries. In Benson and de la Fuente 1996.

——. 1996c. "The Olmec." In *Olmecs: Special Edition, Arqueología Mexicana*, pp. 12–23.

——. 1997. "Olmec Archaeology: A Half Century of Research and Its Accomplishments." *Journal of World Prehistory* 11 (1): 51–101.

——. 2000. "Faces of the Earth at Chalcatzingo, Mexico: Serpents, Caves, and Mountains in Middle Formative Period Iconography." In Clark and Pye 2000a, pp. 277–295.

——. 2006. "Chalcatzingo y la 'Cultura Tlatilco' en el Preclásico de Morelos." In *Jornadas académicas en homenaje a Eduardo Matos Moctezuma*, edited by Leonardo López Luján, Davíd Carrasco, and Lourdes Cué, pp. 103–111. Mexico: INAH.

——. 2007. "Stirrup Spout Vessels and Carved Stone Monuments: The Many Faces of Interregional Interactions in Formative Period Morelos." In Lowe and Pye 2007, pp. 209–227.

——. n.d. "The Middle Preclassic Period Paintings of Oxtotitlan Cave, Guerrero." Available online at http://www.famsi.org/research/grove/ (accessed May 9, 2010).

Grove, David C., and Jorge Angulo V. 1987. "A Catalog and Description of Chalcatzingo's Monuments." In Grove 1987, pp. 114–131.

Grove, David C., Kenneth G. Hirth, and David E. Bugé. 1987. "The Physical and Cultural Setting." In Grove 1987, pp. 6–13.

Guernsey, Julia, and F. Kent Reilly III, eds. 2007. *Sacred Bindings of the Cosmos: Ritual Acts of Bundling and Wrapping in Ancient Mesoamerica*. Barnardsville, NC: Boundary End Archaeology Research Center Press.

Guzmán, Eulalia. 1934. "Los relieves de las rocas del Cerro de la Cantera, Jonacatepec, Mor." *Anales del Museo Nacional de Arqueología, Historia y Etnografía* 1 (2): 237–251.

Heizer, Robert F. 1966. "Ancient Heavy Transport, Methods and Achievements." *Science* 153 (3738): 821–830.

Heizer, Robert F., John A. Graham, and Lewis K. Napton. 1968. "The 1968 Investigations at La Venta." In *Papers on Mesoamerican Archaeology*, pp. 127–153. Contributions of the University of California Archaeological Research Facility 5. Berkeley: University of California.

Heizer, Robert F., Tillie Smith, and Howel Williams. 1962. "Notes on Colossal Head No. 2 from Tres Zapotes." *American Antiquity* 31: 102–104.

Helms, Mary. 1998. *Access to Origins: Affines, Ancestors, and Aristocrats.* Austin: University of Texas Press.

Hill, Warren D. 1999. "Ballcourts, Competitive Games, and the Emergence of Complex Society." PhD diss., University of British Columbia.

Hosler, Dorothy, Sandra L. Burkett, and Michael J. Tarkanian. 1999. "Prehistoric Polymers: Rubber Processing in Ancient Mesoamerica." *Science*, n.s., 284 (5422): 1988–1991.

Houston, Stephen, and Michael D. Coe. 2004. "Has Isthmian Writing Been Deciphered?" *Mexicon* 25: 151–161.

Jiménez Moreno, Wigberto. 1942. "El enigma de los olmecas." *Cuadernos Americanos* 5 (5): 113–146.

Joralemon, Peter David. 1971. *A Study of Olmec Iconography*. Studies in Pre-Columbian Art and Archaeology 7. Washington, D.C.: Dumbarton Oaks.

———. 1976. "The Olmec Dragon: A Study in Pre-Columbian Iconography." In Nicholson 1976, pp. 27–71.

———. 1996. "In Search of the Olmec Cosmos: Reconstructing the World View of Mexico's First Civilization." In Benson and de la Fuente 1996, pp. 51–59.

Joyce, Rosemary A., Richard Edging, Karl Lorenz, and Susan D. Gillespie. 1991. "Olmec Bloodletting: An Iconographic Study." In *Sixth Palenque Round Table, 1986*, edited by Merle Greene Robertson and Virginia M. Fields, pp. 143–150. Palenque Round Table 8. Norman: University of Oklahoma Press.

Justeson, John, and Terrence Kaufman. 2008. "The Epi-Olmec Tradition at Cerro de las Mesas in the Classic Period." In *Classic Period Cultural Currents in Southern and Central Veracruz*, edited by Philip J. Arnold III and Christopher A. Pool, pp. 159–194. Washington, D.C.: Dumbarton Oaks.

Kappelman, Julia Guernsey, and F. Kent Reilly III. 2001. "Paths to Heaven, Ropes to Earth: Birds, Jaguars, and Cosmic Cords in Formative Period Mesoamerica." *Ancient America* 2/3: 33–52.

Kaufman, Terrence, and John S. Justeson. 2001. "Epi-Olmec Hieroglyphic Writing and Texts." Austin: Texas Workshop Foundation. Also available online at http://www.albany.edu/anthro/maldp/EOTEXTS.pdf (accessed May 9, 2010).

Kelemen, Pál. 1943. *Medieval American Art*. 2 vols. New York: Macmillan.

Kelley, David H. 1966. "A Cylinder Seal from Tlatilco." *American Antiquity* 31 (5): 744–746.

Kirchhoff, Paul. 1943. "Mesoamérica: Sus límites geográficos, composición étnica y caracteres culturales." *Acta Americana* 1 (1): 92–107.

———. 1960. "Mesoamérica: Sus límites geográficos, composición étnica y caracteres culturales." *Tlatoani*, supplement no. 3.

Krotser, Ramón. 1973. "El agua ceremonial de los olmecas." *Boletín del Instituto Nacional de Antropología e Historia* 2: 43–48.

Kubler, George. 1962. *The Art and Architecture of Ancient America*. Middlesex, U.K.: Penguin Books.

Kunz, George Frederick. 1889. "Sur une hâche votive gigantesque en jadeite de l'Oaxaca, et sur un pectoral en jadeite du Guatemala." In *Congrès international d'anthropologie et d'archéologie préhistoriques, dixième session*, pp. 517–523. Paris.

———. 1890. *Gems and Precious Stones of North America*. New York: Scientific.

Lacadena, Alfonso. 2008. "La escritura olmeca y la hipótesis del mixe-zoque: Implicaciones lingüísticas de un análisis estructural del monumento 13 de La Venta." In Uriarte and González Lauck 2008, vol. 2: 607–626.

Ladrón de Guevara, Sara. 2008a. "Sobre la cabeza colosal 7 de San Lorenzo." In *El mediterraneo americano: Población, cultura e historia*, edited by Carlos Serrano Sánchez and Marco Antonio Cardoso Gómez, pp. 135–142. XXVII Mesa Redonda de la Sociedad Mexicana de Antropología. Mexico City: Sociedad Mexicana de Antropología, UNAM.

———. 2008b. "Insignias de poder: Permanencia y transformación de monumentos escultóricos." In *Arqueología, paisaje y cosmovisión en Los Tuxtlas*, edited by Lourdes Budar and Sara Ladrón de Guevara, pp. 131–143. Xalapa: Universidad Veracruzana.

Lee, Thomas A., Jr. 1989. "Chiapas and the Olmec." In Sharer and Grove 1989, pp. 198–226.

León, Ignacio, and Juan Carlos Sánchez. 1991–1992. "Las gemelas y el jaguar del sitio El Azuzul." *Horizonte* 1 (5–6): 56–60.

López Austin, Alfredo. 1998. *Los mitos del tlacuache: Caminos de la mitología mesoamericana*. Mexico City: Instituto de Investigaciones Antropológicas, UNAM.

López Luján, Leonardo. 1994. *The Offerings of the Templo Mayor of Tenochtitlan*. Translated by Bernard R. Ortiz de Montellano and Thelma Ortiz de Montellano. Niwot: University Press of Colorado.

Loughlin, Michael. 2004. "Recorrido arqueológico El Mesón." Crystal River, FL: Foundation for the Advancement of Mesoamerican Studies. Available online at http://www.famsi.org/reports/02058/index.html (accessed May 9, 2010).

———. 2009. "The Tres Zapotes Regional Polity: A View from the Hinterland." Paper presented at the 74th Annual Meeting of the Society for American Archaeology, Atlanta, Georgia, April 22–26.

Lowe, Gareth W. 1962. "Algunos resultados de la temporada 1961 en Chiapa de Corzo, Chiapas." *Estudios de Cultura Maya* 2: 185–196.

———. 1969. "The Olmec Horizon Occupations of Mound 20 at San Isidro in the Middle Grijalva Region of Chiapas." Master's thesis, University of the Americas, Puebla, Mexico.

———. 1990. Catalogue entries. In *Mexico: Splendors of Thirty Centuries.* New York: Metropolitan Museum of Art.

———. 1994. "Comunidades de Chiapas relacionadas con los olmecas." In Clark 1994c, pp. 113–127.

———. 1998. *Mesoamérica olmeca: Diez preguntas.* Serie arqueología. Mexico City: INAH.

Lowe, Lynneth S., and Mary E. Pye, eds. 2007. *Archaeology, Art, and Ethnogenesis in Mesoamerican Prehistory: Papers in Honor of Gareth W. Lowe.* Papers of the New World Archaeological Foundation 68. Provo, UT: Brigham Young University.

Luckert, Karl W. 1976. *Olmec Religion: A Key to Middle America and Beyond.* Civilization of the American Indian 137. Norman: University of Oklahoma Press.

Malmström, Vincent Herschel. 1997. *Cycles of the Sun, Mysteries of the Moon: The Calendar in Mesoamerican Civilization.* Austin: University of Texas Press.

Marcus, Joyce. 1989. "Zapotec Chiefdoms and the Nature of Formative Religions." In Sharer and Grove 1989, pp. 148–197.

Martínez Donjuán, Guadalupe. 1994. "Los olmecas en el estado de Guerrero." In Clark 1994c, pp. 143–164.

Matos Moctezuma, Eduardo. 1996. Catalogue entries. In Benson and de la Fuente 1996.

———. 1999. "Una máscara olmeca en el Templo Mayor de Tenochtitlan." In *El Templo Mayor, El recinto ceremonial, Mundo mexica,* edited by Eduardo Matos Moctezuma, pp. 155–163. Vol. 1, bk. 1 of *Obras: Estudios mexicas.* Mexico City: El Colegio Nacional.

———. 2003. *Vida y muerte en el Templo Mayor.* Mexico: Fondo de Cultura Económica. (Orig. pub. 1986.)

———. 2009. "The Coronation of Moctezuma II." In McEwan and López Luján 2009, pp. 56–67.

McAnany, Patricia. 1995. *Living with the Ancestors: Kinship and Kingship in Ancient Maya Society.* Austin: University of Texas Press.

McEwan, Colin, and Leonardo López Luján, eds. 2009. *Moctezuma: Aztec Ruler.* London: British Museum.

Medellín Zeñil, Alfonso. 1960. "Monolitos inéditos olmecas." *La Palabra y el Hombre* 16: 75–97.

———. 1978. "El contorsionista de Las Choapas, Veracruz." *Boletín del Instituto Nacional de Antropología e Historia* 2 (22): 14.

Melgar, José M. 1869. "Antigüedades mexicanos." *Boletín de la Sociedad Mexicana de Geografía y Estadística* 2 (1): 292–297.

Milbrath, Susan. 1979. *A Study of Olmec Sculptural Chronology.* Studies in Pre-Columbian Art and Archaeology 23. Washington, D.C.: Dumbarton Oaks.

Millet Cámara, Luis Alfonso. 1979. "Rescate arqueológico en la región de Tres Zapotes, Ver." Licenciatura thesis in anthropology, Escuela Nacional de Antropología e Historia.

Morley, Sylvanus Griswold. 1915. "An Introduction to the Study of the Maya Hieroglyphs." *Bureau of American Ethnology Bulletin* 57. Washington, D.C.: Smithsonian Institution.

———. 1946. *The Ancient Maya.* Stanford: Stanford University Press.

Navarrete, Carlos. 1971. "Algunas piezas olmecas de Chiapas y Guatemala." *Anales de Antropología* 8: 69–82.

———. 1974. *The Olmec Rock Carvings at Pijijiapan, Chiapas, Mexico and Other Olmec Pieces from Chiapas and Guatemala.* Papers of the New World Archaeological Foundation 35. Provo, UT: Brigham Young University.

Nicholson, Henry B. 1971. "Major Sculpture in Pre-Hispanic Central Mexico." In *Handbook of Middle American Indians,* vol. 10, *Archaeology of Northern Mesoamerica,* pt. 1, edited by Gordon F. Ekholm and Ignacio Bernal, pp. 92–134. Austin: University of Texas Press.

———, ed. 1976. *Origins of Religious Art and Iconography in Preclassic Mesoamerica.* UCLA Latin American Studies 31. Los Angeles: UCLA Latin American Center Publications.

Niederberger, Christine. 1975. "Excavaciones en Zohapilco-Tlapacoya, Mexico." *Actas del XLI Congreso Internacional de Americanistas* 1: 403–411.

———. 1976. *Zohapilco: Cinco milenios de ocupación humana en un sitio lacustre de la Cuenca de México.* Colección Científica 30. Mexico: INAH.

———. 1996a. "The Basin of Mexico: A Multimillennial Development toward Cultural Complexity." In Benson and de la Fuente 1996, pp. 83–93.

———. 1996b. Catalogue entries. In Benson and de la Fuente 1996.

———. 1996c. "Olmec Horizon Guerrero." In Benson and de la Fuente 1996, pp. 95–103.

———. 2000. "Ranked Societies, Iconographic Complexity, and Economic Wealth in the Basin of Mexico toward 1200 BC." In Clark and Pye 2000a, pp. 169–191.

———. 2002. "Nácar, 'jade,' y cinabrio: Guerrero y las redes de intercambio en la Mesoamérica antigua (1000–600 a.C.)." In *El pasado arqueológico de Guerrero,* edited by Christine Niederberger and Rosa Ma. Reyna Robles, pp. 175–223. Mexico: INAH.

Norman, V. Garth. 1976. *Izapa Sculpture, Part 2: Text.* Papers of the New World Archaeological Foundation 30. Provo, UT: Brigham Young University.

Ochoa, Lorenzo, and Marcía Castro-Leal Espino. 1986. *Archaeological Guide of the Park-Museum of La Venta.* Villahermosa: Government of the State of Tabasco.

Ochoa Castillo, Patricia. 1982. *Secuencia cronológica de Tlatilco, estado de México: Temporada IV.* Mexico: Biblioteca Enciclopédica del Estado de México.

———. 1996. Catalogue entries. In Benson and de la Fuente 1996.

———. 2003. *Tlatilco, el lugar donde hay cosas ocultos.* Saltillo, Mexico: Centro Cultural Vito Alessio Robles.

———. 2004. *Preclásico: Museo Nacional de Antropología.* Mexico City: CONACULTA-INAH.

Ochoa Castillo, Patricia, and Oscar Orueta Cañada. 1994. *La sala del Preclásico del Altiplano.* Mexico City: INAH.

Olivier, Guilhem, and Leonardo López Luján. 2009. "Images of Moctezuma and His Symbols of Power." In McEwan and López Luján 2009, pp. 78–91.

Ortíz Ceballos, Ponciano. 1975. "La cerámica de los Tuxtlas." Master's thesis, Escuela de Antropología, Facultad de Humanidades, Universidad Veracruzana, Xalapa.

——. 1980. "Laguna de Los Cerros y su área de interacción cultural: Propuesta de investigación." Archivo Técnico del IAUV. Xalapa.

Ortíz Ceballos, Ponciano, and Ma. del Carmen Rodríguez M. 1989a. *Proyecto Manatí: Segunda temporada de campo*. Archivo Técnico del Centro Regional Veracruz. Mexico: INAH.

——. 1989b. "Proyecto Manatí 1989." *Arqueología* 2 (1): 13–22.

——. 1992. *Proyecto Manatí: Informe de la temporada de campo de 1992*. Archivo Técnico del Centro INAH Veracruz. Mexico: INAH.

——. 1994. "Los espacios sagrados olmecas: El Manatí, un caso especial." In Clark 1994c, pp. 69–91.

——. 1995. *Proyecto Manatí: Informe técnico temporada 1994*. Archivo Técnico del Centro INAH Veracruz. Mexico: INAH.

——. 1996a. "El Manatí, Veracruz." In *Olmecs: Special Edition, Arqueología Mexicana*, pp. 38–41.

——. 1996b. *Proyecto Manatí: Informe técnico de la temporada 1996*. Archivo Técnico del Centro INAH Veracruz. Mexico: INAH.

——. 1997. *Proyecto Manatí: Propuesta para la temporada 1998: Recorrido en las márgenes y tierra adentro de los ríos Coachapa y Cahuapa*. Archivo Técnico de la Coordinación Nacional de Arqueología. Mexico: INAH.

——. 1998. *Proyecto Manatí: Informe técnico de la temporada 1998*. Archivo Técnico del Centro INAH Veracruz. Mexico: INAH.

——. 2000. "The Sacred Hill of El Manatí: A Preliminary Discussion of the Site's Ritual Paraphernalia." In Clark and Pye 2000a, pp. 75–93.

Ortíz Ceballos, Ponciano, Ma. del Carmen Rodríguez M., and Alfredo Delgado C. 1997. *Las investigaciones arqueológicas en el cerro sagrado Manatí*. Universidad Veracruzana. Xalapa: INAH.

Ortíz Ceballos, Ponciano, Ma. del Carmen Rodríguez M., and Daniel Nahmad. 1988a. *Proyecto Manatí: Rescate arqueológico*. Archivo Técnico del Centro Regional Veracruz. Mexico: INAH.

Ortíz Ceballos, Ponciano, Ma. del Carmen Rodríguez M., and Paul Schmidt. 1988b. "El proyecto Manatí: Informe preliminar." *Arqueología* 1 (3): 141–154.

Ortíz Ceballos, Ponciano, Ma. del Carmen Rodríguez M., Paul Schmidt, Alfredo Delgado C., Luis Heredia, Lourdes Hernández, Inés Gheno et al. 1989. *Proyecto Manatí 1988: Informe final de temporada*. Archivo Técnico del Centro Regional Veracruz. Mexico: INAH.

Ortíz Ceballos, Ponciano, Ma. del Carmen Rodríguez M., Paul Schmidt, Alfredo Delgado C., Lourdes Hernández, Luis Heredia, Ricardo Herrera et al. 1990. *Proyecto Manatí: Informe final, temporada 1989*. Archivo Técnico del Centro Regional Veracruz. Mexico: INAH.

Paillés Hernández, María de la Cruz. 2007. "Las Bocas, Puebla, Archaeological Project (2000)." Available online at http://www.famsi.org/reports/99041/index.html (accessed May 9, 2010).

Paradis, Louise Iseult. 1981. "Guerrero and the Olmec." In Benson 1981a, pp. 195–208.

——. 2008. "Contribución del Guerrero antiguo a la civilización olmeca." In Uriarte and González Lauck 2008, pp. 533–546.

Pasztory, Esther. 1983. *Aztec Art*. New York: Harry N. Abrams.

——. 1993. "Semiprecious Stone Objects." In Berrin and Pasztory 1993, pp. 176–183.

——. 2000. "The Portrait and the Mask: Invention and Translation." In Clark and Pye 2000a, pp. 265–275.

Peres, Tanya. 2009. "Fishing and Hunting for the Family Larder: Olmec and Epi-Olmec Subsistence Strategies at Tres Zapotes." Paper presented at the 74th Annual Meeting of the Society for American Archaeology, Atlanta, Georgia, April 22–26.

Pérez de Lara, Jorge. n.d. "Olmec Discovery at Zazacatla." Mesoweb Report. Available online at http://www.mesoweb.com/reports/zazacatla.html (accessed May 9, 2010).

Pérez Suárez, Tomás. 1994. "Breve crónica de la arqueología olmeca." In Clark 1994c, pp. 21–29.

——. 2008. "Un nuevo monumento olmeca en el oriente de Tabasco." In Uriarte and González Lauck 2008, pp. 113–124.

Piña Chan, Román. 1955. *Las culturas preclásicas de la Cuenca de México*. Mexico: Fonda de Cultura Económica.

——. 1958. *Tlatilco*. 2 vols. Serie Investigaciones 1. Mexico City: INAH.

——. 1960. *Mesoamérica: Ensayo histórico cultural*. Memorias del Instituto Nacional de Antropología e Historia 6. Mexico: INAH.

Piña Chan, Román, and Luis Covarrubias. 1964. *El pueblo del jaguar*. Mexico City: Museo Nacional de Antropología.

Piperno, Dolores R., and Kent V. Flannery. 2001. "The Earliest Maize (*Zea mays L.*) from Highland Mexico: New Accelerator Mass Spectrometry Dates and Their Implications." *Proceedings of the National Academy of Science* 98 (4): 2101–2103.

Pires-Ferreira, Jane W., and B. J. Evans. 1978. "Mössbauer Spectral Analysis of Olmec Iron Ore Mirrors: New Evidence of Formative Exchange Networks in Mesoamerica." In *Cultural Continuity in Mesoamerica*, edited by David L. Browman, pp. 101–154. The Hague: Mouton.

Pohl, Mary D., Kathryn Josserand, Kevin O. Pope, and Christopher von Nagy. 2008. "La U olmeca y el desarrollo de la escritura en Mesoamérica." In Uriarte and González Lauck 2008, vol. 2: 685–694.

Pohl, Mary D., Kevin O. Pope, and Christopher von Nagy. 2002. "Olmec Origins of Mesoamerican Writing." *Science* 298: 1984–1987.

Pohorilenko, Anatole. 1990. "La estructura del sistema representacional olmeca." *Arqueología* 3: 85–90.

——. 1996. "Portable Carvings in the Olmec Style." In Benson and de la Fuente 1996, pp. 119–131.

——. 2008. "Cultura y estilo en el arte olmeca: ¿Un estilo, muchas culturas?" In Uriarte and González Lauck 2008, pp. 65–88.

Pool, Christopher A. 2000. "From Olmec to Epi-Olmec at Tres Zapotes, Veracruz, Mexico." In Clark and Pye 2000a, pp. 137–153.

——, ed. 2003. *Settlement Archaeology and Political Economy at Tres Zapotes, Veracruz, Mexico*. Monograph 50. Los Angeles: Cotsen Institute of Archaeology, University of California.

——. 2007. *Olmec Archaeology and Early Mesoamerica*. Cambridge: Cambridge University Press.

——. 2008. "Architectural Plans, Factionalism, and the Protoclassic-Classic Transition at Tres Zapotes." In *Classic Period Cultural Currents in Southern and Central Veracruz*, edited by Philip J. Arnold III and Christopher A. Pool, pp. 121-157. Washington, D.C.: Dumbarton Oaks.

——. Forthcoming. "Stone Monuments and Earthen Mounds: Polity and Placemaking at Tres Zapotes, Veracruz, Mexico." In *The Place of Stone Monuments: Context, Use, and Meaning in Mesoamerica's Preclassic Transition*, edited by Julia Guernsey, John E. Clark, and Barbara Arroyo. Washington, D.C.: Dumbarton Oaks.

Pool, Christopher A., and Michael Anthony Ohnersorgen. 2003. "Archaeological Survey and Settlement at Tres Zapotes." In Pool 2003, pp. 7–31.

Pool, Christopher A., and Ponciano Ortíz Ceballos. 2008. "Tres Zapotes como centro olmeca: Nuevos datos." In Uriarte and González Lauck 2008, pp. 425–443.

Pool, Christopher A., Ponciano Ortíz Ceballos, and Ma. del Carmen Rodríguez M. Forthcoming. "The Early Horizon at Tres Zapotes: Implications for Olmec Interaction." *Ancient Mesoamerica*.

Porter, James B. 1989. "Olmec Colossal Heads as Recarved Thrones: 'Mutilation,' Revolution, and Recarving." *Res: Anthropology and Aesthetics* 17/18: 22–29.

Porter, Muriel Noe. 1953. "Tlatilco and the Pre-Classic Cultures of the New World." Viking Fund Publications in Anthropology 19. New York: Wenner Gren Foundation for Anthropological Research.

Porter Weaver, Muriel. 1967. *Tlapacoya Pottery in the Museum Collection*. Indian Notes and Monographs 56. New York: Museum of the American Indian, Heye Foundation.

Princeton University. 1995. *The Olmec World: Ritual and Rulership*. Princeton, NJ: Princeton University Press.

Proskouriakoff, Tatiana. 1968. "Olmec and Maya Art: Problems of their Stylistic Relation." In Benson 1968, pp. 119–134.

Pugh, Marion Stirling. 1981. "An Intimate View of Archaeological Exploration." In Benson 1981a, pp. 1–13.

Pye, Mary E., and Gerardo Gutiérrez. 2007. "The Pacific Coast Trade Route of Mesoamerica: Iconographic Connections between Guatemala and Guerrero." In Lowe and Pye 2007, pp. 229–246.

Ramírez, Felipe, Lorena Gámez, and Fernán González. 2000. *Cerámica de Temamatla*. Mexico: Instituto de Investigaciones Antropológicas, UNAM.

Rathje, William L., Jeremy A. Sabloff, and David A. Gregory. 1973. "El descubrimiento de un jade olmeca en la Isla de Cozumel, Quintana Roo, México." *Estudios de Cultura Maya* 9: 85–89.

Reilly, F. Kent, III. 1994. "Cosmología, soberanismo y espacio ritual en la Mesoamérica del Formativo." In Clark 1994c, pp. 239–259.

——. 1995. "Art, Ritual, and Rulership in the Olmec World." In Princeton University 1995, pp. 27–45.

——. 1997. "Die Olmeken." In Rickenbach 1997, pp. 25–42.

——. 1999. "Mountains of Creation and Underworld Portals: The Ritual Function of Olmec Architecture at La Venta, Tabasco." In *Mesoamerican Architecture as a Cultural Symbol*, edited by Jeff K. Kowalski, pp. 14–39. New York: Oxford University Press.

——. 2002. "The Landscape of Creation: Architecture, Tomb, and Monument Placement at the Olmec Site of La Venta." In *Heart of Creation: The Mesoamerican World and the Legacy of Linda Schele*, pp. 34–65, edited by Andrea Stone. Tuscaloosa: University of Alabama Press.

——. 2005. "Olmec Ideological, Ritual, and Symbolic Contributions to the Institution of Classic Maya Kingship." In Fields and Reents-Budet 2005, pp. 30–36.

——. 2007a. "Introduction to Bundling Special Section." In Guernsey and Reilly 2007, pp. 1–12.

——. 2007b. "Middle Formative Origins of the Mesoamerican Ritual Act of Bundling." In Guernsey and Reilly 2007, pp. 13–34.

Reilly, F. Kent, III, and James F. Garber. 2003. "The Symbolic Representation of Warfare in Middle Formative Mesoamerica." In *Ancient Mesoamerican Warfare*, edited by M. Kathryn Brown and Travis W. Stanton, pp. 127–148. Walnut Creek, CA: AltaMira Press.

Reyna Robles, Rosa Ma., and Paul Schmidt Schoenberg. 2006. "El estilo olmeca en Guerrero." *Arqueología Mexicana* 82: 38–41.

Rickenbach, Judith, ed. 1997. *Mexiko: Präkolumbische Kulturen am Golf von Mexiko*. Zürich: Museum Rietberg.

Rodríguez M., Ma. del Carmen, and Ponciano Ortíz Ceballos. 2000. "A Massive Offering of Axes at La Merced, Hidalgotitlán, Veracruz, Mexico." In Clark and Pye 2000a, pp. 155–167.

Royal Academy of Arts. 2002. *Aztecs*. London: Royal Academy of Arts.

Rust, William F., III. 1992. "New Ceremonial and Settlement Evidence at La Venta, and Its Relation to Preclassic Maya Cultures." In *New Theories on the Ancient Maya*, edited by Elin C. Danien and Robert J. Sharer, pp. 123–130. Philadelphia: University Museum, University of Pennsylvania.

Sahlins, Marshall David. 1985. *Islands of History*. Chicago: University of Chicago Press.

Sánchez-Martínez, Fernando. 1996. "The Rubber Tree." In *Olmecs: Special Edition, Arqueología Mexicana*, pp. 82–84.

Saturno, William. 2006. "Dawn of Maya Gods and Kings." *National Geographic Magazine* 209 (1): 68–77.

Saville, Marshall H. 1900. "A Votive Adze of Jadeite from Mexico." *Monumental Records* 1: 138–140.

——. 1929. "Votive Axes from Ancient Mexico, pts. 1 and 2." *Indian Notes* 6: 266–299, 335–342.

Scarborough, Vernon L. 1998. "Ecology and Ritual: Water Management and the Maya." *Latin American Antiquity* 9 (2): 135–159.

Schele, Linda. 1995. "The Olmec Mountain and Tree of Creation in Mesoamerican Cosmology." In Princeton University 1995, pp. 105–117.

Schele, Linda, and Mary Ellen Miller. 1986. *The Blood of Kings: Dynasty and Ritual in Maya Art*. Fort Worth, TX: Kimbell Art Museum.

Schmidt, Peter, Mercedes de la Garza, and Enrique Nalda, eds. 1998. *I maya*. Milan: Bompiani-CNCA INAH.

Seler-Sachs, Caecilie. 1922. "Altertümer des Kanton Tuxtla im Staate Vera-Cruz." In *Festschrift Eduard Seler*, edited by Walter Lehmann, pp. 543–556. Stuttgart: Verlag von Strecker & Schroeder.

Sharer, Robert J., and David C. Grove, eds. 1989. *Regional Perspectives on the Olmec*. Cambridge: Cambridge University Press.

Sociedad Mexicana de Antropología. 1942. *Mayas y olmecas: Segunda reunión de mesa redonda sobre problemas antropológicos de México y Centro América*. Mexico City: Talleres de la Editorial Stylo.

Solís Olguín, Felipe, ed. 2004. *The Aztec Empire*. New York: Guggenheim Museum Publications.

——. 2009. "Family Histories: The Ancestors of Moctezuma II." In McEwan and López Luján 2009, pp. 24–41.

Stark, Barbara L. 2000. "Framing the Gulf Olmecs." In Clark and Pye 2000a, pp. 31–53.

Stirling, Matthew W. 1939. "Discovering the New World's Oldest Dated Work of Man." *National Geographic Magazine* 76: 183–218.

——. 1940a. "An Initial Series from Tres Zapotes, Vera Cruz, Mexico." *National Geographic Society, Contributed Technical Papers, Mexican Archaeology Series* 1 (1): 1–15.

——. 1940b. "Great Stone Faces of the Mexican Jungle." *National Geographic Magazine* 78: 309–334.

——. 1941. "Expedition Unearths Buried Masterpieces of Carved Jade." *National Geographic Magazine* 80: 278–302.

——. 1942. "Recientes hallazgos en La Venta." In Sociedad Mexicana de Antropología 1942, pp. 56–58.

——. 1943. "Stone Monuments of Southern Mexico." *Bureau of American Ethnology Bulletin* 138. Washington, D.C.: Smithsonian Institution.

——. 1947. "On the Trail of La Venta Man." *National Geographic Magazine* 91 (2): 137–172.

——. 1955. "Stone Monuments of the Río Chiquito, Veracruz, Mexico." *Bureau of American Ethnology Bulletin* 157. Washington, D.C.: Smithsonian Institution.

——. 1964. "The Olmecs, Artists in Jade." In *Essays in Pre-Columbian Art and Archaeology*, edited by Samuel K. Lothrop, pp. 43–59. Cambridge, MA: Harvard University Press.

——. 1968. "Early History of the Olmec Problem." In Benson 1968, pp. 1–8.

Stirling, Matthew W., and Marion Stirling. 1942. "Finding Jewels of Jade in a Mexican Swamp." *National Geographic Magazine* 82 (5): 635–661.

Stuart, George E. 1993. "The Carved Stela from La Mojarra, Veracruz, Mexico." *Science* 259: 1700–1701.

Sullivan, Timothy D. 2002. "Landscape of Power: A Spatial Analysis of Civic-Ceremonial Architecture at Tres Zapotes, Veracruz, Mexico." Master's thesis, Southern Illinois University.

Symonds, Stacey. 2000. "The Ancient Landscape at San Lorenzo Tenochtitlán, Veracruz, Mexico: Settlement and Nature." In Clark and Pye 2000a, pp. 55–73.

Symonds, Stacey, Ann Cyphers, and Roberto Lunagómez. 2002. *Asentamiento prehispánico en San Lorenzo Tenochtitlán*. Mexico: Instituto de Investigaciones Antropológicas, UNAM.

Tate, Carolyn E. 1995. "Art in Olmec Culture." In Princeton University 1995, pp. 47–67.

——. 2009. "The Colossal Fetuses of La Venta and Mesoamerica's Earliest Creation Story." In *Imagining the Fetus: The Unborn in Myth, Religion, and Culture*, edited by Vanessa R. Sasson and Jane Marie Law, pp. 223–258. American Academy of Religion Cultural Criticism Series. New York: Oxford University Press.

Taube, Karl A. 1995. "The Rainmakers: The Olmec and Their Contribution to Mesoamerican Belief and Ritual." In Princeton University 1995, pp. 83–103.

——. 1996. "The Olmec Maize God: The Face of Corn in Formative Mesoamerica." *Res: Anthropology and Aesthetics* 29/30: 39–81.

——. 2000. "Lightning Celts and Corn Fetishes: The Formative Olmec and the Development of Maize Symbolism in Mesoamerica and the American Southwest." In Clark and Pye 2000a, pp. 297–337.

——. 2003. "Ancient and Contemporary Maya Conceptions about the Field and Forest." In *The Lowland Maya Area: Three Millennia at the Human-Wildland Interface*, edited by Arturo Gómez-Pompa, Michael F. Allen, Scott L. Fedick, and J. J. Jiménez-Osornio, pp. 461–492. New York: Haworth Press.

——. 2004. "Olmec Art at Dumbarton Oaks." *Pre-Columbian Art at Dumbarton Oaks* 2. Washington, D.C.: Dumbarton Oaks.

——. 2005. "The Symbolism of Jade in Classic Maya Religion." *Ancient Mesoamerica* 16: 23–50.

——. 2007. "La jadeíta y la cosmovisión de los olmecas." *Arqueología Mexicana* 15 (87): 43–48.

Taube, Karl, and William Saturno. 2008. "Los murales de San Bartolo: Desarrollo temprano del simbolismo y del mito del maíz en la antigua Mesoamérica." In Uriarte and González Lauck 2008, pp. 287–318.

Thompson, J. Eric S. 1941. "Dating of Certain Inscriptions of Non-Maya Origin." *Theoretical Approaches to Problems* 1. Cambridge, MA: Division of Historical Research, Carnegie Institution of Washington.

Thomson, Charlotte W. 1987. "Chalcatzingo Jade and Fine Stone Objects." In Grove 1987, pp. 295–304.

Tolstoy, Paul. 1989. "Coapexco and Tlatilco: Sites with Olmec Materials in the Basin of Mexico." In Sharer and Grove 1989, pp. 85–121.

Tolstoy, Paul, and Louise I. Paradis. 1970. "Early and Middle Pre-Classic Cultures in the Basin of Mexico." *Science* 167: 344–351.

Uriarte, María Teresa, and Rebecca B. González Lauck. 2008. *Olmeca: Balance y perspectivas: Memoria de la Primera Mesa Redonda,* 2 vols. Mexico: UNAM, New World Archaeological Foundation, Brigham Young University.

Uriarte, María Teresa, and Leticia Staines Cicero, eds. 2004. *Acercarse y mirar: Homenaje a Beatriz de la Fuente*. Estudios y fuentes del arte en México 74. Mexico: INAH, UNAM, Instituto de Investigaciones Estéticas.

Vaillant, George C. 1932. "A Pre-Columbian Jade: Artistic Comparisons Which Suggest the Identification of a New Mexican Civilization." *Natural History* 32 (6): 512–520, 557–558.

Valverde Valdés, María del Carmen. 1992. *Chiapa de Corzo: Épocas Prehispánica y Colonial*. Chiapas: Gobierno del Estado de Chiapas.

Venter, Marcie. 2008. "Community Strategies in the Aztec Imperial Frontier: Perspectives from Totogal, Veracruz, Mexico." PhD diss., University of Kentucky.

Wauchope, Robert. 1950. "A Tentative Sequence of Pre-Classic Ceramics in Middle America." *Middle American Research Records* 1 (14): 211–250.

Wedel, Waldo R. 1952. "Structural Investigations in 1943." In *La Venta, Tabasco: A Study of Olmec Ceramics and Art*, pp. 34–79. *Bureau of American Ethnology Bulletin* 153. Washington, D.C.: Smithsonian Institution.

Weiant, Clarence Wolsey. 1943. "An Introduction to the Ceramics of Tres Zapotes, Veracruz, Mexico." *Bureau of American Ethnology Bulletin* 139. Washington, D.C.: Smithsonian Institution.

———. 1952. "Reply to 'Middle Tres Zapotes and the Preclassic Ceramic Sequence.'" *American Antiquity* 18: 57–59.

Wendt, Carl J. 2003. "Buried Occupational Deposits at Tres Zapotes: The Results from an Auger Testing Program." In Pool 2003, pp. 32–46.

Wendt, Carl J., and Lu Shan-Tan. 2005. "Sourcing Archaeological Bitumen in the Olmec Region." *Journal of Archaeological Science* 33: 89–97.

Weyerstall, Albert. 1932. "Some Observations on Indian Mounds, Idols, and Pottery in the Lower Papaloapan Basin, State of Vera Cruz, Mexico." In *Middle American Papers: Studies Relating to Research in Mexico, the Central American Republics, and the West Indies*, pp. 27–69. New Orleans: Tulane University of Louisiana.

Whiting, Thomas A. Lee. 2007. "Los olmecas en Chiapas." *Arqueología Mexicana* 15 (87): 66–70.

Wichmann, Søren, Dmitri Beliaev, and Albert Davletshin. 2008. "Posibles corelaciones lingüísticas y arqueológicas vinculadas con los olmecas." In Uriarte and González Lauck 2008, pp. 667–683.

Wicke, Charles R. 1971. *Olmec: An Early Art Style of Precolumbian Mexico*. Tucson: University of Arizona Press.

Williams, Howel, and Robert Fleming Heizer. 1965. *Sources of Stones Used in Prehistoric Mesoamerican Sites.* Contributions of the University of California Archaeological Research Facility 1, pp. 1–39. Berkeley: University of California.

Winter, Marcus. 1994. "Los Altos de Oaxaca y los olmecas." In Clark 1994c, pp. 128–141.

Front and back cover: Consejo Nacional para la Cultura y las Artes—Instituto Nacional de Antropología e Historia—México—Javier Hinojosa

Frontispieces, pages 2, 4: Consejo Nacional para la Cultura y las Artes—Instituto Nacional de Antropología e Historia—México—Javier Hinojosa; 88–89, 234–235: Richard H. Stewart, National Anthropological Archives, Smithsonian Institution (stirling_24, stirling_20); 94–95: Michael Calderwood; 118–119: © Charles and Josette Lenars / Corbis; 196–197: © Richard Hewitt Stewart / National Geographic Society / Corbis

Figures 1, 7–10, 19, 41, 51: Consejo Nacional para la Cultura y las Artes—Instituto Nacional de Antropología e Historia—México—Javier Hinojosa; 2: Matthew W. Stirling / National Geographic Stock; 3–4: Michael Calderwood; 5, 34: Kenneth Garrett / National Geographic Stock; 11–15, 43, 49: © Marco Antonio Pacheco / *Arqueología Mexicana* / Raíces; 16–18, 20–25: National Anthropological Archives, Smithsonian Institution (heizer_1291, heizer_921, heizer_616, heizer_809, heizer_1449, heizer_099, heizer_1164, heizer_280, heizer_017); 26: Richard Hewitt Stewart / National Geographic Stock; 27–28, 30: Christopher A. Pool; 29: courtesy the New World Archaeological Foundation; 31–33, 35–36: courtesy David C. Grove; 37: © 1970 Dumbarton Oaks Research Library and Collection, Trustees for Harvard University, original artwork by Felipe Davalos; 38: courtesy the John Carter Brown Library at Brown University; 39: © Biblioteca Nacional de España; 40: Consejo Nacional para la Cultura y las Artes—Instituto Nacional de Antropología e Historia—México—Luis Martín Martínez García; 42: Markus Gruber, 2006, © Museum der Kulturen, Basel, Switzerland; 44: Werner Forman / Art Resource, NY; 45, 47: © Dumbarton Oaks, Pre-Columbian Collection, Washington, D.C.; 46: Musée du Quai Branly / Scala / Art Resource, NY; 48: © Gerardo Montiel Klint / *Arqueología Mexicana* / Raíces; 50: courtesy the Brooklyn Museum; 52: Consejo Nacional para la Cultura y las Artes—Instituto Nacional de Antropología e Historia—México—Michel Zabé; 53: Michel Zabé / Art Resource, NY

Plate 1: © Marco Antonio Pacheco / *Arqueología Mexicana* / Raíces; 2: courtesy the Division of Anthropology, American Museum of Natural History; 3: image #5747, American Museum of Natural History Library; 4–23, 26–32, 34, 37–87, 99–101, 107, 110–111, 113–114, 119–130, 133–134, 136–140, 142–145, 147–148, 151, 153–154: Consejo Nacional para la Cultura y las Artes—Instituto Nacional de Antropología e Historia—México—Javier Hinojosa; 24, 94, 96, 105–106, 115–118, 141, 146: digital image © 2009 Museum Associates / LACMA / Art Resource, NY; 25, 132: Joseph McDonald, courtesy the Fine Arts Museums of San Francisco; 33: Consejo Nacional para la Cultura y las Artes—Instituto Nacional de Antropología e Historia—México—Rafael Doniz Lechon; 35–36: © Carlos Blanco / *Arqueología Mexicana* / Raíces; 88–89: Consejo Nacional para la Cultura y las Artes—Instituto Nacional de Antropología e Historia—México—Luis Martín Martínez García; 90, 103, 109: image © The Metropolitan Museum of Art / Art Resource, NY; 91, 97–98, 104, 149–150: © Dumbarton Oaks, Pre-Columbian Collection, Washington, D.C.; 92, 95, 102, 108: © The Cleveland Museum of Art; 93: image courtesy Dallas Museum of Art; 112: Michael Cavanagh and Kevin Montague, © 2010 Indiana University Art Museum; 131: courtesy the Bowers Museum, Santa Ana, CA; 135: Consejo Nacional para la Cultura y las Artes—Instituto Nacional de Antropología e Historia—México—Michel Zabé; 152: courtesy the Peabody Museum of Archaeology and Ethnology, Harvard University

A

Acosta Lagunes, Agustín, 60
altars:
  altar (Aztec), 82, **82**
  Altar 4 [La Venta], 27, 48, **48**, 64, 109, 148, 150
  Altar 5 [La Venta], **2**, 46, 48, 72, **72**, 150, **151**, 193, 231
  functioning as thrones, 150; *see also* thrones
Alvarado Stela, 65
andesite, 26
  standing figure [Ojo de Agua], 74, 229, 231, **231**
Antonio Plaza, "The Wrestler," 178
Arroyo Pesquero, 118
  masks, 28, 167, **167**
Atlihuayan, personage of Atlihuayan, 114, **114**, **115**, 117
axes, *see* celts
Aztec culture:
  altar, 82, **82**
  Coyolxauhqui (colossal head), 81, **81**
  Huitzilopochtli (god of war), 28, 81, **81**, 83–84
  jadeite, 166
  jaguar, reclining, 83, **83**
  knife [Templo Mayor], 84, **84**
  mask [Templo Mayor], 30, 79, 236, **236**
  Moctezuma Xocoyotzin, **76**, 77–78, **78**
  Olmec parallels with, 80–84
  rain deities, 83–84
  Templo Mayor site, 12, 28, 30, 236
  Tlaloc vase [Templo Mayor], 84, **84**
  Tonatiuh (sun god), 80, **80**

B

"baby faces," 27, 61, 69–70, 71, 212
baby figure, hollow, 224, **225**
ballcourts, 130, 232
  ballplayer relief sculpture [Tonalá], 74, 232, **233**
  rubber balls [El Manatí], 35, 130, 132, **133**
Baltazar, Miguel, 239
basalt, 26, 88
  colossal heads, *see* colossal heads
  monuments, *see* monuments
  sources of, 19, 37, 59, 94, 118
  tools, 37
bench figures:
  Monument 40 [La Venta], 193
  Río Arriba, 193
  San José Pinula, 193
  seated figure [Mexico], 192, **192**
  seated figure holding infant [Tabasco], 193, **193**
Benson, Elizabeth, 20, 247
Beverido Pereau, Francisco, 59
Beyer, Hermann, 10
bird-shaped effigy vessel [Los Molinillos], 107, **107**
Blom, Frans, 10, 20, 45, 86, 148

C

cacao (chocolate), 132
calendars, Mayan, 65; sacred, 234
Campbell, Lyle, 20
Cantón Corralito, 71
Caso, Alfonso, 88
Cassedy, E. G., 57
Castro-Leal, Marcía, 250
celts (axes):
  axes and axe fragments [El Manatí], 132, **136**, 137, **137**, **138**, **139**, 182
  axe with footprint [El Manatí], 135, **135**
  Aztec and Olmec styles, 84
  "El Bebé," *see* Monument 2 ("El Bebé")
  celt pendant [Mexico], 28, 82, **82**, 184, **184**
  celt with carved human profile [Simojovel], 28, 190, **190**
  celt with deity [Guerrero], 28, 100, 184, **184**, 194
  celt with incised human profile and hand motif [Tabasco], 28, 183, **183**
  incised celt [Guerrero], 28, 185, **185**
  incised celts [La Venta], 22, 28, 46, 118, 182, **182**, 231, 248
  Kunz Axe (votive axe) [Oaxaca], 92, **92**, 93
  Monument 2 ("El Bebé") [La Merced], 29, 140, **143**
  "The Ocelot" [La Merced], 140
  Offering 2 [La Venta], 51, **51**
  Offering 4 (group of standing figures and celts) [La Venta], 29, 46, 51, **51**, 160, **161**, 186
  Offering 10 [La Venta], 51, **51**
  selection of axes [La Merced], 140–141, **142**, 143, 182
  votive axe [La Venta], 46, 83, **83**, 164, **165**
Central Highlands:
  bottle with carved relief, 69, 116, **116**, 241
  hollow-baby figures, 224
  jar, 222, **223**
  seals, 218, **218**, **219**, 247
  zoomorphic vessel in the form of an opossum, 113, **113**
  see also specific sites
Central Veracruz, stela depicting royal figure, 250, **251**
ceramics:
  bird-shaped effigy vessel [Los Molinillos], 107, **107**
  bottle with carved relief [Central Highlands], 69, 116, **116**, 241
  bowl carved with image of a celestial being [Las Bocas], 69, 71, 117, **117**, 241
  effigy head brazier [Oaxaca], 236, **237**
  female figure carrying child [Tlatilco], 208, **209**
  female figure with elaborate hair and headdress [Tlatilco], 210, **210**
  female figure with incised flaring skirt [Tlatilco], 70, 208, **209**
  female figure with topknot coiffure [Tlatilco], 70, 208, **209**
  female figurine with mirror [Tlatilco], 70, 211, **211**
  figural jar with lid [Guajilar], 228, **228**
  fish effigy vessel [Tlatilco], 106, **106**
  gourd-shaped bowl (*tecomate*) [La Merced], 140, **141**
  gourd-shaped bowl (*tecomate*) [Tlatilco], 214, **214**
  hollow-baby figure holding ball [probably Las Bocas], 69–70, 71, 224, **225**
  incised bottles [Tlatilco], 216–217, **216**, **217**
  incised bowl [Morelos], 71, 206, **206**
  incised bowl [Tlatilco], 215, **215**
  incised vessel [Valley of Mexico], 185, 220, **221**
  jar [Central Highlands], 222, **223**
  personage of Atlihuayan [Atlihuayan], 114, **114**, **115**, 117
  plate with cut shells [Tlatilco], 105, **105**
  plate with two fish [Zohapilco], 104, **104**
  roller seals [Central Highlands], 218, **218**, **219**
  seated figure with head resting on hand [Las Bocas], 71, 222, **222**
  with "spider" supports, 217
  tripod vessel with incised design [Teotihuacan], 241, **241**
  twin figures [Tlatilco], 212, **212**, **213**
  vessel with spout [Tlatilco], 215, **215**
  zoomorphic effigy vessel [Tlapacoya], 112, **112**
  zoomorphic vessel in the form of an opossum [Central Highlands], 113, **113**
Cerro de las Mesas:
  anthropomorphic figure, 79, **238**, 239
  canoe-shaped pectoral, 79, 239, **239**
  Monument 2, 234, **234–235**
  stelae, 27, 250
Chalcatzingo, 72–73, 204, 206
  Monument 1, 48, 72, **72**, 207
  Monument 16 (seated headless figure), 207, **207**
  Monument 22 (throne), 72
  Relief I-B-2, 109
  standing figure, 204, **205**, 226
Chiapa de Corzo, Stela 2 (with portion of Long Count date), 59, 244, **245**
Chiapas, 71, 74, 168, 226
  ballcourt, 130

Page numbers in **bold** refer to illustrations.

pendant with two men wearing bird masks, 109, **109**, 185
see also specific sites
clamshell pendant [La Venta], 46, 52, 110, 162, **162**
Classic period, 30, 64, 79
Clewlow, C. William, 86
Coe, Michael, 22, 93, 100, 126, 130, 180, 246
colossal heads, 26–27, 70, 88
Colossal Head 1 ("El Rey") [San Lorenzo], **18**, 19
Colossal Head 4 [San Lorenzo], 36, 40, 81, 120, **121**
Colossal Head 5 [San Lorenzo], **26**, 27, 36, 40, 81, 122, **123**, **124**, **125**
Colossal Head 7 [San Lorenzo], 27
Coyolxauhqui (Aztec), 81, **81**
of La Venta, 48, 52
Monument 1 [La Venta], 47, 118, **118–119**
Monument 2 [Cerro de las Mesas], 234, **234–235**
Monument 89 [San Lorenzo], 27, **34**, 35, 40
Monument A [Tres Zapotes], 27, 57, **57**, 59, 60, 61, 64, 90
Monument Q [Tres Zapotes], 27, 56, 59, 60, 64, 81, **81**, 90, **91**
recarved from monuments, 40
of San Lorenzo, 118
sizes and weights of, 26
contortionist [Las Choapas], 181, **181**
Contreras, Eduardo, 160
Cortés, Hernán, 77, **78**
Costa Rica, Olmec links to, 92
Covarrubias, Miguel, 20, 25, 70, 88, 116, 198, 203
chart, Olmec influence on evolution of jaguar mask into rain gods, **24**, 25, 32, 84
Coyolxauhqui (Aztec colossal head), 81, **81**
Cruz del Milagro, Monument 1 (seated figure), 27, 178, **179**
cult of the dead, Tlatilco, 106
Cyphers, Ann, 34–43, 47, 86, 100, 120, 126, 144

D
dates, note on, 20
de la Fuente, Beatriz, 10, 20, 25, 85, 86, 120, 130
Diehl, Richard A., 76–85, 126, 180
Draper, Perry, 172
Drucker, Philip, 52, 59, 60, 110, 172, 239, 242

E
earflares [La Venta], 46, 52, 110, **111**, 158, 163
Early Classic period, 66, 79
Early Formative (Preclassic) period, 20, 37, 47, 61, 69, 70–71
ceramics, 70, 71, 106, 107, 112, 113, 218, 220
cult of the dead, 106
Easby, Elizabeth, 92
Ejido Ojoshal, scepter, 191, **191**
El Azuzul, *see* Loma del Zapote-El Azuzul
El Manatí, 12, 37, 132
axes and axe fragments, 132, **136**, 137, **137**, **138**, **139**, 182
axe with footprint, 135, **135**
human busts, 22, **22**, 132, **134**, 135
ritual symbols of, 22, 28, 132, 137, 182
rubber balls, 22, 35, 130, 132, **133**
seated figure, 135, **135**
shrines of, 22, 118
El Mesón:
Stelae 1 and 2, 65
Tres Zapotes Plaza Group (TZPG) plan of, 64
epi-Olmec period, 20
stelae, 27, 62
in Tres Zapotes, 62, 63–64, 168

F
Fields, Virginia M., 246
figurines, 10, 28–29, 30, 37, 52, 61, 70, 71, 112, 118, 126, 158, 160, 167, 186, 192, 193, 208, 215, 218, 232
fish effigy vessel [Tlatilco], 106, **106**
Formative (Preclassic) period, 52, 69, 116
full-length figures, 26, 27–28

G
Gallegos, Roberto, 96
García Cook, Ángel, 60
García Moll, Roberto, 181
González Lauck, Rebecca B., 20, 47, 49
greenstone, 19, 28, 29, 30, 70, 88
axes and axe fragments [El Manatí], **136**, 137, **137**, **138**, **139**, 182
figure wearing incised loincloth [Puebla], 247, **247**
head [Tabasco], 186, 187, **187**
mask [Guerrero], 200, **200**
mask with incised design [Oaxaca], 248, **248**
Monument 1 ("El Señor de Las Limas"), 29, **29**, 193
necklace, 77–78, **78**
pectoral [La Encrucijada], 108, **108**
pectoral [Soconusco], 74, 226, 227, **227**
plaque with carved human profile [Gulf Coast], 189, **189**
seated figure [El Manatí], 135, **135**
sources of, 167, 196
symbolic value of, 167
see also jadeite
Grove, David C., 63, 68–75, **68**, 102, 172, 206, 207, 230
Guajilar, figural jar with lid, 228, **228**
Guerrero, 198, 236
celt with deity, 28, 100, 184, **184**, 194
incised celt, 28, 185, **185**
Juxtlahuaca cave mural, 74
masks, 200, **200**
see also specific sites
Gulf Coast:
ceramics, 215, 218
exchange networks of, 22, 196
flora and fauna of, 21
languages of, 20
plaque with carved human profile, 189, **189**
sacred calendar, 234
see also specific sites

H
Heizer, Robert, 59, 150
hollow-baby figure holding ball [probably Las Bocas], 69–70, 71, 224, **225**
Hueyapan de Ocampo, mask, 28, 166, **166**
Huitzilopochtli (Aztec god of war), 28, 81, **81**, 83–84

I
ilhuitl (opposing volutes), 106
Instituto Nacional de Antropología e Historia (INAH), 60–61, 96, 206
Introduction to the Study of the Maya Hieroglyphs, An (Morley), 58
Izapa:
Miscellaneous Monument 2, 65
Stela 5, 65

J
jade, 26, 30; *see also* jadeite
jadeite, 79, 88, 166
anthropomorphic figure [Cerro de las Mesas], 79, **238**, 239
axe with footprint [El Manatí], 135, **135**
canoe-shaped pectoral [Cerro de las Mesas], 79, 239, **239**
celt pendant [Mexico], 28, 82, **82**, 184, **184**
celt with incised human profile and hand motif [Tabasco], 28, 183, **183**
earflares [La Venta], 46, 52, 110, **111**, 158, 163
fragmentary figure [Mexico], 81, **81**, 186, 188, **188**
head fragment with incised design [Mexico], 186, 187, **187**
incised celt [Guerrero], 28, 185, **185**
Kunz Axe (votive axe) [Oaxaca], 92, **92**, 93
La Venta figures, 204
mask [Arroyo Pesquero], 28, 167, **167**
mask [Hueyapan de Ocampo], 28, 166, **166**
mask [Mexico], 186, **186**

pendant with were-jaguar head framed with cleft elements [San Gervasio], 30, 79, 238, **238**
seated female figure with polished hematite disk [La Venta], **4**, 46, 52, 158, **159**
seated zoomorph with crest and pleated ear decorations [Necaxa], 93, **93**
standing figure [La Venta], 46, 163, **163**
standing figure [Ocozocuautla], 74, 226, **226**
votive axe [La Venta], 46, 83, **83**, 164, **165**
jaguar, 26, 27–28, 82–83
anthropomorphic jaguar figure [Tuxtla Chico], 74, 230, **230**
dance of, 32
Monument 7 (small feline) [Loma del Zapote-El Azuzul], 28, 41, 144, **145**
Monument 10 (large feline) [Loma del Zapote-El Azuzul], 28, **28**, 41, 144
Monument 107 [San Lorenzo], 32, 39, **39**, 83, **83**
Painting 1-d (human and jaguar) [Oxtotitlan], 73, **73**
pendant with were-jaguar head framed with cleft elements [San Gervasio], 30, 79, 238, **238**
reclining jaguar (Aztec), 83, **83**
"were-jaguars," 30, 92, 172
jaguar faces, 58
jaguar masks, evolution into rain gods, **24**, 25, 32, 84
jaguar-men, 26
Joralemon, Peter, 92, 100, 109
Justeson, John, 65

K

kaolin, 10, 214
jar [Central Highlands], 222, **223**
seated figure with head resting on hand [Las Bocas], 71, 222, **222**
Kaufman, Terrence, 20
kneeling figure, 201, **201**
knuckledusters:
"manoplas," 128, 192, 194
Monument 10 (seated figure with knuckledusters) [San Lorenzo], 36, 128, **128**, **129**, 184
Kunz, George, 92
Kunz Axe (votive axe) [Oaxaca], 92, **92**, 93

L

Lacadena, Alfonso, 242, 244
Ladrón de Guevara, Sara, 24–33
La Encrucijada, pectoral, 108, **108**
La Farge, Oliver, 10, 45, 86, 148
Laguna de los Cerros, 40, 118
Monument 1 (head of supernatural being), 174, **174**, **175**
Monument 2, 174
Monument 19 (standing figure), 176, **177**, 186
La Merced:
axe ("El Bebé"), *see* Monument 2 ("El Bebé")
axe ("The Ocelot"), 140
gourd-shaped bowl (*tecomate*), 140, **141**
Monument 1, 140, 191
Monument 2 ("El Bebé"), 29, 140, **143**
ritual symbols of, 28, 140, 167, 182
selection of axes, 140–141, **142**, 143, 182
shrines of, 22, 118
La Mojarra Stela, 27, 65, 66
Las Bocas, 71, 215, 216, 224
bowl carved with image of a celestial being, 69, 71, 117, **117**, 241
hollow-baby figure holding ball, 69–70, 71, 224, **225**
seated figure with head resting on hand, 71, 222, **222**
Las Choapas, contortionist, 181, **181**
Las Limas:
Monument 1 ("El Señor de Las Limas"), 29, **29**, 193
"were-jaguar" baby, 172
Late Classic period, 66
Late Formative period:
ceramics, 59, 63–64
Tres Zapotes, 59, 62, 63–64, 65, 168
Late Preclassic period, 58
La Venta, 19, 44–53, 118
aerial view, 94, **94–95**
Altar 4, 27, 48, **48**, 64, 109, 148, 150
Altar 5, **2**, 46, 48, 72, **72**, 150, **151**, 193, 231
apogee of, 45
and Chalcatzingo, 72–73
clamshell pendant, 46, 52, 110, 162, **162**
colossal heads, 52
Columnar Tomb, 158, 163, 164, **196–197**; *see also* Tomb A
decline of, 63
earflares, 46, 52, 110, **111**, 158, 163
enclosed court, 50, 51, 52
excavations, **47**, 47–49, 50, **50**, **51**, 196, **196–197**
incised celts, 22, 28, 46, 118, 182, **182**, 231, 248
iron-oxide ores, 162
jadeite figures, 204
Massive Offering 2, 52
mirror, 46, 52, 110, 162, **162**
Monument 1 (colossal head), 47, 118, **118–119**
Monument 11 (seated supernatural being), 154, **155**
Monument 13, 242, **243**
Monument 40, 193
Monument 44, 47, **47**, 66
Monument 59 (throne), 46, 48, 102, **102**, **103**
Monument 77 (seated figure wearing cape), 46, 49, 80, **80**, 93, 108, 152, **152**, **153**, 194, 248
monumental head of supernatural creature, 156, **157**
Monuments 25/26 and 27, 191
mosaic masks, 50, **50**
Offering 2, 51, **51**
Offering 4 (group of standing figures and celts), 29, 46, 51, **51**, 160, **161**, 186
Offering 10, 51, **51**
pyramid, 27, 49, **49**, 52, 94, **94–95**, 231
rise of, 20, 47, 70, 118
ritual symbols of, 28, 29, 167, 231
sarcophagus, 117
seated female figure with polished hematite disk, **4**, 46, 52, 158, **159**
site map, **46**
standing figure, 46, 163, **163**
Stela 1 (female figure), 46, 50, **50**, 148, **149**, 158
Stela 2, 10, **44**, 45, 47, 191
Stela 3, 65
Tomb A, 52, 110, 118
votive axe, 46, 83, **83**, 164, **165**
Loma del Zapote, 41, 86
Monument 12 (head), 126, **127**, 186
see also Loma del Zapote-El Azuzul
Loma del Zapote-El Azuzul, 27–28, 118
Monument 7 (small feline), 28, **28**, 41, 144, **145**
Monument 8 (Twin I), 28, **28**, 41, 144, **146**
Monument 9 (Twin II), 28, **28**, 41, 144, **147**
Monument 10 (large feline), 28, **28**, 41, 144
Long Count dates, 65, 170, 244
López Luján, Leonardo, 12
Los Molinillos, bird-shaped effigy vessel, 107, **107**
Lowe, Gareth, 109, 191
Luckert, Karl, 93

M

Magaloni Kerpel, Diana, 10–13
maize and maize gods, artistic depictions of, 82, **82**, 182, 183, 191, 194, 248
maps:
La Venta site map, **46**
The Olmec World, **16–17**
San Lorenzo site map, **36**
Tres Zapotes site map, **56**
masks:
basalt, recarved monument [Medias Aguas], 31, **31**
greenstone [Guerrero], 200, **200**
greenstone, with incised design [Oaxaca], 248, **248**
hornblende [Templo Mayor], 30, 79, 236, **236**

jadeite [Arroyo Pesquero], 28, 167, **167**
jadeite [Hueyapan de Ocampo], 28, 166, **166**
jadeite with traces of cinnabar [Mexico], 186, **186**
serpentine [probably Guerrero], 200, **200**
stone, 28, 79
Matos Moctezuma, Eduardo, 12, 236
Maya:
calendar, 65
carved slab monuments, 148
cosmology of, 38
cross-legged figures, 192
jadeite, 166
Long Count, 244
maize rituals and gods, 183, 248
Olmec influence on, 30
Popol Vuh (sacred book), 28, 144
stelae, 27, 250
turtles depicted in art, 108
Uaxactun site, 58
Medellin Zeñil, Alfonso, 122, 174, 178, 180, 181
Medias Aguas, large mask (recarved monument), 31, **31**
Melgar, José, 57
Mexico, riverine landscapes in, **21**
Mezcala, bowl, 198, **199**
Middle Formative period, 20, 61–63, 64, 70, 71–74
ceramics, 59, 236
jadeite figures, 186
Middle Preclassic period, 30, 105, 107
Mije-Zoque languages, 20, 242
Millet Cámara, Luis, 59–60, 61
mirror [La Venta], 46, 52, 110, 162, **162**
Mixteca Alta, hollow baby, 224
Moctezuma: Aztec Ruler (exhibition, British Museum), 80
Moctezuma Xocoyotzin, **76**, 77–78, **78**
monuments:
carved monument [Tiltepec], 248, **249**
Monument 1 [Chalcatzingo], 48, 72, **72**, 207
Monument 1 [La Merced], 140, 191
Monument 1 (colossal head) [La Venta], 47, 118, **118–119**
Monument 1 (composite creature) [Chiapas], 74, 229, **229**
Monument 1 (crouching figure with headdress and ceremonial staff) [San Martín Pajapan], 10–11, **11**, 12
Monument 1 (head of supernatural being) [Laguna de los Cerros], 174, **174**, **175**
Monument 1 (seated figure) [Cruz del Milagro], 27, 178, **179**
Monument 1 ("El Señor de Las Limas"), 29, **29**, 193
Monument 1 (victor and captive) [San Lorenzo], 92, 180, **180**
Monument 2 ("El Bebé") [La Merced], 29, 140, **143**
Monument 2 [Cerro de las Mesas], 234, **234–235**
Monument 7 (small feline) [Loma del Zapote-El Azuzul], 28, 41, 144, **145**
Monument 8 (Twin I) [Loma del Zapote-El Azuzul], 28, 41, 144, **146**
Monument 9 (Twin II) [Loma del Zapote-El Azuzul], 28, 41, 144, **147**
Monument 9 (waterbird) [San Lorenzo], 36, 98, **98**, 99
Monument 10 (large feline) [Loma del Zapote-El Azuzul], 28, **28**, 41, 144
Monument 10 (seated figure with knuckledusters) [San Lorenzo], 36, 128, **128**, **129**, 184
Monument 11 (seated supernatural being) [La Venta], 154, **155**
Monument 12 [Loma del Zapote], 126, **127**, 186
Monument 13 [La Venta], 242, **243**
Monument 16 (seated headless figure) [Chalcatzingo], 207, **207**
Monument 19 (standing figure) [Laguna de los Cerros], 176, **177**, 186
Monument 22 (throne) [Chalcatzingo], 72
Monument 34 (half-kneeling figure) [San Lorenzo], 36, 130, **131**
Monument 40 [La Venta], 193
Monument 44 [La Venta], 47, **47**, 66
Monument 52 (zoomorphic sculpture) [San Lorenzo], 36, 100, **101**, 108, 172, 184
Monument 58 (relief of composite creature) [San Lorenzo], 36, 96, **97**
Monument 59 (throne) [La Venta], 46, 48, 102, **102**, **103**
Monument 77 (seated figure wearing cape) [La Venta], 46, 49, 80, **80**, 93, 108, 152, **152**, **153**, 194, 248
Monument 89 [San Lorenzo], 2, **34**, 35, 40
Monument 102 (decapitated bird) [San Lorenzo], 39, **39**
Monument 104 (earth monster) [San Lorenzo], 37–38, **38**
Monument 105 (mutilated head) [San Lorenzo], 39, **39**
Monument 107 (composite feline and descending ballplayer) [San Lorenzo], 32, 39, **39**, 83, **83**
Monument A (colossal head) [Tres Zapotes], 27, 57, **57**, 59, 60, 61, 64, 90
monumental head of supernatural creature [La Venta], 156, **157**
Monument C (box with elaborate carving) [Tres Zapotes], 22, 56, 57, 60, 65, 168, **169**
Monument I [Tres Zapotes], 64
Monument M (anthropomorphic head) [Tres Zapotes], **54**, 55, 56, 63, 172, **173**
Monument Q (colossal head) [Tres Zapotes], 27, 56, 59, 60, 64, 81, **81**, 90, **91**
Monuments 7–10 [Loma del Zapote-El Azuzul], installation of, 28, **28**, 41, 144
Monuments 25/26 and 27 [La Venta], 191
mutilations of, 207
naming of, 86
Morelos, 70, 72–73
incised bowl, 71, 206, **206**
see also specific sites
Morley, Sylvanus G., 58

N

National Geographic Society, 57, 59, 79
Navarette, Carlos, 191, 231
Necaxa, seated zoomorph with crest and pleated ear decorations, 93, **93**
Nestepe Monument 1 (Tres Zapotes Monument Q), 90, **91**
Nicholson, H. B., 80
Niederberger, Christine, 186

O

Oaxaca:
effigy head brazier, 236, **237**
hollow baby [Mixteca Alta], 224
Kunz Axe (votive axe), 92, **92**, 93
mask with incised design, 248, **248**
Ocozocuautla, standing figure, 74, 226, **226**
Ojo de Agua, standing figure, 74, 229, 231, **231**
Olman, use of term, 88
Olmec:
history of term, 20, 53n1
meanings of name, 35, 69, 88, 93
Olmec culture, 19–20
Aztec parallels with, 80–84
chronological parameters of, 20, 30–31, 59, 78
defining royal authority in, 109, 118, 122, 144, 182, 194, 247
heirlooms, 78–80
as "mother culture" of Mesoamerica, 10, 88
origins of, 35
religious ideology, 22, 83, 94
sacred calendar, 234
of water, 40–41
Olmec dragon, 116
Olmec style:
defining, 25–32, 53n1, 69, 88
"flame eyebrows," 92, 112, 114, 117, 164
geographic area of, 10, **16–17**, 19, 30, 53n1, 198
influence of, 10, 20, 30, 76–85, 88, 240

"*manoplas*" (knuckledusters), 128, 192, 194
outside Olman, 68–75
prototypical features of, 10–11, 117, 206
variations in, 20
Ortíz Ceballos, Ponciano, 12, 22, 59
Oxtotitlan:
cave mural, 27, 64, **68**, 69, 73–74, **74**, 102, 109, 192
Painting 1-d (human and jaguar), 73, **73**

P

pars pro toto, 27
Paso de la Amada, ballcourt, 232
pectorals:
[La Encrucijada], 108, **108**
[Soconusco], 74, 226, 227, **227**
canoe-shaped pectoral [Cerro de las Mesas], 79, 239, **239**
pendants:
celt pendant [Mexico], 28, 82, **82**, 184, **184**
clamshell pendant [La Venta], 46, 52, 110, 162, **162**
pendant with two men wearing bird masks [Chiapas], 109, **109**, 185
pendant with were-jaguar head framed with cleft elements [San Gervasio], 30, 79, 238, **238**
Pepper, George, 112
Pijijiapan, relief sculptures, 231
Piña Chan, Román, 106, 117
Pool, Christopher A., 20, 54–67, 86
Popol Vuh, 28, 144
Porter, James, 86, 168
Postclassic period, 32, 59
"pretty lady" style, 70, 208, **209**, **210**, 211, **211**
Proskouriakoff, Tatiana, 148
Protoclassic period, 64, 65, 66, 79
Puebla, 215
figure wearing incised loincloth, 247, **247**
hollow-baby figure holding ball, 69–70, 71, 224, **225**
see also specific sites

R

rain gods:
Aztec, 83–84
evolution from jaguar masks into, **24**, 25, 32, 84
standing figure [Ojo de Agua], 74, 229, 231, **231**
Reilly, F. Kent III, 44–53, 64
Río Pesquero, celts, 64
Rivera, Diego, 70
Rodríguez M., Ma. del Carmen, 12, 22
roller seals [Central Highlands], 218, **218**, **219**, 247
rubber balls [El Manatí], 35, 130, 132, **133**

S

Sahlins, Marshall David, 10
San Andres, roller stamp, 247
San Bartolo, Guatemala:
creator god figure, 30
mural, 108
San Gervasio, pendant with were-jaguar head framed with cleft elements, 30, 79, 238, **238**
San Lorenzo, *see* San Lorenzo Tenochtitlán
San Lorenzo Tenochtitlán, 21–22, 34–43, 118
Colossal Head 1 ("El Rey"), **18**, 19
Colossal Head 4, 36, 40, 48, 81, 120, **121**
Colossal Head 5, **26**, 27, 36, 40, 81, 122, **123**, **124**, **125**
Colossal Head 7, 27
decline of, 20, 41–42, 63
Group E plateau architecture, 38–39
maximum splendor of, 37, 69, 118
Monument 9 (waterbird), 36, 98, **98**, 99
Monument 10 (seated figure with knuckledusters), 36, 128, **128**, **129**, 184
Monument 23, 130
Monument 34 (half-kneeling figure), 36, 130, **131**
Monument 52 (zoomorphic sculpture), 36, 100, **101**, 108, 172, 184
Monument 58 (relief of composite creature), 36, 96, **97**
Monument 89 (colossal head), 27, **34**, 35, 40
Monument 102 (decapitated bird), 39, **39**
Monument 104 (earth monster), 37–38, **38**
Monument 105 (mutilated head), 39, **39**
Monument 107 (composite feline and descending ballplayer), 32, 39, **39**, 83, **83**
political system of, 41, 126
productive activities in, 40
Red Palace, 39
religious festivities of, 41, 118
settlement of, 37–40
site map, **36**
social zoning, 38–39
water culture of, 40–41, 98, 118
in wider perspective, 40–42
San Martín Pajapan, Monument 1 (crouching figure with headdress and ceremonial staff), 10–11, **11**, 12
Saville, Marshall, 92
scepter [Ejido Ojoshal], 191, **191**
Seler, Eduard, 57
Seler-Sachs, Caecilie, 57, 168
serpentine, 26
axes and axe fragments [El Manatí], **136**, 137, **137**, **138**, **139**, 182
mask [probably Guerrero], 200, **200**
Massive Offering 2 [La Venta], 52
Offering 4 (group of standing figures and celts) [La Venta], 29, 46, 51, **51**, 160, **161**, 186
pendant with two men wearing bird masks [Chiapas], 109, **109**, 185
seated figure holding infant [Tabasco], 193, **193**
standing figure [Chalcatzingo], 204, **205**, 226
Simojovel, celt with carved human profile, 28, 190, **190**
Smithsonian Institution, 57, 79
Soconusco, pectoral, 74, 226, 227, **227**
Solís Olguín, Felipe, 80, 85
Squier, Robert, 59
stelae, 26, 27
Alvarado Stela, 65
La Mojarra Stela, 27, 65, 66
Mayan, 27, 250
Monument 23 [San Lorenzo], 130
recarved and reused, 31
Stela 1 (female figure) [La Venta], 46, 50, **50**, 148, **149**, 158
Stela 2 [La Venta), 10, **44**, 45, 47, 191
Stela 2 (with portion of Long Count date) [Chiapa de Corzo], 59, 244, **245**
Stela 3 [La Venta], 65
Stela 5 [Izapa], 65
Stela A [Tres Zapotes], 62, **62**, 64
Stela C [Tres Zapotes], 22, 56, 57–58, **58**, 59, 60, 64–65, 66, 170, **171**, 244
Stela D [Tres Zapotes], 65, 88, **88–89**
stela depicting royal figure [Central Veracruz], 250, **251**
Stelae 1 and 2 [El Mesón], 65
Stewart, Richard H., 57
Stirling, Marion, 57, 58–59, 170, 239
Stirling, Matthew W., 52, 57, 58–59, 60, 63, 66, 79, 86, 92, 98, 100, 110, 120, 126, 128, 168, 170, 172, 180, 188, 239, 250

T

Tabasco, 10, 167
aerial view, **45**
celt with incised human profile and hand motif, 28, 183, **183**
head, 186, 187, **187**
seated figure holding infant, 193, **193**
see also specific sites
Taube, Karl, 117, 181, 184, 188, 191, 194, 246, 247
Templo Mayor, Tenochtitlan, 12, 28, 30, 83–84
knife, 84, **84**
mask, 30, 79, 236, **236**
Tlaloc vase, 84, **84**
Tenochtitlan, 28
Olmec mask, 79
see also San Lorenzo Tenochtitlán

Teopantecuanitlán, 73, 198
ballcourt, 130
Sculpture 4, 73, **73**
Teotihuacan:
as pilgrimage site, 12
standing figure with cupped hands, 240, **240**
Tepantitla murals, 12
tripod vessel with incised design, 241, **241**
Thompson, J. Eric S., 58
Thomson, Charlotte W., 204
thrones, 26, 27, 70
altars functioning as, 150; *see also* altars
Monument 22 [Chalcatzingo], 72
Monument 59 [La Venta], 46, 48, 102, **102**, **103**
recarved and reused, 31
Tiltepec, carved monument, 248, **249**
Tlacotepec:
small yoke, 203, **203**
small yoke with carved face and incisions, **202**, 203
Tlaloc (Aztec rain god), 83–84
vase, 84, **84**
Tlapacoya, 70–71, 206
plate with two fish, 104, **104**
zoomorphic effigy vessel, 112, **112**
Tlatilco, 70–71, 107, 208, 211
acrobat figure, 181
cult of the dead, 106
cylinder seal, 247
female figure carrying child, 208, **209**
female figure with elaborate hair and headdress, 210, **210**
female figure with incised flaring skirt, 70, 208, **209**
female figure with topknot coiffure, 70, 208, **209**
female figurine with mirror, 70, 211, **211**
fish effigy vessel, 106, **106**
gourd-shaped bowl (*tecomate*), 214, **214**
incised bottles, 216, **216**, 217, **217**
incised bowl, 215, **215**
opossums depicted in, 113
plate with cut shells, 105, **105**
twin figures, 212, **212**, **213**
vessel with spout, 215, **215**
Tlatilco panel, 106
Tokovinine, Alexandre, 246
Toltec civilization, Olmec link to, 92
Tonalá, ballplayer relief sculpture, 74, 232, **233**
Tonatiuh (Aztec sun god), 80, **80**
Tres Zapotes, 19, 54–67, 118
chronology, 58–59, 65, 67n3, 118, 170
cooperative government in, 64–65
decline of, 66
Group 2, **55**
growth of, 61–63, 118
influence of, 64–65, 70, 118
Monument A (colossal head), 27, 57, **57**, 59, 60, 61, 64, 90
Monument C (box with elaborate carving), 22, 56, 57, 60, 65, 168, **169**
Monument I, 64
Monument M (anthropomorphic head), **54**, 55, 56, 63, 172, **173**
Monument Q (colossal head), 27, 56, 59, 60, 64, 81, **81**, 90, **91**
PATZ archaeological project, 60
Plaza Group (TZPG) plan, 63–64, 66
Protoclassic reorganization, 66
RATZ archaeological survey, 60
removal of objects from, 60
rise of, 20
site map, **56**
Stela A, 62, **62**, 64
Stela C, 22, 56, 57–58, **58**, 59, 60, 64–65, 66, 170, **171**, 244
Stela D, 65, 88, **88–89**
Stela F, 62, 64
unanswered questions, 60
Tribes and Temples (Blom and La Farge), 45
Tuxtla Chico, anthropomorphic jaguar figure, 74, 230, **230**
Tuxtla statuette, 30, 65, 66

U
Uaxactun (Mayan site), 58
Uriarte, María Teresa, 12

V
Vaillant, George, 20, 93
Valley of Mexico, incised vessel, 185, 220, **221**
Vasconselos, Atanacio, 144
Veracruz, 10
seated figure wearing elaborate headdress and cape, 194, **195**
stela depicting royal figure, 250, **251**
see also specific sites
Villaflores, Monument 1 (composite creature), 74, 229, **229**

W
Wedel, Waldo, 242
Weiant, Clarence W., 57, 59
Weiant, Marian, 57
Wetmore, Alexander, 57
Weyerstall, Albert C., 57, 86, 168
Williams, Howel, 59, 150
winged plaque [Mexico], 30, 79, 246, **246**
wooden busts [El Manatí], 12, 22, **22**, 132, **134**, 135
writing, origins of, 234

Z
Zazacatla:
chronology of, 206
stone figure, 206, **206**
Zohapilco (Tlapacoya), 70–71
figurine, 104
plate with two fish, 104, **104**
zoomorphic effigy vessel [Tlapacoya], 112, **112**
zoomorphic sculpture (San Lorenzo Monument 52), 36, 100, **101**, 108, 172, 184
zoomorphic vessel in the form of an opossum [Central Highlands], 113, **113**

This catalogue was published by the Fine Arts Museums of San Francisco and the Los Angeles County Museum of Art on the occasion of the exhibition *Olmec: Colossal Masterworks of Ancient Mexico*.

Hardcover edition published in association with
Yale University Press
302 Temple Street
P.O. Box 209040
New Haven, CT 06520-9040
www.yalebooks.com

Exhibition Itinerary:

Los Angeles County Museum of Art
October 2, 2010–January 9, 2011

de Young Museum, San Francisco
February 19–May 8, 2011

This exhibition was organized by the Fine Arts Museums of San Francisco and the Los Angeles County Museum of Art in collaboration with the Consejo Nacional para la Cultura y las Artes—Instituto Nacional de Antropología e Historia de México.

Instituto Nacional de Antropología e Historia

Consejo Nacional para la Cultura y las Artes

This exhibition is supported by an indemnity from the Federal Council on the Arts and the Humanities.

The San Francisco production of the exhibition is wholly funded by and attributed to the Phyllis C. Wattis Fund for Traveling Exhibitions.

The catalogue is published with the assistance of the Andrew W. Mellon Foundation Endowment for Publications.

Photography credits appear on p. 265.

Olmec: Colossal Masterworks of Ancient Mexico was produced through the Publications Department of the Fine Arts Museums of San Francisco:

Ann Heath Karlstrom, Director of Publications
Karen A. Levine, Editor in Chief

Fine Arts Museums of San Francisco
Golden Gate Park
50 Hagiwara Tea Garden Drive
San Francisco, CA 94118-4502

Edited by Jennifer Boynton
Designed by Tracey Shiffman and Alex Kohnke with Deanne Oi, Shiffman & Kohnke
Translations from the Spanish by Debra Nagao and Rose Vekony
Index by Nancy Wolff
Maps by Anandaroop Roy
Color separations by Echelon
Printed in Singapore by CS Graphics Pte Ltd

Library of Congress Cataloging-in-Publication Data

Olmec : colossal masterworks of ancient Mexico / edited by Kathleen Berrin and Virginia M. Fields.

p. cm.

"This catalogue was published by the Fine Arts Museums of San Francisco and the Los Angeles County Museum of Art on the occasion of the exhibition *Olmec: Colossal Masterworks of Ancient Mexico*"—Colophon.

Includes bibliographical references and index.

ISBN 978-0-300-16676-7 (hardcover) — ISBN 978-0-88401-131-6 (pbk.)

1. Olmec art—Exhibitions. 2. Olmecs—Antiquities—Exhibitions. 3. Mexico—Antiquities—Exhibitions. I. Berrin, Kathleen. II. Fields, Virginia M. III. Fine Arts Museums of San Francisco. IV. Los Angeles County Museum of Art.

F1219.8.O56O465 2010

972'.01—dc22

2010015664

Front and back cover:
MONUMENT 1 (SEATED FIGURE)
Mexico, Veracruz, Municipality of Sayula de Alemán, Cruz del Milagro, 1200–900 BC
Basalt
49 3/16 x 33 1/16 x 39 3/8 in. (125 x 84 x 100 cm)
Museo de Antropología de Xalapa, Universidad Veracruzana (Reg. 49 P.J. 4023)
See pl. 85

Frontispiece, page 2:
ALTAR 5
Mexico, Tabasco, La Venta, 900–400 BC
Basalt
61 x 80 x 60 1/4 in. (155 x 203 x 153 cm)
Parque Museo de La Venta, Villahermosa, Tabasco (PMV-012)
See pls. 64–66

Frontispiece, page 4:
SEATED FEMALE FIGURE WITH POLISHED HEMATITE DISK
Mexico, Tabasco, La Venta, Mound A-2, Tomb A (Columnar Tomb), 900–500 BC
Jadeite and hematite
3 x 1 7/8 x 1 1/2 in. (7.7 x 4.7 x 3.8 cm)
Museo Nacional de Antropología, Mexico City (10-9652)
See pl. 71